THE WEST

The West

THE HISTORY OF AN IDEA

GEORGIOS VAROUXAKIS

PRINCETON UNIVERSITY PRESS
PRINCETON & OXFORD

Copyright © 2025 by Georgios Varouxakis

Princeton University Press is committed to the protection of copyright and the intellectual property our authors entrust to us. Copyright promotes the progress and integrity of knowledge created by humans. By engaging with an authorized copy of this work, you are supporting creators and the global exchange of ideas. As this work is protected by copyright, any reproduction or distribution of it in any form for any purpose requires permission; permission requests should be sent to permissions@press.princeton.edu. Ingestion of any PUP IP for any AI purposes is strictly prohibited.

Published by Princeton University Press
41 William Street, Princeton, New Jersey 08540
99 Banbury Road, Oxford OX2 6JX

press.princeton.edu

GPSR Authorized Representative: Easy Access System Europe - Mustamäe tee 50, 10621 Tallinn, Estonia, gpsr.requests@easproject.com

All Rights Reserved

ISBN 9780691177182
ISBN (e-book) 9780691272368

British Library Cataloging-in-Publication Data is available

Editorial: Ben Tate and Josh Drake
Production Editorial: Nathan Carr
Jacket/Cover Design: Chris Ferrante
Production: Danielle Amatucci
Publicity: Alyssa Sanford and Carmen Jimenez

This book has been composed in Minion 3

Printed in the United States of America

10 9 8 7 6 5 4 3 2 1

To Bella and Alexander

'Words, as is well known, are the great foes of reality.' Joseph Conrad, *Under Western Eyes*, p. 3

'A idées nouvelles, mots nouveaux, d'où la création significative des vocables' (For new ideas, new words [are required], hence the meaningful creation of terms.) Jane [Jeanne] Nardal, 'Internationalisme noir', *La Dépêche africaine*, 15 February 1928

'[T]he "Defence of the West" [. . .] is a subject about which everyone thinks he has something to say.' T. S. Eliot to Geoffrey Faber, 4 September 1926, in Eliot and Haffenden, *Letters of T. S. Eliot*, vol. 3, p. 273

CONTENTS

Preface xv

1 Introduction: 'The West' 1
   I. The West, 'from Plato to NATO'? 5
   II. A Russian Import, or a Substitute for 'Whiteness'? 9
   III. A Gradual Growth, Consummated in Paris,
      rue Monsieur-le-Prince 13
   IV. This Book 19

2 'The West' as an Alternative to 'Europe' in the Nineteenth Century 25
   I. Heeren of Göttingen 26
   II. From North–South to East–West: Mme de Staël and
      the View of Russia 28
   III. Les Deux Mondes: Saint-Simon and the Saint-Simonians 30
   IV. Greeks Bearing Gifts? Or 'la garantie véritable de l'Occident
      contre l'Orient' 35
   V. Fear of Russia Intensifies: 'the West' Must Unite… 38
   VI. The East of Xerxes or the East of Christ? 42
   VII. The Unlikely Godfather: Auguste Comte and the Substitution
      of Occident for Europe 48
   VIII. Comte's Political Project: The 'Republic of the West' 52
   IX. From L'Europe to L'Occident 60
   X. Positivist Contributions after Comte 63
   XI. Conclusion 66

3 Insular Britain Joins the West   69
    I. Insular Britain versus Continental Occident   70
    II. Early Uses of 'West' and 'Western'   71
    III. 'Europe' and 'the Liberties of Europe'   72
    IV. Different 'Others': 'The West' versus 'Northern'/'Eastern' Russia, 'Oriental' Jews, and Turkey   75
    V. Edward Freeman and the 'Eternal' Struggle of 'the West' against 'the East'   81
    VI. The British Comtists' West   84
    VII. The Novelty of 'the West' in English   90
    VIII. The Wages of Foreign Influence   91
    IX. Conclusion   93

4 Ex Germaniae lux? How Did the Idea of 'the West' Reach America?   94
    I. Heidelberg, Göttingen, Halle, Berlin...   96
    II. From Franz Lieber to Francis Lieber   99
    III. The Need 'to have a distinct name for the indicated group': 'Western'? 'Occidental'? 'Cis-Caucasian'?   103
    IV. 'Orientalism' and 'Occidentalism': America, 1853   107
    V. European Immigrants and Eastern Questions   110
    VI. Occidentalism versus Orientalism (and Yet Another German-Educated American Academic)   113
    VII. 'The Meeting of the Orient and the Occident, Long Foreshadowed': Academic Political Science and 'Western Civilisation'   115
    VIII. Afro-American Radicalism versus Russian Menace? (And Japan as a Beacon of Hope)   119
    IX. Civilisations and Civilisationism: Alexander Crummell, William H. Ferris, W.E.B. Du Bois   121
    X. Conclusion   128

5 The War of Words: 'Western Civilisation' and 'the West', 1914–1919   130
   I. 'We shall carry on this war to the end as a *Kulturvolk*': German Professors and 'the Civilised World'   131
   II. 'We are Europeans': America 'taken back into the fold'   136
   III. 'If not civilization, at least our civilization is at stake': The West according to 'the Zelig of twentieth-century politics'   139
   IV. Rabindranath Tagore on East and West   145
   V. Black America as the 'acid test for occidental civilization'   151
   VI. Thomas Mann's 'monstrous article'; and His *Reflections*   156
   VII. Conclusion   162

6 From 'Decline of the West' to 'Defence of the West': The Interwar Years and the Crisis of Civilisation   165
   I. *The Spengler Affair:* The Decline of the West   167
   II. From Harlem to Paris (via Berlin, Munich, and Luxor): Black Intellectuals and Western Civilisation   171
   III. 'Nordic' Supremacists and Responses to Them   175
   IV. *The Massis Affair:* Defence of the West   176
   V. German East-Mania after the Great War   181
   VI. Anglo-American Responses to Massis   182
   VII. 'Bis auf weiteres möchten wir Abendländer bleiben': German-Speaking Reactions to Massis, and Alternative Visions for Germany   186
   VIII. More Criticism of Massis; and Alternatives for Jazz-Age France   192
   IX. 'A new West, […] by an act of further creation'   194
   X. The Sufi Convert on East and West: René Guénon/ Abd al-Wāḥid Yaḥyá and Traditionalism   195
   XI. Defence of the West Continued: the 1930s and the Clouds of War   197
   XII. Conclusion   199

7	The Second World War and Ideas of 'the West'	202
	I. 'Western civilization will be saved.' Or Was 'the prevailing education [...] destroying it'?	203
	II. A 'tear for France'	206
	III. Guerres franco–françaises under Occupation: Civilisation européenne or Civilisation occidentale?	209
	IV. Europe between East and Extreme West: from Simone Weil to Albert Camus	212
	V. 'Pour l'alliance de l'Occident', or a 'Latin Empire'? Raymond Aron's versus Alexandre Kojève's Postwar Order	217
	VI. The Atlantic Community	220
	VII. When Peoples Meet: Alain Locke and 'the Achilles of the West'	221
	VIII. Conclusion	224
8	The Cold War and Its 'Wests'	227
	I. Lippmann's 'natural allies' and the Atlantic Community	229
	II. A 'spiritual consolidation of western civilization': Made in Britain	231
	III. 'It is twenty-five o'clock': Europe 'between the barbarians of the East and those of the West'?	233
	IV. '[T]o swing the spiritual balance in favor of the US': Henry Kissinger's '"Western" or "Occidental" civilization'	237
	V. The Gospel(s) according to Arnold Toynbee	242
	VI. 'Freunde, die Freiheit hat die Offensive ergriffen!' Those Who Said, 'I Choose the West'	247
	VII. Hannah Arendt and 'the famous "decline of the West"'	249
	VIII. Return to the Principles of Western Civilisation: Athens and Jerusalem	254
	IX. The 'true Westerner' par excellence: Raymond Aron's Cold War	257
	X. 'Last call [...] to the moral conscience of the West': Richard Wright, Empathetic Westerner 'ahead of the West'	261
	XI. The 'vitality of the so-transgressed Western ideals': James Baldwin's Parisian Encounters	275
	XII. 'Liberalism is the ideology of Western suicide.'	278

	XIII. Cultural versus Political West: Milan Kundera's and Czesław Miłosz's 'Kidnapped West'	280
	XIV. Post-mortem: Victorious America Conquered by Germania capta?	283
	XV. Conclusion	287
9	What Is 'the West' after the Cold War?	291
	I. 'The Triumph of the West, of the Western idea' according to Francis Fukuyama	292
	II. Professor Schlesinger's Reflections on a Multicultural Society	294
	III. Trotskyite (Critical) Defence of the West: Cornelius Castoriadis	298
	IV. 'The West Unique, Not Universal': Samuel Huntington and 'the Clash of Civilizations'	301
	V. '[A]uf die Seite des Westens': Jürgen Habermas, Heinrich August Winkler and the Western Wertegemeinschaft	307
	VI. American Anticivilisation versus All Civilisations? Huntingtonism after Huntington	314
	VII. A Tale of Three Speeches: Who Spoke Better in Warsaw— Bush or Trump?	318
	VIII. The End of the West, version Michel Houellebecq	325
	IX. Conclusion: What 'West' for the Post-Post-Cold War Era?	330
10	Conclusion: Words, Ideas, and Why They Matter	335
	I. Alternatives at the Gates?	339
	II. '[O]nly something which has no history can be defined.'	340
	III. Why Does Any of This Matter?	342
	IV. Classicists Bearing Gifts?	346
	V. What Is To Be Done?	350

Acknowledgements 357

Notes 363

Bibliography 409

Index 467

PREFACE

THE WEST PUZZLED me from an early age. I grew up in a village in Crete. I was seven when Turkey invaded Cyprus, in July 1974. Cyprus was an independent state. Crete, the other large-ish island in the eastern Mediterranean, was part of Greece. After the invasion, Greece went on a war footing and my father was mobilised. War between Greece and Turkey in relation to Cyprus seemed more than likely. Meanwhile, democracy was being restored in Greece after seven years of rule by vulgar military clowns. I needed to understand it all. There were no books whatsoever in our house. And my whole family were impeccably innocent of any educational influences. What had just happened made me both anxious and curious. I began to watch the news on television and to read serious newspapers. As other children noticed that I was hopeless at football but more and more immersed in politics, they nicknamed me 'the politician' (ο πολιτικός). As a result of that interest in politics I noticed that the man who had been flown back from exile in Paris late one night (in Valéry Giscard d'Estaing's presidential aeroplane), to take over as provisional prime minister, Constantinos Caramanlis, kept declaring in his speeches that 'we belong to the West'. I began to wonder what that meant—and why on earth it was so important. For it was contested by opposition politicians, who argued that 'the West' was responsible for what had happened in Cyprus.

As I grew older, meanwhile, I acquired new nicknames. One of them was 'Mustafa'—because of my keenness to dance to a song of that name (known to me in at least three versions). I was told that I was good at belly-dancing and I most certainly enjoyed dancing to Middle Eastern music. Did that make me 'Eastern'? But then, I was passionately in agreement with the aforementioned prime minister when he tried, and managed, in 1981, to make Greece the tenth member of the EEC, which was a clearly 'Western' group of countries, from Ireland to West Germany and Italy. Surely that meant that Greece was 'Western', as a member of both NATO (which it had joined in 1952) and the European Community of Western European democracies?

But was it that simple? There were other things, besides the political alignment of the country in Cold-War Europe. My paternal grandfather had been born before Crete joined Greece in 1913 (when the island was autonomous but still under the suzerainty of the Ottoman Empire). He would occasionally refer to himself as Roman ('Romios'). That was the way Greeks in the Ottoman Empire (which in turn called them 'Rum') self-identified. They saw themselves as the descendants of the conquered Greek-speaking, Orthodox Christian, Eastern Roman Empire, with its capital in Constantinople, the New Rome. It was the 'Eastern' Roman Empire, and the Church in which I was baptised was the 'Eastern' Greek Orthodox Church. Its doctrine was obviously Christian and to that extent very close to that of churches further west, but its chants and music sound unmistakeably 'Eastern'. So too does the Cretan folk music I grew up with.

Meanwhile, I was taught at school—a lot—about ancient Greek history, philosophy, literature and art, Athenian democratic politics and how they affected Europe and the West. Growing up in Crete, I was also taught, of course, about the 'Minoan' civilisation that predated the Greeks. And according to ancient Greek mythology, it was to Crete that Zeus took Europa—the Europa after whom a continent was named. But it would be much later that I would realise, among other things, how important Minoan Crete would become for Afro-American and Asian thinkers and activists in the early twentieth century, as the crucial link mediating between Egyptian, Phoenician and Greek cultures. As a glance at the map can remind one, Crete lies at the intersection between three continents in the eastern Mediterranean.

To be Greek was to inhabit a complex mix of heritages. Later, as I studied at university, first in Athens and later at University College London, there came the historiography and political thought I was studying, enjoying and admiring. At some point John Stuart Mill and other major modern political thinkers entered my life and thoughts. They and their ways of thinking were 'Western'. Did I have to choose between being Western and being Eastern? Were these self-contained entities with different essences, or were they just words, sweeping generalisations, or at least changeable, flexible narratives? Could one have multiple identities, or did one have to choose? The matter was ... well, existential. All these questions—and many others—are both raised and, I hope, answered in this book. I have asked a great number of highly sophisticated women and men who have reflected on related questions what they thought of these issues and dilemmas, and their answers are in the following pages.

This book may well challenge more or less everything the reader thought about the idea of the West. It will certainly surprise those who thought that 'it' always existed, or at least existed 'from Plato to NATO'. But it will meanwhile challenge the assumptions of those who thought that it must have emerged after World War II with the onset of the Cold War. It will also surprise those with more specialist knowledge, who have read in the extant scholarly literature that the idea of the West emerged in the West in the 1890s or thereabouts. It will most certainly give second thoughts to those who assumed that the idea of the West emerged in juxtaposition to Asia, or Islam. It will also present a challenge to those who thought (and have been told routinely in the academic literature) that the idea of the West arose to cater to the needs of high imperialism. Such readers will certainly be intrigued to read of the extent to which the first explicit and thorough articulation of the idea of the West emerged as part of a staunchly anti-imperialist theory and political programme. Similar surprises await those who take for granted that the idea of the West inherently involves adherence to liberal democracy, rights, individualism and the like. The book will also take issue with the impressions of those who take for granted that the idea of the West had Anglo-America at its core and is simply an extension of the so-called Anglosphere. As T. S. Eliot put it, the West is 'a subject about which everyone thinks he has something to say'. And this book is likely not to conform to existing preconceptions about what constitutes it. It is not a history of the West, but rather a history of what many different people have understood 'the West' to be. That is, however, an important history.

The book endeavours to reconstruct the history of when, how, and why 'the West' emerged as a sociopolitical concept, to what uses it has been put in the two centuries since its emergence, how many different things it has meant, and what the implications and repercussions of each of the different meanings are. The task is daunting, for the meanings and uses have been many and diverse. But I can at least say with confidence that no work exists that remotely matches this one in terms of tracing the many different uses of the concept, connecting them to their respective historical contexts, and analysing the significant implications and consequences of each of them. If this book provokes others to come up with more meanings and uses, or with better analyses of their respective contexts of emergence, then it will have fulfilled its ambition of alerting readers to the inadequacy of our current understanding of a long, complex and certainly fascinating story.

I have made a deliberate decision to avoid 'academese', including extensive methodological discussions. They are very important, and I have played my own small part in inflicting them on hundreds of intelligent and patient MA students for the best part of the last two decades. But I think the reader would hardly wish this book to be any longer than it is already. And there are others who have written on these methodological questions with much more authority and eloquence than I can ever aspire to. The reader will glean my methodological approaches through the result. Meanwhile, there is an important argument that many of the methodological writings stress about the importance of the uses of language in politics: words do matter; and re-descriptions and redefinitions of words to mean what the user (speaker, author) may wish them to mean can help people win arguments in debates, and followers in political and ideological battles. I fully subscribe to the validity of this argument, and this book will contribute a striking example of why and how words matter, and hence of why not letting others own or monopolise the meanings of words matters. Precisely for this reason, a good history is needed.

Author's Note on Quotations

For quoted passages, where reference is not given to a published translation in English, translations from French, German, Greek (ancient and modern) or Turkish are my own. Italic emphasis in quotations follows the original in cases where it is not indicated in an endnote as added.

THE WEST

1

Introduction

'THE WEST'

'Only where the word for the thing has been found is the thing a thing [...;] the word alone gives being to the thing.'

MARTIN HEIDEGGER, 'THE NATURE OF LANGUAGE', P. 62

'Words are not definitions of the meanings to which they refer. The meanings of the words cannot be discovered by simply knowing their etymologies.'

ZIYA GÖKALP, *THE PRINCIPLES OF TURKISM*, P. 298

THIS IS A HISTORY of the idea of the West. It does not purport to be a history of 'the West' per se. It does not take for granted any unit in history or part of the world as being 'the West' and study 'its' history. Instead, the book first seeks to understand when, how and why the term 'the West' came to be used to refer to a social or political entity based on cultural commonality. It then follows the many and often surprising changes in the uses and meanings of the term, and the different intentions and important repercussions related to contested uses, definitions and membership lists.

I take issue with two different extreme positions. There are those who assume that people have always talked of 'the West' as a civilisational and sociopolitical concept (or at least, have done so since the time of the ancient Greeks or the Romans) and hence take the term and its meaning to be more or less eternal. A recent example (among many) of how an East–West distinction is projected onto ancient Greek texts can be observed in the following instance of translation: 'πῶς εἶπας; οὐ γὰρ πᾶν στράτευμα βαρβάρων περᾷ τὸν Ἕλλης πορθμὸν Εὐρώπης ἄπο;' This has been translated as, 'What do you mean? Hasn't the whole of the Eastern army crossed back from Europe over the straight of Helle?'[1] Aeschylus wrote 'barbarian army'. The reader of the translation is told that he wrote 'the Eastern army'. The two words do not mean the same thing, and Aeschylus would as likely have called 'barbarian' an army coming from west of Greece as any from the east. Through an anachronistic translation, however, a distinction from an 'East' is projected, and an entirely unwarranted sense of Aeschylus's own 'Westernness' is assumed. No wonder it can still be asserted in a serious (and otherwise fascinating) recent book that 'Athens saw in itself a West opposed to the despotic Persian East'.[2]

There are also those who argue, by contrast, as Kwame Anthony Appiah recently did, that 'the very idea of the "West", to name a heritage and object of study, doesn't really emerge until the 1880s and 1890s, during a heated era of imperialism'.[3] As we will see, Appiah follows the now established scholarly orthodoxy with regard to the timing of the emergence of the idea of the West. Both approaches described above are flawed. I will establish both the correct timing and the reasons behind the emergence of the idea of 'the West' in the modern world. But that will be only the beginning of this book's contribution to the subject. The full intellectual history of the idea of the West that I pursue here permits both its current plethora of meanings and its potential for future meanings to be brought to the fore. The majority of current theories as to when 'the West' began and what it is can be shown to be emphasising, selectively, disproportionately and often polemically, only particular layers of the different meanings of the concept during its protracted history. By the end, this book will have produced a variety of recommendations for the present and future, arising from its critical study of the long journey traced in these pages.

The book distinguishes between 'the West' and 'Europe'—partially overlapping concepts, but by no means identical. Indeed, it shows that the use of 'the West' emerged precisely from the need to avoid the confusing or unwanted consequences of the use of 'Europe', as perceived by those who began deliberately to employ and promote the alternative term. For, from the 1820s and 1830s, 'the West' was beginning to be employed more and more frequently, and for a particular reason: that is, the elephant, or rather the bear, in the room at the Congress of Vienna—Russia. The standard distinction within Europe until the eighteenth century had been between North and South. Russia was, since it joined the 'European' system under Peter the Great, a 'Northern' power. That began to change in the couple of decades following the end of the Napoleonic wars. Most of those who would begin talking of Russia as 'Eastern' after the Congress of Vienna were invoking its Easternness in order to defend themselves against Russian domination of Europe, by creating a new, 'Western' alliance against what they saw as the Russian menace.

The persistence of the importance of Russia for the idea of the West is one of the themes that the *longue durée* approach of this book will allow me to highlight. There were of course various 'others' against whom the peoples now seen as 'the West' collectively defined themselves at different stages, or even, often, simultaneously. But to all these different 'others' (Arabs, Ottomans, indigenous Americans, Islam, China, India, Africa; to name but a few) it was, until the early nineteenth century, still possible, and common practice, to juxtapose 'Europe' or 'Christendom' as the unit or identity encompassing those who observed or opposed them. It was only when a differentiation was deemed necessary in opposition to 'others' who could also be called Christian, and part of Europe, that the need for a novel concept arose: hence the need for the invocation of 'the West', vis-à-vis the Eastern Roman (later baptised 'Byzantine') Greek Orthodox Christians, first, and Orthodox Russia subsequently. And it was this latter distinction, vis-à-vis Russia, that resulted in the modern idea of the West.

I show that, after some early attempts by others in the 1820s and 1830s, it was the French philosopher Auguste Comte and his successors who first consciously and systematically made such a choice. (That, far from 'the West' being invented in the 1880s–1890s to cater to the needs of British imperialism, as current scholarship tends to argue, Comte's 'Western Republic' was designed in the 1840s to abolish all empires of conquest and be an altruistic peaceful federation, is one of the many interesting twists in the story). Comte's Positivists were explicit that 'Europe' was confusing, because it included Russia, and hence a different name was needed. So was Oswald Spengler, when he argued, seven decades later, that the word 'Europe' ought to be struck out of history, because it had led people to associate Russia with the West in an utterly baseless unity.

But there were other agendas as well. For many French authors and politicians, a major factor was fear of German ascendancy (and already in the 1730s, Montesquieu was noting that 'France is no longer in the middle of Europe; it is Germany').[4] That fear intensified with the rise of Prussia and subsequently with German unification in 1871. Such anxieties led to recurring attempts by French (and Francophile) authors to promote an idea of a 'West' that put France at its centre—as opposed to a 'Europe' whose centre would inevitably be Germany. I analyse many such instances in this book (including even within German-occupied and Vichy-governed France during World War II).

Meanwhile, intra-German debates as to the meaning of 'the West' and whether Germany was part of it have been long and fascinating. Thomas Mann was not untypical when, in his 1918 *Betrachtungen eines Unpolitischen* (*Reflections of a Nonpolitical Man*), he proclaimed Germany and its *Kultur* to represent the eternal 'protest' and resistance to the universalising/homogenising tendencies of Rome and then of 'the West'. Much was to change after systematic Westernisation efforts following World War II. The German Federal Republic's *Westbindung* has had many valiant defenders, including Jürgen Habermas, Ralf Dahrendorf and Heinrich August Winkler. (Meanwhile, however, the fact that the members of Patriotische Union—arrested in December 2022 for plotting a coup d'état to subvert the Federal Republic and restore the German Reich—evoked, as Thomas Mann had done, the Battle of the Teutoburg Forest [9 CE], when Germanic Hermann/Arminius defeated the Roman legions, may mean that the idea of German 'protest', against 'the West', the EU or the modern world, has not completely disappeared.)

The book also analyses the alternatives proposed in each phase of the story. These have involved various proposals for the unity of 'Europe' rather than 'the West', and often included Russia in that Europe. For a while—very briefly—Russia was even included in what was meant by 'the West'. Such an exception lasted for a handful of years, during and immediately after the Second World War. The Soviet Union, as an indispensable ally and then a crucial contributor to victory, was then widely talked of as part of 'Western civilisation'. The onset of the Cold War as of 1947 changed all that very fast. And for the bulk of the past two centuries, Russia—imperial, Soviet, or post-Soviet—has not been considered part of the West, within the West, but rather as the 'other'. Thus, in the overwhelming majority of cases 'the West' was used in contradistinction to Russia, while it usually included some Slavic-speaking countries but not others. The list of the latter varied, but a country almost always included as 'Western' was Poland. This book's long-term approach allows it to highlight the importance of constantly recurring themes such as the role assigned to Poland and other Central or Eastern European countries as 'Western' and as ramparts of the West against 'Eastern' Russia. During the Cold War they could be seen as a 'kidnapped West', as Milan Kundera famously put it. Meanwhile the role of Eastern or Central European (including some Russian-born) thinkers and émigrés in definitions and understandings of 'the West' is one of the major themes throughout the book: from the relentless activism of Polish refugees such as Adam Czartoryski and many others in London, Paris and German lands in the 1830s to the impact in more recent times of Czesław Miłosz and many others in Paris, London and the USA. And one of the themes in the concluding chapter will be that of how definitions and membership of 'the West' have been reassessed, since February 2022, to consider Ukraine, and the potential for future redefinitions.

I. The West, 'from Plato to NATO'?

The concept of 'the West' was not used by Plato, Cicero, Locke, Mill and other canonised figures of what is today called the 'Western' tradition. While 'west' pertaining to geographical location is as old as any language, use of 'the West' to refer to a sociopolitical concept or a political association based on cultural commonality is relatively modern. (I am referring to uses of 'the West' as a sociopolitical category rather than to whether or not there was an east–west orientation in people's geographical consciousness. The latter was the case in Greek and Roman antiquity, when 'from Cadiz to the Ganges' was the usual way of speaking of the whole *oikoumenê*.[5] But by the early modern era, and emphatically throughout the eighteenth century, it was a distinction between North and South that dominated people's mental horizons).

There were of course earlier uses of the word in different senses, that were later to be co-opted as historical antecedents of modern identities. For 'the West' came to be employed as of 395 CE to describe the Western Roman Empire, once the Empire was divided between the two sons of Emperor Theodosius. But the Western Empire collapsed not long afterwards, conquered by Germanic so-called 'barbarians'. Later, as of 800 CE, the empire of Charlemagne claimed to be the successor to the Roman Empire. However, there was already in existence another Roman empire, the part of the two earlier-divided entities that had not been conquered by Germanic invaders, with its capital in Constantinople. That it was briefly (797–802) headed by a woman (Irene of Athens) was used in an attempt to delegitimise that empire. But success in this was limited, not least when she was succeeded by a man. At best, Charlemagne's empire could only call the Eastern Roman Empire of Constantinople the 'Greek' empire, and claim the mantle of the Roman Empire of the West. Charlemagne's empire thus began to be referred to as 'the Empire of the West', or, simply, 'the West'. By the eleventh century, with a definitive schism occurring between the churches of Rome and Constantinople, 'West' could also refer to the Latin (Catholic) Church as opposed to the 'Eastern' Greek Orthodox Church. The different (and limited) meanings of such earlier uses can be found in dictionaries in their entries for 'the West', 'l'Occident' or 'das Abendland' (and the differences between the very short entry 'L'Occident' in the eighteenth-century *Encyclopédie*, written by its co-editor d'Alembert himself, and the much longer entry in Larousse's dictionary of 1866–79 are telling as to when the concept began to acquire its sociopolitical meanings).[6]

These earlier uses, though they may have provided the word with useful historical antecedents for later adoption through elective affinities, do not amount

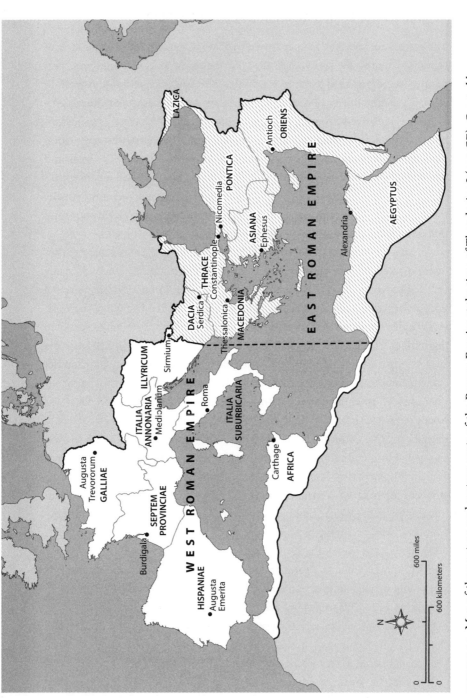

FIGURE 1.1. Map of the western and eastern parts of the Roman Empire at the time of Theodosius I (379 CE). Created by NeimWiki. *Source:* https://commons.wikimedia.org/wiki/File:4KTHEODOSIAN.png

to the same concept as 'the West' of today. According to Martin Lewis and Kären Wigen, '[t]he East–West division is many centuries old, and has had at least three distinct referents'. The first of these—'[t]he original and persistent core of the West', is said always to have been 'Latin Christendom, derived ultimately from the Western Roman Empire—with (ancient) Greece included whenever the search for origins goes deeper'. Thus 'the most significant historical divide across Europe was that separating the Latin church's *Europa Occidens* from the Orthodox lands of the Byzantine and Russian spheres'. As for the 'second referent', it arose as a result of the European expansion and diaspora from the sixteenth to nineteenth centuries, when 'divisions within European Christendom began to recede in importance' and instead 'the idea of a supra-European West, encompassing European settler colonies across the Atlantic, increasingly took hold'. The authors add that '[t]his sense of an expanded West was greatly strengthened after World War II'.[7] Now, it is a sweeping leap from the medieval division between Western Catholic and Eastern Orthodox Christians to the 'expanded West [...] after World War II'; and, while it may be broadly true that 'the idea of a supra-European West, encompassing European settler colonies across the Atlantic, increasingly took hold', the questions then arise of when, why and how exactly this came about. It may seem to us now obvious that, once the New World had been discovered, some term or concept like 'the West' would be invented; but was it indeed inevitable? And if so, was it equally inevitable that that particular name should be adopted? In this book I explore the when, the why and the how of this, and what the alternatives were. For no matter how much sense it may make to us, retrospectively, it did not occur to people in the newly independent United States to talk of themselves as part of a 'West' that included themselves and the Western Europeans. And it did not occur to Western Europeans to talk of themselves and their cousins in the New World as 'the West' until well into the nineteenth century. This book begins by tracing the crucial missing links between the medieval Catholic *Europa Occidens* and 'the idea of a supra-European West, encompassing European settler colonies across the Atlantic'.

There were many uses of the term 'the West' in the eighteenth century and in the early decades of the nineteenth century. But in almost all cases, with variations of greater or lesser inconsistency, authors were using 'the West' either in purely geographical terms, or as a historical term, when discussing previous centuries of European history, in reference to the Western Roman Empire and its successor states in the same geographical area. But that was not 'the West' as understood today. It was a historical use, not a term describing a politico-cultural community in the present or a programme for a common future.

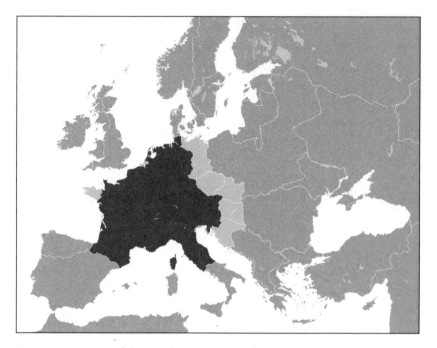

FIGURE 1.2. A map of the Carolingian Empire (a.k.a. Francia; the Frankish Empire) within Europe, ca. 814 CE. Created by Alphathon. *Source:* https://upload.wikimedia.org/wikipedia/commons/thumb/6/66/Francia_814.svg/1920px-Francia_814.svg.png

This latter use began to emerge gradually from the 1820s in the writings especially of French and German thinkers—though still interchangeably with 'Europe'. The deliberate substitution of 'the West' for 'Europe' was then made for the first time explicitly and thoroughly (too thoroughly, in exasperating detail) in the voluminous writings of the French philosopher Auguste Comte (1798–1857). We can follow in Comte's writings the gradual abandonment of 'Europe'—which he employed in his earlier works—and its replacement by 'the West', as well as his reasons for consciously deciding that a new term was needed: because 'Europe' was too confusing for what he was describing (as well as prescribing).

To put it simply, for now, let us go back to Lewis and Wigen's first two referents: the Latin church's *Europa Occidens*, and a 'supra-European West, encompassing European settler colonies across the Atlantic'. Wishing to propose a particular reorganisation for the latter, Comte decided that the name of the former would suit his proposed new entity, and the specific identity he wanted to cultivate for it, much better than the available alternatives, 'Europe' or 'Christendom'. (Typical was the title of Novalis's essay of 1799, 'Christianity or Europe.')[8] Up to, and during, his own time, when people wanted to talk about both sides of the Atlantic, they talked of 'Christendom', or 'the civilised world'. Meanwhile, for Americans themselves, 'the West' meant something different, located on their shifting frontier. In Europe 'the West' was available as a historical term to refer to the Western Roman Empire or Charlemagne's later empire, but—casual instances here and there notwithstanding—it had not been explicitly or consistently adopted to describe a clearly defined contemporary and future sociopolitical entity until Comte chose to promote its use in this sense assiduously; indeed, relentlessly.

Before we go into more detail as to how these changes came about, it should be noted that some fascinating definitions of, and debates about, 'the West' are to be found among thinkers and writers in China, Korea, Japan, India, Turkey or Russia. However, my focus here is upon 'the West' as a self-description: 'the West's West'. When, and why, did thinkers and writers in the core of what others saw as 'the West'—France, Britain, the German lands and America—start referring to such an entity and calling it 'the West'? For most of their history the peoples now retrospectively seen as constituting the West referred to themselves by other terms—latterly 'Christendom', 'Europe', or 'the civilised nations'. And yet it is commonplace to find self-styled histories of 'the idea of the West' anachronistically projecting what nineteenth- or twentieth-century thinkers and historians co-opted as their preferred collective past and referring to it as 'the West', no matter what the self-identifications of the earlier people concerned might have been. (This is often referred to as the 'from Plato to NATO' narrative.)[9] That said, when the ideas of people from outside 'the West' become involved in or impinge upon debates and definitions within it, these will be analysed in the relevant parts of this book. Thus, in some of the chapters that follow we will consider too some highly interesting Russian, Greek, Turkish, Indian, Caribbean, African, Chinese and Japanese contributions to the discussion.

II. A Russian Import, or a Substitute for 'Whiteness'?

There are a very few works that do not succumb to anachronistic accounts such as those I complain of above, and instead try to study the actual uses of 'the West' historically. But even these still fail to trace the concept's history accurately. Thus, it has been repeatedly asserted that the first sustained elaboration of 'the West' as a politico-cultural entity was that found in books published by the British Social Darwinist thinker Benjamin Kidd in 1894 and 1902. Moreover, some of the scholars in question attribute the emergence of the idea of the West to causes that may indeed have conduced to an expansion in its uses, but by no means account for its emergence, as they argue. One such claim was made, influentially, by Christopher GoGwilt, who maintained that '[t]he idea of the West has a recent history, emerging around the turn of the [twentieth] century from the combined and related phenomena of European imperial expansion and the crisis of democratic politics'. In trying to explain 'the shift from a European to a Western identity', GoGwilt, besides attributing that shift to the needs of imperialism, also asserted that it was the Russian debates between Slavophiles and Westernisers, most notably as of the 1860s, that decisively influenced the self-descriptions of Western Europeans in the following decades, and led to their adoption of the term 'the West' in place of 'Europe'.[10] According to GoGwilt, it was 'only relatively recently—between the 1880's and the 1920's—that formulations of "the West" came to mean a relation between a structure of international political power, an imagined cultural identity, and a discrete historical development within world history'. GoGwilt is in no doubt that he has an explanation for 'the invention of the West': 'With both Toynbee and Spengler there is good reason to emphasize [. . .] the deciding factor of the Bolshevik revolution of 1917 in determining the boundaries—both political and historical—of "the West."' Thus he argues that '[r]eaction to the Bolsheviks crystallized an idea of the West that had, already since the 1880's, begun to emerge from responses to Russian ideas'.[11]

A similar claim about the importation of the concept of 'the West' from Russian debates was advanced by Peggy Heller.[12] Her argument is, *prima facie*, most appealing. It corresponds with our wish 'to be open to the possibility that "non-Western" discourse is contributive as well as derivative'.[13] It is, however, misleading as far as the emergence of the modern concept of the West is concerned. The Russian debates of the mid-nineteenth century in which, it is claimed, the concept of 'the West' finds its origin, were themselves heavily influenced by Western European thought.[14] Moreover, the very thinker taken in recent scholarship to have initiated the use of 'the West' (that was then to permeate the later fierce debates between Westernisers and Slavophiles), Petr [Peter] Chaadaev (1794–1856),[15] was clearly strongly influenced by French philosophy and philosophy of history (not least by de Bonald, Balanche, de Maistre, Chateaubriand and Lamennais).[16] Chaadaev was also following François Guizot in his main argument about the causes of Russian stagnation and about the family resemblance of 'the European peoples'. (Guizot's *History of Civilisation in Europe* had been published in 1828, the year before Chaadaev's 'First Philosophical Letter' was written.)[17]

Use of 'the West' was not, then, Chaadaev's invention, to be succeeded by the Slavophiles-versus-Westerisers debates, and then exported to the West, as Heller has claimed (and others have followed her in asserting).[18] Chaadaev, besides the impact of his own sojourn in Western Europe, was deeply influenced by the Catholic thinker Joseph de Maistre (1753–1821), whom he had probably met in person when de Maistre lived in St Petersburg.[19] For de Maistre spent fourteen years (1803–17) in Russia as ambassador of the Kingdom of Piedmont-Sardinia, and had reflected and written extensively on the differences of Russia and its Orthodox Church from Western Europe.[20] In his book *Du pape*, whose manuscript he had completed whilst in Russia, and then published in 1819, de Maistre used the terms *Occident* and *les Occidentaux* extensively. (In just one of many such instances he complained as follows, in the last chapter of the book, of the modern Greece that he expected was about to emerge: 'It styles itself *the East*, whilst as regards the real East, it is only a point of the West, and to us it is scarcely visible.').[21]

In fact, there was another, unnoticed, Russian (or at any rate Orthodox) connection, much earlier than Chaadaev's 'Letter'. De Maistre was clear in his correspondence that he wrote Book 4 of *Du pape*, where most of his references to '*l'Occident*' occur, as the 'anti-Stourdza', as he put it. Alexander Stourdza, son of a Moldovan father and descended on his mother's side from a Constantinople Greek aristocratic ('Phanariot') family, was an adviser to the Russian czar. In 1816 he published, in French, a book on the doctrine and the spirit of the Orthodox Church.[22] The book had been written at the request of Czar Alexander I, who paid 20,000 rubles for its publication.[23] Among other things, Stourdza's book was intended as a deterrent to Catholic conversion temptations (promoted by de Maistre whilst an ambassador in St Petersburg) in Russian high society. It was vehemently critical of Catholicism, 'l'église d'Occident', 'l'Occident' and 'les Occidentaux'. Among other accusations, Stourdza claimed that 'the blind hatred of the barbarians of the West' (la haine aveugle des barbares de l'Occident) had contributed to the fall of the Eastern Roman or Byzantine Empire. De Maistre felt obliged to respond; hence the passionately anti-Eastern Church and particularly anti-Greek tone of Book 4 of *Du pape*. In his correspondence he had explicitly noted the East–West division highlighted by Stourdza and the anti-Western language the latter had employed. Referring to Stourdza he wrote that '[a] man whom I esteem immensely, who belongs to Greece by birth [...] has just published against the Catholic Church a work written with remarkable bitterness'. For example, he went on, 'to express [...] our well-known incapacity in any kind of science, he calls us the SIMPLE-MINDED Westerners.'[24] All this does not mean that 'the West' was 'invented' by Stourdza either, of course. The ecclesiastical distinction between Eastern and Western Christian churches was centuries old, and the Greek Orthodox spoke of 'Western' 'Franks' long before Stourdza or de Maistre.[25]

In any case, the novelty of Chaadaev's use of 'the West' has been greatly exaggerated. Although he did use the term in the 'First Philosophical Letter' (written in 1829 and first published in Russia in 1836), it was employed interchangeably with 'Europe', and the terms 'Europe' and 'European' were used vastly more often than 'the West' in that text.[26] Others had done likewise long before him, in France in particular. Moreover, given that GoGwilt's argument is that it was the later debates (ignited by Chaadaev) between Westernisers and Slavophiles in Russia in the 1860s that first alerted Western thinkers to the potential of the term 'the West', it may not be out of place to mention that those Russian controversies were themselves very much influenced by French and German philosophers and debates. One of the strongest influences by then, moreover, was that of Auguste Comte, whose positivist philosophy was being widely discussed by the 1850s and 1860s and had been making converts in Russia for some decades prior to that. Besides Comte's claim later that he had been informed already in 1836 of the impact his ideas were having in Russia, we know that Valerian Maĭkov (1823–1847) had been promoting Comte's thought in Russia in the 1840s. His influence clearly had become very widespread by the late 1850s and 1860s, and continued spreading thereafter.[27] As I will show in the next chapter, Comte and his disciples had been elaborating upon and propagating his detailed definition and analysis of 'the West' for quite some time before the Russian debates of the 1860s and 1870s intensified. And he had no need of Russian predecessors to inspire him in the use of the term. Condorcet and de Maistre, as well as one of his favourite historians, Arnold Heeren, had done so much earlier, as had his erstwhile friends and collaborators, Henri de Saint-Simon himself and the Saint-Simonians.[28]

In saying all this, I am not suggesting that the debates between Slavophiles and Westernisers and the prodigious philosophical and literary output in nineteenth-century Russia had no influence in Western Europe, especially Germany, later in the nineteenth century and into the twentieth. (Nikolai Danilevsky's thought and its echoes in Oswald Spengler would be one of several examples, as we will see in chapter 6; and Czesław Miłosz was not necessarily exaggerating when he wrote that Dostoyevsky 'had an influence like none of his contemporaries, with the exception of Nietzsche, on the thinking of Europe and America'.)[29] But I am arguing that it is far from being the case that Chaadaev was the first author to use 'the West' in the sense the term acquired in the following two centuries. My claim is that Chaadaev himself had found uses of the term among French and German authors who wrote before him, and that it was available before he wrote his 'First Philosophical Letter'. Thus the early cases of uses of 'l'Occident' that we will discuss in chapter 2, by people such as—to name but a couple of examples—Benjamin Constant in 1825 or Dominique de Pradt in 1822, 1823, 1824, 1825 and 1828, did not owe anything to a piece that Chaadaev wrote in 1829 and which was not published until 1836.

Another argument regarding the emergence of the idea of the West has been contributed by the geographer Alastair Bonnett, who agrees with GoGwilt's assertion that the first sustained elaboration of 'the West' as a politico-cultural entity was that of Benjamin Kidd, and then attributes the emergence of the idea at that time to the impasses into which 'narratives of racial whiteness' had run. Thus, according to Bonnett, 'the West, in the West, emerged in the context of the inadequacies and contradictions of a more racially explicit discourse' between 1890 and 1930.[30] Again, this may be an interesting contribution to explaining the increase in the employment of the term, but by no means establishes the origin of the idea of the West in English, let alone in 'the West' more generally. As I will show in chapter 3, sustained elaborations of 'the West' in English had been supplied by Comte's British disciples for some decades before Kidd (himself steeped in Comte)[31] wrote the works that Bonnett focuses upon.

The periodisation proposed by GoGwilt and Bonnett, and the claim that '[t]he category of "the West" or "the Western world" [...] does not appear [...] before the 1890s', were also adopted recently by Jürgen Osterhammel, who references Bonnett specifically.[32] Similarly, Arthur Herman, speaking of 'Arnold Toynbee, Oswald Spengler, Benjamin Kidd, or any number of other gloomy prognosticators' in the first decades of the twentieth century, claimed that those very writers, 'in fact, had *originally coined* the term "Western" to describe a faltering European civilization that, they believed, was steadily fading away'.[33] Much more recently, Naoíse Mac Sweeney has stated that 'the rise of the West as a concept, and the invention of its history as Western Civilisation, was at the outset [...] an ideological tool deployed in the service of empire'; and as we have already seen, Kwame Anthony Appiah has also argued that 'the very idea of the "West," to name a heritage and object of study, doesn't really emerge until the 1880s and 1890s, during a heated era of imperialism'.[34]

III. A Gradual Growth, Consummated in Paris, rue Monsieur-le-Prince

I take issue with the assertions cited above, and will show that the use of the idea of the 'West' to name 'a heritage and an object of study', as well as an elaborate and detailed political project, arose much earlier in the nineteenth century and in a very different historical and intellectual context—with different causes, intentions and implications. As should be clear by now, I make no claim that there was but one idea of the West, fully articulated at some point by a single individual. My endeavour is rather to study different uses of 'the West', the intentions with which the relevant ideas and terms have been employed, and the implications in each case.[35] But certain steps and contributions were nevertheless decisive. There have been related myths, such as the tradition of *translatio imperii*, or heliotropic myth (the notion that human beings and their civilisation are involved in the movement of the sun from east to west), with its origins in the early Christian era, when the linear theory of historical progression replaced the cyclical theory of the ancients.[36] Use of 'the West' to describe the Western Roman Empire, or the Latin (Catholic) Church as opposed to the Greek ('Eastern') Orthodox Church remained significant, too. But these differed greatly from what 'the West' came to mean in the nineteenth and twentieth centuries.

'The West' as a potential political entity based on civilisational commonality is a modern idea that arose in the first half of the nineteenth century. I will show in chapter 2 that, after some incipient uses of 'the West' by various authors in the 1820s and 1830s, the first elaborate articulation of such a concept was provided by Auguste Comte, writing reclusively in his rue Monsieur-le-Prince flat in Paris.[37] Before then, and still in the eighteenth and much of the early nineteenth century, the terms 'Christendom' or 'Europe' were those used in the main to self-identify a cluster of like-minded peoples who wished to differentiate themselves from the rest of the world. One book that arguably influenced the historical imagination decisively for some decades was François Guizot's *Histoire de la civilisation en Europe*, first published in 1828 and translated into several languages. Besides contributing a highly influential definition of 'civilisation', it offered an equally influential argument as to what had made the civilisation of Western Europe 'steadily progressive' for the past fifteen centuries, since the fall of the Western Roman Empire.[38] Guizot was talking of the history and civilisation of the very part of the world—Western Europe—that constituted the core of what would soon, with increasing frequency, be referred to as 'the West'. But he used what was then (and would continue to be for some more time) the standard name for it, 'Europe', and called its civilisation 'European civilisation'. (Meanwhile, in 1851, the Spanish Catholic thinker Donoso Cortés's main complaint against Guizot's book was that the French Protestant historian ought to have acknowledged that it had been 'the Church alone' that 'had made it one' and 'gave it its essential character'. Hence, Donoso Cortés argued, 'it was and is called Catholic civilisation.')[39].

FIGURE 1.3. Auguste Comte. Lithograph by Johan Hendrick Hoffmeister, known as the 'Dutch portrait' (*portrait hollandais*), from a daguerreotype of 1849 (Den Haag, 1851). Maison d'Auguste Comte collection, Paris. *Source:* https://commons.wikimedia.org/wiki/File:Auguste_Comte.jpg

There have in fact been various versions of the 'from east to west' tradition previously mentioned. The best known is the formulation by Georg Wilhelm Friedrich Hegel, who wrote that '[w]orld history travels from east to west; for Europe is the absolute end of history, just as Asia is the beginning'.[40] Yet 'west' was used in a geographical sense here, and it was 'Europe' that was claimed to constitute the culmination of history in the very same sentence. As Alastair Bonnett correctly remarked, 'despite elaborating at length on the Oriental world,

Hegel had little to say about the West as a unity'. Thus Hegel 'had scant interest in developing an explicit or overarching sense of Western identity' (though he did have strong views on what he called 'the Germanic World', as the group of nations that shaped modern Europe).[41] We will see in the next chapter that what has thus been remarked of Hegel cannot be said of Comte, who had rather a lot to say about the West as a unity, and a more than pronounced interest in developing an explicit and overarching sense of Western identity. He even coined a word for this latter: *occidentalité*. Comte's writings have been completely ignored in existing histories of 'the idea of the West'; yet, in what was the very core of what outsiders saw as 'the West', it was Comte and his followers who first adopted the term deliberately and programmatically in order to describe in great detail (as well as prescribe) a political entity, based on cultural commonality.

Before the nineteenth century, however, when people made distinctions *within* Europe it was decidedly a North–South division that prevailed.[42] By the eighteenth century, with people clear by then about the locations of the North and South poles, Edward Gibbon could confidently write (in 1790 or 1791) in the margin of his own famous book, 'The distinction of North and South is real and intelligible; and our pursuit is terminated on either side by the poles of the Earth. But the difference of East and West is arbitrary, and shifts round the globe.'[43] And such statements are redolent of a long tradition. In 1576, Jean Bodin was merely rehearsing, and summarising longstanding medieval theories when in his *Six Books of the Republic* he insisted that (and explained why) the North–South divide was much more significant than that between West and East.[44]

It cannot indeed be emphasised enough that the transitions (from 'Europe' to 'West' and from North–South to East–West distinctions) were not sudden, straightforward, coherent or unanimous.[45] The same Alexander Stourdza whom we saw making distinctions, in 1816, between East and West while focusing on the churches, their doctrines, and the historic grudges of post-Byzantine Greeks and Russians against 'les Occidentaux', would still refer to Russia as 'North' many years later in his memoirs.[46] In French writings, references to Russia as part of 'Northern Europe' continued to be very common well into the 1880s.[47] Similar attitudes were typical of British thinkers, too. When the former Saint-Simonist Gustave d'Eichthal sent his friend John Stuart Mill his book *Les Deux Mondes*, the two worlds alluded to in the title were *l'Orient* and *l'Occident*. And yet, so deeply ingrained in Mill's mind were the notions of Europe, 'European' and the north–south distinction that, in acknowledging receipt of the book he commented, '[Y]our views respecting the differences between the Oriental and the *European* character, seem to me perfectly just. I quite agree with you that an infusion of the Oriental character into that of the nations of *northern* Europe would form a combination very much better than either separately.'[48] Mill was typical. 'The West' and 'Western' were used rarely in English in the early to middle decades of the nineteenth century. Where 'West' and 'Western' might have been expected to feature *par excellence*, given the Crusading theme of the novel, in Disraeli's *Tancred*, the terms used most often to denote the antithesis of the East are mainly 'Christendom', and 'the north' or 'the northern tribes'.[49]

However, there was a difference in France, where *l'Occident* and *occidental/e* were used much more often than the equivalent terms in English. France had been at the heart of Charlemagne's 'Empire d'Occident' and thus the latter word was more familiar and available in French, being integral to what the French saw as their own history. Henry Laurens has argued that Nicolas de Condorcet was probably the first to use the term in its modern sense, at the end of the eighteenth century.[50] But this use was interchangeable with that of *l'Europe*, which appeared overwhelmingly more often than *l'Occident* in Condorcet's *Esquisse*.[51] It is also rewarding to pay close attention to exactly how and where 'the West' was used in this work. Almost all references appear in the parts of the essay dealing with 'the sixth epoch' and 'the seventh epoch',[52] concerning the fall of the Western Roman Empire ('the West') to the Germanic 'barbarians', and then the Crusades. More generally, the term is used primarily to distinguish between developments in the two parts of Europe at particular times in the past. Meanwhile, neither in the *Esquisse* nor in any of his writings directly dealing with America and its influence on Europe did Condorcet (though he was 'perhaps the most brilliant of all the Americanists')[53] refer to 'the West' in any sense that included both Europe and America.[54] Similarly, the term *Occident* appears only once in the whole third volume of Diderot's *Œuvres* (on *Politique*)—in his *Encyclopédie* entry on the Crusades, to distinguish the western Christian crusaders from their eastern Christian brethren. The term *Europe*, on the other hand, appears sixty-eight times, and *européen(s)* at least fourteen.[55]

Even earlier, Montesquieu had sometimes used *Occident* when the contradistinction was with the *Orient* and the person speaking was purportedly an Oriental—this was the case particularly in his epistolary novel *Lettres persanes* (*Persian Letters*).[56] However, that did not alter the fact that whenever he spoke of the supranational entity, culture or wider society that he lived in, he would call it 'Europe': 'A prince thinks he will be made greater by a neighboring State's ruin. On the contrary! Things in Europe are such that States depend on each other. France needs the opulence of Poland and Muscovy, just as Guyenne needs Brittany, and Brittany, Anjou. Europe is one State composed of many provinces.'[57] And the main distinction within 'Europe', was clear: 'In Europe, there is a sort of balance between the peoples of North and South.' The vast majority of eighteenth-century thinkers and writers would go on thinking and speaking in terms of North and South. Another characteristic example was the—highly influential—Johann Gottfried Herder (1744–1803). Some interesting instances occur in his 1774 *Auch eine Philosophie der Geschichte zur Bildung der Menschheit* ([Yet] another philosophy of history for the education of mankind), where such language was conspicuous.[58]

The most fascinating case in the eighteenth century, however, is probably that of Voltaire. Larry Wolff, whose *Inventing Eastern Europe* was an attempt to show that an idea of Eastern Europe was invented in the eighteenth century, was surely right in observing that '[n]o one held more tenaciously to the rubric of "the north" than Voltaire, who himself emptied the concept of its significance in discovering Eastern Europe'.[59] And that is characteristic more generally of the state of play in the eighteenth century. Many authors and travellers had begun to stress differences between what they called 'Europe', by which they usually meant (geographically) western, or north-western, Europe, and another 'Europe' to their east, that they considered alien, or at least insufficiently 'European'. They had not, however, come up with neologisms that would express in concrete terms the differences so inchoately conceived. Thus, Voltaire was typical in speaking constantly of 'North' and 'South' when he was dealing with Europe. He wrote a sympathetic history of the Russia of Peter the Great, celebrated Russia's advances in civilisation, and was notorious for flattering the empress Catherine the Great in their correspondence:[60] he was not likely to envisage and articulate a 'West' that would exclude Russia. (Meanwhile, Voltaire is unusual among eighteenth-century authors in another respect. He did use the words '*Occident*' and '*occidentaux*' extensively when he was differentiating between Western Europe, on the one hand, and China, the Arabs or the Ottoman Empire on the other. In making such distinctions most people in his century would differentiate rather between 'Europe' and 'the East'. Voltaire would do so as well at times, but he would also, quite often, use *Occident* rather than *Europe*.[61] In many such comparisons Voltaire was determined to highlight positively the cultural achievements of the Chinese in order to hit hard at Bible-centric, so-called universal histories.[62] And although some of his uses of *Occident* might be taken to be primarily geographical, in others a sense of civilisational commonality is implied.)[63]

Though Voltaire did not deviate from the standard categorisation of Russia as 'Northern', others would soon begin to do so. As we will see in the next chapter, references to Russia as 'oriental' or 'semi-Asiatic' were to intensify spectacularly in the early decades of the nineteenth century.

IV. This Book

In what follows, I will first (chapter 2) trace the gradual emergence of 'the West', particularly in continental European languages and writings, where it first started to be employed, during the nineteenth century—from its first more or less casual appearances in the 1810s, through the intensification of such uses, especially in juxtaposition to Russia in the 1820s and 1830s, to its omnipresence by the end of the century. A number of thinkers, especially writing in French or German, will be studied, with some excursions also into Russian and Greek authors and arguments. They include Arnold Hermann Ludwig Heeren; Mme [Germaine] de Staël; Henri de Saint-Simon and some Saint-Simonians, not least Gustave d'Eichthal and Michel Chevalier; Benjamin Constant; the abbé Dominique de Pradt; the Marquis [Astolphe] de Custine; Jakob Philipp Fallmerayer; Gustav Diezel; Friedrich Nietzsche; Aleksei Khomyakov; Markos Renieris; Auguste Comte; Émile Littré; and Pierre Laffitte. In the latter part of the chapter, I analyse in particular, and in detail, the writings of Comte, the French philosopher and founder of Positivism and sociology, and subsequently those of some of his French disciples. It was in an attempt to preserve the cultural coherence of the entity they were proposing (and for that reason primarily to exclude Russia from it) that Comte and then his followers insisted on the name 'the West'—*l'Occident*—as opposed to 'Europe'—which latter, to their chagrin, was seen as including Russia since the time of Peter the Great.

In chapter 3, we cross the English Channel to focus on when and how 'the West' began to be used in Britain. A brief pre-history identifying a few rare seventeenth- and eighteenth-century instances is followed by an analysis of the intensification of use that occurred as of the 1830s, and increasingly thereafter. Alternative (and sometimes contradictory) uses of the term, during a time of inchoate early meanings, are juxtaposed. Authors or politicians discussed in the chapter include John Milton, Francis Bacon, Thomas Hobbes, John Toland, Adam Smith, Oliver Goldsmith, Edward Gibbon, Thomas Arnold, Lord Palmerston, Henry Thomas Buckle, David Urquhart, Karl Marx, George Eliot (Mary Ann Evans), Harriet Martineau, Richard Monckton Milnes (Lord Houghton), Edward Augustus Freeman, Henry Maine, Richard Congreve, Frederic Harrison, F. S. Marvin, James Ramsay MacDonald, Benjamin Kidd and others. The bewilderment with which both translators and reviewers initially reacted to the neologism 'the West' when it was first promoted explicitly and vociferously by the British Comtists is underscored, with some striking examples. The crucial role of intellectual and cultural exchanges and interactions with continental Europe is highlighted.

Chapter 4 takes us on a transatlantic journey, to the United States—and back to Europe, from time to time, given how interconnected American culture was, during the nineteenth century, with European (not least German) universities. The peculiarities of America's situation are highlighted first. 'The West' meant something else in America, referring to its own ever-shifting western frontier and the ideas associated with those who lived there. And a strong sense of American exceptionalism and difference from European imperialistic and aristocratic states also prevented any notion of a transatlantic 'West' from emerging during the first decades of the American republic's existence. But things started to change as the nineteenth century advanced. Many thinkers are discussed who were important in the development of the concept of the 'West' in the sense of a transnational cultural and potentially political entity that included the Americas (or North America, at least), Europe (or at least Western and Central Europe) and other settler populations with a European core origin. The chapter makes the case that most of these thinkers were either themselves born and raised in Europe before they migrated to America, or were Americans who had studied in European, and particularly German, universities. Francis (formerly Franz) Lieber receives particular attention, precisely because of how explicit he became about the need for a distinct name for the group or civilisation in question, and his own assiduous attempts at defining it. There were a number of visions for the future of America in the nineteenth century and until the Great War, and most of these, until the late nineteenth century, posited an America that was born of principles different to those of the states of the Old World; hence its exceptionalism, rather than its commonality with Europe, tended to be stressed. There were others—fewer—who highlighted affinities with Europeans; and others still who sought to increase, celebrate and entrench those commonalities in people's consciousness. Nobody was a more ardent member of this last category than Francis Lieber; and given his multiple important roles in American intellectual life, his role is not a negligible one. It is very telling, meanwhile, that in 1853 and in 1859 he complained as explicitly as he did of the absence of a commonly agreed term to describe the civilisational grouping for whose existence he always argued, and which comprised the Europeans, the Americans and other peoples descended from European settlement.

Chapter 5 studies the crucial developments in the meanings and uses of 'the West' and 'Western civilisation' from the outbreak of the Great War in the summer of 1914 to the first phase of analysis of its repercussions at the time of the peace treaties in 1919. The 'war of words' between German academics and official propaganda and their counterparts in France, Britain and America was heated. But above and beyond the exploitation of words and concepts by the two sides in order to gain advantage, a number of contributions were articulated by both 'Western' and 'non-Western' people, who began to reconsider the very validity, as well as the actual meaning, of 'Western civilisation'. The chapter begins and ends with juxtapositions of German self-perceptions as bearers of a deeper 'culture' [*Kultur*] as against a superficial 'civilisation' [*Zivilisation*] that they saw as characteristic of their Western neighbours. Even if the manifestos of German academics for the purposes of the war effort were to be dismissed, the passionate outpourings of Thomas Mann in his wartime writings arguably had deeper roots, as well as an afterlife. German ambivalence about, and resistance to, 'the West' became major topics of discussion in France, Britain and in the (initially neutral) United States. During such discussions, some American commentators passionately pleaded for America to stop boasting about its exceptionalism and 'return to the fold' of Europe and its civilisation, with John Jay Chapman being the most vociferous among them. Meanwhile the most consequential advocate of America's alignment with the Entente allies in a 'Western' or 'Atlantic' community turned out to be the young Walter Lippmann. Undoubtedly the longer-term consequences of the Great War were game-changing. The unprecedented scale of its mechanised slaughter discredited the standing of 'civilisation', along with the related notion that 'Western civilisation' in particular was superior because it was technologically so advanced. The terrifying results of those technological advances as displayed during the war turned the tables for many, both within 'Western' countries and beyond. Something was wrong with Western civilisation as a whole, many thought, and the industrial-scale massacre that started in August 1914 was the most striking proof of that. Some of these critics came from colonised peoples, or from groups that felt marginalised in their own countries, not least in the United States. They were all inspired by Rabindranath Tagore's utterances during his widely publicised series of lectures on nationalism around the globe in 1916–17. And some serious rethinking began among Afro-American thinkers, from the beginning of the war. Of these, the chapter pays particular attention to the contributions of Alain Locke and W.E.B. Du Bois.

Chapter 6 analyses the consequences of these initial debates and challenges for the interwar period, which proved to be profound. The publication of Oswald Spengler's *Der Untergand des Abendlandes* (*The Decline of the West*), and its spectacular popularity in Germany and later elsewhere, both captured and further galvanised the *Zeitgeist*. Spengler came at the end of the Great War to say that not just defeated Germany, but the whole of the West (which, for him, included Germany), was already in its phase of decline. It had stopped being a living, organic 'culture', and had passed to the stage of a petrified 'civilisation'; it was thus inexorably on its way to being superseded by another culture eventually (probably the Slavic). The debates and reactions Spengler's thesis generated were immense. It also provoked, in 1927, a vociferous and sustained response from the pen of the French conservative Catholic intellectual Henri Massis, *La Defense de l'Occident*. Already before the publication of his book, Massis had been writing articles advancing the idea that Germany and Russia were not parts of 'the West', but rather semi-Asiatic Trojan horses posing lethal threats to it. Massis defined the West as Mediterranean, inspired by classical Greece and Rome, and Catholic—and, needless to say, with France as its core. The chapter will follow the impressive diffusion of Massis's ideas in many countries and the reactions of followers and critics. Related pronouncements of a number of fascinating characters and authors are analysed in the rest of the chapter. W.E.B. Du Bois, Jessie Fauset, Alain Locke, Leo Frobenius, Madison Grant, T. Lothrop Stoddard, José Vasconcelos, Antonio Gramsci, T. S. Eliot, John Gould Fletcher, Max Rychner, Ernst Robert Curtius, Georg Moenius, Ernst Troeltsch, Carl Schmitt, Jane (Jeanne) Nardal, René Maran, René Gillouin, Wyndham Lewis, René Guénon (Abd al-Wāḥid Yaḥyá after his conversion to Islam) and Aurel Kolnai, among others, will command attention.

Chapter 7 moves to debates about and articulations of the meaning of 'the West' or 'Western civilisation' during the Second Word War. The tables were turned between the Molotov–Ribbentrop Pact of August 1939 (at which point the Western democracies could argue that the totalitarian dictators were all on the other side) and Hitler's invasion of the Soviet Union in 1941 (which turned the latter into an inevitable as well as indispensable ally of those same Western democracies). These developments, as well as the shockingly rapid defeat of France in the summer of 1940, the subsequent collaboration under the Vichy government, the entry of the United States into the war and plans for a postwar world that would avoid repetition of the destructive patterns of previous decades, were all elements of the context in which 'the West' and 'Western civilisation' were discussed between 1939 and 1945. The chapter focuses on the perspectives of different thinkers, from highly established figures to some of the most marginalised, including in particular analyses of contributions by, among others, Walter Lippmann, Simone Weil, Alain Locke, Jacques Maritain, Louis T. Achille, Gonzague de Reynold, André Siegfried, Albert Camus, Raymond Aron, Alexandre Kojève, Hannah Arendt, Paul Valéry, George Orwell and Aldous Huxley.

Chapter 8 analyses the multiple and decisive ways in which the Cold War impacted definitions, and 'membership lists', of 'the West'. The chapter pays particular attention to the early years of the Cold War, and shows how inchoate and fluid uses and definitions of the term were at that time, before the crystallisation of the binary distinction that later emerged as a result of the Cold War confrontation. Sources of different genres from several different countries are cited in order to make sense of the fermentations that took place at that turbulent time. From government policies in foreign ministries and diplomatic planning; through highly influential highbrow journalism; best-selling novels expressing the main anxieties of European or American readers; a young Henry Kissinger's Harvard Summer School planning; the widely publicised historiographical and public pronouncements of Professor Arnold Toynbee; the cultural Cold War conducted by networks such as the Congress for Cultural Freedom; the writings of European émigrés turned influential American academics such as Hannah Arendt and Leo Strauss; the relentless activism and writings of Raymond Aron; the ever-increasing disillusionment with 'the West' manifested by W.E.B. Du Bois, and his role during the early Cold War; the passionate quest of Afro-American novelist Richard Wright to understand the deeper meaning of 'Western civilisation' and to warn 'the West' not to waste its last chance; James Baldwin's early Cold War reflections; James Burnham's denunciations of Liberalism as the 'ideology of Western suicide'; Milan Kundera's and Czesław Miłosz's laments for the 'kidnapped West' of Central and Eastern Europe; through to the student revolts of the 1960s and the reactions to them of the likes of Allan Bloom and other followers of Leo Strauss, who warned that defeated Germany had conquered America through its pernicious intellectual influence: a cornucopia of arguments will be scrutinised, and the multiplicity of meanings and evaluations of 'the West' will be brought into sharp relief.

Chapter 9 focuses on the changes to the meanings of 'the West', and the widely differing prognoses as to its future, once the Cold War was over. The initial relative optimism (though not without some hints at drawbacks) associated with Francis Fukuyama's 'triumph of the West' and 'end of history' thesis was very soon challenged from various quarters. Besides an early warning from veteran academic and political insider Arthur Schlesinger, who focused on culture wars within the United States, the most influential response came from Fukuyama's former teacher, Samuel Huntington, with his 'clash of civilisations' thesis. Huntington's recommendation was that 'the West' should be seen and cherished as a unique civilisation that had to learn how to live in the midst of other (increasingly powerful and assertive) ones, and that beliefs in the universalisability of Western civilisation were to be regarded as dangerous chimeras. Meanwhile, the chapter also analyses the arguments with respect to what was peculiar about the

West, among thinkers as diverse as Cornelius Castoriadis, Jürgen Habermas and Heinrich August Winkler—the latter two considered in the highly interesting context of German debates about their country's *Westbindung* during and after German reunification. The fraught issue of American leadership or conversely abandonment of the West after the Cold War is then analysed from various angles, including some fascinating debates that arose after a controversial speech by President Trump in 2017—which in some sense brought the discussion back to the Fukuyama-versus-Huntington dilemma as to whether the West should look after itself and its interests or aspire to universalisation of its model and principles. Some important themes addressed not just in chapter 9 but in the book as a whole are brought together in the final section of the chapter, which focuses on the notion of the end of Western civilisation that has been omnipresent in Michel Houellebecq's novels during the past decades. That Houellebecq takes us back not just to René Guénon, but also all the way to Auguste Comte and Joseph de Maistre, is another reminder of the rewards of the *longue durée* approach adopted here.

In the concluding chapter, I highlight further advantages to be derived from that *longue durée* perspective. I discuss examples of arguments, debates, stereotypes and much else, that can perhaps only be truly understood and appreciated after having absorbed what the book has to say. Some of the issues analysed in earlier chapters will be revisited, and arguments presented concerning the best way forward. A final discussion follows, about 'the West', 'Western values' and our potential futures. An argument is advanced regarding realistic ways of defending desirable principles, without the distortions caused by disputes over the ownership of such principles or values; accompanied by a further argument, about the dangers of throwing away babies along with the bathwater. The repercussions of the war in Ukraine since February 2022 are then assessed. Finally, we will return to some reflections of the French philosopher Raymond Aron, as well as to some of the far-sighted thoughts articulated by Richard Wright, the Afro-American self-defined Westerner who thought that he was 'more advanced than the West'.

2

'The West' as an Alternative to 'Europe' in the Nineteenth Century

'[T]oute la politique européenne n'a plus qu'un seul objet, *l'opposition à la Russie.*'

DOMINIQUE DE PRADT,
DU SYSTÈME PERMANENT DE L'EUROPE (1828), P. 34

WE HAVE SEEN that the eighteenth century was the century of 'Europe', as far as supranational self-identifications were concerned. Though the word 'West' was used in various contexts and senses, especially in historical texts, it had not come to be employed extensively to describe a current, or a future, entity or identity. That was going to change in the nineteenth century. And though the changes would be gradual and take time to become generalised, they began from the very first decades of the nineteenth century, especially in France. French interest in 'the East' (including Africa) increased strikingly as a result of Napoleon's expedition to Egypt at the very end of the eighteenth century. (Constantin-François Volney's groundbreaking works on the East were not unrelated to that expedition.)[1]. Meanwhile, debates on the presumed primacy of India or Egypt (or Ethiopia) in the genesis of world religions and civilisation were not immune from political considerations (with the British in India, and the French in Egypt, for instance) or personal biases, as a concerned Benjamin Constant was confiding to his diary whilst staying in Mme de Staël's house at Coppet in 1804. Such Anglo-French rivalry over the 'Orient' was not new, nor was it at all innocent of domestic political implications.[2] Interest in, and discussions of, the 'East' intensified in the course of the early decades of the nineteenth century. The Greek

Revolution that began early in 1821, along with the new phase of the 'Eastern Question' that it gave rise to, was to make such discussions more urgent.

The most crucial issue, however, turned out to be Russia, and how the rest of Europe might deal with it. It was primarily in contradistinction to Russia that ther term 'the West' was to be needed, to replace 'Europe': as Russia's political, military and diplomatic weight on the European scene loomed ever larger after the defeat of Napoleon and the Congress of Vienna, 'Europe' was becoming more and more problematic for more and more people. Now Mme de Staël—one of the very first authors to do so—spoke sympathetically of the 'Easternness' of the Russians, and of the Slavs and of the East more generally. But others, the vast majority, who would begin talking of Russia as 'Eastern' after the Congress of Vienna (and the subsequent congresses that consolidated the centrality of Czar Alexander's Russia in the European state system and his initiative in establishing, and leadership of, the 'Holy Alliance'), were invoking the Easternness of Russia in order to exclude it from the 'European' system, by creating a new, 'Western' alliance against the Russian menace. The issue arose in the first place from the success of Peter the Great, in the early eighteenth century, in having Russia accepted as a 'European' state in terms of international politics and law.[3] The question then became much more acute with the success of Alexander I in making his country not only accepted as part of 'Europe', but central to the new European dispensation after the defeat of Napoleon; for one of Alexander's achievements had been 'to put Catholicism, Protestantism, and Orthodoxy on the same footing'.[4] On top of increasing anxiety about this enhanced power and importance, moreover, the succession to the throne of the arch-authoritarian Nicholas, when Alexander died in 1825, served only to make Russia ever more unpopular abroad.

I. Heeren of Göttingen

Arnold Hermann Ludwig Heeren (1760–1842) was a very important historian during his own time, when it could confidently be asserted that '[t]out le monde connaît [everyone knows] M. Heeren'.[5] He developed an elaborate theory explaining what he saw as the superiority of Europeans (including their descendants overseas) to all other peoples in history.[6] Interchangeably with 'Europe' and 'Europeans' Heeren also used 'the West' and 'Westerners' quite often: 'Even in the centuries of the middle age, when the intellectual superiority of the Europeans seemed to have sunk, the nations of the East attempted to subjugate them in vain.' Thus 'the Arabs desired to overturn the West [*den Westen*]; the sword of Charles Martel compelled then to rest contented with a part of Spain; and the chivalrous

FIGURE 2.1. The old Göttingen university campus and library building, called the Collegiate Building, ca. 1815. Copper engraving by H. Chr. Grape. *Source:* https://en.wikipedia.org/wiki/University_of_G%C3%B6ttingen#/media /File:Grape_-_G%C3%B6ttinger_Universit%C3%A4ts-_und_Bibliotheksgeb %C3%A4ude_1815.jpg

Frank, under the banner of the cross, soon bade them defiance in their own home.' Heeren included Russia among the 'European' powers whose successes he celebrated, meanwhile: 'The new world [...] became their prey; more than a third part of Asia submitted to the Russian sceptre; merchants on the Thames and the Zuyder See seized on the government of India.'[7] Raising an issue that was discussed by many before (Voltaire included) and after (Francis Lieber included), Heeren highlighted the significance of monogamy versus polygamy in differentiating 'Westerners' from others: 'Does not the wall of division which separates the inhabitants of the East from those of the West [zwischen dem Orientaler und Occidentaler],[8] repose chiefly on this basis?' It could not be doubted, in his opinion, that Westerners' 'better domestic institution was essential to the progress of our political institutions'.

Heeren also addressed the division between North and South within Europe, primarily in order to celebrate the extent to which the—formerly rustic—northerners had more than caught up with the earlier-civilised southerners. Though 'the nations of the South' had 'preceded' those of the North; and though these latter 'were still wandering in their forests' when the southern

Europeans 'had already obtained their ripeness', the northern peoples 'finally made up for their dilatoriness. Their time also came; the time when they could look down on their southern brethren with *a just consciousness of superiority*'.[9] This is an important dimension. For *translatio imperii* did not just move from east to west. It also moved from south to north—or, combining the two, from south-east to north-west. Which means that, by the beginning of the nineteenth century, 'North' was coming to signify highly advanced and civilised: at the top of civilisational hierarchies. This may not be unconnected to the embryonic tendency to dispute the description of Russia as 'northern' and to talk of it instead as 'eastern'.

II. From North–South to East–West: Mme de Staël and the View of Russia

Louise Germaine de Staël-Holstein (1766–1817), better known as Mme de Staël, was the daughter of Jacques Necker, the Genevan banker who became the minister of finance of King Louis XVI of France, and Suzanne Curchod-Necker, a woman of letters who held one of the most famous and influential intellectual salons in pre-revolutionary Paris.[10] Through a combination of her talents, drive and family connections Mme de Staël met more or less everyone who was anyone in Europe at the time. Napoleon was correct in sensing that she was an influence to be reckoned with. As one of her contemporaries put it, 'there are three great powers struggling against Napoleon for the soul of Europe: England, Russia, and Mme de Staël'.[11] Her interest in nationalities and national characteristics did not go unnoticed among contemporaries. Around a year after her death, a writer in a British magazine was to observe, 'The sciences have always owed their origin to some great spirit. [Adam] Smith created political economy; Linnaeus, botany; Lavoisier, chemistry; and Madame de Staël has, in like manner, created the art of analysing the spirit of nations and the springs which move them.'[12] De Staël's *De l'Allemagne* (On Germany) (1810) caused a real sensation. It encouraged an interest in, and indeed a fashion for, German culture, in France, in Britain and, not least, in the United States. The book was initially printed (ten thousand copies) in Paris, in 1810. But Napoleon ordered all copies to be destroyed and banned the book, as he considered it to be too subversive and anti-French. It was then published in London in 1813. An English translation was also published that year, with the title *Germany*. Its impact on the popularisation of romanticism was considerable. It is also credited by many with having encouraged a far-reaching fashion for young graduates of Harvard College, Massachusetts, followed by other Americans, to make the pilgrimage to Göttingen, Heidelberg or Berlin, to obtain a doctorate from a German university.

What is more, De Staël offers a fascinating example of the transition from thinking in traditional eighteenth-century terms of North–South to the emerging nineteenth-century East–West division. The transition became explicit in her later work, *Dix années d'exil*, in the early nineteenth century. And it was, significantly, related to Russia. 'The Russians', she wrote, 'have, in my opinion, much greater resemblance to the people of the South, or rather of the East, than to those of the North. What is European in them belongs merely to the manners of the court, which are nearly the same in all countries; but their nature is eastern.'[13] South and East are interestingly conflated here initially, but by the end of the same sentence the Russians (who were then generally categorised as of 'the North' or a 'northern' power) are declared to be 'eastern'. The same theme was taken up in the Marquis de Custine's immensely influential four-volume book of 1843, *La Russie en 1839* (and no doubt plagiarised; de Custine knew Mme de Staël, whose daughter he almost married, and mentioned her on other occasions in his book.). As de Custine was to put it, the Russians were 'an Oriental people, long ago led astray by their chiefs, who lost their road in the migration, and forced towards the north a race born for the sun.'[14]

The way Mme de Staël proceeded to elaborate on her statement was also characteristic of the vagueness or inchoateness of meanings at that time: a certain 'Kalmuck prince, to whom wooden houses appeared a residence too delicate in the middle of winter, gave diamonds to the ladies who pleased him at a ball' and, given that verbal communication was not possible, 'he substituted presents for compliments, in the manner practised in India and other silent countries of the East, where speech has less influence than with us'. De Staël then goes on the mention that the Russian general who had narrated to her the story of the Kalmuck prince had invited her to a ball 'at the house of a Moldavian princess', to which she much regretted not being able to go. An exoticising remark follows: '[a]ll these names of foreign countries and of nations which are scarcely any longer European, singularly awaken the imagination'; all of which caused her to conclude, 'You feel yourself in Russia at the gate of another earth, near to that East from which have proceeded so many religious creeds, and which still contains in its bosom incredible treasures of perseverance and reflection.'[15] There was quite a distance between Moldavia and India, but in De Staël's imaginary they were both alien or exotic enough to evoke 'the East'.

FIGURE 2.2. Mme de Staël. *Anne Louise Germaine de Staël-Holstein*, portrait in oils by Vladimir Borovikovsky (1812). State Tretyakov Gallery, Moscow. *Source:* https://en.wikipedia.org/wiki/Germaine_de_Sta%C3%ABl#/media/File:Germaine_de_Sta%C3%ABl_by_Vladimir_Borovikovsky.png

III. *Les Deux Mondes*: Saint-Simon and the Saint-Simonians

Henri de Saint-Simon (1760–1825) was one of the most influential thinkers of the nineteenth century. He gave his name to a movement, and that movement continued to have a great impact on the world for decades after the dissolution of the group named 'the Saint-Simonians'.[16] Among other things, Saint-Simon had a vision for European unity, and in the autumn of 1814 he hastily proposed a way forward toward European federation—just in time for it to influence, he hoped, the leaders to be assembled in Vienna in order to rebuild the European order after the Napoleonic wars.[17] The plan involved an Anglo–French union, that would later admit the German lands as well. This was a very different conception of 'Europe' from the one that actually emerged from the deliberations of the Congress of Vienna, with Russia and its Czar Alexander I at the very centre. Both before and after that time, Saint-Simon often referred to 'Europe' or 'Western Europe' as being composed of the peoples he often invoked as follows: 'French, English, Belgians, Dutch, Danes, Swedes, Germans, Italians, Spaniards and Portuguese[: . . .] it is to you collectively that this work addresses itself.'[18] He referred to these same peoples or countries collectively as 'l'Occident de l'Europe', 'l'Europe occidentale', or 'la grande nation des Européens occidentaux'.[19] On one occasion in 1822 (at the time when a young Auguste Comte was still his secretary) Saint-Simon used both terms, addressing the peoples he had enumerated earlier as 'Européens, Occidentaux'.[20] The comma marks a difference from his usual references to 'les Européens occidentaux' and turns 'Occidentaux' into a noun in this case, and thus into an alternative collective appellation for the nations he referred to. But otherwise he persisted in talking of 'l'Europe' and 'les européens'. Saint-Simon, who often changed his mind, came up with slightly different membership lists at different times;[21] but, minor differences notwithstanding, his Europe does sound quite close to that later described by Comte, and meanwhile he did display a certain indecisiveness about whether to call it 'l'Europe', 'l'Occident' or 'l'Europe occidentale'. Overall, the first and the last of these alternatives prevailed by far in his writings. What is clear is that his Europe was based mainly on Charlemagne's former empire (Saint-Simon claimed that he himself was descended from Charlemagne and that he had apparitions of Charlemagne encouraging him in his philosophical ambitions), to which were added Britain and the Iberian peninsula.[22]

Besides Saint-Simon, there were many others who began talking of 'l'Occident' in the early nineteenth century. Debates over the 'Eastern Question' (la question d'Orient), which increased significantly during the Greek Revolution of the 1820s, invoked 'l'Orient' ever more frequently, and references to 'l'Occident' increased accordingly, at least to an extent.[23] Some good examples occur in speeches and articles by Alphonse de Lamartine;[24] these contain references to 'l'Europe' in far greater abundance, however, and it is 'la civilisation européenne' that he proposes to promote in the Ottoman Orient and a new 'système politique européen' that he wants to see created.[25] Similar things can be said of some of the Saint-Simonians, most notably Michel Chevalier, Gustave d'Eichthal, Émile Barrault and Ismaÿl [Thomas] Urbain (this last converted to Islam). Saint-Simonians were in the early 1830s obsessively trying to bring together opposites, such as matter and spirit, woman and man, *Orient* and *Occident*, as they put it.[26]

One of these Saint-Simonians who used 'l'Occident' extensively from early on had a special relationship with Auguste Comte. Gustave d'Eichthal had been Comte's first disciple. Whilst in Germany, d'Eichthal had given one of Comte's early essays to none other than Hegel to read. Similarly, d'Eichthal later introduced the British philosopher John Stuart Mill to Comte's work. Meanwhile, he did much to explain German philosophy (notably Hegel, Kant and Herder) to Comte, including sending him handwritten translations of texts by German thinkers.[27] He later emancipated himself and joined the Saint-Simonian 'sect', to Comte's great chagrin.[28] Despite their subsequent estrangement, d'Eichthal sent his book *Les Deux Mondes* (1836) to Comte and the latter replied that he was keen to read it.[29] In *Les Deux Mondes*, d'Eichthal wrote of Christianity moving from its cradle, Jerusalem,[30] through Athens to Rome. Then the German race came from the plains of Germany and, mingling in France with the Roman and Gallic populations, formed there 'the mixed Western race, the most Christian people' (la race mixte occidentale, le peuple très chrétien). To the French went the honour of having accomplished the greatest deeds of Christian civilisation (which d'Eichthal enumerated, from the time of Charlemagne to the French Revolution and Napoleon).[31]

D'Eichthal drew up an extensive list of differences between 'l'Orient' and 'l'Occident'. Though human nature was no doubt in general the same in both 'great divisions of our planet', there existed a diversity between West and East that consisted in the predominance of certain characteristics in each of them. According to d'Eichthal, '[m]aterial life' dominated in the East, while 'spiritual life' dominated in the West. (This was the exact opposite of what the Slavophiles would assert later in Russia, or Asian thinkers would say of the differences between East and West). The one was 'pantheist', the other 'anthropomorphist'. The East 'adores fatality and the unchanging laws that preside in the development of external phenomena', whereas the West 'is in love with the liberty that reigns in the actions of intelligent beings'. The East was 'essentially continental', the West 'essentially maritime'. In the East, 'the race dominates, it is what classifies man according to the fatality of birth'. The West, on the other hand, 'gives superiority to the principle of education, it seems to think that all men are born equal, whatever their origin might be, and that only education makes the difference'. The East 'divides the human species into families and castes; the West has founded its *universal* church, open to all men, without distinction of family, nor birth, whether they are from East or from West, and from that religious equality was born [...] civil equality'. In the East 'man belongs first of all to his family', whereas in the West, 'on the contrary, man belongs first of all to the nation; his duties as citizen are his first duties, those of the family come afterwards'. In the East, 'man is a slave to beauty, which he prefers to "l'esprit" and even to talent; nature and its simple pleasures have more hold on him than the marvels of art and civilisation; he loves pleasure'. On the other hand, the man of the West 'prefers the advantages of intelligence to those of beauty; the glory of work [...] has the upper hand, in his eyes, over the sweetness of pleasure and the charms of leisure'. He likes 'to foresee the future, to anticipate unfavourable chances; he leaves nothing to fortune and what he can snatch from it by consultation or by foresight'. The man of the West 'thinks that God has given man in his reason a second providence: "Help yourself, and heaven will help you"; that is his great maxim'. He is 'prodigious with calculations and with combinations; and with him social progress is always being prepared and is accomplished in an incessant and continuous manner'.[32]

D'Eichthal also offered his readers a map with clear lines of demarcation. His median line dividing West and East almost coincided with the lines drawn by major rivers (and separated 'la race allemande' from the 'races slave et hongroise'). It then left the continent of Europe, traversing Malta and going through Africa from the Cape of Tunis to the Cape of Good Hope. The details show that d'Eichthal took the distinction too literally in geographic terms, in a way Comte (who did not use any maps) would never do. Some of the oppositions he outlines had already been formulated by Michel Chevalier in 1832 (Chevalier had also invoked the oppositions feminine–masculine and matter–spirit, each as characterising East and West respectively). But d'Eichthal went into much more detail and came up with more binary distinctions. Though the intention and the argument in the case of both of these Saint-Simonians were the union, association and combination between the West and the East in the interests of universal harmony, there was an implied hierarchical evaluation of the traits of each group.

It needs to be stressed, however, that the authors who used 'l'Occident' in the first decades of the nineteenth century by no means all meant the same thing by the term. Sometimes the same author meant different things by it in different works, or even within the same work. This is not unrelated to the fact that *l'Orient* did not have a clear meaning. The prominence of the Eastern Question meant that the Ottoman lands were quite commonly called 'l'Orient'. But then there was a deeper 'Orient', stretching to India, China and Japan. Michel Chevalier alluded to the confusion when he wrote, in 1836 that '[t]he peoples that we are used to calling Orientals, but who are but of the *Minor* Orient, have ceased to be formidable adversaries for Europe'. They had 'irrevocably surrendered their swords' to Europe 'in Heliopolis, in Navarin, in Adrianople'. He distinguished that '*Petit*

Orient' from 'le *Grand* Orient' that was further east.[33] But things were still further complicated by the fact that more and more people in the nineteenth century began to draw a vague distinction *within* Europe between East and West (as opposed to the earlier intra-European distinction between North and South, as already mentioned). This means that *l'Occident*, as the opposite of *l'Orient*, could mean a number of things, from Western Europe as opposed to Eastern Europe, to Europe as a whole as opposed to 'the East' or the rest of the world.

An additional complicating factor was America. We can discern the confusions and the inconsistency in the use of the terms even in the writings within a handful of years of writers related to and cross-referencing each other. Thus, in *Lettres sur l'Amérique du Nord*, published in 1836, Michel Chevalier refers approvingly to the first edition of Gustave d'Eichthal's *Les Deux Mondes*,[34] published earlier that year. They both spoke extensively of 'l'Occident' and its relation to 'l'Orient'. Yet by 'l'Occident', did they both mean the same entity? Sometimes yes and sometimes no. In the *Lettres*, Chevalier speaks of the two 'hémisphères', in the sense that we would understand today, with America occupying a different hemisphere from Europe and the 'Old World'.[35] When d'Eichthal talked repeatedly of the two 'hémisphères' in *Les Deux Mondes*, however, he was distinguishing between Western and Eastern Europe (with the Ottoman Empire as part of the latter), and, as already mentioned, included a map with detailed delimitations of the separation. Yet both authors talked of the need for unity, or marriage, between East and West—whatever each meant by these terms. Chevalier had used the marriage metaphor earlier in arguing that the Mediterranean Sea would become 'le lit nuptial [marriage bed] de l'Orient et de l'Occident'.[36] When Chevalier wrote that sentence (quoted approvingly by d'Eichthal in *Les Deux Mondes* four years later), both men were active members of the Saint-Simonian 'sect' and they both were (and would remain) enthusiasts for the Mediterranean. The union between the West and the East that they were both recommending as necessary to humanity's peaceful future may have seemed straightforward to them. But when one of d'Eichthal's German relatives criticized his *Les Deux Mondes* as being typically French, in that it was 'looking too much towards the South', he replied that it was up to others to write on other parts of the world, and that it was true that an appreciation of Germany was entirely missing from his book, as was an appreciation of England, America, Spain and so on; to which he added, 'You may know the work of my friend Michel Chevalier on North America, which it would have been better to entitle *On the West*.'[37] Why would d'Eichthal think that Chevalier's book ought to have been entitled '*Sur l'Occident*'? Presumably North America was now 'the West' in a geographical sense, or a major part at least of 'the West' in a wider sense.[38]

But *Occident* could also be used in a much more restricted sense. Thus, in 1857, a French author was urging 'the reconstitution of the empire of the West, through the voluntary and peaceful union of the Latin races' (*la reconstitution de l'empire d'Occident, par l'union volontaire et pacifique des races latines!*)[39] What the West meant for this writer seems to be simply the geographical space of Western Europe, where he wanted to see a French-dominated enlarged state that would unite France, Italy and Spain. He was calling for a Latin union of the three neo-Latin peoples of Western Europe (as Alexandre Kojève was to do again in 1945),[40] but could not resist claiming for it the mantle of the ancient Roman Empire of the West.[41] Meanwhile, in a statement already quoted above, d'Eichthal seemed to refer simply to France when he invoked 'la race mixte occidentale, le peuple très chrétien'. (This is one more indication that the reason why *Occident* was always available in France, and used sporadically, is that France had come to see itself as the centre of Charlemagne's 'Empire d'Occident'.).

IV. Greeks Bearing Gifts? Or 'la garantie véritable de l'Occident contre l'Orient'

There were, meanwhile, many other early uses among French thinkers, besides those of Saint-Simonian inspiration. A man whose life had been intimately linked with that of Mme de Staël for many years was Benjamin Constant (1767–1830). Also born elsewhere (in Lausanne), Constant first came to France with Mme de Staël in May 1795. He eventually became a French citizen and was to end his days as a liberal member of the French Chamber of Deputies during the early months of the July Monarchy. During the Greek Revolution, a crucial year in terms of developments in French philhellenism was 1825.[42] Constant, a member of the French National Assembly at the time, wrote an important pamphlet that year, the *Appel aux nations chrétiennes en faveur des Grecs*. It was published on behalf of the Comité des Grecs of the Société de la morale chrétienne. Constant's pamphlet employed many different arguments, but the Greeks being Christians fighting against Muslim conquerors was the main one. The 'West' made an appearance as well, though. Constant complained that the military instruction, tactics and knowledge 'of Europe' were penetrating the Turkish empire through the route of Egypt (it was a common complaint of French philhellenic agitation that the military instruction provided by French former soldiers to Egypt's Pasha

Mehmet Ali was being used to suppress the Greek Revolution on behalf of Mehmet Ali's suzerain, the Ottoman sultan). Frenchmen disowned by France were going, in exchange for money, 'to train and discipline the murderers of Christians'. 'That way', Constant added, 'disappears or is enfeebled the real guarantee of the West against the East [la garantie véritable de l'Occident contre l'Orient], of civilisation against the semi-savage state that some unexpected fanaticism may suddenly arm and render invincible.' It was not the Turkish empire itself, in its current feeble state, that Constant feared as a future danger to Europe. But from some unknown horde could rise a new Mohamed, and Europe ought to know what such a man could do to it. Who could have guessed thirty years earlier, Constant elaborated, the degree to which Europe would tremble in front of a single man, going on to cast Napoleon Bonaparte in the guise of an 'oriental' threat: 'Cet homme [Napoleon] avait quelque chose d'oriental dans son genie' (That man had something oriental in his essence). Europe should therefore not exaggerate her forces of resistance: 'softened, faithless, bastardised by pleasures, disarmed by industry itself, incapable of conviction and sacrifice', the European peoples were 'still good for attack, because attack hopes for success; but they are no longer good for defence, when setbacks manifest themselves'. And that is where the Greeks turned out to be a godsend: Providence, which did 'not want Christendom to succumb', had 'raised a people that has two qualities that polished Europe no longer has, faith and readiness to die'. That people, the Greeks, was placed at the entrance to Europe. It opposed to Asia a political and religious rampart. It was admirable for its courage, its devotion, its enthusiasm, and for its heroic defiance of death. And so, 'La cause des Grecs est la nôtre' (The Greek cause is our own).[43]

There were many others who pleaded with the French and West European publics in support of the Greeks during the 1820s. None is more interesting from our point of view than the abbé de Pradt. De Pradt, like Constant, was adamant that his main worry was not the Ottoman Empire. But rather than any hypothetical new oriental danger that might arise in the future, he identified a real and present peril for Western Europe. And that was Russia. In the early nineteenth century, de Pradt took a great interest in both the independence of various republics in the Americas and the Greek Revolution of the 1820s. He wrote several books on each of these areas. Some of his books directly connected developments in the Americas and in Greece.[44] He was a maverick in many ways, but also representative of the tendencies of the times, and hence a notably popular author, whose books sold well. He has been aptly described as 'a prolific writer with particularly sharp antennae for international developments'.[45] He insisted that his outlook was not narrowly French, but more broadly European. From that point of view, there were two 'others' for de Pradt. On the one hand there were the Ottoman Turks; and he spoke of the Greeks—in juxtaposition to the Turks—as being part of 'the West'. The Greeks were 'Westerners living on the soil of Turkey, as the Turks were Orientals entrenched on the land of Europe'. The consequence was that the Greeks were susceptible to all the social progress made by the West and equipped to make use of it. Their history was the proof of that.[46] But—like many others—de Pradt regarded the Ottoman Empire as moribund. His main anxiety was who would succeed it in the lands it occupied in Europe.

And that was where the other 'other', the really serious danger, came in. De Pradt made it clear in his books in the 1820s, time and again, that it was exactly because Russia had mastered 'civilisation' during the past century that he considered it the greatest danger to the rest of Europe. Russia had become civilised and powerful, besides being enormous. The most pressing evil for Europe, 'one could not tire of repeating', was the supremacy of Russia ('Le mal le plus pressant, le plus poignant de l'Europe, on ne peut se lasser de le dire, est la suprématie de la Russie.'). And given that Russia was lethally dangerous, and the Ottoman Empire was too effete meanwhile to play the role of rampart of buffer state against Russia, the emergence of the Greeks was an inestimable boon. In such a position, the states of Europe ought to regard it as a great blessing of fate that a new people was arriving on the scene to replace a depleted one—and, to boot, 'a European people succeeding an Asiatic people, a civilised people occupying the vacancies left by a nomadic people'. For that was exactly what Greece had come to offer Europe. Given the weakness of Turkey, there was a dangerous void in the vaunted barrier against Russia, and it was very important that it be filled. A point of resistance needed to be created, so that the whole responsibility would not fall 'on the side of the West abandoned to itself' (du côté de l'Occident abandonné à lui-même). As things stood at the time, it was the 'West' that had to shoulder the entire burden; Turkey had nothing to contribute. Thus, 'from the point of view of the safety of Europe,' de Pradt was convinced, 'if the Greek revolution had not happened, it would have had to be invented' ([e]n prenant ainsi la question du côté des sauvegardes de l'Europe, on se convaincra que, si la révolution de la Grèce n'existait pas, il faudrait l'inventer).[47]

Near the end of the Greek war of independence, in 1828, de Pradt wrote that Russia was so powerful that it had divided Europe into two parts, the East and the West. The whole of the East belonged to it, and that fact rendered the West in a state of blockade by the Eastern power. Every time Russia moved, the West would shake. Surely that was not real independence. Obsequity towards Russia was too generalised as a result.[48] The solution de Pradt proposed to the Russian problem was for Western Europe to form itself into a federative system: 'The European system is divided into two branches, one defensive and the other offensive; [...] the former is that to which Western Europe is obliged and the latter is that of Russia.' Each particular state was 'too weak to resist Russia, and hence arises the necessity of a federative system, whose indispensable basis has to be the guarantee of all by all'. Russia, by forming itself into a homogeneous body of power, in all respects, had 'taught Western Europe [l'occident de l'Europe] that, for its own preservation, it too must form itself into one defensive body'. It was the 'force of things', therefore, that was leading to a federative system among all these Western powers ('La force des choses crée donc entre toutes les puissances occidentales un système fédératif').[49] The conclusions followed, first, that a federative system was the only means of preservation that remained to 'the rest of Europe' against Russia; second, that that system had to be and could not but be defensive; third, that it had to be permanent; fourth, that, in the state of respective forces as between the two 'divisions européennes', it would be barely sufficient; fifth, that 'the diversity of elements in that system, in the interests, in the mores, in the laws, in the cults of those destined to form that federation, gave great advantages to Russian power, which was homogeneous in all its parts, and thus the western part of Europe, even if it formed a perfect union, would still be inferior to the eastern part'; and sixth, finally, that European politics as a whole no longer had any object other than opposition to Russia.[50]

V. Fear of Russia Intensifies: 'the West' Must Unite...

Though already obvious in the 1820s, fear of Russia intensified in the 1830s and continued to increase thereafter. Meanwhile, after the July Revolution of 1830, France and Britain could be said to have relatively similar constitutional liberal regimes. That also encouraged talk, in both France and Britain, of a 'Western' alliance against despotic 'Eastern' powers.[51] Then the publication in 1843 of the Marquis (Astolphe) de Custine's *La Russie en 1839* marked a further crucial step.[52] It is striking how often de Custine used the terms *l'Occident*, or *civilisation occidentale*, in his four-volume book. *La Russie en 1839* was one of the main milestones in the consolidation of a distinction between a 'West' of Europe and an 'oriental' Russia.[53] De Custine emphatically warned of Russia's inevitable designs to conquer Western Europe. The book was soon translated into other European languages (as well as being favourably reviewed in many countries).[54] By the 1850s, Russia would be paying the price of its ever-increasing unpopularity, as the Crimean War was to show.[55]

And it was not just French and British radicals and liberals (highly influenced by the activities and lobbying of Polish exiles) who were complaining about the behaviour of Russia. The German lands were experiencing similar developments. Jakob Philipp Fallmerayer (1790–1861) was a most vociferous Cassandra with regard to the Russian menace. Fear of Russia was directly related to the work for which he is best known today, a two-part study published in 1830 and 1836 that tried to warn that European philhellenism was fatally misguided. According to Fallmerayer, the inhabitants of the Greek peninsula were mainly descendants of Slavic migrations during the Middle Ages, and had little to do, genetically, with the ancient Greeks. To his mind, this meant that the modern Greeks were bound to be allies of Russia.[56] Fallmerayer went on to write extensively on topics related to Russia, including a long review of de Custine's book of 1843.[57]

German liberals were also very resentful of the Russian intervention to suppress the revolutions of 1848.[58] Some of the German 'Forty-Eighters' were to be particularly active in warning of the Russian menace during the next decade, and a clear and explicit distinction between Russia and 'the West' was part of their ammunition. In book after book, Gustav Diezel was vociferous about Russia's 'Eastern' nature and how much of a threat it was to the 'Western' nations. As he put it in 1853, the Russian state seemed to be 'growing every day more powerful, more oppressive, and more overbearing, as also more threatening to the independent development of the Western nations [der westlichen Nationen], and particularly of Germany'.[59] Having expanded upon how far Russia was from being homogeneous, Diezel reflected, 'Does this state of things represent an incomplete fusion likely to be consummated in future, or a hopeless attempt to blend elements which can never enter into intimate union?' The question seemed to him worth examining, for on the answer depended the most important conclusions relative to the future prospects of the Western nations ('für unsere ganze abendländische Zukunft bedingt').[60] According to Diezel, the Russians had 'been called an Asiatic people, and if by this it is meant to describe their chaotic, massive, inorganic nature, in opposition to the individual, organic, and fully developed nature of the Western races [des Abendlands], the expression is undoubtedly well chosen'.[61] He conceded that '[i]n its infancy' the Russian state had been 'connected with the West [mit dem Westen], whence it derived its being, and it could in consequence lay claim to be a member of the family of European states'. Russia then forfeited this claim 'in the progress of ages by a practical disseverance of the connexion, and a relapse into the Asiatic slough, but subsequently renewed by reknitting the bond in a peculiar manner, and one which has hitherto been singularly successful'.[62] Diezel is highly interesting, as, in his case, the

Crimean War 'prompted a recoding of the mental map. Previously convinced that a united Germany could only be realised "in a battle against East and West", he came then to argue 'that Germany was part of a "West"—a "Romano-Germanic West"—that was fighting against the "Slavic East".'[63]

And still, two decades later, after the Franco–Prussian war and when the newly formed German Empire was about to annex Alsace and Lorraine, the SDAP (Social Democratic Workers' Party of Germany) leaders Wilhelm Liebknecht and August Bebel were declaring in a pamphlet (that was to lead them to be tried for treason), 'The German workers, in the interest of France as well as Germany, in the interest of peace and freedom, in the interest of Western civilisation against Cossack barbarism [im Interesse der westlichen Civilisation gegen die kosakische Barbarei], will not tolerate the annexation of Alsace and Lorraine'.[64] It is telling that they felt the need to define 'Western civilisation' in opposition to 'Cossack barbarism'.

The juxtaposition was to continue in nineteenth-century German thought, including among thinkers to whom German Socialism was far from congenial. It would be an understatement to say that Friedrich Nietzsche was a complex thinker. His thought developed and changed much; he wrote in aphorisms that sometimes sounded deranged (and he did literally go mad in the last eleven or so years of his life, from 1889 to 1900). A whole industry of commentary has been dedicated to trying to explain or explain away much that he wrote. His sister's Nazi sympathies and the distortions she encouraged constituted only one of the many problems involved in interpreting his writings. But certain things can be established and made sense of. When, late in his (sane, pre-January 1889) intellectual evolution, Nietzsche came to develop a political project, the lineaments of its international dimension were relatively clear. He had come to believe that a united continental European entity was needed, to defend European high culture from the twin dangers of 'English' herd, philistine, utilitarian 'slave morality', on the one hand, and the Russian menace on the other. But given that the greater threat came from Russia, some 'understanding' with Britain was needed, so that a united continental Europe could protect its high culture under a hierarchical organisation, led by a transnational and transracial elite. Moreover, Nietzsche explicitly wished the Russian threat to become so overwhelming as to convince 'Europe' to abandon the petty politics of the *Kleinstaaterei* and unite.[65] His elite he famously called 'the good Europeans', in various late works and unpublished notes. One of the things that had created the European high culture that he wanted to defend (and hoped would, in the twentieth century, conquer the whole world), was the combination of 'southern' and 'northern' traits that had been achieved in western continental Europe. That combination was most notably exemplified in France. One of the (three) reasons he adduced to defend French superiority in the Europe of his time was that 'in the French nature there exists a half-achieved synthesis of north and south which makes them understand many things and urges them to do many things which an Englishman will never understand'.⁶⁶ As perhaps befits someone who spent as many years as he did in the in-between city of Basel, Nietzsche's use of the language of South–North was striking. (Spengler was later to refer to him as the 'last victim of the South'.)⁶⁷

And yet, though 'Europe', 'good Europeans' and North–South constituted the predominant building-blocks of his thinking, Nietzsche's language takes an interesting turn when it comes to juxtaposition with Russia. He speaks innumerable times of 'Europe', 'European civilisation', and 'we Europeans' in *On the Genealogy of Morality* (1887). But when he wants to differentiate between 'us' and the Russians, he uses another term to describe his own side: 'For millennia, wrong-doers overtaken by punishment [. . .] submitted to punishment as you submit to illness or misfortune or death, with that brave, unrebellious fatalism that still gives the Russians, for example, an advantage over us Westerners in the way they handle life'.⁶⁸ And here is what he had to say in *Twilight of the Idols* (1888), in a paragraph headed 'Critique of Modernity': 'For there to be institutions there must be a kind of will, instinct, imperative, which is anti-liberal to the point of malice: the will to tradition, to authority, to centuries of responsibility to come, the will to *solidarity* of generational chains stretching forwards and backwards *in infinitum*.' His next remark is revealing:

> If this will is there, then something like the *imperium Romanum* is founded: or like Russia, the *only* power nowadays which has endurance, which can wait, which still has promise—Russia, the conceptual opposite of Europe's pitiful petty-statery and nervousness [Russland der Gegensatz-Begriff zu der erbärmlichen europäischen Kleinstaaterei und Nervosität], which has reached a critical condition with the founding of the German Reich [. . .]. The whole of the West has lost those instincts from which institutions grow, from which *future* grows [Der ganze Westen hat jene Instinkte nicht mehr, aus denen Institutionen wachsen, aus denen Zukunft wächst]: nothing perhaps goes against the grain of the 'modern spirit' so much. People live for today, they live very quickly—they live very irresponsibly: and this is precisely what is called 'freedom'.⁶⁹

It has been remarked that '[f]or Nietzsche, "the West" was a cipher for modernity and progress; and Germany, alas, was part of it'.⁷⁰ That may well be so, but it is noticeable that 'the West' appears only once in *Twilight of the Idols*, and where it appears is no accident: in the part of the book, that is, where Nietzsche is drawing a contradistinction between an 'all European party-system and neurasthenia', on the one hand, and Russia, on the other. The current chapter shows that this should be no surprise. It was as opposed to Russia, primarily, that 'the West' emerged and gained a meaning.[71]

VI. The East of Xerxes or the East of Christ?

What did people in Russia make of the relationship? We noted in chapter 1 that Petr Chaadaev published his 'First Philosophical Letter' in 1836. He profoundly shocked Russian society with his verdict that, by opting for the Orthodox branch of Christianity, Russians had cut themselves off from the unity of the Christian world that he saw as represented by Catholicism, and thus missed the chance of participating in the developments that had made modern Europe what it was. The problem was that the Russians had 'never marched with the other peoples'. They did not 'belong to any of the great families of the human race'. 'We are', Chaadev wrote, 'neither of the West nor of the East, and we have not the traditions of either. Placed, as it were, outside of time, we have not been touched by the universal education of the human race.' His compatriots lived 'in a narrow present, without a past as without a future, in the midst of a dead calm, com[ing] into the world like illegitimate children, without a heritage, without any ties binding us to the men who came before us on this earth, carry[ing] in our hearts none of the lessons preceding our own existence. [...] Our memories go back no further than yesterday; we are, so to say, strangers to ourselves.' The Russians were 'an exception among peoples; [...] one of those nations which do not appear to be an integral part of the human race, but exist only in order to teach some great lesson to the world'. No doubt the lesson they were destined to teach would 'not be wasted'; but who knew 'when we shall rejoin the rest of mankind, and how much misery we must suffer before accomplishing our destiny?' In the West were certain crucial ideas, that made a world of difference. These were the ideas 'of duty, justice, right, and order'. They derived 'from the events which have formed European society; they are part and parcel of the social fabric of these countries'. That was 'the atmosphere of the West; it is more than history, more than psychology—it is the very physiology of European man'. The Russians, by contrast, were a people 'which cannot link its thinking to any sequence of ideas progressively developed by society and slowly succeeding each other, which has taken part in the general movement of the human mind only by a blind, superficial, and often clumsy imitation of other nations'. 'We are alone in the world,' Chaadev concluded, no less devastatingly: 'we have given nothing to the world, we have taught it nothing. We have not added a single idea to the sum total of human ideas; we have not contributed to the progress of the human spirit, and what we have borrowed of this progress we have distorted.'

As we saw in chapter 1, Chaadaev started a debate that was to intensify in the decades to follow. Slavophiles confronted Westernisers in a battle for Russia's soul and future. Westernisers would castigate Russian despotism and backwardness, and propose modernisation and liberalisation. Slavophiles would blame all Russia's current problems on the fact that it had been, ill-advisedly, imitating the West. The common denominator of Slavophile descriptions of the West was that it focused only on matter, and neglected the spiritual side of life (hence its success in material advances, but at a terrible price). The Slavophile recipe for a better balance was Orthodoxy, the 'right' kind of Christianity. Meanwhile, Russian thinkers were of course well aware of how they were perceived and talked of in Western Europe. The ever-increasing perception of Russia as Eastern, and the concomitant dualism of uses of 'the East', did not escape Russian contemporaries. An interesting formulation of the implied conundrum was to be found in the thought of the leading Russian Slavophile Aleksei Khomyakov (1804–1860). The East comprised two parts, 'the East of Xerxes and the East of Christ'. Ultimately, 'Russia was the East of Christianity, and in this respect essentially it had much in common with the West'.[72] (We will see in chapter 3 how vividly that dualism was reflected in, for instance, the many writings of the British historian Edward Freeman.)

Meanwhile, the degree to which the orientalising of Russia had advanced by 1842 (even before de Custine's seminal book was published) can be seen in the juxtapositions formulated by the Greek philosopher of history Markos Renieris. That year Renieris published an article with a strikingly explicit title: 'Τι είναι η Ελλάς; Ανατολή ή Δύσις;' (What is Greece, East or West?).[73] That question was the most important of all the issues generated by the 'resurrection' of the Greek nation in the nineteenth century. 'Any statesman who should fail to solve this question would resemble a sailor who sailed in the ocean without map and compass.' If Greece was East, the political implication would be that her national character (εθνισμός) was Eastern as well, and therefore 'opposed and averse' to Western civilisation. And, if that were the case, by receiving her institutions from Western Europe, Greece was 'committing political suicide, renouncing her national character and adopting alien features which would little by little stifle the innate ones, the end result being that Greece would henceforth live a borrowed

FIGURE 2.3. Aleksei Khomyakov. *Self-portrait* in oils (1842). Abramtsevo Museum-Reserve, Khotkovo (Russia). *Source:* https://en.wikipedia.org/wiki/Aleksey_Khomyakov#/media/File:KhomyakovA_AvtoportretABR.jpg

life.' On the other hand, if Greece was of the West, 'by receiving Western civilisation and adopting the political and procedural laws, the administrative organisation, social liberties, philosophical systems, science and art of the Western nations', she was 'not adopting foreign elements, but rather familiarising herself with her own patrimony; she is not relinquishing her national character but complementing it, she is developing herself rather than committing suicide, she is progressing rather than regressing.'[74] Far from being merely an academic issue, this inherent dilemma and the diverse views associated with it had led to the emergence of the two 'parties' into which the nation was divided. Maintaining that Greek civilisation was Western, the supporters of the first 'party' advocated that Greece should look to Britain and France as her archetypes. Their opponents, on the other hand, considered Greek civilisation to be Eastern, and therefore believed that the Greeks should look to Russia as their model. (The new alignments were especially obvious after 1830, when France had become recognisably a constitutional monarchy.)

Renieris suggested that best entitled to give an answer to that vexing question was Greece herself and her history. He went on to claim that 'Ancient Greece was the Orient's very antithesis in that it made the individual the centre of the universe, which constituted the *kat' exochen* [preeminent] trait of Western civilisation, while the quintessence of Oriental civilisation was the individual's absorption by—and submergence into—the mass and the negation of individuality'. That meant, in other words, that 'Hellas gave birth to the very distinction East–West, by being herself the West and by assuming the "mission" of westernising the East [να δυτικήση την Ανατολήν] [and of] distinguishing and exalting human individuality from the chaos of Oriental pantheism'. Renieris then presented a historical outline of the process whereby 'Greece found herself in the centre of the absolute monarchy of Constantine's successors'. He attributed the gradual stifling of 'the nature' of ancient Hellenism to barbarian invasions, to the 'slavish spirit that emanated from the Byzantine court' and to the 'Oriental customs regulating the relations between subjects and monarch' in the Greek-speaking Byzantine Empire. It was 'from this cause, rather than from religious disputes, that the great antipathy between the West and Greece stemmed during the Byzantine era', and it was due to this antipathy that Greece suffered many misfortunes. Renieris considered the enmity inevitable, in view of the 'profound cultural differences' between Byzantines and Westerners. Offering an account of the cultural shock felt by the two groups on their first encounter during the Crusades, he goes out of his way to praise the chivalrous qualities of the 'free and independent' Occidentals and deplore the faults of the despotism-trodden Byzantines. It should come as no surprise that he cites the bible of Byzantium-bashing, Gibbon's *Decline and Fall of the Roman Empire*, to prove the validity of his contrast. Thus, for Renieris, it was only natural that the Crusaders should destroy the Byzantine Empire. The wars of the Crusades were part of 'the eternal struggle of the West against the East'. While 'Europe was crossing Greece she found out that Greece was Orient, and therefore she included Greece in the destruction of the Orient'. An idealised account of that age of 'chivalry' follows, which is telling as to Renieris's cultural predilections.[75] The subsequent Turkish conquest plunged Greece once more into the dark ages. Finally, the regeneration of Greece in the modern era was achieved thanks to the appeal of Western ideas to young Greeks who went to the West for commerce or study. The most prominent example of these was Adamantios Koraïs.[76] He was the great interpreter of the West to Greece.[77]

While Koraïs in Paris was laying the foundations of this grand enterprise, 'the last vestiges of the Byzantine spirit' were forming another 'school' opposed to that of Koraïs. Its main characteristic was 'repulsion for the West, inherited from the Byzantines'. Laudable as the strict adherence of its supporters to 'our Eastern Orthodox Church' might be, 'their religious fanaticism makes them mistake all the creations of Western intellect for threats against our sacred religion'. These were the two parties of modern Greece, formed even before independence had been achieved. Renieris likened them to two angels, that of the East and that of the West, fighting to hold sway over the infant to be born. As soon as the baby was born it pronounced on its predilections. Its first utterances were the (remarkably liberal) constitutions of the Greek war of independence. 'Far from hurling curses against the West in the manner of the Byzantines, the newly born infant translated into the language of Demosthenes the liberal principles of the French Assembly.' Thus, 'as soon as she was resurrected, Greece on her own initiative proclaimed herself offspring of the West [τέκνον της Δύσεως] and had no memory for the implacable enmity that once was between herself and the West'. Renieris summed up: 'Greece, by her nature, by her civilisation, and by her historical mission, is West and not East.' During 'the age of decline and corruption, at the time of the Byzantines, she seemed to transfigure herself into her opposite. Once resurrected, however, she is returning to her previous orbit, and promises to become the leader of the West in the task of the moral conquest and regeneration of the East.' His conclusion read as a paean to Westernisation and its inevitability.[78]

Meanwhile the Easternisation of Russia had advanced still further by the time of the Crimean War, as can be seen in a later essay by Renieris. Regarding the position of his compatriots, Renieris was to change his tune in 1853, and argue that the Greeks were not 'Western' but rather ecumenically combined Western and Eastern civilisation, having given birth to the civilisations of both the Latino-Germanic West and the Slavic East. It would seem that, as political situations and needs changed, his interpretation of history must follow suit. The context now was the ambition of the tiny Kingdom of Greece to expand in territories populated by Greek-speaking or Orthodox populations under Ottoman rule, and the objections of Britain and France to any such expansion at the expense of the Ottoman Empire. Renieris's article was published in French, in September 1853, in the—interestingly baptised—magazine he co-edited, *Le Spectateur de l'Orient*.[79] Renieris argued that in Greece there were only two real political parties, 'le parti oriental' and 'le parti occidental'. As he put it, Europe was divided between two rival civilisations: on the one hand, 'la civilisation latino-germanique ou occidentale', and on the other, 'la civilisation slave ou orientale'. The two civilisations, having grown next to each other in different directions and almost without touching each other, had ended up, in his day, entering into contact—and were engaged, moreover, in a collision with each other because of the Eastern Question (la question d'Orient). That Eastern Question could be summarised in a few words: were the countries about to escape Ottoman rule, thanks to the rapidly proceeding decadence and dissolution of Turkey, destined to be the recipients of Latino-Germanic/Western or of Slavic/Eastern civilisation?[80] Now, given that in most of the lands occupied by the Ottoman Empire in Europe it was 'the Greek race' (la race grecque) that by its numbers, traditions, intelligence and civilisation was the preponderant element, and that as a consequence the future of 'the East' was sleeping in its womb, it was important to examine what the correlation was between that 'race' and the two rival civilisations that were to dispute between themselves, through propaganda, ideas, or through the force of arms, the heritage of the Ottoman Empire. What was missing in all related discussions, according to Renieris, was the realisation that the two rival civilisations ready to tear each other apart, 'la civilisation occidentale' and 'la civilisation slave', were sisters, and that both were descended from Greek civilisation.

Thus, Renieris was anticipating the later theory of that most influential historian of civilisations, Arnold Toynbee, who described both what he called the 'Western Civilisation' and what he called the 'Orthodox Christian Civilisation' as 'affiliated' to the earlier 'Hellenic Civilisation'. That meant, according to Toynbee, that the 'Orthodox Christian Society' was 'clearly twin offspring with our Western Society, of the Hellenic Society'.[81] Around a century earlier, Renieris was arguing that it had been Greece that, by its sciences, its letters and its arts, the charm of its genius and the spread of its philosophy, had transformed the West. In that way, at the time of the Roman conquest, from conquered, Greece had become conqueror. Then, under the Roman Empire, the word of Jesus Christ was spread by means of the Greek language, and the emperor moved to Byzantium; and subsequently, in the fifteenth century, Greeks from Constantinople galvanised the Renaissance. Meanwhile, in the ninth and tenth centuries, poor Greek monks had accomplished an immense labour, whose consequences would possibly change the face of the world: they transplanted Greek civilisation and religion onto Slav civilisation in Bulgaria, in Moravia, in Russia—and thus removed 'la race slave' from Latin influence. This was one of the greatest events in history; for had Western missionaries been faster than the Byzantine missionaries, and the Slavs thus become Latins, the whole future of humanity would have been changed.

Given the affinities and literal parenthood of both 'Western' and 'Eastern' civilisations that Renieris claimed for Greek civilisation, his next assertion was that Greece could not, therefore, be repulsed either by Latino-Germanic or by Slavic civilisation. On the contrary, the Greek element was the common denominator of the two. Western civilisation, on the one hand, could not but call itself 'Greco-Latin'; and Oriental civilisation, on the other hand, proudly proclaimed itself 'Greco-Slavic'. When all was said and done, it was 'the Greek who is the most universal man, the only truly catholic one of Europe'.[82] As a consequence, ran Renieris's argument, the Eastern Question was wrongly formulated, and that was why no solution had so far been found. Its presupposition was that the countries involved did not possess any original civilisation: that they constituted a tabula rasa, upon which either the Russians would prevail, and thus the populations concerned would become Slavs, or France and Britain would prevail, and they would become Catholic and Protestant. Renieris begged to differ, on the grounds that the countries in question possessed in fact 'the most ancient, the most original, and the most tenacious civilisation of Europe, Greek civilisation'; that civilisation was 'neither Eastern nor Western exclusively'; it was, rather, 'more perfect, more universal, more catholic than the two sisters which owed their birth to it'; it was 'ecumenical'.[83] What is striking in all this is that 'the East of Xerxes' is not even mentioned. 'Eastern civilisation' is equated with Russia and the Slavs, *tout court*.

VII. The Unlikely Godfather: Auguste Comte and the Substitution of *Occident* for *Europe*

There is a single monument in the Place de la Sorbonne in front of Paris's historic university. It is dedicated 'À AUGUSTE COMTE'. On the reverse side one reads,

FAMILLE
PATRIE
HUMANITÉ[84]

These were the three units of social organisation, or communities, according to Comte. But he came up with a fourth as well. For he highlighted an indispensable intermediary between *Patrie* and *Humanité*, which he called *l'Occident* (the

West). The monument is no random memorial. Comte was considered an extremely prominent figure until the early decades of the twentieth century. His thought and writings loomed large for all thinkers of the second half of the nineteenth century, and for many into the early twentieth century, either as an influence or as an opponent they felt the need to refute. Marx realised that he had to read him in the 1860s because the British and the French were 'making so much fuss about him', though he ultimately preferred Hegel to Comte. The comparison is telling in itself, and Marx was very far from alone in making it.[85] The extent of Comte's readership was astonishing. Some of these readers were more admiring than others, but his reach was undeniably immense.[86]

It is my argument that Comte was the first political thinker to elaborate an explicit and thorough sociopolitical idea of 'the West'—both as a supranational cultural identity and as a proposed political entity, based on civilisational commonality and shared historical antecedents.[87] The attribution of such a role to Comte leads me to argue, further, that the modern political idea of 'the West' was anything but an imperialistic project in its inception, despite widespread arguments in the literature that attribute its emergence to the needs of high imperialism. Comte made a conscious decision to substitute the term 'the West', *l'Occident*, for 'Europe', in order to avoid the confusions to which he thought the latter term led. His proposed entity included most of the peoples of Western Europe plus the peoples 'descended from' them in the Americas and Australasia. By proposing the new name in place of 'Europe' he attempted to safeguard the cohesiveness of his proposed sociopolitical entity for the immediate future, in the interests of the radical reorganisation that he was proposing. I am by no means claiming that Comte was the first person to use *the term* 'the West'. As we have seen above, the word was used from time to time (not least in expressions such as 'in East and West' or 'from East to West' and the like, or as a historical term to describe the Western Roman Empire and/or the kingdoms that succeeded it). But in these casual instances it was far from being consciously the denominator of a new entity or of any coherent political proposal for the future. Although the term had been used before Comte, especially in French and German, it was employed interchangeably with 'Europe', and the latter designation always predominated in the very texts that sporadically featured 'the West'. But 'Europe' was a geographical expression, referring to a conglomeration of states that included countries that Comte thought did not form part of the 'vanguard of Humanity' he was keen to see reorganised (while simultaneously excluding populations than Comte thought did belong to the group he had in mind, in the Americas and Australasia). It was in order to avoid such confusions, and to promote instead a

FIGURE 2.4. Auguste Comte monument, designed by Jean-Antoine Injalbert, Place de la Sorbonne, Paris (erected 1902). Photograph by Georgios Varouxakis.

distinct and precisely defined new entity, as well as to prescribe a new supranational identity and allegiance for it, that Comte opted for the term *l'Occident*. He also coined the term *occidentalité* (Westernness) to describe the new identity and supranational allegiance in question.

In seeking to establish the long-ignored origin of the first explicit and elaborate modern sociopolitical idea of the West, this book challenges a currently prevalent historiographical narrative regarding not only the timing, but also the intentions leading to, the emergence of that idea. In what he called 'A Brief Genealogy of the West', Christopher GoGwilt argued, as already mentioned, that the idea of the West emerged at the turn of the twentieth century, and that the first context in which it arose was 'that of the British imperial rhetoric during the 1890's, at the height of jingoism, propaganda, and politics of the "new imperialism"'.[88] That timing and the association with imperialism have been widely accepted and reproduced in subsequent scholarship, as we saw in chapter 1. And yet, the first elaborate articulation of a sociopolitical concept of 'the West' emerged from the pen of Comte, as part of a thorough proposal for the reorganisation of the existing world order. That new world order was designed, among other things, to abolish empires of conquest and establish a 'Western Republic' that would, first, organise the most advanced part of the world on a new basis internally. It would then radically alter the way the 'vanguard of Humanity' dealt with the rest of the world. It would offer to those outside it sympathy, example and assistance, on a strictly voluntary basis; but all forceful interference in the affairs of other countries or civilisations, not to speak of imperial conquests, would be excluded. And it would, in the long term, eventually admit those countries and civilisations, if and when they were willing and ready to join it.

I am therefore arguing that 'the West' as a self-conscious and explicitly political proposal originated in a vociferously anti-imperialist project aimed at abolishing the European empires and replacing them with an altruistically inclined 'Western Republic'. Meanwhile, there were other features of that Western Republic that would make it unattractive to most liberal-minded people (then or now); but my aim is neither to resuscitate Comte's overall political project nor to rehabilitate his reputation. It is rather to establish the real historical origins of the modern idea of the West, and to challenge some prevalent perceptions as to its meaning or content. It is an important (though ignored) part of those origins that, instead of being a product of imperialist plans and rhetoric around the turn of the twentieth century, as current scholarship would have one believe, 'the West' as a deliberate political project was, on the contrary, fiercely anti-imperialist. It represented, certainly, a road not taken, in that here was a self-assured, conscious and fully articulated proposal for the development of a 'Western' identity and commonwealth, which, however, would deal with the rest of the world in a way completely different from many of the attitudes and practices that actually prevailed in the nineteenth and twentieth centuries.[89] The notion of 'the West' was of course used later to justify imperialist projects, among other things. But that was far from being at the root of its inception.

Meanwhile, Comte's project was Western Europe–centric and Latin Europe–centric. This leads us to a further reminder of how partial current mainstream understandings of the idea of 'the West' are. Establishing that the first, as well as the most thorough, modern articulation of the idea of 'the West' as a sociopolitical concept was that contributed by Comte and propagated by his disciples is a healthy antidote against the all too frequent equation of 'the West' with the so-called Anglosphere. Comte's Latin-centric 'West', explicitly relegating Britain and the United States to important but non-hegemonic roles, certainly amounted to another road not taken. In all this, I am not proposing a 'correct' definition of 'the West'. But I do aim to contribute to our understanding of a complex history, which, thus far, has been surprisingly limited.

VIII. Comte's Political Project: The 'Republic of the West'

Comte is mainly seen as a philosopher who made important contributions to the history and philosophy of science and as the founder of sociology. Yet he himself regarded his life's work as primarily political, and as a project for social and political reorganisation after the cataclysm of the French Revolution.[90] He regarded his scientific and epistemological work as a parenthesis (admittedly longer than planned) that would corroborate his political project.[91] Many commentators have interpreted his work as being divided into two phases. The first (scientific) phase culminated in the six-volume *Cours de philosophie positive* (1830–42). The second was preoccupied by the development of his political project, accompanied by his elaboration of the 'religion of Humanity'. The major work of that period was the *Système de politique positive*, published in four volumes between 1851 and 1854. This sharp division of Comte's life and work into two distinct periods is almost always accompanied by the judgement that his best work and thought was contributed during the first phase, while the second is seen as the period of his intellectual and mental decline, when—to be blunt—he more or less went mad.[92] Today most Comte scholars reject the thesis that his career underwent an overwhelming change in his last decade or so. Instead they stress that he had already formulated his plans and ambitions for the political and social reorganisation of European society in his early writings of the 1820s (the *opuscules de jeunesse*).[93]

Around the middle of the 1840s Comte's mind took a religious turn, and the 'religion of Humanity' was born. Comte attributed his religious emphasis to his meeting in late 1844 with the much younger Clothilde de Vaux, and her untimely death little over a year later. Be that as it may, from 1847 onwards Comte was to elaborate at great length upon the religion of Humanity, which he formally founded in 1849.[94] But the religious focus was already in evidence by 1845. On 14 July 1845 Comte wrote to John Stuart Mill that he had dedicated the previous

FIGURE 2.5. Church of Humanity: Positivist temple in Porto Alegre, Brazil. Courtesy of User: Tetraktys. *Source:* https://commons.wikimedia.org/wiki/File:Templo_positivista.jpg

two months to special studies of medieval Catholicism, and mainly to reading, for the first time, Augustine's *City of God*.[95]

Besides whatever personal or biographical dimension came into play, Comte had a more theoretical reason to create his new religion. He had initially been very hostile to religion.[96] From the mid-1840s, however, he began to see the establishment of a religion as a logical consequence of his establishment of the new science that he baptised 'sociology'. He now came to believe that a genuine society cannot exist without being 'linked together' (*liée*).[97] A strong 'glue' was needed; and the way for that to be achieved was for all its members to agree upon a certain truth. He was convinced that, in his time and in the future, the truth in question could only be that of science, and therefore, he thought, he needed to found a 'scientific religion'.[98] As Étienne Gilson has put it, this was for Comte a simple 'deduction': he 'wanted to establish a universal society founded on the acceptance of a truth common to all people, and as he did not recognise any [such truth] other than that of science, it was upon this that he relied in order to construct his work'. Put simply, '[f]or science to become a social bond, it had to become philosophy, then religion'.[99] The religion of Humanity would, Comte hoped, unite people not just in getting to know Humanity (that was the function of sociology), but also in coming to love Humanity. He defined the 'Great Being' (Humanity) as 'the whole constituted by the beings, past, future, and present, which co-operate willingly in perfecting the order of the world'.[100] Given that the dead (*la Priorité*) and those yet to be born (*la Posterité*) were incomparably more numerous than those alive at any given time, the religion of Humanity was much more preoccupied with the past and the future than with the present. Comte believed that it was crucial to re-establish the feelings of continuity with the whole chain of Humanity's existence that people in the West had broken. In fact, this was the *maladie occidentale* (the Western disease).[101] 'Gradually developed by Protestantism, by deism and by scepticism, the Western disease consists in a continuous revolt of individual reason against the totality of human antecedents.'[102] Individualism was the direct result of that contempt for the past and neglect of the future.

According to the founder of Positivism, 'the fundamental problem' was that 'of reconciling Order and Progress'. He thought that all other schools of thought of his time were utterly incapable of achieving such a reconciliation.[103] On the one hand there were the supporters of eighteenth-century revolutionary principles. Such critical or negative revolutionary principles had completed their work of undermining the *ancien régime* with the French Revolution. In the nineteenth century they no longer had a reason for being. Their continuation led only to the destruction of any principle of order, and hence to anarchy. On the other hand, there was the reactionary or retrograde party, which went to the other extreme out of fear of the anarchical tendencies of their opponents. Such reactionaries wanted to undo everything the French Revolution had achieved and stood for. It was obvious to Comte that both were wrong.[104] His own motto was 'Order and Progress'. He insisted that progress was only the development of order, and that order and progress were not possible without each other.[105]

Comte had a radical solution. He advocated the introduction of a new 'spiritual power' that would oversee 'the spiritual reorganisation of society' and a corresponding separation between the spiritual and the temporal powers. He was inspired by his understanding of the role of the separation of spiritual from temporal power in Western Europe's Middle Ages. In adopting the latter idea, he was influenced by Joseph de Maistre's *Du pape*. Comte thought that the Catholic Church and its pontiff had played a beneficial role during the Middle Ages by exercising a spiritual power that both curbed the excesses of the secular rulers and kept the peoples of Western Europe together in a spiritual unity despite their fragmentation into separate political jurisdictions. During the Middle Ages the human mind was not ready for anything better than the dominance of the spiritual domain by the

Catholic clergy. But in Comte's own time, things were different, and the 'positive' age ought to usher in a different political arrangement.

This brings us to one of Comte's most cherished ideas, his 'law of the three states'.[106] Though it is reminiscent of various similar eighteenth-century schematic conjectures of the course of human history, Comte was proud of what he saw as the originality of his 'law' and often insisted that he had 'discovered' it as early as 1822.[107] He argued that humankind had gone through three stages of evolution, in relation to the development of the human mind in particular. The first stage he called 'theological', when people attributed everything that happened in the natural world to direct divine intervention. Then came the 'metaphysical' state, when gods were replaced by abstract entities and substances as explanations for phenomena. The final state of the human mind was the 'positive' state, which was characterised by scientific explanations and by a quest for relative knowledge, and laws of explanation (as opposed to the quest for absolutes and for ultimate causes that had characterised the previous states). The first stage was one of offensive war or conquest; the second, transitional, stage was one of defensive war; the third, positive, stage was industrial and peaceful.[108] Thus, in the positive state, war and conquest would be seriously anachronistic. This had deep repercussions with regard to Comte's, and Positivism's, attitude towards empire and imperialism.

The positive state would be the final and permanent state of the human mind and human society. Comte thought that what he saw as the most advanced part of the world, 'the élite of humanity', ought to be organised in a particular way that would overcome the anarchy that had resulted from the 'metaphysical' politics of the previous centuries of critical upheaval. This much-needed reorganisation was possible in his time, thanks to his systematisation of Positivism and his elaboration of sociology. He argued that the most advanced part of the world was ready for that new dispensation, which would recreate the salutary separation of spiritual from temporal power, but, crucially, without any need to believe in the existence of God. He envisaged the 'theoretical' class (*les savants*), the scientist-thinker-philosophers, forming themselves into an organised body and constituting the 'spiritual power' for the whole of the advanced world (as of 1848 Comte decided to stop calling the power in question 'spiritual' and to use 'moderating power' in its stead).[109] Meanwhile, temporal power would be in the hands of members of the capitalist class in each distinct temporal republic.

Comte also introduced another very significant stipulation: the temporal states in question had to be small in size for them to be well governed and for the spontaneous and 'organic' feelings of patriotism to arise (given his firm belief that 'what sociability gains in breadth, it loses in energy'.[110]). For example, France would have to be decomposed into seventeen smaller republics;[111] Ireland, Scotland, England and Wales would be separated, Britain would have to relinquish all its transmarine dependencies, France would relinquish Algeria, and so on. Each state would have to be roughly of the size of Belgium, Corsica or Tuscany. Comte went to great lengths to provide exact details of the size and population of each of the states, as well as the ideal social and occupational composition of each population. Given the small size of the proposed temporal states, and the restriction of their powers to the 'temporal' functions that Comte had reserved for them, it is hardly an exaggeration to claim that he was proposing a 'withering away of the state'.[112]

The most crucial aspect of Comte's political scheme was that the scale over which the temporal power and the spiritual (or moderating) power would repectively operate would not be identical.[113] The temporal governments would control the industrial organisation of each of the small states of the size of Tuscany or Belgium. The spiritual power, however, would be one alone for the whole of the Western Republic (*la République occidentale*), which would include the five great 'national'—or, more accurately, linguistic/cultural—groupings of Western Europe (French, Italian, Iberian, British, German) as well as their colonial transplantations in the Americas, Australia and so on. (The full title of Comte's 1848 *Discours* is indicative of the membership he had in mind. It makes up in explicitness for what it lacks in brevity: *A General View of Positivism: Or, Summary Exposition of the System of Thought and Life Adapted to the Great Western Republic, formed of the Five Advanced Nations, the French, Italian, Spanish, British and German, which, since the time of Charlemagne, have always constituted a Political Whole*). Whereas the temporal power would take care of solidarity between the members of each limited state, the spiritual power would preserve continuity between the dead, future generations, and those living in the present.[114] The spiritual power would be charged with the education of youth, but also with the continued education and moral guidance of people throughout life, as well as with keeping the temporal power in check. The capital of the new supranational entity united by the spiritual power, that is, 'the West', was to be, 'naturellement', Paris. Comte went into meticulous detail to describe exactly the composition of the 'Western Republic', the reasons for inclusion or exclusion, the primacy of France within it, the hierarchical precedence he accorded to the other two southern, Catholic, Latin, nations or groups (Italy and Spain) over the northern, Protestant ones ('England' and Germany); and much else.

This is how Comte delineated what he meant by 'the West' in the 1848 *Discours*: 'Since the fall of the Roman Empire, and more especially from the time of Charlemagne, France has always been the centre, socially as well as geographically, of this Western region which may be called the nucleus of Humanity.' Now, north and south of this 'natural centre', there were 'two pairs of nations, between which France will always form an intermediate link, partly from her geographical position, and also from her language and manners'. One pair was for the most part Protestant. It comprised, first, 'the great Germanic body, with the numerous nations that may be regarded as its offshoots; especially Holland'; and second, 'Great Britain, with which may be classed the United States, notwithstanding their present attitude of rivalry'. The other pair was 'exclusively Catholic': it consisted of 'the great Italian nationality' and 'the population of the Spanish Peninsula (for Portugal, sociologically considered, is not to be separated from Spain), which has so largely increased the Western family by its colonies'. Finally, '[t]o complete the conception of this group of advanced nations, we must add two accessory members, Greece and Poland, countries which, though situated in Eastern Europe, are connected with the West, the one by ancient history, the other by modern'.[115]

Comte was to elaborate much more upon the details of membership of his Western Republic and, even more, upon how exactly it was to be governed during the following few centuries of 'transition' to the 'normal' state of Humanity. For the Western Republic was not to be the final stage of his plan. It was merely required in order to prepare and lead the transition of the whole of Humanity to the future that Comte thought the scientific laws of his sociology had prescribed for it: the 'positive' and permanent state. The West would eventually disappear and be merged into a greater republic that would encompass the whole of Humanity. When that transition was completed (it would take around seven centuries, Comte calculated), the capital would move from Paris to Constantinople, which would become the permanent seat of the spiritual power and the centre of Humanity.[116] Comte again developed in great detail the plans for the transition, including which groups could be admitted first and which later—depending on their civilisation, religion and consequent degree of susceptibility to the 'positive' message. He was keen to point to shortcuts that would spare major parts of humankind the need to go through the turbulent evolution that the West had experienced and instead would allow them to pass straight from the state they found themselves in to the positive state. It was in this vein that he wrote to Czar Nicholas in 1852 that Russia might be spared the anarchic revolutionary upheavals that had afflicted Western Europe and pass one day straight to the positive state.[117]

Given that Comte deliberately chose to substitute 'the West' for 'Europe' not least in order to exclude Russia from the advanced transnational entity he envisaged, there is an irony in the fact that in scholarship on French attitudes to

Russia, Comte is presented as one of those authors who were positive towards it, unlike the majority of liberals, radicals and socialists, who were staunchly against it.[118] Such readings are infelicitous, their view being based solely on Comte's public letter to Czar Nicholas. However, even in that letter, Comte's message was not exactly complimentary towards Russia. Thanks to its backwardness, the country had been spared the revolutionary and anarchic upheavals of the more advanced West, and the czar was advised to keep it clear of such influences. But Comte was also adamant that his projected institutions were proposed only for France for the next half-generation, and after that only for the remainder of the five 'nations' of 'the West'. Russia, the rest of Eastern Europe and countries further east would have to wait much longer, as they were far from ready to be assimilated by the most advanced part of the world. Near the end of his letter, Comte also advised the czar to start adhering to the lessons of positivist analysis by freeing Poland, which was really part of 'the West'.

Thus, Comte's 'West' was a complex 'sociological' notion, and certainly not a geographical entity. He set out to study the historical development of the part of humankind that was most advanced, 'the avant-garde of Humanity'. Through that history he arrived at his 'scientific' interpretation of the past and future of Humanity—which he elaborated through his new science of *sociologie*. That avant-garde of Humanity was ready to receive Comte's proposed 'positive' reorganisation. However, for that reorganisation to succeed, the cohesion of the most advanced part of Humanity—the only part of the world ready, in his time, for the new, 'positive', dispensation—had to be safeguarded. Hence his concern to exclude for the time being more backward components of humankind from the proposed unit that had to be reorganised. Those 'backward' elements included Russia and most of Eastern Europe. The use of the name 'Europe' in reference to the countries that he included in the vanguard of Humanity (by more or less everyone else until, and during, his own time) led inevitably to confusion, and indeed contradiction, Comte decided. 'Europe' was seen—since the time of Peter the Great, at least—as including Russia, and consequently also the lands between Russia and Western Europe. Meanwhile, 'Europe' did not include populations that Comte thought belonged to the vanguard of humanity: peoples descended mainly from the 'five great nations' but living outside geographical Europe, in the Americas, Australia or New Zealand.

Now, these latter populations were often included (along with Europeans), in Comte's time, under the name 'Christendom'. But Christendom would not do either. First, it was still confusingly over-inclusive, as the populations of most of Eastern Europe and Russia were also Christian. Second, Christianity (and—crucially—more precisely Catholic Christianity, with its spiritual unity under one pope and one sacerdotal organisation) had been only one of the many elements or phases that had shaped the vanguard of Humanity. The other formative influences had been the incorporation of the populations in question under the Roman Empire, medieval feudalism, the unity of (most of) those populations under Charlemagne, and the revolutionary 'metaphysical' upheavals of the previous five centuries, culminating in the French Revolution. It was the populations that had shared in all or most of those successive experiences that had become the vanguard of Humanity, according to Comte, and it was through an analysis of their history that he formed his 'scientific' laws of sociology.

Comte's project was utopian, but he considered it, unlike the Saint-Simonians' and others' utopian schemes, to be based on 'scientific' foundations, and on his analysis of the past to yield valid prescriptions as to what was needed for the present and the future. What is remarkable about the whole scheme of Comte and his disciples was the combination of the striking Eurocentrism (and Francocentrism) it displayed, on the one hand, with a desire to be inclusive and universal and open to different civilisations and cultures, on the other. *Prima facie* it would be plausible to suggest that Comte's whole international vision was but one more version of the 'transnational projects of empire in France' brilliantly analysed by David Todd.[119] Certainly Giuseppe Mazzini was speaking for many in the nineteenth century when he complained in 1847 that several French 'political and philosophical schools' had recently begun by 'disdainfully shrugging their shoulders at the very word *nationality* or *country*' but meanwhile 'they ended up placing *their own* country, and even *their own* town, at the center of their theoretical edifice'.[120] Reinhold Niebuhr made a similar comment, directly aimed at Comte, a century later.[121] To see only the Francocentrism of the Comtean project would be unfair and one-sided, however: for it comprehended in the articulation of the religion of Humanity a genuine and consistently sustained attempt at inclusiveness of non-Western cultures and religions and an attempt at universality—admittedly combined with a striking degree of Eurocentrism, Francocentrism, Paris-centrism and rue-Monsieur-le-Prince-centrism. And there was a strong anti-imperialist thrust in Comte's Positivism, both in his own case and in that of the majority of his loyal disciples.

The overall project of the political and social reorganisation of the vanguard of Humanity was already conceived by Comte by the mid-1820s, and had been explained in his several early works, the *opuscules de jeunesse*. Though he was to add vast numbers of detailed stipulations in his later works (particularly in the *Système de politique positive*), the major building blocks and proposals were already there in the 1820s. What did change between the *opuscules* of the 1820s and the *Discours* of 1848 was the name of the entity in question. The 'Europe' of the 1820s was renamed 'the West' in the 1840s.

IX. From *L'Europe* to *L'Occident*

As early as 1816 Comte had displayed a sense of the unity of the five 'nations' he was later to include as the core of the West. 'J'aimerais mieux vivre médiocrement en Amérique que de nager dans l'opulence dans l'Anglo-Germano-Latino-Hispano-Gaule' (I would rather live modestly in America than swim in opulence in Anglo-Germano-Latino-Hispano-Gaul)', wrote the eighteen-year-old Comte on 29 October 1816.[122] (At that time he was seriously contemplating to move to the United States[123]). This was written before he met Henri de Saint-Simon and became his secretary in 1817. The lumping together of the nations in question was shared by Comte's new master. As we saw, Saint-Simon also referred to 'Europe' or 'Western Europe' as being composed of the same peoples. Comte had displayed a similar indecisiveness, and indeed explicit uneasiness, at least once, with regard to the use of the term 'Europe' to describe the supranational unit that he was talking about. In the 1826 'Considerations on the Spiritual Power', while describing the supranational authority of the 'spiritual power' to which he was allocating an overarching role, transcending state jurisdictions, he wrote in a footnote,

> Obliged to employ one or other of two expressions, *European* or *universal*, in order to designate that part of the functions of the spiritual power which is exerted over international relations [sur les relations de peuple à peuple], I prefer the former as being the most accurate and consecrated by past usage, *although probably it is at once too large and too narrow*. But I employ it without prejudice to the territorial extension which the spiritual power shall some time or other attain.[124]

Later Comte clearly realised that there was a third option, and that he did not have to use either 'European' or 'universal'. That third option was to use 'Western'. His uneasiness seems to have come to a head by early 1842. Already in the last volume of the *Cours* Comte began to display indecision regarding what to call the historic entity composed of the 'five great nations'. Mostly he used 'Europe', but 'Western Europe' (l'occident européen) was being employed with growing frequency by the end.

There have been some sophisticated analyses related to Comte's ideas on the West or on Europe contributed by Comte scholars in French in the last two decades or so.¹²⁵ Tonatiuh Useche Sandoval has produced an excellent analysis of the meaning and role of 'l'Occident' in Comte's overall system.¹²⁶ He notes that in the last lessons of the *Cours*, Comte began treating Europe as a 'republic' and that he hesitated between the adjectives *européen* and *occidental*, but that the former predominated by far. He then remarks that it is not until the publication of the *Système* (1851–54) that *européen* gives way to *occidental*.¹²⁷ And this is roughly true as far as published works are concerned—though the first published work in which *l'Occident* was formally proclaimed, however, was the *Discours* of 1848: not only was the word used innumerable times in the book, but the top of the front page announced, 'RÉPUBLIQUE OCCIDENTALE: Ordre et Progrès'.

We can trace the victory of *l'Occident* and *occidental* more closely, however, by following Comte's correspondence (which Useche Sandoval does not use in this context, with the exception of one rather later letter, of 1846). In his first letter to J. S. Mill, in 1841, Comte wrote that he was just then finishing, in his latest volume of the *Cours*, the elaboration of the proposal for the spontaneous institution 'of a European committee' (d'un comité européen), aiming to coordinate the common movement of philosophical regeneration, once positivism had planted its flag thanks to the publication of his work. That permanent committee, composed of thirty members, would represent the populations of Western Europe ('de l'Occident européen'), which, since Charlemagne, had 'always advanced more or less in synergy'. All the rest of Europe and the rest of the world would have to remain for a long time 'outside this association, which makes up the elements of the great European republic [la grande république européenne] of which we are both fellow-citizens'.¹²⁸ Thus the term 'European' prevailed in November 1841, though 'Western Europe' was mentioned as well. In the next letter, of 17 January 1842, ambivalence is obvious, with both 'the great European republic' (la grande république européenne) and 'the whole Western community' (toute la communauté occidentale) coinciding on the same page. Similar ambivalence within a single sentence occurs on 4 March when Comte talks of 'the new European synergy of the five great Western populations' (la nouvelle synergie européenne des cinq grandes populations occidentales).¹²⁹ In May, Comte wrote to Mill that '[t]he more our century advances, the more one will feel everywhere that all West Europeans are, in fact, fellow citizens'.¹³⁰ Comte's see-saw between 'Europe' and 'Western Europe' continued for some months.¹³¹ But he seems to have made up his mind by the end of 1842, when he wrote of the 'phase currently reached by the totality of the European, *or rather Western*, revolution' (phase actuellement atteinte par l'ensemble de la révolution européenne *ou plutôt occidentale*).¹³² In the remainder of his letters to Mill, from 1843 to 1846, 'l'Occident', 'en Occident', 'dans l'ensemble de notre Occident', 'occidentales', 'concert occidental', 'les mœurs occidentales' were the expressions that would clearly prevail.[133] Similarly, he wrote of 'la grande famille occidentale' and 'l'ensemble de l'Occident' to other British correspondents in the same period.[134]

Comte had also begun using in his correspondence a term pointing towards his coinage, by 1848, of the noun *occidentalité*. At some point Mill took issue with Comte's insistence that the English were the most prone to nationalistic prejudices among the five 'advanced' populations and retorted that the knowledgeable portion of the English were cosmopolitans ('cosmopolites') beyond what Comte could imagine.[135] The Frenchman replied that such 'vague' cosmopolitanism, that led people (such as the English cosmopolitans) to place on the same level the French or the Germans, on the one hand, and the Turks or the Chinese, on the other, was not conducive to real political cooperation. Such cooperation required habitual sentiments of more complete sympathy. He explained, 'The basic situation of the elite of humanity urgently requires everywhere the preponderance, not of an insufficient cosmopolitanism, but of an active Europeanism, or rather of *a profound Occidentalism* [non d'un insuffisant cosmopolitisme, mais d'un actif européanisme, ou plutôt d'*un profond occidentalisme*], corresponding to the necessary solidarity of the various elements of the great modern republic'—after which he repeated the historical antecedents that he regarded as binding together the five 'elite' populations.[136] Comte explicitly considered and then abandoned the term *européanisme*, opting instead for *occidentalisme*. (In this he departed from his former master, who had used *européanisme*, more or less equating it with cosmopolitan Christian morality or philanthropy: thus Saint-Simon was conflating the European and the universal, between which Comte was clear that he had to choose in 1826).[137] Comte insisted that an intermediate level of allegiance to the Western family of nations, the 'Western Republic', would be necessary in order for the urgently needed social and political reorganisation of the vanguard of Humanity to take place. Once that reorganisation was achieved, the vanguard of Humanity (the West) could help others and gradually accept them one by one (eventually merging itself and them into 'Humanity'). He named this supranational intermediate allegiance *occidentalisme*, and then *occidentalité*.

The latter concept is explained further in Comte's *Discours* of 1848 (and then in the *Système*) in a passage that makes clear both the medieval inspiration of the notion and the completely new character that it needed to assume in the 'positive' era:

> Between the simple nationality, which the social spirit of antiquity never superseded, and Humanity in its definitive conception, the Middle Ages

instituted *an intermediary conception too little appreciated today, by founding a free occidentality*. Our first political duty now consists in reconstructing it [occidentality] on unshakeable bases, by putting right the anarchy generated by the extinction of the Catholic and feudal regime.[138]

Comte did not insist on the need to cultivate an allegiance to 'Westernness' due to any desire for permanent exclusions. It was simply a matter of time and readiness. To the extent that the systematisation and reorganisation that he was proposing would be accomplished, he continued, that reorganisation would show that 'Westernness' (*l'occidentalité*) constituted merely a last preparation for genuine 'Humanity' (*Humanité*). For the fundamental laws of human evolution, which were the philosophical basis of the final regime, 'applied necessarily to all climates and to all races, except for simple inequalities of speed'.[139]

In other words, the 'Westernness' that had emerged in the Middle Ages needed to be reconstructed on new 'positive' bases, and until that reconstruction was complete it would be necessary for the West not to be adulterated by the inclusion of peoples that did not share the same degree of advancement and cohesion as the five 'advanced' or 'elite' populations (with the minor exceptions of Poland and Greece). But once the reconstruction of the vanguard of Humanity, the West, was complete, the positive laws established scientifically would be able to be applied to the rest of Humanity and bring the more backward populations into the fold, at their own pace and on their own initiative. That process once achieved, Humanity would be complete in its 'normal' and 'permanent' state.

Once Comte had adopted the term *l'Occident* to describe the entity he was envisaging he did make the most of it. From July 1848, when he published the *Discours sur l'ensemble du positivisme*, all books and circulars produced by the rue Monsieur-le-Prince publishing concern were headed 'RÉPUBLIQUE OCCIDENTALE'. The shared Navy that would replace standing armies would be called the 'Western Navy'. Comte was very alert to the importance of symbols.[140] He therefore also designed a common Western currency, a Western flag, and much more. In all these endeavours he went into astonishing degrees of detail—for, as Mill observed, he could 'not bear that anything should be left unregulated'.[141]

X. Positivist Contributions after Comte

As has been mentioned already, Comte was, for some decades, strikingly influential around the world. His disciples were to be found 'dispersed as far apart as Newcastle and Rio de Janeiro'. And '[h]is followers were to be instrumental in the establishment of republics not only in France but also in Brazil, Portugal, and

FIGURE 2.6. The flag of Brazil, with the motto *Ordem e Progresso* (Order and Progress), inspired by Auguste Comte's motto of Positivism. *Source:* https://en.wikipedia.org/wiki/Auguste_Comte#/media/File:Flag_of_Brazil.svg

Czechoslovakia'.[142] Positivism was particularly popular in Latin America, India and Turkey.[143] Still today, the national flag of Brazil bears Comte's motto *Ordem e Progresso* (Order and Progress), adopted when the Brazilian Republic was founded by Comtist Positivists, in 1889.[144]

Around the revolutionary year 1848, Comte's ideas were being spread (more effectively than through his own wooden prose) thanks to a series of articles in the highly influential paper *Le National*, by one of his—then—disciples, Émile Littré.[145] Littré was a major figure in French philosophical life. He was to abandon ship a few years later, disappointed by Comte's opportunistic appeal to conservatives, including his approval of Louis-Napoleon Bonaparte's coup d'état. But during the ferment of the 1848–49 debates, Littré repeated time and again the message of the need for a federation that he, following Comte, called the 'République occidentale'.[146]

After Comte's death, his successor in France (and hence pontiff of Humanity, in light of France's 'presidency' over 'the Western Republic') was Pierre Laffitte. It was in his introduction to the French translation of an essay written by his British counterpart, Richard Congreve, that Laffitte first contributed, in 1858, one of his clarifications on the meaning of *l'Occident* and *république occidentale*, characteristically entitled 'Ce qu'on entend, dans le Positivisme, par le mot de république occidentale' (What 'Western Republic' means in Positivism). As Laffitte put it, 'the epithet "European" was too vague, as it included populations that ought not to be part of it, for example Russia'.[147] And much later, in 1881, Laffitte would still be writing, 'With the spread of Positivism, the use, as a political expression, of the purely geographical term "European" must be dropped: for it was applied in an utterly irrational way to an assemblage of very distinct and dissimilar peoples.' As used, 'the appellation errs at once by excess and by defect'. He explained that '[d]emocratic hallucinations notwithstanding, there is no United States of Europe; for this portion of the world comprises Oriental populations, such as Turkey and Russia, while it does not include the various colonial extensions of the West, especially the Americans, who manifestly form part of it.'[148] This, surely, is what Comte had meant already in 1826, when, as we have seen, he remarked of the term 'European' that it was 'at once too large and too narrow'.[149]

'Europe' was not, moreover, the only term that must be superseded and replaced by 'the West'. In 1861 Laffitte stressed 'the need there is for setting on foot a reasonable and moral policy for regulating the relations of the West with the rest of the World'. There was a pressing preliminary need, however: 'before the group formed by the advanced populations can adopt a proper policy towards the rest of the world, a change must be brought about in its way of looking at itself'. That change consisted 'in dropping the notion of *Christendom*, and adopting in place of it, the notion of *Westerndom* [*occidentalité*] or *The West*'. Laffitte defined what he was talking about: 'By the term *Westerndom*, or the *Western Commonwealth* [*république occidentale*], I mean to indicate the group of the five leading peoples [...] as identified by Auguste Comte.' 'The West' was preferable because it was more precise, for the reason already explained (exclusion of Eastern Christians), as well as because it represented fully 'the whole set of antecedents that [had] helped to mould this memorable group'. The word 'Christian' referred only to one of those antecedents. 'Westerndom', however, owed its formation 'to its conquest by the Romans more than to anything else; and the formative process was completed by the policy of Charlemagne, by the sway of the Catholic Church, by the incomparable influence of Feudalism, and the revolutionary developments of the last five centuries'. But the substitution of 'Westerndom' for 'Christendom' would also have a salutary influence on the group's external policy: for the Christian point of view, 'which so profoundly vitiates our appreciation of the other peoples of the world', would, if 'Westerndom' were adopted in its stead, stop being a barrier to Westerners' capacity to understand other peoples accurately.[150]

XI. Conclusion

I have followed, through the writings of a number of French- and German-speaking thinkers, with some reinforcements from Russia and Greece, the gradual progression of uses of 'the West' and the meanings attached to the term in the course of the nineteenth century. We traced the steps whereby an earlier distinction between North and South started to be relaced by one between East and West, and we saw Russia moving from being considered a 'Northern' power to being seen as an 'Eastern' one. We also saw that uses of 'the West' were often confusing and inconsistent, not least because of varying understandings of what was meant by 'the East'. Sometimes the latter term referred to the Ottoman Empire, sometimes to the Far East, beyond. But when it came to juxtaposing an opposing entity against such an East, the term 'Europe' was still available, and often invoked. It was when the need arose for juxtaposition against a fellow 'European' power, however, that 'the West' became indispensable. We noted its occurrence already in the second decade of the nineteenth century, in the case of Mme de Staël, although in that instance Russia was depicted sympathetically. But by the 1820s, with writers such as the abbé de Pradt, Russia was being discussed as a lethal threat to the rest of Europe, and the need for a Western federation in order to resist the Eastern danger coming from Russia was being explicitly expressed. Besides various French versions, we followed some striking examples among German-speaking authors, culminating in Nietzsche's uses of 'West' when the discussion concerned the danger that he too saw coming from Russia. A brief discussion of the way things were viewed by some thinkers in Russia itself, and in the young Kingdom of Greece, allowed us to consider some alternative perspectives on the same issues. Some of the thinkers concerned were more consistent than others, and some more explicit than others. But the general picture of a growing deployment of the idea of 'the West' is clear.

It is also clear that no one was more explicit and more systematic in this regard than Auguste Comte. Comte was original, and important to this story, because he made a conscious decision to abandon 'Europe' and substitute 'the West' to designate an entity that he described in meticulous detail. Others who employed the term before him or contemporaneously with him were neither precise nor consistent in their use of it. D'Eichthal is typical of such inconsistency: few people had cited *l'Occident* as early, and as often, as he did. However, in later years he proceeded to promote 'l'unité européenne' and a 'confédération européenne' based explicitly on the kind of pan-Christian unity sponsored by the Holy Alliance, on Russia's initiative, and of course including Orthodox

Russia.¹⁵¹ That inclusion was anathema to Comte, who strongly advocated a more restricted 'membership list', based primarily on Charlemagne's Europe, or pre-Reformation Catholic Europe: the Europe envisaged by de Maistre, de Bonald and Saint-Simon, with the addition of the extra-European colonial offshoots of the peoples in question. In order to avoid the contradictions and confusions arising from the use of the much vaguer term 'Europe', Comte decided to name his supranational entity 'the West'. Thus the various recent theories about the history of the modern idea of 'the West' in the West have missed the most important link in the story. That link consists in the writings and tireless propagandising efforts of Auguste Comte. It was Comte who first developed a thorough and explicit idea of 'the West' as a sociopolitical concept, basing it on a historical analysis of the development of what he saw as the 'elite' of Humanity, and proposing an elaborate plan for the reconstruction of that part of the world prior to it enabling the rest of Humanity to achieve the same 'positive' state of development. I have followed in some detail the gradual adoption of *l'Occident* to replace *l'Europe*, and found the decisive developments to have occurred in the course of the year 1842: implying that his notion of the West was adopted and developed by Comte well before his religious turn a few years later, and was therefore independent of the latter. Once he had invented his religion, of course, 'the West' and the 'religion of Humanity' became closely associated; but the timing that I have established means that they were neither coeval nor necessarily inextricably linked.

To the extent that the idea of 'the West' tends to be associated with 'democracy, individualism and liberalism',¹⁵² meanwhile, the attribution that I have argued for here of a crucial role to Comte complicates the picture. The West envisaged by Comte was designed as anything but democratic, individualistic or liberal. This need not change our understanding of the meanings and associations acquired by the concept through its later uses, but it shows that such meanings and associations were neither inherent to it nor coeval with its emergence. Comte's diagnosis of the problem of modernity was that, in its recent revolutionary and 'metaphysical' phase, the 'vanguard of Humanity' had fallen victim to individualistic neglect of the past and of historical antecedents, which he called the 'Western disease' (*la maladie occidentale*).¹⁵³ That is why his proposed spiritual power would be preoccupied with establishing continuity with past and future generations, why his 'religion of Humanity' was to cultivate reverence for past benefactors of Humanity, and the Positivists' motto 'Vivre pour autrui' (Live for others) would promote altruism (itself a term coined by Comte). In order to combat 'metaphysical' revolutionary notions such as individual rights, Comte proposed a deeply illiberal programme of moral regeneration through religiously inculcated altruism and love of Humanity.

Far from its emergence being related to the needs of European imperialism, then, as has often been argued, the modern idea of the West had clearly anti-imperialist origins. Though strikingly Eurocentric, Comte's long-term utopian plan was meant to become universal and inclusive, aiming to encompass the whole of Humanity. And no matter how patronising it may appear to us today, if judged against any proposed alternatives in the nineteenth century, Comte's scheme was a plea for the Western nations to associate with the rest of the world 'on terms of mutual courtesy and fair reciprocity of advantage'.[154]

3

Insular Britain Joins the West

'Ideas are extraterritorial, and pay no duty as they pass from land to land.'
JOHN E. E. DALBERG-ACTON, *SELECTED WRITINGS OF LORD ACTON*, VOL. 3, P. 644

'We of the West, the advanced guard of Humanity, are citizens of no mean city; not lowered by narrow and local aspirations; not isolated by national selfishness; [...] We cease to be solely or primarily members of such or such a Western nation, England or France. We become primarily Western, with an immunity from all the evils which have clung around the exclusive prominence given to the more restricted associations; [...] The ties and obligations of the new relation exert a healthy influence on all our thought and action, not extinguishing, nor even lessening our love of our separate countries or states, but correcting its excess, and by placing it in its due subordination, at once purifying and strengthening it.'
RICHARD CONGREVE, 'THE WEST' (1866), PP. 39–40

IT IS TAKEN for granted by many, in the English-speaking world, at any rate, firstly that America and Britain are *the* leading members of 'the West' or 'Western civilisation'; and secondly that the quintessence of the West is a staunch attachment to liberty, democracy, human rights and related so-called 'Western values'. Both assumptions need to be challenged. In this chapter I wish to argue against a number of misrepresentations regarding both when a sociopolitical concept of the West as a supranational self-description based on civilisational commonality emerged in English, and what it meant when it entered the political and cultural vocabulary.[1]

In the following pages I will argue, first, that there were, already in the eighteenth century, some incipient attempts that groped towards a term denoting a distinctive West European cultural unity, especially as a response to the entry of Russia into the political and cultural system of 'Europe' since the time of Peter the Great. I further argue, that these uses were rather casual and always accompanied by, and interchangeable with, overwhelmingly more references to 'Europe' as the supranational civilisational entity that the authors identified with, until, roughly, the middle of the nineteenth century. Such instances intensified as of the early nineteenth century, without directly or explicitly opposing themselves to the dominant collective self-description of 'Europe'. They coexisted with 'Europe' and were employed in parallel with it. However, the first conscious and sustained attempts in Britain to articulate a distinctive 'Western' identity and a concept of the West that was promoted as an actual alternative to the allegedly confusing term 'Europe' came as of the 1850s and 1860s, thanks to the relentless activism of the British followers of Auguste Comte. A third and related argument is that, besides Positivism itself having been imported from France, the authors who had most often used 'West' or 'Western' in English (no matter how casually or inconsistently), before the conscious propagation of these terms by the Comtists, were people who had lived in continental Europe or were deeply influenced by continental thought and had mastered one or more of the continent's languages.

What emerges in this chapter is a complex picture, which challenges dominant stereotypes. While some of the first uses of 'the West' in a sociopolitical sense conform to the widespread picture of celebrating a liberty-cherishing West, others—those, moreover, representing the most sustained and consistent articulations of an idea of the West—were inspired by an overtly illiberal project. Meanwhile, to add to the paradoxes or surprises, the rival or alternative supranational self-description 'Europe' had emerged in late seventeenth-century England as part of an explicitly Whig political discourse promoting William III as the defender of 'the liberties of Europe'.

I. Insular Britain versus Continental Occident

It is important to stress from the beginning that there is a clear difference between uses of 'the West' in English on the one hand, and uses of equivalent terms in French or German on the other. In the latter languages, uses of *l'Occident* or *der Okzident/das Abendland* were much more common in the eighteenth and early nineteenth centuries, as well as occurring earlier.[2] As already mentioned, I attribute the difference to the fact that, given that neither England nor Britain as a whole was part of Charlemagne's empire (nor of the later Holy Roman Empire of the German Nation), the word was less available and less attractive, in terms of associations with the country's own past, than it was in Germany or in France. It is probably not accidental that, in the nineteenth century, French authors would come up with federal solutions to Europe's problems that would take the form of the resurrection of the 'Western Empire', with France as its leader.[3] It had by then (not least through Napoleon's efforts) become entrenched in French national mythology that France was the descendant and successor of Charlemagne's 'Empire of the West' (while France was simultaneously claiming the older mantle of Latin Rome).[4] 'The West' or 'the Western Empire' was part of what nineteenth-century French thinkers or politicians regarded as their own national past (some of the statements from Gustave d'Eichthal's *Les Deux Mondes* that we encountered in chapter 2 are typical in this respect). Similar attitudes can be attributed to German-speaking authors. Such co-option through elective affinities was less tempting for insular Britons.

II. Early Uses of 'West' and 'Western'

Of course, 'west' and 'western' had long been used in English (or in Latin texts written by English authors) in what was clearly a geographical sense. John Milton, for instance, referred to 'this goodly tower of a Common-wealth, which the *English* boasted they would build, to overshaddow kings, and be another *Rome* in the west'. Moreover, when on the same page Milton referred to the supranational community before which the English should beware of being ridiculed, it was 'the common laughter of *Europ*' that he was worried about.[5] The geographical sense also prevailed when Adam Smith wrote that 'Greece, and the Greek colonies in Sicily, Italy, and the Lesser Asia, were the first countries which, in these western parts of the world, arrived at a state of civilized society'.[6] There do exist some few examples where, besides geography, historical or cultural similarities among the nations of 'western Europe' might be implied. Francis Bacon referred to 'nos, occidentales [...] Europæ nationes' or 'nos Europæos occidentales'.[7] In the Conclusion to the Second Part of *Leviathan* (1651), Thomas Hobbes referred to 'these Western parts, that have received their Morall learning from *Rome*, and *Athens*'.[8]

Some uses that do grope towards a distinction between *Western* Europe and other parts, beyond, did begin to emerge more clearly in the latter part of the eighteenth century. They appeared in the context of suspicion of the newcomer on the political and cultural scene of 'Europe': Russia. One of the most striking instances occurs in an epistolary novel, *The Citizen of the World*, by the Irish writer Oliver Goldsmith. The novel began being published in instalments in the

Public Ledger in 1760. (Thus it appeared earlier than Jean-Jacques Rousseau's expression of deep pessimism about the long-term prospects of Peter the Great's reforms in *Du contrat social* [1762])[9]. The international context was the Seven Years' War. Even in Goldsmith's novel, the main comparisons are between the Chinese and 'the Europeans', or between China and 'Europe'. When a juxtaposition with Russia was the subject, however, uses of 'Europe' alternated with uses of 'the western parts of Europe'. In 'Letter LXXXVII' we read one putative Chinese correspondent censuring 'the people of Europe' for their tendency, when at war with one another, to 'apply to the Russians, their neighbours and ours, for assistance'. The Chinese correspondent was critical of the habit, because he judged that all subsidies that 'the people of Europe' paid for such aid were strengthening the Russians; and that was a bad idea, given that he could not 'avoid beholding the Russian empire, as the natural enemy of the more western parts of Europe.'[10] As he added, 'It was long the wish of Peter, their great monarch, to have a fort in some of the western parts of Europe; many of his schemes and treaties were directed to this end; but, happily for Europe, he failed in them all.' Success would have been fatal, because '[a] fort, in the power of this people, would be like the possession of a flood-gate', as 'they might then be able to deluge *the whole western world* with a barbarous inundation'.[11] Even here, in the most striking case of a differentiation between two parts within (the author's contemporary) Europe, there is no gainsaying the easy alternation between 'Europe' and 'the western parts of Europe' to denote the advanced part of the world that was threatened by alleged Russian designs. There was as yet no fully fledged distinction between 'Western Europe' and 'Eastern Europe', let alone any fully articulated concept of 'the West'.

The distinction introduced (even partially and inconsistently) by Goldsmith was rather unusual for the mid-eighteenth century, but it was to become progressively much more common in the nineteenth. It was a distinction *within* Europe between Western Europe and Eastern Europe. Following Peter the Great's reforms, Russia had been admitted as part of 'Europe'. Those who were uneasy with Russia being thus identified as 'European' began to look for ways to distinguish between themselves and the political-cum-cultural newcomer.

III. 'Europe' and 'the Liberties of Europe'

The term 'the West' does appear in one major and influential a work in the late eighteenth century: Edward Gibbon's *History of the Decline and Fall of the Roman Empire* (1776–88). And it appears with a vengeance, innumerable times. However, it is used in a specific sense (similarly to what we have seen in the case of

Condorcet et al.). 'The West' begins to appear in Gibbon's narrative once the Roman Empire is divided into Western and Eastern Empires (395 CE), to denote the Roman Empire of the West. It then continues to be used with reference to the Germanic conquests in the territories of the former Western Empire and subsequently the pretender successor realms in Western Europe, Charlemagne's empire and the later Holy Roman Empire of the German Nation, as well as the French kingdom. Gibbon chose to concentrate in the last two volumes of his *History* on the Eastern Empire.[12] But even with that eastern focus, 'the West' is ubiquitous through its interactions with the empire of Constantinople—the Crusades being among those interactions. In other words, Gibbon's 'West' was part of a (long) phase in the history that he was narrating. It was used in contradistinction to the Eastern Roman (Byzantine/Greek) Empire.

Gibbon did not use 'the West', however, to describe the supranational civilisational entity to which he felt he himself belonged in the eighteenth century. For that, there was another word. At the end of his third volume (1781), Gibbon inserted his 'General Observations on the Fall of the Roman Empire in the West'.[13] There he proposed to enquire whether such a re-barbarisation of his part of the world could occur again:

> It is the duty of a patriot to prefer and promote the exclusive interest and glory of his native country: but a philosopher may be permitted to enlarge his views, and *to consider Europe as one great republic*, whose various inhabitants have attained almost the same level of politeness and cultivation. The balance of power will continue to fluctuate, and the prosperity of our own, or the neighbouring kingdoms, may be alternately exalted or depressed; but these partial events cannot essentially injure our general state of happiness, the system of arts, and laws, and manners, which so advantageously distinguish, above the rest of mankind, the Europeans and their colonies.

He went on to concede that '[t]he savage nations of the globe are the common enemies of civilized society; and we may enquire with anxious curiosity, whether Europe is still threatened with a repetition of those calamities, which formerly oppressed the arms and institutions of Rome'. His verdict was that there were crucial differences between the Romans of old and the Europeans of his own time, and those differences led him to argue that the latter were safe. The Romans had been 'ignorant of the extent of their danger, and the number of their enemies'. Beyond the Rhine and the Danube, 'the northern countries of Europe and Asia were filled with innumerable tribes of hunters and shepherds, poor, voracious, and turbulent; bold in arms, and impatient to ravish the fruits of industry'. But in his own time, such 'formidable emigrations no longer issue[d] from the North'. Instead of 'some rude villages', Germany could display 'a list of two thousand three hundred walled towns'; and even Russia now 'assume[d] the form of a powerful and civilized empire'. In addition, Europeans were in his time living in separate and diverse states, and could not be conquered in one go as Rome had been. All this meant that, '[i]f a savage conqueror should issue from the deserts of Tartary, he must repeatedly vanquish the robust peasants of Russia, the numerous armies of Germany, the gallant nobles of France, and the intrepid freemen of Britain; who, perhaps, might confederate for their common defense'.[14]

Clearly, when he wrote his 'General Observations' in the early 1770s, Gibbon did not share Goldsmith's or Rousseau's apprehensions about Russia a decade earlier. On Peter's reforms, he was rather with Voltaire, the author of the *Histoire de l'Empire de Russie sous Pierre le Grand* (1760–72).[15] In this instance at least, Gibbon talked of Russia as part of the civilised Europe that he was optimistic about—and he even included it as one of the countries that 'perhaps, might confederate for their common defense', along with Germany, France and Britain.

Interestingly, more than a century later, one of Comte's British disciples saw Gibbon as a precursor of the founder of Positivism in conceptualising Europe as a republic. But he also noted crucial differences, remarking that Comte gave the idea 'a definiteness, an exactness, which Gibbon's language does not express, and which cannot be realized except by reference to Comte's theory of history'.[16] And, even more tellingly,

> It is, however, essential to remember that the republic thus alluded to is the republic of *Western* Europe—is limited, that is, to the nations which had been more or less *Catholicised*; whereas Gibbon speaks loosely of 'Europe'—a geographical term which would embrace Russia and Turkey; is incompatible with any idea of republican community of thought and life; and has not the historical significance attaching to Comte's definition.[17]

What has been said above does not mean that Gibbon did not have a Western-Europe-centric view of history. He did, and as Karen O'Brien has shown, one of the features that distinguishes him from his Scottish contemporaries was his refusal fully to accept most of the Scottish Enlightenment thinkers' generic 'progress of society' (or stadial-historical) explanations that could apply potentially to all societies. Gibbon thought, rather, that the history of the 'Europe' that emerged from the merger of the ruins of the Western Roman Empire with the Germanic 'barbarians' who conquered it was a contingent and unique story of a singularly progressive civilisation.[18] But he followed the common practice of his contemporaries, and called the eventual outcome of that West European story 'Europe'.[19]

In talking in terms of 'Europe', Gibbon was typical of eighteenth-century British thinkers. Now, 'Europe' had been used from time to time sporadically in earlier centuries as well.[20] But the dominant self-descriptor used to name the overarching supranational cultural entity or wider community that West European thinkers identified with, certainly until the end of the seventeenth century, had been 'Christendom'. From then onwards, however, 'Europe' came to compete with—though by no means completely to supersede—'Christendom'. One explanation for the popularity of 'Europe' as of the late seventeenth century is that it reflected a process of secularisation.[21] But in Britain in particular, the popularity of 'Europe' was also related to the need for the Whigs to find a term other than Christendom, given that the king of France was presented by his English allies—the Whigs' (Jacobite) opponents—as the defender of Christendom, 'the Most Christian King'. In response, the Whigs began to call William III the defender of the 'liberties of Europe'.[22] John Toland was only one of many who referred to William III as 'both the restorer and supporter of the Liberty of *Europe*'.[23]

While the epithet 'western' in contradistinction to 'eastern' might appear from time to time, used in a geographical sense, and while 'western parts' or 'western world', to identify the part of the world one was referring to, would sometimes be used, sociopolitical uses of 'the West' or 'Western civilisation' were very rare in early to mid-nineteenth century British writings. In his widely discussed *History of Civilization in England*, of which the first volume was published in 1857, H. T. Buckle nowhere mentioned 'Western civilisation' or 'the West'. Besides talking rather of national civilisations ('English', French, American, German), his major generalisation was that referring to the differences between 'European civilization' and 'the non-European division' of civilisation (or between 'the East' and 'Europe').[24] Though it was in that very year that the Comtist leader Richard Congreve published two pamphlets promoting a different term,[25] Buckle's use was still the norm.

IV. Different 'Others': 'The West' versus 'Northern'/ 'Eastern' Russia, 'Oriental' Jews, and Turkey

Meanwhile, there were some early manifestations of usages that were to become much more common some decades later; and there was a particular context in which these arose, as of the early 1830s. Russia had become very unpopular abroad because of the way it suppressed the Polish uprising of 1830–31 and then suspended the Kingdom of Poland's special constitutional status stipulated by the Treaty of Vienna of 1815. One of the factors that would affect debates in Britain and France from 1831 onwards would be an immense sympathy for Poland in both countries and the assiduous campaigning of great numbers of Polish refugees (many of them highly sophisticated and well-connected members of the Polish aristocracy).[26] Then, in 1833, Russia provoked shockwaves of anxiety in the other powers by managing to capitalise on the threat posed to the Ottoman Empire by the latter's own vassal, Mehemet Ali, pasha of Egypt, and provisionally turn the Sultan to all intents and purposes into Russia's protégé. For a short period Russia was allowed to station military forces around Constantinople, and then signed the Treaty of Unkiar Skelessi (Hünkâr İskelesi) with the Ottoman Porte.[27] Two decades later, the Crimean War would be both a result and an additional cause of unpopularity for Russia among most British commentators.[28]

Thus, in most of the limited number of cases when the terms 'West' and 'Western' were used in Britain in the 1830s and 1840s the reason involved (a juxtaposition with) Russia. For a short time the foreign secretary Palmerston spoke of the treaty of alliance that he forged between Britain, France, Spain and Portugal in 1834 as 'a quadruple alliance among the constitutional states of the West, which will serve as a powerful counterpoise to the Holy Alliance of the East' (or as 'a formal union between the four constitutional states of the West to drive absolutism out of the [Iberian] Peninsula').[29] It is likely that the usage was imported from the discourse of Palmerston's French interlocutors and allies, who were talking much of a 'Western' alliance between the constitutional powers of France and Britain at the time in question. Like the expression 'the Eastern Question' itself, it is possible that reference to a 'Western' alliance was derived by Palmerston from the language of his French counterpart, the Duc de Broglie, and the French ambassador in London, Talleyrand, with whom he was in constant negotiation throughout that period.[30] Another continental source of Palmerston's language may have been Prince Adam Czartoryski, the Polish leader living in exile in London and Paris after the suppression of the Polish uprising of 1830–31 and assiduously advising Palmerston on the unavoidable struggle between what he described as the liberal West and the despotic East.[31] At any rate, Palmerston alternated between calling the other side (Russia, Prussia and Austria) 'the Eastern Powers' and 'the three Northern Powers'[32]—typically displaying the inchoateness of these distinctions in the early nineteenth century. Most others also referred to Russia, Prussia and Austria as 'the Northern Powers' or 'Northern Courts' at the time.[33]

One of those who sometimes employed the term 'Western' from early on was the highly idiosyncratic activist and politician David Urquhart. His distrust of Russia became almost proverbial as of the 1830s.[34] His impact was considerable, and those captivated by the charms of his magnetic personality included King William IV. Urquhart referred to 'the Empires of the West', 'the Western nations' or 'the Powers of the West' when he wanted to make a distinction between France and Britain on the one hand, and Russia (which he loathed) or the Ottoman Empire (which he admired) on the other.[35] He did convince many of the Russian danger and of Palmerston's allegedly pro-Russian stance, including—for a while, and partially—Karl Marx. Marx eventually saw through him, though: 'He [Urquhart] is a romantic reactionary—a Turk, and would gladly guide the West back to Turkish standards and structures.'[36] The German-born and London-based Marx, meanwhile, was one of the authors writing in English, not least for the *New York Tribune*, in the 1850s who used 'West' and 'Western' much more extensively than did most native English speakers (either in Britain or in the United States) at that time.[37]

Sometimes 'West' or 'western' would be used in contradistinction to 'Oriental' Jews. Dr. Thomas Arnold was a major figure in his overall impact on nineteenth-century British culture.[38] He wrote to a correspondent that Providence had communicated 'all religious knowledge to mankind through the Jewish people', and 'all intellectual cultivation through the Greeks'. A propos, he remarked that he had 'occasion in the winter to observe this in a Jew, of whom I took a few lessons in Hebrew, and who was learned in the writings of the Rabbis, but totally ignorant of all the literature of the West, ancient and modern'. The man in question was, Arnold continued, 'consequently just like a child'. He meant by that that the man's mind was 'entirely without the habit of criticism or analysis, whether as applied to words or to things'.[39]

But not all depictions of Jews were negative, and their role could also be seen as that of a bridge between East and West (rather than simply as being 'Orientals'). Certainly that was an idea highlighted in George Eliot's novel *Daniel Deronda*, published in 1876. George Eliot (Mary Ann Evans; 1819–1880) of course became famous as a novelist, but before achieving such success she worked as a translator of major works of continental European philosophy, and as the virtual co-editor of the highly influential *Westminster Review*. Her command of philosophical systems was striking and her talent prodigious. She did much research while writing *Daniel Deronda* between 1872 and 1876, including extensively into Jewish history and culture, which also involved her learning Hebrew.

The novel was first publishing in instalments in *Blackwood's Edinburgh Magazine* from February to September 1876.⁴⁰ The most interesting passages appear in chapter 42, where Mordecai expands on his hopes for a Jewish state in Palestine:

> There is store of wisdom among us to found a new Jewish polity, grand, simple, just, like the old—a republic where there is equality of protection, an equality which shone like a star on the forehead of our ancient community, and gave it more than the brightness of Western freedom amid the despotisms of the East. Then our race shall have an organic centre [. . .]. And the world will gain as Israel gains. For there will be a community in the van of the East which carries the culture and sympathies of every great nation in its bosom; there will be a land set for a halting-place of enmities, a neutral ground for the East as Belgium is for the West.⁴¹

What Mordecai envisaged, in Eliot's novel, was 'a new Judaea, poised between East and West—a covenant of reconciliation.'⁴²

Some of the most striking early uses of 'the West', meanwhile, bring us back to Russia as the main 'other', followed by the Ottoman Empire. In the middle of the nineteenth century, the social theorist Harriet Martineau found herself writing to the poet and politician Richard Monckton Milnes 'to ask a favour':

> I want—much—to read again a political article of yours in a quarterly review—but cannot remember which review it was, nor its title. It is the article in wh[ich] you gave a broad & striking view of the conflict, natural & future—of the barbaric Eastern, with the civilized Western mind & empire. [. . .] I <u>think</u> a review of Custine.⁴³

The article Martineau wished to read again was indeed striking in its juxtaposition of Russia with what the author repeatedly referred to as 'Western civilization'. Milnes opined that despotic power had always been 'repugnant to western civilization'. On the other hand, what he wanted to draw attention to with regard to the Russians' attitude to power was 'its Oriental character'.⁴⁴ And after treating his readers to a long list of features in Russia that he considered typically 'Eastern', Milnes added,

> And, above all, there is the strange and complicated array of the same feelings with which all these races have regarded Western civilization; the same ambitious hatred which precipitated Xerxes on Greece, the Turks on Europe, *and the Czar on Poland*; the same desire of rivalry which sent Peter

FIGURE 3.1. Harriet Martineau. Portrait in oils by Richard Evans (1834). National Portrait Gallery, London. *Source:* https://en.wikipedia.org/wiki/Harriet_Martineau#/media/File:Harriet_Martineau_by_Richard_Evans.jpg

into the Dutch dockyards, and has now filled Russia with copies [...] of Italian art, of French manners, of English intelligence—just as it has dressed the Turkish army in stocks and trousers [...]: the same jealous animosity of all that is felt to be beyond their reach; [...] Let, then, this consideration of the Oriental characteristics of the Russian people and institutions never be lost sight of.[45]

It would have been tempting to argue that Milnes used 'Western' as much as he did in this review article simply because he was borrowing the language of the French book that he was commenting on, Astolphe de Custine's *La Russie en 1839* (1843). This is *prima facie* plausible, given how strikingly often the Marquis de Custine used *l'Occident*, or *civilisation occidentale* in his four volumes, as we saw in chapter 2 above. And yet, Milnes's is a more interesting instance than being simply a case of him translating terms from the particular French work that he was reviewing. (In the other major British review of de Custine's book, the West-versus-East focus is absent.)[46] In 1832 Milnes had travelled to Greece, then at the very beginning of its independent existence.[47] Some of the poems he wrote and published subsequently are striking in relation to what I am discussing here. This is how one of them ended:

> O breezes of the wealthy West!
> Why bear ye not on grateful wings
> The seeds of all your life has blest
> Back to their being's early springs?
> Why fill ye not these plains with hopes
> To bear the treasures once they bore,
> And to these Heliconian slopes
> Transport civility and lore?
>
> For now, at least, the soil is free,
> Now that one strong reviving breath
> Has chased that Eastern tyranny
> Which to the Greek was ever death:
> Now that, though weak with age and wrongs,
> And bent beneath the recent chain,
> This motherland of Greece belongs
> To her own western world again.[48]

This was unusual. For the philhellenic British men of letters of the previous decade, the motto had been *The Cause of Greece, the Cause of Europe*—as the characteristic title of a pamphlet published in 1821 put it.[49] In that widely circulated pamphlet alone,[50] there were literally dozens of evocations of the specifically 'European' character and civilisation that the Greeks had in common with the people being addressed (the European public), and a smaller number of references to their shared belonging to Christendom (the author was a professor of theology at Leipzig). There was not a single mention of 'the West'.[51] And the

Greek Declaration of Independence, issued at the beginning of 1822, also tried to appeal to the European and Christian commonalities between the Greeks and their desired audience, but not a word appeared about the West. The exceptions and early references appeared in France, in the writings of Constant and especially of de Pradt, as we saw in chapter 2. In Britain, the 'Western' dimension that Milnes was to apply to the new Greek state, and to the community it was rejoining, was an innovation.

V. Edward Freeman and the 'Eternal' Struggle of 'the West' against 'the East'

Another case of frequent use of 'the West' was that of the historian Edward Augustus Freeman, from the mid-1850s onwards. But even in the texts where he most solemnly posited an eternal struggle between 'the West' and 'the East', Freeman's use of the terms was peculiar, and not consistent. He argued that 'the whole history of Europe forms the record of one long struggle, a struggle of which the earliest known phases will be found in the opening chapters of Herodotus, while the latest as yet will be found in the morning's telegrams'. It was, he noted, 'the present Lord Derby who, in a sneering fit, first spoke [...] of "the eternal Eastern question"'. In so doing, His Lordship had 'stumbled on the happiest epithet that man ever lighted on'. For Freeman, 'The strife' was 'indeed eternal'. It was 'the strife between light and darkness, between freedom and bondage; [...] the strife between the West and the East, between Europe and Asia, the strife which in its earliest days took the shape of the strife between Greek and barbarian, the strife which, for the last twelve centuries, has been sharpened to its keenest as the strife between Christendom and Islam'. The tale was 'the same in all ages, from the Plataean who gave his life for right at Marathon to the Russian who gave his life for right at Plevna'. It is clear from the reference to the battle of Plevna during the Russo–Turkish War of 1877–78 that Freeman included Russia in 'the West' whose eternal struggle against 'the East' was the most striking feature of 'the unity of history' regarding which he was so vociferous. Indeed, he explicitly stated that he knew some would be surprised that an Englishman could 'speak well of Russia'; but to him it seemed that Russia and its rulers were 'simply like any other nation and its rulers, capable of righteous action at one moment and of unrighteous action at another'.[52]

Freeman wrote of 'the strife of East and West' in several other works.[53] Though he is not discussed in her work, he exemplifies what Holly Case has aptly referred to as the 'misdating' of 'questions' during what she calls 'the age of questions': 'at the very instant they were born, questions were often endowed with a history that backdated them by decades, sometimes centuries, before their actual emergence.'[54] Freeman backdated the 'Eastern Question' and the 'strife of East and West' by millennia. He was, and is, in good company.

Meanwhile, however, when addressing distinctions within Europe and within Christendom, Freeman would use 'Western' in contradistinction to the Eastern Roman Empire. He was unusually sympathetic to the empire of Constantinople. He complained of many of his contemporaries

> showing how little they know of that mighty Empire which for so many ages cherished the flame of civilization and literature when it was well nigh extinct throughout Western Europe—which preserved the language of Thucydides and Aristotle, and the political power of Augustus and Constantine, till *the nations of the West* were once more prepared to receive the gift and to despise the giver.[55]

This did not mean that he ranked the Eastern Empire above the modern 'Teutonic' realms, of course: 'essentially conservative and unprogressive, it had not the same hope for the future which dwelled in the vigorous barbarism of the Western nations'. Thus, the Eastern Empire lived on, in old age, 'alongside of the youth of the Western nations, till they had sufficiently advanced to give the world a lesson in a higher, and we trust, more enduring civilization.'[56] Clearly, in Freeman's hierarchy, some of the 'Western' nations (the 'Teutonic' ones especially) were superior, not least thanks to the free institutions they developed (with the 'English' and their brethren in America leading the way). 'Western' was in these contexts used to distinguish between the two Roman empires and their respective later successor states. However, these were both 'European-Aryan', in Freeman's terms, and, therefore, *both* 'Western' in the other sense in which he used the term, when it came to universal history's 'eternal strife'. That 'West' was represented (or led) by different actor-peoples in each epoch, including, successively, the ancient Greeks, Alexander's empire and both Roman empires, Western and Eastern (and, in his own time, the successors to both, including the Balkan Christians as well as their Russian would-be protectors). Thus, writing of the Eastern Roman Empire's 'great war with Persia' in the early seventh century CE, Freeman commented, 'The Roman had succeeded the Macedonian as the champion of the West against the East, and the work of that championship was as worthily done from the New Rome as from the Old.'[57] The New Rome was, of course, Constantinople. The 'Emperor of the East' (as far as the intra-Roman, or intra-European, division went), the so-called Byzantine emperor, was 'the champion of the West against the East' in the broader, universal-historical, eternal 'strife between East and West'. (The distinction is reminiscent of the one that in chapter 2 we saw being drawn by Aleksei Khomyakov, between the East of Xerxes and the East of Christ.)

That was not a widespread view among 'Teutomaniacs' at the time.[58] Charles Kingsley, regius professor of modern history, told his Cambridge students in 1864 that the Muslim invaders had saved 'Europe' by distracting the Eastern Roman Empire and preventing it from defeating their (the students', that is) Teutonic ancestors during the centuries of their weakness from 550 to 750: 'and if you hold (with me) that the welfare of the Teutonic race is the welfare of the world; then, meaning nothing less, the Saracen invasion, by crippling the Eastern Empire, saved Europe and our race'.[59] Freeman relished the chance to ridicule this argument in his devastating—anonymous—review of Kingsley's book.[60]

Moreover, the 'West' of the 'eternal strife' included the Slavs. Time and again in his writings on the Eastern Roman Empire Freeman wistfully commented how differently things would have turned out had the Slavs conquered Constantinople during one of their attempts—instead of the Ottoman Turks. He repeatedly drew an analogy between the renewal of the Western Roman Empire by the conquering youthful Teutons and the (counterfactual) would-be renewal of the Eastern Roman Empire by the conquering youthful Slavs.[61] Elsewhere, Freeman explained that, despite the initial racial or linguistic kinship of all Aryans, the 'Western Aryans' who lived in Europe had developed a different civilisation from the 'Eastern Aryans' ('the Persian and the Hindoo'). The Western Aryans 'all form part of one historic world, the world of Rome. They all share, more or less fully, in the memories which are common to all who have been brought within the magic influence of either of the two seats of Roman dominion'; thus 'All Europe, Eastern and Western' had 'a common right in Rome and in all that springs from Rome'. There had been two centres of Roman influence, Old Rome and New Rome: 'from the city of Romulus and from the city of Constantine, has come the civilization which distinguishes Europe from Africa and Asia. In that heritage all Europe has a share.'[62] In the 'eternal strife', Freeman's 'West' was 'Aryan Europe', which included the Russians and other Slavs.

Freeman sometimes jested about his lack of interest in other parts of the world. But, he retorted, the part he did study was not negligible in its extent: 'Indian things are commonly beyond me. I am parochially minded; but my parish is a big one, taking in all civilized Europe and America.'[63] He often referred to America alongside Europe, as an extension of Europe and a 'third home' to the

Teutonic English nation.⁶⁴ However, he did not use the term 'the West' to lump Europe and America together, as Comte and his followers did. Meanwhile, the fact that an author who used 'the West' as frequently as Freeman did should include within its ambit Byzantium and Russia (when speaking of the 'eternal struggle') is telling indeed with regard to the different, and often conflicting, meanings of the term in the nineteenth century.⁶⁵

VI. The British Comtists' West

And yet, there had emerged at around the same time a very different 'West'. For meanwhile Comte (as of the 1840s) and some of his British followers (as of the 1850s–1860s) opted for the term 'the West' to describe the entity they proposed to reorganise, instead of the hitherto used term 'Europe', precisely because 'Europe' was simultaneously too broad (insofar as it included Russia and Eastern Europe), and too narrow (insofar as it did not include the two Americas and Australasia). One could adduce further examples of early uses of 'the West', some more casual than others, some more consistent than others. But the first conscious decision made by a group of British thinkers and political activists systematically to substitute 'the West' for 'Europe,' and to define it in exhaustive detail in contradistinction to 'Europe,' was that of the British Comtists when they published their long volume on *International Policy* (1866), headed by 'The West' signed by their leader, Richard Congreve.⁶⁶ There had previously been no such explicit and thorough definition in English of what 'the West' meant and what it ought to become. The closest anyone had come had been in contributions by Congreve himself a decade earlier.⁶⁷ Similarly, in the future, it was only to be rivalled in the following decade by the English edition of Comte's four-volume *System of Positive Polity* (1875–77), the translators of which included some of his own leading British disciples (John Henry Bridges, Frederic Harrison, Edward Spencer Beesly, Vernon Lushington, Godfrey Lushington, Fanny Hertz, Samuel Lobb, Richard Congreve, Henry Dix Hutton). There were disagreements among the British Comtists, especially about the particular ways in which the leader Congreve was promoting the cause, already in 1856.⁶⁸ 'He [Congreve] has no shadow of an idea that does not come straight from "the system"', Harrison complained of Congreve's pamphlet *Gibraltar*.⁶⁹ But dissensions notwithstanding, they all followed Comte in using 'the West' to describe the supranational 'vanguard of Humanity' that they wanted to reform.

It is important to emphasise in this context how astonishingly widely known Comte's work was, and how vociferous were his British followers. As Terence

FIGURE 3.2. Frederic Harrison. Photograph by Alexander Bassano (1901), in Frederic Harrison, *Autobiographic Memoirs*, vol. 1: *1831–1870*, frontispiece. Source: https://upload.wikimedia.org/wikipedia/commons/f/f0/Photo_of _Frederic_Harrison.jpg

Wright has shown, 'nearly all the major British thinkers of the second half of the nineteenth century seem to have studied Comte'. Thus, '[n]o student, it was claimed, could "pass through the 'sixties untouched by curiosity about the new philosophical system" [...] and from 1860 to 1880 it seemed impossible for any major "literary or scientific figure who ventured into public controversy" not to "defend his position in relation to Positivism"'. Hence, in the later nineteenth century, 'it became almost impossible for educated people *not* to have encountered Comte's ideas'.[70] The British Comtists had a high platform from which to promote their ideas and vocabulary, and punched way above their mere

FIGURE 3.3. George Eliot. Portrait in chalk by Frederick William Burton (1865). The National Portrait Gallery, London. *Source:* https://en.wikipedia.org/wiki/George_Eliot#/media/File:George_Eliot_7.jpg

numerical weight. It was one of their assets that the place of Frederic Harrison in British intellectual life was significant for some decades.[71] Besides the dedicated core followers who formed the Church of Humanity (though they ended up splitting into two churches later, as the younger generation found Congreve too prescriptive), there were many others who had read Comte extensively. The historian J. R. Seeley was one of them (and in his best-known book, *The*

Expansion of England, he frequently deployed the language of 'the West' and 'Western civilisation'). After thorough study of the Frenchman's works some were critical, not least John Morley. Others were much more sympathetic, including George Eliot, a close friend of both Harrison and Congreve.[72]

'The West' as a term was used routinely by the British Comtists. Besides constant references, however, they proceeded to define and elaborate on what it meant directly and in detail. As mentioned previously, in 1866 a group of British Comtists published *International Policy: Essays on the Foreign Relations of England* (there would be a second edition in 1884). The first essay, signed by Congreve as leader of the British Comtists at the time, was entitled 'The West'. According to Congreve, the decline of the power of Catholicism, and the consequent disunion of medieval Europe, were 'first evidenced by disorder in the international relations of its constituent states'. By the same token, it was 'in the same international relations that the restoration of order must begin, as the first step to the reorganisation of modern Europe on a sound basis; to the reconstitution of a new union analogous to, not identical with, that offered by Catholicism'. Congreve argued that ever increasing contact between peoples had led to a growing sense of mutual interdependence. The latter engendered the conception of a common interest, which led in sum to the conception of the unity of the human race. Humanity had to be united, but on two conditions: first, that the power which attempted its unification should be 'duly subordinated to the larger whole' (Humanity) on whose behalf it did it; and second, that the agent must be complex, like the larger body on which it was to act—constituted by several nations 'differing greatly from one another'. In that way, no mere national interest could gain ascendancy and there would be 'ample provision for a larger range of sympathies with those outside, and a just mutual control with reference to those within'. The familiar units of social organisation were:

- the family
- the country
- Humanity

For the new dispensation that the Comtists envisaged, one more unit was necessary, between the country and Humanity: this unit would be, on the one hand, broader than the country or state, and thus not as isolated or selfish as the state; while, on the other hand, it would be less extensive than Humanity, and thus not as powerless for action and practical purposes as Humanity at large. The intermediate unit needed was 'the West'. Thus, social existence would be organised along the lines:

- the family
- the country
- the West
- Humanity

According to Congreve, 'the leadership of the human race is invested in the West'. But here we come to the crucial issue of the name of the unit in question: 'The actual consciousness of the world accepts this term Europe as a whole.' However, 'Europe' would not do. It needed 'still further clearing and definition'; and this would follow 'if we attempt to get a clear conception of what the term *the West* means, how far it is synonymous with, how far different from, Europe'. In other words, Congreve continued, 'let us seek an adequate answer to the question— What constitutes the West?'

Referring to the post-1815 Concert of Europe, this leading Positivist noted that '[t]he actual, the official state-system of Europe is a heterogeneous aggregate'. Since the Peace of Vienna (1815), five great powers, France, England, Austria, Prussia and Russia had 'virtually constituted Europe'. This was the old order that desperately needed changing. The first step required was one of exclusion: '*The elimination of Russia from the system is the first great rectification. She is an Eastern, not a Western power, or more Eastern than Western.*' This, in turn, raised the question, '[W]herein lies the difference, what grounds are there in reason or history for asserting such a distinction?' Congreve's answer was that the criterion for membership was 'participation directly or indirectly, completely or incompletely, in the progressive civilisation which, since the repulse of the theocracy of Western Asia by Greece, has characterised Europe' (comprehending 'the intellectual cultivation of Greece'; 'the social incorporation of Western Europe by Rome'; 'the Catholic-Feudal organisation of medieval Europe'; and the revolutionary upheavals of the previous five centuries).[73] For Congreve, thus, exclusion of Russia was 'a cardinal point'—because Russia was not 'Western', but mainly 'Eastern', and its contact with European history had only recently begun.

Another interesting testing ground was Ottoman Turkey, which according to Congreve was 'more Western than Russia'. It was 'far more intimately bound up with the history of Europe than is Russia, whose admission to that history is barely a century old'. Besides this historical argument, there was also a far from unimportant political one: 'It is her religion which would make me wish for her admission, were it legitimate on other grounds.' Every recognition of Turkey, down to the latest, at the time of the Crimean War, had been 'valuable as a protest against the spirit of religious exclusiveness', and 'distinctly set aside the claim of Christian nations, as such, to domineer over others in the name of an inherent superiority conferred on them by their religion'. It was 'an acknowledgement that there may be common human and political action in spite of the barriers raised by differences of faith'. It would be ideal in this respect to have Turkey included simultaneously with the exclusion of Russia. However, this could not be: 'Whatever the advantages of such a view, they must be foregone rather than weaken by any immature concession the cohesion of the Western body, already far too weak.' Revealingly, Congreve added that the advantage of removing Russia and Turkey was that such a removal rectified 'a not uncommon error': the perceived centrality of Germany. For in 'the true Western Europe', the centre was France. Those who thought otherwise, including Heeren, were wrong, according to Congreve.[74]

Congreve also stressed that for the Positivists, followers of Comte's precept of 'altruism' and 'living for others', the way forward was 'sympathy'. Thus he defined as the 'aim' of the West 'the peaceful action on the rest of the [human] race, with the purpose of raising, or enabling its various constituents to rise, in due order to the level it has itself attained'. Such a body would 'stand forth as the model at once and director of the rest. Thus, '[d]uly organised within, conscious of its functions and obligations, it would appreciate the wants and situation of those without it'; and, 'without any pressure or unwarranted interference with their legitimate independence of action, it would be ready to help them in their onward course.'[75]

The article concluded with a six-page 'Note on the United States of America'. Congreve appears to have realised that he could not get away with publishing such an essay on 'The West' in 1866, following the Union victory in the Civil War, and mention the USA as little as Comte had done in the 1840s and 1850s (mainly as an 'offshoot' of 'England'). Thus he starts almost apologetically: 'In the preceding Essay [...] I have given but a few lines to the United States [...]. Many reasons seem to conspire to claim more for it.' The whole tone shows a growing unease (obvious in British thought more generally by the 1860s) about the rise of the USA and its increasing assertiveness following the Civil War. For, although the USA deserved much more attention as part of the West than it had so far received, Congreve was adamant that one should not meanwhile admit 'her claim to be the latest outcome of the mature political wisdom of the race, the type to which all others must eventually conform'. The problem, he added, was that 'America claims no less, it would seem'. On one point only could he admit that claim: 'America stands before the world as the representative of republican government.' But, 'this [...] conceded to America, in her further claims we cannot acquiesce. We cannot recognise any general leadership vested in her.' Those who would reorganise the West should not take the American social order as their model: 'America must weigh heavily in the scales of international policy; but she weighs by her mass, not by her ideas'. This meant that 'she will receive far more than she can give; be guided rather than lead; be influenced rather than influence'. Importantly, 'in the domain of the intellect, in relation to all the more general and higher conceptions of man, whether scientific, philosophical, or religious, America can claim, and, speaking broadly, does claim, no initiative'. He imagined that 'all cultivated Americans' would agree with him. It was 'from Western Europe that any impulse to progress in these departments must in the main originate'. To demonstrate this, he added, 'Nothing can be a clearer proof of this than the evidently greater influence in America than in Europe of the religious ideas of the past'.[76] American reviewers of Congreve's article—even those otherwise positive overall—were not amused by the part that concerned themselves.[77]

VII. The Novelty of 'The West' in English

Throughout the correspondence that I discussed (in chapter 2) between Comte and Mill, the British thinker remained remarkably unconverted to Comte's new lexical preferences and continued to reply using 'Europe' or 'European' whenever Comte had used 'West' or 'Western'.[78] That was typical. It is even more telling how, initially, even some of Comte's disciples or translators were not sure how to handle the conceptual innovation that he had introduced. The novelty of the term in English is obvious both from the way Congreve introduced his definition in 1866 and from the way reviewers commented on it. 'What is meant by the West is defined in the preliminary Essay by Mr. Congreve,' noted an American reviewer.[79] British reviewers found Congreve's definition and membership list of 'the West' idiosyncratic, and some protested against his (and Comte's) exclusion of some Christian nations from membership of 'the West'.[80] Reviewers explicitly took exception to the replacement of 'what once was Christianity till essayists found out a better name for it'.[81] Others commented on 'what he calls the West' referring to Congreve as 'paradoxical'.[82] A *Westminster Review* author referred to '"the West", as Comtists affectedly chose to call Europe at large', and went on to observe that '[t]he West being a new general term, admits of a fresh definition better than could be easily supplied of that for which it stands', and then hastened to complain against 'the arbitrary manner in which every European influence is discarded from the definition of "the West" that cannot be traced back to the times of Imperial Rome'.[83] Meanwhile, a sympathetic reviewer explained that '[t]he idea of Humanity, which has become too familiar to need any exposition here, has given birth to an offshoot which may be called "the West", or "Occidentality".'[84]

Earlier, Harriet Martineau, in her free translation of Comte's *Cours*, was unable to follow Comte in his linguistic innovations, which, as we have seen, were incipient in the last lessons of the *Cours* (written at the end of 1841 and in early 1842). She translated 'qu'aucune autre branche de la grande famille occidentale' as 'than any other branch of the great family', thus avoiding translation or acknowledgement of 'occidentale'. And where Comte had written 'tendant à isoler profondément le peuple anglais de toute le reste de la famille occidentale', Martineau translated 'which tend to separate the English people from the rest of the European family'. She did not translate 'dans le reste de notre Occident' at all; and further on, where Comte had written 'la république occidentale', Martineau translated, 'the great European commonwealth'. The omission of the 'Western' dimension becomes even more striking near the end of Lesson 57, where Comte had written about his projected 'Comité positif occidental'. Martineau completely ignored the emphasis on the supranational, 'occidental' character of the proposal outlined in the original text.[85]

The reluctance became bewilderment when it came to translating Comte's new coinage, *occidentalité*. J. A. Bridges clearly hesitated in his first translations of the *Discours* of 1848. For example, in a crucial text already quoted, Comte's original read 'le moyen âge a institué un intermédiaire trop méconnu aujourd'hui, en fondant une libre occidentalité'.[86] In his translation of 1865 Bridges rendered the text, 'the Middle Ages introduced the intermediate conception of Christendom, or Occidentality'.[87] However, that translation was completely inconsistent with Comte's intention, which was specifically to reject 'Christendom' as a collective description, and stress the 'Occidentality' developed only among Catholic Western Christians. But the neologism seems to have been too much for Bridges, so he added in the older term, which was at least more familiar. Clearly, 'the West' needed some getting used to.

VIII. The Wages of Foreign Influence

In the Conclusion of her article arguing for a Russian origin of the idea of the West in the West, Peggy Heller wrote that 'even in the British context, the West did not emerge simply out of the discourse of imperialists, but played an important role in anti-imperialism'. In a note attached to that statement Heller added that '[t]he anti-imperialism of some of the early accounts of Western civilisation, such as Francis Sydney Marvin's [...], has not been appreciated in the work of GoGwilt or Bonnett'. (She then went on to suggest a probable Russian influence again, calling for further research to establish it).[88] Heller was right to point to a significant anti-imperialist current of thought among people who wrote much on 'the West' and 'Western civilisation' around the time of the First World War, but was mistaken in looking to Russian connections for the sources of the combination of anti-imperialism with a focus on 'the West'. One of the most prolific authors writing on Western civilisation in the Great War period was indeed Francis Sydney Marvin. He was also a well known and highly active Comtist (already as a student in Oxford he co-founded, with the classicist Gilbert Murray, an Auguste Comte discussion society, and he later contributed more than a hundred articles to the Comtist *Positivist Review* between 1893 and 1925).[89] Besides books on *The Unity of Western Civilization*, and similar titles,[90] he authored a volume on Comte, in which he discussed quite explicitly Comte's projected 'Western Republic' and assessed the chances of implementation of Comte's plans in the real world and through the League of Nations.[91] Thus my own argument is that the link between British anti-imperialism and British writings on the West and Western civilisation in the early twentieth century was Auguste Comte. Marvin's case is characteristic, and he is yet another example of how the idea of 'the West' came to be used in English since it was first systematically propagated by an earlier generation of Comte's disciples in the 1850s and 1860s. More broadly, it may or may not be coincidental that the three British thinkers whom Bonnett identifies as the first to develop the idea of the West in the late nineteenth and early twentieth centuries all had close connections to varying degrees with Comtean Positivism.[92] Ramsay MacDonald had links with the Comtists, and referred to their *International Policy* in his writings.[93] Benjamin Kidd was deeply indebted to Comte's ideas and writings.[94] And, as we have just seen, Francis Sydney Marvin (whose name appears in front of more titles than any other in Bonnett's bibliography) was a leading and highly active Comtist.[95]

One more general observation suggests itself in the light of what this chapter has shown. Comtist Positivism had come to Britain from France. In the seventeenth century, Thomas Hobbes had lived for years in France before he published *Leviathan* (a book in fact written in France); in the eighteenth, Oliver Goldsmith spent some years in the Netherlands and other parts of continental Europe before he wrote *A Citizen of the World*. Edward Gibbon had spent many years in Switzerland and his continental credentials were impressive. Richard Monckton Milnes, besides other long sojourns on the Continent, had studied in Bonn before his first visit to Greece.[96] David Urquhart had lived in Switzerland and France for several formative years, and 'his education and whole experience were continental'.[97] Karl Marx was German. J. R. Seeley was steeped in German thought, but also an avid reader of Comte. Thomas Arnold was immersed in German thought and strongly influenced by Barthold Georg Niebuhr, Christian von Bunsen and other German scholars. So was his staunch admirer, Edward Augustus Freeman.[98] And Henry Maine's debts to the German historical school of law of Friedrich Carl von Savigny, to Georg Ludwig von Maurer and to Niebuhr's *Roman History* are well known.[99] The 'comparative method' so dear to Freeman and Maine owed its appeal to the philological researches into the 'Aryan' languages of Bunsen and Friedrich Max Müller, both Germans based and highly influential in Britain.[100] George Eliot's command of continental European languages, cultures and philosophical movements was striking (and she was also a strong admirer of Auguste Comte and his works and close friend of several of the British Comtists). These examples may at least indicate that the earliest uses of 'the West' and 'Western' came to Britain from continental European languages and discourses, in which they were much more common. Lord Acton was of course right that ideas are 'extraterritorial'. As far as John Bull's isle was concerned, the idea of the West was a case of *ex oriente lux*.

IX. Conclusion

It should be clear from the evidence adduced in this chapter that there were several different uses of 'the West' in British thought in the nineteenth century, and that they did not all mean the same thing or denote the same entity. It should also be clear by now that most of them were as yet inchoate or incoherent uses, which juxtaposed an undefined 'West' (most of the time used interchangeably, without any differentiation, with 'Europe') against various others (the Eastern Roman Empire of the medieval 'Greeks', or Russia, or the Jews, or the Saracens, or 'the Turk') with often contradictory criteria of selection or membership. The only conscious and thorough attempt at a comprehensive definition of an entity that it was proposed should be called 'the West' was that undertaken by the Comtists, in the footsteps of their French master. There is an irony in all this. As we noted (in section II above), most of the first uses of 'Europe' as a supranational self-description arose in England in the late seventeenth century very much in relation to defences of liberty. But when 'the West' came to be programmatically promoted, it was for very different purposes. The truth, far from conforming to the widely held belief that Britons invented 'the West' to celebrate their primacy in liberal credentials or to legitimise their empire, is that the first time a coherent and thoroughly elaborate idea of the West was explicitly promoted in Britain, it was as part of the 'liberticide' as well as anti-imperialist system proposed by Comte. If I may quote Richard Wright, from a different context, 'history is indeed a strange story'.

4

Ex Germaniae lux? How Did the Idea of 'the West' Reach America?

'Europe, and not England, is the parent country of America. This new World hath been the asylum for the persecuted lovers of civil and religious liberty from *every part* of Europe. [...] In this extensive quarter of the globe, we forget the narrow limits of three hundred and sixty miles (the extent of England) and carry our friendship on a larger scale; we claim brotherhood with every European Christian, and triumph in the generosity of the sentiment.'

THOMAS PAINE, 'COMMON SENSE' (1776), IN PAINE, *WRITINGS*, VOL. 1, P. 87

'But one can forgive Dr. [Madison] Grant; he is a good American, and good Americans [...] are usually fifty years behind the English, who, in turn, are usually twenty years behind the Germans.'

HUBERT HARRISON, '*THE RISING TIDE OF COLOR AGAINST WHITE WORLD-SUPREMACY* BY LOTHROP STODDARD' (*NEGRO WORLD*, 29 MAY 1920), IN J. B. PERRY, *A HUBERT HARRISON READER*, P. 307

IN THIS CHAPTER I will show that both those who take the existence of 'the idea of the West' for granted as a given of the historical conscience of North Americans and those who claim that such an idea first emerged in America as a result of the 'Western Civ[ilization]' curricula of American universities following the Great War (or—for some—even later, after the Second World War), miss the full picture. I trace the gradual and slow emergence and increase in the uses of the concept of 'the West' in its civilisational-cum-political sense throughout the nineteenth century. And I argue that the evidence suggests that such usages were introduced to America and proliferated through the influence of Europeans, particularly of German descent, who had recently migrated to the United States, or of Americans who had lived and studied in Europe, particularly in German universities, for extended periods of time.

Though the Atlantic Ocean is immense, there cannot be an exception to the rule of which Lord Acton reminded us in the epigraph to the last chapter. Meanwhile, there are two factors peculiar to the young American polity that initially militated against uses of 'the West' and 'Western' in a civilisational or sociopolitical sense as a self-descriptor (to refer, that is, to a supranational entity that included America along with Europe, or at least with parts of Europe). In the first place, 'the West' meant something concrete in America, and it was something distinctly different. The term was widely used as a—primarily and initially— geographical term that indicated the shifting frontier of the Americans' own country. And the whole westward expansion was associated with older myths and traditions, not least the 'heliotropic myth' of *translatio imperii*, which was interpreted as leading to the culmination and end of history in the millennial achievement of the American republic.[1] In the second place, the existence of that other 'West', of the American shifting frontier, was a factor contributing to the cluster of ideas and myths that had, in combination with fervent Protestant millenarianism and a republican historical perspective, created a narrative of American exceptionalism and a belief in the existence of a fundamental divergence from Europe and its history. 'Unlike the nations of the past, America would never grow old'; rather, Americans 'could relegate history to the past while they acted out their destiny in the realm of nature. They could develop in space rather than in time.'[2]

The two issues were far from unrelated. For the American West was not just a geographical notion, but, in the words of the best-known proponent of the 'frontier thesis', Frederick Jackson Turner, 'a phase of social organization'. The West in that intra-American sense was 'preëminently a region of ideals, mistaken or not'. Thus, the 'Western man believed in the manifest destiny of his country'. And crucially, the West was 'more American, but less cosmopolitan than the seaboard'. Furthermore, '[t]he separation of the Western man from the seaboard, and his environment, made him in a large degree free from European precedents and forces'. As Turner went on to argue, the 'Western' man 'looked at things independently and with small regard or appreciation for the best Old World experience'. Thus he 'had no ideal of a philosophical, eclectic nation', that should advance civilisation by 'intercourse with foreigners and familiarity with their point of view, and readiness to adopt whatever is best and most suitable in their ideas, manners, and customs'. Instead, his ideal was that of 'conserving and developing what was original and valuable in this new country'. And the West was the opposite of conservative: 'buoyant self-confidence and self-assertion were distinguishing traits in its composition. It saw in its growth nothing less than a new order of society and state.'[3]

Both these factors, American belief in American exceptionalism and superiority to aristocratic and imperialistic old Europe, on the one hand, and the use of 'the West' in its concrete intra-American meaning to refer to an ever-shifting frontier part of the United States itself, on the other, made it difficult, in America in the early decades of its existence as an independent country, to use 'the West' in a civilisational or sociopolitical sense to refer to a supranational entity or identity. In *Democratic Vistas*, the bard of American democracy wrote, 'If a man were ask'd, for instance, the distinctive points contrasting modern European and American political and other life with the old Asiatic cultus, as lingering-bequeath'd yet in China and Turkey, he might find the amount of them in John Stuart Mill's profound essay on Liberty in the future.'[4] We might have expected (were we to indulge in anachronistic thinking) that in juxtaposing 'modern European and American political and other life' with 'Asiatic' practices from China to Turkey, Whitman would have used the word 'Western' to describe the former. Yet he did not. It was simply not available in late-1860s America in the way it is today. The term meant something completely different in the United States then, and for some further decades. The *Encyclopædia Britannica* (which had turned Anglo-American from the beginning of the twentieth century), contained no entry on 'the West' until the fourteenth edition, of 1929; even that entry, however, refers exclusively to the US 'West' in the intra-American sense.[5] None of this means that Acton was wrong. Ideas did travel, and with them the uses of words.[6] And the story of how this particular idea gradually gained currency in America is a fascinating one.

I. Heidelberg, Göttingen, Halle, Berlin...

There were several avenues whereby ideas could cross borders and oceans, and travelling was only one of them. A crucial way in which nineteenth-century American culture was influenced by European culture and thought was through the attractiveness of German universities to young Americans (to be followed by deliberate attempts by American university presidents—not least President Eliot of Harvard—to model their institutions on those universities).[7] As Ralph Waldo Emerson noted, 'Our young men went to the Rhine to find the German genius which had charmed them [...]. They hunted for it in Heidelberg, in Göttingen,

FIGURE 4.1. Göttingen University, university anniversary student parade, 17 September 1837. Coloured lithograph by Carl I. Rohde (ca. 1838). *Source:* https://en.wikipedia.org/wiki/University_of _G%C3%B6ttingen#/media/File:Goettingen_-_Kirchenzug_der _Studenten_anlaesslich_des_Universitaetsjubilaeums_(1837).png

in Halle, in Berlin'.[8] As has been aptly observed, although they were keen to jettison 'Old World modes', those who wished to establish a national literature in America in the decades before the Civil War 'were not blind to the fact that certain critical principles and literary developments currently dominant in Europe afforded a salient re-enforcement for their designs and aspirations'. Hence, in the years around 1815–20, George Bancroft, Edward Everett, Frederic Henry Hedge, George Ticknor and many other young Americans studying in German universities 'were introduced to literary doctrines which were thoroughly congenial to the buoyant nationalism of America after the War of 1812'.[9]

It may therefore not be too surprising to find the odd reference to 'the west' (the frequency of use of lower-case 'w' indicating the casualness of the use) in American publications of the time. Readers of the *North American Review* could find references to 'the literature of the west' in a review of works by Herder as early as 1825.[10] The same author was to use the word repeatedly in an essay on Russia in 1829.[11] That young author was the future famous historian and diplomat George Bancroft. He had studied in Germany, receiving his doctoral degree from the 'Georgia Augusta' University of Göttingen in September 1820,[12] and had returned from Europe in the summer of 1822, a couple of years before he wrote the review article on Herder.[13] Such examples of casual uses, by people with extensive European connections and sojourns, especially when a contradistinction was made with 'the East', could be proliferated.

Another interesting early case is another American review of a German author's work. It has been wrongly attributed to George Bancroft; in fact it was written by Edward Everett.[14] Everett was the first American ever to be awarded a Ph.D. That the studies that led to his doctorate also took place in Göttingen is part of a story this chapter aims to highlight. Everett's fellow Göttingen graduate Bancroft had translated a work of his former German professor, Arnold H. L. Heeren: his *Reflections on the Politics of Ancient Greece*. Everett published an anonymous review of the translation upon its publication in 1824. Among other things, Everett signalled his distance from the German professor's celebration of Europe as the apogee of world history. He supposed that nobody would 'be inclined to deny the justice, with which the superiority of Europe is here maintained', but he immediately began to qualify and undermine that statement: 'unless there may be some who think that Europe has only for two or three thousand years had *its turn*; that the Eastern nations had theirs earlier, and attained a perfection, in many of the arts and improvements of life, of which the monuments have perished, and the tradition is lost'. In other words, he invited the reader to reflect on the possibility 'that the European superiority seems to us decisive, because we survey it from a nearer point of view, while it is out of our power to take a station, from which we can penetrate to the unrecorded ages of Oriental achievement'. Everett commented that this latter, alternative way of looking at the question 'has something to recommend it, especially if we consider the forgotten greatness of the East, and the present predominance of Europe, as two acts in the history of man'.

Moreover, Everett then came up with some remarks that were unmistakably suggestive of the ineluctable logic of *translatio imperii*—and this time Europe was not to be a beneficiary of the transfer, but its victim. When one looked towards the future, a pattern was clear. The past history of the world did not encourage 'the belief, that while such a vast development of energy is taking place in the continents of America, no diminution will result of that, which is in action in the old world'. In Roman and Greek antiquity, 'national character, glory, and power appeared necessarily to gather about one centre. The sceptre seemed literally to pass from one to another.' Clearly, 'a high degree of eminence could be attained

FIGURE 4.2. The Old University Observatory in Göttingen, designed by Georg Heinrich Borheck and completed in 1816. Photograph by Daniel Schwen. *Source:* https://en.wikipedia.org/wiki/University_of_G%C3%B6ttingen#/media /File:Goe_Sternwarte_pano.jpg

only by one political community, at a time'. Thus, 'there must be a limit to the multiplication of powerful nations'. That meant that, inexorably, 'while political power and national wealth are increasing, with a rapidity we can hardly compute in this hemisphere,[15] it is scarcely possible that the seeds of their decline should not be sown in the eastern'. The corollary to that historical rule was ineluctable, according to Everett: 'Perilous conflicts must in time follow, and vast rivalries grow up; and in that condition of the world's politics, it is plain that the complicated enginery of the old world must give way in the collision with the new.' As for the Old Continent, Everett's prediction was painful: 'Europe is hereafter, like Asia, to exhibit monuments where she now exhibits trophies, and furnish themes for speculation, not on national superiority, but national decline.'[16]

We will see in the next two sections that not everyone in America thought that the American hemisphere was bound to replace Europe in the leadership of the world. There was at least one American thinker whose thoughts turned instead to partnership between Europe and the United States, in terms that directly anticipate what is now called 'the West'.

II. From Franz Lieber to Francis Lieber

The most striking case is that of Francis Lieber. Lieber's importance in nineteenth-century American intellectual history can hardly be overestimated. He is generally recognised to be the founder of American political science.[17] But that was only one of many contributions to the country he came to as a migrant in the summer of 1827, after spending the first decades of his life in Germany (as Franz Lieber) and being educated in German universities. To begin with, he edited the first American encyclopaedia, starting work less than a year after he arrived in Boston.[18] The encyclopaedia in question (later known as *Appleton's American Encyclopedia*) would go through many editions and inform American readers for decades. Lieber gave America 'an encyclopedia which did not follow the pattern of those in common use at the time'. It was not irrelevant 'whether a people that does not possess an encyclopaedia of its own uses a British, a French, or a German one'; and Lieber's 'German birth and education accounted for an emphasis on German civilisation that was lacking in earlier encyclopaedias.' Thus, 'the wide circulation of this work served as a means by which a strong element of the German spirit was injected into the American mind.'[19] Importantly, Lieber's was not just a German encyclopaedia translated—far from it. Though initially envisaged to correspond closely to the Brockhaus *Conversations-Lexicon*, in the end 'Lieber had in truth edited an American encyclopedia', the *Conversations-Lexikon* serving as 'no more than a basis'. The editor eventually decided to have '[a]lmost all the significant articles' either new or rewritten 'from the American point of view'.[20]

One of the earliest uses of 'Western civilization' to appear in the United States in more or less the sense the term has today was, in fact, to be found in Lieber's *Encyclopaedia*, in a volume first published in 1833. Under the entry 'Woman' one reads,

> With the two most polished and interesting nations of the ancient world, the female sex was on a very different footing, but in both less highly respected and less justly estimated, than with the polished nations of modern times. Greece, situated on the borders of Asia, then the seat of civilization, presents a singular mixture of Oriental manners with European institutions and habits. The condition of the Grecian women accordingly resembles this general condition of society, in a union of something of Eastern restraint and seclusion, with somewhat of the moral virtues and brilliant qualities of Western civilization.[21]

This was an early reference indeed, and it is no coincidence that it was published in an encyclopaedia edited by the German-born Lieber and based on a German model. For 'West' and 'Western' (in a sense that was no longer geographical and restricted to the western hemisphere, but referred to the transatlantic and cultural West), were surreptitiously beginning to enter the register. Most often, it was continental Europeans or Americans who had studied in German universities who were doing the registering. Thus Lieber used 'the West' in a lecture he delivered before the Boston Society of Useful Knowledge as early as 1829, a version of which he then published as an article for 'the sanctum of the New

England intellect', the *North American Review*. One reads there that the Turkish system of distributing land in 'timars' might appear to have been more equitable than the hereditary feudalism of Western Europe. That would be a wrong inference, however. For it had been to 'the feudal system of the West' that 'we owe the enlightened freedom of modern times', according to Lieber. That freedom had arisen from 'the conflicts between the interests of different classes of society, placed, by the natural operation of that system, in a state of direct and perpetual hostility to each other, and from the formation and growth of cities, the immediate results of those conflicts'.[22]

But an even more striking reference to a civilisational 'West' that most explicitly included both Europe and its 'descendants' overseas, came a decade later, from the same pen. In 1841 Lieber wrote that *'the Western World—all Europe, with her many descendant nations'*—acknowledged monogamy to be of the utmost importance for 'the cause of human advancement'. (As we saw in chapter 2 above, this was a theme Lieber's German compatriot Heeren had earlier highlighted). Further on, Lieber wrote that '[t]here have been periods in the history of Europe, indeed, in which the inquiring spirit of the Western race was greatly fettered by the dogmas imposed upon it by an extensive system of theology, and a philosophy closely interlinked with it'. Nevertheless, 'the European mind' had 'always resumed its free inquiry, especially so after the restoration of learning and the reformation of religion'. And since 'these two great events' had 'exercised their powerful influence *upon the great family of Western nations'*, a 'boldness and activity' had been the result, with 'the extent of research [...] widened in such a degree, that men have sometimes fallen into the extreme opposite to that of the spellbound Asiatic'. Lieber also asserted that such things as the security of the acquisition and transmission of property—'the consciousness of holding property by an inherent natural right, and not simply at the mercy of the ruler'—constituted 'the striking difference between man as he appears in Asia, and the western man'. Such references to 'the Western World—all Europe, with her many descendant nations' or to 'the great family of Western nations' constituted a novelty in America at the time—and we will see very soon (in section III below) how painfully aware of this Lieber was, and would continue to be well into the 1850s and beyond. When people in eighteenth- or early-nineteenth-century America spoke of 'the Western world' or 'these western parts', they were not referring to 'all Europe, with her many descendant nations', as Lieber was to come to define the 'Western World'. They were talking in a geographical sense, referring to their own part of the globe.[23]

There was more to Lieber's thought on the group to which he saw himself as belonging than simply a binary distinction. As he was (unhappily) a professor in the American South (in South Carolina) at a time when the issue of 'race' was becoming explosive, there are some highly relevant comments in his correspondence. He wrote in 1850,

> I am far from joining in the wholesale declamation about races. We have nowadays always the Caucasian race in our mouths. If that *race* is so pre-eminently superior, how did it happen that civilization flourished on the Ganges thousands of years before the Caucasian race began to work itself out of the mire of barbarism? How did it happen that Egypt was in a high state of civilization when the Caucasians were mere brutes, and that Egypt gave the germs of all civilization to Greece? If the Caucasians are the peers of mankind in virtue of their race, how does it happen that a few nations of that race only have arrived at civilization, and that the Wallachians, Croatians, and many Sclavonians are sheer barbarians to this day? And how does it happen that the genuine Caucasians are no better?

(Presumably 'the genuine Caucasians' refers to the inhabitants of the Caucasus region). Lieber's answer to his own question was that people talked of 'the Caucasian race' as they often did of 'France, England, Italy', when in reality they meant 'Paris, London, or Rome'. People, in other words, were generalising through synecdoche. For his part, he believed 'only in certain favorable elements which, under certain circumstances, can produce certain results; and no one can say what certain conditions of geographic and chronologic position, of intellectual succession, &c., &c., will produce'. The 'Caucasian race' had 'produced some great nations, but *very late* indeed'. He proceeded to ask, 'It is continually said that we have more brain. But if this had been so from the beginning, why then did this brain not produce great effects before the Hindoo brain, the Egyptian brain?' There was 'a great deal of idle talk now everywhere about this subject'.[24] A few months later he was again complaining about people who forgot that 'it is not the white race that stands pre-eminent in history, but only a few, very few, nations of that race, and those only in recent history'. And it was the case that 'the working out of barbarism into light belongs altogether to other races; and innumerable Caucasian tribes continue to live in begrimed, dark, and dull savagery, as the Croatians'.[25] Thus, his insulting comments on Slavs and other East Europeans aside, Lieber was in essence criticising the increasingly popular racial theories of the mid-nineteenth century. Rather than 'the white race', it was a particular sub-group that he identified as having produced an advanced civilisation—and only in recent history, civilisational primacy having earlier been achieved by Indians, Egyptians and others. Crucially, that was a subgroup for which Lieber was to persist in trying to find a common name.

FIGURE 4.3. Francis Lieber. Photograph by Mathew Benjamin Brady (ca. 1860). Library of Congress Prints and Photographs Division, Washington, DC: Brady-Handy Photograph Collection. *Source:* https://en.wikipedia.org/wiki/Francis_Lieber#/media/File:Francis_Lieber_-_Brady-Handy.jpg

III. The Need 'to have a distinct name for the indicated group': 'Western'? 'Occidental'? 'Cis-Caucasian'?

It is clear that Lieber had strong views regarding the civilisational unit that he saw himself and his compatriots (both his current American and his former German ones) as belonging to. It was not the whole 'white' or 'Caucasian' so-called race, but a sub-group thereof. And it badly needed a name for itself. There is no mistaking his frustration that no agreed name existed in mid-nineteenth-century

America. It is most telling that he felt the need to write the following explanation in one of his most successful books, in 1853:

> I ask permission to draw the attention of the scholar to a subject which appears to me important. *I have used the term Western History, yet it is so indistinct that I must explain what is meant by it. It ought not to be so.* I mean by western history, the history of all historically active, non-Asiatic nations and tribes—the history of the Europeans and their descendants in other parts of the world. In the grouping and division of comprehensive subjects, clearness depends in a great measure upon the distinctness of well-chosen terms. Many students of civilization have probably felt with me the desirableness of a concise term, which should comprehend within the bounds of one word, capable of furnishing us with an acceptable adjective, the whole of the western Caucasian portion of mankind—the Europeans and all their descendants in whatever part of the world, in America, Australia, Africa, India, the Indian Archipelago and the Pacific Islands. It is an idea which constantly recurs, and makes the necessity of a proper and brief term daily felt. [...] In my private papers I use the term Occidental in a sufficiently natural contradistinction to Oriental. But Occidental like Western, indicates geographical position; nor did I feel otherwise authorized to use it here. [...] That some term or other must soon be adopted seems to me clear, and I am ready to accept any expressive name formed in the spirit and according to the taste of our language.[26]

In the second edition (1859), he had come up with a proposal, for he added, 'As the whole race is called the Caucasian, shall we designate the group in question by the name of Cis-Caucasian?' He went on, 'It is more important for the scholar of civilization to have a distinct name for the indicated group, than it was for the student of [...] natural history [...] to adopt the recently formed term of prognathous tribes, in order to group together all the tribes with projecting jaws.'[27]

Lieber had a strong penchant for coining new words (and prided himself on having invented quite a few in his new language). It is not surprising therefore that he went on for the rest of his life trying to promote the term 'Cis-Caucasian' to describe the discrete civilisational unit that he insisted should be recognised.[28] (Meanwhile, the complication created by the existence of the American sense of 'the West' as the shifting frontier is underscored by the fact that, after his first visit to some western states, Lieber wrote, in 1848, a long poem singing the praises of what he had seen. Its title was *The West: A Metrical Epistle*). Referring in 1856 to 'our western Caucasian race', Lieber attached a footnote: 'By this term I mean the

Europeans and their descendants in other parts of the globe, a portion of our species for which we stand in need of a proper term, as I have elsewhere expressed (in my Civil Liberty and Self-Government).'[29] As he put it again elsewhere, 'The multiplicity of civilized nations, their distinct independence (without which there would be enslaving Universal Monarchy), and their increasing resemblance and agreement, are some of the great safeguards of our civilization.' Thus,

> [m]odern nations *of our family* have come to agree in much, and the agreement is growing. We have one alphabet; the same systems of notation, arithmetical and musical; one division of the circle and of time; the same sea-league; the same barometer; one mathematical language; one music and the same fine arts; one system of education, high and low; one science; one division of government; one domestic economy; one dress and fashion; the same manners, and the same toys for our children (Asia and Africa have no toys); we have a united mail system, and uniting telegraphs; we have an extending agreement in measures, weights, coinage, and signals at sea, and one financial conception [...]; we have a rapidly extending international copyright; perfectly acknowledged foreign individual property; we have a common international law, even during war. Add to this, that we really have what has been, not inaptly, called an international literature, in which a Shakspeare [sic] and a Kepler, a Franklin, Humboldt, Grotius, and Voltaire belong to the whole Cis-Caucasian race; we have a common history of civilization; and Columbus and Frederick, Napoleon and Washington, for weal or woe, belong to all.[30]

Here was a paean to transatlantic Western unity and shared civilisation (with the twist that Lieber was hoping to endow it with the more precise name 'Cis-Caucasian'). There is no mistaking Lieber's belief in the existence of multiple layers of belonging, multiple groups and identities to which individuals could attach themselves. He wrote that the 'national society ought not to be the all-absorbing one, nor is the jural society the only important society to which the individual of our race belongs'. Thus, he explained, people in modern times 'belong to societies of great importance, which are narrower than the state, and to others which extend far beyond it', as was testified by the existence of 'the religious society or church, the œconomical society or society of production and exchange, the society of comity, the society of letters and science' (his examples here being pre-unification Germany, and the society of letters and science that covered 'England and the United States')—and 'the international society embracing all the Cis-Caucasian people.'[31]

Lieber saw the 'Cis-Caucasian' or 'Western' nations as forming a commonwealth of equals or near-equals in a joint enterprise, rather than as succeeding one another in the primacy of world history. He rejected, in other words, the logic of *translatio imperii*. He argued that 'while in antiquity we find a strict succession of one civilized nation to another, the succeeding one improving on the antecedent, and predominating for a time over the others—a monarchical principle, as it were, in the line of succession', there was a significant difference 'in modern times'. What one witnessed in modern times was 'rather a commonwealth of civilized nations'. It was, he argued, 'Christianity and the broad universal character of modern knowledge, closely connected with Christianity' that had rendered possible that 'striking phenomenon'. As he explained, '[w]ith the ancients everything was strictly national; religion, polity, knowledge, literature, art, acknowledgment of right, all were local'. On the other hand, 'with us, the different colors on the map do not designate different districts of religion, knowledge, art, and customs'.[32] As he also wrote to a correspondent in 1867, 'Among the ancients one state always ruled; but we, the Cis-Caucasian race, are becoming more and more united in one great confederation, binding together all nations.' To another he wrote that 'the co-existence of many leading nations, united by the law of nations and a common civilization, is the characteristic of the present political dispensation'.[33] For, in his opinion, the three 'main characteristics of the political development which mark the modern epoch' were, firstly, '[t]he national polity'; secondly, '[t]he general endeavour to define more clearly, and to extend more widely, human rights and civil liberty;' and thirdly, 'the decree which has gone forth that many leading nations shall flourish at one and the same time, plainly distinguished from one another, yet striving together, with one public opinion, under the protection of one law of nations, and in the bonds of one common moving civilization'.[34] He kept repeating the same idea on every possible occasion.[35]

Lieber also advanced a view that would be echoed later by the anarchist geographer Élisée Reclus:[36] 'Even the course which civilization has steadily taken for thousands of years, from the southeast to the northwest, has ceased.' Instead, Lieber claimed, civilization 'now spreads for the first time in all directions, and bends its way back to the Orient. The old historic belt between 30 and 50 northern latitude, within which the great current of events has flown, shall confine history no more.'[37] Apparently, then, he disagreed with Edward Everett's remarks in the latter's review of Heeren's book, regarding the inevitability of America superseding the European powers in leading the world, and the European powers' concomitant decline.

Lieber's hopes, meanwhile, were not restricted to the prospects of the 'Cis-Caucasian' nations only. In 1868 he was to be found commenting on the 'propitious and civilizing interdependence among nations'. In his view, '[t]he civilized nations have come to constitute a community, and are daily forming more and more a commonwealth of nations, under the restraint and protection of the law of nations'—which latter, moreover, had 'begun to make its way even to countries not belonging to the Christian community, to which the law of nations had been confined'. Lieber, who had already distinguished himself as one of the most important contributors to the advancement of international law, went on, 'Our Wheaton's Law of Nations has been translated into Chinese, and is distributed by the government of the empire among its high officials. Soon it will form a subject of the Chinese higher state examination.' That year many in America were excited about the prospects of China opening up to the world. The previous year, in 1867, an American diplomat (and former congressman), Anson Burlingame, resigned his post as United States minister to China and became the leader of a Chinese delegation pursuing treaties with the United States and the European powers. Early in 1868 'the colourfully garbed delegation set out with circus-like fanfare for the United States'.[38] It was in that context that Lieber wrote, 'The leading nations—the French, the English, the German, the American—they draw the chariot of civilization abreast, as the ancient steeds drew the car of victory.' And those very pages were being written, Lieber went on, at the time 'when a citizen of the American republic has entered our city, at the head of a Chinese embassy, sent to the great western powers in America and Europe, for the avowed purpose of attaching China to that union of nations among whom the law of nations has its sway in peace and in war.'[39]

Lieber had an acute sense of a civilisational unity among the peoples that he alternated between calling 'Western' and 'Cis-Caucasian'. At the same time, he was thinking in terms of that civilisation being in the vanguard of global progress, and thought it desirable and likely that the rest of the world might gradually join it. Many were to follow in his footsteps.

IV. 'Orientalism' and 'Occidentalism': America, 1853

Lieber's explicit complaint about the need to agree on a word to describe the civilisation and peoples he was talking about was telling; yet in that very year, 1853, some increase in the uses of 'Western' or 'western' could be registered. The Eastern Question was again topical, which may not be unrelated, and it was only very recently that Commodore Matthew C. Perry had paid his first visit to Japan and promised to return with more gunboats next time.[40] In June the New York magazine *The Knickerbocker* published an article entitled 'Orientalism', which did precisely what in most of the existing scholarly literature we are told was to happen only come the 1890s: it assertively claimed a piece of the imperial pie for the United States, referring repeatedly to that country as a 'western' power (and used the term 'western civilization'). According to the article's rationale, it was exactly by dint of its 'Westernness' that America must take part in 'rescu[ing] from eternal anarchy, stagnation, and despotism, the magnificent domains of the East.'[41]

The article first surveyed the state of the Ottoman Empire. After having discussed 'the scenery, the history, the mind, and the religions of the Orient', the anonymous author came to the most important part of the essay: 'It remains to consider how and with what results these will be modified and changed by western civilization.' For no one could fail to notice 'that with the decay of the old civilization of the orient', a 'new and more energetic civilization' was entering the East. The first 'energetic display of European power toward Turkey' in modern times had occurred 'when she lost the best part of Greece'. Russia, England and France, 'for the first time joining forces, reddened the bay of Navarino with Ottoman blood'. Now, 'Navarino was a severe lesson'; 'the Turk', however, sulked so much that '[h]is ire [...] had prevented this display of western power from having its due impress'. Instead, 'he immediately rushed into a war with Russia'. In a rather crude, but fairly typical, display of climatic determinism the article went on to comment, 'He forgot that the hardy Turk, who had been nurtured amid the snows of the Caspian, and had followed the fierce Mahmoud to victory, had been gradually melting under the sun of the Mediterranean.' Meanwhile, 'the hardy Russian, like his victorious ancestors, had been nurtured under the frosts of northern winters'. Inevitably, then, the Ottomans were defeated by 'northern courage and western science'; and Russia was 'about to swallow the Orient'. The article went on to predict that while Turkey was 'thus dissolving, new elements will enter into her body politic'. And as a result, 'the Turkey of the twentieth century, while she may have lost her baggy trousers and ample turban with her nationality, her intolerance and her religion, and her exclusiveness with her ignorance, may reveal new glories and resources under the auspices of western civilization.'[42]

The article then moved to the history of the British in India, castigating the hypocrisy of the English newspapers when they accused the United States of 'lust of annexation and dominion'. The Americans were simply doing what their 'mother' had been doing. The article was adamant that it criticised the hypocrisy of the British only insofar as the latter were accusing the Americans of what they themselves had been doing on a huge scale; but it was equally adamant that it was by no means critical of imperialism per se: 'We are not of those who would arraign England for grasping India and opening Asia. There is a higher law than the law international for that.' And, no less explicitly, 'GOD gives the intelligent and civilized *power*, not to prey upon the weaknesses of his creatures, but to elevate them in the scale of being, to rescue from eternal anarchy, stagnation, and despotism, the magnificent domains of the East.' It was by that same 'right' that 'America may unfurl the stripes and stars in the harbor of Jeddo, and open Japan to the world', and that 'western powers may divide the Mahometan world, displace sterility with cultivation, ignorance with refinement, and rapine with protection, but not the converse'.[43] A Lockean justification for imperialism was adduced:[44] 'That right is supported by this reason: that no nation has aught independently of another; but that all is held in trust for the common weal of GOD's creatures.' Now, God had given Turkey 'the finest of climates', fertile Mesopotamian plains and 'her Grecian isles as the resorts of commercial millions—all in trust for his creatures, and for their best uses.' If, however, Tukey 'fails in her efforts to execute his trust, according to the requirements of this century, the conscience of the world will sanction its partition among powers having higher civilization'.

It was in that context that the crucial question was then asked: 'In conclusion: What part have we of America in the Orient?' The answer began with the remark that 'never, till this golden era, has any great power turned its eyes to the lonely Pacific'. Lands that had been for a couple of centuries 'undisturbed by miners and untilled by husbandmen, seem to have been reserved by PROVIDENCE for the meeting-place of the Anglo-Saxon, on his eastern and western path of empire'.[45] California and Australia were meeting in the Pacific. The 'destiny of the Orient' was bound to be 'influenced by these new-born nations'. Chinese emigration was already notable: 'Sydney and San Francisco receive ship-loads of Celestials.' On their return, their influence and example were bound to 'react upon China'.[46] It was, therefore, 'not by Russia, nor by England, that eastern China and Japan are to be affected'. How long would it be, therefore, 'before the stars and stripes are planted upon the opposite coast of Asia?' For '[t]he thirty millions of Japan await the key of the western Democrat to open their prison to the sun-light of social interchange'. The Pacific would 'become to modern civilization what the Mediterranean was to the ancient, and our rail-road will become to the world what the Roman highway was of old—the great artery of national aggrandizement and power'. All things considered, 'no power but the ALMIGHTY can prevent the Democratic element of America from making its impress upon the Orient'.[47]

It has been remarked, quoting historian Reginald Stuart, that '[t]he American destiny did not seem so manifest in the 1850s'.⁴⁸ To the *Knickerbocker* correspondent of 1853, however, America's destiny was already then clear: to be a leading 'western' power providentially bound to build an empire in the Pacific and share the cake in Asia. And it was, according to that author, precisely America's participation in 'Western civilization' that awarded it that destiny.

V. European Immigrants and Eastern Questions

As we saw, Lieber was keen to highlight the commonalities between his new country and the old continent he came from. But other migrants from Europe were keener to highlight the differences, and America's exceptional nature. *The New Rome; Or, The United States of the World* was a remarkable book, co-authored by Theodore Poesche, a German migrant, and Charles Goepp, an American of English background (but it was made clear in the Preface that the bulk of the book had been drafted by the German). It was a striking statement of American destiny, published, like the *Knickerbocker* article, in 1853. Another recent migrant from Europe, Adam Gurowski, was also to sing the praises of American exceptionalism and manifest destiny, though he was simultaneously a Panslavist. Even in a century replete with idiosyncratic characters and prophets Gurowski stands out: the story of his legendary itinerary from Polish nationalist to Russian Panslavist *and* American nationalist has been recounted, and it is a fascinating one.⁴⁹ He migrated to the United States in November 1849; when he died in 1866, the American friends and luminaries attending his funeral included Walt Whitman, who reported that 'all the big radicals were there'.⁵⁰ Gurowski had studied for four years in German universities, as well as in Paris, where he came under the influence of the ideas of Saint-Simon, Comte and Fourier. Since he 'could not live happily unless he was embroiled in a controversy', he had to change countries many times before he reached America—where, of course, he continued to be so embroiled. But he also won many people over, because he was 'about the most entertaining man going [...] despite the difficulties of his jargon of French and German and villainous English'. He met the great and the good of Massachusetts intellectual life (the poet Longfellow became one of his many friends); after two years there, in Cambridge, and unsuccessful attempts to obtain an academic post at Harvard, he moved to New York City in November 1851. He was soon employed on the editorial staff of Horace Greeley's *New York Daily Tribune*, the paper Karl Marx too was writing for, from London, during the 1850s. Gurowski wrote primarily on foreign politics 'and frequently on his favorite theme, the advocacy of Russia's

Slavic leadership'. The *Tribune* at that time 'approached its peak of national influence', and in many parts of the northern United States it was 'a political bible'.[51]

As Russia and Turkey went to war in what became known as the Crimean War, Gurowski was frantically writing in support of Russia and predicting its victory. Besides many articles in Greeley's highly influential paper, Gurowski published three books in 1854 and 1855.[52] In *Russia As It Is*, he predicted that the Russian people would eventually get rid of their autocratic rulers and expand into Asia. But first of all he explained why he had abandoned his earlier Polish nationalism and converted to Russian-led Panslavism: 'Russia alone represented the Slavic vitality in the moving complications of Europe and the Western world.' Being himself by birth a Slav, Gurowski wrote, he had 'looked around to see where was alive the powerful trunk of my race, and found that Russia alone represented it. Thus originated with me the idea of Panslavism.' Its meaning, to his mind, was 'the union of disseminated Slavic families—some of whom vegetate miserably under the foreign dominion of the Magyars, Turks and Germans, into a homogeneous whole, around one mighty stock'. But he stressed that this creed harboured no aggressive designs against Western Europe (though he conceded that Panslavism did have a defensive attitude to Western encroachments at its expense): 'Panslavism does not aim to give laws to Western Europe, but only not to receive any from her, or from Ouralian invaders.'[53] There would therefore be no conflict with the West, because the expansion of Russia and the Slavs was bound to be eastwards. By conquering Constantinople, meanwhile, the people of Russia would 'find a mighty opening valve, for through this channel the nation would be connected with Europe and the world, for the first time, both commercially and culturally'. Moreover, 'Western ideas would stimulate the empire, and the masses would no longer be isolated and suspicious of everything foreign'.[54]

That same year Gurowski also published *The Turkish Question*. The Ottoman Tanzimat reforms had been a sham, in his opinion. 'Aiming at violently Europeanizing the Turks, these reforms have rather, miserably bastardized the whole race; making them neither Christians nor Mohammedans; neither Asiatics nor Europeans.' According to Gurowski, every intelligent man knew that 'the difference between the state of civilization and culture'—between 'the social and civil institutions of any state of Europe whatever, and that of Turkey'—was 'radical, enormous, and most deeply rooted'. Thus, 'wholesale importations of the implements and instruments of European civilization, will not give life to a corpse; they will alter neither personal disposition nor social institutions'.[55] He again predicted a Russian victory in the Crimean War.

Gurowski soon found an opportunity to defend Russia and Panslavism again, in an insidious and characteristically bizarre way. The *New York Daily Tribune*'s correspondent in Europe, Karl Marx, sent nine articles on Panslavism (in fact written by his friend Friedrich Engels) for publication. However, the timing turned out to be unfortunate for Marx and Engels. Their fierce attacks on Panslavism were destined not to have any chance of influencing the American reading public. Gurowski saw to that. For an extended period in 1855–56, while Greeley was away and Charles A. Dana was performing Greeley's editorial duties, Gurowski as Dana's friend had plenty of scope both considerably to modify the first two Marx-Engels articles on Panslavism, and to prevent the following seven from ever being published. For he did not approve at all of their critical attitude towards Russia.[56] In the *Tribune* of 7 May 1855, with considerable cheek, Gurowski inserted into Marx's article a tribute to himself and his sound interpretation of Panslavism, which Marx never wrote (nor read, apparently):

> Panslavism as a political theory has had its most lucid and philosophic expression in the writings of Count Gurowski. But the learned and distinguished publicist, while regarding Russia as the natural pivot around which the destinies of this numerous and vigorous branch of the human family can alone find a large historical development, did not conceive of Panslavism as a league against Europe and European civilization. In his view the legitimate outlook for the expansive force of Slavonic energies was Asia. As compared with the stagnant desolation of that old continent, Russia is a civilizing power, and her contact could not be other than beneficial.[57]

We already saw Russia presented in a favourable light in the 1853 *Knickerbocker* article. As distinct from what was the case in Western Europe, such an attitude was more general in America at the time. It seems fair to say that Gurowski's endeavours in favour of Russia in the *Tribune* and in his three books 'were significant in shaping public opinion in America and maintaining the friendship of the United States and Russia, which had originated in mutual hatred of England'.[58] (Meanwhile, another European migrant—Lieber—was unhappy with Gurowski's success in that respect: 'To those things which have given me a shock of late [...] I must now add the grand spectacle of American would-be republicans siding with Russia.'[59]).

The Ottoman Empire was also to be talked of as the main 'other' during the new phase of the 'Eastern question' around the time of the Bulgarian crisis. At that point, the most relevant contribution came from another immigrant—Irish, this time—who ended up becoming America's most influential journalist for some decades: Edwin Lawrence Godkin (1831–1902). The earlier surfacing of the Eastern Question that led to the Crimean War had seen Godkin being sent to the front as the London *Daily News*'s special correspondent in Turkey. He spent much time in the Balkans and Russia, familiarising himself with parts of Europe that were relatively unknown to most Western Europeans (let alone Americans). Then, in the autumn of 1856, a twenty-five-year-old Godkin arrived in America.[60] His 1877 essay on 'The Eastern Question' for the *North American Review* was a *longue durée* analysis of the famous 'question'. It is hard not to notice the interchangeability in Godkin's language between 'Christendom'/'Christian', 'Europe' and 'the Western powers', often on a single page.[61] The 'other' was, throughout Godkin's article, the—overrated and to his mind over-indulged—Ottoman Empire. In contrast to what was increasingly the case in Western Europe from the 1820s, Russia was not—yet—unpopular in the United States. That was to change by the end of the century.

VI. Occidentalism versus Orientalism (and Yet Another German-Educated American Academic)

The Ottoman Empire was neither the only, nor the main 'other' to be reckoned with. Once it had been (as was widely expected) defeated or eclipsed, the question would become that of which among the great powers would emerge more powerful; and clearly Russia was feared the most. Benjamin Ide Wheeler was professor of Greek and comparative philology at Cornell, and then president of the University of California. Like many of those discussed in this chapter, he had studied (for four years) in German universities. The Greco–Turkish War of 1897 led him to write a series of articles on the 'perennial' Eastern Question. Like Edward Augustus Freeman, he considered it 'not a question of to-day nor of yesterday. When European history first began to be written, it was already there'. It had already begun 'before there was any Russia, or any Turkey, or any England'. Indeed, Greece 'sprang into being as a nationality out of its discordant elements in order to face the Eastern Question'. It was a question which in reality concerned 'the perennial antithesis between Occidentalism and Orientalism'. And, what it meant in practice for Americans was, 'Who is to lead, who is to champion, who is to represent Occidentalism in its inevitable conflicts with Orientalism?' That is what Wheeler called 'the Greater Eastern Question'.[62]

According to Wheeler, when one crossed the Aegean, or the Bosphorus, one was 'made aware that he has passed out of one world into another. He has passed out of the Occident into the Orient'. A long list of differences and (mostly stereotypical) descriptions of 'Oriental' and 'Occidental' characteristics followed. And a long history also followed, of the ebbs and flows in the relations between East and West as interpreted by this classicist, with Alexander's conquests featuring prominently as 'the richest victories of Occidentalism ever won'. Now, in Wheeler's own time, Turkey was still in Europe 'because the forces of modern Occidentalism are not united under leadership'. The mutual suspicions of the Great Powers, 'the forces of Occidentalism', were permitting the survival of Turkey in Europe. However, 'when the leader emerges, Occidentalism will straightway push out over Alexander's track to the Persian Gulf'. The question was, 'Who is to be that leader? Who is to be Occidentalism's champion in the twentieth century?'[63]

The occasion for the article was the war between the little Kingdom of Greece and the Ottoman Porte, following yet another insurrection in Crete aiming at union with Greece. Inevitably then, Wheeler's contemporary Greeks were discussed. They were 'a people that must, at least to some extent, be reckoned with in the future settlement of Eastern questions'. They were 'thoroughly Occidental, and their antagonism to Orientalism, both in spirit and in the concrete forms of Turkey and the Turks, is deep-seated'. The conflict between the two would 'last to the death, because it is grounded in an indestructible difference of thought, mood, and character'.[64] He went on to analyse the role of the Armenians, the Bulgarians and some of the Great Powers. But one of these powers loomed largest. Wheeler gave a number of indications of how powerful and well placed Russia was, in the context of the succession to the Ottomans in the Balkans and the long-coveted possession of Constantinople. Among other things, the 'awful consistency of her foreign policy, ruthless of right, reckless of truth, framed on a plan that spans generations, conceived in terms of world-empire, may well appall us'. Anticipating an observation concerning the long-term history of Russian–American relations that Walter Lippmann was to make forty-five years later, Wheeler asserted, 'That policy long ago assigned the United States to the list of traditional friends. The purpose was to alienate us from her future rival, England.' And foreshadowing what Paul S. Reinsch was to write three years later,[65] he also remarked that Russia was 'strong, furthermore, in a certain sympathy her semi-barbarism has with that of the border peoples of Asia'. The peoples of the East had 'always preferred the Russian to the Englishman'.[66]

Under the circumstances, 'England' was 'preparing for an inevitable conflict'. That conflict concerned the question, 'Who is to be the leader and champion of Occidentalism in the twentieth century—shall it be the Anglo-Saxon or the Slav?' A question that immediately proved to be rhetorical followed: 'Has Russia the natural right to be the leader of Occidentalism?' Of course not: 'Occidentalism grounded itself in the right of the individual personality and the individual community to find the law of its action in its own purposes of being.' Russia, on the other hand, represented 'government from above and from outside'. The situation at that moment was that the battle was 'being arrayed'. The prize of victory was going to be 'the leadership of Occidentalism'. It would be 'a battle between the Slav and the Anglo-Saxon; and when it comes, the Anglo-Saxon world must not be divided against itself'. Wheeler obviously had in mind the recent controversy between Britain and the United States over Venezuela, and wished for arbitration between them to work. The Anglo-Saxon mission shared by America and Britain meant '[e]qual justice, personal rights, distributed government, immanency of law'; that was 'the Occidental idea which the Anglo-Saxon spirit offers to champion before the world'.

Finally, the logic of *translatio imperii*, the movement of civilisation westwards, was also on display:

> The issue is stated in terms of Greece, but it is written in terms of the succession to her ancient leadership in human civilization. In the spoils of the battle little Greece will have small part; but then, it is only one more illustration of the fate of history that has left her desolate, while her ideas have gone forth into the great world, following the course of the wick, and shedding their light through the lamps of others whose strength avails to set them higher and give their beams a wider and a surer reach.[67]

This is only a sample of similar arguments Wheeler repeatedly deployed in a number of other publications around that time.[68]

VII. 'The meeting of the Orient and the Occident, Long Foreshadowed': Academic Political Science and 'Western Civilisation'

Paul Samuel Reinsch (1869–1923) had been a Ph.D student of the famous historian Frederick Jackson Turner. Awarded his doctorate at the University of Wisconsin in 1898, Reinsch was soon offered an academic post there and established the first course in international politics. The credentials he acquired by his academic publications led to him later (in 1913) being appointed United States minister in China.[69] These credentials derived most notably from the book he published in 1900, with a characteristic title: *World Politics at the End of the Nineteenth Century as Influenced by the Oriental Situation*. What would happen in China was to determine the future not only of world politics, but of civilisation, the book argued. The focus may not be surprising, in light of the Boxer Rebellion of 1898–1901.[70]

According to Reinsch, '[t]he meeting of the Orient and the Occident, long foreshadowed, has finally taken place, and the settlement of accounts between the two civilizations cannot be longer postponed'. Whenever 'the Orient' and 'the Occident' had met before, it had 'always been in a life-and-death struggle for leadership in civilization'. Some much-rehearsed examples followed. It was at Marathon that 'the West' had 'first saved itself from Oriental dominion'. Later, Alexander 'carried Western influences far into the Orient'. However, 'the wave swept back, and the European nations were again in turn forced to fight for their existence against Moors, Tartars, and Turks'. But the struggle was not over yet. On the one hand, 'Western civilization, now fully developed, and rich in the accumulated wealth and wisdom of centuries, stands panoplied in all the glories of history'. On the other, '[t]he Orient, which believes that it has learned ages ago the sum of knowledge and the essence of truth, is still animated with the same social and political institutions that existed at the beginning of the Christian era'. Though these two civilisations had 'in some degree reacted upon each other', they still maintained 'a distinct character, with little real mutual understanding'. Hence the 'great question': 'Is the Western spirit to conquer or to be conquered, or is there to be a peaceful union of the two ancient civilizations, combined into a higher harmony?' Reinsch contributed a stereotypical enumeration of the traits that were supposed to characterise each of the two civilisations. The Orient had 'the pessimism of complete knowledge and disillusionment: it is quiet and serene, because it sees nothing worth striving for: individual existence is unimportant'. The West, by contrast, was 'intensely individualistic, and filled with an optimistic energy which leads it to believe in an evolution of higher forms and in progress to a higher civilization'. Though 'not always clear as to the final aim', it yet believed 'above all in upward struggle', and took for granted 'that humanity can progress'.[71]

The meeting between the two civilisations had 'long been foreshadowed in philosophy and in general thought'. The 'opening of India to the nations of Europe introduced the Western mind to the treasures of Eastern philosophy'. For example, Schopenhauer was a Buddhist, and derived 'from oriental ideas the life and spirit of his pessimistic philosophy'. And, last but not least, '*Russia, the chief Western exponent of Orientalism*, has loomed larger and larger in men's minds, and the strange fascination which her power exercises in modern political life is due in no small measure to the anti-individualistic tendencies of her civilization'.[72]

The ambiguity with which Russia was viewed is typified in the awkward way Reinsch spoke of it as 'the chief Western exponent of Orientalism'. The reasons why the ambiguity mattered, and why Russia inspired deep anxiety, are elaborated upon: 'Moreover, the Russian spirit will be present there [in China] to act as an interpreter and mediator between the two civilizations'; and if Russia were to succeed 'in assimilating large areas of the Chinese Empire', Orientalism would acquire 'a strong political organization to aid it in impressing its character upon the world'.[73]

Given that the future of China was the decisive factor, Reinsch was keen to stress that the most momentous question at that time concerned 'the influence of Western industrial, political, religious, and intellectual forces on China'. His prediction was that, '[s]hould the empire remain intact, and should friendly relations continue to be fostered, much of Western civilization would imperceptibly creep in and become a part of Chinese life'. If, on the other hand, the ill-advised policy of partition which had been advocated in some quarters were to be pursued, it was bound to lead to 'terrible conflicts between the far East and the West'. To his mind, therefore, the 'broadest interests of civilization' demanded 'that the Western powers should exert all their influence in maintaining intact and open to Western thought and life the greatest empire of the East'.[74]

Reinsch was aware that some 'pessimistic spirits have already prophesied a conquest of our civilization by Oriental ideals'. They believed that it was becoming 'untrue to itself', and was 'beginning to worship at the shrine of Oriental fatalism'.[75] He conceded that there had, indeed, been a 'deepening and broadening of Western thought within the last few decades'. This was 1900 after all, and Swami Vivekananda and many others had been travelling around spreading their message for some years (to say nothing of other, earlier and later, influences, from Raja Ram Mohan Roy to Keshub Chunder Sen, the Tagores or Helena Blavatsky's Theosophy).[76] Thus Reinsch was bound to acknowledge that the 'influence of Indian philosophy and religion on Western life can have escaped no one'. His main worry was that, 'unhappily', an Orient-inspired 'return to reverence for the deep, mysterious forces of nature and of life' was accompanied, for many, by 'a discountenancing of scientific methods in the field of knowledge and an impatience with liberal ideas in the field of politics; a return to mystic romanticism in fiction—to a worship of half-understood symbols which are dealt out to the faithful as the essence of knowledge and experience'. The 'slow, painful methods of acquiring knowledge by scientific investigation' were 'viewed with impatience'. In the same vein, the 'imperial idea' was invoked 'in a movement to endow nations with world domination through manifestoes supported by brute force'. The 'simple ideals of democracy, of social equality, of the coöperation of the governed in matters that most concern them' were 'in some quarters beginning to be brushed aside' and were giving way to 'a claim of the right of the stronger to govern as he pleases'. The upshot was that Western civilization had, it must be admitted, 'lost its harmony and cohesion'.[77]

It was at such a juncture that the East, 'with its swarming hordes living a listless life from century to century', and the West, 'with its energetic, individualistic impulses, but without any consistent philosophy of civilization', were meeting face to face. It was evident that all this threatened 'to accentuate the reactionary forces, to strengthen autocracy and brute force, and to weaken everything that bases itself on reason, reflection, and individual right'. Reinsch summarised the 'unfavorable influences that are to be expected from Oriental civilization':

> a pessimistic view of life; an undervaluing of individual rights and the power of individual initiative; a caste spirit which looks upon men as mere incomplete portions of a larger unity in which their existence is entirely swallowed up; the degradation of women, whom Western ideals have placed on an equal intellectual and moral footing with men; a lack of sympathy; the preponderance of theocracy; and absolutism.

For it was the case, he stressed, that, for all its individualism, the West was 'more sympathetic than the East'. He attributed that 'sympathy' largely to the impact of the Christian religion. Meanwhile '[t]hroughout the Orient, man is singularly apathetic and untouched by the woes of his fellows'. But there were also some 'favorable influences that may be exercised by the meeting of the older and younger civilizations'. The latter, younger ('Western'), civilisation could gain 'a deeper insight into the mystic elements of life, more serenity, and greater quiet and self-possession'. For he conceded that '[o]ur civilization is too materialistic, and lays too much emphasis on mere machinery'. The Oriental was entitled to ask, 'Why do you hurry, and struggle, and make inventions, and reduce life to an endless scramble, when you have not time left to think about the deepest questions of the human soul?'[78] (M. K. Gandhi was to elaborate upon what he saw as the 'Western' mania for speed—to say nothing of what he saw as the materialistic nature of modern 'Western civilisation'—less than a decade later, in his *Hind Swaraj*.)

All great powers were 'straining every nerve to gain as large a share as possible of the unappropriated portions of the earth's surface'. In that contest, Asia was 'the principal prize', because with 'its marvellous resources' and 'its great laboring population' it was bound to become 'the industrial centre of the future'. And interest in that contest was increased 'when men become conscious that the questions to be solved involve not merely commerce and industry, but the deeper interests of civilization as well'—because, to Reinsch's mind, '[t]he whole cast of thought that characterizes the West, its ideals and principles, may be modified by the intimate contact with the Orient into which it is now being brought by imperial expansion'. And here, once more, the role of a particular power loomed largest: 'On account of her mediating position between the Orient and the West, the character and policy of Russia are at present of the greatest importance to the world.' These were the reasons why Russia's 'civilizing capacity, her true aims and ideals, her attitude toward Oriental and Western civilization, the scope of the means at her disposal' were matters 'of supreme importance to every thoughtful man'. Given that situation, it was, he noted elsewhere, 'unfortunate that all these developments tend to emphasize the Asiatic character of the Russian Empire and to estrange it more and more from Western, and especially English, civilization'. In a number of ways, 'the semi-Asiatic character of Russia' was 'becoming still more Oriental'. Oriental influences in Russia were 'more and more predominant'. The 'unconscious instinct of the masses' had been 'a foremost guide in Russian politics' and that consideration was 'of prime importance in judging of the respective positions of England and Russia in China'. The difference was crucial: 'Russia assimilates, while England merely superimposes her authority'; the prospects were alarming. If the Russian advance were allowed to proceed 'naturally and gradually' as it had in the past, 'the power of that nation in Asia would become almost irresistible'; and 'England in opposing her would have the unfortunate position of Carthage'. For Britain would have to rely for her defence 'on unassimilated subject nations, while Russia could summon against her the vast masses that will gradually become penetrated with the spirit of Russian polity and civilization'.[79] The future looked gloomy indeed.

VIII. Afro-American Radicalism versus Russian Menace? (And Japan as a Beacon of Hope)

We saw how deeply worried about Russia Benjamin Wheeler was in the late 1890s. We have just seen how deeply worried about Russia Paul Samuel Reinsch was in 1900. Anxiety about Russia and an impending confrontation between 'Slav' and 'Anglo-Saxon' was widespread at the time.[80] The West Indian-born turned American activist Hubert Harrison (who would later play a major role in the Garveyite movement), was also writing on the 'The Russian Menace', in a letter to the *New York Times* published on 4 January 1904. His letter was prompted, he explained, by the imminence of war between Russia and Japan, which was bound to turn out to be 'a world-drama, with England, Japan, China, and Russia as the principal actors'. As a recent student of his thought has put it, '[h]e began curiously, with a statement imbued with assumptions of racial superiority similar to those dominant in the United States and similar to those that he would regularly challenge'. According to Harrison, '[b]y superior force the nobler races have impressed their civilization [...] on the baser peoples, and so made for the elevation of humanity'. But 'sometimes the advance of civilization has been seriously checked by the force of barbaric hordes and the fate of humanity has trembled in the balance until the nobler races reasserted their superiority'. Making his case more concrete, he asserted that 'the Slavonic race, or, to be more exact, the Russian nation, is the most serious menace to advancing civilization'. Its political system was 'based on the groveling subservience of the people, and the entrenched despotism of their rulers'. And with such a system, Russia was pursuing the 'final absorption of China' in order to create 'a Cossack world'.[81] The solution Harrison proposed to the menace was to 'look to the German races'. He recommended that the 'three great Germanic nations' (Britain, the United States and Germany) should 'exert their combined commercial and military powers to defeat the arms of Russia'. What was at stake in the East was 'an approaching struggle, not merely between two nations [...] but between two races'. It was not just an opposition between Russia on the one side and 'Japan supported by England' on the other, but rather 'between the Slavonic and Germanic civilizations, to decide for the coming generations whether this shall be a world of bureaucratic despotism or of free institutions'. Harrison expressed the hope that 'when the decisive struggle comes [...] God grant that the sceptre of civilization may remain in the hands of the Germanic race!'[82]

Whatever Harrison's reasons for such prognostications,[83] the Russo–Japanese war of 1904–1905 ended in victory for Japan. This outcome was seen as an—in modern times at least—unprecedented victory of a non-white, or non-European, power over a white European one. It therefore unleashed huge waves of enthusiasm across Asia, from the Ottoman Empire to India and beyond. Afro-Americans rejoiced as well. W.E.B. Du Bois was speaking for many when he wrote,

> For the first time in a thousand years a great white nation has measured arms with a colored nation and been found wanting. The Russo–Japanese War has marked an epoch. The magic of the word 'white' is already broken, and the Color Line in civilization has been crossed in modern times as it was in the great past. The awakening of the yellow races is certain. That the awakening

of the brown and black races will follow in time, no unprejudiced student of history can doubt.

The only question then was, 'Shall the awakening of these sleepy millions be in accordance with, and aided by, the great ideals of white civilization, or in spite of them and against them?' This was 'the problem of the Color Line'. Might things change? 'Force and Fear have hitherto marked the white attitude towards darker races; shall this continue or be replaced by Freedom and Friendship?'[84]

IX. Civilisations and Civilisationism: Alexander Crummell, William H. Ferris, W.E.B. Du Bois

Du Bois had good reasons, of course, to wonder and be concerned. The—once upon a time highly popular—American poet Henry Wadsworth Longfellow has been praised for his universalist cosmopolitanism and 'the multicultural version of America in which he so fervently believed', as opposed to the nationalism of authors such as Emerson or Melville.[85] Such comments were made with particular reference to the following passage from Longfellow's 1849 novel *Kavanagh: A Tale*:

> 'But, at all events,' urged Mr. Hathaway, 'let us have our literature national. If it is not national, it is nothing.'
>
> [Mr. Churchill] 'On the contrary, it may be a great deal. Nationality is a good thing to a certain extent, but universality is better. All that is best in the great poets of all countries is not what is national in them, but what is universal. [. . .] I was about to say also that I thought our literature would finally not be wanting in a kind of universality.
>
> As the blood of all nations is mingling with our own, so will their thoughts and feelings finally mingle in our literature. We shall draw from the Germans tenderness; from the Spaniards, passion; from the French, vivacity, to mingle more and more with our English solid sense. And this will give us universality, so much to be desired.[86]

Inevitably, Afro-Americans might not find much comfort in reading Longfellow's conception of how American literature would become 'universal', by adopting German, Spanish and French influences, in addition to English. Nor could they be blamed for feeling excluded from Thomas Paine's emphatic declaration that serves as an epigraph to this chapter. Feelings of exclusion and the concomitant resentment were evident, for example in a collective protest at the way Black Americans were (not) represented in the 1893 Chicago Exhibition.[87] Hence some of them started exploring alternatives. Afro-American thinkers were inevitably faced from early on with the question of their relation to 'Western' or 'European' civilisation. They were Americans, some very recently liberated and others previously free, but all facing the predicament of finding themselves in a country whose majority identified with a civilisation purportedly originating in Western Europe and claimed as the heritage of white Americans of European origin. The strategies Afro-American thinkers and activists developed in order to cope with that predicament differed widely and evolved over time. They generated a range of cultural and intellectual responses. One strategy was to demand to be allowed equal and unsegregated educational opportunities to share in that 'European' culture, seen as higher, and prove their worth within and through it. Education was seen as key to 'the advancement of the race'. Another strategy was to opt for more or less complete rejection of 'European' cultural norms and search for inspiration and pride through a 'return' to African art, folklore and music. And still another was to attempt to prove that 'Western' civilisation had originated in Africa, and therefore to claim respect for Afro-Americans as co-owners of the cultural heritage of that civilistion. Each of these strategies encompassed a vast array of combinations and nuances. One of the most interesting responses was the attempt to claim superiority of empathy for African Americans because of their ability to understand both the 'white' vantage points of their fellow Americans and another vantage point that was unique to themselves. This 'double vision' with which, thanks to their predicament, Afro- Americans were endowed, was proposed as a unique advantage through which they could make their distinct contributions to 'Western civilisation'.

A major source of inspiration for several late nineteenth- and early twentieth-century thinkers was the thought of Alexander Crummell (1819–1898).[88] New-York born Crummell had studied in England, at Queens' College, Cambridge, between 1848 and 1853. He then went to Liberia as a missionary for twenty years. In 1873 he returned to the United States and continued his activities as a Protestant minister and leading intellectual light of Afro-American activism. He disagreed with Frederick Douglass's assimilationism and was (for much of the time) in favour of Black American separatism. Shortly before his death he founded the 'American Negro Academy'. During his studies in Cambridge, Crummell had been influenced by the ideas on civilisation of the French Protestant historian François Guizot. In *Civilization, the Primal Need of the Race* (1898), Crummell argued that '[w]hat ['the Negro'] needs is CIVILIZATION. He needs the increase of his higher wants, of his mental and spiritual needs'. It has been justly said of Crummell that he 'tended to see blacks as aesthetically gifted people, strongly

FIGURE 4.4. Alexander Crummell. Frontispiece photograph from Alexander Crummell, *The Greatness of Christ* (1882). *Source:* https://en.wikipedia.org/wiki/Alexander_Crummell#/media/File:Alexander_Crummel_(cropped).png

enthusiastic, but lacking in discipline'. Wilson Jeremiah Moses finds him to have been 'representative of a number of black intellectuals who publicized throughout the nineteenth century the idea that civilization is a universal absolute toward which all people should strive and that it had found its highest expression among the Western European peoples'. And Crummell was convinced that 'in order to command the respect that is due to civilized people, Africans would have to make a collective effort under elite leadership to contribute to the world's cultural wealth in a way that could be described as definitely "Negro"'.[89]

In 1877 Crummell delivered a sermon entitled 'The Destined Superiority of the Negro'. He remarked that it had been 'now nigh five hundred years since the breath of the civilized world touched, powerfully, for the first time, the mighty masses of the Pagan world in America, Africa, and the isles of the sea'. And the outcome had been, 'almost everywhere, that the weak, heathen tribes of the earth have gone down' before its presence, 'tribe after tribe!' The 'Negro', however, was destined not only to survive, but to come out on top eventually. Christianity and civilisation would lead 'him' to great things in the future. He had the crucial qualities that warranted 'the expectation of superiority'. These qualities were 'plasticity, receptivity, and assimilation'. And moreover these 'peculiarities' implied 'another prime quality, anticipating future superiority [. . . :] imitation'. According to Crummell, 'the Negro, with a mobile and plastic nature, with a strong receptive faculty, seizes upon and makes over to himself, by imitation, the better qualities of others'. In that 'he' resembled the most successful peoples in history. The ancient Greeks and Romans turned out to be the 'great nations' they were because they became 'cosmopolitan thieves'. By that Crummell meant that they adopted whatever they found useful from other cultures. Therein lay the justification for his ambitious prophecy: 'In the Negro character resides, though crudely, precisely the same eclectic quality which characterized those two great, classic nations; and he is thus found in the very best company.'[90] There were, too, obvious religious overtones to the claim that the past suffering of Crummell's people was proof not of God's disfavour, but rather of the contrary.[91]

One of Crummell's staunch admirers was William H. Ferris. In an important and characteristically titled book, *The African Abroad: Or, His Evolution in Western Civilization, Tracing His Development under Caucasian Milieu* (1913), Ferris came up with some of the most often to be repeated arguments regarding the contributions of Africa to 'Western civilisation'.[92] He quoted extensively from European sources, both older ones such as Constantin-François Volney and recent scholarship. A contemporary authority adduced on African prehistory was the German-born Columbia University anthropologist Franz Boas. Many other contemporary anthropologists and specialists in other disciplines were cited for corroboration of Ferris's arguments, including, unsurprisingly, the German maverick Leo Frobenius (invoked by most of those who tried to vindicate Africa's contributions to civilisation).[93]

As Moses has observed, '[a]lthough he was interested in Egypt, and while he accepted the opinion of Volney that the ancient Egyptians had been black, Ferris was far more interested in Ethiopia.'[94] Curiously, Moses does not mention the crucial older source that Ferris used extensively to corroborate his thesis about the Ethiopian origins of Egyptian, and hence also of 'Western', civilisation: the Göttingen historian Arnold H. L. Heeren (see Section I above).[95] To the evidence represented by the monuments unearthed by archaeologists were added testimonies to '[t]he fame of the Ethiopians', Herodotus having described them as the 'tallest, the most beautiful and long-lived of human races', and Homer, before Herodotus, in even more flattering language, as 'the most just of men, the favorites of the gods'. In addition, in the 'Mosaic records', while they were 'described as the most powerful, the most just, and the most beautiful of the human race, they are constantly spoken of as black, and there seems to be no other conclusion to be drawn than that at that remote period of history *the leading race of the western world was a black race*.'[96]

Besides his importance as author of the 1913 book, Ferris (a clergyman, and the holder of MA degrees from both Yale and Harvard) went on to occupy important roles, not least as literary editor of the Marcus Garvey movement's newspaper, *Negro World*, during the 1920s. The tension between his Afrocentrism and his cosmopolitanism is illustrative of broader stresses and even contradictions affecting many in a similar predicament before, during and after the Great War. While, on the one hand, '[t]ypical of the African vindicationists of his generation', Ferris 'experienced the Garveyite impulse to repudiate the Western tradition in order to defend the African', he was on the other hand 'in the habit of using his Afrocentric arguments to demonstrate the participation of black people in the common heritage of Western civilization'.[97]

Another admirer of Crummell was the man Ferris had debated with at the first meeting of the 'American Negro Academy', in 1897, W.E.B. Du Bois (1868–1963).[98] A major difference between Ferris and Du Bois was that the latter went on to live a long life, in the course of which much would happen to affect his attitudes (especially after 1945). It was crucial to Du Bois's development that he was advised by his teacher at Great Barrington, Massachusetts, to study classics, and he did. This provided him with the educational opportunities that he deserved, as well as a special and complex relationship with 'Western civilisation'.[99] It is important to note too that, like many educated nineteenth-century Americans, Du Bois spent time studying in Europe, in Berlin (1892–94). He clearly relished both the experience and the superior vantage point he felt it gave him once back home: *ex Germaniae lux*, once again. A lecture Du Bois gave to an African American audience in 1900, after his second sojourn in Europe, is striking in that respect:[100] he proposed to analyse 'the trend and meaning of modern European civilization'. He pointed out that the 'civilization of the 20th century centres in Europe'—meaning that 'the organization of European states and their development for the last four centuries has been the pattern and norm of the civilization of the world'. As he would do many times in the future, he pointed to African contributions to the ancestry of that civilisation. His Francophilia was also already evident, in the comments he made on Paris, 'the metropolis of the modern world' (not to mention his remark that 'the man or woman in the civilized world who has not at least a distant acquaintance with the language of the Parisians dare not claim a pretense of liberal culture').[101]

Du Bois emphasised that the point of his long survey of Europe was to make his audience 'realize that after all America is not the centre of modern civilization'. 'What', he wanted to know, was 'the spirit of modern Europe?' His answer was that 'Europe today represents in her civilization five leading ideas: Continuity of Organization, Authority of government, Justice between men, Individual Freedom and Systematic Knowledge'. After elaborating on the meaning of each of these leading ideas, he declared, 'In short, Europe today stands for a systematic and continuous union of individual effort to promote Justice and Freedom by means of Knowledge and Authority'. He then preemptively commented on the potential objection that '[i]t may easily be said that this is after all the end and striving of all civilization, no matter how imperfectly realized in particular societies'. But here his response was that this was 'both true and false: true that the same ideals which Europe today clearly recognizes were more or less dimly seen in Egypt, Persia and Judea'; but 'false to think that *ever before in human history these ideals of society ever stood in such clean light, or came so near realization*'. The important thing to understand, therefore, amounted to 'a question of method': what were 'the method and means' by which Europe had attained its ends? The answer lay in Europe's full awareness that 'no army march [sic] faster than its rear guard, that the civilization of no community can outstrip the same community's barbarism, that knowledge is measured by the amount of ignorance abroad in the land, that the culture of every nation and city is measured by its slums'. For Du Bois, that 'idea of social solidarity and social responsibility'—that 'recognition of the fact that human life is not an individual foot race where the devil takes the hindmost'—was 'the central idea of the 20th century and woe to the race or individual that does not recognize its power'.[102]

Speaking before an 'all-Black audience in Louisville, Kentucky', Du Bois next turned to the relevance to them in particular of what he had said up to that point: 'What lesson, has all this to us?' he asked. His reply was that the students of Louisville were 'part of the advance guard of the new people'; and he added, '*These ideals differ in no respect from the ideals of that European civilization of which we all today form a part*'. Hence his advice: 'our watch word today must be Social Solidarity—Social Responsibility: Systematic and Continuous union of our individual effort to promote Justice and Freedom among ourselves and throughout this land by means of knowledge and authority'. That meant, to his mind, that '[y]oung men and women who would serve the Negro race must bravely face the facts of its condition: the ignorance, the immorality, the laziness, the waste, and the crime'. His final admonition was, 'Here are the paths which civilization points out and in these paths we must plod'. They could do little about 'the unfortunate surrounding prejudice', beyond 'a quiet and dignified protest'. Meanwhile, however, 'within our own ranks lies work enough—a people who are training up far

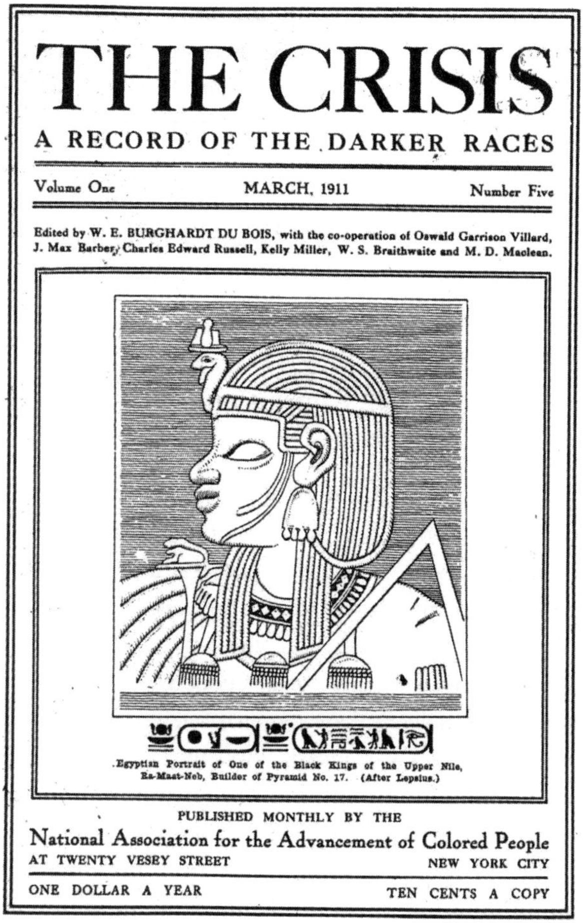

FIGURE 4.5. Front cover of *The Crisis*, vol. 1, no. 5 (March 1911), depicting 'Ra-Maat-Neb, one of the black kings of the Upper Nile', a copy of the relief of Nebmaatre I on Meroe pyramid 17. *Source:* https://en.wikipedia.org/wiki/The _Crisis#/media/File:Bois.jpg

more than their proportion of criminals—who are scattering disease and death, whose ignorance threatens the foundations of democratic government—such a people have a task before them calculated to keep their hands busy and their eyes open for a century to come'.[103]

This was a man still closely following the civilisationist message of Alexander Crummell, who two years earlier had written, 'What ["the Negro"] needs is CIVILIZATION.' And 'European civilization' was still 'that European civilization of which we all today form a part'. As Du Bois was to put it much later in one of his autobiographies, 'In the folds of this European civilization I was born and shall die, imprisoned, conditioned, depressed, exalted and inspired.'[104] Du Bois's attitudes towards 'European' or 'Western' civilisation were to change considerably during his life, along with subtle changes to the meanings attached to these terms themselves between the 1890s and the 1960s. But this early Du Bois was a long way indeed from the Du Bois who was to denounce the 'reeking West whose day is done' in a 1962 poem.[105] Much was to happen in the interim. For Du Bois as for most other people, few milestones were as important as the Great War, to which we will turn in the next chapter.

X. Conclusion

There were differing visions for the future of America in the nineteenth century and up to the Great War. Most of those who enunciated these juxtaposed to old, corrupt, imperialist Europe an America born of principles different from those of the states of the Old World. Hence it was America's exceptionality that was stressed, rather than its commonality with Europeans. There were others, fewer, who highlighted the commonalities; and others still who actively sought to enhance awareness of these. In this last category, nobody outranked Francis Lieber; but, always more of an academic than a populariser, he chose to promote a strikingly odd-sounding term. 'Cis-Caucasian' was never likely to, and never did, excite enthusiasm. Meanwhile, the fact speaks for itself that as late as 1853 and 1859 he publicly complained as explicitly as he did of the absence of a commonly agreed term to describe the civilisational grouping, comprising the Europeans, the Americans and other peoples descended from European settlement, for the existence of which he always argued.

Let me conclude this chapter with a brief sample of the kind of scholarship with which I take issue. In his otherwise brilliant biography of the Boston intellectual Charles Eliot Norton, James Turner entitled the penultimate chapter 'The Invention of Western Civilization'. There one reads, 'So Norton invented Western civilization (more precisely, he conceived the concept, not the phrase, typically speaking not of "Western" but of "our" civilization: "our" referring to Europeans and Americans).'[106] We have seen already in the introductory chapter above that the chronology advocated by Turner is widely shared in the existing scholarship. Yet there had in fact been a long story both of the gradual 'invention' of the concept and of uses of the crucial word or phrase, even in America. And, like much else, the idea had come to the Western hemisphere from Europe: *ex oriente lux*, as it were—or, alternatively (depending on what one thinks of the idea of 'the West'), corruption of the young republic by influences from the Old World.

By the time Herbert Croly, founding editor of *The New Republic*, published *The Promise of American Life* (1909),[107] 'the West', 'Western' and 'Western civilisation', or alternatives thereof, were no longer exotic neologisms to be defined and promoted in the way Lieber had tried to do a few decades earlier. The work had been done. That Herbert Croly was the son of two devotees of Auguste Comte's 'religion of Humanity', initiated from childhood into all its 'sacraments', may or may not be relevant to his uses of the term 'Western'.[108] It is noticeable that in many cases, even among people who used 'the West' and 'Western civilisation' or 'Occidentalism', there was a strong identification with Anglo-American leadership of the world, or Anglo-Saxonism, rather than the notion of common 'Western' (or 'Western Caucasian/Cis-Caucasian') unity and leadership that one finds in Lieber.[109] The rise in American power and self-confidence after the Civil War made American assertiveness more likely, while the increase in the currency of racial theories in the second half of the nineteenth century made 'Anglo-Saxonism' more plausible and attractive. But new alliances, and with them new configurations of what was 'the West' and who was 'Western', were to arise during the Great War. To that cataclysmic time we must now turn.

5

The War of Words

'WESTERN CIVILISATION' AND 'THE WEST,' 1914–1919

'Each country believes that it is fighting for civilisation. But what does it mean by civilisation? There, inevitably, peoples differ: and on these different conceptions, we can be taught by the books published since the beginning of the war.'
ÉLIE HALÉVY TO XAVIER LÉON, 27 JUNE 1915, IN HALÉVY, *CORRESPONDANCE (1891–1937)*, P. 485

'Germany [...] does not know what it has done against herself, by giving France the certainty that she is the soul of the West, and by giving to the whole West the consciousness that its soul is France. At last, that West that France had hoped for and which France has so much sought to achieve for centuries, here it is, being created.' (L'Allemagne [...] ne sait pas ce qu'elle a fait contre elle-même, en donnant à la France la certitude qu'elle est l'âme de l'Occident, et en donnant à tout l'Occident la conscience que son âme est la France. Enfin, cet Occident qui était dans les vœux de la France et qu'elle a tant cherché depuis des siècles, le voici qui se constitue.)
ANDRÉ SUARÈS, *OCCIDENT* (1915), P. 84

'First of all, I must know what you mean when you speak of civilization. [...] I hate the twentieth century, as I hate rotten Europe and the whole world on which this wretched Europe is spread out like a spot of axle-grease.'
GEORGES DUHAMEL, *CIVILIZATION 1914–1917* (1919), PP. 271–72

THE GREAT WAR would affect decisively the ways in which 'the West', 'Western civilisation' and 'civilisation' more generally were talked of. Major controversies arose, and these did not merely regard who was fighting for 'civilisation' and what each who claimed to be doing so meant by it—though they did that as well, as the statement by Élie Halévy quoted as the first epigraph above suggests. Rather, the very concept of civilisation was contested and problematised. There were many reasons for this. One was that the unprecedented scale of mechanised slaughter discredited the very notion that 'civilisation' was a good thing, or the— related—notion that 'Western civilisation' in particular was superior because it was so technologically far advanced. The terrifying results of those technological advances displayed during the war led to a turning of the tables for many, both within 'the West' and beyond. The reactions of people in the rest of the world, as well as of marginalised groups within 'Western' countries, faced believers in the assured progress of 'civilisation' with ineluctable challenges to their self-confidence (and we will see much more on this type of reaction in chapter 6 below, as well). In the United States in particular, the unavoidable debate that began with the outbreak of the war, as to who was to blame and who deserved support, led, by the time America joined the combatants in 1917, to serious soul-searching that resulted in many voices vociferously asserting that America must abandon isolationist illusions and take its place as a leading member of 'the West'. But from the very beginning of the war, long before the painful consequences of deadlocked trench warfare became fully apparent, there was also much controversy as to whether 'civilisation' was a good thing in the first place. And in that early debate, Germany was central.

I. 'We shall carry on this war to the end as a *Kulturvolk*': German Professors and 'the Civilised World'

Some weeks after the successive declarations of war, a manifesto signed by ninety-three German academics and artists was published and soon translated in the press of different countries into their respective languages. It first appeared in German on 4 October 1914.[1] In America it was published on 10 October as 'An Appeal to the Civilized World!' (Significantly—as we shall see—the word, and its cognates, used in the original was not 'civilisation', but rather 'culture': 'An die Kulturwelt!'.) In France it was on 13 October that *Le Temps* published the manifesto. The German professors did more than defend the German kaiser from any guilt for the outbreak of the war and the German army from early accusations of atrocities (not least in Belgium in August 1914). They also deflected the accusations of barbarism raised against Germany back onto their western neighbours, on account of the latters' choice of wartime allies and associates: 'Those who have allied themselves with Russians and Servians [sic], and present such a shameful scene to the world as that of inciting Mongolians and Negroes against the white race, have no right whatever to call themselves upholders of civilization.'[2] (In the 'improved' English version 'European civilization' was substituted for plain 'civilization', which was more faithful to the original 'europäischer Zivilisation'.)

Such charges would be raised in all manner of pronouncements by German intellectuals and politicians in the early stages of the Great War. (Once the Ottoman Empire had joined the war on the German side in October 1914, and the sultan declared 'holy war' [jihad] in November, newspapers in the Entente countries would soon reciprocate of course by blaming German 'barbarians' 'for conceiving the idea of raising the Muslim East against Christian Europeans'.)[3] A further articulation of the German charge had been levelled by two professors in August: they complained particularly about the instigation by the British of the Japanese 'to undertake the detestable raid upon the German territory in China, which needs must end in strengthening the power of that Mongolian nation at the costs of Europeans and Americans'. Their main concern was how it was possible 'for a nation that in such a way has betrayed precious interests of Western culture as soon as it seems to benefit them, [...] for these accomplices of the Japanese robbery' to 'put on the air of being the guardians of morality?'[4] A couple of months later, in October, Romain Rolland was explicit about such accusations coming from Germany, and about the very different perspectives of the two sides as to who was defending what: 'Barbarous despotism, the worst enemy to liberty, is exemplified *for us Frenchmen, Englishmen, men of the West*, in Prussian Imperialism.' Meanwhile, however, for the Germans, 'the monster [...] which threatens civilization is Russia, and the bitterest reproach which the Germans hurl against France is our alliance with the Empire of the Czar. I have received many letters reproaching us with this.'[5]

The initial German reaction to Britain's participation in the war against them had been one of great shock, and thus an upsurge of anti-British feeling set the tone. '*Gott strafe England* (God punish England)' was 'the most popular German slogan in 1914'. But as the prospect of victory against Britain steadily receded, the Germans shifted to different arguments regarding their war aims. The new line was that Germany was fighting to save the whole of 'Europe' from 'barbaric', 'Asiatic' Russia.[6] One of the first to articulate this notion had been the philosopher Max Scheler, in a book he hastily wrote in the autumn of 1914.[7] Scheler proclaimed that it was Germany's task to unite the whole continent against Russia: only a strong Germany stretching from the Baltic to the Mediterranean could protect Europe against the deadly Russian danger.[8]

Nevertheless, anti-British fervour meanwhile often went hand in hand with (or was generalised into) a rejection of 'Western' models. Werner Sombart's *Händler und Helden* was one particular example:[9] the leading economist contrasted the British nation of 'shopkeepers' with the German nations of 'heroes'. He emphasised 'the ancient and dominant German tradition of love for war', condemning Immanuel Kant's pacifist writings as 'senile'. He declared in 1915 that German thought and feeling, 'express themselves in the unanimous rejection of everything that even distantly approximates English or western European thought and feeling'. The 'German spirit' had 'risen against the ideas of the eighteenth century which were of English origin'. Echoing much that Nietzsche had written, he noted that every German thinker had 'always resolutely rejected all utilitarianism and eudaemonism [...]. We must recognize everything which resembles western European ideas or which is even distantly related to commercialism as something much inferior to us,' he declared.[10]

As Sombart's book highlights, one of the features both of the manifesto of the ninety-three professors and of other German intellectuals' output at the beginning of the war was a celebration of German militarism (Germans were, after all, Sombart's 'heroes'). The ninety-three declared that, were it not for German militarism, German culture 'would long since have been extirpated. For its protection it arose in a land which for centuries had been plagued by bands of robbers as no other land has been.'[11] (We will see in the final section of this chapter that the novelist Thomas Mann would take things even further.)

Now, that connection was not lost upon the recipients of the professors' manifesto abroad. French intellectuals too thought that German *Kultur* was the root cause of German militarism. Thus, 'if Fichte and Hegel could be identified as the intellectual architects of the movement, then they could also be held responsible (at least indirectly) for the aggression.'[12] Others in France were also to blame Fichte's intellectual hero Immanuel Kant as ultimately the root of the poison. So did many in Britain, as well as in neutral America, not least the distinguished Pragmatist philosopher and educationalist John Dewey.[13] Meanwhile, one of France's veteran specialists on German thought was giving his verdict on the war to the French public. Émile Boutroux (1845–1921), long before he became a Sorbonne professor, had studied in German universities, and drew authority from his experiences there. The Germans were not merely proving, Boutroux opined, that despite all their science, they were, deep down, not very civilised after all. No: things were even worse, because their brutality was calculated and systematic.

It was, indeed, 'une barbarie savante'. In other words, the Germans' violations of the laws of the civilised world were not despite their culture, but rather, precisely because of it. 'Ils sont barbares parce qu'ils sont supérieurement civilisés.' Then Boutroux set about explaining the seeming paradox by blaming Johann Gottlieb Fichte's *Reden an die Deutsche Nation* (Addresses to the German nation) of 1807–1808. Fichte's notion of *Deutschheit* led to 'la théorie du germanisme, ou *Deutschtum*', which provided, to Boutroux's mind, the explanation of the connection the Germans were trying to establish between culture and barbarism. Boutroux undertook to define how the Germans understood civilisation. Nations in general, and particularly 'Latin' nations, saw as the essence of civilisation the 'moral element' of human life, and 'the mellowing of mores'. On the other hand, according to 'la pensée germanique', mellowing, sweetness and goodness were equated with weakness and impotence. Only force was powerful ('Seule, la force est forte'). And the force *par excellence* was science. The Germans saw themselves as the master-nation, and believed that they were proven to be God's chosen people since the time when Hermann (Arminius) defeated the Roman Varus in the forest of Teutoburg in the ninth year of the Christian era.[14]

The world, looking on meanwhile, was wondering with anxiety what relations it might be able to have with Germany after the war. Consciously and systematically, 'Germany will have opposed to our Hellenic, Christian, human civilisation, the destructive fury of the Huns'. German culture was in reality but a scientific barbarism. Boutroux concluded with a trope that was to be much repeated, both during and after the Great War: namely, the idea of the two Germanies. The Germany of open-minded thinkers such as Leibnitz or Kant or later (Swiss-born) Johann Caspar Bluntschli, had been defeated by the Prussian Germany, the Germany of arch-nationalists such as Treitschke.[15] Moreover, a West–East logic was explicit in the analysis. Thus, in a second instalment on the same topic, two years later, Boutroux declared that 'Greece had applied itself to dethroning Oriental fatalism, while Germany [...had] allocated itself the task of re-establishing Oriental fatalism in all its sovereignty.' (In a related move, Maurice Barrès had, at the beginning of the war, called the Germans 'Orientals'.)[16]

Similarly, one of the most vociferous critics of the flaws of German *Kultur* was the highly influential philosopher Henri Bergson. Pursuing an argument already advanced earlier by Boutroux (as well as quoting his phrase), Bergson made a great impact on French intellectual circles by accusing the Germans of 'scientific barbarism' (Boutroux's 'barbarie savante').[17] He was to remain extreme in his assessment of Germany for the rest of the war. Even as sympathetic and Francophile an observer (from a still, at that stage, neutral country) as Walter

Lippmann found himself commenting in a private letter, after having lunch with Bergson, 'The function of philosophy in wartime appears to be confined to making terrible faces at the enemy. Lord knows, I don't feel a bit neutral between the Western Powers and Germany, but can't believe that Germany is the last and most elaborate effort of Satan to destroy God. I don't understand Bergson.'[18]

But not everybody in France had gone along with the demonisation of Germany. In the midst of intense fighting (with the Gallipoli campaign in the balance) in October 1915, Boutroux's old student Élie Halévy was writing, 'Our role [...] will be unenviable. We are intelligent enough to know that all of us, French, English, Germans, we are the inheritors and transmitters of one and the same civilisation.' They were also, Halévy went on, 'intelligent enough to understand that European civilisation takes a national, not an international, form, and that it is in the context of the French nation that our action needs to be exercised for it to be effective'. It was going to be 'a difficult role to play, in a combination of circumstances that will not at all resemble those in the midst of which we grew up, where France will no longer be a fallen great nation, but a nation of an extremely fearful secondary rank.'[19]

There were other reactions as well. One of the most striking for our purposes came from the writer André Suarès. He argued that Germany was effectively scoring a major own goal by starting the war. As we can see from Suarès's statement quoted as an epigraph to this chapter, his view was that Germany had awarded France the certainty that it was the 'soul of the West', and the whole of 'the West' the 'consciousness that its soul is France': That West that France had so wished to create for centuries was now finally coming into being.[20] (Suarès thus resembles Richard Congreve in the explicitness with which he celebrated the way 'the West' had advantages for France's leadership ambitions vis-à-vis Germany.)

In Britain, meanwhile, there was the inevitable anti-German feeling and propaganda.[21] But there were also some who were trying to think of the future in terms of 'The Unity of Western Civilization'—the title of a collection of essays by a great number of participants in the summer schools at the (Quaker) Woodbrooke Settlement, near Birmingham, in the summer of 1915. We have already seen that F. S. Marvin was a passionate and prolific Comtist, and Comtist ideas as well as vocabulary permeate his works. Not least among the ideas he focused upon was that of 'the West'. Circumstances in 1915 were very different from those prevailing when Comte was writing in the 1840s, of course, and Marvin adjusted to his times. But his aim remained the unity of humanity, through the action of its Western 'vanguard', and the first step in attempts to bring about such unity must be greater emphasis on science and scientific advances in the teaching of history. Besides Marvin himself, contributors to the 1915 volume included well-known political thinkers or academics such as J. A. Hobson, L. T. Hobhouse and Ernest Barker. As Marvin put it in the Preface, the contributors may have differed in details,

> [b]ut they agree in thinking that while our country's cause and the cause of our Allies is just and necessary and must be prosecuted with the utmost vigour, it is not inopportune to reflect on those common and ineradicable elements in the civilization of the West which tend to form a real commonwealth of nations and will survive even the most shattering of conflicts.

And the fact that 'we on the Allied side stand fundamentally for this ideal is one of our most valuable assets'. It was clear, Marvin thought, that '[w]e need [...] to associate ourselves mentally with others in order to realize the common elements which underlie the seeming diversity in the civilization of the West'.[22]

II. 'We are Europeans': America 'taken back into the fold'

A rewarding way of beginning to examine reactions to the Great War in the United States is by following the activities and utterances of the writer John Jay Chapman (1862–1933). Towards the close of 1914 Chapman published a very interesting book (though he understandably referred to it near the end as 'a symposium', given the extent to which it was a reproduction of other people's statements). In that volume he collected and commented on some of the utterances of prominent German intellectuals, politicians and generals on the war that had recently broken out. (His method was 'to let the Germans damn themselves by their own apologia'.)[23] America was then neutral—and Chapman at that stage thought it best for it to remain so; but he thought he should nevertheless warn the American public of the nature of the German peril.

Chapman advanced a straightforward argument. The scary ways in which the Germans were behaving could be attributed neither to economic nor to any 'racial' factors. What accounted for the Germans' conduct was the kind of education they had received. The recent generations of Germans had been overworked and overspecialised. That made them inflexible, dogmatic, nervously strained and, worst of all, docile towards their militarist leaders. 'Germany then has been suffering and causing us to suffer from the fact that she never became properly a part of the Roman Empire, but has been living in spiritual isolation since the dark ages.' Therefore, Germany's cure would come 'through her entry into the modern world'. Germany's citizens needed to 'adopt the ideals of Western Europe' and 'learn its forms of Government and its modes of thought'.²⁴ To all intents and purposes, Chapman was proposing what later came to be called the 'Westernisation' of Germany. (What he did not know then of course was that it would take yet another world war for—most of—Germany to go through such a process).

Chapman's close engagement with the war had begun from very early on. In August 1914 his son, Victor, had left for France to fight as a volunteer against the Germans. Chapman himself was in England at the time, and had an article published by the London *Times* of 5 August (the issue that informed people of Britain's declaration of war), entitled 'An Appeal to Americans'. Then on 12 August, in a 'Memorandum on Compulsory Disarmament', he presented the need for disarmament after the war. It was his conviction that some form of international government would be needed. It would become necessary to police Germany and prevent her from rearming; but the Allies needed to 'exclude [. . .] all ideas of national aggrandizement', if they wanted to avoid yet another war. It was crucial for Great Britain to refrain from taking over the former German colonies.²⁵ At the beginning of September Chapman returned to America, and in a journal entry made on board the ship taking him home, he questioned whether his disarmament ideas were not like 'reaching for the moon'. Perhaps America had to go through with this experience 'to be melted into modern Europe', and become 'an integral conscious portion' of it. On the other hand, he could see advantages in America remaining neutral, as it could in that case stand convincingly for peace and disarmament.²⁶ This latter was a widely shared belief, and many American intellectuals and publicists were arguing that America had unique characteristics that rendered it the ideal nation to take the lead for world peace.²⁷

By the end of the year, having become convinced that the Germans had no respect whatsoever for international law, Chapman had published *Deutschland Über Alles or Germany Speaks*. As German submarines increasingly provoked a withdrawal from the isolationist tendency in America, 'a cohort of Progressive historians ([Frederick Jackson] Turner among them) renounced exceptionalist separatism'.²⁸ Finally, by February 1916, John Jay Chapman was delighted to declare that

> [t]he myth of America as promised land is finished. *We are going to be taken back into the fold. We are Europeans, European history, both past and present, is our history, and Europe's future is our future.* The thought of this allies us with every form of intellectual life in Europe and destroys at a blow the mind-killing theory on which we have all been brought up—namely that America has a private destiny of her own, a fate distinct from Europe's fate.²⁹

The same Chapman—who had meanwhile lost his volunteer pilot son in France—was to publish his 'Ode on the Sailing of Our Troops for France' (dedicated to President Wilson), in the *North American Review* in November 1917. His exhortations included verses such as

> Go fight for Freedom, Warriors of the West!
> At last the word is spoken: Go!
> Lay on for Liberty. 'Twas at her breast
> The tyrant aimed his blow;
> And ye were wounded with the rest
> In Belgium's overthrow. [...]
> The Old World and the New shall live apart no more.
> Awake! the Future claims you. Europe's soul
> Hangs in the balance, and the gods contrive
> That without *her* thou never canst be whole,
> Nor she without thee save her soul alive. [...]
> Go, Western Warriors![30]

Chapman was of course far from alone. As the historian John A. Thompson has remarked, '[t]he shock with which Americans responded to the outbreak of the First World War reflected not only their innocent optimism but also their underlying sense of involvement with the old world'. And for some American intellectuals there was a concrete manifestation of that involvement, 'by their physical presence; as well as [Charles Edward] Russell and [Walter] Lippmann, [Randolph] Bourne, [Norman] Hapgood, and [Lincoln] Steffens were in Europe in August 1914'.[31] As we have seen, so was Chapman; and as we will see below, so was Alain Locke. Thompson further notes that some of the Americans 'were soon caught up emotionally in the cause of one of the belligerent countries'. There were many (especially young) American intellectuals who supported the Entente powers because of their love of France, whose artistic and cultural contributions they rated very highly.[32] Chapman clearly shared in that response. But as Thompson observes, the most salient reaction was 'distress at the very fact of the war itself and its consequences for Europe as a whole'.[33] The initial editorial line of the recently launched review representing young reformers, the *New Republic*, edited by the more senior Herbert Croly, was to condemn the war 'as "murderous, damned nonsense," "the sum of all villainies," "insane, brutal, hideous,"' and 'it blamed the belligerent powers when the Turks resorted to massacres again'. The *New Republic*'s rationale was that '[t]he tortured Armenians are a reminder of what a price the makers of this war are asking us to pay. By embroiling the western world in what is essentially a civil war they have let loose anarchy in all the ends of the earth.'[34] Meanwhile Croly had earlier written in an editorial that '[i]ndependence in the sense of isolation has proved to be an illusion' and that America could no longer assume that it could control its own destiny through 'merely the renunciation of European entanglements'.[35] These had already been Croly's views before the war, argued forcefully in *The Promise of American Life* in 1909. Now they were to be shared by many.

III. 'If not civilization, at least our civilization is at stake': The West according to 'the Zelig of twentieth-century politics'

> 'At the depths of the depression (if my memory is correct), the *New Yorker's* "Talk of the Town," commenting on the reported formation of a Monarchist party in the United States, said that many Americans would be glad to settle for Walter Lippmann as king.'[36]

One of the younger contributors and editors of Croly's *New Republic* deserves particular attention here. Walter Lipmann (1889–1974) was much more than just America's undisputedly leading journalist for several decades—active from before the Great War until the late 1960s. He was arguably the twentieth century's most influential newspaperman. A brilliant Harvard graduate, he served for a year as George Santayana's philosophy assistant in the same institution, before deciding that he preferred to make his mark outside the walls of academe. But his philosophical education was far from wasted, and many of his books and essays clearly bear its imprint. Lippmann was much more philosophically ambitious than the average highbrow journalist. From his highly influential articles in Croly's *New Republic* during the First World War to his last 'Today and Tomorrow' newspaper columns in the 1960s, he was an author whose pronouncements were carefully read and noticed by millions, including US presidents and presidential candidates—whose popularity depended much on Lippmann's endorsement. A number of his books, too, were widely discussed and celebrated in their time.[37] Meanwhile, Lippmann was possibly involved in more of the momentous events of his century than anyone else one might name. As David Runciman puts it, felicitously, 'Lippmann is the Zelig of twentieth-century politics. He turns up everywhere, at all the important moments, though in retrospect it's easy to miss him. It's the people he is standing next to who get remembered.'[38]

FIGURE 5.1. Walter Lippmann (Los Angeles, 1936). *Los Angeles Times* Photograph Collection, UCLA. *Source:* https://en.wikipedia.org/wiki/Walter_Lippmann#/media/File:Walter_Lippmann_at_his_desk,_1936.jpg

This was a time of *Großräume* thinking, and many people had begun to talk in terms of continents.[39] Lippmann was instead looking at things in terms of oceans. He saw himself as a thinker with a deep sense of history (the trait he most admired in others such as General de Gaulle). As a consequence, he often spoke in emphatically civilisational terms, and he was one of the first American authors to write widely on 'the West' and 'Western civilization', long before the famous 'Western Civ' curricula in American elite universities made discussion of such notions widespread.[40] Lippmann was assessing the possibility and desirability of 'a unification of western civilisation' into a 'Great State' as early as 1915, and of a 'western alliance' during the Great War well before the United States joined it as a belligerent. His preoccupation with the meaning, membership and prospects of 'the West' and 'Western civilization' was to remain constant throughout the following six decades.

Besides his many contributions to the *New Republic* and other magazines, in 1915 Lippmann published a bold book on international politics, *The Stakes of Diplomacy*. There he argued that a noticeable enlargement of the circle of people's fellow-feeling—or patriotic allegiances—was taking place at the time: 'loyalty overflows the national state because in the world to-day the national state is no longer a sufficient protection'. People wanted 'to be members of a stronger group'. This proved, according to Lippmann, 'that patriotism is not a fixed quantity, that it is not attached to the map as it was drawn when we were at school, and that it is not only capable of expansion, but is crying for it'. That was hardly surprising. It had almost always been fear that played 'a large part in welding states together'. Thus, in the same way that the existence of 'an enemy' tended 'to blot out political differences within a nation', the appearance of such a potential enemy would 'often unite a number of nations'. And that had recently happened in a concrete case. 'The rise of Germany had that effect on the Great Powers of Europe; the fear of her created a league almost coextensive with western civilization.'[41]

Lippmann also discussed 'a new issue' that had arisen on the rim of the Pacific, and which opened up 'difficulties far greater than those which have hitherto troubled diplomacy'. For the imperial clashes of the time, 'the intrigues and competitions and wars that harass our world', revolved around 'the spread of western commerce among backward peoples'. But 'a new problem' had arisen 'in California, Canada, Australia, infinitely more painful than the struggle of empires': that was, 'a real friction of peoples who do not know how to live together and are forced therefore to compete for territory'. He described the 'Hindus who cannot settle in Canada, the Japanese and Chinese excluded from the United States' as 'the first symptoms of a world problem to which no man has proposed a satisfactory answer'. And to his mind, it was an East–West problem:

> As the pressure of the East upon the West becomes more intense, as the East becomes stronger, prouder, and better organized, men may wonder how they could ever have fought suicidal wars over the present stakes of diplomacy. Differences which once seemed 'vital' may appear in a new perspective, *and those who plead for a unification of western civilization be listened to with a more urgent interest*. Out of the desire to preserve western power in Asia, and

out of the fear of Asiatic aggression, may come some of the strongest *incentives to the creation of a super-national state.*

Lippmann elaborated upon 'the kind of Great State which is at present humanly possible'. It would not include the whole world, governed by 'a world government, elected by the equal suffrage of the inhabitants of the globe'. Instead, it would be 'some kind of federation of existing Powers, and probably not an equal federation at that'. Its core force might be 'some coalition of western states, acting towards the world a little, it may be, as Prussia has acted towards the other German states, or England towards the Empire'. There would 'unquestionably be an effort to keep the power in the hands of western peoples, but among those western peoples there is every reason to expect jealousy and what is called "politics".' They would 'hold together as best they can to preserve their dominion and prevent aggression'. Thus, the realistically feasible 'greater state' would 'at the utmost probably not be more extensive than western commercial civilization'. In other words, 'the larger state' likely to emerge in the real world would 'for a long time bear slight resemblance to the Federation of Mankind'.[42]

But Lippmann had become much more concrete and less speculative by the next year. In an important article published in the summer of 1916, with America still neutral, he asked, 'What program shall the United States stand for in international relations?' He described as follows the membership of the alliance that he envisaged, which he referred to as 'the west': 'The kind of world we desire, a world of stable, autonomous, interdependent democracies acting as the guardians of less developed peoples—that vision depends upon the coöperation of the United States and Great Britain.' But then, 'France and Latin America, perhaps Italy, too, would be magnetized to it, and we should have established a mighty area of security'. Again, he tried to be realistic: 'No one need pretend that within it complete justice would prevail. The American negro, the Hindu, the Irish, the Egyptian would still suffer oppression. But if there were enough freedom from external danger, the mind of the west would be freed for the solution of those questions.' Lippmann had another important recommendation (reminiscent of Reinsch's plea in 1900): 'If internationalism means anything real, it means above all that China must not be disintegrated and destroyed.' What China needed was 'time to develop, time to modernize herself, time to find her own strength'. But America could not help in that direction if she remained alone: 'We cannot from our isolation challenge the ambitions of Japan. That must be done if at all by the united western nations, and the core of that unity is Anglo-American coöperation.'[43]

Lippmann was meanwhile recommending a generous policy towards (a putatively defeated) Germany: 'After the war, the best allies the German oligarchy will have are the bogeys of England and Russia.' The plausibility of any such appeals to hatred for Britain and Russia by 'the German oligarchy' should be eroded: 'Dispel those bogeys by a generous policy [: . . .] give the German democracy air, and instead of a Germany frightened into aggression, there may arise a new Germany with which the western world can live at peace.' The alliance he had in mind would inevitably be messy, but it could work, as its very heterogeneity would prevent it from becoming despotic.[44]

The most crucial part of the vision Lippmann was proposing involved his emphasis upon sea power. He had accepted Admiral Alfred Thayer Mahan's theories on the importance of the latter,[45] and he was adapting the idea to his aspirations for the future of 'the liberal powers of the west': 'All larger schemes, such as those for a League of Peace with Permanent Courts of Arbitration and Conciliation must rest it seems to me on the unity and supremacy of sea power concentrated in the hands of the liberal powers of the west.' The schemes would be 'workable only if the British Empire, the United States, France, Pan-America, and ultimately Germany are knit together, their economic conflicts compromised, their military resources pooled, their diplomacy in a league of the west'. What the world needed was not so much international machinery, as 'a cohesion of power'. No 'machinery' one could suggest, nor rule of international law one could propose had a chance of survival 'unless the liberal world represents a sufficient union of power to make it a shield for men's protection, and a standard to which the people can rally'.[46] Lippmann was envisaging a close Anglo–American alliance, which he meanwhile saw as the core of a wider 'western' alliance.

More was to come a year later, with America still (just about) neutral. In what his biographer calls 'one of the most important editorials he ever wrote, one that governed his approach to foreign policy for the rest of his life', Lippmann '[coined] a phrase that was to stick—the "Atlantic community".'[47] He did indeed use the phrase 'the Atlantic community', once, and 'the Atlantic world' another couple of times. What his biographer fails to report, however, is that Lippmann also used 'the West', or a variation thereon ('western world', 'western nations'), around a dozen times. He unequivocally recommended that America should join the war on the side of the 'Western' allies. And he went to great lengths to justify the proposal in civilisational as well as security terms. He argued that America was right to be accepting the British blockade of Germany while defying the German submarines' attempts to stop traffic in the Atlantic, *'because the war against Britain, France, and Belgium is a war against the civilization of which we are a part. To* be *'fair' in such a war would be a betrayal.'* America needed 'to keep open the seas that lead to the western Allies'. Only by clearly grasping the 'gigantic consequences' of the situation could Americans steer their course in the future. 'The world's highway shall not be closed to the western Allies if America has power to prevent it.' As he emphatically declared, 'The safety of the Atlantic highway is something for which America should fight.' His rationale was that 'on the two shores of the Atlantic Ocean there has grown up a profound web of interest which joins together the western world.' He enumerated the members of that 'web': 'Britain, France, Italy, even Spain, Belgium, Holland, the Scandinavian nations, and Pan-America are in the main one community in their deepest needs and their deepest purposes.' For this reason, he thought, '[w]e cannot betray the Atlantic community by submitting. *If not civilization, at least our civilization is at stake.'*[48]

On the other side were what might be classed as 'the wrong kind of Germans': 'A victory on the high seas would be a triumph *of that class which aims to make Germany the leader of the East against the West*, the leader ultimately of a German-Russian-Japanese coalition against the Atlantic world.' It would be, therefore, 'utter folly not to fight now to make its hopes a failure by showing that in the face of such a threat the western community is a unit.' Meanwhile, magnanimity towards 'the right kind' of Germany was also urgently recommended:

> It would be a great mistake to suppose, however, that we are dealing with a single-minded Germany. We wage war on Germany as long as she commits her destiny to those who would separate her from the western world. By rights Germany should be a powerful and loyal member of the Atlantic world, and she will be if this war is effectively fought and wisely ended. Our aim must not be to conquer Germany as Rome conquered Carthage, but to win Germany as Lincoln strove to win the South, to win her for union with our civilization by the discrediting of those classes who alone are our enemies. It is no paradox and no sentimentality to say that we must fight Germany not to destroy her but to force her and lure her back to the civilization to which she belongs. She is a rebel nation as long as she wages offensive war against the western world.

If America were to add her strength on the side of the Allies, as Lippmann urged, that would represent 'a German failure indeed because it would be clear then that the assault on the West had merely doubled the power of the West'. When all was said and done, Lippmann's rationale for America to join the war was, 'What we must fight for is the common interest of the western world, for the integrity of the Atlantic Powers. *We must recognize that we are in fact one great community and act as a member of it.'* America's entrance into it 'would weight it immeasurably in favor of liberalism, and make the organization of a league for peace an immediately practical object of statesmanship. By showing that we are ready now, as well as in the theoretical future, to defend the western world, the cornerstone of federation would be laid.'[49]

Now, the issue of blame for the Great War was, among other things, dividing American intellectuals along generational lines, as Henry May has shown. The older 'custodians of culture' preferred to blame the war on Germany, because otherwise they would have had to accept that the whole European civilisation that they admired was at fault.[50] But there were many others who were prepared to say exactly that. Something was wrong with European or Western civilisation as a whole, they thought, and the industrial-scale massacre that started in August 1914 was the most striking proof of that. Many of these critics came from colonised peoples, or from groups that felt marginalised in their own countries, not least in the United States.[51] All were attentive to the utterances of Rabindranath Tagore.

IV. Rabindranath Tagore on East and West

Rabindranath Tagore (1861–1941) was a man of many parts and talents. He published some two hundred books, including poetry, songs, plays, short stories, novels and essays. He became, more literally than most people, a global figure for some time, and his pronouncements were widely read and commented on in different countries and continents. He was the first 'non-white' man to receive a Nobel Prize, and he had many staunch admirers in the West and in the rest of the world. Tagore was critical of the British administration of India. But he was nevertheless at pains 'to dissociate his criticism of the Raj from any denigration of British—or Western—people or culture'. According to Amartya Sen, 'unlike Gandhi, Tagore could not, even in jest, be dismissive of Western civilization.'[52] Tagore believed that there were some extremely valuable things about Western culture and influences. At the same time he was vehemently against mere aping of the West and the rejection out of hand of India's own heritage. He thought that Indian culture could be enriched by contact with the West, and the West by contact with India.

In his lectures on 'Nationalism', delivered in Japan and in the United Sates in late 1916 and early 1917, and the book *Nationalism* that resulted from them, composed of a selection of three lectures, Tagore spoke of 'the Nation' in terms that sound similar to how other people might describe the State. And some of his references to nationalism resemble definitions of what historians came to call 'High Imperialism'. That is hardly surprising, if we bear in mind that he was giving those lectures in the midst of the Great War, a war that he saw as being the result of the imperial competition of major European 'Nations' or States. Much of his criticism of 'the Nation' juxtaposed its mechanical, artificial character against what was 'natural' in his eyes: 'society' or *samaj*. Tagore's lectures caused quite a sensation in the countries where they were delivered, and generated much coverage in the press.[53] His reputation at the time was such that comments on his pronouncements were legion, both during the Great War and for years afterwards. From Du Bois reporting on Tagore's wartime lectures and interviews in *The Crisis*, to René Maran's quoting him on 'Civilization' in his incendiary introduction to his novel *Batouala* (1921), to Tagore's lionisation for a week in the Baltic Count Keyserling's 'Schule der Weisheit' (School of wisdom) in Darmstadt, to innumerable other invitations and citations, Tagore's statements were seen as oracular. A few years later Henri Massis even added an Appendix to his *Défense de l'Occident* to attack what he saw as Tagore's dangerous undermining of Western civilisation. (And yet, arguably, if Tagore was its greatest enemy, Western civilisation would have been perfectly safe.)

In a lecture that he delivered in Japan, Tagore tried to cajole and persuade his hosts to avoid becoming nationalist imperialists themselves and instead adopt a different way of being a powerful modern country. (He was, meanwhile, well aware that they had gone a long way down the former path, and disappointed by what he saw as their intense nationalism).[54] Referring obviously to Japan's spectacularly rapid modernisation after the so-called Meiji restoration of 1868, Tagore commented that Japan 'in giant strides left centuries of inaction behind' and joined the modern world very fast. That had 'broken the spell under which we lay in torpor for ages, taking it to be the normal condition of certain races living in certain geographical limits'. He distinguished what we might call 'modernisation' from Westernisation. The whole world was waiting to see 'what this great eastern nation is going to do with the opportunities and responsibilities she has accepted from the hands of the modern time'. If it were to be 'a mere reproduction of the West, then the great expectation she has raised will remain unfulfilled'. For there were 'grave questions that western civilization has presented before the world but not completely answered'.[55]

Tagore remarked that the 'political civilization' which had emerged from Europe was 'based upon exclusiveness'. That political civilisation was 'scientific, not human'; and in a statement reminiscent of similar comments by Russian Slavophiles in the nineteenth century, Tagore added that it was powerful because

FIGURE 5.2. Rabindranath Tagore. Photographer and date unknown (pre-August 1941). *Source:* https://commons.wikimedia.org/wiki/File:Rabindranath_Tagore.jpg

it concentrated 'all its forces upon one purpose, like a millionaire acquiring money at the cost of his soul'. Meanwhile, he did not wish to be one-sided: 'I must not hesitate to acknowledge where Europe is great, for great she is without doubt.' Indeed,

> [w]e cannot help loving her with all our heart and paying her the best homage of our admiration—the Europe who, in her literature and art, pours out

an inexhaustible cascade of beauty and truth fertilizing all countries and all time; the Europe who, with a mind which is titanic in its untiring power, is sweeping the height and the depth of the universe, winning her homage of knowledge from the infinitely great and the infinitely small, applying all the resources of her great intellect and heart in healing the sick and alleviating those miseries of man which up till now we were contented to accept in a spirit of hopeless resignation.[56]

This latter statement was in direct opposition to the attitude towards medicine proposed by Gandhi a few years earlier in *Hind Swaraj* (and later to be practised by the Mahatma when his wife was about to die).[57] Tagore's differences from Gandhi are also evident in his statement regarding 'the Europe who is making the earth yield more fruit than seemed possible, coaxing and compelling the great forces of nature into man's service'. Tagore's judgement was that '[s]uch true greatness must have its motive power in spiritual strength'. And he offered what looked like an explanation: 'In the heart of Europe runs the purest stream of human love, of love of justice, of spirit of self-sacrifice for higher ideals. The Christian culture of centuries has sunk deep in her life's core.' In Europe there were 'noble minds who have stood up for the rights of man irrespective of colour and creed'. There were 'these knight-errants [*sic*] of modern Europe who have not lost their faith in the disinterested love of freedom, in the ideals which own no geographical boundaries or national self-seeking'. Such people existed and proved that 'the fountainhead of the water of everlasting life has not run dry in Europe, and from thence she will have her rebirth time after time'. Tagore's verdict was that Europe was 'supremely good in her beneficence where her face is turned to all humanity; and Europe is supremely evil in her maleficent aspect where her face is turned only upon her own interest, using all her power of greatness for ends which are against the infinite and eternal in Man'.[58]

He returned to cautioning that his Japanese audience should form a balanced judgement on 'the West' later on: 'But while trying to free our minds from the arrogant claims of Europe and to help ourselves out of the quickness of our infatuation, we may go to the other extreme and bind ourselves with a wholesale suspicion of the West.' There was the understandable 'temptation of wishing to pay back Europe in her own coin, and return contempt for contempt and evil for evil'. But that attitude would amount to imitating Europe 'in one of her worst features'. Instead of making one-sided judgements, he advised, '[w]hen we really know that Europe which is great and good, we can effectively save ourselves from the Europe which is mean and grasping'. There was 'a living soul in the West which is struggling unobserved against the hugeness of the organizations' that he had been castigating. For it was obvious to him that '[t]he West could never have risen to the eminence she has reached if her strength were merely the strength of the brute and the machine'. In fact, he added, 'The divine in her heart is suffering from the injuries inflicted by her hands upon the world—and from this pain of her higher nature flows the secret balm which brings healing to these injuries.' That was why '[t]ime after time she has fought against herself and has undone the chains which with her own hands she fastened round helpless limbs'. Therefore, he urged, 'It would be altogether unjust both to us and to Europe, to say that she has fascinated the modern eastern mind by the mere exhibition of her power.' Because, besides cannons and machines, Europe had 'brought to us the ideal of ethical freedom, whose foundation lies deeper than social conventions and whose province of activity is worldwide'. In addition, 'Europe has been teaching us the higher obligations of public good above those of the family and the clan, and the sacredness of law, which makes society independent of individual caprice, secures for it continuity of progress, and guarantees justice to all men of all positions in life'. And, above all, 'Europe has held high before our minds the banner of liberty, through centuries of martyrdom and achievement—liberty of conscience, liberty of thought and action, liberty in the ideals of art and literature.'[59] Finally, there was

> one safety for us upon which we hope we may count, and that is that we can claim Europe herself as our ally in our resistance to her temptations and to her violent encroachments; for she has ever carried her own standard of perfection, by which we can call her before her own tribunal and put her to shame—the shame which is the sign of the true pride of nobleness.[60]

In one of the lectures Tagore gave in America, published as 'Nationalism in the West', he emphasised that the West was 'necessary to the East'. Thus, 'We are complementary to each other because of our different outlooks upon life which have given us different aspects of truth'. And when Indians were to become 'able to assimilate in our life what is permanent in western civilization we shall be in a position to bring about a reconciliation of these two great worlds. Then will come to an end the one-sided dominance which is galling'. Indians were suffering from the conflict between 'the spirit of the West' and 'the Nation of the West'. The 'benefit of western civilization' was 'doled out to us in a miserly measure by the Nation, which tries to regulate the degree of nutrition as near the zero-point of vitality as possible'. The portion of education allotted to Indians was 'so raggedly insufficient that it ought to outrage the sense of decency of western

FIGURE 5.3. Rabindranath Tagore with Mohandas and Kasturba Gandhi at Shantiniketan, Bengal, in 1940. Photographer unknown. *Source:* https://en.wikipedia.org/wiki/Rabindranath_Tagore#/media/File:Gandhi-Tagore-cropped.jpg

humanity'. And the 'Nation of the West' was adding insult to injury: 'While depriving us of our opportunities and reducing our education to the minimum required for conducting a foreign government, this Nation pacifies its conscience by calling us names, by sedulously giving currency to the arrogant cynicism that the East is east and the West is west and never the twain shall meet.' One had to acknowledge a paradox: 'that while the spirit of the West marches under its banner of freedom, the Nation of the West forges its iron chains of organization which are the most relentless and unbreakable that have ever been manufactured in the whole history of man'. The lesson of the war then raging among European powers ought to be clear, though: 'Has not this truth already come home to you now, when this cruel war has driven its claws into the vitals of Europe?' To those who asked what she had done to deserve this, Tagore's answer was that 'the West has been systematically petrifying her moral nature in order to lay a solid foundation for her gigantic abstractions of efficiency. She has all along been starving the life of the personal man into that of the professional.'[61]

In another lecture delivered in the United States, published as 'Nationalism in India', Tagore opined, 'If it is given at all to the West to struggle out of these tangles of the lower slopes to the spiritual summit of humanity then I cannot but think that it is the special mission of America to fulfil this hope of God and man.'

This was because America was 'the country of expectation, desiring something else than what is'. That is why Tagore told his American audience that 'America is destined to justify western civilization to the East'. Europe had 'lost faith in humanity', and had become 'distrustful and sickly'. America, on the other hand, was 'not pessimistic or blasé.'[62]

V. Black America as the 'acid test for occidental civilization'

Though most of them admired Tagore, Afro-American thinkers were much less sure about his prediction that America was 'destined to justify western civilization to the East'. For them, it was America that was the most tainted of the countries of 'the West'. Despite their important differences, and despite their deep links to Europe, people such as W.E.B. Du Bois, Jessie Fauset, Alain Locke and many others would see a potential opportunity in the shock caused by the war.

Alain Locke had been the first Black Rhodes scholar at Oxford. He also travelled extensively to continental Europe every year. Locke was one of the many American writers caught in Europe during the summer when the war broke out. Almost as soon as he returned to the USA he gave a lecture to the 'Negro Society for Historical Research' in Yonkers, New York, on 23 September 1914.[63] Locke argued that 'the real cause, and the real issue is a war to the death rivalry between two arms of the same civilization[,] the same race'. Defining his terms, he continued, 'With Gallic civilization as a dueling ground, Anglo-Saxon civilization is engaged in a duel to the death.' One cannot help noticing the equation of 'civilization' and 'race' in the above statement. But which 'race' and/or which 'civilization' was it that Locke was referring to? In the very next sentence one might think we have a gesture towards an answer:

> My friends, I am too sensible of our personal and racial debt to European civilization and culture to use this inopportune moment to put it to disadvantage, but for years [...] I distinctly claimed that we should be prouder as a people of having acquired this civilization and culture than of having it as an inheritance. I said this first in the interests of sincerity[.] I thought our culture would be sounder if we made no false claims to it, and had a sense of our own racial and ethnic past as a foundation upon which to rear it[.] But now not merely for our own pride's sake[,] but to avoid their shame, let us realize and confess that the civilization which is at war with itself is not ours in the intimate sense that we owe it a blood debt or even an irrevocable allegiance.

Two things stand out so far. First, Locke talks about the war being a war of a 'civilization' (or was it a 'race'?) with itself, and refers to that 'civilization' initially as 'Anglo-Saxon' and then as 'European'. Second, he is telling Black Americans that they have no concern in that war. He goes on to highlight the imperialist character of the conflict and the lessons to be drawn from it. For one of 'the predictable results of the war' would be 'its inevitable lesson to other races and alien civilizations that I trust will forever make impossible the Frankenstein of the nineteenth century—the pretensions of European civilization to world-dominance and eternal superiority'. Meanwhile, the 'civilization' that was at war with itself suddenly ceased to be 'European' and became 'Anglo-Saxon' again: 'Up to a few days ago England[,] America[,] and Germany were custodians of Anglo-Saxon civilization'; but now, 'before the youngest [the USA] as a neutral spectator, the elder partners [Britain and Germany] struggle in [a] death-grip', and one of them moreover was 'treacherously inviting the assistance of the civilization that has threatened us a thousand years—*the byzantine, Slavic oriental culture*—[and thus was] willing to pull the house over its head if it cannot win its feud by any other means'.⁶⁴

That Alain Locke was echoing here almost verbatim what German war propaganda repeatedly claimed about the treachery of the British in allying themselves with 'the byzantine, Slavic oriental culture' (many Germans' favourite ways of referring to Russia) is not surprising.⁶⁵ Not only was Locke pro-German and keenly wished for (as well as expected) a German victory at this stage. He (and his mother) had also spent the first four weeks of the war trapped in Berlin, where he had gone that summer with the intention of acquiring a Ph.D.⁶⁶ He no doubt heard these arguments made repeatedly whilst in Berlin—which he was only able to leave on 25 August 1914, less than a month before he delivered the 'Great Disillusionment' lecture.

Locke was pleased to report to his mother that his 23 September Yonkers lecture had received enthusiastic approval and cries of 'Better than Du Bois'. That was praise indeed. For Dr. Du Bois was indisputably the intellectual leader of African Americans at the time, compared to whom Locke was painfully aware of his 'invisibility'.⁶⁷

But what was the older man saying? As editor of *The Crisis*, Du Bois started writing about the war in civilisational terms from very early on (and long before American participation was an issue). He also soon took a side; and it was not with the same side as Alain Locke's that Du Bois's sympathies lay. Although he had been educated in Berlin in the 1890s and had loved the experience, Du Bois preferred the Entente powers to Germany. One reads as follows in his editorial

FIGURE 5.4. Jessie Redmond Fauset. Photograph from Robert T. Kerlin, *Negro Poets and Their Poems* (1923), p. 160. Courtesy of Library of Congress. Source: https://en.wikipedia.org/wiki/Jessie_R._Fauset#/media/File:Negro_Poets_and _Their_Poems-0182.jpg

'World War and the Color Line', of November 1914: '[W]here should our sympathies lie? Undoubtedly, with the Allies—with England and France in particular.' Not that these nations were 'innocent'. He was clear about their imperialist sins. 'But the salvation of England is that she has the ability to learn from her mistakes. To-day no white nation is fairer in its treatment of darker peoples than England.' Thus, 'as compared with Germany England is an angel of light'.[68] As for France, she 'is less efficient than England as an administrator of colonies and has consequently been guilty of much neglect and injustice; but she is nevertheless the most kindly of all European nations in her personal relations with colored folk. She draws no dead line of color and colored Frenchmen always love France.'[69]

In 'The African Roots of War' published in *The Atlantic* in May 1915, Du Bois wrote in a register addressing not so much his fellow Afro-Americans, as he did in *The Crisis*, but more broadly his fellow Americans:

> We, then, who want peace, must remove the real causes of war. We have extended gradually our conception of democracy beyond our social class to all social classes in our nation; we have gone further and extended our democratic ideals not simply to all classes of our nation, but to those of other nations of our blood and lineage—to what we call 'European' civilization. If we want real peace and lasting culture, however, we must go further. We must extend the democratic ideal to the yellow, brown, and black peoples.[70]

Even more explicitly civilisational is Du Bois's analysis in 'The Battle of Europe', written in September 1916. There the addressees were fellow Afro-Americans:

> The civilization by which America insists on measuring us and to which we must conform our natural tastes and inclinations is the daughter of that European civilization which is now rushing furiously to its doom. This civilization with its aeroplanes and submarines, its wireless and its 'big business' [...]. Behind all this gloss of culture and wealth and religion has been lurking the world-old lust for bloodshed and power gained at the cost of honor. The realization of all this means for us the reassembling of old ideals. [...] Brothers, the war has shown us the cruelty of the civilization of the West. History has taught us the futility of the civilization of the East. Let ours be the civilization of no *man*, but of *all men*. This is the truth that sets us free.[71]

As mentioned in the previous section, Du Bois also wrote reports on Rabindranath Tagore's wartime lecture tour and interviews, and among other things, he noted in December 1916 Tagore's answer when asked what was needed for the healing of the nations: 'The great problem of man's history has been the race problem. Western civilization, particularly as exemplified in Germany, has been based upon exclusiveness. [...] This attitude must change, if peace is to come and endure upon the earth.'[72]

Despite all the grievances of Afro-Americans as a result of their treatment in the United States, when America itself joined the war, Du Bois (at the cost of much criticism from some quarters) asked his brethren to 'close ranks' and fight for the right side in that war.[73] His hope was that by displaying their patriotism during the war and contributing to the common struggle, Afro-Americans would be appreciated and rewarded after it. He also undertook extensive research in order to write a book on the contribution of Black soldiers to the Great War, a book he never managed to finish.[74] Sadly the opposite of what he had hoped happened, partly by reaction on the part of many white Americans against the increased assertiveness of Afro-Americans on the basis of their war efforts (and because of how differently from back home Black soldiers serving in France found they were treated, as we will see shortly).[75]

Even before the end of the war, however, signs of what was to come were becoming obvious. It was during the Great War that an argument that was to be used even more extensively later, during the Cold War, was first deployed in no uncertain terms. I refer to the warning about what its treatment of its Black population was doing to America's international reputation, as well as to its internal health as a society. The Afro-American activist Jessie Fauset, an intimate of Du Bois, novelist and literary editor of *The Crisis*, concluded as follows her letter to the editor of *The Survey*, in protest against the East St. Louis pogroms of African Americans:

> [I]it is senseless to suppose that anarchy and autocracy can be confined to only one quarter of a nation. [...] Turkey has slaughtered its Armenians, Russia has held its pogroms, Belgium has tortured and maimed in the Congo, and today Turkey, Russia, Belgium are synonyms for anathema, demoralization and pauperdom. *We, the American Negroes, are the acid test for occidental civilization.* If we perish, we perish. But when we fall, we shall fall like Samson, dragging inevitably with us the pillars of a nation's democracy.[76]

The same effort of persuasion included another line of argument. One way, already alluded to above, whereby African Americans complained against their lot in the United States was by highlighting the (incomparably better) way Black American soldiers had been treated in France during and immediately after the Great War. The argument went in parallel with a more general comparison between the respective attitudes towards race and racial mixing between the 'Anglo-Saxons' on the one hand, and the 'Latin' peoples and empires on the other. The number of references to France in the aftermath of the war, from the enthusiastic to the ecstatic, in Du Bois's editorials and notices in *The Crisis* is striking. 'It was France—almighty and never-dying France leading the world again. The day was given to honor the black men and yellow men who gave their lives for a country they are proud to call theirs and which is equally proud to claim them.'[77] In 1919, after he came back from the First Pan-African Congress that he had co-organized in Paris the previous February, Du Bois was to write, 'We are returning from war! *The Crisis* and tens of thousands of black men were drafted into a great struggle. For bleeding France and what she means and has meant and will mean to us and humanity.'[78]

Such attitudes towards France and francophone Black brethren also led Du Bois to write, in a piece in *The Crisis* entitled 'French and Spanish', in April 1919,

> ONE result of seemingly secondary, but really of prime, importance should come out of this war: the American Negro should speak French. It is idiotic for any modern man to be unilingual. [...] But more important than this is the fact that the only white civilization in the world to which color-hatred is not only unknown, but absolutely unintelligible is the so-called Latin, of which France and Spain are leading nations. [...] *Today the greatest threat on the earth's horizon is the possible world domination of the 'nigger'-hating Anglo-Saxon idea.* Only the world union of African, Latin, Asiatic, and possibly Slav and Celt can stop this arrogant tyranny—this death to human aspiration. [...] It is high time that, armed with modern tongues, we tried a counter-propaganda and a positive spiritual alliance with the best culture of the modern world.[79]

Such efforts and proposed alliances on the part of Du Bois would continue and intensify in the 1920s, as the onslaught of the 'Nordics' was becoming, if anything, more aggressive, as we will see in the next chapter.

When all is said and done, the most important outcome of the Great War for Afro-American thinkers was what Wilson Jeremiah Moses calls 'the decline of the civilizationistic pattern' in their thinking. Moses concedes that it would be 'too much of an exaggeration to say that they emerged as cultural relativists'. And yet, 'surely the tendency of the Jazz Age to glorify the primitive, the emotionally exuberant stereotypical Harlem Renaissance Negro, must be attributed at least in part to a disillusionment with the standards of industrial civilization and the idea that black people should slavishly conform to them'.[80]

VI. Thomas Mann's 'monstrous article'; and His *Reflections*

But 'the West' was challenged also from another quarter, during the Great War. Even Romain Rolland, famously trying to stay 'above the fray', was shocked: 'When I wrote this I had not yet seen the monstrous article by Thomas Mann (in the *Neue Rundschau* of November 1914), where, in a fit of fury and injured pride, he savagely claimed for Germany, as a title to glory, all the crimes of which her adversaries accuse her.' Rolland was disturbed to observe that Mann 'dared to write that the present war was a war of German Kultur "against Civilization," proclaiming that German thought had no other ideal than militarism'.[81]

FIGURE 5.5. W.E.B. Du Bois. Photograph by Cornelius Marion Battey (1919). Library of Congress. *Source:* https://en.wikipedia.org/wiki/W._E._B._Du_Bois#/media/File:W.E.B._(William_Edward_Burghardt)_Du_Bois,_1868-1963_LCCN2003681451.jpg

In the 'monstrous article' Rolland complained of, Mann declared that '[c]ivilization and culture are not only not the same, they are opposites.' An example he used to explain his distinction was, 'No one would deny that Mexico had a culture when it was discovered by Europeans. But who would argue that it was civilized?' For in fact 'culture' was often 'just stylish savagery, not the contrary of barbarism'. Culture represented 'a particular intellectual-spiritual organization of the world, no matter how adventurous, bizarre, wild, bloody, and terrible'. On the other hand, civilisation involved 'reason, enlightenment, moderation, moral education, skepticism—in a word, spirit'. And spirit was 'civil and burgherly—and the sworn enemy of the drives and the passions'. It was thus 'hostile to genius.' On the other hand, '[a]rt, like all culture, is the sublimation of the daemonic'. And art was, to Mann's mind, a matter of culture, rather than of civilisation. Art was certainly 'more accustomed to the passions and nature than to reason and the spirit'. Moreover, art was closely related to war. 'How the poets' hearts caught fire when the war broke out!'[82]

Another way of illustrating his contrast was to compare Frederick of Prussia with his friend 'whom he both admired and scorned, and who in turn both admired and scorned the king'. The friend in question was Voltaire, 'writer, *haut bourgeois*, son of the spirit, father of the enlightenment and all antiheroic civilization'. Voltaire and Frederick represented, respectively, 'reason and the daemonic, spirit and genius, dry light and beclouded fate, bourgeois morality and heroic duty'. (Mann referred to France in extremely scornful terms, including as 'the filthy plutocratic bourgeois republic whose capital is still venerated as the "Mecca of civilization".')[83]. Another formulation of the difference was,

> One thing is certainly true: Germans are not nearly as enamored of the word 'civilization' as [their] Western neighbors are. They do not toss it around as the French do for prestige, nor in the bigoted English way. Germans have always preferred 'culture' as a term and concept. Why? Because it has purely human content. 'Civilization' has a more sober, political feel that makes it seem important and honorable to us but not the highest thing. That is because this inward-looking people, a nation of metaphysics, pedagogy, and music, is a people morally rather than politically oriented.

And 'German militarism' was 'really the form and expression of German morality'. The crux of the matter was one of depth versus superficiality: 'The German soul is too deep for civilization to be its highest value.' The German soul 'finds the corruption and disorder of embourgeoisement dreadful and laughable'. Moreover, 'the same kind of deep, instinctive aversion rises up against civilization's pacifist ideal'. The German soul was 'warlike out of morality, not vanity or a yearning for glory or imperialism'. There was nothing surprising about what the Western allies were pursuing: 'For our Western enemies, this war is really about forcing Germany to become "civilized".'[84]

Most revealingly, perhaps, Mann concluded, 'Who would deny that the German condition is problematic! It is not easy being German.' In fact, the German people 'have a hard time with themselves and feel a bit dubious, almost to the point of disgust.' Yet, both in the case of individuals and in the case of peoples 'the most valuable ones are those who have the roughest time of it. Whoever would wish that Germanness would simply vanish from Earth in favor of *l'humanité, la raison*, or plain cant *committeth an iniquity*.' It was true that 'depth and irrationality suit the German soul, which shallower peoples find disturbing, strange, disgusting, even savage'. It was the Germans' '"militarism," their ethical conservatism, their soldierly morality, that daemonic and heroic something[,] that resists accepting the civilian spirit as the highest human ideal.' It was, as he had stated from the beginning, a matter of the antithesis between 'culture' and 'civilization': 'Only the completely ignorant deny that the Germans are highly cultivated. However, the Germans do not want to succumb to the civilizing process and have no taste for making a hypocritical or vain fuss about it.'[85]

Thomas Mann had no interest in politics before the Great War. It was the war that made him begin to write essays and books and give lectures on political matters. His battle lines were clearly drawn in October 1916, when he playfully boasted in a letter,

> 'Car il est plus Allemand et moins Latin que vous ne pourriez le croire de premier abord. C'est là son originalité.' [For he is more German and less Latin than you could believe him to be at first. In that lies his originality.] That was once written about me in a French periodical before the war, and it has been demonstrated and confirmed in the course of the war—to the embitterment of our radical literati, who naturally are doing everything in their power to contribute to Germanophobia and arouse *sympathy for the Roman West*, and with whom I have extremely tense relations.[86]

He was soon to coin a term for 'our radical literati'. That was to appear in the most notorious of his wartime productions, the (characteristically entitled) *Betrachtungen eines Unpolitischen* (*Reflections of a Nonpolitical Man*), written between 1915 and early 1918 and published in October 1918 (very shortly before the end of the war).[87] It has correctly been called 'a work of great weight and substance' which 'presents the most brilliant and penetrating summation of antiwestern and antiliberal German nationalist sentiment written in the twentieth century'. As its title suggests, it was not intended to be a political work, but was rather 'a metapolitical philosophy of history, civilization, and the German mind'.[88] What in other hands might have been simply platitudes, Mann's pen (and authority) turned into a powerful articulation of a vision of Germanness. There was no mistaking its passionate tone; for the matter was, literally, personal. The main target of Mann's *Betrachtungen* was the German intellectual admirer of France and 'the West', who wished Germany to be defeated and to become a 'Western democracy' ('our radical literati' of the 1916 letter). Mann's new term coined in order to ridicule the pro-Western German intellectual was *Zivilisationsliterat* (literary prophet of civilisation/civilization's literary man).[89] And it was no secret that the picture of the *Zivilisationsliterat* Mann drew was a portrait description of his elder brother, Heinrich.[90]

The first chapter was entitled 'The Protest'.[91] Here, Mann extensively and approvingly quoted Fyodor Dostoyevsky's 1877 ruminations on Germany.[92] The Russian thinker had reflected on Germany's '*eternal* protestantism, her *eternal* protest as it began with Arminius against the Roman world, against everything that was Rome and Rome's mission, and later against [...] all nations that received the Roman idea, formula, and element, *protest* against the heirs of Rome and against everything that constitutes this heritage'.[93] Mann applauded Dostoyevsky's remark. In his opinion there had been

> the most complete unanimity from the first moment that the intellectual roots of this war [...] lie in Germany's inborn and historical 'protestantism', that this war is essentially a new outbreak, perhaps the grandest, the final one, as some believe, *of Germany's ancient struggle against the spirit of the West*, as well as the struggle of the Roman world against stubborn Germany. ['des uralten deutschen Kampfes gegen den Geist des Westens, sowie des Kampfes der römischen Welt gegen das eigensinnige Deutschland bedeutet'].[94]

Mann argued that the Entente, 'America included, is the unification of the Western world, of the heirs of Rome, of "civilization" against Germany, against the Germany that is now protesting with more primeval power than ever before'. Returning to the distinction he had drawn in his 1914 article, he wrote, 'What we call "civilization," and what calls itself civilization, is nothing more than precisely this victorious advance, this propagation of the [...] middle-class spirit, its colonization of the inherited areas of the globe.' Moreover, he argued, '[t]he *imperialism of civilization* is the last form of the Roman idea of unification against which Germany is "protesting."' That was Germany's 'mission, her eternal and innate mission'.[95]

A year later, with Germany having lost the war, Mann was commenting, with a certain degree of resignation, in a letter beginning with this retrospective assessment of what he had tried to do in writing the *Reflections*,

> Our entire national existence [...] condemned as guilty and erroneous—that is what my *Betrachtungen* would not concede, long before people imagined that we might ever come to such a pass. That the great tradition of Germanism

from Luther to Bismarck and Nietzsche should be refuted and discredited—this is the fact which is *hailed* by many among us, the fact which is laid down in many a carefully considered paragraph of the peace conditions, and the fact which I was opposing in my fight against the 'civilization literatus' [*Zivilisationsliterat*]. It lay in the nature of things that my opponents would triumph; I recognized that early and said as much.

As for the future,

> One must take a contemplative, even a resignedly cheerful view, read Spengler and understand that the victory of England and America seals and completes the civilizing, rationalizing, pragmatizing of the West *which is the fate of every aging culture* [Spengler lesen und verstehen, daß der Sieg England-Amerika's die Civilisierung, Rationalisierung, Utilarisierung des Abendlandes, die das Schicksal jeder alternden Kultur ist, besiegelt und beendigt]. More and more I see this war [...] as a vast quixotism, a last mighty effort to rear up and strike a blow on the part of the Germanic Middle Ages, which remained astoundingly well preserved before collapsing with a rattle of bones.

Anyone who has seen Jean Renoir's film *La Grande Illusion* may sense what Mann meant here. At any rate, the future was clearly going to be very different:

> What's coming now is Anglo-Saxon dominance of the world, that is, perfected civilization [die vollendete Civilisation]. Why not? We will discover that it is quite comfortable to live under. The German spirit need not even die—on the contrary, there are signs that under the pressure of unparalleled dishonor this spirit will recollect itself and want to keep alive. The denigration of the great tradition of Germanism will diminish as conditions improve—the whole thing may even turn out to be highly interesting. But Germanism will probably play a predominantly romantic role—representing *the nostalgia* of an old, clever civilization *for its youth, when it had been a true culture* and that culture had been German [die Rolle der Sehnsucht einer alten, klugen, civilisierten Kultur nach ihrer Jugend, die deutsch war].[96]

Mann was now investing words with novel meanings and nuances. He had begun reading Spengler's *Decline*, as his diaries show,[97] and this subtly affected what he wrote in his letter. Although the Americans and British still represented 'civilisation', there was more to this equation than the distinction Mann had drawn in 1914. Civilisation and culture were now spoken of less in geographical-national (American/British/French 'civilisation' versus German *Kultur*), and more in temporal terms. Civilisation, in the letter of 5 July 1919, was spoken of as the inevitable outcome, or next stage, after a culture had matured so much that it ceased in fact to be a Culture ('civilisierten Kultur'). In other words, Mann was now speaking the language of Oswald Spengler's recently published book when he talked of 'the civilizing, rationalizing, pragmatizing of the West which is the fate of every aging culture', or of an old civilisation that was nostalgic for its youth, when it was 'a true culture'. These are novel uses of the familiar terms. And the new distinction, introduced by Spengler, we shall discuss in the next chapter.

VII. Conclusion

The war of words during the Great War took many forms and had several outcomes. German academics and writers habitually complained of the hypocrisy of the purported defenders of Western or European civilisation who meanwhile allied themselves with 'Byzantine', 'Asiatic' Russia and 'Mongolian' Japan to hit at Germany. French authors missed no opportunity to highlight the 'Easternness' of Germany and the centrality of France for the West: Boutroux did so in his wartime articles, though clearly nobody was more tellingly explicit than André Suarès—who thanked the Germans for enabling France to build 'the West' that it had been trying to create for centuries, a 'West' with France as its heart. In Britain, anti-German feeling and propaganda against the 'Huns' was notorious, of course. There were, however, interesting voices calling for a postwar future of peaceful cooperation under the auspices of 'Western civilisation'. That those initiatives were animated and coordinated by staunch admirers of Auguste Comte may not surprise readers of this book.

The most consequential developments, though, took place in the United States. American intellectuals were confronted by a painful challenge. They dealt with it in differing ways, and they argued a lot before their own country joined the war in 1917. Those who identified with the cause of the Anglo-French Entente had to justify their preference, and the defence of 'Western civilisation' came to be used as their main argument. Among the most vociferous in their identification with Europe's fate were staunch Francophiles such as John Jay Chapman. But the most strikingly explicit evocations of Western civilisation as a community Americans ought not only to join, but also to fight for, came from the pen of the young Walter Lippmann. Also important was Lippmann's proposed attitude towards Germany. Like Boutroux, he discerned the existence of two Germanies. But rather than despairing over the predominance of the 'wrong' (Prussian, 'Eastern')

Germany, Lippmann recommended a wise and generous policy towards the Germans after an Entente victory, so that Germany could be lured back to the Western civilisation to which it truly belonged.

For Afro-American thinkers, the dilemmas raised by the war were, if anything, even more complicated. We saw samples of two different initial responses, in the shape of pro-German Locke and pro-Entente Du Bois. But whatever they thought of the rights and wrongs of the war and the likely victors, Afro-American thinkers and activists saw it as an opportunity for the improvement of their own people's lot in the United States. At the war's end, such hopes were to be bitterly disappointed. Meanwhile—and crucially, for what was to emerge in the 1920s— the attractiveness and prestige of 'Western civilisation' had suffered irrevocably. The wartime lectures delivered by the Indian poet Rabindranath Tagore, widely commented on all over the world, reinforced the critical mood towards Western civilisation, Tagore's own carefully balanced attitude notwithstanding. He was at pains to distinguish between 'the spirit of the West', that he admired and praised, and 'the Nation of the West', whose mechanised focus on industrial-scale exploitation or slaughter he castigated. But the message readers noticed most of all was that '[a]ll the great nations of Europe have their victims in other parts of the world'. Meanwhile, Tagore's attempt to cajole Americans into 'justify[ing]' western civilization to the East' sounded less than convincing to Afro-Americans facing worse treatment by the end of the war than before. In light of the declining fortunes of the civilisationist perspective that most Afro-American thinkers had previously adopted, a number of alternative approaches and strategies would emerge in the highly fertile 1920s, as we shall see in the next chapter.

The German dualism that Boutroux and Lippmann noted (the intra-German battle that Lippmann hoped might be resolved by Germany's return to the Western fold), was both symbolised and enacted within the Mann family during the war. Against Francophile Westerners committed to liberal democracy, such as his own brother Heinrich, Thomas Mann launched a visceral and desperate onslaught. Resuscitating (as many had done before and would later do again) the memory of the stubborn and victorious resistance of Arminius/Hermann against the mighty Romans in the year 9 CE, Mann declared that Germany's eternal mission was to resist the homogenising and 'civilising' encroachments of Rome and Rome's successor, 'the West'. Mann presented Germany as conducting a noble anti-imperialist struggle against the 'imperialism of civilisation' represented by the West.

When that battle was finally lost, Mann initially tried to console himself by endorsing what he understood of Oswald Spengler's redescription of the situation. Acceptance of Spengler's diagnosis made Germany's predicament seem relatively more palatable. Crucially, Spengler's reframing involved using the terms 'culture' and 'civilisation' in new ways. Instead of viewing Germany and its distinctive *Kultur* as defeated, Spengler's analysis moved the discussion onto the plane of a much more dramatic, longer-term development. That development was the decline and petrification of the whole of 'Western culture' (including Germany, which was part of Spengler's West/*Abendland*) by the end of the eighteenth century. Since that time, the West had passed into its final stage of decline, which Spengler called 'civilisation'. We will see much more on that distinction, on Spengler's overall theory, and on the reception it met with, in the chapter that follows.

6

From 'Decline of the West' to 'Defence of the West'

THE INTERWAR YEARS AND THE CRISIS OF CIVILISATION

'Down the dim dusk of the ages the man from Africa appears as the burden bearer of Western civilization. Long ago, while yet the world was wrapped in ignorance and slavery, he laid in ancient Ethiopia the sure foundations of Egyptian culture, as Egypt's own sons have confessed.... There, as the Father of History has told us, did white Greece come to learn letters and law, religion and art, science and philosophy; to light her torch of culture at the resplendent blaze built by the black and brown children of the land of Khem and from this torch to kindle the fire of civilization upon the altars of barbarian Rome, whence sottish Saxon and brute German, wild Celt and wandering Goth have taken tribute of light and heat to warm themselves and enlighten the world of the present.'

HUBERT H. HARRISON, 'THE BLACK MAN'S BURDEN: MEDITATIONS OF MUSTAPHA AS TRANSLATED BY HUBERT H. HARRISON', *THE NEGRO WORLD*, 20 SEPTEMBER 1920, QUOTED IN J. B. PERRY, *HUBERT HARRISON: THE STRUGGLE FOR EQUALITY*, PP. 271–72

'And first we will destroy this civilization that is so dear to you [...]. Western world, you are condemned to death. We are the defeatists of Europe, beware [...]. We will ally ourselves with all your enemies [...]. We will awaken everywhere the germs of confusion and malaise. We are the agitators of the spirit. [...] We are those who will always give our hand to your enemy.'

LOUIS ARAGON, 'FRAGMENTS D'UNE CONFÉRENCE', *LA RÉVOLUTION SURRÉALISTE*, NO. 4 (15 JULY 1925), P. 25

THE PREVIOUS CHAPTER began and ended with Germany. This one too must begin with a German author: one who was to mark the whole climate of discussion for decades. He published the first instalment of his book at a time when it was bound to be noticed, and he chose a title that captured the *Zeitgeist*. The Great War was so cataclysmic that it would inevitably change how people thought about history, progress or civilisation. One of the most discussed questions in its immediate aftermath was whether it had signalled the end of 'Western civilisation'. Of the innumerable contributions to such debates, two in particular stand out in terms of the responses they generated. One came from Munich and the other from Paris, authored by Oswald Spengler and Henri Massis respectively. But the collapse of self-confidence in 'the West' among 'Western' elites reflected by these works was only one of the outcomes of the Great War. The other side of the coin was of course the striking degree to which both non-Westerners and minority Westerners came to assert themselves against the previous cultural and political hierarchies. We will follow the multifaceted verdicts on what the Great War had proved in an array of very different authors.

Meanwhile, as a direct result of US participation in the Great War, the country's whole outlook was about to change after it ended. American universities would begin to teach undergraduates the famous 'Western Civ[ilization]' curricula that built a particular understanding of the world for at least two generations of educated Americans. That understanding was a 'grand narrative' of a Western civilisation that started with Socrates and Athens and, by way of selected milestones such as the Renaissance, the Reformation, the Enlightenment and the American and French Revolutions, led to a modern world culminating in democratic twentieth-century America.[1] As one of those best qualified to comment on them, historian William W. McNeill, himself a prolific textbook author, was to put it much later, '[t]he courses and curricula in the history of Western Civ that became ubiquitous from about 1930 to 1960 were first crafted in response to U.S. belligerence in 1917.' It was rather simple and inevitable that '[i]nitially, at least at Columbia University, Western Civ was designed to teach soldiers what it was they would be fighting for in Flanders Fields.'[2] To a great extent, the wishes of John Jay Chapman and Walter Lippmann were being fulfilled. America was at last talking of itself as part of the West and Western civilisation, and accepting its 'destined' leadership role. Yet, as we will see in this chapter, some Americans felt excluded from the story, and started thinking of alternatives.

In Britain, meanwhile, the historian Arnold Toynbee began to publish his analyses of civilisations and the results of civilisational contact that were to affect the way civilisations in general, and Western civilistion in particular, were to be talked about for some decades to come. One of the earliest instalments came in 1922, with *The Western Question in Greece and Turkey: A Study in the Contact of Civilizations*. Toynbee insisted there that 'Western society is a unity—a closer and more permanent unity than either the independent states that form and dissolve within its boundaries or the Empires compounded of Western and non-Western populations'.[3] He also emphasised the importance of 'the shadow of the West' for the rest of the world (and the huge potential for misunderstandings and mistakes related to that shadow). He was to elaborate on the definition of civilisations, which he insisted were the main meaningful units of historical study, in 1934, in the first instalment of his monumental, twelve-volume *A Study of History*. There Toynbee explained again that 'the intelligible unit of historical study is neither a nation state nor (at the other end of the scale) mankind as a whole but a certain grouping of humanity' which he called 'a society' or 'a civilization'. He discerned five such societies or civilisations 'in existence to-day, together with sundry fossilized evidences of societies dead and gone'.[4] He would proceed to elaborate upon these categories and terms, with considerable publicity, until the tide of his popularity began to ebb more than two decades later. Toynbee had been highly impressed, and his outlook decisively affected, by his reading (in the summer of 1920) of the work of Oswald Spengler.[5]

I. The Spengler Affair: *The Decline of the West*

The most discussed book on 'the West' in the interwar period was Oswald Spengler's *Der Untergang des Abendlandes* (translated as *The Decline of the West*). Though the first of its two volumes was published in July 1918, shortly before the end of the Great War, it had basically been written before the war started, between 1911 and 1914. The outbreak of hostilities delayed publication, and its appearance near the end of the cataclysm lent the book a sense of timeliness, and a popularity, that it might not otherwise have received. The second volume appeared in 1922, and a revised edition of the first in 1923. Its success in the German-speaking world was spectacular. By 1926 an authorised English translation of the first (and more crucial) volume had appeared, to be followed in 1928 by a translation of the second. There were also translations into French, Spanish, Italian, Russian and Arabic. As a result, in the late 1920s and early 1930s 'Spengler's theories had become a fashionable topic for semi-intellectual conversation'. For they 'admirably fitted the prevailing temper of a rather callow scepticism'.[6]

Spengler challenged the whole way history was studied and its periodisation into ancient, medieval and modern. But he was not simply arguing that one could not know 'world history' by following the co-opted self-centred trajectory of Western Europeans and Americans who selectively studied what they called 'ancient', 'medieval' and 'modern' history. He was also saying (to adapt Rudyard Kipling's famous line), 'What do they know of the Occident who only the Occident know?' By studying the West—*Abendland*, in Spengler's vocabulary—as one part only of a history of different 'cultures' as self-contained organisms, each with its own life, growth and maturity, passing into the stage of static, no longer creative 'civilisations', and finally death, its real historical cycle would be shown in its unmistakable 'destiny', including—crucially—its future. According to Spengler's calculations regarding the life span of each 'culture' and his analysis of the 'analogies' with previous cultures, the *Abendland* had already exhausted its creative juices by the end of the eighteenth century. It had entered, since then, its last stage, that of having become a static 'civilisation': no longer a living, growing 'culture.' The Westerners of the centuries between, roughly, 1800 and 2000 stood vis-à-vis their ancestors of the centuries between the tenth and the eighteenth in the same relation as the Romans had stood vis-à-vis the Greeks, in the history of the ancient Greco-Roman culture that Spengler referred to as 'Apollinian'. He boldly stated at the very beginning, 'In this book is attempted for the first time the venture of predetermining history, of following the still untravelled stages in the destiny of a Culture, and specifically of the only Culture of our time and on our planet which is actually in the phase of fulfilment—the West-European-American [der westeuropäisch-amerikanischen].'[7] He identified that 'West-European-American', or Western, culture-turned-civilisation as 'Faustian'.

Spengler insisted that the whole approach to history had to change. The search for 'causes', in the manner of the natural sciences, was not applicable to history and not relevant to historical study. For there was, he insisted, 'besides a necessity of cause and effect—which I may call the *logic of space*—another necessity, an organic necessity in life, that of Destiny—the *logic of time*'. He emphasised that Westerners had a peculiar historical sense and attitude to time, very different from that of the people living in the Classical or 'Apollinian' Culture (Greeks and Romans): 'We men of the Western Culture are, with our historical sense, an exception and not a rule. World-history is *our* world picture and not all mankind's.' By contrast, 'Indian and Classical man formed no image of a world in progress, and perhaps when in due course the civilization of the West is extinguished, there will never again be a Culture and a human type in which "world-history" is so potent a form of the waking consciousness.'[8]

Commenting on Western schemes of history from 'the great Joachim of Floris (c. 1145–1202)' to Hegel, Spengler noted that '[i]t would appear, then, that the

Western consciousness feels itself urged to predicate a sort of finality inherent in its own appearance.'[9] And yet, he found it 'quite indefensible' to 'begin by giving rein to one's own religious, political or social convictions and endowing the sacrosanct three-phase system with tendencies that will bring it exactly to one's own standpoint'. It amounted to 'making of some formula—say, the "Age of Reason", Humanity, the greatest happiness of the greatest number, enlightenment [die Aufklärung], economic progress, national freedom, the conquest of nature, or world-peace—a criterion whereby to judge whole millennia of history'. And then 'we judge that they were ignorant of the "true path", or that they failed to follow it, when the fact is simply that their will and purposes were not the same as ours.'[10] Some kind of criticism of this sort had of course already been raised in the late eighteenth century by thinkers such as Herder. But Spengler was keen to stress his own originality (and sometimes clearly exaggerated it).

To the linear understanding of history seen as tending towards 'progress' or whatever else, Spengler retorted, '"Mankind", however, has no aim, no idea, no plan, any more than the family of butterflies or orchids.' 'Mankind' was simply 'a zoological expression'. But if one were to 'conjure away the phantom', one would be able to see instead 'an astonishing wealth of *actual* forms'. Thus, 'in place of that empty figment of *one* linear history which can only be kept up by shutting one's eyes to the overwhelming multitude of the facts', Spengler saw, rather, 'the drama of *a number* of mighty Cultures, each springing with primitive strength from the soil of a mother-region to which it remains firmly bound throughout its whole life-cycle'. Each of those cultures had been 'stamping its material, its mankind, in *its own* image; each having *its own* idea, *its own* passions, *its own* life, will and feeling, *its own* death'. What was lacking to the Western thinker was 'insight into the *historically relative* character of his data, which are expressions of one *specific existence and one only*; knowledge of the necessary limits of their validity'; also, the 'conviction that his "unshakable" truths and "eternal" views are simply true for him and eternal for his world-view'; and the 'duty of looking beyond them to find out what the men of other Cultures have with equal certainty evolved out of themselves.'[11]

Now, as Comte had done in the mid-nineteenth century, Spengler (who had of course read, and extensively cited, Comte) also took issue with the use of the term 'Europe' to describe a culture/civilisation. He blamed 'the subdivision of history into "Ancient", "Mediæval" and "Modern"—an incredibly jejune and *meaningless* scheme, which has, however, entirely dominated our historical thinking', for the fact that 'we have failed to perceive the true position in the general history of higher mankind, of the little part-world which has developed on

West-European soil from the time of the German-Roman Empire, to judge of its relative importance and above all to estimate its direction.' To the phrase 'on West-European soil', Spengler attached the following footnote:

> Here the historian is gravely influenced by preconceptions derived from geography, which assumes a *Continent* of Europe, and feels himself compelled to draw an ideal frontier corresponding to the physical frontier between 'Europe' and 'Asia.' *The word 'Europe' ought to be struck out of history* [Das Wort Europa sollte aus der Geschichte gestrichen werden]. There is historically no 'European' type, and it is sheer delusion to speak of the Hellenes as 'European Antiquity' (were Homer and Heraclitus and Pythagoras, then, Asiatics?)[12] and to enlarge upon their 'mission' as such. [...] *It is thanks to this word 'Europe' alone, and the complex of ideas resulting from it, that our historical consciousness has come to link Russia with the West in an utterly baseless unity* [Es war allein das Wort Europa mit dem unter seinem Einfluß entstandenen Gedankenkomplex, das Rußland mit dem Abendlande in unserm historischen Bewußtsein zu einer durch nichts gerechtfertigten Einheit verband]—a mere abstraction derived from the reading of books—that has led to immense real consequences. In the shape of Peter the Great, this word has falsified the historical tendencies of a primitive human mass for two centuries, whereas the Russian *instinct* has very truly and fundamentally divided 'Europe' from 'Mother Russia' with the hostility that we can see embodied in Tolstoi, Aksakov or Dostoyevski. *'East' and 'West' are notions that contain real history, whereas 'Europe' is an empty sound* [Orient und Okzident sind Begriffe von echtem historischem Gehalt. 'Europa' ist leerer Schall].[13]

As already observed in chapter 5 above, a crucial distinction Spengler introduced was that between 'Civilization' and 'Culture': 'Looked at in this way, the "Decline of the West" comprises nothing less than the problem of *Civilization*. We have before us one of the fundamental questions of all higher history. *What is Civilization, understood as the organic-logical sequel, fulfilment and finale of a culture?*'[14] The American historian Stuart Hughes (in an otherwise outstanding analysis of Spengler and his context) was incorrect to write of Spengler's distinction as being the same as Thomas Mann's and other Germans' distinction between *Kultur* and *Zivilisation* (the distinction that we discussed in chapter 5).[15] For Spengler goes on to clarify that he is using the distinction in a new way, not in the sense of the contrast routinely employed by his contemporaries in Germany.[16] He could not have been more explicit. For having asserted that 'every Culture has *its own* Civilization' he emphasised that '[i]n this work, for the first time the two words, hitherto used to express an indefinite, more or less ethical, distinction, are used in a *periodic* sense, to express a strict and necessary *organic succession*'. For Spengler, '[t]he Civilization is the inevitable *destiny* of the Culture'. Civilisations are 'a conclusion, the thing-become succeeding the thing-becoming, death following life, rigidity following expansion, intellectual age and the stone-built, petrifying world-city following mother-earth and the spiritual childhood of Doric and Gothic'. They were 'an end, irrevocable, yet by inward necessity reached again and again'.[17]

Thanks to his scheme whereby each 'Culture' was inexorably succeeded by its own corresponding 'Civilization' in an overall life span of roughly a thousand years, Spengler claimed, 'for the first time, we are enabled to understand the Romans as the successors of the Greeks, and light is projected into the deepest secrets of the late-Classical period'. For him, this could be the only meaning of the fact 'that the Romans were barbarians who did not *precede* but *closed* a great development'. His estimate of the Romans was that, '[u]nspiritual, unphilosophical, devoid of art, clannish to the point of brutality, aiming relentlessly at tangible successes, they stand between the Hellenic Culture and nothingness'. He summarised it thus: 'In a word, Greek *soul*—Roman *intellect*; and this antithesis is the differentia between Culture and Civilization. Nor is it only to the Classical that it applies'.[18]

Spengler of course had many predecessors who had already been predicting civilisational decline and doom.[19] But the fundamental idea of Spengler's book, regarding the existence of separate and largely incommensurable cultures, had been anticipated primarily by the Russian Panslavist Nikolai Iakovlevitch Danilevsky (1822–1885). So had the prediction that the culture of the West was on its way out, and that the one most likely to succeed it as dominant and about to thrive was the Slavic.[20] But the timing of his book's publication, following the Great War, meant that Spengler made much more of an impression than any of his predecessors. It received literally hundreds of reviews. The specialist academics were almost unanimously critical. His impact on popular audiences was immense, however; first in Germany, and then in the rest of the world.[21]

II. From Harlem to Paris (via Berlin, Munich, and Luxor): Black Intellectuals and Western Civilisation

The generally perceived decline of 'the West' may have been a regrettable fact of 'Destiny' for Spengler, but for others it presented serious opportunities and hopes. The man who would soon become known as the father of the 'Harlem Renaissance', Howard University's philosophy professor Alain LeRoy Locke, was on a quest for an alternative route to construct an African American self-understanding. Though almost as attached to Europe as the young Du Bois had been, Locke came to see new possibilities for building the self-confidence and self-respect of Afro-Americans. Whilst spending some months in Vienna attending lectures and reading the latest works of Leo Frobenius and Sigmund Freud, Locke tried to get permission to translate one of Frobenius's works into English. He began to envisage the possibility of Egypt's ancient civilisation serving as an alternative classical past for Afro-Americans. In that spirit Locke undertook his long-postponed first visit to Africa in October 1923, during which he would eventually go to Luxor and inspect the excavation of King Tut's tomb (which was completed with the opening of the sarcophagus in February 1924, after Locke had left). No sooner had Locke arrived in Alexandria, however, than he had set off in a different direction: that he combined his first visit to Africa with a trip to Constantinople, the historic capital of the Eastern Roman or 'Byzantine' Empire, leads his biographer to comment, 'Although reluctant to go directly to Africa, he was also intellectually alienated from West. So, Locke split the difference and journeyed to Constantinople, the capital of a Byzantine tradition that was non-Black and non-Western.'[22] (Marcus Garvey presumably had a similar idea when he turned to Eastern, Greek Orthodox Christianity for strategic reasons and created a new African Orthodox Church that would associate his movement more directly with the historic religion of Ethiopia).[23]

In one of Locke's articles written shortly after his return from Egypt,[24] he emphasised that instead of looking to West Africa as their place of origin (due to the fact that the enslaved were transported to America from West African ports), Afro-Americans ought to consider the whole of Africa as their 'especial patrimony [...] if we ever had one'. As Jeffrey Stewart notes, 'That last hint of irony—or was it sarcasm—suggests he knew that a direct African heritage for twentieth-century American Negroes was an imagined tradition. But including Egypt in the African American "patrimony" made it easier for his Afro-Anglo Saxon audience to identify with Africa.' Stewart remarks that Locke was 'still not ready to identify with the non-literary, non-scholarly, and non-linear cultures of West Africa'. The solution he chose was 'to identify with the more Europeanized Africa'. This was because the ancient cultures of Egypt and Ethiopia 'were both part of the Western tradition and precursors of it—alternatives to the modern Western European narrative that all that was civilized was White'. Egypt stood for 'cultural traditions that could stand up to Europe, indeed, prefigure Europe's historicity, spirituality, and, most important, social and political order'. Thus it was simple: 'Anglo-Americans might claim an undocumented lineage to the Greeks; Locke would match their hybris and claim

FIGURE 6.1. Alain Locke. [Monochrome reproduction of] *Alain Leroy Locke*, portrait in oils by Betsy Graves Reyneau (1944). Original at the National Portrait Gallery, Smithsonian Institution, Washington, DC (gift of the Harmon Foundation). US National Archives at College Park (NARA Archives II), College Park, MD. *Source:* https://commons.wikimedia.org/wiki/File:Alain_Locke_-_NARA_-_559203.jpg

African Americans as the heirs of Egyptian civilization and dare anyone to prove him wrong.'[25]

At that same time Locke took the initiatives that led to the publication of the *New Negro* special issue of the magazine *Survey Graphic*, and then, in book form, *The New Negro: An Interpretation*, which appeared in December 1925.[26] The publication of the 'New Negro' volumes and the whole 'Harlem Renaissance' were of course part of broader cultural and intellectual developments. For one of the results of recent trends had been what the historian Wilson Jeremiah Moses calls the 'anti-modernist paradox' of 'Modernism as Primitivism'. Thus, 'Afrocentrism, a movement that places such absolute value on the quality of Africanness, is ironically indebted to the ideology of cultural relativism, which arose at the beginning of the twentieth century'. Cultural relativism was 'the theory, associated with anthropologist Franz Boas and the sociologist William Graham Sumner, that every culture should be viewed as a rationally integrated world view, and that no culture should be condemned by the standards of another'. (Again, it deserves to be noted that Johann Gottfried Herder had already tried to convince people to view cultures in such a way, in the eighteenth century; but the idea was to become much more popular in the early twentieth.) Moses is right in stressing the extent to which the idiosyncratic German anthropologist Leo Frobenius 'did much to champion this view with his treatment of African cultures, particularly their erotic beliefs' (and Suzanne Marchand has shown the extent of Frobenius's impact, beyond doubt).[27] With Boas's view of culture established, and once 'the Freudian view of sexual repression had been promulgated, the celebration of African eroticism as represented in the writings of Frobenius became fashionable'.[28] As Moses further notes, '[i]nspired by the Dionysian spirit of modernism and the Harlem Renaissance, the French negritude poets sought in artistic primitivism a positive affirmation of a Negro Personality'; and even prior to the Négritude movement, Afro-American artists and intellectuals had begun taking 'a perverse pleasure in depicting themselves as exotic savages, or Calibans, cursing an oppressive Western civilization'.[29] Similar trends were observable at the same time in Latin American intellectual life, not least in Brazil, with a revolt against traditions of European origins and provocative celebrations of 'cannibalism', among other features.[30]

Now, between the United States and Latin America stood 'Latin America's capital', Paris.[31] Though there were very close transatlantic links and exchanges between African diaspora thinkers, the context for French-speaking Black intellectuals was quite distinct. There was no official segregation in metropolitan France, as there was in the United States. Meanwhile, there was a French Empire. Early in the aftermath of the Great War, in 1921, a major sensation was caused in France by the publication, by a Martinican who had served as a colonial civil servant for France in Africa, René Maran, of *Batouala, véritable roman nègre*. In November that year it was awarded the prestigious Prix Goncourt. Stormy reactions followed from self-appointed defenders of the honour of France, who were outraged by the Goncourt Academy's decision to award the prize to a book whose preface had bitterly denounced the French colonial system. Meanwhile, the award of France's most prestigious literary prize to a Black man caused excitement on the other side of the Atlantic. The number of enthusiastic reviews Maran's novel elicited in the Afro-American press (it received no less than six reviews in Marcus Garvey's *Negro World* alone) is characteristic of the close and increasing contacts between activists on the two sides of the Atlantic.[32] Some of the outcomes of those contacts will emerge in the pages that follow.

III. 'Nordic' Supremacists and Responses to Them

The people Du Bois, Locke, and many others were fighting against in the United States—the racist theorists most vociferous and influential in the early decades of the twentieth century—were not just arguing that whites were superior to non-whites. They were equally if not more concerned about the 'contamination' of America by 'inferior' whites, and wanted to preserve the predominance of the 'superior' 'Nordic', 'Anglo-Saxon' or 'Teutonic' type. One of their major spokesmen, Madison Grant, first published *The Passing of the Great Race; or, The Racial Basis of European History* in October 1916. The focus of the book was on the superiority of the 'Nordic race' over not just non-white 'races' but also what Grant called the 'Mediterranean' and 'Alpine' (white) 'racial' groups. Among his many critics was the German-born and leading American cultural anthropologist Franz Boas, who exposed the book's untenable premises as well as its striking contradictions (So did John Jay Chapman).[33] Yet Grant's influence was considerable, and not just among American followers. After his book appeared in a German translation, it became the 'Bible' (as he wrote in a fan letter to Grant) of a young Austrian named Adolf Hitler.[34] Grant's protégé T. Lothrop Stoddard soon afterwards published (with a preface by Grant) *The Rising Tide of Color: The Threat against White World-Supremacy* (1920), which made him the leading apostle of Nordic racial supremacy in the United States. Stoddard's views were very widely publicised.[35]

This was the context in which Du Bois wrote articles such as 'Americanization', when Harvard College started trying to restrict its number of Jews as well as segregate Black students in dormitories. In a climate where Jews too were unwelcome, Du Bois made common cause with them.[36] The 1920s saw the peak of 'Nordic' assertiveness. Thus, the passage of the draconian 1924 Immigration Act was far from being random;[37] nor is it coincidental that in Latin America, the Mexican politician José Vasconcelos's most influential reaction to Anglo-Saxonist

'Nordic' rhetoric came in 1925. In an attempt to turn the tables, Vasconcelos argued that the future of the world was bound to see the dominance of a mixed 'race': the 'cosmic race'. Indeed, given how open to racial mixing the Latin American peoples had been, they were ahead in the game of the future, compared to their North American neighbours with their fixation on Nordic racial purity.[38]

Such a context may explain some of Du Bois's other utterances. Describing later what had been his thoughts and feelings in 1924, when he first visited Africa via France and Portugal, he proclaimed,

> I began to notice a truth as I entered southern France. I formulated it in Portugal. I knew it as a great truth one Sunday in Liberia. And the Great Truth was this: efficiency and happiness do not go together in modern culture. Going south from London, as the world darkens it gets happier. Portugal is deliciously dark. Many leading citizens would have difficulty keeping off a Georgia 'Jim Crow' car. But, oh, how lovely a land and how happy a people! And so leisurly. [...] How delightfully angry Englishmen get at the 'damned, lazy' Portuguese! But if this is Portugal, what of Africa? Here darkness descends and rests on lovely skins until brown seems luscious and natural. [...] And laziness; divine, eternal, languor is right and good and true.[39]

There is no mistaking a 'Southern' dimension to Du Bois's thinking here. If the enemy was claiming superiority for Nordics, he would claim a different superiority for darker, happier, sexier and relaxed Southerners.

But there was also a particularly vociferous and widely discussed 'Latin' response to both Spengler's pessimism and to Nordic supremacy theories. Unsurprisingly, perhaps, it came from the self-appointed capital of 'Latin' and 'Western' civilisation, Paris.

IV. The Massis Affair: *Defence of the West*

For Spengler's *Decline of the West* did not attract criticism only on account of its fatalism, obsession with 'time' or its often cryptic prose.[40] It was also castigated for its Germanness. The most sustained attack came from the French conservative Catholic intellectual Henri Massis and his circle associated with the *Revue universelle*, which he co-founded in 1920. Massis initially wrote several articles related to what he called 'Defence of the West'.[41] Though forgotten now, the Massis affair was arguably as important for debates on 'the West' as the Spengler affair. Moreover, it explicitly emerged as a response to the pessimism and resignation that Massis saw as the main corollary of Spengler's message. If Spengler diagnosed inevitable decline and recommended accepting the inexorable fact, Massis proposed instead a 'defence of the West'. He would go on volunteering advice on how to save 'the West' all the way into the early decades of the Cold War.

Unlike Spengler—a loner who wrote a book that happened to hit a nerve at the time of its publication—Massis, a very different kind of intellectual, was a particularly effective cultural-political operator, who managed to appeal to a younger generation in ways most other, more senior, conservative thinkers such as Maurice Barrès or Charles Maurras could not. He played a crucial role as a link both between generations and between the politics-first movement centred around Charles Maurras's Action Française movement and Catholic intellectuals who were more focused on achieving a cultural impact, not least the Thomist philosopher Jacques Maritain.[42] Massis also had a talent for drafting manifestos and petitions. His role as an organiser and mobiliser was considerable, and arguably catalytic in terms of the outcome of intellectual warfare: it was largely as a result of his endeavours that writers on the right and extreme right took the upper hand in French intellectual debates in the interwar period.[43] On the back of the success of his manifesto 'Pour un parti de l'intelligence' in Le Figaro of 19 July 1919, some of the signatories of that manifesto founded the *Revue universelle*, which began publication in April 1920. Massis served as chief editor and Jacques Maritain was responsible for the philosophy section. The *Revue universelle* became the right-wing counterpart of *La Nouvelle Revue française*, the major organ of the interwar intellectual left in France.

Like most uses of 'the West' that we have seen so far, Massis's employment of the term had a particular angle and purpose. (After all, André Suarès alerted us to that dimension as explicitly as possible in the previous chapter). Massis's *Occident* was not exactly Spengler's *Abendland*. Rather, he defined the 'West' in such a way as for it (or at least its core) to coincide with the Catholic and 'Latin-Mediterranean' world inspired by Greece and Rome, and to exclude Germany and Russia as half-Asiatic Trojan horses that were turning more and more 'Oriental' in the wake of the 1917 Bolshevik Revolution (in case of the latter) and defeat in the Great War (in the case of the former).

Massis saw no reason to understate what was at stake, at the very beginning of his 'Defence of the West': 'The future of western civilisation, indeed the future of mankind, is to-day in jeopardy.' He hastened to clarify that he was not indulging in the defeatist exaggerations of 'weak minds': it was, rather, specifically against their incipient state of resignation that he was writing. But the 'tragic greatness of the danger' was plain to see. 'The crisis of Western civilisation and the danger of Asiaticism are no longer questions reserved solely for the meditations of men of intellect.' Even politicians were at last waking up to the danger.⁴⁴ It was 'the soul of the West that the East wishes to attack, that soul, divided, uncertain of its principles, confusedly eager for spiritual liberation'. Thus, 'a certain kind of Asiaticism is disposing us to the final dispersal of the heritage of our culture and of all that which enables the man of the West still to keep himself upright on his feet'. The 'root-ideas' of the West were '[p]ersonality, unity, stability, authority, continuity'. Yet, Westerners were 'asked to break these to pieces for the sake of a doubtful Asiaticism in which all the forces of the human personality dissolve and return to nothingness'.

That 'new assault by the East on the Latin inheritance' found its natural allies, Massis opined, 'in those newly formed nations who have not kept step with the others in the march of human civilization, *and who belong only in an artificial and incomplete manner to the body of the West*'. The first of the nations in question was Germany, 'which is perpetually hesitating between Asiatic mysticism and the Latin spirit, and which is *in a state of permanent protest against the Roman idea*'. After the Great War, Germany in defeat was 'regaining touch with her native East, which presents remarkable affinities with her own thought'. As a result, '[n]o other nation was [...] more eager than Germany to prophesy the "downfall of the West", the West, the mastery of which had slipped from her hands'.⁴⁵ After quoting some characteristic statements by Walter Rathenau a few months before his tragic death, Massis came to the names of his major targets:

> The Germany of 1918, frustrated in her ambition for spiritual hegemony, proclaimed, by the voice of [...] Spengler, the downfall of Europe, and greeted the advent of a new religious faith in the East. At Darmstadt, Count Hermann Keyserling opened a School of Wisdom, the disciples of which looked to the *yoghis* to satisfy the needs of their uneasy spiritual state. At Munich, frenzied crowds were seen following the Bengali poet, Rabindranath Tagore, and his fakir-like stammerings were well adapted to soothe their wounded pride. Defeated Germany, faithful to the pessimism of Schopenhauer, found once more in Chinese and Indian texts that contradictory philosophy, with its infinite perspectives, that idealistic pantheism, which slumbers in the depths of her being.

There was in Germany 'a veritable craze for books on the language, the philosophy, the art and the peoples of Asia'.⁴⁶ Beneath that 'return to Asia' may be discovered 'a sort of grudge, of bitter resentment, a secret aversion from the culture, the spirit, that has conquered'. And the Germans 'devoted themselves to discrediting it even at the risk of seeing civilization itself disappear in the crash foretold by their gloomy philosophy.' He went on,

> This obscure will to destruction which pierces through Spengler's book, *Der Untergand des Abendlandes*, flattered the German in his taste for the confused, the unfinished, the thing which is not, the novelty which has no name, the chaos from which anything may emerge, where the imagination may dream without end, where nothing possesses either form or limit. But under cover of a romanticism that proclaims the ruin of material culture, repudiates the worship of organisation, and exalts the inward contemplation of the Orient, *it is her intellectual revenge on the classic West that conquered her*, that Germany is seeking to prepare. The whole philosophy of a Spengler, for example, is a historico-metaphysical edifice, hastily constructed to liberate modern thought from Hellenism.[47]

And Spengler's 'too famous book would never have had such a success, if, more or less consciously, Germany did not hope for great things from this liberation.' (Massis was not of course the only one to notice what has aptly been referred to as the 'tyranny of Greece over Germany.')[48]. And in an astute remark, he added, 'Even those who, like Thomas Mann, are to-day denouncing these Asiatic tendencies as a danger to the German national spirit, are also asking whether the humanist tradition of classicism is important to humanity as a whole'. Mann's ambiguity even after he had converted to supporting the Weimar Republic did not escape Massis.[49]

But the feeling of defeat was 'not enough to explain the sudden aversion shown by Germany for Western humanity, for the Latin races in which it is embodied, for all that Germany once took so much trouble to understand, to imitate, and to organise with so determined and intent a method'. No, there was more to the problem. The reason the Germans were so keen to 'dewesternise' themselves was that 'civilisation', and 'the intellectual, social and moral progress' that it represented, did 'not operate in the Germanic race as a result of an inner development'. It had not been 'the product of an "indigenous progress", a progress inwardly accomplished'. In other words, Greco-Latin culture was 'not Germany's own proper possession, the foundation of her humanity'; it was 'an acquisition of her learned men, her philologists'; it was 'not a fundamental asset of civilisation for the German, since he has not shared its past to the point of becoming identified with it'.[50] The implication was clear, of course. French ownership of the Greco-Latin heritage by dint of France's Latinity and Mediterraneanness was the unmissable message.

The problem was not just Germany, however. Massis identified a similar phenomenon in the case of Russia. After 'two centuries of forced Europeanisation', Russia was 'returning to its Asiatic destinies, and rousing itself and all the Asiatic races against the civilisation it endured only under compulsion and in a spirit of bitter resistance'. Despite superficial appearances, so-called 'Marxian or Western elements' in the Russian Revolution should not conceal what was the main meaning of the Bolshevik takeover: 'the end of the epoch of Peter the Great, which was captivated by Western liberalism, the end of the European epoch in Russia, which [...] is again turning its face towards the East'. And 'the struggle between "slavophils" and "Occidentalists", the bloody episodes of which fill the annals of modern Russia', was 'to some extent a foreshadowing of the great drama in which the East and the West come to grips'. Massis proceeded to quote extensively from Chaadaev's 'First Philosophical Letter', which we discussed above in chapters 1 and 2, and by the end had also cited approvingly the Marquis de Custine's comments on the 'oriental' character of Russia.[51] In recent treaties signed and statements made by Russian officials Massis saw evidence that there was 'an attempt to form a Germano-Asiatic *bloc*'. The striking rapidity of the progress of that bloc in the previous five years, he thought, was due to the fact 'that the Soviets, as seen from the East, look like an Asiatic reaction against European civilisation'. Such were 'the facts'; such was 'the reality that is hidden in the Bengalee poetry of a Tagore, the Tolstoyan gospel of a Gandhi'. And Massis's exhortation was urgent, because the enemy was within: 'It is in the West that we must first look for the ideologists who, on the pretense of opening up to us the ideas of the East, are betraying civilisation, and their own vocation'. For 'these pseudo-Asiatic ideas would certainly not exist if they were not in a way galvanised into life by contact with Western heresies, mainly of Germanic or Slav origin'.[52]

Another theme Massis identified in 'these doctrines of dissolution which they are trying to acclimatize among us under cover of Asiaticism', was that of 'the materialism of Western civilisation'. But here he clarified that he had no desire to defend the West's actual defects. 'Before the gloomy spectacle of Europe' as it was in his day, he could not 'dream of bringing forward in her favour the homicidal benefits of her puny mastery over matter'. Instead, 'when we desire to defend the West against its detractors, it is not our aim to apologise for its defects, its excesses, its surrenders, but to restore the essential principles, the true traditions of our civilisation, that may save it and the human race with it'. In other words, the West was indeed in urgent need of moral regeneration. But the reason why Massis expected no help from Asia in that 'necessary recovery', was that 'the pseudo-Orientalism of its defenders' was 'most often only an exotic form of the return to nature, of the "Rousseauism" that, with progressive intentions, has led to a general retrogression'. It was 'the same distrust of civilisation, the same hatred of society and of law'. Leaving aside how unfair that comment may be with regard to Rousseau's message and intentions, it is noteworthy that Massis added, 'Rabindranath Tagore denounces the misdeeds of Western machinery and technique in the same tone in which Rousseau condemned the corruption of Athens, the decadence of Rome, the humanism of the Renaissance, in order to exalt the Scythians, the Early Persians and the Germans of Tacitus.'[53] It is odd that Massis chose Tagore as his target here. To cite Gandhi's *Hind Swaraj* (1909), with its denunciation of doctors and medicine along with everything else it associated with 'modern' or 'Western' civilisation, would undoubtedly render Massis's parallel with Rousseau (who had written very similar things against the need to use doctors in the 'Second Discourse') more plausible than does his onslaught upon the much more nuanced utterances of Tagore. But then, it was Tagore in particular who was being lionised in Germany at the time; hence he had to be the target.

Massis had touched a nerve. Even his critics and targets in France could not but agree with some of his premises and arguments, as a review in the rival (left-wing) *Nouvelle Revue française* by André Malraux testifies.[54] In the colder climes of Wilno/Vilnius, meanwhile, a seventeen-year-old Czesław Miłosz was also deeply struck. The impression was to be a lasting one, as he was to reflect from his new Californian home some decades later.[55]

V. German East-Mania after the Great War

Massis was not just making up—or even particularly exaggerating—the 'dewesternisation' tendencies in Germany that he so passionately decried. Suzanne Marchand has shown beyond doubt the extent to which, before, during and after the Great War, German academics, and then more popular writers, turned towards the East for a number of reasons. She felicitously names the phenomenon 'the *furor orientalis*'. Some of the major targets of Massis's criticisms were indeed instrumental in the changes that emerged in German thought at the time. Hermann Hesse and Thomas Mann (initially at least) were among them. But most of all, Hermann Graf Keyserling attracted Massis's ire. That was only to be expected. What Marchand calls 'vitalist orientalism' had 'many manifestations on the Weimar era'. Marchand convincingly argues that 'Spengler's *Decline of the West* would be [...] unthinkable without the radical historicization of European history produced in large part by orientalist critiques'. And she adds, 'Less well known, but deserving of more study, is the work of Hermann Graf Keyserling, author of the *other* great prophecy of Western decline in the postwar period, the *Travel Diary of a Philosopher*.' Keyserling's 'set of philosophical ruminations on his prewar travels in India and China was published in 1919 and sold nearly as well as Spengler'. As Massis noted, in the aftermath of the Great War, Keyserling founded the Schule der Weisheit (School of wisdom) in Darmstadt. According to Marchand, Keyserling's School 'brought together a huge number of vitalistically-inclined intellectuals [...] and aimed at cultural goals that were just as "revolutionary" in their way as those of the other Frankfurt-area school'. For 'Keyserling's crowd sought to reconstruct Western self-formation not by reviving Greek and Christian norms, but by juxtaposing German and oriental Geist'. Tellingly, '[e]ven the former kaiser Wilhelm II, in exile, took up the study of the Orient'. He 'furiously exchanged letters with the esoteric ethnologist Leo Frobenius on the "cultural morphology" of Africa and Asia'. Marchand highlights, moreover, that, in a 1928 letter to Frobenius, the former emperor of Germany 'reported a recent conversation with Oswald Spengler in which Wilhelm had tried his best to convince the herald of Western doom that "we are *orientals* [*Morgenländer*] and *not* westerners [*Abendländer*]"'. The East, after all, had some prospect of revitalization.'[56] No wonder, then, that Keyserling was to receive even more (critical, it goes without saying) attention in the book, *Defense de l'Occident*, that Massis published in 1927.[57]

VI. Anglo-American Responses to Massis

In Britain meanwhile, T. S. Eliot, American-born but turned Euro-patriot,[58] for his own reasons was keen to promote Massis's writings.[59] As a result, long before his book was itself published in either the French original or in English translation, Massis had ignited a debate in Britain. His articles on the West in his *Revue universelle* in the first part of the 1920s had attracted the attention of Eliot, who requested permission to have 'Defence of the West' published in English in the magazine he edited, *The Criterion*.[60] Massis obliged, and an English version of the article was published in two instalments, in the April and June 1926 issues.[61] These provoked numerous responses, published by the magazine over several months. Among others, the Indian polymath Vesudeo B. Metta contributed 'In Defence of the East'. When in 1927 Massis published a book on the subject, *Defense de l'Occident*, its translation into English generated a new round of reviews and articles in both Britain and the United States.[62]

Though keen to start a debate, Eliot was not uncritical of the Frenchman's arguments. As he wrote to Herbert Read in January 1927, Massis's 'propaganda' was 'a good icebreaker to move ahead of us, but there are plenty of difficulties behind'. The point had to be made clear 'that *the "occident" is a bad term if it includes both Europe & America. In some ways America is more like Asia than it is like Europe*'. In any case, the world could 'no longer be divided into "East & West", [for] there is a third position now. *It does not seem to me that much of what is worth preserving in the "occident" exists in America*.'[63] And while encouraging Vasudeo Metta to write 'a "Defence of the East", but certainly with some allusion to Massis', Eliot warned him that 'one must avoid Massis's own difficulties—i.e. he covers far too much ground, for him the East is now Russia (which is largely a product of European-Jewish influence in its present condition), now India, now China; all of which are as different from each other in many ways as "Europe" from "Asia"'.[64] In another letter Eliot put his finger on the main problem, as well as the main allure, of the subject: 'I think that something can be done by emphasizing [in the *New Criterion*] the element of "discussion", even to the extent of including a larger amount of correspondence; the "Defence of the West" has had a success of this kind exceeding its merits; it is a subject about which everyone thinks he has something to say.'[65]

Another London-based American poet, John Gould Fletcher, wrote a letter to the editor that was published in the October 1926 issue of the *Criterion*. He complained that Massis was 'deeply infected with the Mediterraneanism of M. Charles Maurras and other Frenchmen'. The symptoms of that disease were 'supposing that the Greeks were alone enlightened, that Græco-Roman culture is the only classic culture, that Italy and France are the great centres of culture, that every other race and nation, Eastern or Western, is *per se* barbarian'. Fletcher clearly had no time for 'this faith which has been dignified with the expressive name of humanism'.[66] He was granted the opportunity to elaborate further upon his criticisms. In August 1927 he sent Eliot what the editor of the *Criterion* referred to as Fletcher's 'essay on Massis',[67] which was published as 'East and West'.[68] There he argued that the people who were most alarmed at the interest in Oriental thought manifested recently, particularly in Germany, were 'the scholars and politicians to whom the Greco-Roman tradition is something sacred in itself'. That tradition accepted 'largely, as the basis for values, the institutions of codified law, ecclesiasticism, the plastic arts, logic, and the Agora'. Meanwhile, in 'Anglo-Saxon and Scandinavian countries' there were 'probably others to whom the Teutonic-Norman tradition of common law, anticlerical independence, the arts of literature and music, metaphysics, and the free parliament are sacred things. The

FIGURE 6.2. T. S. Eliot. Photograph by Ottoline Morrell (1923). National Portrait Gallery, London. *Source:* https://en.wikipedia.org/wiki/T._S._Eliot#/media/File:T.S._Eliot,_1923.JPG

former class have found able spokesmen in France in Messieurs Massis, Maurras, and Maritain.' In a rather odd statement, given how rampantly theories on the superiority of 'the Nordics' were spreading in the 1910s and 1920s, Fletcher added that '[t]he latter class needs a champion still; when he comes, I do not doubt that he will be able to put up as good a case for his side, the Protestant side of the West, as these champions have for theirs'. To Fletcher's mind, 'all these discussions of the primacy of Western Culture over Oriental, *or of one half of the West over the other part*' were 'highly artificial and sentimental'.[69]

Fletcher correctly identified Massis's 'main problem' as being 'the question of the Oriental tendency that the chief leaders of thought and culture have recognized as existing in Germany since the end of the War'. Here Fletcher had a history lesson of his own: 'Since the conclusion of the barbarian invasions, that is to say from about the eighth century of our era, Europe has been roughly divisible into two halves: *the Northern* and *the Southern*'. These divisions had been 'largely psychological and racial'. On the one side, there was 'the Latin Mediterranean civilization of Italy, Spain, Southern and Central France [sic], Bavaria, Austria, a civilization largely Catholic, Classical and concrete in tendency and thought'. On the other side, 'in Northern Germany, the "Low Countries", and in Central France [sic] and Scandinavia, you get a civilization largely Nordic, Gothic, and abstract'. Fletcher criticised Massis on the grounds that 'by his insistence that European culture can only exist under the direct influence of Greco-Roman ideas', he revealed 'the real cause for his falsification of history'. The problem was that the Holy Roman Emperors were 'Germans'. And 'to men of M. Massis' stamp naught save sweetness and light ever came from the Mediterranean, naught save demoniac darkness from Germany'.[70] Fletcher was thus anticipating the analysis of the German sociologist Wolf Lepenies, who recently paid some attention to Massis in his study of projects for alternative, Mediterranean-centred 'Europes' developed in response to anxieties about German domination by French thinkers and politicians from the Saint-Simonians to Nicolas Sarkozy.[71]

The English translation of Massis's book soon attracted attention also in the United States.[72] A critical review was contributed by the associate editor of *The Nation*, Joseph Wood Krutch. He remarked, in relation to recent American debates, 'Perhaps, indeed, the skeptic anxious not to be taken in by any sophistries however modish would do well to ask himself whether the whole pother over "the Western mind" be not, in part at least, merely a more intellectually respectable analogue of the now subsiding furore over "Nordic" superiorities'. And if one were to do so, one would 'be struck by the fact that whereas the proponents of the last-mentioned theory were compelled to prove that the Germans were not really Nordic the supporters of the Western mind must now maintain that this same unhappy people, whom no one seems to want, are not really Western either'. (Krutch must have had Madison Grant's widely discussed theories in mind. Especially as of the second edition of his book, once America had joined the Great War against Germany, Grant had used all his ingenuity to prove that the real Nordics were not in Germany.)[73] Krutch's next comment is relevant not only to Massis's biases, but also to much of what the present book has been discussing:

> Any argument which is based upon the supposed existence of entities as ill-defined as the Nordic race or the Western mind must indeed end in something

no better than the calling of names. Who shall say that the Middle Age was more characteristically 'Western' than the Renaissance? In all such discussions the truly 'American', 'Nordic', 'Democratic', or 'Western' is likely to be merely what one happens to like. What one does not like is 'Un-American', not 'Nordic', 'Bolshevistic', or 'Eastern'.[74]

VII. 'Bis auf weiteres möchten wir Abendländer bleiben':[75] German-Speaking Reactions to Massis, and Alternative Visions for Germany

As we have seen, Massis was reacting to persistent German manifestations of a non-Western self-identification. Most of the Germans he had in mind tended to identify themselves as 'European', but defined 'Europe' as a culture and identity separate from those of both 'the West' and 'the East'. One of the most vociferous articulations of the views of German nationalists came in 1923, from the pen of the man who coined the term 'Third Reich', Arthur Moeller van den Bruck:[76] 'The German nationalist [...] sees through the humbug of the fine words with which the peoples who conquered us ascribed a world mission to themselves.' And the German nationalist knew 'that within the radius of *these people's civilization, which they so complacently describe as western*, humanity has not risen but has sunk'. In the midst of that 'sinking world', the German was seeking 'his salvation. He seeks to preserve those imperishable values, which are imperishable in their own right. He seeks to secure their permanence in the world by recapturing the rank to which their defenders are entitled.' But there was more to his claim: '*At the same time he is fighting for the cause of Europe*, for every European influence that radiates *from Germany as the centre of Europe* [daß er zugleich für alles kämpft, was von Deutschland aus europäische Reichweite hat].'[77] Germany's mission was to be the heart of a 'Europe' defined against both Russia and 'the West'.

That was written before Massis's diatribe against Germany in *Defense de l'Occident*. Early reactions by German-speakers to Massis's arguments about the essence of 'the West' and his assertion that Germany did not really belong to it also preceded the publication of his 1927 book, appearing in response to his earlier articles on the theme. Two of the German-speaking contributors to Eliot's *Criterion* took up the challenge. The Swiss intellectual Max Rychner used his 'German Chronicle' regular feature to expand on his objections. (Eliot encouraged such articles with comments on the Massis thesis from different national points of view and in that effort also solicited—unsuccessfully—an article from the famous Spanish author and editor of the *Revista de Occidente*, Ortega y Gasset.)[78] Rychner began by conceding that it was 'well known' how 'helplessly the youth of Germany after the war faced the question of the spiritual course they were to follow'. Many of them thought 'salvation' would come from the East. Yet he argued that the 'turning to the East [...] affected not only Germany but the whole of Europe'. Thus, even in France there was 'an intense preoccupation with the idea (compare, e.g., the special number of the *Cahiers du mois*, 'Les Appels de l'Orient', the writings of René Guénon, etc.).' But the main line of defence was that 'the anti-toxins' against the danger in Germany were being prepared simultaneously. Some '[c]onvinced Europeans' had already 'raised their voices in warning', including Ernst Robert Curtius and Wilhelm Worringer. Rychner referred to several recent books that showed 'that in Germany the halo of light from the East has been cracked'. The upshot was clear: 'There is then a spiritual Germany which is convinced that it belongs to the domain of the former *imperium romanum*, and that its ancestors had their place within the *limes*.' Meanwhile, it was 'not only permissible but necessary to have an interpretation of the "West" which includes the province of German culture'. His counter-argument was that the 'differences between Romance and Germanic culture [...] become of less importance when the opposition between East and West, Europe and Asia, enter into the discussion'. Thus, '[c]ontrasted with this opposite pair of ideas, Germany undoubtedly belongs to the West, in spite of Rathenau, Hesse and Oswald Spengler!'[79]

Rychner meanwhile conceded that German culture was not 'a homogeneous unity [...] everywhere ranked in opposition to the East'. There was, on the one hand, 'the South-West of Germany', which, 'in its development through a thousand years of Germano-Roman union has produced humanism and classicism'. On the other hand, 'in the North-East, a district originally Slav colonised by the Germans in the thirteenth century, romanticism sprang from this Germano-Slav blend'. But he tried to turn that tension into a quintessential trait of Europeanness, for that 'striving after a synthesis seems to me to be an essentially European characteristic'.[80]

The most important German contributor to this debate was the senior literary scholar Ernst Robert Curtius, whose Western credentials were in no doubt.[81] He had a particular interest in France and in being a bridge-builder between Germany and France. Both through his own writings and through doctoral dissertations he encouraged and guided,[82] Curtius was a crucial interpreter of French ideas of *civilisation* to the German public.[83] He was among the first to castigate the fascination of German youth by Eastern cultural attractions, insisting instead on Germany's 'Western' identity. His complaints about the fads of German youth were quoted in the observations adduced by Massis to corroborate his case. Presumably Massis would be less receptive to Curtius's criticisms of his own restrictive and excessively 'Latin' definition of 'the West'. Curtius's initial sally against Massis came in a characteristically entitled article, 'Französische Civilisation und Abendland' (French *civilisation* and the West) in the *Europäische Revue*, in June 1927. He elaborated there upon relations and mutual perceptions and misunderstandings between France and Germany, and the possibility of harmonising the German idea of culture with the French idea of civilisation. He ended the article with some unequivocally disdainful comments regarding 'die Idee von dem civilisatorischen Monopol Frankreichs' (the idea of France's civilisational monopoly), taking issue explicitly with Massis's *Defense de l'Occident* and castigating the latter's attempt to distinguish between the 'West' (*Abendland*) and 'Deutschtum, Slawentum, Asiatismus'. He asked whether 'Leibniz, Winkelmann, Goethe, Wilhelm von Humboldt, Hölderlin, Mozart, Beethoven, Nietzsche' were humanist Westerners (*Abendländer*), or not; and concluded that Massis's albeit brilliant plea had not decided the verdict, as far as Germans were concerned: 'Until further notice we would like to remain Western. If the West (*das Abendland*) is to be defended today, that must happen *with* Germany, not *against* Germany.'[84]

In another article published in various languages Curtius commented on the need for 'people of a synthetic consciousness' on whose shoulders rested 'the responsibility for the preservation, the recovery and the renovation of Europe'; to which he added that '[s]een from this point of view, neo-classicism or neo-Thomism, and such like, are merely specimens of ingenious carpentry'. They had 'only a special interest, only a local significance'. They were 'the provincial games of the Latins—*if indeed there are still Latins in existence (but perhaps Latinity is only a fine word behind which unadapted Europeans can take refuge)*'.[85] And there is no doubt who was meant by 'Latins' or 'unadapted Europeans': earlier in the same article he had written, 'We hear much about a return to Classicism. In France Cocteau raises the cry: *Retour à l'Ordre* and Massis would save us by the combination of *latinité* and Thomism'. But, Curtius commented, 'we must have a united European front in which all the great powers in the world of culture can participate'.[86]

Curtius went on trying to explain the very different understandings of *civilisation* and *Kultur* entertained by the French and Germans, and to mediate against the fatal misunderstandings arising from such differences. In 1930 he published a book entitled *Die Französische Kultur: Eine Einfürung* (French culture: an introduction).⁸⁷ There he reiterated that the German and the French 'conceptions of civilization differ fundamentally'. He also stressed that the question was not simply theoretical: far from it, given how, during the Great War, 'the misunderstanding of mutual ideals of civilization in France and in Germany gave rise to an interminable controversy which also expressed itself politically in propaganda among the neutral nations'. The difference 'came to a head in the antithesis: *Kultur* and *Civilisation*'.⁸⁸ Putting his finger on a major difference, Curtius explained that 'when we speak of *deutscher Kultur* and the Frenchman translates this into *culture allemande*, in his mind this seems like a negation of the idea of "civilization" altogether'. In the eyes of the French, '*Kultur* must be something essentially universal; it must have a pan-human content. How then, thinks the Frenchman, can one proclaim and propagate a national "culture"?' For French sentiment that was 'a contradiction—indeed it is a challenge. When France identifies herself with the idea of civilization she never speaks of "French civilization" but of *civilisation* in general'. In so doing, Curtius argues, 'the French national consciousness broadens out into the universal. It attains the dignity of a human value. France feels herself as a nation, and, at the same time, as a nation she is the bearer of this universal idea'. Then came a disclaimer which, again, leaves no doubt as to what Curtius thought of the writings of Massis: 'I would like to state most definitely that the cultivated minds in the France of the present day have overcome this idea of France as the supreme representative of civilization'. It was of course true that that idea still appeared 'in popular forms of public opinion'. But among 'the intellectual class of leaders it only occurs now among those of the extreme Right. In saying this I am thinking of a critic like Massis, who sees in France the bulwark of the Western spirit over against Germany, Russia and Asia.'⁸⁹

Crucially, coming to the peculiarly restricted meaning of *Zivilisation* in German usage, Curtius opined, 'To a very great extent the misunderstanding which exists between the German and French idea of civilization is based upon the fact that by civilization we [Germans] mean exclusively, or almost exclusively, these new achievements of the machine-age.' Inevitably, he thought, '[i]f the idea is thus restricted of course there must be opposition to the idea of civilization itself. Civilization then becomes the materially mechanized existence, the hostile force which menaces the sphere of the soul, of art, of the intellect.'⁹⁰ As we saw in chapter 5 above (and as Curtius stressed at the beginning of his book), that restricted meaning had played a major role during the Great War.

Now, besides German-speaking authors who defended Germany's place in 'the West' and meanwhile protested against Massis's characterisation of Germany as 'dewesternising' and half-Eastern, the Frenchman did have some admirers in Germany. Not least among them was Dr. Georg Moenius, a Catholic priest, who translated Massis's *Défense de l'Occident* into German in 1930 as *Verteidigung des Abendlandes* (as well as defending it in an almost book-length introduction).[91] And in 1931 we find another inhabitant of Munich, Oswald Spengler, bitterly complaining about 'that Moenius', who in his newspaper was incessantly striking out against anything that was called Germany and German ('unaufhörlich gegen alles loszieht, was Deutschland und deutsch heißt'), and extolled the Versailles Treaty as just punishment.[92] But other contemporaries, more critical of German nationalism than was Spengler, had very different comments on 'Georg Moenius, the pro-Western Bavarian priest who has edited Henri Massis's *Defence of the West* in German'.[93] Moenius was one of a group of staunchly pro-Western German Catholic thinkers, promoters of Romano-German symbiosis and the ideal of *Romanitas*. To such minds, Germany should abandon its historical refusal to join the Roman world and cease to vacillate between East and West. It should join *Romanitas*, which would immediately assure the pacification of Europe. Rome was the European solution to all questions.[94]

So Moenius was not alone. He was to become the editor of the *Allgemeine Rundschau* in 1929, a paper which had from the beginning of the decade emerged as 'one of the most important organs of South German federalism'.[95] In September 1923, its then editor Otto Kunze 'reasserted the guiding principles of the *Allgemeine Rundschau* as: "Catholic–Occidental–Greater German [*Großdeutsch*]."' Here is how he elaborated upon the second of these principles:

> Occidental: we fight against the catch cry of the 'Decline of the West'. Rome lies in the Occident, the focal point of Christendom. Rome and with it the Occident, will remain if it focuses itself upon Rome and permits the sources of its cultural life power, Catholic Christendom, once again to flow freely. All efforts which lead and advance the culture of the Occident in this manner will be attentively followed and enthusiastically supported. From here follows the struggle against Bolshevism in every form and disguise and further the representation of the Papal Peace Policy.[96]

Once he became its editor, Moenius continued and intensified the Western orientation of the *Allgemeine Rundschau*. He had already written extensively on the importance of *Romanitas* following his long sojourns in Italy and then France, where he frequented Charles Maurras's Action Française circles.[97] Besides the extended circle of intellectuals around the *Allgemeine Rundschau*, there were also the pro-Western Catholic intellectuals around the *Abendland* review.[98]

Even Massis acknowledged the efforts of 'le docteur H. Platz et ses collaborateurs d'*Abendland*'.⁹⁹

Nor were those who wished Germany to abandon antagonism to 'the West' all Catholic. The Protestant theologian Ernst Troeltsch made an important intervention in such debates when he tried to take stock of what had been happening in German history and what ought to be the Germans' attitude in 1922:

> Above the practical and temporary questions with which we are confronted to-day, there rises the theoretical and permanent problem of the difference between the German system of ideas—in politics, history and ethics—and that of western Europe and America. [...] The same contrast also appears, in an acute form, in our own internal political struggles. It supplies telling catchwords to those who seek to interpret the obvious fact of a real and practical struggle, between the different classes and interests in the nation, as a conflict of moral and theoretical principles [...]. *The designation of 'western' has thus come to be applied (as it is in Russia) to all movements in favour of democracy, or pacifism, or national self-determination, or a League of Nations, or the attainment of international understanding*; and such movements are then opposed to the specifically 'German' way of thought, with its historical and organic character. This is simply the old external contrast reappearing in a new and internal form; and it is applied by the very same means which were used by the propaganda of the Entente in the War. The war-cries which then divided the nations are being imported to-day into our midst.¹⁰⁰

Meanwhile, Troeltsch was not an admirer of Spengler: 'When we look at a book such as Spengler's *Decay of Civilisation*, which is fundamentally inspired by Nietzsche, and reflect on the enormous impression which it has made, we have to admit that the current is flowing in the opposite direction to that which has just been suggested.' (There is an error in the translation here: the original read, 'Ein Buch wie das Spenglersche Untergangsbuch';¹⁰¹ clearly by 'Spengler's Decline-book' Troeltsch was referring to *Der Untergand des Abendlandes*.) According to Troeltsch, Spengler's book was encouraging 'scepticism', 'amoralism', 'pessimism', 'belief in the policy of force', 'cynicism.' Inevitably, he considered it 'an absolute confirmation of the reproaches which western Europe brings against us.'¹⁰²

But that same year, 1922, perhaps the most spectacular manifestation of German conversion to 'the West' (or at least willingness to accept the inevitability of the defeat of 'resistance to Rome') came from none other than the very man who had most vociferously proclaimed the revolt against 'the West' in 1918. Though a certain ambiguousness was never entirely absent in his case, by 1922 Thomas Mann had decided to defend the Weimar Republic—and, along with it, Germany's belonging to the West. It was during that year that he wrote, 'A Russian writer [...] recently spoke about the fate that awaited intellectuals in his homeland, a tense and dangerous existence in a way *that we in the West can hardly imagine*' (and the word for 'West' that Mann used in German on this occasion was unequivocal: 'von der *wir im Westen* uns schwer eine Vorstellung machten').[103]

VIII. More Criticism of Massis; and Alternatives for Jazz-Age France

Massis's book was even being read and commented upon in an Italian prison in the year of its publication. Antonio Gramsci wrote to a correspondent on 8 August 1927,

> I was very disappointed by the highly touted book by Henri Massis, *Défense de l'Occident*. [...] What makes me laugh is the fact that this worthy Massis, who is terrified that the Asiatic ideology of Tagore and Gandhi may destroy the Catholic rationalism in France, is quite unaware that Paris has been colonized by Senegalese intellectuals and that the number of half-castes in France is increasing. It could be argued, as a joke, that, if Germany is the farthest outpost of Asiatic ideology, darkest Africa begins in France and the jazz band is the first molecule of a new Euro-African civilization.[104]

Gramsci may have been joking about the 'new Euro-African civilization', but others at that very time were coining terms representing similarly hyphenated civilisational syntheses. Around four months later, in December 1927, a Martinican classics student at the Sorbonne, Jane (Jeanne) Nardal (1902–1993), was writing to Alain Locke to ask for his permission to translate his 1925 *New Negro* collection into French. Wishing to convince the Afro-American professor of her credentials, she evoked her 'Afro-Latin' identity ('en ma qualité d'Afro-Latine') as enabling her to choose the excerpts that might best interest a francophone readership.[105] And a few weeks later Nardal was offering the new term 'Afro-Latinity' to the world in public. Neologisms are needed for new ideas, as she explicitly put it: 'À idées nouvelles, mots nouveaux, d'où la création significative des vocables: Afro-Américains, Afro-Latins.' (For new ideas, new words [are required], and thus the meaningful creation of terms: Afro-Americans,

Afro-Latins).[106] Nardal did not recommend biological assimilation, but rather acculturation within a context of colony–metropole migration.[107]

Jane Nardal's thought and her proposal for the celebration of an Afro-Latin identity had been galvanised by the publication and, as we saw, surprising success in 1921, of the novel *Batouala*, by the (also Martinican) René Maran. In a book published a year after Nardal's article, in 1929, René Gillouin included an essay expressing his objection to the award in 1921 of the prestigious Prix Goncourt to that novel, whose preface had been strongly critical of the French empire.[108] The first essay in Gillouin's book, however, which gave its name to the collection, was 'Le Destin de l'Occident', and this was dedicated to an attack on Massis, as the most typical example of a fashionable tendency that Gillouin found unpalatable. Gillouin was, like Massis, conservative, but, unlike Massis, he was a French Protestant. The people he labels 'nos néomédiévistes' (our neo-medievalists) rejected the Renaissance, the Reformation and the Revolution *en bloc* and completely. They thought that the modern world had gone wrong simply by dint of breaking with the eternally valid principles of the Middle Ages. (He included Paul Claudel and Jacques Maritain, as well as Massis, in this category). What such authors had in common was their passionate hatred of Protestantism. But 'la fureur antiprotestante' was not the only 'psychosis' of the French *néomédiévistes*. It was doubled by their 'fureur antigermanique' (which they confounded with their other psychosis, he added, 'as they reduce the whole of Germany to Luther'.). Gillouin emphasised that it was because of the excessive popularity of Massis's book (and the fact that a hot-headed younger generation had made of that 'philosophy' its bible), that he had to underline its weaknesses. By far the greatest of these was the arbitrariness with which it defined 'the West', in a way that excluded Protestantism (which represented 'in number, half, and in power, three and a half quarters' of those who actually belonged to the West).[109]

Gillouin then offered his own definition and analysis of what the West was, and his vision of its past and future. The West was based on three traditions: a scientific, philosophical, aesthetic and moral tradition of Hellenic origin; a juridical and political tradition of Roman origin; and a religious tradition of Hebraic origin. Certainly, there were tensions between these three sources, but the tension was conducive to the strength of 'our civilization'. And turning the tables against the pessimism that he had accused Massis and the other Catholics of spreading, Gillouin claimed that the current crisis was perhaps a blessing in disguise, offering a major opportunity for the West.[110]

IX. 'A new West, [...] by an act of further creation'

Meanwhile, in Britain, the highly idiosyncratic artist-philosopher Wyndham Lewis (1882–1957) published in 1929 a highly idiosyncratic book entitled *Paleface: The Philosophy of the 'Melting-Pot'*.[111] A section in the latter part of the book bore the title 'What Is "the West"?' There Lewis wrote against 'a belief, or prejudice, that you cannot be a good plastic artist and at the same time "a good European"'. In his opinion, '[i]t would be an important step in the reform and rejuvenation of our beliefs if we could overcome such prejudices'. Thus, '[t]he appreciation of the formal beauties of Mexican pottery, for instance, does not in any way involve enthusiasm for Mexican gods'; which was why he ranged himself, he went on, 'in some sense, with the modern scholastic teachers'. This did not, however, 'at all mean that I share their historical prejudices, any more than it means that I share their dogmas'. As he elaborated, '"Classical" is for me *anything* which is nobly defined and exact, as opposed to that which is fluid—of the Flux—without outline, romantically "dark", vague, "mysterious", stormy, uncertain.' Lewis entitled the next section of his book 'The Necessity for a New Conception of "the West", and of "the Classical"'. There he explained that '[t]he opposition, as it is understood here, is not between the Roman Cult and Aristotle on the one hand, and the "modernist" disorder of Nineteenth Century "romantic", "revolutionary", European thought, on the other.' Rather, it was 'a universal opposition; and the seeds of the naturalist mistakes are certainly to be found precisely in Greece'. He believed that instead 'we should use the *Classical* Orient (using this distinction in the sense of Guénon) to rescue us at length from that far-reaching tradition'.[112] But Lewis's most interesting argument comes next:

> 'European' does not mean for me a fixed historical thing, for it is so little that, in any case, if you tried to make of Gaelic chivalry and Italian science, German music and Norse practical enterprise, *one* thing, that would be a strange monster. Which is demonstrated by Mr. Massis in his *Défense de l'Occident*, where his 'West' is confined to the Latin soil. This is an evasion only of the problem. It is just against that separatism as between the different segments of the West that we have to contend. We should have—should we not?—our local melting-pot.

The upshot was a radical proposal on Lewis's part: 'It is *a new West*, as it were, that we have to envisage.' A new West 'that, we may hope, has learnt something from its recent gigantic reverses. For it is only by a fresh effort that the Western

World can save itself: it can only become "the West" at all, in fact, in that way, by an act of further creation.' He elaborated upon how that 'act of further creation' might be feasible. There were 'a great many common traditions and memories and considerable consanguinity: that is the "material", at least, for one "West". And yet, as things were in his time, 'not only such people as Spengler, but also (but with better motives, and perhaps inevitably) the catholic thinkers and the best of the "patriots", insist on regarding the problem historically, in terms of a rigid arrest'. As a result,

> 'The West' is for almost all of those a *finished* thing, either over whose decay they gloat, or whose corpse they frantically "defend". It never seems to occur to them that the exceedingly novel conditions of life today demand an entirely new conception: in that respect they are firmly on the side of those people who would thrust us back into the medieval chaos and barbarity.[113]

X. The Sufi Convert on East and West: René Guénon/ Abd al-Wāḥid Yaḥyá and Traditionalism

We have seen Max Rychner in *The Criterion* referring to 'the writings of René Guénon' as evidence that the 'turning to the East' affected the whole of Europe. And we have just seen Wyndham Lewis referring to 'the *Classical* Orient (using this distinction in the sense of Guénon)'. Around that same time, in autumn 1927, T. S. Eliot was reading some of the Frenchman's books and recommending them to others.[114] René Guénon (1886–1951), who was to end his days as Abd al-Wāḥid Yaḥyá, and as a Muslim convert in Egypt, held an important place in the study of the East and its religions in the interwar years. Even if his claim to be the only person who explained the East to the West may indicate that a surfeit of modesty was not his greatest failing,[115] his role was remarkable.[116] In his book *East and West*, published in 1924, Guénon declared that he was 'not attacking the West in itself, but only, which is quite different, the modern outlook, in which we see the cause of the West's intellectual ruin'. In his opinion, 'nothing would be more desirable [. . .] than the reconstitution of a truly western civilization on normal foundations, for the diversity of the civilizations, which has always existed, is the natural outcome of the mental differences which characterize the races'. But 'diversity on the forms' did not exclude 'agreement on the principles'; and 'concord and harmony do not mean uniformity'. He then declared that a 'normal civilization' would 'always be able to develop itself without being a danger to other civilizations'. It would 'not create any antagonism', because it would 'not have any pretension towards taking the lead, and because it [would] abstain from all proselytizing.'117

In the year Massis's *Defense* was published in book form, 1927, Guénon was complaining that much of what he had written in *East and West* three years earlier had been misrepresented, and he had to come back to some of the same issues. He insisted that it was the West that was aggressively taking over the rest of the world and destroying cultures, not the other way round (as Massis had recently claimed). According to Guénon, none of the 'moralistic pretexts' routinely evoked could 'gainsay that Western encroachment is the encroachment of materialism'. And it was 'extraordinary' that the very moment when Western encroachment was penetrating everywhere 'is the moment chosen by some people to raise a cry against the peril [...] of a supposed infiltration of Eastern ideas into the West'. A 'recently-published book by Henri Massis entitled *Défense de l'Occident*' was 'one of the most characteristic manifestations of this frame of mind'. According to Guénon, it was 'a book full of confusion and contradiction'. Massis had attributed to the East all sorts of unfounded conceptions, and based them on 'quotations taken from certain more or less "official" orientalists, in which the Eastern doctrines are—as usually happens—deformed to the point of caricature'. Pointedly, Guénon also asked Massis (a fellow traditionalist) 'whether he really considers it advisable to attack tradition abroad while striving to restore it at home.'118

Here Guénon introduced a footnote, in which he declared, 'We know that Massis is not unacquainted with our works, but he carefully avoids making the least allusion to them, since they would tell against his thesis.'119 Guénon argued that among the 'propagandists' of Eastern ideas in the West that Massis had in mind, he could distinguish two groups, and the first of them he saw as 'exclusively composed of Westerners'. And, like Eliot, he took exception to the all-inclusiveness of Massis's 'East': 'to see Germans and Russians included among the representatives of the Eastern outlook would be truly ludicrous, if it were not a sign of the most deplorable ignorance of all that concerns the East'. As for the second group, Guénon noted that one found in it several of the people he had earlier called 'Westernized Easterners'. In Guénon's view, such people were 'as ignorant of Eastern ideas as are the first group, and they would therefore be quite incapable of spreading them in the West even should they wish to do so'. They were 'a danger only to the East, and not to the West, of which they are a mere reflection.'120

Guénon stressed that the reason why he made an exception to his rule of not referring to individuals in order to quote Massis was that Massis represented 'a part of the contemporary mentality, a part that must be taken into account in the present study of the state of the modern world'. He elaborated: 'How can this low-grade and to a large extent artificial traditionalism, with its narrow horizons and lack of understanding, offer any real and effective resistance to an outlook, so many of whose prejudices it shares?' That 'inadequate reaction' was of no other interest than that it showed 'a certain dissatisfaction with the present state of things among some of our contemporaries'.[121] Guénon was not entirely inconsistent in evincing a certain sympathy for Massis, despite his criticisms. They did share a deep antipathy to modernity.[122]

Guénon's battle with Massis was significant because, in an important sense, it was a civil war between traditionalists who both rejected materialism, secularism and the other accompanying traits of modernity. Guénon promoted *philosophia perennis* and insisted that it was less important which religion one professed than that one professed a traditional religion—and his own choice for Islam, once he was in Egypt, was simply a practical one, he insisted. He believed strongly in the role of an initiated elite that would elaborate and promote the fundamental traditional principles. His influence has been far-reaching, and continues to increase today. The availability of all his books in English translation (from a publishing house named Sophia Perennis) and in open-access editions, is interesting and probably not by chance. He is widely considered to be one of the major inspirations behind contemporary influential figures, from Steve Bannon (Donald Trump's former adviser and speech writer) to Aleksandr Dugin, Vladimir Putin's purported ideological guru.[123] We will see in chapter 9 that the controversial French novelist Michel Houellebecq has noticed him as well.

XI. Defence of the West Continued: the 1930s and the Clouds of War

Meanwhile, Massis continued to plead the same cause. While being as anti-German as it gets, he and his *Revue universelle* began displaying more and more admiration for Italian Fascism. It was, after all, a 'Latin' movement. And the matter became seriously controversial when Mussolini's Italy invaded Ethiopia. Ethiopia, being a member of the League of Nations, received support from the League, and sanctions were imposed on Italy. Massis used his skills, again, to organise like-minded intellectuals. And the irresistible title was invoked, once again, in a manifesto 'pour la défense de l'Occident', authored by Massis himself. A counter-manifesto of the left followed, as well as a different one by other Catholic intellectuals.[124] Eliot and *The Criterion* took notice, though more discreetly than during the previous decade (no names were mentioned).[125] It may not be coincidental that, that same year, the British diplomat Gladwyn Jebb christened his solution to Britain's defence challenges 'The Defence of the West'.[126] It is even more telling that in a related memorandum Jebb used French to conclude, 'This is what is meant by the "Défense de l'Occident"'.[127] Massis's watchword (though not necessarily his recipe to achieve the desired outcome) had crossed several borders.

The language of 'Western civilisation' and the distinction between West and East were also employed in relation to theories on, and attitudes towards, the role of the state in the 1930s, and not least by the ubiquitous Walter Lippmann. In the middle of the decade Lippmann was warning of the major threat posed by an importation 'alien to western civilization'. That was 'the idea that the security and happiness and glory of the individual man are to be found in surrendering to the compulsion of mass feeling and the domination of omnipotent states'. According to his reading of history, Lippmann continued, that idea was 'native in the eastern world' and had 'inspired the long series of oriental despotisms from the Egyptian Pharaohs to the present day'. Like Massis, Lippmann saw the main danger as coming from semi-Eastern Russia and Germany: 'It was in this borderland that bolshevism and fascism appeared. They are two sprouts from the same stem.' Though they employed 'some of the same apparatus of western civilization, in their essence they are nothing but another manifestation of the ancient despotism of the east'. To his mind, such ideas were 'alien to western civilization' and had been 'rejected by the genius of all those from Socrates through St. Thomas Aquinas to the English and French and American thinkers who have made articulate the western way of life'.[128]

Meanwhile, it was not just in France that Hitler's rise to power raised problems for groups on the right. Eliot's *Criterion* was only one small part of this story. A number of influential and vociferous British conservatives, grouped around a monthly edited by Douglas Jerrold, *The English Review*, had built very strong ties with German counterparts in the 1920s and early 1930s. Not all of them were able to maintain such links as the nature of the Nazis' domestic activities and foreign policies became increasingly clear.[129] For the Nazis were taking things too far. In 1938, the exiled Hungarian philosopher Aurel Kolnai published his passionate condemnation of the Nazi onslaught on 'the West', entitled *The War against the West*.[130] Kolnai, of Jewish origins, had converted to Catholicism a decade earlier and was an Austrian citizen, but had to leave Austria in 1937 due to the Nazi danger. Employing a strategy similar to that adopted during the First World War by John Jay Chapman, he assembled an astonishing number of statements by academics, intellectuals and politicians of the Third Reich (or close sympathisers) to show that theirs was a deliberate assault on 'the West' and what it stood for. Kolnai's book did not meet the academic standards of another exile from *Mitteleuropa*, Harvard's Professor Carl J. Friedrich,[131] but in the main thrust of his argument about the anti-Westernism and anti-Romanism of most Nazi sympathisers he clearly had a point.

XII. Conclusion

The aftermath of the Great War witnessed a veritable explosion of commentary on the future (and past) of 'the West' and 'Western civilisation'. Virtually all had something to say about Spengler's best-selling book, not least the main message conveyed by its title. The West was perceived to be in terminal decline—though most commentators missed the difference between long decline and imminent death that Spengler had posited in his book. One of the two most sustained developments of this period was surely the new assertiveness of people from marginalised groups, who witnessed a collapse of both the cultural prestige and the perception of invincibility surrounding 'the West' in the midst of a war of unprecedented destructiveness.

The other major development was an enhancement of the established perception of Russia as alien and non-Western, now seriously reinforced in the eyes of many by the new Bolshevik regime and its choices. It may be fitting here to add one more striking case of a thinker viewing Russia as the very antithesis of 'the West' in the interwar years: that of the German jurist Carl Schmitt. Overlooked by most of the ever-expanding scholarship on Schmitt (overshadowed, no doubt, by his notorious anti-Jewish focus), Schmitt's fear of Russia was overwhelming—and echoed similar fears expressed by two of his main intellectual heroes, Joseph de Maistre and Juan Donoso Cortés. (In fact, one of the things Schmitt praised emphatically in his essays on Donoso Cortés was that the Spaniard realised in the middle of the nineteenth century that a new enemy of European civilisation had appeared: the possible union of revolutionary socialism and Russian politics ('Jetzt erscheint ein neuer Feind der europäischen Zivilisation: die Möglichkeit einer Verbindung von revolutionären Sozialismus und russischer Politik.')[132]

Schmitt began an important 1929 lecture in Barcelona with the portentous statement,

> We in Central Europe live 'sous l'oeil des Russes'. For a century their psychological gaze has seen through our great words and institutions. Their vitality is strong enough to seize our knowledge and technology as weapons. Their

prowess in rationalism and its opposite, as well as their potential for good and evil in orthodoxy, is overwhelming. They have realised the union of Socialism and Slavism, which already in 1848 Donoso Cort[é]s said would be the decisive event of the next century.[133]

(It is noteworthy that, writing in 1929, Schmitt referred to the Russians' gaze 'for a century'—that is, since the 1820s, precisely when, as we have seen, anxiety about Russia was increasing, leading to calls for a united 'West'.) Some years earlier, in 1923, Schmitt had concluded his idiosyncratic book on the political role of Catholicism with some even more idiosyncratic remarks on the Russianness of Bakunin, and on the Westernness or Marx and Engels, as explaining the vehemence with which the latter two rejected Bakunin (as well as the Silesian—and to that extent 'Eastern'—Ferdinand Lassalle).[134] He also commented that, since the nineteenth century, there had been 'two great masses to whom the traditions and culture of Western Europe are absolutely foreign, two mighty torrents lashing against their embankments—the proletariat of the great cities with their class antagonism, and the Russian element turning its back more and more on Europe'. In Schmitt's opinion, from the point of view of 'traditional Western civilisation', both were 'barbarian, and where they display a self-conscious sense of power they even pride themselves on being barbarian. That they met on Russian soil in the Russian Soviet has its profound justification in the history of ideas.' The whole book was a reflection on the past role of Catholicism as underpinning the ideal political order, and in the final paragraph Schmitt asserted his belief that 'in that skirmish of Bakunin's the Catholic Church and the Catholic conception of humanity were on the side of Thought and Western European civilisation.'[135]

Around the same time (1923) Schmitt was similarly writing in *Die geistesgeschichtliche Lage des heutigen Parlamentarismus* of 'the Russian hatred for the complication, artificiality, and intellectualism of Western European civilization'. He also stressed that the myth of class consciousness was transformed, when it travelled from west to east, into a Russian nationalism that rejected 'West European intellectualism'. As a result, 'Russia again could be Russian, Moscow again the capital, and the Europeanized upper classes who held their own land in contempt could be exterminated. Proletarian use of force had made Russia Muscovite again.'[136]

Nor was the comment on Lassalle as 'Eastern' in the eyes of the 'Westerners' Marx and Engels, because Lassalle was from Silesia, a merely casual observation. Schmitt had a keen sense of his own Westernness or 'proper Europeanness' compared to East Prussian Germans at that time. 'The city is very interesting,' he wrote to a friend about Berlin, 'but it is not in Europe. As someone from the Mosel, I cannot get over that fact.' And still in January 1933 he was writing, 'This Berlin is a vacuum between East and West.'[137] References to 'the dichotomy between the West and the East' or 'a deep opposition between East and West', which 'runs right across the middle of Germany, halfway through Germany's heart', are ubiquitous in his writings and interviews throughout his life.[138] As for 'Eastern' Russia, in his 1927 essay 'Donoso Cortés in Berlin', Schmitt stressed that the task was 'to save Europe from the Russian danger' and to form, despite all inner differences, a unifying European alliance against the 'enemy of European civilization'.[139] (It may come as no surprise to readers of chapter 2 above that elsewhere Schmitt praised Auguste Comte as 'a man endowed with great historical intuition'.)[140]

Now, considering how Russia was spoken of by the two most influential authors discussed in this chapter, Spengler and Massis, as well as by Carl Schmitt (and countless others), it becomes obvious that the following statement by a sophisticated historian, made in 1952, was hardly accurate:

> In viewing Russia as a nation [...] with a destiny separate from that of Western Europe, Spengler's theory [...] is far more likely to find a sympathetic hearing today [1952] than it was at the time Spengler originally conceived it. *Then most educated Europeans simply assumed that Russia belonged to the West.*[141]

Both the present chapter, and this book more broadly, should serve as a corrective to such sweeping statements. For most of the time between the 1820s and today, it clearly cannot be stated with such certainty that 'most educated Europeans simply assumed that Russia belonged to the West'. However, one of the short periods that could be said to constitute a partial exception was a few years in the mid-1940s; and that was as a result of the prestige the Soviet Union gained due to its role in defeating Hitler during the Second World War. To that war we now turn.

7

The Second World War and Ideas of 'the West'

'The task of Britain and France is to assert the tested values of Western civilization, and to give new life to its cultural inheritance from Greece and Rome, from Christianity and from modern science. The sharpness of the Nazi threat has shown that this inheritance cannot be defended as a static ideal, but must be given fresh and dynamic expression.'

'AFTER THE WAR: ANOTHER CHANCE TO REBUILD THE FOUNDATIONS OF FEDERALISM', *THE TIMES*, 3 NOVEMBER 1939

'This retribution [...] which operates automatically to penalize the abuse of force, was the main subject of Greek thought. It is the soul of the epic. Under the name of Nemesis, it functions as the mainspring of Aeschylus's tragedies. To the Pythagoreans, to Socrates and Plato, it was the jumping-off point of speculation upon the nature of man and the universe. Wherever Hellenism has penetrated, we find the idea of it familiar. In Oriental countries which are steeped in Buddhism, it is perhaps this Greek idea that has lived on under the name of Kharma. The Occident, however, has lost it, and no longer even has a word to express it in any of its languages: conceptions of limit, measure, equilibrium, which ought to determine the conduct of life are, in the West, restricted to a servile function in the vocabulary of technics. We are only geometricians of matter; the Greeks were, first of all, geometricians in their apprenticeship to virtue.'

SIMONE WEIL, 'THE *ILIAD* OR THE POEM OF FORCE' [1940] (TRANSLATED BY MARY MCCARTHY [1945]), IN WEIL, *SIMONE WEIL: AN ANTHOLOGY*, PP. 182–215, AT P. 195

IT WAS INEVITABLE that there would be much talk of 'the West' or 'Western civilisation' during the Second Word War. The initially clear moral dichotomy between Western democracies and totalitarian regimes that the Molotov–Ribbentrop Pact of 1939 had resulted in was blurred once Hitler invaded the Soviet Union in 1941 and the latter turned into an ally of the Western democracies. Meanwhile, the rapid fall of France in the summer of 1940 evoked remarkable expressions of sympathy from all sorts of quarters, in agreement that France was 'indispensable to [...] Western civilization'. Within France itself there were intense debates as to the merits of 'Western' versus 'European' civilisation; for one factor adding to the timeliness of references to 'the West' and 'Western civilisation' was that the Nazis used 'Europe' as their watchword, and proclaimed that they were aiming to create a 'New Europe'. That confronted even collaborating French intellectuals with painful dilemmas—to say nothing of those who were opposed to the Nazis. And on the other side of the English Channel, French thinkers such as Simone Weil and Raymond Aron had strong views as to how postwar Europe ought to relate to 'the West'. In America, meanwhile, the 'Atlantic Community' was being promoted and redefined not only by Henry Luce and his highly influential magazines, but even more by the man who had coined the term already during the First World War, Walter Lippmann. At the same time Alain Locke was proposing the application of democratic principles to the whole of the postwar world irrespective of 'race' or 'colour', and castigating the internal sins of the 'Achilles of the West', whose heel would prove fatal if racial equality were not imminently implemented. Clearly, the future of 'Western civilisation' was to be the subject of intense contemplation at the war's end.

I. 'Western civilization will be saved.' Or Was 'the prevailing education [...] destroying it'?

After France and Britain declared war on Germany in September 1939, following the latter's invasion of Poland, the French Catholic theologian Jacques Maritain published a short article, 'To My American Friends', in the US Catholic magazine *Commonweal*. He explained there that, earlier, he and his American friends had been asking each other 'what could be the destiny of Europe,' and sometimes they wondered 'if Western civilization, our common Christian civilization,' finding itself 'caught between two equally monstrous forms of slavery and scorn for the human conscience—the totalitarianism of the Communist State and the totalitarianism of the racist State—could withstand the forces of spiritual disintegration which threatened it'. He now had an answer: 'Well, the thing which I want to say at once and that I want to cry from the house tops is that the spiritual situation of Europe has completely changed and that the salvation of Europe has begun.' Now he was 'absolutely convinced that Western civilization will be saved. To be more precise, it is already saved.' He knew that the price would be 'mass sacrifice' and 'torrents of blood', but he also knew 'that this night is not a night of despair but a night of resurrection'. What led him to say that 'the spiritual situation of Europe has completely changed' had been the Russo-German alliance. That alliance had 'completed the unmasking of the enemy'. For a long time people had been asking themselves whether they were 'not forced to choose between Communism and Hitlerism'. As a result, following the '"principle of the lesser evil," falsely applied', many crimes had been excused. The illusion had now been dispelled.[1]

On 14 November 1939 Walter Lippmann was writing to Maritain, 'Your article in the *Commonweal*, written when the war began [...] seemed to me profoundly right and I myself have no doubt that, in your meaning of the words, western European civilization has already been saved.' One could see that even in America, Lippmann noted. 'For however much the Hitler-Stalin agreement may have complicated the diplomatic and military problems of the world, it has enormously simplified and clarified the spiritual problem.' The Allies were 'lucky that their negotiations with Russia failed' and the reason, their 'refusal to betray the Polish and Baltic peoples', was most commendable. In the United States that outcome had had 'a very important practical result as well'. Lipmann seriously doubted 'whether the arms embargo would have been repealed had Russia been signed as an ally of France and Great Britain'; because, in such a case, 'those of us who favored repeal would have found it almost impossible to convince the people of this country that there was any deep moral difference between the warring powers'.[2]

Lippmann mentioned himself as one of those in America 'who favored repeal' of the arms embargo. While Congress was debating repeal, that same November 1939, the Soviet Union demanded of Finland that it cede to them bases and territory along the Finnish-Soviet frontier. Finland refused. The Russians moved troops to the border and threatened to seize the Finnish bases. In his 'Today & Tomorrow' column on 10 December 1939, Lippmann declared, 'Here in the making is one of the most dreadful catastrophes which has menaced Western civilization since the armed might of Islam invaded Europe.' The Finns might have to fight and by so doing would be 'resisting the advance of another Genghis Khan'. Lippmann urged German conservatives to purge themselves of the Nazis 'so that Germany could return to its natural role as "defender of the West" against Eastern barbarism'.[3]

In a book he published in March 1940, Lippmann wrote that this was '*a civil war of the western world* resulting from the anarchy which has followed the breakdown of the centers of authority and order'. That anarchy would continue, and it would 'expand and become even more destructive, unless there is forged in the fires of the war itself—under the pressure of necessity and in the mood of heroic devotion—the hard core of an enduring union.'[4] He was to elaborate during the rest of the war upon what that enduring union would look like. Meanwhile, he was soon to express even darker thoughts on the deeper roots of the 'civil war of the western world'. In a lecture he delivered at the annual meeting of the American Association for the Advancement of Science, on 29 December 1940, he propounded 'a thesis about the state of education in this troubled age'. His thesis was that 'during the past forty or fifty years those who are responsible for education have progressively removed from the curriculum of studies the Western culture which produced the modern democratic state'. As a result, 'deprived of their cultural tradition', Western men who received their education recently no longer possessed 'the ideas, the premises, the rationale, the logic, the method, the values or the deposited wisdom which are the genius of the development of Western civilization'. It was part of his thesis, further, that 'the prevailing education is destined, if it continues, to destroy Western civilization and is in fact destroying it'. All that meant that 'our civilization cannot effectively be maintained where it still flourishes, or be restored where it has been crushed, without the revival of the central, continuous, and perennial culture of the Western world'.[5]

It was a 'plain fact' in Lippmann's judgement, that 'the graduates of the modern schools are the actors in the catastrophe which has befallen our civilization'. Lippmann accepted that he had to 'define and identify' what he meant by 'Western culture'. The 'institutions we cherish—and now know we must defend against the most determined and efficient attack ever organized against them' were, he emphasised, 'the products of a culture which, as [Étienne] Gilson put it, "is essentially the culture of Greece, inherited from the Greeks by the Romans, transfused by the Fathers of the Church with the religious teachings of Christianity"' and subsequently 'progressively enlarged by countless numbers of artists, writers, scientists and philosophers from the beginning of the Middle Ages up to the first third of the nineteenth century'. The authors of the American Constitution and the Bill of Rights had been educated 'in schools and colleges in which the classic works of this culture were the substance of the curriculum'. Modern education, however, was based on 'a denial that it is necessary or useful or desirable for the schools and colleges to continue to transmit from generation to generation the religious and classical culture of the Western world'. It rejected and excluded from the curriculum 'the whole religious tradition of the West'. And it 'abandons and neglects as no longer necessary the study of the whole classical heritage of the great works of great men'. Lippmann's main target was now identified: the vacuum was filled with 'the elective, eclectic, the specialized, the accidental and incidental improvisations and spontaneous curiosities of teachers and students'. There was 'no common faith, no common body of principle, no common body of knowledge, no common moral and intellectual discipline'. The school had inevitably ended up being 'a mere training ground for personal careers. Its object must then be to equip individual careerists and not to form fully civilized men'.[6]

The former philosophy assistant to George Santayana at Harvard came at last to his crucial point: 'In abandoning the classical religious culture of the West the schools have ceased to affirm the central principle of the Western philosophy of life—that man's reason is the ruler of his appetites'; they had 'reduced reason to the role of servant of man's appetites'. It had been that 'specialized and fundamentally distorted development of knowledge which [had] turned so much of man's science into the means of his own destruction'. Lippmann wound up by urging the rationale and the need for a tradition, given that 'what enables men to know more than their ancestors is that they start with a knowledge of what their ancestors have already learned'. A society could be 'progressive' only if it conserved its tradition. 'In developing knowledge men must collaborate with their ancestors. Otherwise they must begin, not where their ancestors arrived but where their ancestors began.'[7]

II. A 'tear for France'

Meanwhile, during that fateful year of 1940, some three weeks after the fall of France, Walter Lippmann advised his American readers in his column that 'in the misfortune of France it should be our fierce pride to be the last to forget the greatness of France'. Americans 'must wish to be the first to remember [...] that France is indispensable, as indispensable to the maturity of Western civilization as Hellas was to its birth—and as imperishable'.[8]

Lippmann was far from alone. We have already seen (in chapters 5 and 6) that even among fierce critics of European empires, France was seen as special. Lawrence D. Reddick, Afro-American curator of the Schomburg Center in Harlem, published a poem in *The Crisis* in August 1940, reflecting on the new war in Europe and the fall of the great powers:

In a few days
>Holland was gone,
>Belgium was gone,
>France was gone,
>English doom seems near.
I can not shed a tear for Holland.
>I remember the Dutch East India.
>I remember how the Boer drove my people into the earth.
I can not shed a tear for Belgium. [...]
I can not shed a tear for England. [...]
I shed *one* tear for France.
>For tho she like the rest wrung sweat from blood
>Yet never did she preach that men be brutes or insist
>>upon it.⁹

And when the Trinidadian Pan-Africanist George Padmore claimed, also in an article in *The Crisis*, that examples of brutality could indeed be found in the French empire, the Martinican Louis Achille (cousin of Jane and Paulette Nardal, and a long-time member of their salon in Paris, but by this time living in the United States) felt the need to defend France. In a contribution to the June 1940 issue of the magazine, he started by trying to be pragmatic, but he also wanted to stress that he, Padmore and *The Crisis* all themselves belonged to the civilisation that was under scrutiny:

> First, so far as colonization is concerned, it is too late to prevent French imperialism: the conquest and colonization of Africa is a historical fact. Western civilization, with its search for material power and wealth, has exposed this whole planet to a general hunt for raw material destined for man's alternating comfort and destruction. Woe to those peoples that are rich in natural resources but weak in defensive power! This has been the predominant trend in the history of this Western civilization of which Mr. Padmore and I, and *The Crisis*, are a part.¹⁰

But the Catholic Martinican thinker wanted to make a much stronger case for the French empire. Students of colonisation were 'usually economists, sociologists or historians', and they tended to 'ignore or belittle the important moral and spiritual factors that enter into it'. If they had been 'philosophers, psychologists or moralists, they would less often characterize colonization exclusively as an economic, political and military exploitation'. This bias was 'particularly dangerous and misleading in the case of a nation such as France, whose life, literature and civilization are so rich in spiritual contents':

> French colonization has done much more than exploit natural resources and put the natives to work; it has awakened in their consciences the dignity of the human personality, slumbering under the spell of ancestral traditions often exacting and totalitarian; it has invited them, originally by force, to enter into the modern civilized world of the automobile and the radio, by the regal road of French democracy where man is most respected regardless of his race, and adopt as their own a legion of heroes, from Vercingetorix to Pasteur, not to mention Joan of Arc and Voltaire. Forced into this empire, now the colonial peoples want to remain parts of it, with a loyalty that defies economic 'laws' and speaks highly of their feeling for the greatest values of human life. Often their wholehearted devotion to France's national heroes and glories is an inspiration to the French who have become blasé about them. This, a foreign observer can seldom notice and appreciate at its real value. A spirit cannot be seen or explained: it must be felt and learned by personal experience. The family spirit of the French empire escapes the stranger, often not without puzzling and tantalizing him.[11]

When, four years later, Paris was liberated, *Life* magazine declared, 'Paris is like a magic sword in a fairy tale—a shining power in those hands to which it rightly belongs, in other hands tinsel and lead.' 'Whenever the City of Light changes hands,' the editorial proceeded, 'Western civilization shifts its political balance. So it has been for seven centuries; so it was in 1940; so it was last week.' Unsurprisingly, then, '[t]he civilized world went wild with joy when Paris was freed. Paris is the second capital of every nation.'[12] That same year, the British politician Sir Edward Grigg was writing that 'the West can never be safe against Germany without loyalty to its cause in its central citadel, which is France.'[13] The following year Hannah Arendt, writing in the *Partisan Review*, was to be found explaining to her American readers that, in the midst of the catastrophes and evident inadequacy of the nation states, the European resistance movements coalesced surprisingly rapidly towards 'a positive political slogan which plainly indicated the non-national though very popular character of the new struggle. That slogan was simply EUROPE.' And the 'centre of gravity' for all these fighters of resistance movements was 'France, the country which has truly been, culturally as well as politically, the heart of Europe for centuries and whose more recent contributions to political thought have again put her *at the spiritual head of Europe*'. In that connection it was, she argued, 'more than significant that the liberation of Paris was celebrated in Rome with more enthusiasm than even its own liberation; and that the message of the Dutch Resistance to the French Forces of the Interior after the liberation of Paris concluded with the words "So long as France lives, Europe will not die."[14]

Clearly, from the beginning to the end of the Second World War, people around the world felt that France was special to 'Western civilisation'. But France was defeated in that summer of 1940, and had to live under direct German occupation in parts of the country, or under a collaborationist regime based in Vichy in the south. What was the fate of 'the West' and 'Western civilisation' among those experiencing the war in France?

III. *Guerres franco–françaises* under Occupation: *Civilisation européenne* or *Civilisation occidentale*?

The reader who followed the discussion of the Massis affair in the previous chapter may not be too surprised to learn that, in the essays and articles published in occupied and Vichy-ruled France from early 1941, a cleavage occurred between uses of 'Europe' and 'West' as between defenders of 'European civilisation' and of 'Western civilisation' respectively.[15] The German victors were promoting the idea of a 'New Europe' dominated by themselves.[16] The Maurrasian *Revue universelle* had now moved to Vichy, and, while supporting the Vichy regime, it was against collaborationism with the Germans—who, as we have seen, were never popular with Latino-Mediterranianists such as Maurras and Massis in the first place. As of the beginning of 1941 the *Revue universelle* started featuring articles by the influential Swiss historian Gonzague de Reynold (1880–1970).[17] In an early example entitled 'Qu'est-ce que l'Europe?', he left no doubt where he stood when he concluded, 'The European Europe, the original Europe, is the West. Thus, when we speak of European civilization, we must mean by that, exclusively, Western civilization.'[18] That civilisation had its roots in the Mediterranean, according to de Reynold. The thesis advanced in this article received wide publicity in the pages of *Le Temps* and *Le Figaro*, before appearing in a longer form as a book a few months later. De Reynold was not the only author at that time to broach this 'far from innocent subject'.[19] A great number of related articles followed.[20]

André Siegfried (1875–1959) was one of the most prominent figures in French life and thought for some decades with regard to matters of national identities, national characteristics and civilisational comparisons and definitions.[21] That 'Western civilisation' or 'the West' appears in the titles of around a dozen of his works between the 1930s and 1950s makes him particularly relevant here.[22] Among other things, in 1941 Siegfried wrote a long article in the *Revue des deux mondes* entitled 'La Civilisation occidentale'.[23] He began by stating, 'Western civilisation, mistress of the world [maîtresse du monde], is juxtaposed to rival civilisations, which may tomorrow contest its supremacy.' He offered a history of what he called Western civilisation. It was possible for a long time, he noted, to merge, in the same association of ideas, 'Europe', 'the white race (at least the most important part of the white race)' and 'Western civilisation'. That was the case until the great discoveries. After white people dispersed in the world, beginning in the fifteenth century, the two expressions 'Europe' and 'Western civilization' ceased to be synonyms. North America even became such an important part of the Western system that one could ask oneself whether she was not to become its centre. Meanwhile, Asians were patiently planning their own course: 'Asia has never admired Western civilisation, but she has understood that our technology was placing her at the mercy of our power: it is in order to defend herself that she borrows it.' Asia thus calculated that she could doubly prevail, because she believed that she had preserved an integrity of a spiritual life that she was convinced the West did not possess.[24]

Siegfried is seen by some historians as incarnating the ambiguities whereby certain features of the republican tradition of the Third Republic produced some of the unpalatable traits of the Vichy regime in the early 1940s. Others defend him from such accusations.[25] Bernard Bruneteau in particular defends him from the charges brought against him most notably by Zeev Sternhell. The latter interpreted Siegfried's works during the German occupation as serving the purposes of the occupiers by highlighting the civilisational contributions of the European section of the 'white race'; whereas Bruneteau argues that Siegfired's definitions of 'the West' and 'Western civilisation' were designed precisely to mark a distance from the Nazis' 'New Europe'.[26] Notwithstanding the undeniably distasteful racial language used by Siegfried, a careful perusal of his works during the war justifies Bruneteau's view. In German-occupied France in September 1941, Siegfried's greatest worry was that 'the extra-European section of the white race live now in a geographical context whose structure no longer resembles that in which European civilisation was formed: that is the case in America, in Australia, in Africa'. In the United States, for example, the vast scale of the geographical environment was so disproportionate (*démesuré*) as to deprive Protagoras's famous saying about man as the measure of things of any sense. The prestige enjoyed by quantity in America was notorious, and came at the expense of the development of a civilisation of quality. 'A structure different from ours, involving an abandonment of the Mediterranean and Greek tradition, is being built.'[27] Meanwhile, the different climate was bound to modify the 'white race' established in new lands.

FIGURE 7.1. André Siegfried in 1910. Photographer unknown. *Source:* https://en.wikipedia.org/wiki/Andr%C3%A9_Siegfried#/media/File:Andr%C3%A9_Siegfried.jpg

'The Greek tradition has not crossed the Atlantic: the Americans are far from it, do not understand it; it is not for them a living principle.' Conformism was, in North America, 'a common attitude', befitting the instinctive tendencies of a regime that increasingly based itself on the directed masses.

But Siegfried had more immediate reasons to emphasise the danger in all this. It was an indirect way to hit out at the Nazis' 'New Europe'. Although Germany is nowhere mentioned by name, it was clearly the elephant in the room, and hence his concluding paragraph was brave, under the circumstances: Europe would orientate itself in a direction ever more similar to that of America if, united in its turn by a hegemonic master-power, it were to unite in a single *faisceau offensif* (attacking cluster) the dispersed forces that had hitherto maintained its fruitful diversity. 'As Macedonia led the whole of Greece in a war of revenge and conquest, but did so by making it lose a large part of its ancient personality', similarly, 'a militarisation, which would unify the Old Continent, would increase its force, but do so by transforming its old character'.[28] As we shall see in chapter 8 below, Siegfried would continue to fear and resent such transformations even after the Nazis were defeated (the suspected culprits subsequently being the Americans and the Russians).

IV. Europe between East and Extreme West: from Simone Weil to Albert Camus

Some French thinkers had fled and worked for General de Gaulle's Free French. Two of the most interesting, Simone Weil and Raymond Aron, found themselves eventually in London. Others, such as Albert Camus, found ways to join the Resistance, first in Algeria and Vichy territory, later in German-occupied Paris. Some had as well—like Siegfried—concerns about the 'Extreme West' during the war, as it turned out. Simone Weil (1909–1943) was a literally extraordinary philosopher. She stands out in many respects—and not just because she is widely seen as a kind of 'saint', on account of her biographical itinerary and the way in which she died. A number of religious experiences in the 1930s led to her adoption of a deep Christian faith, though she never joined the Catholic Church, which she thought suffered from being too 'Romanised' (an important problem and the source for her of baneful consequences).[29]

Besides her earnest research on different traditions of religious thought (she learned Sanskrit in order to study the *Bhagavad-Gita*, for instance), Weil had a profound interest in the classics and developed strong views with regard to the merits and demerits of the legacies of ancient Greece and Rome respectively.[30] Her metaphysical, theological, philosophical and political interests coalesced into some remarkable arguments on what was wrong with mainstream French patriotism, and led to her articulating an alternative, very different, type: patriotism as compassion for one's own country—as well as for everyone else's. That she did so most prominently in *L'Enracinement* (*The Need for Roots*), a report she had been asked to write for de Gaulle's Free French while she was working with them in England for the liberation of France, is one of the many manifestations of her indomitable courage and relentless honesty—de Gaulle was one of the most vociferous proponents of the idea of *la France eternelle*,[31] which Weil denounced passionately in her report. (That she was asked to write it as a diversion that might stop her from implementing her plan to be parachuted to occupied France to fight with the Resistance is further suggestive of her spirit.)[32]

One of Weil's many striking ideas was that what had gone wrong with French patriotism (and with the West more generally) was its adoption of the 'Roman' idea of glory: glory based on conquest and force.[33] Sadly for her, that meant that

FIGURE 7.2. Simone Weil. Photographer and date unknown. *Source:* https://en.wikipedia.org/wiki/Simone_Weil#/media/File:Simone_Weil_04_(cropped).png

French patriotism up to then had based itself on the same core idea as 'Hitlerism'. What France had done to the colonised peoples under its rule had been no better than what the Nazis were doing to the countries they had conquered in Europe. 'The fact is', she wrote in 1943, 'that Hitlerism consists in the application by Germany to the European continent [... of] colonial methods of conquest and domination.'[34] This is an idea now associated primarily with one of the leaders of the Négritude movement, Aimé Césaire, but Weil had articulated it a decade earlier.[35] She developed it in several essays and in *L'Enracinement*, but its most striking formulation can be found in an essay she wrote around the same time, in London, on 'The Colonial Question and the Destiny of the French People'. Weil castigated the treatment of colonised non-European peoples by the French empire and recommended a radical change in the relationship after the war. Returning to the status quo was not an option. And it would be sharing the logic of Hitler to discuss it as if it concerned only the French: 'The problem concerns [...] the whole world, and first and foremost the subject populations.'[36] Colonialism's greatest sin was to deprive the colonised peoples of their past, which was the worst thing anyone could do to anyone else—and the reason why (some of) the French were resisting the Germans at that very time.

Besides articulating some powerful and original arguments against colonialism, Weil connected the whole question to the relationship between East and West. She pointed out that 'Europe is situated like a kind of proportional mean between America and the East'; and, she warned, 'We know very well that after the war the Americanization of Europe will be a very grave danger, and we know very well what we would lose if that came about.' In fact, what Europeans would lose was 'that part of ourselves that is very close to the East'. Europeans looked upon Orientals, 'quite wrongly, as primitives and savages', and moreover told them so. Meanwhile, 'Orientals look on us, not without some reason, as barbarians, but they don't tell us'. And Europeans tended 'to see America as having no real civilization', while Americans believed Europeans to be 'primitives'. Yet, if an American, an Englishman and a 'Hindu' were to be put together, the first two would 'have in common what we call Western culture, that is, a certain participation in an intellectual atmosphere composed of science, technical expertise, and democratic principles'.[37] The Hindu was 'a stranger to all that'. But that was not the end of the story; for, on the other hand, the Englishman and the Hindu had in common 'something of which the American is totally deprived. That something is a past.' Their pasts were indeed different, but 'much less than one might believe'. What did all this mean? Europeans fighting against Germany talked a lot about their past, Weil noted. This was because they were afraid of losing it. 'Germany wanted to snatch it from us; American influence threatens it. We are only hanging onto it by a few threads. We do not want those threads to be cut. We want to put down roots into it again.' She had a solution to the problem of identifying and reinforcing those all-important roots: '[W]hat we are insufficiently conscious of is the fact that our past comes in great measure from the East.'

Weil took issue with the 'commonplace' assertion 'that our civilization, being Greco-Latin in origin, is in opposition to the East'. She begged to differ: 'As with many commonplace sayings, it is erroneous. The term Greco-Latin does not mean anything precise.' In a statement similar to the arguments advanced some years earlier by a man who was later to admire her deeply, Albert Camus,[38] Weil argued, 'The origin of our civilization is Greek. From the Romans we have inherited only the notion of the state, and the use we make of it leads one to believe that it is a bad inheritance. [. . .] In all other areas, their creative contribution has been nil.' As for the Greeks, who were 'the authentic source of our culture', they had 'received from elsewhere what they transmitted to us. Until the pride of military success made them imperialist, they acknowledged it openly.' Thus, Herodotus was 'outstandingly clear on the subject'. There had been, 'before historical times, a Mediterranean civilization whose inspiration came above all from Egypt, and secondly from the Phoenicians'. And the Greeks 'always had toward Egypt an attitude of filial respect'.[39] In addition, the 'oriental origin of Christianity' was obvious. As for the Middle Ages, 'its moments of brilliance were those in which Eastern culture came again to enrich Europe, by the intermediary of the Arabs and also by other mysterious paths, because they were injections from Persian traditions'; and the Renaissance 'in particular was in part caused by the stimulus of contacts with Byzantium'. All these remarks were made in corroboration of the following argument: 'To sum up, it would seem that Europe periodically needs real contact with the East in order to remain spiritually alive.' It was 'true that in Europe something is opposed to the spirit of the East, something that is specifically European' (*sic*: 'European' here mistranslates *occidental* [Western] in the original text, which makes better sense: 'Il est exact qu'il y a en Europe quelque chose qui s'oppose à l'esprit d'Orient, quelque chose de spécifiquement occidental').[40] But that 'something' was 'to be found in its pure form and to the power of two in America and is threatening to devour us'. As Weil went on to put it, 'European civilization is a combination of the spirit of the East with its opposite, a combination in which the spirit of the East has to be present in a fairly large proportion.' That proportion was 'far from being realized today'; what was needed was 'an injection of the spirit of the East'. Her verdict was that 'Europe has perhaps no other means of avoiding disintegration through American influence except by a new, real, deep contact with the East'. Going back to her example of bringing together, 'an American, an Englishman, and a Hindu', the American and the Englishman would, at that time, 'fraternize in exterior fashion, each regarding himself as vastly superior to the other, and [. . .] leave the Hindu to himself'. It was urgent for that to change, in Weil's opinion: 'The progressive appearance of an atmosphere in which the reflexes are different is perhaps, spiritually, a question of life and death for Europe.'[41]

After all, Weil thought, some humility on the part of Westerners was long overdue: 'Over the last few years we have felt very deeply that the modern Western world, including our conception of democracy, is insufficient. Europe suffers from a number of maladies so severe that one hardly dares to think about it.' Therefore, 'we can no longer say or think that we have received from on high the mission to teach the universe how to live'. In spite of all that, 'we have doubtless certain lessons to give. But we have many to receive from ways of life which, however imperfect, bear nevertheless within their age-old past the proof of their stability.' In a statement that could have been written by Guénon, Gandhi or Tagore, she also noted that '[t]he age-old civilizations of the East, in spite of great differences, are much closer to our Middle Ages than we ourselves are. By warming ourselves in the dual radiance of our past and those things in the present that are a transposed image of it, we can find the strength to prepare a future for ourselves.' It was not a trifling matter: 'What is at stake is the destiny of the human species'; for 'just as the Hitlerization of Europe would doubtless set the scene for the Hitlerization of the terrestrial globe [...] so an Americanization of Europe would set the scene without doubt for an Americanization of the terrestrial globe'. The second evil was 'less than the first, but not by much. In both cases, the whole of humanity would lose its past.'[42]

Meanwhile, in *The Need for Roots*, Weil repeatedly stressed that the fact that 'Europe' was then the watchword of the Nazis should not avert people from the 'idea of Europe, of European unity' after the war.[43] She was far from alone in protesting against the use to which the Nazis had put 'Europe' and 'European'; nor was she alone in envisaging a different kind of united Europe emerging after the war. The man who would soon come to admire her as 'the greatest spirit of our time' (and become instrumental in persuading Gallimard to publish her works), Albert Camus (1913–1960), entertained similar thoughts, while resisting the occupier and writing for *Combat* in occupied Paris. His *Letters to a German Friend* were composed between 1943 and 1945 (and until the liberation of Paris in August 1944 had to be published underground). Camus wrote in the 'Third Letter' (April 1944), 'During all the time when we were obstinately and silently serving our country, we never lost sight of an idea and a hope, forever present in us—the idea and the hope of Europe. To be sure, we have not mentioned Europe for five years. But this is because you talked too much of it.' It went without saying, Camus added, that 'our Europe is not yours'. Instead, 'for us Europe is a home of the spirit where for the last twenty centuries the most amazing adventure of the human spirit has been going on.' Europe, for Camus, was 'the privileged arena in which Western man's struggle against the world, against the gods, against himself is today reaching its climax.' Not that the future would be straightforward: 'And, finally, I know that all will not be over when you are crushed. Europe will still have to be established. It always has to be established. But at least it will be Europe.'[44]

Such establishing was never going to be easy. In many an article in *Combat* in the last year of the war Camus showed how aware he was that the great powers had other plans. When initial reports of what had been agreed at Yalta were published, he warned that 'the whole future of the world hangs in the balance'. The veto upon decisions of the proposed international organisation of the future that five powers alone were reputed to have been allocated appalled him, and led him to comment that 'it would effectively put an end to any idea of international democracy'. It was 'a question of choosing between international democracy on the one hand and recognition of imperialism on the other'. That France was to be one of those five powers was no consolation for Camus: 'And since some would speak to us of grandeur, let us continue to say that if our grandeur is to be built on the misfortune of others, we want no part of it.'[45]

V. 'Pour l'alliance de l'Occident', or a 'Latin Empire'? Raymond Aron's versus Alexandre Kojève's Postwar Order

There was another French thinker in London, like Weil working for the Free French, who was less apprehensive about America than Weil might have been. That thinker was Raymond Aron (1905–1983). In January 1944 Aron published 'Pour l'alliance de l'Occident' (For the aliance of the West). He was adamant that in the postwar world France would be too small to defend itself alone. It needed to be part of a larger entity.[46] And he was equally adamant that that entity had to be much more than an alliance of the old type. What would be needed, at the very least, would be a 'Western entente' (*entente occidentale*) with permanent coordination of the economies and the diplomacy of its members, and unification of their armed forces. He considered alternatives proposed by others, particularly under the guise of a Latin bloc (*bloc latin*) comprising France, Italy and Spain (a version of the idea Alexandre Kojève was to propose the following year). But Aron saw two objections to that alternative. The first was that the *bloc latin* would lack that most indispensable resource, coal. The second was that Belgium and Holland would never involve themselves in a permanent organisation in which both France and Great Britain did not figure simultaneously. Therefore, an agreement between France and Britain constituted, more than ever, the only possible basis for an *entente occidentale*. To that *entente*, the United States would offer a moral support and be an indispensable complement. The USA did not have any interest in Europe beyond the extension of its trade and the spread of its culture, except the need to prevent the unification of the old continent by violence under the laws of a conqueror. Aron's concluding remarks leave no doubt as to how he envisaged the alliance of the West. Great Britain and France had 'deepened in our days their spiritual affinity'. In both countries, the essential will and the supreme task were the same: 'to safeguard, in the age of mechanisation and collective organisation, the values of liberal civilisation'. The Franco–British alliance was not going to be 'one more diplomatic combination, superficial and transient; it would, instead, endeavour to re-establish the equilibrium, today broken, between the culture incarnated by the West and the power [the West] disposes of'.[47]

More than a year later, Aron was still proposing the 'Western' alliance, meaning by the term a close alliance of Western European countries led by Britain and France. In June 1945, he elaborated upon his recommendations for the security and defence of France in the future. In that article, 'Western' (*occidental/e*) referred to 'West-European', while the alternative alliance that would include America as well as Western Europe is referred to as 'what Walter Lippmann has called the Atlantic community'. When French people were asked about their preferences in matters of foreign policy the response left no room for doubt, Aron wrote. 'A majority of the French wish for the country to belong to the ensemble that Walter Lipmann has called the Atlantic community'. Meanwhile, 'a good number are equally favourable to a Western federation or a Western bloc'. But, he went on, 'a minority of French people, whose influence is due less to their number than to their organisation and to their ascendancy over the working class, is ferociously opposed to any version of a *bloc occidental*'. Now, the prestige of Russia, and the influence of the Communist Party on the proletariat were such that a French government would find it difficult to risk formulating a diplomatic programme that would directly clash with the minority that was inclined towards a 'continental' solution instead of the 'Western' bloc or federation solution. Thus, while he was strongly recommending a constant and close cooperation between Great Britain and France (i.e., the 'Western' option) as indispensable, Aron stressed that it mattered how *not* to call that cooperation: The less one were to speak of the 'Western bloc', the better, as the expression raised too many passions and objections. ('Moins on parlera du bloc occidental, mieux cela vaudra: la formule soulève trop de passions et d'oppositions.')[48] As we will see in the next chapter, during the Cold War, Aron's use of 'West' would change to include the United States under the same name.

Meanwhile, later that same summer of 1945, a Russian-born philosopher turned French civil servant, Alexandre Kojève (1902–1968), was also planning the postwar future.[49] His proposal was entitled 'An Outline of a Doctrine of French Policy'. Kojève agreed with Aron's (and Orwell's and many other contemporaries') assessment, that the coming era would be an age of empires (or superstates). But his solution for France's security in that new era diverged from that proposed by Aron. (There can in fact be little doubt that he developed it specifically it in opposition to plans for a 'Western union': a dossier was found along with his typed 'Outline' containing articles from *Le Monde* reporting from London on plans for a 'project of Western association' involving Great Britain, France, the Netherlands, Belgium and Luxembourg—exactly the kind of

FIGURE 7.3. Alexandre Kojève, Berlin, 1922. Photographer unknown. *Source:* https://en.wikipedia.org/wiki/Alexandre_Koj%C3%A8ve#/media/File:Alexandre_Koj%C3%A8ve.jpg

association London-based Aron was proposing at that time.) Kojève's recommendation for France was that it should become the leader (*primus inter pares*) of a 'Latin empire' that would unite it with Italy and Spain. The three countries were already associated by a similar mentality and by Catholicism. Together they would still be too weak to threaten the other two 'empires' that would dominate *de facto* the postwar world, the 'Anglo-Saxon' or Anglo-American, and the Russian-Slavic. But they would be strong enough to exist, assert their culture and prevent a resurgent and rearmed Germany from being a threat to France.[50]

The world was witnessing 'a decisive turning point in history', according to Kojève. The nation states that had been formed since the end of the Middle Ages were now themselves 'irresistibly [...] gradually giving way to political formations which transgress national borders and which could be designated with the term "Empires"'. Thus, in order to be 'politically viable, the modern State must rest on a vast "imperial" union of affiliated [*apparentées*] Nations'. The State in his time was 'only truly a State if it is an Empire'. The Latin Empire that he was proposing could be 'strong enough to establish its neutrality and thus to save the circumference of the Mediterranean and the entire West—the Latin West and also the rest of it—from ruin'. That meant that, if France were to engender the Latin Empire 'in order to prolong, in the future, the autonomy and greatness that its purely national present can no longer support, she does so in her quality as a leading European power, responsible for the conservation of a civilization which she largely created'. And it could thus be said that 'the final goal of Latin imperial policy is maintaining peace in the European West'.[51]

VI. The Atlantic Community

We saw above Raymond Aron referring to what Walter Lippmann called 'the Atlantic community', and that Lippmann had been talking of such a community, as a promising young journalist, since the First World War. By the Second World War he was America's most authoritative publicist. In the summer of 1943 he published a book on *U.S. Foreign Policy*.[52] That same spring (April 1943) Wendell L. Willkie's *One World* had appeared, and its popularity was instant and spectacular. Willkie was promoting global universalism and a world federation. The message appealed to many Americans; Lippmann, however, thought that more down-to-earth planning would be needed for the postwar world. Such planning involved choosing the right allies. It was, he conceded, 'impossible to prepare efficiently against every contingency and all conceivable combinations'. But that was exactly why it was the business of diplomacy 'to reduce the uncertainty by forming dependable alliances, in order to limit the number of potential opponents against whom it is necessary to prepare our armaments'. In a chapter entitled 'The Atlantic Community' Lippmann tried to contribute to such planning. What he called 'The British–American Connection' was indispensable. He was adamant that 'the British vital interest and the American vital interest' were 'complementary and inseparable'. But such a connection was, emphatically, not 'a plan for the combined domination of the world by the English-speaking nations'. It was rather a defensive imperative. For the geostrategic needs of defending America involved much more than an alliance with the British Empire: 'The fall of France in 1940 was a conclusive demonstration that France is a member of the great defensive system in which the American republics live'. Thus France was 'primarily a member of the same community to which the United States belongs'. The same was true of Spain and Portugal. The Netherlands, Belgium, Denmark, Iceland and Norway were added as 'members of the same community of interest'. The upshot was that '[i]f we re-examine the catalogue of nations which are involved in the same system of security, we come upon an interesting and, I believe, a very significant fact'; that is, that 'the nations of the New World are still vitally related to precisely those nations of the Old World from which they originated'. The 'original geographic and historic connections across the Atlantic' had persisted. The Atlantic Ocean was 'not the frontier between Europe and the Americas'. Rather, it was 'the inland sea of a community of nations allied with one another by geography, history, and vital necessity'. An emphatic remark followed: 'Not what men say, not what they think they feel, but what in fact when they have to act they actually do—that is the test of community'. And '[b]y that test there is a great community on this earth from which no member can be excluded and none can resign. This community has its geographical centre in the great basin of the Atlantic.'[53] It is striking how matter-of-fact and geopolitical was Lippmann's reasoning in *U.S. Foreign Policy*. He was to come back to defining the Atlantic community in 1947, and some interesting changes had occurred by then (including the smuggling back in, up to a point, of the Germans); but to that we will return in chapter 8.

Lippmann was of course not the only one thinking of a Western or Atlantic community in wartime America. Henry Luce and his magazines were working hard at it as well.[54] One of the main contributors of crucially influential articles to Luce's magazines was Lippmann himself, however; and, as we saw in chapter 5 above, Lippmann had coined the term 'Atlantic community' long before, during the Great War. Though Luce's magazines were important in popularising the message, that message was not invented by Luce himself, notwithstanding the attention his 1941 article 'The American Century' has received.[55] In one of Luce's popular magazines, shortly before the outbreak of the Second World War, Lippmann had been as explicit as it gets as to what his vision of the 'American Destiny' was: 'In the lifetime of the generation to which we belong there has occurred one of the greatest events in the history of mankind. The controlling power in western civilization has crossed the Atlantic'. Thus America, once 'a colony on the frontiers of Europe, is now, and will in the next generations become even more certainly, the geographic and the economic and the political center of the Occident'. And it was not a matter of choice: 'There is no way to refuse this destiny.'[56]

VII. When Peoples Meet: Alain Locke and 'the Achilles of the West'

The postwar world was of course also being contemplated by many others on the western side of the Atlantic. The 'father of the Harlem Renaissance' chose the magazine that had published the '*New Negro*' issue in the 1920s, the *Survey Graphic*, to publish, in November 1942, 'The Unfinished Business of Democracy'.

Alain LeRoy Locke assessed the prospects of the United States for 'leadership in an emancipated world' after the war—and urged that America should be careful, as must the rest of the Western nations. For, '[a]s Walter Lippmann [...] put it', the allied nations had 'found themselves in a position where they could be accused, not without warrant, of fighting to preserve the rule of the white man over the peoples of Asia and of being committed at fearful cost to a war for the restoration of empire'. But, as Locke continued, quoting Lippmann, 'the Western nations must now do what hitherto they have lacked the will and the imagination to do: they must identify their cause with the freedom and security of the peoples of the East, putting away the "white man's burden" and purging themselves of the taint of an obsolete and obviously unworkable white man's imperialism'. Radical solutions were needed after the war, not just sticking-plasters and palliatives, Locke insisted; because otherwise, 'Western color prejudice' would be 'corroding with suspicion the confidence of India, China, and other non-white peoples in the common democratic cause'. Moreover, '[w]orst irony of all, observe the same undemocratic behavior, venting itself in a southern lynching or a midwestern riot, boomeranged back at American democracy in mocking and insidious Japanese propaganda'. It should be obvious that, 'if we would effectively stave off totalitarian tyranny, democracy itself must first be universalized'.[57]

All that having been said, *prima facie*, America had a lot going for it as a potential leader of a better postwar world:

> Moreover, the United States with its composite populations sampling all the human races and peoples, is by way of being almost a United Nations by herself. We could so easily and naturally, with the right dynamic become the focus of thoroughgoing internationalism—thereby realizing, one might say, our manifest destiny. [...] But over against all this, there stands one tragic but not irremedial [sic] liability. In the neglected and unsolved problem of the Negro in America, the Achilles of the West has a dangerously vulnerable heel. At any time in any critical position requiring moral authority before the world, this threatens to impair our influence as an exemplar of democracy. It has already done so.[58]

That year, 1942, also saw the publication of a remarkable volume that Locke had been proposing and preparing for some years. *When Peoples Meet* was edited by Locke, of Howard University, and Columbia University's Bernhard Stern. Financed by the Progressive Education Association, the volume was presented as 'a resource on global intercultural problems for teachers'. It was a kind of anthology of writings already published by (mostly) senior scholars and writers in anthropology, history, sociology, political science and international relations. These included such academic luminaries as Margaret Mead, Ruth Benedict, Franz Boas, Hans Kohn and Arnold Toynbee.

Locke himself wrote the introduction and 'the substantial headnotes to each section of readings', commenting on each piece.[59] It was in these that he deployed his long experience in reflecting on the interactions between 'culture' and 'race' and how these concepts were used or abused. The major objectives of those who abused them were 'the justification of conflict and exploitation through the disparagement of other group cultures and the promotion of prestige and group morale through self-glorification and claims of superiority'. The history of racist theory in Europe for the previous century presented, Locke remarked, 'a contradictory cavalcade of superiority claims and shifting "superior" races;—in turn it has been Latin, Aryan (Old Style), Teutonic, Anglo-Saxon, "Nordic," European, Caucasian ("white") and Aryan (New Style),—all competing in obvious theoretical inconsistency and practical self-contradiction'. (Presumably he would no longer confound some of these himself, as he had in his September 1914 lecture that we discussed in chapter 5.)

But racism was 'only one of the fictions involved in current false perspectives of human history'. According to Locke, the 'prevailing notion of separate, distinctive and ethnically characteristic cultures is another example, and it, too, is shown by broad historical analysis to be contrary to fact'. Culture, to his mind, was 'not related functionally to definite ethnic groups or races', but varied independently: 'Races change their culture on many historic occasions and various culture advances are made independently by different racial stocks.' Furthermore, each 'dynamic and constantly changing' culture had 'an increasing tendency, on the whole, to become more and more composite, in the sense of incorporating aspects of other cultures with which it comes to contact'. Thus, 'the older a culture, the more composite it usually is'. In Locke's view, '*No group has proprietary hold on the culture that it originates, and at any moment of its history, most of its own culture will be found to be a composite of culture elements from all the centuries and from the rest of the world*.' In fact, progress, in some cases seemed 'proportional to the degree to which a society has a many-sided cultural exposure. Provided it can integrate them, a variety of culture contacts is a favorable situation for any culture.' For groups did, of course, 'differ widely in their susceptibility to cultural change, but none are so conservative as to be completely resistant'. Meanwhile, '[t]he realization of the composite character of civilization [...] does not gainsay the fact of the distinctive character of individual cultures'; it would, however, be 'a misapplication of this truth to regard it as sanctioning a uniformitarian theory or criterion of culture'. In sum, '[v]ariation is at the root of cultural change, and cultural diversity is conducive to it'.[60]

Locke also wrote that a 'common civilization tolerantly supporting a variety of cultures is at least not an impossibility; and can readily take shape where intercultural tolerance permits'. That 'possibility of cultural pluralism' was 'an important lesson for the Western world to learn, since in spite of its traditional cultural illusions, this is a world where no one general form of culture has a clear or permanent majority'. In that context, Locke gave pride of place to Arnold Toynbee's criticisms of the pretensions of European civilisation in 'egotistically identifying itself with human civilization'.[61] Locke continued to write on intercultural exchanges and their implications during the rest of World War II,[62] and went on to expand on such arguments shortly after the war.

VIII. Conclusion

Upon the outbreak of World War II, clear 'civilisational' lines could easily be drawn, Hitler's Germany and Stalin's Russia having signed a pact. We have seen Jacques Maritain and Walter Lippmann celebrating the moral clarity that that development conferred upon the cause of the Western allies: 'Western civilisation' was already saved, as it would not have to compromise itself by alliance with one of the totalitarian regimes. And yet, all that was to change once Germany invaded Russia in 1941, and the Soviet Union became a crucial ally against Hitler. By the end of the war, the monumental sacrifices Soviet Russia had suffered and its indispensable contribution to the defeat of Nazism had given it enormous prestige (and left a substantial chunk of Central and Eastern European territory under its military control). What would happen next?

In planning for the reconstruction of the postwar world, 'Western civilisation' was all too frequently evoked among the major considerations, as something either to be saved or to be reformed. Pope Pius XII's fear of Communism had been a significant factor throughout the war, making him reluctant to go along with the efforts of US President Roosevelt to improve relations with Stalin's Soviet Russia in the interests of the conduct of the war.[63] Henry Luce's magazines highlighted the religious dimension throughout the war. In September 1944, *Life* published a long article by the American diplomat William C. Bullitt, reporting from Rome on the anxieties of the Vatican about the Communist danger.[64]

> What is that picture as seen from Rome? It is an old picture which has been familiar to Romans since the time of the Caesars—a picture of western Europe

and Western civilization threatened by hordes of invaders from the East. The task of the Caesars was to hold back those hordes and preserve within the limits of the Roman Empire that civilization which had its source in Athens and its strength in Rome. In the end [...] they failed. [...] The barbarians in successive waves rolled over Western Europe and through the Dark Ages the light of Western civilization was preserved only by the Church. Today, when the moral unity of Western civilization has been shattered by the crimes of the Germans [...] Rome sees again approaching from the East a wave of conquerors. And dominating the hearts and minds and, indeed, the talk of all men throughout Italy is the question: 'Will the result of this war be the subjugation of Europe by Moscow instead of by Berlin?'[65]

The main point made by Bullitt was also confirmed a few years later, when the French ambassador to the Vatican, the same Jacques Maritain with whom this chapter began, was giving an account of his three years at the Holy See to his foreign minister. Pius XII, Maritain informed Georges Bidault, 'believed it was his duty as pope to act as the defender of Western civilization'.[66]

Also in 1944, an Austrian exile, the libertarian economist Friedrich Hayek, was alarmed at what he saw as the 'entire abandonment of the individualist tradition which has created Western civilization'.[67] 'Western civilisation' was on everybody's lips. In the British Foreign Office, when he was not being disconcerted by the plans of the head of the Foreign Research and Press Service (Professor Arnold Toynbee) for 'world government', Gladwyn Jebb was denouncing 'in unmeasured terms' the isolationist policy of the colonial secretary, 'the formidable Leo Amery', who was proposing that Britain and America should not concern themselves with 'Europe', and that Britain rather 'should occupy itself with the British Commonwealth'. For Jebb, following Amery's policies would mean that 'there would be a good chance, not of a happy Europe, based on the essential tenets of Western civilization, but a Sovietized Europe, and of a pretty anti-British one into the bargain'.[68] Meanwhile, a fellow ex-Etonian, Eric Blair (1903–1950), alias George Orwell, was also busy planning the postwar future. When, in 1941, with Tosco Fyvel, Fredric Warburg and Sebastian Haffner, he started the series of short 'Searchlight Books', they announced that it was the aim of these volumes 'to do all in their power to criticise and kill what is rotten in Western civilization and supply constructive ideas for the difficult period ahead of us'.[69] Meanwhile, there clearly were things worth preserving. In what was intended to be the preface to *Animal Farm* (1945), Orwell noted that 'intellectual liberty [...] without a doubt has been one of the distinguishing marks of western civilization'.[70]

But who was included in, or who was to be the saviour of, 'Western civilisation', was not at all static. The war inevitably affected affiliations, alliances and membership lists. In 1939, Paul Valéry could speak of the Germans' attitudes towards their leaders, and then juxtapose in contradistinction, 'But we in the West can tolerate neither the suppression of thinking individuals—to be replaced by automatons—nor an unreasoning and unlimited obedience to some precise and necessary aim requiring that.'[71] Walter Lippmann would include Latins, Dutch, Belgians, Norwegians and Danes in his 'Atlantic community', but Germans were conspicuously absent. (It will be instructive to see, in the next chapter, how he would describe his proposed 'Atlantic' community four years later).

The most obvious and immediate question was that concerning the future relationship between the powers that had fought on the Allied side, given that these included Soviet Russia. Aldous Huxley thought he knew the answer. The consequences of the bombing of German cities by the British and Americans would most likely turn the Germans towards Russia, 'as being, in their eyes, the most humane of the victor nations, inasmuch as the only one that did not use saturation bombing'. (Presumably California-based Huxley had not heard of the industrial-scale rape of German women by Russian soldiers.) Moreover, Russia would probably be the only power able 'to offer the Germans bread—which will be given, out of the conquered wheatlands, in exchange for political and economic collaboration'. He thought that, when the Russians' ways of ingratiating themselves with the Germans had succeeded, the balance of power in Europe would be 'more completely gone than it is even at present'. His comment was, 'Let's hope that the Western nations may have the sense to accept the inevitable and come to terms with those whom population, birth-rate, resources and territory predestine to be the masters of Asia and Europe.' Their best course was to '"agree with thine enemy while thou art in the way with him", and not run the risk of being knocked to pieces by a power that is now of positively cosmic proportions'.[72] Incidentally on the very day that Huxley wrote this to his brother Julian (27 May 1945), *The Observer* published a piece by George Orwell, whose prognosis was: 'Certain dangerous illusions—for instance, the widespread idea that the U.S.S.R. and the Western Powers will be at war in the near future—have sprung up and need to be contradicted by the highest authorities.' He was to be much more pessimistic two years later, however.[73]

A world had to be rebuilt. The future was full of possibilities, and full of dangers. That the end of the war would rather soon lead to another kind of war, baptised by George Orwell a 'Cold War',[74] came as a surprise to some, but not to all. To that other war and the new alignments and definitions it led to, we turn in the next chapter.

8

The Cold War and Its 'Wests'

'Two things stood out at the Rencontres de Genève [September 1946]. One was that the intellectuals of Europe are now as divided politically as the politicians themselves. [...] The other is that we deceive ourselves in Europe, speaking of the East and the West, if we mean that the West has any unity. The West only exists in opposition to the East. Otherwise it consists of areas such as the American, British, and French zones of Germany, Italy, France, Spain, Great Britain, the Lowlands, Scandinavia, part of the Balkans, Eire, etc. What unity is there in the West? Absolutely none.'

STEPHEN SPENDER, 'THE INTELLECTUALS AND EUROPE'S FUTURE', *COMMENTARY*, JANUARY 1947, PP. 10–11

'It's been a pretty good civilization, ours; it's a pity it's all over. You realize that by the end of 1957 Western civilization as we know it will have finished.'

HAROLD MACMILLAN, NOVEMBER 1956, QUOTED IN STEEL, *WALTER LIPPMANN*, PP. 506–7

'Most Asian and African writers I have been in contact with are steeped in religious feeling, and their works and political struggle are suffused with their religious conceptions. This seems somewhat strange to an American Negro like me: in the United States, we fight for a real application of the Constitution, which is not the case in African nations. We fight to become part of a civilization which we accept. We do not oppose the West; we want the effective application of Western principles of freedom.'

RICHARD WRIGHT, 'INTERVIEW WITH RICHARD WRIGHT', *L'EXPRESS*, 479 (18 AUGUST 1960), PP. 22–23; REPRINTED IN KINNAMON AND FABRE, *CONVERSATIONS WITH RICHARD WRIGHT*, PP. 201–2

PRECONCEIVED NOTIONS pose a serious challenge in general for this book. In this chapter, however, the problem we face in terms of preconceived understandings of what 'the West' is taken to mean is particularly acute. The Cold War is part of many people's living memory, and it crystallised eventually into a binary distinction between two sides with established names. This latter fact may easily leave people under the highly misleading impression that, during the Cold War, 'the West' meant what they remember understanding as 'the West' in 1989 or 1990. The reader needs to unlearn what she knows, 'un-remember' what she remembers, and look afresh at what people thought of the world and themselves between the end of the Second World War and the end of the Cold War. What came to be seen more or less unproblematically as 'the West' in 1989 was the result of what happened in the previous decades. The whole period is of interest, but most particularly the decade or so from the end of the Second World War to the numerous crucial events that took place in the mid-1950s and in various ways shaped how people came to understand their world, and what they came to mean by 'the West'. Meanings and distinctions were much more fluid and inchoate in the beginning of the period than they came to be by its end.

In November 1946 Du Bois could still write, 'How can we forget [. . .] that it was the Russian people and their army which saved Western civilization in the Second World War?'[1] And Karl Jaspers could say, in a lecture delivered in Geneva on 13 September 1946, '*America and Russia, the two last great structures of Western civilization*, are becoming the masters of the world.' Jaspers added that, given the weakness of Japan, '[f]or the time being, the political course of the world is still set *by Western countries—America and Russia*.'[2] The year before, the French historian André Siegfried had similarly told the audience of his Romanes Lectures in Oxford that 'Western civilisation' was bound to be modified by the dominance of the United States and the Soviet Union, and repeatedly referred to the Soviet Union as belonging to it.[3]

Around a year after Du Bois's and Jaspers's statements, however, in 1947, most of those who talked of Western civilisation had come to assign a very different place to the Soviet Russians and their army. The latter were now seen rather as the overwhelming threat to that very civilisation. And this is possibly the most succinct way to summarise the onset of the Cold War.

Fear of Soviet Russia mounted after the breakdown of negotiations over the future of occupied Germany. Over dinner with the American secretary of state, George C. Marshall, the UK's foreign secretary Ernest Bevin declared the need for 'a *spiritual* consolidation of western civilization' which would be 'backed by the United States and the Dominions'.[4] The Western democracies should form a 'spiritual federation of the West', Bevin told General Marshall.[5] Tensions had been rising between July and November 1947, when a meeting of the Council of Foreign Ministers in London failed to reach agreement on divided Germany. It was that summer that George Orwell, contemplating (in *Partisan Review*) whether 'the present "cold war"' with the USSR would continue, proposed a Socialist United States of Europe, though admitting that it was highly unlikely to happen in the foreseeable future.[6] There was a bewildering number of proposals for European unification at the time.[7] But what would be the Europeans' relationship with the power on the other side of the Atlantic?

I. Lippmann's 'natural allies' and the Atlantic Community

For very soon it became explicitly apparent that there was indeed a 'Cold War' going on.[8] The cultural/civilisational uses of the terms 'West' and 'Western' were now to be either superseded, or complemented, by (and often confused with) more strictly political uses and definitions. A particularly interesting case of the continuing relevance of older civilisational affinities being invoked as crucial to the new political divisions and antagonisms arose in the very essay that is credited with being one of the first to use the phrase 'Cold War' (as already mentioned, Orwell is credited as having been *the* first). Walter Lippmann took up his pen to criticise the recommendations of 'Mr. X' for 'containment' of the Soviet Union wherever the latter might try to encroach. Everyone already knew that 'X' was the diplomat George Kennan.[9] What exercised Lippmann most was his (erroneous) conviction that it was Kennan who had fathered the 'Truman doctrine' as promulgated in the American president's speech of 12 March 1947.[10] (Lippmann was not happy that the president promised to defend Greece and Turkey, among other commitments. But nor was he correct in his interpretation of what exactly the 'X' article was proposing.)[11]

Lippmann wrote fourteen columns in all attacking 'Mr. X' in the *New York Herald Tribune* (the first of these appearing 2 September 1947), which were widely reproduced in other papers, and then published as a book entitled *The Cold War*. The crucial question for him was, '[C]an the western world operate a policy of containment?' According to Lippmann, 'the kind of strength we have and the kind of resourcefulness we are capable of showing are peculiarly unsuited to operating [such] a policy'. A constitutional democracy could not act as fast as a dictatorship and a free economy could not plan and rationalise its resources in the way the Soviets could do. But, most fatally, the policy of containment and the Truman doctrine were committing the United States to defending the wrong kind of allies. 'There is still greater disadvantage in a policy which seeks to "contain" the Soviet Union by attempting to make "unassailable barriers" of the surrounding states.' Those states were 'admittedly weak'. And a weak ally was a liability; but '[w]orst of all, the effort to develop such an unnatural alliance of backward states must alienate *the natural allies of the United States*'. Here was the crux of the matter:

> The natural allies of the United States are the nations of the Atlantic community: that is to say, the nations of western Europe and of the Americas. The Atlantic Ocean and the Mediterranean Sea, which is an arm of the Atlantic Ocean, unite them in a common strategic, economic and cultural system. The chief components of the Atlantic community are the British Commonwealth of nations, the Latin states on both sides of the Atlantic, the Low Countries and Switzerland, Scandinavia and the United States.[12]

In the next paragraph Lippmann's criteria for inclusion display a tiny bit more flexibility: 'The boundaries of the Atlantic community are not sharp and distinct, particularly in the case of the Germans and the western Slavs and the dependencies and the colonies of western Europe.' But this did not change the fact that

> *the nucleus of the Atlantic community is distinct and unmistakable*, and among the nations that are indisputably members of the Atlantic community there exists a vital connection founded upon their military and political geography, the common tradition of western Christendom, and their economic, political, legal, and moral institutions which, with all their variations and differences, have a common origin and have been shaped by much the same historical experience.

And yet, the 'policy of containment' proposed by 'Mr. X' was 'an attempt to organize an anti-Soviet alliance composed [...] of peoples that are either on the shadowy extremity of the Atlantic community, or are altogether outside it'. The architects of that theory had been 'concerned immediately with the anti-Soviet parties and factions of eastern Europe, with the Greeks, the Turks, the Iranians, the Arabs and Afghans, and with the Chinese Nationalists'. The result was that '[i]nstead of becoming an unassailable barrier against the Soviet power, this borderland is a seething stew of civil strife.'[13]

At the very same time as the 'Cold War' was becoming fully explicit and official, there were voices warning that the main problem for the United States lay at home. In 'An Appeal to the World' that he sent to the United Nations in October 1947, W.E.B Du Bois argued, 'It is not Russia that threatens the United States so much as Mississippi; [...] internal injustice done to one's brothers is far more dangerous than the aggression of strangers from abroad.'[14] The message was not heeded, and it would resurface and be used extensively to criticise the US by both friend and foe. (As late as 1977 the Soviet leader Brezhnev would be using James Baldwin's letter to US president Jimmy Carter on racial injustice to hit back at American scolding on the human rights record of the USSR.)[15]

II. A 'spiritual consolidation of western civilization': Made in Britain

We have seen 'the West' used by French thinkers to promote a European or world order that would put France at its centre (or at least enhance France's role). That was not, of course, an exclusively French sport. Some of the British tried it in the immediate postwar years.[16] It was arguably the failure of that version of 'Western civilisation' (in the aftermath of the Suez crisis of 1956) that Harold Macmillan was lamenting in the conversation quoted in one epigraph to this chapter.[17] We saw earlier how Ernest Bevin evoked 'Western civilization' in his discussions with his American counterpart. What he shared with the Americans and what he had in mind and shared with his Foreign Office officials and the Cabinet did not always coincide, however. After all, what Bevin had liked most about Marshall's famous speech at Harvard on 5 June 1947 (announcing what became the Marshall Plan for Europe) had been that the US secretary of state stressed that '[t]he initiative, I think, must come from Europe.'[18] Bevin needed American support and 'Western civilisation' was a good umbrella term covering that. But when he was using the 'spiritual' survival of Western civilisation as an argument to his own Cabinet, it was in order to promote a British-led Western Europe as a 'Middle Power' that would save Western civilisation from Russians and Americans alike. Having been '[g]iven the nod by Bevin at the end of 1947', British diplomats and civil servants prepared the rationale for Britain to take a lead in Europe through a customs union. According to the biographer of one of them, Gladwyn Jebb's contribution offered 'a glimpse into the immediate difficulties surrounding European co-operation as well as those which would still resonate decades later'. For Jebb explained that a customs union 'would only make sense if it led to "the creation of some federal entity" of the Western European states and their colonial dependencies'. If, despite the odds, such a federal entity were to be achieved, however, 'it would restore the balance *in the current bi-polar system centred on what Mr. Toynbee calls the two "semi-barbarian states of the cultural periphery"*'. It would 'raise living standards to American levels whilst *enhancing West European "spiritual and cultural values"*'. Jebb's verdict was that the chances of achieving union were 'slim, yet the alternative to attempting to create a "Middle Power" would be having to make the "dismal" choice between being a Soviet satellite or an American dependency', and he therefore was 'in favour of making the effort'.[19] Thus,

> [t]he burden of the key Cabinet paper, pointedly titled 'The First Aim of British Foreign Policy', was not that Britain must secure the protection of the USA, *but that she should remain independent of any major Power by seizing the leadership of Western Europe and supplying (mentioned five times in the paper) a 'spiritual' rallying point.* Short-term American material aid would be indispensable, but this would be offset by *a philosophical alternative to what was on offer from either capitalist America or communist Russia.* The countries of Western Europe, it was confidently affirmed, '*which despise the spiritual values of America will look to us for political and moral guidance* and for assistance in building up a counter attraction to the baleful tenets of communism'.

Once he obtained the approval of the Cabinet, Bevin 'gave his first public airing, suitably shorn of comments adverse to Washington, to what he called his "Western Union" policy' in the House of Commons on 22 January 1948.[20] The foreign secretary's emphasis in such a public statement was bound of course to differ from that used in internal Foreign Office and Cabinet papers. While calling for a union of Western Europe to repair a war-damaged continent, he paid tribute to the generosity of the United States, as displayed in Marshall's Harvard speech the year before. He declared that '[t]he United States and the countries of Latin America are clearly as much a part of our common Western civilisation as are the nations of the British Commonwealth'. But he also felt the need to add, 'When I speak of the United States, I am not thinking of the country misrepresented in propaganda as a sort of Shylock of Wall Street, but a young, vigorous, democratic people'; which speaks volumes, of course, as to what the perception of the United States then was. 'To conclude', then, the British government had 'striven for the closer consolidation and economic development, *and eventually for the spiritual unity, of Europe as a whole.*' In Eastern Europe, however, one was 'presented with a fait accompli'. Eastern European countries were not free to choose what they wanted. The sovereignty of the Eastern European nations was 'handicapped'. As far as Western Europe was concerned, on the other hand, '[n]either we, the United States nor France is going to approach Western Europe on that basis. *It is not in keeping with the spirit of Western civilisation, and if we are to have an organism in the West it must be a spiritual union.*'[21] (That ubiquitous word, 'spiritual', again!).

Things continued to look dark though, and became darker a month later. On 25 February 1948 a Communist coup was staged in Prague and took Czechoslovakia to the other side of the Iron Curtain. Intense fears were also raised by the prospects of the Communists in Italian elections due that April. Anxieties were mounting in the British Foreign Office and '[a] momentous Cabinet paper' drafted in the light of the Prague coup by Gladwyn Jebb for Bevin 'offered, under the austere heading "The Threat to Western Civilization", the most desolate survey of the international scene which he was ever to produce'.[22]

Clearly 'Western civilisation' was a handy concept to deploy for two parallel purposes. On the one hand it was an obvious way to legitimise closer bonds with America and convince America to invest both its money and its military resources in defence of Western Europe. But simultaneously it could be evoked to highlight British 'moral' and 'spiritual' leadership of that civilisation, given the widespread perception of the Americans 'as a sort of Shylock of Wall Street' or one of the two 'semi-barbarian states of the cultural periphery'.[23]

III. 'It is twenty-five o'clock': Europe 'between the barbarians of the East and those of the West'?

It was not only Arnold Toynbee who spoke in those terms; and not only in Britain that anxieties about the influence and dominance of the American 'extreme West' were growing, leading to ideas of establishing a European 'third force' or 'middle force'—or simply to despair. German Social Democrats, most of them recently affected by exile in Britain or America, were particularly busy planning a European federation as a third force between East and West. It would take some years before they were to accept the Federal Republic's orientation or binding to 'the West' (*Westbindung*) promoted by the Christian Democrat chancellor, Konrad Adenauer.[24] France, for its part, was a particularly challenging case. Anti-Americanism was part of a longer tradition of attitudes to *les Anglo-Saxons*, and more recently the popularity of Marxism and the Soviet Union had become rather pervasive in French intellectual circles. Altogether, this meant that America had very few friends in late 1940s France. André Malraux could be added to Raymond Aron, but they were very far from typical.[25] Paris was known as the capital of Communism's fellow-travellers.[26] The hostile reception of Czesław Miłosz, freshly defected from Communist Poland in early 1951, on the part of the 'Leftist *bien pensants*' in Paris was just one more case in point.[27]

The climate can be gauged by the extraordinary popularity of a—now completely forgotten—novel. The Romanian author Constantin Virgil Gheorghiu (1916–1992) wrote *Ora 25* in his native language during his life in exile, but it had to wait until after the fall of Nicolae Ceaușescu in 1989 for a Romanian edition to appear. Instead, it was first published in his adopted country, France, in October 1949, as *La Vint-cinquième Heure*. An English translation, *The Twenty-Fifth Hour*, was published in 1950. Within months it had become spectacularly popular around Europe. In its first year it sold 175,000 copies in France, 'more than any other book of fiction since the war'; and within a year or so it had been 'translated into fourteen languages and published in eighteen countries, with total sales exceeding a million'. In addition, more than a thousand newspaper articles had been written on it by the summer of 1951, according to a contemporary Canadian reviewer, besides it having also 'been the subject of scores of speeches and sermons'. It had clearly been 'taken up [...] enthusiastically as a tract for the times' and it was because of that reaction that *The Twenty-Fifth Hour* 'takes on a significance greater than its literary merit indicates'.[28] Its popularity was seen as so alarming from an American point of view that it was mentioned as part of the rationale for the creation of the Foreign Student Project that a young Ph.D researcher named Henry Kissinger and his supervisor were proposing to set up in 1951 (on which more in the next section). Though they exculpated themselves from the ignominy of actually having read the novel by mistyping its title, they were sufficiently perturbed to write of the 'significant example [of] the tremendous critical and popular success of the book *The Twenty-Fifth House*, which states Europe's dilemma as a choice between the barbarians of the East and those of the West'.[29]

The Twenty-Fifth Hour was hailed as admittedly 'a gripping and strangely disturbing book', upsetting 'because we fear that Gheorghiu is right when he says that our civilization has already passed the time when we might have averted disaster'. For Gheorghiu's main thesis was that 'today man is no longer an individual but merely a slave of the machine society'. The villains in the novel were not just Nazis or Fascists or Communists, but rather 'bureaucrats who regard men as categories rather than as individuals'. The Romanian novelist portrayed that attitude as characteristic of the US Allied occupation authorities no less than of the Nazi officials who controlled Europe before the 'liberation'. He saw 'the complicated centralized government of all modern nations as a great machine that is squeezing men into rigid moulds and destroying all the qualities that make them human'. Therefore 'the machine, and man's subjection to it, is the crux of our present woes'.[30] The message of *The Twenty-Fifth Hour* was that all individual values had been wiped out by a technological civilisation which could deal only with quantitative units. Men had become the 'apes of robots'.[31]

What was more, Gheorghiu's novel expressed strong views as to what 'Western civilisation' meant and the place of the Soviet Union, not beyond, but within it: '"Don't be misled by words, Mr. Lewis" [warns the character Nora]. "This so-called Third World War is not a war of West against East."' It was not, properly speaking, a war at all: '"This war is nothing but an internal revolution within the framework of the civilization of the West; a mere internal revolution, entirely and exclusively Western."' The American officer Lewis objects that they are 'fighting against the East, against the whole of eastern Europe'. His delusions are promptly corrected, however: '"You are wrong," said Nora. "You, the West, are fighting against an offshoot of your own civilization."' To the American's reply that they were 'fighting against Russia' Nora, the Romanian refugee, retorts,

> 'Russia, since the Communist Revolution, has become the most advanced branch of Western Technological Civilization. It has taken up all the theories of the West and put them into practice. It has reduced man to zero, in accordance with the doctrine of the West. It has transformed society into one vast machine, in accordance with the doctrine of the West. [...] [Y]ou are at war with this particular aspect of Western civilization—its Communist aspect. That is why your Third World War is simply a revolution that has broken out and is following its course within the limits of the Technological Civilization of the West. [...] The East has nothing to do with this internal upheaval of the West.'

The American is puzzled, so his interlocutor enlightens him further: '"[I]t is very simple," said Nora. [...] "In the Technological Civilization of the West men live, like the early Christians, in catacombs, prisons, churches, and ghettos, on the fringes of life."'[32] According to Nora, '[m]en must hide the fact that they are human. They have to behave according to technical laws, like machines.'[33]

The ubiquitous 's'-word could not of course be missing from such a novel. A (European, obviously) refugee's eyes observed by Nora hold a sad expression: '"There is a certain sadness that is akin to spiritual greatness [Il y a une mélancholie qui tient à la grandeur de l'esprit]," she said to herself [...]. His sadness was not merely of the flesh but of the spirit.' And though they are desperate to be accepted by the American soldiers in order to escape the Russians, the refugees cannot bring themselves to pretend to fight for 'civilization' and 'the West': '"Please accept us," he said. "We are hard-working, honest people." Petru had taught him many other things to say, but he did not want to say them.' He simply 'could not bring himself to affirm his belief in civilization, in the West, and all the rest of it. It would not come. His lips refused to pronounce the words.'[34]

While the first part of the novel was about the inhumanity of the mechanical 'Western' civilisation shared by Soviets and Americans, the second part was mainly focused on highlighting the chasm that separated Americans from Europeans. The climax comes in the long Epilogue, when the American officer asks the Romanian widow to marry him. She flatly refuses, and he wants to hear the reason. 'If you really want to know—because of the difference in age between us.' The startled American, having seen her papers, knows that she is one year younger than himself. Thus he challenges her, asking how old she is. Her reply? 'I am nine hundred and sixty-nine years old, but don't forget that women always make themselves out to be younger than they really are. Actually I am much older than that.' The puzzled American persists; so does Nora: '"I've told you already—difference in age," she said. "You are a nice, selfish, charming young man, just like every other young man, whereas I am a woman from another world."' To his reply, that he doesn't understand, she retorts, '"It is quite natural that you shouldn't understand. I have lived through a thousand years and more. A thousand years of experience that have made me what I am today. You have nothing behind you. You have the present and the future, perhaps."' Sensing how uncomfortable she had made the American feel, Nora explains to him that after 'listening to words of love uttered by Petrarch and Goethe, Byron, Pushkin' and so on, she could not take his professions of love as amounting to anything. He sadly came from a superficial world without history or depth.[35]

Though the literary merits involved are worlds apart, the condescending attitude of a European towards the 'young' Americans with their innocence of historical depth depicted in Gheorghiu's novel was also evinced by the young Czesław Miłosz when he first resided in America as a Polish diplomat in the late 1940s. There was of course much that he did like in the United States; '[a]ll the same, America was difficult to get used to'. His circumstances brought about 'an acute recurrence' of his 'old sickness'—'a disturbance in one's perception of time. The sick man constantly sees time as an hourglass through which states, systems, and civilizations trickle like sand; [...] being is unreal, only movement is real.' Milosz could not stop his mind 'from coursing through the ages like a projectile, seizing general characteristics and lines of development, speeding up the processes of becoming'. In other words, he was 'troubled by an excess of what the Americans so strikingly lack'. As for them,

> Americans accepted their society as if it had arisen from the very order of nature; so saturated with it were they that they tended to pity the rest of humanity for having strayed from the norm. If I at least understood that all was not well with me, they did not realize that the opposite disablement affected them:

a loss of the sense of history and, therefore, of a sense of the tragic, which is only born of historical experience.³⁶

Nor was it only the Lithuanian-Polish-born Miłosz, or the Romanian-born Gheorghiu, who thought in that way about America and its distance from Europe. We saw in chapter 7 above what Simone Weil thought in 1943. Meanwhile, the foremost interpreter of America to the French public since the interwar years had been André Siegfried.³⁷ We have already encountered some of his wartime reflections. His verdict immediately after the end of the Second World War was that 'Western civilisation' was being de-Europeanised by moving away from its historic centre of gravity (Europe, and more specifically the Mediterranean) and instead being squeezed between the United States and the Soviet Union. And what was the problem with these influences? Sheer size, and mechanisation, beyond measure.³⁸ These two powers, emerging victorious from the war, were about to exert an enhanced influence on the 'orientation of our civilization'. Both were 'extra-European powers'. Their geographical structure, being that of great spaces, predisposed them to massiveness.³⁹ The ancient Greek maxim according to which man is the measure of things 'no longer has a meaning in the Russian steppe or in the American prairie'. Inevitably, then, one might wonder whether, under the influence of such leaders, Western civilisation was not in danger of relying for inspiration upon massiveness, on colossal hyper-organisation, 'at the expense of individualism, of measure, and of diversity'. 'Europe' and 'the West' (*Occident*) had been for a long time synonymous terms, but such assimilation was now out of the question. It seemed to Siegfried obvious that '[b]y being de-Europeanized, Western civilization could well change in character'. His conclusion expressed his trepidation in 1945: 'Under these new influences, it is inevitable that Western civilization will change. The fact that its centre of gravity can no longer be the same is, in that respect, decisive. A new chapter is beginning. Let us hope that the unity of the book might be maintained.'⁴⁰

IV. '[T]o swing the spiritual balance in favor of the US': Henry Kissinger's '"Western" or "Occidental" civilization'

Faced with such levels of suspicion (or worse) in Europe about American domination or influence (and concomitant attraction to ideas of 'a third force', or neutralism), many Americans were alarmed. What was their recourse? Once more, 'Western civilisation'. A telling example is the 'Harvard International Seminar' that another European immigrant to America, the young Henry Kissinger (then a Ph.D candidate), and his supervisor, William Yandell Elliott, set up as part of the Harvard Summer School, beginning in 1951 (the correspondence in Kissinger's papers shows that the planning had started in 1950).[41] A related initiative was their launching, the year after, of the magazine *Confluence*. The rationale can be followed through the archives of both initiatives, and it is highly instructive. While he and his supervisor were preparing what became the Harvard International Seminar in 1951, Kissinger typed a seven-page 'Informal Memorandum for Professor Elliott'. Under 'Objectives of the Program' he first articulated the 'General Principles':

> [T]he program can constitute *a spiritual link* between a segment of the foreign youth and the US. Among a generation for which, both in Europe and Asia, war has come to be a normal state and power the only criterion of political decision, cynicism and indeed nihilism is obviously rampant. In the groping for certainty in a world, in which American material aid represents frequently only an allieveation [sic] of misery and can therefore never supply the ultimate answer, the greater humanity of the American principles does not always suffice *to swing the spiritual balance* in the favor of the US. The determination of the Communists, their show of interest in the souls of the young generation constitutes a powerful appeal. It is primarily *in the spiritual field* that American stock is lowest in overseas countries due to a combination of Nazi and Communist propaganda which pictures the US as bloated, materialistic and culturally barbarian. A proper psychological understanding on the part of US agencies, the very fact of concern for foreign students as personalities, may therefore constitute a more powerful appeal than much of the, however well-intentioned, material assistance.

Then the young Ph.D candidate explained the objectives that he proposed for the programme: 'To create nuclei of understanding of the true values of a democracy and *of spiritual resistance to Communism*.' If the summer at Harvard became an experience, rather than just a course of study, 'one could expect that contact among former students might be maintained', and a 'basis for international understanding would thus be created among groups of promising young individuals'. The course programming must constantly keep 'the basic objective' in mind. Thus, subjects that were also available at European universities would not be included. Instead, '[e]mphasis should be placed on studies in American History, Literature, Political Theory and related fields'.[42]

Most of these suggestions were adopted and went into the 'Preliminary Statement of Objectives and Program of the Harvard Summer School Foreign

Student Project'–signed by the 'Director: Professor William Y. Elliott'. There, one reads under '1. General Principles' that

> [t]he Harvard Summer School Foreign Student Project represents an attempt to strengthen *the spiritual link between Europe and the United States*. Among a generation of Europeans [...] American material aid frequently represents only an alleviation of misery and *leaves the spiritual void unfilled*. Communism tends to become the residuary legatee. [...] This argument regarding the essentially poetic nature of the Communist appeal to many young Europeans was well stated in a recent article by Barbara Ward in the *New York Times Magazine*. Perhaps a more significant example is the tremendous critical and popular success of the book 'The Twenty-Fifth House,' [*sic*] which states Europe's dilemma as a choice between the barbarians of the East and those of the West.[43]

(The latter reference was, as we have seen, to Gheorghiu's novel; the former was to a British *Economist* magazine journalist and prolific author. Ward was constantly emphasising that 'the Western powers are engaged—if they will see it so— in an absorbing *contest of spiritual vitality*.')[44] Now, the Harvard Summer School Foreign Student Project could 'assist in counteracting the tendencies of concern 'by giving active, intelligent young Europeans an opportunity to observe the deeper meaning of United States democracy'. It was hoped that 'contact with intense young Americans may demonstrate to foreign participants that a concern for abstract problems is no European monopoly and that the United States does not exhaust its aspirations in material prosperity'.[45]

It is clear from both Kissinger's informal memorandum to Elliott and from the formal proposals that he and Elliott submitted that they wanted initially to attract promising young Europeans (only in later years was the Project opened up to future leaders from Asia as well), and to impress upon such guests a sense of the quality of American political thought and institutions. Kissinger showed himself particularly concerned to avoid appearing patronising, or overtly propagandising: he reflected constantly on the strategies required to avoid generating such an impression; and here, '"Western" or "Occidental" civilization' came very handy. A particularly revealing document is a sheet containing Kissinger's handwritten notes on the content and structure of the seminar:

> Why not make the proposed course of study one on 'Western' or 'Occidental' civilization + govt?
> American + Western European civilization are but branches off the same tree.

To point to the overall problems of Western thought and institutions, to undertake a comparative study of Western developments in general
Would   a) make us appear less egocentric
b) include Europe and thereby make the European student more eager and more personally concerned re the subject
c) permit us to point out in the most natural manner possible, certain differences that do exist between the civilizations of both sides of the Atlantic.

Imagine, for ex[ample], the attraction of a series of lectures and seminars on:
'Nihilism and Despair in US and European Literature since 1900'
or: Factors of strength and health in the US + European body politic in the age or relativism + cynicism
or: Comparative Govt of the US, UK, France, Germany'[46]

Having thought through the rationale, the main courses, as well as the—very important, he insisted—social aspects of the experience to offer, Kissinger paid particular attention to planning the selection process.[47] He took over much of that responsibility personally and went to Europe to interview candidates. He must have done some things right, given that the people selected to attended the programme eventually included a future president of the French Republic (Valéry Giscard d'Estaing), prime minister of the Turkish Republic (Bülent Ecevit), Japanese prime minister (Yasuhiro Nakasone), Malaysian prime minister (Mahatir bin Mohamad) and Belgian prime minister (Leo Tindemans), to name but a few.[48]

The magazine *Confluence* was a related initiative begun by Kissinger and Elliott at about the same time as the Foreign Student Project was launched. A mission statement in the first issue shows what they were after:

> Are there any really common values that underlie the civilization of the West, *and by the West we certainly mean a broader community than just those countries that now form part of the NATO organization*? What of the others who constitute the wider Atlantic community and for that matter the rest of the free world that extends beyond those regional confines? Is there a positive moral content to freedom in our Western tradition that rests upon *spiritual values* for which men not only will die, but for which they will live with devotion and sacrifice? How can we bring the streams of national cultures into a sufficiently common channel to give, once more, hope and faith and the requisite strength to face the prospects of our times?[49]

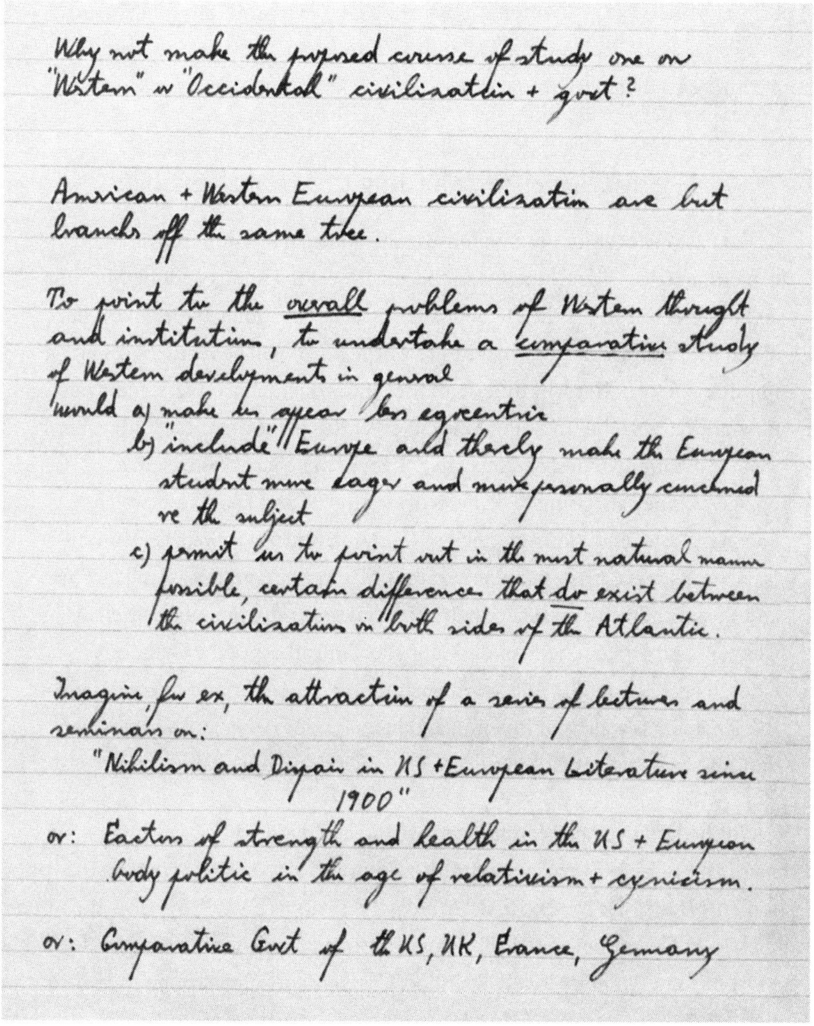

FIGURE 8.1. Handwritten note by Henry Kissinger, ca. 1951. Beinecke Rare Book and Manuscript Library, Yale University Library: Henry A. Kissinger Papers, part 2: series 1 (early career and Harvard University), box 132, folder 6 ('Seminar beginnings'), p. 3. The author is grateful to Dr. Kissinger's literary representative for kind permission to reproduce this image.

Henry Kissinger had been thinking about 'Western' or 'Occidental' civilisation for some time. His recently submitted (and notoriously over-lengthy) undergraduate thesis at Harvard had been on the problem of determinism and freedom in the approaches to history of Immanuel Kant, Oswald Spengler and

Arnold Toynbee.⁵⁰ The former two would have been familiar already from Kissinger's early years in Weimar Germany. The latter had very recently become something of a celebrity in America.

V. The Gospel(s) according to Arnold Toynbee

[T]he past histories of our vociferous, and sometimes vituperative, living contemporaries—the Chinese and the Japanese, the Hindus and the Muslims, and our elder brothers the Orthodox Christians—are going to become a part of our Western past history in a future world which will be neither Western nor non-Western but will inherit all the cultures which we Westerners have now brewed together in a single crucible. Yet this is the manifest truth, when we face it. Our own descendants are not going to be just Western, like ourselves. They are going to be heirs of Confucius and Lao-Tse as well as Socrates, Plato, and Plotinus; heirs of Gautama Buddha as well as Deutero-Isaiah and Jesus Christ; heirs of Zarathustra and Muhammad as well as Elijah and Elisha and Peter and Paul; heirs of Shankara and Ramanuja as well as Clement and Origen; heirs of the Cappadocian Fathers of the Orthodox Church as well as of the African Augustine and our Umbrian Benedict; heirs of Ibn Khaldun as well as of Bossuet; and heirs [...] of Lenin and Gandhi and Sun Yat-sen as well as Cromwell and George Washington and Mazzini.⁵¹

It was in the last week of March 1947 that the abridged edition of the first six volumes of the British historian Arnold J. Toynbee's *A Study of History* was published in New York by Oxford University Press (the UK edition had been published in December 1946). The timing proved felicitous. As a result, for a few years from 1947, America loved Toynbee. Conveniently, he happened to be in the United States (and later in Canada) for lectures during and following the date of publication, so he was able to give many interviews.

A couple of weeks earlier, on 12 March 1947, President Truman had asked Congress to approve funding to support the governments of Greece and Turkey against Communist threats. Five days later, Henry Luce's *Time* magazine undertook to explain to the American public what was at stake. On the cover they put a portrait of Toynbee, accompanied by the comment, 'Our civilization is not inexorably doomed.' An extraordinarily influential article in that issue of the magazine, written by the repentant ex-Communist Whittaker Chambers, was meant to translate to the readers the complex message of the first six volumes of Toynbee's *Study of History*. It began by referring to Britain's withdrawal from

Greece and the Empire as 'a crisis in Western civilization itself'. As a result, '[t]he U.S. must, in Britain's place, consciously become what she had been in reluctant fact, since the beginning of World War II: the champion of the remnants of Christian civilization and history'. Such publicity at such a time did the publication of the abbreviated edition of Toynbee's extant volumes (to be published a week or so later) no harm at all. Sales were beyond anyone's expectations, and continued so with every new printing. Yet this was the same Toynbee who thought as poorly of the Americans in cultural terms as is indicated by the 'semi-barbarian [...] on the cultural periphery' statement that we earlier saw quoted by Gladwyn Jebb. But then, *Time* magazine had sufficiently distorted Toynbee's message to make it sound like what Americans needed to hear.[52] (Chambers was to continue his crusade with a seven-part series on the history of Western culture, stressing the role of 'America as heir and hope of the West's civilization' for Henry Luce's *Life* magazine in 1947 and 1948).[53]

Time's founder, Henry Luce, had liked Toynbee and his recently found religiosity when they met in 1942. Luce had a—literally—missionary zeal to promote America's destiny. Later he would realise that Toynbee was not as keen on that part of his thinking as he was himself: 'But then, five or six years later, when Toynbee became famous, I knew that I disagreed with him on one point, the critical point for now. Toynbee regarded America as simply a peripheral part of European civilization. I regarded America as a special dispensation [*sic*]—under Providence—and I said so.'[54] That is why they parted company eventually, though not before Luce's magazines (*Time*, *Life* and *Fortune*) had made of the British professor a major celebrity in the United States and, in time, in the rest of the world.

But while Toynbee came to be lionised in America as a beacon of optimism fighting for the survival of Western, Christian civilisation, he was soon to find himself in trouble in Britain (and being accused of the exact opposite). He was asked by the BBC to deliver the prestigious Reith Lectures for 1952. The lectures were broadcast and printed in *The Listener*, and then published as a book, entitled *The World and the West*, in 1953. Toynbee argued that in 'the encounter between the world and the West that has been going on by now for four or five hundred years' it had not been the West that had been 'hit by the world'. Rather, 'it is the world that has been hit—and hit hard—by the West'. He then asked Westerners to try briefly to 'slip out [of their] native Western skin and look at the encounter between the world and the West through the eyes of the great non-Western majority of mankind'. That was important, in light of what the Westerner would learn by adopting such a perspective. For no matter how different the 'non-Western peoples' were in other respects from one another, they would nevertheless all inform him that '[t]he West [...] has been the arch-aggressor of modern times, and each will have their own experience of Western aggression to bring up against him.' One of the things that particularly annoyed critics was Toynbee's assertion that '[t]he Russians will remind him that their country has been invaded by Western armies overland in 1941, 1915, 1812, 1709, and 1610.' People should remember, Toynbee maintained, 'that the Germans, who attacked their neighbours, including Russia, in the First World War and again in the Second World War, are Westerners too'; but also 'that the Russians, Asians, and Africans do not draw fine distinctions between different hordes of "Franks"— which is the world's common name for Westerners in the mass'.[55] That Toynbee should state that 'Russia is part of the world's great non-Western majority' and attribute that classification to the fact that Russia had been converted not from Rome, but from Constantinople, would have come as no surprise to anyone who had read the first part of his *Study of History* and his classification of civilisations there.[56] Meanwhile, the fact that he needed so explicitly to assert and justify that categorisation during the Reith Lectures may not be unrelated to the ambivalence we have noted earlier in this chapter, that led many in the aftermath of World War II to speak of the Soviet Union as part of 'Western civilisation'.

The other part of Toynbee's argument that was painful referred to the 'spiritual' advantage that he claimed Russia had gained over the West through Communism, 'a weapon of Western origin' that the Russians were now using against the West. The Russians had in the past (under Peter the Great and under Stalin) used technological/industrial Westernisation in order to defeat the West, but now they were using a much more dangerous weapon: '[A]ll tools are not of the material kind; there are *spiritual tools* as well, and these are the most potent than Man has made.' A creed could be a tool, and 'in the new round in the competition between Russia and the West that began in 1917, the Russians this time threw into their scale of the balances [a creed that] weighed [...] heavily against their Western competitors' material tools'. Communism, invented by Westerners Marx and Engels, was 'particularly well suited to serve Russia as a Western weapon for waging an anti-Western *spiritual warfare*'. For the new creed, in the West where it had arisen, was 'a heresy'. It was 'a Western criticism of the West's failure to live up to her own Christian principles in the economic and social life of this professedly Christian society'. It was 'just the *spiritual weapon* that an adversary of the West would like to pick up and turn against its makers'. With this Western weapon in her hands, Russia could carry her war with the West into the enemy's country on the spiritual plane. Thus, '[i]n [...] threatening to undermine the Western civilization's foundations on the West's own home ground, Communism has already proved itself a more effective anti-Western weapon in Russian hands than any material weapon could ever be'; and besides that undermining within the West, Communism was moreover serving to bring into the Russian camp 'the Chinese quarter of the human race, as well as other sections of the majority of mankind that is neither Russian nor Western.'[57]

Clearly for Toynbee, for the time being at least, 'the spiritual initiative, though not the technological lead' had passed 'from the Western to the Russian side'; and (as if he had not yet sufficiently invoked the 's'-word) he went on to declare that 'the present encounter between the world and the West is now moving off the technological plane on to the spiritual plane.'[58] He announced that he had '[s]ome light on this chapter of the story' to offer, by way of analysing the history of 'the world's earlier encounter with Greece and Rome'.

That 'light' came in the last chapter of *The World and the West*. Toynbee tried there to establish an analogy between the impact of the Greco-Roman civilisation on the rest of the world in antiquity and the impact of the West on the rest of the world over the past four or five centuries. Given that the relationship of 'the West' to 'the world' was a work in progress, the only historical precedent to which one could turn for clues to understanding it was that of the Greco-Roman civilisation's relationship to 'the world'. (The logic of parallels and analogies is unmistakably similar to Spengler's.) Toynbee identified a 'spiritual vacuum' in the Greco-Roman world in the second century CE. The civil servants and philosophers were 'still unaware that any such question' was 'on the agenda'. Instead, the people who had 'read the signs of the times' and had 'taken action in the light of these indications' were 'the obscure missionaries of half-a-dozen Oriental religions'. These preachers of strange religions had 'gently stolen the initiative out of Greek and Roman hands'. This counter-offensive was looming, but not yet recognised for what it was, for it was being 'launched on a different plane'. The original offensive had been 'military, political and economic'; the counter-offensive was religious. Toynbee's conclusion was indicative of what he prophesied as the most likely outcome for the future of the West's encounter with 'the world': 'After the Greeks and Romans had conquered the world by force of arms, the world took its conquerors captive by converting them to new religions which addressed their message to all human souls without discriminating between rulers and subjects or between Greeks, Orientals, and barbarians.' Was something like that also to be 'written into the unfinished history of the world's encounter with the West?' He could not 'foretell the future'; but we could 'see that something which has actually happened once, in another episode of history, must at least be one of the possibilities that lie ahead of us.'[59]

The 1952 Reith Lectures caused a scandal in Britain.[60] Given prime listening time on the BBC, they commanded a large audience and 'stirred considerable indignation among patriotic Englishmen who felt that Toynbee's portrait of the British Empire [...] was utterly unfair'—on account of his dwelling upon 'the West's aggressiveness in times past and on the pain and indignation Western superiority had created in Asian minds, while saying nothing of the benefits, or presumed benefits, that westerners had brought to their colonial subjects'.[61] The part that received the most negative attention was of course the treatment of Russia, both as a victim of past Western aggression and as currently holding the upper hand in the 'spiritual' battle, because of the appeal of Communism as a substitute for the West's own lamentably abandoned Christian heritage. *The Times*'s comment on the first lecture shows what the take-away lesson was: 'The World and the West: Russian Capture of Initiative—Prof. Toynbee on the Spiritual Issue'.[62] Besides reporting on each Reith lecture individually, *The Times* dedicated a long editorial to Toynbee's argument after the last lecture had been delivered, entitled 'As Others See Us'. Though sympathetic in general, the article was critical of Toynbee's presentation of Russia as a victim of aggression, retorting—in Toynbee's register—that Russia had been 'far more "western" in behaviour than Mr. Toynbee suggests', given its steady self-aggrandisement through conquest. But another question went deeper. 'Anxious over the West's failure to live up to its Christian ideals and desirous of emphasising the spiritual element in Communism, he tends in places to reduce the clash between the West and the East into one between western force and eastern religion.' Yet there had been quite a bit of force used by the Soviet army in imposing Communism upon Eastern Europe, the article reminded its readers.[63]

When Douglas Jerrold's 'response' to Toynbee, *The Lie about the West*, was published in 1954, it was favourably reviewed in the *Times Literary Supplement* (*TLS*). A long debate ensued, focused around a series of letters to the *TLS*.[64] For some two months Toynbee was obliged to clarify further what he had meant in the Reith Lectures. Challenged by the *TLS* reviewer to declare his own guess about the prospect of new religions from the East conquering the West as their predecessors had conquered Rome, Toynbee responded, 'I guess that the West is going to be converted to some religion which, like Mayayanian Buddhism, Mithraism and Christianity, calls on us to worship a god who is not a deification of our human selves.' He also guessed 'that this will be the Christian religion that came to the Greeks and Romans from Palestine, with one or two elements in traditional Christianity discarded and replaced by a new element from India'. More concretely: 'I expect and hope that this avatar of Christianity will include the vision of God as being Love. But I also expect and hope that it will discard the other traditional Christian vision of God as being a jealous god, and that it will reject the self-glorification of this jealous god's "Chosen People" as being unique.' This was 'where India comes in, with her belief (complementary to the vision of God as Love) that there may be more than one illuminating and saving approach to the mystery of the universe'.[65]

Toynbee's frequent utterances about his preferred syncretic religious future came at a price. The final straw as regards Toynbee's reputation in Britain came with a bitingly mocking article in *Encounter* on Toynbee's prophetic role in inaugurating a new religious era. Written by Oxford University's regius professor of history, Hugh Trevor-Roper, it proved fatal to Toynbee's academic standing.[66]

VI. 'Freunde, die Freiheit hat die Offensive ergriffen!'[67] Those Who Said, 'I Choose the West'

A fascinating aspect of the intellectual history of the Cold War is the role played by the front organisations that both sides used to promote their own image and undermine that of their opponent. One of the most successful such operations was the Congress for Cultural Freedom that began in Berlin in 1950. The CCF was crucial in the 1950s and 1960s in promoting contacts and activities among mainly left-wing intellectuals who rejected (or, all too often, came to reject, having initially been Communists) the ideology of the Soviet Union. Much of the historiography on the CCF has understandably been preoccupied with the details of how it was secretly funded by the CIA, something that was only revealed in the late 1960s.[68] But the story of the ideas generated, exchanged and promoted through many magazines supported by the Congress and its international gatherings is no less fascinating. It was a catalyst in efforts at 'Westernising' West Germany, and it was no coincidence that it began its life with a huge gathering in West Berlin under the auspices of the magazine *Der Monat*, then published from the American High Commission.[69] Unsurprisingly, most of those with pivotal roles in the initiative were refugees from either Russia or other Eastern European countries, or came from families of refugees. (As Edward Shils was to put it much later—referring to Estonian-born Michael Josselson and the Jewish-American, of Russian origin, Melvin Laski—'these two Russian Jews decided to save Western civilisation'.[70]).

The CCF was far from being a monolith with a particular 'line'. There were many and passionate, often acrimonious, disagreements within it. But what it did manage collectively to do was give a forum to many intellectuals, artists and politicians of various hues of the left who could not be comfortable with conservatives and yet rejected Stalinism. One of the most tangible results of the debates and publications related to the Congress or its members was the emergence of the idea of the 'end of ideologies' by the mid-1950s. Magazines established by the CCF in several countries and languages spread ideas and built strong networks. *Preuves* from Paris and *Encounter* from London were among the most influential, but there were several others, in German, Italian, Spanish and later other languages. By the mid-1950s the meetings of the CCF had started including notable numbers of people from what was then called the 'Third World'—not least the Milan meeting of 1955. Decolonisation meant that competition intensified for the loyalties of people in the newly independent counties that were rapidly proliferating. Marxism held strong attractions for African, Asian and Latin American intellectuals, and the Soviet Union made sure to enhance those attractions by propaganda, networks and front organisations, with particular attention paid to writers and intellectuals. The Paris Secretariat of the CCF in particular began to turn its attention to 'the Third World'. While for the moment Europe remained the centre of the CCF's cultural activities, by the 1960s more and more attention was being paid to the non-European world.[71]

But in its early hectic days, a notable manifestation of the climate that the CCF encouraged was that all sorts of intellectuals, by various kinds of extreme-left itineraries, ended up declaring, as did former Trotskyite Dwight Macdonald in 1952, 'I choose the West.'[72] By the winter of 1952 the battle lines were clear. In a debate at Mt. Holyoke College with Norman Mailer (whose position instead was 'I cannot choose'),[73] Macdonald's verdict was, 'I choose the West—the US and its allies—and reject the East—the Soviet Union and its ally, China, and its colonial provinces, the nations of Eastern Europe.' He hastened to clarify: 'By "choosing" I mean that I support the political, economic and military struggle of the West against the East. I support it critically [...] but in general I support Western policies.' He justified this choice as follows:

> I choose the West because I see the present conflict not as another struggle between basically similar imperialisms as was World War I but as a fight to the death between radically different cultures. In the West, since the Renaissance and the Reformation, we have created a civilization which puts a high value on the individual, which has to some extent replaced dogmatic authority with scientific knowledge, which since the 18th century has progressed from slavery and serfdom to some degree of political liberty, and which has produced a culture which, while not as advanced as that of the

ancient Greeks, still has some appealing features. I think that Soviet Communism breaks sharply with this evolution, that it is a throwback not to the relatively humane middle ages but to the great slave societies of Egypt and the Orient.

Meanwhile he was not blind to the lethal dangers posed by McCarthyism in America at the time: 'In choosing the West, I must admit that already the effects on our own society of the anti-Communist struggle are bad: Senator McCarthy and his imitators are using lies to create hysteria and moral confusion in the best Nazi-Communist pattern.' In short, America was 'becoming to some extent like the totalitarian enemy we are fighting, but (1) being on the road is not the same thing as being there already [...] and (2) this malign trend can be to some extent resisted'.[74]

The American intellectual historian Christopher Lasch commented more than a decade later that 'Macdonald was much influenced by Hannah Arendt's researches into Nazi Germany', noting that Macdonald referred to Arendt as early as 1945. Later Macdonald 'read with admiration' Arendt's *Origins of Totalitarianism*. Lasch commented, 'The only trouble with this theory is that Miss Arendt and her admirers fell in love with it. The effect of this attachment was to blind them to the differences between Stalin's Russia and Hitler's Germany.' For Lasch, 'Macdonald's choice of the West and his general political despair rested in part on a theory of the nature of totalitarianism which events later showed to have been too rigid. In this sense his despair, like that of so many others, was premature.'[75] Others have criticised Lasch and his narrative of the early Cold War from a left-wing point of view, for underestimating the urgent need to fight it.[76] But whatever the merits of Lasch's latter judgement, he was undoubtedly right about Hannah Arendt's influence on many thinkers at the time.

VII. Hannah Arendt and 'the famous "decline of the West"'

Hannah Arendt (1906–1975) was haunted by the theme of the 'decline of the West' or 'decline of the Occident' (she used both phrases interchangeably).[77] And her references to 'the famous "decline of the West"' were not just for rhetorical effect. She was herself deeply immersed in the search for a more satisfactory answer to the question represented by the 'famous'—and at the time ubiquitous—phrase. Born in Germany in 1906 to a Jewish family, Arendt spent some years in France, fleeing the Nazis, before she managed to escape to America in 1941. Once in the United States, she wrote a lot about Europe for American magazines. She took issue with the widespread interpretations of Nazism as a German phenomenon, as a product of the peculiarities of German history and 'national character'. Instead she accounted for the rise of Nazism as being a result of the vacuum left by the collapse of the European order following the Great War. Her explanations were complex, and developed over time, but they all included an insistence that Nazism was a European, not just a German, phenomenon. And a clear corollary for her was that a return to the prewar order of sovereign nation states would lead again to problems similar to those that led to the rise of Nazism in the 1930s. The solution for Arendt was to be found in the direction of European federalism, as many of the European resistance movements were proposing (which meanwhile would provide the best chance for Jews, in her opinion, besides being the best hope for Europe in general).[78]

Many of the explanations and arguments Arendt had used in her articles of the 1940s found their way into her 1951 magnum opus *The Origins of Totalitarianism* (or *The Burden of Our Time*, as the first British edition was titled). That book amplified the search for wider European roots for Nazism as well as Stalinism, under the broader term 'totalitarianism', which had been in circulation since the 1920s, but acquired much greater resonance after the publication of Arendt's book.[79] The totalitarian regimes were explained through a long analysis of developments in Europe and European empires since the last two decades of the nineteenth century, and connections were drawn between European imperialism and the rise of totalitarianism in Europe. (This may be why, after reading *The Burden of Our Time* in the mid-1950s, Richard Wright thought that, along with the Swedish economist Gunnar Myrdal's work, Arendt's was part of 'this new literature which is destined to modify the attitude of white men toward themselves'.)[80] Arendt tried, in her most famous work, to understand what happened to 'the great political and philosophical traditions of the West'. She used 'the West', 'Western civilization' and 'Western tradition' extensively to refer to a long philosophical tradition since Socrates and Plato and a political-institutional tradition since ancient Rome. To refer to the side she preferred during the Cold War she tended to use 'free world'.

Like Francis Lieber in the nineteenth century, Hannah Arendt could not help thinking of both her new and her old countries (and continents) simultaneously; and she worried that their inhabitants did not realise the extent to which their story was one and the same and their fates intertwined. In September 1954 she published in the liberal Catholic *Commonweal* magazine three articles based on her lecture at Princeton University at a conference on 'The Image of America Abroad'.[81] These lectures gave her an opportunity to summarise what she had concluded from her recent extended sojourn in Europe in the spring and summer of 1952.[82]

FIGURE 8.2. Hannah Arendt in 1933. Photographer unknown. *Source:* https://en.wikipedia.org/wiki/Hannah_Arendt#/media/File:Hannah _Arendt_1933.jpg

Arendt agreed with Alexis de Tocqueville's understanding of America as the culmination of the previous seven hundred years of European history, and to that extent as 'an older and more experienced country than Europe herself'. As she put it, the American Republic 'owes its origin to the greatest adventure of European mankind, which, for the first time since the Crusades [...] embarked upon a common enterprise whose spirit proved to be stronger than all national differences'. De Tocqueville, meanwhile (in his *Democracy in America* [1835–40]), was 'the greatest but not the only author' of the nineteenth century who 'saw the New World as the outcome of an old history and civilization'. Things had changed, however, and in her own time that view was 'the element conspicuously missing in Europe's image of America'. Instead 'today the U.S. is considered to have no more relationship with Europe than any other country, and frequently considered less than Russia or even Asia, both of which are being Europeanized through Marxism for a considerable segment of European opinion—by no means including only Communists or fellow-travellers'. (To confine ourselves to people already discussed or mentioned here, T. S. Eliot and Herbert Read in the 1920s, Oswald Spengler in the 1930s, and Simone Weil, Virgil Gheorghiu and André Siegfried in the 1940s immediately come to mind as having said more or less what Arendt was reporting.) Anti-American feeling was of course, Arendt noted, exploited by Communist propaganda, but it was far from being simply a product of that propaganda. It had popular roots. In Europe, it was 'well on the way to becoming a new *ism*. Anti-Americanism [...] threatens to become the content of a European movement'. The image of America then current in Europe 'may well become the beginning of a new pan-European nationalism'. Thus the 'hope that the emergence of a federated Europe and the dissolution of the present nation-state system will make nationalism itself a thing of the past may be unwarrantedly optimistic'. The resulting situation alarmed Arendt: 'Americanism on one side and Europeanism on the other side of the Atlantic, two ideologies facing, fighting and, above all, resembling each other as all seemingly opposed ideologies do—this may be one of the dangers we face.'[83]

In another article in the same series Arendt commented that Europeans had 'engaged in the now-familiar debates about the soullessness of a country dominated by modern technology, the monotony of the machine, the uniformity of a society based upon mass-production, and the like for many years'.[84] However, things were becoming more dangerous than the repetition of stereotypes. For, in her own day, the 'intimate connection between modern warfare and a technicalized society has become obvious to everybody, and as a result large segments of the population—and not only the intellectuals—are passionately opposed to, and afraid of, technological progress and the growing technicalization of our world'.[85] Now, Arendt noted that technology and the way it had been transforming the world were 'so clearly part and parcel of European history since the beginning of the modern age that it is obviously absurd to blame its consequences on America'. In the past, Europeans 'used to see technical progress in America as Tocqueville saw the progress of American democracy': in other words, 'as something which fundamentally concerned Western civilization as a whole, though for certain specific reasons it had found its first and clearest expression in the United States'. That attitude, she noted, changed once the atomic bomb had been dropped on Hiroshima. Since then, 'there has been a growing tendency both to look upon all technical achievements as inherently evil and destructive and to see in America chiefly, and in Russia sometimes, the epitome of destructive technicalization which is hostile and alien to Europe'.[86]

And yet, the truth was that 'the process which Europeans dread as "Americanization" is the emergence of the modern world with all its perplexities and implications'. And it was, she suggested, 'probable that this process will be accelerated rather than hindered through a federation of Europe, which is also very likely a condition *sine qua non* for European survival'. Her prediction was that '[w]hether or not European federation will be accompanied by the rise of anti-American, pan-European nationalism', as she feared it might, 'unification of economic and demographic conditions is almost sure to create a state of affairs which will be very similar to that existing in the United States'. The upshot was that, while '[o]ne hundred and twenty years ago the European image of America was the image of democracy' and '[t]hough not all Europeans could love it, they had come to terms with it because they knew quite well that it presented part and parcel of the history of the West', in her own time, the image of America was 'modernity'. Currently the world's central problems, Arendt thought, were 'the political organization of mass societies and the political integration of technical power'. Given the 'destructive potentialities inherent in these problems', Europe was 'no longer sure whether she can come to terms with the modern world at all'. As a result, Europe was trying 'to escape the consequences of her own history under the pretext of separating herself from America'. In sum, Arendt concluded, '[t]he image of America which exists in Europe may not tell us much about American realities [...] but] it may tell us something about the justified fears of Europe for her spiritual identity and her even deeper apprehensions about her physical survival'. Nor were these fears and apprehensions 'specifically European, no matter what Europeans may tell us. They are the fears of the whole Western world, and ultimately of all mankind.'[87]

Meanwhile, Arendt had strong views on whether or not the 'free world' ought to combat the Communist threat through an emphasis on religion.[88] When fellow German-Jewish émigré Henry Kissinger asked her to contribute to *Confluence* magazine a paper she gave at a Harvard conference on the topic, he clearly interfered too much with her text, and the editorial liberties he took annoyed her. At any rate, in the full text as she intended it, through a typically Arendtian analysis of Plato, Augustine and half of 'the tradition', she wound up arguing strongly against using religion to fight Communism. The corollary was that the political consequence of the secularisation of the modern age had been 'the elimination from public life, along with religion, of the only *political* element in traditional religion, the fear of Hell'. Now, 'from a viewpoint of mere usefulness, nothing could compete better with the inner coercion of totalitarian ideologies in power over man's soul than fear of Hell'. But it was too late for that: 'no matter how religious our world may turn again, or how much authentic faith still exists in it, or how deeply our moral values may be rooted in our religious systems, the fear of Hell is no longer among the motives which would prevent or stimulate the actions of the majority'; and 'under these circumstances religion was bound to lose its primary political element, just as public life was bound to lose the religious sanction of a transcendent authority'. That separation, moreover, had its 'singular advantages for religious as well as irreligious people'. Modern history had shown that 'alliances between "throne and altar" can only discredit both'. Arendt's ultimate message regarding the Cold War dilemma was, 'Confronted with a full-fledged ideology, our greatest danger is to counter it with an ideology of our own.' If those in the free world were to 'try to inspire public-political life once more with "religious passion" or to use religion as a means of political distinctions, the result may very well be the transformation and perversion of religion into an ideology and the corruption of our fight against totalitarianism by a fanaticism which is utterly alien to the very essence of freedom'.[89]

VIII. Return to the Principles of Western Civilisation: Athens and Jerusalem

Hannah Arendt was far from being alone among German-born American thinkers in considering that Spengler's title, *The Decline of the West*, should be taken seriously. One of those who shared such concerns with her also held a distinctive position on the relationship of religion to Western civilisation. A German-Jewish refugee from Nazism, Leo Strauss (1899–1973) became one of America's major academic influences in the twentieth century.[90] His views were aired in many places, but the 1952 text 'Progress or Return? The Contemporary Crisis in Western Civilization' is particularly relevant to our concerns. In a discussion on the delusions of a belief in progress, Strauss argued that 'the incredible barbarization' which people had witnessed in the twentieth century had led to serious reconsideration: 'I think that we all have now become sufficiently sober to admit that whatever may be wrong with Spengler—and there are many things wrong in Spengler—that the very title, in the English translation especially, of the work is more sober, more reasonable, than these hopes [for progress] which lasted so long.' The 'barbarization' was, Strauss claimed, 'not altogether accidental'. In fact, what had taken place in modern times had been 'a gradual corrosion and destruction of the heritage of Western civilization'. In his view, the 'soul of the modern development', as it were, was 'a peculiar "realism," the notion that moral principles and the appeal to moral principles—preaching, sermonizing—is ineffectual', and the concomitant belief that 'one has to seek a substitute for moral principles which would be much more efficacious'. Now, such substitutes 'were found, for example, in institutions or in economics, and *perhaps the most important substitute is what was called "the historical process"'*. That change manifested itself in changes in the use of language, not least 'in the substitution of the distinction between progressive and reactionary for the distinction between good and bad'. The implication was, Strauss believed, 'that we have to choose and to do what is conducive to progress, what is in agreement with the historical trends, and it is indecent or immoral to be squeamish in such adaptations'. The traumatic events of the twentieth century made it clear, however, that 'historical trends are absolutely ambiguous and therefore cannot serve as a standard'; differently put, that 'to jump on the bandwagon or the wave of the future is not more reasonable than to resist those trends'. The result was that 'no standard whatever was left'. For the facts themselves, 'understood as historical processes, indeed do not teach us anything regarding values, and the consequence of the abandonment of moral principle proper was that value judgments have no objective support whatsoever'. The predicament became that 'the values of barbarism and cannibalism are as defensible as those of civilization'.[91]

The obvious conclusion was that the 'crisis of modernity' had to lead 'to the suggestion *that we should return. But return to what?*' Strauss's answer to that last question was, 'Obviously, *to Western civilization in its pre-modern integrity, to the principles of Western civilization.*' But there was a catch.

Yet there is a difficulty here, because Western civilization consists of two elements, has two roots, which are in radical disagreement with each other. We may call these elements [. . .] Jerusalem and Athens or the Bible and Greek philosophy. This radical disagreement today is frequently played down, and this playing down has a certain superficial justification, for the whole history of the West presents itself at first glance as an attempt to harmonize or to synthesize the Bible and Greek philosophy. But a closer study shows that what happened and has been happening in the West for many centuries, is not a harmonization but an attempt at harmonization.

These attempts at harmonisation were 'doomed to failure' for a clear reason: 'each of these two roots of the Western world sets forth one thing as the one thing needful, and the one thing needful proclaimed by the Bible is incompatible, as it is understood by the Bible, with the one thing needful proclaimed by Greek philosophy, as it is understood by Greek philosophy'. For 'the one thing needful according to Greek philosophy is the life of autonomous understanding'; while '[t]he one thing needful as spoken by the Bible is the life of obedient love'.[92]

Strauss argued that if that antagonism was considered 'in action', the obvious conclusion was that 'the core, the nerve of Western intellectual history, Western spiritual history [...] is the conflict between the biblical and the philosophical notions of the good life'. From this derived his most crucial claim, that '*this unresolved conflict is the secret of the vitality of Western civilization*'. He conceded that the recognition of 'two conflicting roots of Western civilization' was initially 'a very disconcerting observation'. But that was not all, because that realisation had 'also something reassuring and comforting about it'. This was because

> [t]he very life of Western civilization is the life between two codes, a fundamental tension. There is therefore no reason inherent in the Western civilization itself, in its fundamental constitution, why it should give up life. But this comforting thought is justified only if we live that life, if we live that conflict. No one can be both a philosopher and a theologian, nor, for that matter, some possibility which transcends the conflict between philosophy and theology, or pretends to be a synthesis of both. But every one of us can be and ought to be either one or the other, the philosopher open to the challenge of theology or the theologian open to the challenge of philosophy.[93]

As Mark Lilla has summarised it, Strauss himself 'chose Athens over Jerusalem. But as a proud Jew who respected his people's belief, he also appreciated what religion at its highest development could offer as a way of life, especially for ordinary, nonreflective people.'[94]

That same year, in the autumn of 1952, Strauss finished preparing for publication a series of lectures that he had delivered at the University of Chicago in 1949. They were published in 1953 as *Natural Right and History*. In the Introduction he made the bold claim that the militarily defeated Germans had defeated 'the West' in the realm of thought. He began by quoting from the American Declaration of Independence: 'We hold these truths to be self-evident, that all men are created equal, that they are endowed by their Creator with certain unalienable Rights, that among these are Life, Liberty, and the pursuit of Happiness.' The nation that emerged by professing that proposition had become, 'no doubt partly as a consequence of this declaration, the most powerful and prosperous of the nations of the earth'. But, he asked, 'Does this nation in its maturity still cherish the faith in which it was conceived and raised? Does it still hold these "truths to be self-evident"?' And then he dropped his bomb. Referring to the 1922 lecture by Ernst Troeltsch that we examined above in chapter 6, Strauss claimed that the historicist relativism of German thought—described by Troeltsch as distinguishing it from the thought of 'the West'—had now come to dominate the social sciences in 'the West', and not least in America. About a generation earlier, according to Strauss, 'a German scholar [i.e., Troeltsch] could still describe the difference between German thought and that of Western Europe and the United States by saying that the West still attached decisive importance to natural right', while, in Germany the very terms 'natural right' and 'humanity' had by then [1922] 'become almost incomprehensible'. Having abandoned the idea of natural right, that same 'German scholar' had gone on to posit that German thought 'was led eventually to unqualified relativism'.[95] Strauss then commented, 'What was a tolerably accurate description of German thought twenty-seven years ago would now appear to be true of Western thought in general.' Adding insult to the injury, he then commented, 'It would not be the first time that a nation, defeated on the battlefield and, as it were, annihilated as a political being, has deprived its conquerors of the most sublime fruit of victory by imposing on them the yoke of its own thought.' For ('[w]hatever might be true of the thought of the American people') it was certain, Strauss argued, that 'American social science has adopted the very attitude toward natural right which, a generation ago, could still be described, with some plausibility, as characteristic of German thought'. Thus, 'present-day American social science [...] is dedicated to the proposition that all men are endowed by the evolutionary process or by a mysterious fate with many kinds of urges and aspirations, but certainly with no natural right'.[96] Here was a challenge indeed for Americans in the early 1950s! As we shall see, it did not go unnoticed.

IX. The 'true Westerner' *par excellence*: Raymond Aron's Cold War

Few people thought as hard about the many issues related to the Cold War as Raymond Aron. He was a towering figure in most phases of Cold War debates, not only in France but everywhere, as befits 'the most cosmopolitan French intellectual of his time'.[97] Not many in France had studied Marx as assiduously and seriously as Aron had. He had also carefully studied Comte, whose entire output he was required to read for his *aggregation* examinations.[98] Aron's subtle analyses of the meaning of 'industrial society' had much to do with his readings of Comte.⁹⁹ He also knew his Tocqueville, his German philosophy and sociology, American thought and social science, and much more. He went out of his way to familiarise himself with every topic that he considered relevant to the pronouncements he had to make. The wish to make informed statements involved him in unusually deep study of several different fields, including economics, sociology, philosophy, international relations, Clausewitz on war, and nuclear technologies, to name but a few. He became one of the godfathers of the idea of 'the end of ideology' in the mid-1950s. Meanwhile, he was a victim of the overwhelming popularity of Communism of various hues among the vast majority of French intellectuals until the late 1970s, and to that extent relatively isolated from them. It was only in the very last years before his death in 1983 that he was accorded ample recognition in his own country. In the earlier decades, however, a slogan even had it that it was better to be wrong with Sartre than right with Aron. Yet he held his nerve and soldiered on with his writings and initiatives. And if there is a brief way to summarise his advice to the West, it is, 'to hold its nerve'. If it could survive without, on the one hand, a mutually suicidal thermonuclear war and, on the other, compromising what made it different and better than its rival, it would have won in the end.¹⁰⁰

A seminal contribution to French debates was Aron's 1955 indictment of what he saw as the follies or hypocritical stances of most French intellectuals who were choosing to be neutralists or fellow-travellers of Communism (his former fellow student, Sartre, being a leading figure among them). It was in that book, *L'Opium des intellectuels*, that Aron offered the following definition: 'The true Communist is the man who accepts the whole of the Soviet system in the terms dictated by the Party. The true "Westerner" is the man who accepts nothing unreservedly in our civilisation except the liberty it allows him to criticise it and the chance it offers him to improve it.'¹⁰¹

Although he disagreed with Hannah Arendt to the extent that he thought that Communism was indeed a secular religion, Aron concurred with her meanwhile that the West should not offer itself as the defender of a 'Christian' civilisation. 'We must be careful not to compromise religion in the struggles of temporal powers, to attribute to the system we defend virtues which it does not possess,' he wrote. To his mind, the liberal democracies did 'not represent a "Christian" civilization'. They had 'developed in societies whose religion was Christian', and they had been 'inspired to a certain extent by the absolute value which Christianity gives to the individual soul'; but that was as far as it went.

FIGURE 8.3. Plaque in rue Raymond-Aron, in the thirteenth *arrondissement* in Paris. Photo by Chabeo1. *Source:* https://fr.wikipedia.org/wiki/Rue_Raymond -Aron#/media/Fichier:Plaque_Rue_Raymond_Aron_-_Paris_XIII_(FR75) _-_2021-06-07_-_1.jpg

> It is not for those of us who belong to no Church to recommend a choice to the believers, but it behoves us all, incorrigible liberals who tomorrow would return again to the struggle against clericalism, to fight today against this totalitarianism from which professing Christians happen to suffer as much as free-thinking scientists and artists. The tyranny we denounce is not solely directed against a faith we do not share; it is one which affects us all. [...] In defending the freedom of religious teaching, the unbeliever defends his own freedom.

What 'essentially' distinguished the West from 'the Soviet universe' was 'the fact that the one admits itself to be divided and the other "politicises" the whole of existence'.[102]

Aron's formulation of a grand strategy for the survival of the West is best epitomised in his 1962 book *Paix et guerre entre les nations* (*Peace and War*). To 'the skeptic or cynic' who might object, '[D]oes the "salvation of the West" ever deserve to be defended at the price of millions, of tens of millions of victims?', Aron had a clear answer:

> This objection is spuriously rational. It is true that the West will not be saved if the thermonuclear war takes place. In the age of the strategy of defense, it was possible to save a nation or a civilization by war. In the age of the strategy of deterrence, it is not possible to save a nation or a civilization by war, but neither is it possible to save them by capitulation. The point therefore is to convince ourselves and others that the values which would perish along with the regime and the civilization of the West justify the danger which we are creating for tens of millions of people, a danger which capitulation would dissipate *temporarily*.[103]

Aron remarked with regard to 'the "leftist intellectual," who is convinced that the Soviet side, because it calls itself socialist, sustains and embodies the hopes of mankind' that 'those intellectuals who seek to be "humanitarians," who claim an association with the tradition of the Enlightenment and who either reserve their sympathy for the Soviet side or else refuse to distinguish between the two giants (or barbarians) seem to me to be suffering from a perversion of the moral sense'. Having said all that, he did not wish to be misunderstood: 'Western societies are imperfect and, in certain regards, perhaps more imperfect than Soviet societies'. Aron had many times made clear that America's race relations or socioeconomic model did not represent any ideal for Europe or anyone else. Thus, he clarified again that, if one were to compare 'the United States and the Soviet Union, perhaps the former has more trouble putting into effect the principle of racial equality than the latter'. Yet his comment was, 'Nothing prevents an observer from hating the commercialized radio and television from across the Atlantic more than the politicized radio and television from behind the iron Curtain'. The difference was that 'criticism of American civilization is an integral part of that civilization itself—which is not the case with Soviet civilization—and above all the negative aspect of the regime is not transformed into a positive one by dialectical jugglery'.[104]

Aron spent much time both in his journalistic writing for *Le Figaro* and in his major books discussing the prospects of decolonisation.[105] He correctly predicted that once decolonisation liberated Western powers from the colonial stigma, nationalism might operate as a problem for the Soviet bloc as much as for the West.

By the mid-1950s decolonisation and the future of newly independent nations were among the hottest topics in town. There were many other people in Paris keenly interested in the matter as well. Among the most interesting was the Afro-American novelist Richard Wright, in self-exile in Paris since 1947.

X. 'Last call [...] to the moral conscience of the West': Richard Wright, Empathetic Westerner 'ahead of the West'

Few people were as preoccupied with the meaning of 'Western civilisation' as Richard Wright (1908–1960). For the poor self-educated boy from Mississippi, become world-famous Paris-based author, the question was existential. It is significant that his friend Gertrude Stein chose to tell him, shortly before she died, that he should go to Spain, because in Spain he would understand the meaning of the Western world.[106] The episode is telling if it actually happened that way—and even more telling if he made it up. (That by chance he spent most of his Paris years in rue Monsieur-le-Prince, two doors away from Auguste Comte's flat, is an entertaining coincidence for readers of this book). Wright was the best-known Black writer in the world in the 1940s and 1950s. The publication of his novel *Native Son* (1940) made him famous. His (first) autobiography, *Black Boy* (1945), was also a major success. Growing up in Mississippi, the most racist state in the American South, he had very poor educational opportunities as a child. Cedric Robinson gave him his due when he pointed out that '[o]nly Richard Wright, among the radical Black thinkers upon whom we shall lay emphasis, came from the Black substratum'.[107] What Wright learned he learned as an autodidact. After moving from the South to Chicago he joined the John Reed Book Club, which gave him a way to read voraciously. Through the club he was recruited to the Communist Party of the United States. By the mid-1940s he had decided that the Communist Party did not have any genuine interest in the plight of Afro-Americans and was simply trying to use them. He broke with the Party and any connection with the Soviet Union, though he continued to believe in the usefulness of Marxism as a method of social analysis. His public declaration of his break with the Party, first published in the *Atlantic* in August 1944 under the title 'I Tried to Be a Communist', caused a sensation. That a few years later it was republished in Richard Crossman's edited volume *The God That Failed: Six Studies in Communism* was another indication of Wright's status as a writer and intellectual—he was the only non-white author in that volume.[108] (Ten years later, however, he refused to participate in an anniversary edition, furious at the way he had been used

FIGURE 8.4. Richard Wright. *Portrait of Richard Wright*, photograph by Carl Van Vechten (date unknown). Van Vechten Collection, Library of Congress, Washington, DC. Photo by Chabeo2. *Source:* https://en.wikipedia.org/wiki/Richard_Wright_(author)#/media/File:Richard_Wright.jpg

in what he saw as Cold War propaganda.) He remained for the rest of his life very critical of both superpowers' methods during the Cold War. He suffered considerably for his criticisms of American policies.[109]

Life in segregated America did not appeal to Wright, and after an extended visit to Paris in 1946, where he was celebrated as a famous author and not judged according to the colour of his skin, he and his wife Ellen decided to move to Paris permanently in 1947. He died prematurely (and suspiciously, for some) in a Paris hospital in 1960. During those Paris years, while continuing to write fiction, he also wrote his most interesting books and essays on political and international subjects. Besides many shorter articles and reviews, and plenty of interviews that he gave in various countries during those years, his most important books include *Black Power: A Record of Reactions in a Land of Pathos* (1954); *The Color Curtain: A Report on the Bandung Conference* (1956); *Pagan Spain* (1957); *White Man, Listen!* (1957); and a sequel to his earlier autobiography *Black Boy*, entitled *American Hunger* (published posthumously in 1977). Wright tried hard to analyse the predicament of Afro-Americans, the psychological results of racism, 'the frog perspective' of feeling looked down upon, and the relation of Afro-Americans to the continent of Africa, among other things. But during his life in Paris he developed much broader, global, interests, and his greatest loyalty turned out to be to the newly liberated or soon-to-be liberated former colonies, the countries of the so-called 'Third World' (courted by both 'the West' and the Soviet 'East'), whose 'Westernised' elites he thought found themselves in a painful predicament. His main theme became highly relevant to the focus of the present book. This is how he put it in an interview, half-way through his Parisian life, in 1953: 'The break from the United States was more than a geographical change [...]. I was trying to grapple with the big problem—the problem and meaning of Western civilization as a whole, and the relation of Negroes and other minority groups to it.'[110] Much of Wright's political writing consisted in attempts to convince the leaders of 'the West' to give the Western-educated elites of Asia, Africa and the Caribbean a proper chance (as well as assistance) to lead their nations to modernisation and progress on their own terms. The dedication page of his book *White Man, Listen!* is telling:

This book is dedicated to [...]

THE WESTERNIZED AND TRAGIC ELITE OF ASIA, AFRICA,
AND THE WEST INDIES—
the lonely outsiders who exist precariously
on the clifflike margins of many cultures—men who are
distrusted, misunderstood, maligned, criticized
by Left and Right, Christian and pagan—
men who carry on their frail and indefatigable shoulders
the best of two worlds—and who,
amidst confusion and stagnation,
seek desperately for a home for their hearts:

a home which, if found,
could be a home for the hearts of all men.[111]

When, encouraged by his friends the Padmores, he first visited Africa (a visit that led to the publication of his *Black Power* in 1954),[112] Wright found himself unable to identify with the continent. The colour of his skin gave him no special access to the ways of thinking of the people he met in Gold Coast (now Ghana). He wrote in his African journal that he saw himself as 'western to the bone', and proud of it.[113]

Jean-Paul Sartre, in his preface to Frantz Fanon's *Les Damnés de la Terre* (*The Wretched of the Earth*), emphasised that, by the time he wrote the book, Fanon had given up on the West and hence it was not addressed to the West, but rather to Fanon's brethren in the colonised world.[114] Such a thing could certainly not be said of Wright. Wright addressed the West directly, hopefully, and urgently. It is little wonder that the—initially highly admiring and complimentary—Fanon ended up criticising Wright for displaying 'an irrational, unjustified confidence in the west's "perspicacity", its "generosity"'.[115] Wright wrote to warn and advise a Western readership to do what he thought was needed to be done before it was too late. The context was of course the Cold War, and time and again in order to make the warning plausible and urgent, he invoked the threat of the Communist bloc, lurking to take advantage of Western short-sightedness, meanness or mistakes. The gist of Wright's message was that the West had to fulfil its promise and live up to its declared principles, for its own sake and the world's as well.

Wright attended the 1955 Bandung Conference and wrote a book-length report on it. The last chapter was entitled 'The Western World at Bandung'. There he asserted that 'if [...] past French and English revolutionaries had had the moral courage to have extended their new and bold declarations of a new humanity to black and brown and yellow men, these ex-colonial subjects would never have felt the need to rise against the West'. He underlined that the Bandung Asian-African Conference communiqué 'was addressed to the West, to the moral prepossessions of the West'. It was his belief 'that the delegates at Bandung, for the most part, though bitter, looked and hoped toward the West'. Accordingly his exhortation was, 'The West [...] must be big enough, generous enough, to accept and understand that bitterness'. The Bandung communiqué was not, to his mind, an appeal to Communism; rather, 'it carried exalted overtones of the stern dignity of ancient and proud peoples who yearned to rise and play again a role in human affairs'. It was also Wright's conviction that, 'if this call went unheeded, ignored, and if these men, as they will, should meet again, their appeal would be different'. Hence his conclusion (printed thus in capitals): 'IN SUM, BANDUNG WAS THE LAST CALL OF WESTERNIZED ASIANS TO THE MORAL CONSCIENCE OF THE WEST!' If the West were to spurn that call, he warned, 'remember that Mr. Chou En-lai stands there, waiting, patient, with no record of racial practices behind him [...]. He will listen.'[116]

Although he was a novelist and not an economist or social scientist, Wright could appear hard-headed in his analysis. He commented that, when Asian and African raw materials were 'processed in Asia and Africa [...] the supremacy of the Western world, economic, cultural, and political, will have been broken once and for all on this earth and *a de-Occidentalization of mankind* will have definitely set in'. As he added in a parenthesis, 'Thus, in time, *the whole world will be de-Occidentalized, for there will be no East or West!*' The bargain seemed to him to be that '[t]o have an ordered, rational world in which we all can share', the 'average white Westerner' would ultimately have to accept that outcome; and, if they were to accept it, they would 'also have to accept, for an unspecified length of time, a much, much lower standard of living, for that is what a de-Occidentalization of present-day mankind will bring about'.[117] Not everyone endorsed Wright's emphasis on the racial focus of the Bandung conference,[118] but Wright had his reasons to issue his 'last warning', and would not miss such an opportunity to tell 'the white West' how serious the danger of catastrophe was. This did not mean that he told his brethren of the African diaspora what they may have wanted to hear either. Far from it, in fact.

Very soon (September 1956) he was to be nothing if not controversial among the vanguard of the world's Black writers and artists. Shortly after he arrived in Paris, Wright had been involved in the founding of the journal *Présence africaine* in 1947.[119] Edited by the Senegalese senator Alioune Diop, the journal had on its editorial board the (also Senegalese) poet Léopold Sédar Senghor and the Martinican poet Aimé Césaire, alongside Wright himself.[120] Then, in 1956 Wright was a member of the committee of intellectuals, affiliated with *Présence africaine*, who organised the first Congrès international des écrivains et artistes noirs, which was to take place at the Sorbonne between 19 and 22 September 1956. It was conceived by Alioune Diop (who, like Wright, had attended the Bandung Conference the year before) as a second, 'cultural Bandung'.

What happened there was vintage Wright. To all intents and purposes, in a friendly and brotherly tone, he told the delegates gathered to discuss ways of reviving and celebrating African culture (who, to his unhappy surprise, turned out to be much more concerned than he was with religion) the equivalent of what

FIGURE 8.5. Plaque commemorating Richard Wright at 14, rue Monsieur-le-Prince, in the sixth *arrondissement* in Paris, where he lived for more than ten years. Photo by Chabe *Source:* https://en.wikipedia.org/wiki/Richard_Wright_(author)#/media/File:Plaque_Richard_Wright,_14_rue_Monsieur-le-Prince,_Paris_6.jpg

Karl Marx had written in the 1850s of the role of the British Empire in India: that the intentions of European imperialists were selfish and greedy, or at best confused, and the justifications they used were irrelevant, but the upshot was that the colonisers had been unwittingly doing the work of history. The human suffering caused was immense and painful to contemplate, but the outcome, all said and done, was rather positive. The Europeans had rid Africans and Asians of their 'irrational' (a crucial word for Wright) traditions and religious handicaps, and created in those countries 'Westernized elites' who were more 'rational' (the other crucial word) than those very Westerners, who had not yet rid themselves entirely of their own religious and other traditional baggage. (As we will see below, three recent research trips to Franco's Spain had convinced Wright of the significance of this insight.)

Wright was to be the last to speak, on a Friday evening. But the tone of what he was to say had become obvious from the first day, when he contributed to the discussion that followed the presentation delivered by Léopold Sédar Senghor. In language adopting essentialist-racial causal explanations of the nineteenth century (even citing approvingly the theories of Arthur de Gobineau),[121] Senghor argued for a revival of the traditions and religions of Africa that colonialism had suppressed. Wright, as respectfully as possible, begged to differ. Everything he had ever written and said, he pleaded, had been 'in defence of the culture that Leopold Senghor describes. Why? Because I don't want to see people hurt; I don't want the suffering to be increased and compounded. And yet, if I try to fit myself into that society, I feel uncomfortable.' He confessed his inability to 'understand and latch onto this culture' that Senghor had been defending; because, he declared, 'my friends, this is not a debate between me and Léopold Senghor; this is a debate between the Western world and the majority of mankind'. And then he threw the grenade: 'Might not the vivid and beautiful culture that Senghor has described [...] have been a fifth column[,] a corps of saboteurs and spies of Europe?' '[W]hen the European guns came in,' he asked, 'did not that [ancestor cult] religion [...] act as a sort of aid to those guns? Did that religion help the people to resist fiercely and hardily and hurl the Europeans out? I question the value of that culture in relationship to the future. I do not condemn it. But how can we use it?' His answer was not going to please most of his audience:

> I [...] want to be free, and I question this culture not in its humane scope, but in relationship to the Western world as it meets that Western world. I have the feeling, uneasy, almost bordering upon dread, that there was a fateful historic complement between a militant white Christian Europe and an ancestral cult religion in Africa. They complemented each other and this morally foul relationship remained for more than five hundred years. I want to see that relationship *ended*. And this is the question I raise generally seeking to offend no-one's sensibilities, but keeping always in mind your freedom and min[e] in relation to the forces that have dominated the West so far, knowing that in that West are some powerful values that Africa must latch onto if Africa is to defend itself.[122]

But that was only the beginning. Late on the last day of the conference, exhausted and stressed by what he perceived to be the dominant atmosphere among the delegates, Wright began to read out his own paper (written the previous summer). He started by complaining about the near absence of women in the deliberations, warning that 'Black men will not be free until their women are free.'[123] Then he proceeded with an attempt to explain his point of view: to clarify where he was coming from, as it were.

Like Du Bois in *The Souls of Black Folk* (1903), Wright saw himself as possessed of 'double vision' (Du Bois had called it 'double-consciousness') due to his predicament as a Black American. But Wright was to be even more emphatic with regard to his peculiar vantage point, focusing explicitly on his relationship with 'the West': '[M]y position is a split one. I'm black. I'm a man of the West [... and]

I see and understand the West; but I also see and understand the non- or anti-Western point of view.' How was that possible? 'This double vision of mine stems from my being a product of Western civilization and from my racial identity.' Thus, '[b]eing a Negro living in a white Western Christian society, I've never been allowed to blend, in a natural and healthy manner, with the culture and civilization of the West'; so now,

> though Western, I'm inevitably critical of the West. Indeed, a vital element of my Westernness resides in this chronically skeptical, this irredeemably critical, outlook. I'm restless. I question not only myself. But my environment. [...] Yet I'm not non-Western. I'm no enemy of the West. Neither am I an Easterner. When I look out upon those vast stretches of this earth inhabited by brown, black and yellow men—sections of the earth in which religion dominates, to the exclusion of almost everything else, the emotional and mental landscape—my reactions and attitudes are those of the West. I see both worlds from another and third point of view.

He added that he was 'numbed and appalled' by the knowledge that 'millions of men in Asia and Africa assign more reality to their dead fathers than to the crying claims of their daily lives: poverty, political degradation, illness, ignorance, etc.' He 'shiver[ed]' when he learned 'that the infant mortality rate, say, in James Town (a slum section of Accra [...]) is fifty per cent'; and he was 'speechless' when he learnt that that appalling condition was 'explained by the statement, "The children did not wish to stay. Their ghost-mothers called them home."' On hearing such explanations he knew 'that there can be no altering of social conditions in those areas until such religious rationalizations have been swept from men's minds'. And yet, this did not prevent him from developing strong sympathies for those he could not identify with: '[B]ecause the swarming populations in those continents are two-time victims—victims of their own religious projections and victims of Western imperialism—my sympathies are unavoidably with, and unashamedly for, them.'[124]

Wright offered a more precise definition of what he meant by 'Western': 'Since I'm detached from, because of racial conditions, the West, why do I bother to call myself Western at all?' He had no choice in the matter, was his answer. 'Historical forces more powerful than I am have shaped me as a Westerner.' What did all this mean for him? 'Hence, standing shoulder to shoulder with the Western white man, speaking his tongue, sharing his culture, participating in the common efforts of the Western community, I say frankly to that white man: "*I'm Western, just as Western as you are, maybe more*; but I don't completely agree with you."' He would not try to define what 'being Western means to all Westerners.' Rather, he was to confine his definition 'only to that aspect of the West with which I identify, that aspect that makes me feel, act, and live Western.' What follows is telling:

> The content of my Westernness resides fundamentally, I feel, in my secular outlook upon life. I believe in a separation of Church and State. I believe that the State possesses a value in and for itself. [...] I feel that man—just sheer brute man, just as he is—has a meaning and value over and above all sanctions or mandates from mystical powers, either from on high or from below. I am convinced that the humble, fragile dignity of man, buttressed by a tough-souled pragmatism, implemented by methods of trial and error, can sufficiently sustain and nourish human life, can endow it with ample and durable meaning. I believe that all ideas have a right to circulate in the market place without restriction. I believe that all men should have the right to have their say without fear of the political 'powers that be,' without having to fear the punitive measures or the threat of invisible forces which some castes of men claim as their special domain—men such as priests and churchmen.

At this point Wright felt the need to add in parenthesis, 'My own position compels me to grant those priests and churchmen the right to have their say, but not at the expense of having my right to be heard annulled.' He expressed too his belief that 'art has its own autonomy, a self-sufficiency that extends beyond, and independent of, the spheres of political or priestly power or sanction'; and furthermore that

> science exists without any a priori or metaphysical assumptions. I feel that human personality is an end in and for itself. In short, I believe that man, for good or ill, is his own ruler, his own sovereign, his own keeper. I hold human freedom as a supreme right and good for all men, my conception of freedom being the right of all men to exercise their natural and acquired powers as long as the exercise of those powers does not hinder others from doing the same.[125]

Wight's lingering Marxist premises may have influenced him still. But most of the elements of his definition of Westernness would be subscribed to by liberals—or, more precisely, Wright would fit perfectly the definition the young Judith Shklar gave in the year following the Sorbonne conference, in her book *After Utopia*, of a radical liberalism based on the Enlightenment. 'The essence of radicalism', according to Shklar, 'is the idea that man can do with himself and his society whatever he wishes.' (Thus, whatever else he may be accused of, Wright cannot be charged with succumbing to what Samuel Moyn recently defined as 'Cold War liberalism.')[126] But, just as Shklar would diagnose lethal threats then facing the Enlightenment-based 'radical aspirations of liberalism', Wright also felt that his assumptions, values and morality were seriously menaced from many sides at the time when he was speaking. His 'decalogue of beliefs' would probably upset those who needed 'external emotional props'—not least, he observed, in the 'Catholic countries of present-day Europe': his recent extended sojourns in Spain no doubt looming large in his mind once more. (It should be noted that Léopold Senghor was Catholic, as was the chairman of the Congress, Alioune Diop.) But Wright could not help such people, he admitted. For his part, it was his 'profound conviction that emotional independence is a clear and distinct human advance'.[127]

Wright then tried to take his audience step by step through the shaping by his experiences of his view of history. His point of view was 'a Western one, but a Western one that conflicts at several vital points with the present, dominant outlook of the West'. Did that mean he was *ahead of or behind the West? My personal judgment is that I'm ahead.* And I do not say that boastfully; such a judgment is implied by the very nature of those Western values that I hold dear.'[128] Having been born 'a black Protestant in that most racist of all the American states: Mississippi', he had to live his childhood under a racial code that he loathed, which was justified in the name of religion. Naturally, he rejected that religion and 'would reject any religion which prescribes for me an inferior position in life; I reject that tradition and any tradition which proscribes my humanity.' (In an essay he wrote on memories of his grandmother nothing is more striking than how deeply he rejected her excessive and resigned religiosity).[129] He became 'passionately curious as to why Christians felt it imperative to practice such wholesale denials of humanity'. His search brought him to the fifteenth century, when the pope divided the world between Spain and Portugal and 'decreed that those two nations had not only the right, but the consecrated duty of converting or enslaving all infidels'. And it so happened that all infidels were 'people of color'. Opposition from Calvin and Luther emerged against the corrupt papal order, but '[t]heir fight against the dead weight of tradition was partial, limited'. The upshot was that 'Calvin's and Luther's rebellious doctrines and seditious actions, hatched and bred in emotional confusion, unwittingly created the soil out of which grew something that Calvin and Luther did not dream of '.[130]

Disarmingly, Wright then exclaimed, 'Perhaps now you'll expect me to pause and begin a vehement and moral denunciation of Europe. No. The facts are complex.' What happened in the history he was describing was that '[t]he irrationalism of Europe met the irrationalism of Asia and Africa, and the resulting confusion has yet to be unraveled and understood'. Neither side understood the real process that was taking place. Wright said that 'the economic spoils of European imperialism' did 'not bulk so large or important' for him. Instead, what fascinated him in that 'clash of East and West' was 'that an *irrational* Western world helped, unconsciously and unintentionally to be sure, to smash the *irrational* ties of religion and custom and tradition in Asia and Africa'. That, to Wright's mind, was the central historical fact. In what could not help being perceived as another direct challenge to what Senghor and others had argued during the previous three days, Wright added that there were 'a few shrewd Europeans who wanted the natives to remain untouched, who wished to see what they called the "nobility" of the black, brown, and yellow lives remain intact'. For Wright, it was obvious that '[t]he imperialist wanted the natives to sleep on in their beautiful poetic dreams so that the ruling of them could be more easily done'.[131]

The paradox Wright kept coming back to was that 'Europe was tendering to the great body of mankind a precious gift which she, in her blindness and ignorance, in her historical shortsightedness, was not generous enough to give her own people!' Thus, there had been 'a boon wrapped in that gift of brutality that the white West showered upon Asia and Africa'; for, 'over the centuries, meticulously, the white men took the sons and daughters of the chiefs and of the noble houses of Asia and Africa and instilled in them the ideas of the West so the eventual Westernized Asian and African products could become their collaborators'. However, they had not given any thought to 'how those Westernized Asians and Africans would fare when cast, like fishes out of the water, back into their poetic cultures. (These unemployed Asians and Africans eventually became national revolutionaries, of course!)' The essence of the story was that '*white Europeans set off a more deep-going and sudden revolution in Asia and Africa than had ever obtained in all of the history of Europe*'.[132] The paradox was that Europeans would not have done all that out of 'merely rational motives': they 'had perforce to believe that they were the tools of cosmic powers, that they were executing the will of God, or else they would not have had the cruel daring to try to harness the body of colored mankind into their personal service'.[133] 'History', Wright reflected, 'is a strange story'; for the end result was that the 'white Western world, until recently the most secular and free part of the earth—with a secularity and freedom that was the secret of its power (science and industry)—labored unconsciously and tenaciously for five hundred years to make Asia and Africa (that is, the elite in those areas) *more secular-minded than the West!*' To which Wright's own response was, 'I say, "*Bravo!*" for that clumsy and cruel deed'—not to the 'all too often ignoble and base' motives, he hastened to add, but '"Bravo!" to all the consequences [...] that created the conditions for the possible rise of rational societies for the great majority of mankind.'

So what, at the time of speaking, was the situation? *'That part of the heritage of the West that I value—man stripped of the past and free for the future*—has now been established as lonely bridgeheads in Asia and Africa in the form of a Western-educated elite, *an elite that is more Western, in most cases, than the West*.' They were '[t]ragic and lonely and all too often misunderstood', these men of the Asian-African elite. The West hated and feared them, and with good reason: 'For this elite in Asia and Africa constitutes islands of free men, the FREEST MEN IN ALL THE WORLD TODAY.' They stood, 'poised, nervous, straining at the leash, ready to go, with no weight of the dead past clouding their minds, no fears of foolish customs benumbing their consciousness, eager to build industrial civilizations.' All that meant that 'the spirit of the Enlightenment, of the Reformation, which made Europe great, now has a chance to be extended to all mankind! A part of the non-West is now akin to a part of the West. East and West have become compounded.'[134]

Wright's historical verdict was, 'I approve of what has happened.' His only regret was that 'Europe could not have done what she did in a deliberate and intentional manner, could not have planned it as a global project.' The question for the future was, 'How can the spirit of the Enlightenment and the Reformation be extended now to all men? How can this accidental boon be made global in effect?' Could 'a way be found, purged of racism and profits, to melt the rational areas and rational personnel of Europe with those of Asia and Africa?' Using (and extending) the metaphor that served him in the title of his Bandung book (*The Color Curtain*), he asked, 'How can the curtains of race, color, religion, and tradition—all of which hamper *man's mastery of his environment*[135]—be collectively rolled back by the free men of the West and non-West? Is this a Utopian dream? Is this mere wishing?' His answer was, 'No. It is more drastic than that. The nations of Asia and Africa and Europe contain too much of the forces of *the irrational* for anyone to think that the future will take care of itself. The islands of *the rational* in the East are too tenuously held to permit of optimism.' And the same was true of Europe. The truth was that 'our world—a world for all men, black, brown, yellow, and white—will either be all rational or totally irrational. For better or worse, it will eventually be one world.'[136]

What is striking here is how, in 1956, a heated Cold War year, Wright talked of East and West in almost completely civilisational terms, as much more important than the other, political-ideological confrontation. To the political 'iron curtain' he was juxtaposing 'the curtains of race, color, religion, and tradition'. No matter how frequently, in his comments on Bandung, he used the danger of Chou En-lai (and behind him his then allies in Moscow) lurking to take advantage, it was the relationship between the former colonial powers of 'the West' and their former colonies in the rest of the world that would decide the future, for Wright: 'Is there no alternative? *Must* there be a victorious East or a victorious West? If one or the other must win completely, then the fragile values won so blindly and accidentally and at so great a cost and sacrifice will be lost for us all.' The crux of the matter was, 'Who is to act first? Who *should* act first?' Obviously, he thought, 'The burden of action rests [...] with the West. For it was the West, however naively, that launched this vast historical process of the transformation of mankind.' He clarified what action was needed. 'The West must aid and, yes, abet the delicate and tragic elite in Asia and Africa to establish rational areas of living'; and, even more emphatically, 'THE WEST, IN ORDER TO KEEP BEING WESTERN, FREE, AND SOMEWHAT RATIONAL, MUST BE PREPARED TO ACCORD TO THE ELITE OF ASIA AND AFRICA A FREEDOM WHICH IT ITSELF NEVER PERMITTED IN ITS OWN DOMAIN. THE ASIAN AND AFRICAN ELITE MUST BE GIVEN ITS HEAD!' An act of faith was required. The West 'must trust that part of itself that it has thrust, however blunderingly, into Asia and Africa'. Therefore Nkrumah, Nasser, Sukarno, Nehru et al., 'the Western-educated heads of these newly created national states, must be given *carte blanche* to modernize their lands without overlordship of the West, and we must understand the methods that they will feel compelled to use'.[137] If the West could not do this, it would mean that it 'does not believe in itself, does not trust the ideas which it has cast into the world'. It was clear that Sukarno, Nehru, Nasser and others would 'necessarily use quasi-dictatorial methods to hasten the process of social evolution and to establish order in their lands'; but '[w]hy pretend to be shocked at this? You would do the same if you were in their place. You have done it in the West over and over again. You do it in every war you fight, in every crisis, political or economic, you have.' And at any rate, the Western-educated leaders, as soon as order had been established, would 'surrender the personal power that they have had to wield'.

Wright explained that he raised 'these points of Western contradictions' because, 'when non-Westerners, having the advantage of seeing more clearly—being psychologically *outside* of the West—what the West did, and when non-Westerners seek to travel the same road, the West raises strong objections, moral ones'. The problem was that, 'if a selfish West hamstrings the elite of Asia and Africa, distrusts their motives, a spirit of absolutism will rise in Asia and

Africa and will provoke a spirit of counterabsolutism in the West. In case that happens, all will be lost.' The result would be that '[w]e shall all [...] be thrown back into an age of racial and religious wars, and the precious heritage—the freedom of speech, the secular state, the independent personality, the autonomy of science—*which is not Western or Eastern, but human*, will be snuffed out of the minds of men.' The problem, Wright concluded, was one of 'freedom from a dead past. And freedom to build a rational future.' 'How much', he asked, 'are we willing to risk for freedom? I say let us risk everything. Freedom begets freedom. Europe, I say to you before it is too late: Let the Africans and Asians whom you have educated in Europe have their freedom, or you will lose your own in trying to keep freedom from them.' Westerners should give the elites of the non-West 'the tools [to] finish the job' that Europe had made only an abortive effort to accomplish.[138]

In order fully to understand what Wright was trying to say at the Sorbonne in September 1956, one has to go to another of his publications of that time, the highly idiosyncratic book *Pagan Spain*. In his own words reproduced on the jacket of the British edition, 'my going to Spain had yet another and deeper meaning, a meaning that I did not know until I got there'. He discovered himself to be 'a man freed of traditions, uprooted from my own racial heritage, looking at white people who were still caught in their age-old traditions. The white man had unknowingly freed me of my traditional, backward culture, but had clung fiercely to his own.' That was 'the point of *Pagan Spain*'.[139] Thus Wright was glad he had followed Gertrude Stein's advice to go there. After three different trips in 1954 and 1955 he came to the conclusion that '[t]hough Spain was geographically a part of Europe, it had had just enough Western aspects of life to make me feel a little at home. But it was not the West. Well, what then was it?' His answer was,

> To be a functioning and organic part of something is to be almost unconscious of it. I was a part, intimate and inseparable, of the Western world, but I seldom had had to account for my Westernness, had rarely found myself in situations which had challenged me to do so. ([...] But Spain was baffling; it looked and seemed Western, but it did not act or feel Western.)
>
> Since I now felt most strongly, in fact, *knew* that Spain was not a Western nation, what then did being Western mean? [...] It was not my task to define the totality of the contents of Western civilization; I was interested only in that aspect of it that engaged my attention in relation to Spain. I was finally led to believe that that difference lay in the area of the *secular* that Western man, through the centuries and at tragic cost, had won and wrung from his own

religious and irrational consciousness. In Spain there was no lay, no secular life. Spain was a holy nation, a sacred state—a state as sacred and as irrational as the sacred state of the Akan in the African jungle. Even the prostitution, the corruption, the economics, the politics had about them a sacred aura. *All was religion in Spain.*[140]

XI. The 'vitality of the so-transgressed Western ideals': James Baldwin's Parisian Encounters

Wright was far from being the only African American at the time who identified himself with 'the West'. James Baldwin attended the 1956 Sorbonne conference and reported on it extensively for *Encounter*.[141] But while Wright had spent his whole lecture ignoring the confrontation with the Soviet 'East', the Cold War dimension in Baldwin's comments could not have been more explicit. And the stakes were high. The atmosphere was 'strange', he reported. 'Hanging in the air, as real as the heat from which we suffered, were the great spectres of America and Russia, of the battle going on between them for the domination of the world.' The resolution of that battle 'might very well depend on the earth's non-European population, a population vastly outnumbering Europe's, and which had suffered such injustices at European hands'.[142] Then there was the fact that the grand old man, the founder of the Pan-African Congresses, had been refused a passport and could not travel to the conference. W.E.B. Du Bois sent a telegram to be read to the delegates, which probably did more damage to the reputation of the United States than anything he might have said had he been present.[143]

Baldwin's judgement was that it had been less Du Bois's message itself which did the damage than 'the incontestable fact that he had not been allowed to leave his country'.[144] That was 'a fact which could scarcely be explained or defended: the very attempt at such an explanation, especially for people whose distrust of the West, however richly justified, also tends to make them dangerously blind and hasty, was to be suspected of "caring nothing about Negroes," of saying what the State Department "wished" you to say'. And therein lay the main problem: 'It was a fact which increased and seemed to justify the distrust with which Americans are regarded abroad, and it made yet deeper, for the five American Negroes present, that gulf which yawns between the American Negro and all other men of colour.' Baldwin's assessment was that this was 'a very sad and dangerous state of affairs, for the American Negro is possibly the only man of colour who can speak of the West with real authority, whose experience, painful as it is, also proves the vitality of the so-transgressed Western ideals.' As it happened, '[t]he fact that DuBois [sic] was not there and could not, therefore, be engaged in debate, naturally made more seductive his closing argument', to the effect that 'the future of Africa being socialist, African writers should take the road taken by Russia, Poland, China, etc., and not be "betrayed backwards by the U.S. into colonialism"'.[145]

Baldwin commented that what distinguished the Americans 'from the Negroes who surrounded us, men from Nigeria, Senegal, Barbados, Martinique' was 'the banal and abruptly quite overwhelming fact that we had been born in a society, which [...] was open, and, in a sense which has nothing to do with justice or injustice, was free'. It was a society in which 'nothing was fixed and we had therefore been born to a greater number of possibilities, wretched as these possibilities seemed at the instant of our birth'. Moreover, he continued, 'the land of our forefathers' exile had been made, by that travail, our home'. That resulted in a psychology 'very different [...] from the psychology which is produced by a sense of having been invaded and overrun, the sense of having no recourse whatever against oppression other than overthrowing the machinery of the oppressor'. African Americans 'had been dealing with, had been made and mangled by, another machinery altogether. It had never been in our interest to overthrow it. It had been necessary to make the machinery work for our benefit and the possibility of its doing so had been, so to speak, built in.' The corollary was that '[w]e could, therefore, in a way, be considered the connecting link between Africa and the West, the most real and certainly the most shocking of all African contributions to Western cultural life'.[146]

Some of Baldwin's comments on the speeches by Senghor and by the Caribbean author George Lemming also display the extent to which he affirmed the 'double vision' concept advanced by Richard Wright during the latter's speech at the Sorbonne.[147] Despite all his criticisms of Wright, Baldwin was in agreement with the older man as regards the Westernness of African American intellectuals, as well as their important role as interpreters of 'the so-transgressed Western ideals'. He was also writing for a magazine (*Encounter*) funded by the Congress for Cultural Freedom that had also paid for Wright's ticket to Indonesia for the Bandung Conference the previous year (none of them being aware at the time that the money ultimately came from the CIA). Moreover, when the publisher Sol Stein, Baldwin's former schoolmate, complained about his description of the confrontation between the United States and Soviet Russia as a battle 'for the domination of the world', Baldwin replied that he meant a battle for ideological domination. He was clear where he himself stood: 'In the case of America vs. Russia, America is the last stronghold of

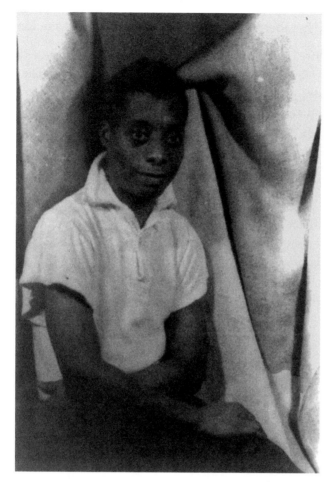

FIGURE 8.6. James Baldwin. Photograph by Carl Van Vechten, 13 September 1955. Van Vechten Collection, Library of Congress, Washington, DC. *Source:* https://en.wikipedia.org/wiki/James_Baldwin#/media/File:Jamesbaldwin.jpg

the Western idea of personal liberty. And I certainly think that this idea *should* dominate the world.'[148] Many other Afro-American thinkers also chose to back the West during the Cold War.[149]

Meanwhile, by the 1960s there were conservatives who thought that the fame and honours awarded to people such as James Baldwin by a self-flagellating liberalism constituted a symptom of what had gone wrong with the West. Outdoing them all in explicitness was James Burnham.

XII. 'Liberalism is the ideology of Western suicide.'

George Orwell was a major admirer of James Burnham's earlier book, *The Managerial Revolution* (1941). But, as the British author put it while reviewing a later book by the American former Trotskyite, 'Burnham seems to me to overstate his case. After all, that is his besetting sin. He is too fond of apocalyptic visions.'[150] True to form, then, Burnham begins his 1964 book *The Suicide of the West* with the crucial premise of what he calls 'the contraction of the West' in the past two generations. Look at an atlas, he suggests. What he calls 'our own Western civilization' (which was 'an observable social formation' by 'about the year A.D. 700 in the center of western Europe') had come to dominate most of the world by 1914. But, beginning in 1917, a contraction started, which had been ongoing and without any reversals until the time of writing in 1964. The process started with Russia in 1917. Although Russia was complicated (not being 'organically part of the West'), it still was the case that 'Peter the Great, the Napoleonic Wars, the Holy Alliance and the influence of Western ideas and technology had brought her in some measure within the Western concert of nations'. But the Bolsheviks at the end of 1917 'broke totally away'. Then, between the two world wars, in a process completed in 1949, 'China shook off what hold the West had established on her territory'. With the end of the Second World War, 'the rate of Western disintegration quickened'. The Communists conquered Eastern and parts of Central Europe. Western power also collapsed 'in the great archipelago of the South Seas' as well as in the Indian subcontinent, and then all the way from Morocco to Indonesia. In 1956 'the Isthmus of Suez, the bridge between Asia and Africa, fell'. From 1957 on, it was the turn of sub-Saharan Africa, until in 1959 'communism's anti-Western enterprise achieved its first beachhead within the Americas' in Cuba. Burnham distinguished between two types of losses: '*a*) the ending of Western dominion over a non-Western society; *b*) the ending of Western domination within a society and region that have been integrally part of Western civilization'. In the latter category, besides the 'special case' of Russia (which admittedly was 'never fully part of the West') he was talking about Central and Eastern European countries 'acquired by the communist enterprise at the end of the Second World War—the Baltic nations, Poland, Hungary, East Germany, Bohemia', which 'had undoubtedly been an integral, and very important, part of the West.'[151]

Why had the West been contracting? Burnham wanted to discard two answers. The contraction could not be explained 'by any lack of economic resources or of military and political power'. According to his analysis of the past five decades, '[t]here *was* no external challenger to be taken seriously, if his assault against Western civilization were mounted solely from the outside'. The conclusion was obvious, for Burnham: that the primary causes of the contraction of the West had been 'internal and non-quantitative: involving either structural changes or intellectual, moral and spiritual factors'. It was a question of 'the will to survive'. The 'community of Western nations' had 'possessed the material means to maintain and even to extend still further its overwhelming predominance, and to beat off any challenger'. And yet, it had not made use of those means. 'The will to make use of the means at hand has evidently been lacking'. Hence he thought he was justified in speaking of the West's contraction as 'suicide', or rather 'potential suicide', or a 'suicidal tendency'. And he could identify a concrete culprit: 'This book is a set of variations on a single and simple underlying thesis: that what Americans call "liberalism" is the ideology of Western suicide.'[152] He explained that he was not suggesting that liberalism was '"the cause" of the contraction and possible, on the evidence probable, death of Western civilization'. He did not profess to know the cause of 'the West's extraordinarily rapid decline', evidenced 'by the deepening loss, among the leaders of the West, of confidence in themselves and in the unique quality and value of their own civilization, and by a correlated weakening of the Western will to survive'. But then he offered some explanations all the same: the cause had 'something to do', he thought, 'with the decay of religion and with an excess of material luxury; and, I suppose, with getting tired, worn out, as all things temporal do'.

There was 'a really dazzling ingenuity in the liberal explanations of defeat as victory, abandonment as loyalty, timidity as courage, withdrawal as advance'. The liberal ideologues proceeded 'in a manner long familiar to both religion and psychology; by constructing a new reality of their own, a transcendental world, where the soul may take refuge from the prosaic, unpleasant world of space and time'. The upshot was that '[l]iberalism permits Western civilization to be reconciled to dissolution'. Thus, 'even if Western civilization is wholly vanquished or altogether collapses, we or our children will be able to see that ending, by the light of the principles of liberalism, not as a final defeat, but as the transition to a new and higher order in which Mankind as a whole joins in a universal civilization that has risen above the parochial distinctions, divisions and discriminations of the past' (a description, incidentally, of exactly what Arnold Toynbee, among others, had been proposing). And Burnham wound up his book as follows: 'But of course the final collapse of the West is not yet inevitable; the report of its death would be premature.' For if a decisive change were to come, 'if the contraction of the past fifty years should cease and be reversed', then the 'ideology of liberalism' would 'fade away, like those feverish dreams of the ill man who, passing the crisis of his disease, finds he is not dying after all'. There were, he noted, 'a few small signs, here and there, that liberalism may already have started fading. Perhaps this book is one of them.'[153]

XIII. Cultural versus Political West: Milan Kundera's and Czesław Miłosz's 'Kidnapped West'

No matter how strongly the Cold War affected perceptions, distinctions and definitions, not everybody accepted the binary definitions of 'West' and 'East' as imposed by the Iron Curtain. We have just seen Burnham referring to the loss, after World War II, of regions which 'had undoubtedly been an integral, and very important, part of the West'. Then there were the emigrants from Central Europe, who considered themselves and their countries Western in cultural/historical terms, and suddenly found themselves in the 'East' by virtue of the Cold War political division. Many of them protested, throughout the Cold War. *Preuves* was replete with articles by Eastern European (and Russian) émigrés in the 1950s.[154] The protest that received the widest attention appeared in the final stages of the Cold War; it was by the Czech-born, Paris-based novelist Milan Kundera (1929–2023). Kundera published a widely discussed essay in Pierre Nora's review *Le Débat* in November 1983, to be translated and published in the *New York Review of Books* in April 1984. 'The Tragedy of Central Europe' touched a nerve, and is claimed to have influenced significantly some French intellectuals' attitudes.[155] Kundera tried to explain to a 'Western' readership what 'Europe' meant 'to a Hungarian, a Czech, a Pole'. In his words, '[f]or a thousand years their nations have belonged to the part of Europe rooted in Roman Christianity'. They had participated 'in every period of its history'. For Hungarians, Czechs or Poles, 'the word "Europe" does not represent a phenomenon of geography but *a spiritual notion* synonymous with the word "West"'. What Kundera went on to say expressed the crux of what happened after the Second World War in the eyes of Central Europeans:

> 'Geographic Europe' (extending from the Atlantic to the Ural Mountains) was always divided into two halves that evolved separately: one tied to ancient Rome and the Catholic Church, the other anchored in Byzantium and the Orthodox Church. After 1945, the border between the two Europes shifted

several hundred kilometers to the west, and several nations that had always considered themselves Western woke up to discover that they were now in the East.

To Kundera's mind, what had taken place in Prague or Warsaw was not 'a drama of Eastern Europe, of the Soviet Bloc, of communism'. It was 'a drama of the West—a West that, kidnapped, displaced, and brainwashed, nevertheless insists on defending its identity'.[156]

Kundera tried to scrutinise his own premises, if only very briefly: 'But am I being too absolute in contrasting Russia and Western civilization? Isn't Europe, though divided into east and west, still a single entity anchored in ancient Greece and Judeo-Christian thought?' His answer was, 'Of course. Moreover, during the entire nineteenth century, Russia, attracted to Europe, drew closer to it.' And the fascination had been 'reciprocated'. No one had escaped 'the impact of the great Russian novels, which remain an integral part of the common European cultural legacy.' All that was true. But it was 'no less true that Russian communism vigorously reawakened Russia's old anti-Western obsessions and turned it brutally against Europe'. At any rate, 'on the eastern border of the West—more than anywhere else—Russia is seen not just as one more European power but as a singular civilization, an *other* civilization'. Here Kundera gave extensive references to some fascinating passages in *Native Realm*, in which Czesław Miłosz had spoken of the alienness of Russia in the eyes of a Polish Balt. For these reasons 'the countries of Central Europe feel that the change in their destiny that occurred after 1945 is not merely a political catastrophe, it is also an attack on their civilization'. The 'deep meaning of their resistance is the struggle to preserve their identity—or, to put it another way, to preserve their Westernness'.[157]

Kundera also made a broader point, beyond the feelings and sensitivities of Central Europeans. He tried to account for what he thought had been happening to 'Europe' as a whole in recent decades. 'Europe hasn't noticed the disappearance of its [Central European] cultural home because Europe no longer perceived its unity as a cultural unity.' In the Middle Ages, European unity was based on a shared religion. In the modern era, religion had 'bowed out, giving way to culture, which became the expression of the supreme value by which European humanity understood itself, defined itself, identified itself as European'. But it now seemed that another change was taking place in the twentieth century, 'as important as the one that divided the Middle Ages from the modern era. Just as God long ago gave way to culture, culture in turn is giving way.' It was not clear 'to what and to whom? [...] Technical feats? The marketplace? The mass media? [...] politics?' Kundera did not profess to know; he knew only 'that culture has bowed out'. Thus the tragedy of Central Europe was that, 'in the eyes of its beloved Europe, Central Europe is just a part of the Soviet empire and nothing more, nothing more'. And that was not surprising: 'By virtue of its political system, Central Europe is the East; by virtue of its cultural history, it is the West. But since Europe itself is in the process of losing its own cultural identity, it perceives in Central Europe nothing but a political regime.' As a result, Central Europe had to fight not only against its big Russian oppressor 'but also against the subtle, relentless pressure of time, which is leaving the era of culture in its wake'. That explained why 'in Central European revolts there is something conservative, nearly anachronistic: they are desperately trying to restore the past, the past of culture, the past of the modern era'.[158] The tragedy of Central Europe, then, was that, while Central Europeans longed to be part of 'Europe', that Europe had been steadily abandoning the culture that constituted the essence of its Europeanness. (Thus it should not perhaps be too surprising that a reversal was to occur a few decades later when, after disappointment with being assessed for progress in 'Europeanness' or 'Westernness', some Central and Eastern European electorates found appealing the message of politicians such as Viktor Orbán, who started to turn the tables by arguing that they were the genuine defenders of Europe and its civilisation against the inroads of Brussels-dictated post-national liberalism and open-border migration).[159]

Kundera advanced similar arguments in other articles, and one of these elicited a powerful rebuttal by the Russian-born and then naturalised American poet Joseph Brodsky. 'The sad truth about [Kundera] (and many of his East European brethren) is that this extraordinary writer has fallen an unwitting victim to the geopolitical certitude of his fate—the concept of an East–West divide.' Brodsky certainly had a point in complaining about the incrimination of the whole of Russian culture and literature for the Soviet behaviour towards Czechs and other Central or Eastern Europeans (and reminded Kundera that in 1938 it had not been a case of the Russians inflicting their 'Eastern' culture on the Czechs).[160] Much more recently, Timothy Garton Ash was also right to observe that Kundera's argument 'carries a strong hint of cultural determinism: your cultural past is your political future. "Western"? Aha, your natural political condition is liberal democracy. "Orthodox"? It's authoritarianism for you, my lad.'[161] Samuel Huntington *avant la lettre*, as it were.

XIV. Post-mortem: Victorious America Conquered by *Germania capta*?

Meanwhile, the 'liberals' of whom Burnham was so critical would be the least of the problems of his version of 'the West' by the end of the 1960s. He would of course say that it had been 'the liberals' who had undermined the fort's resistance. But there were concrete developments that shifted attention. The Cuba missile crisis of 1962 was followed the year after by the signing of a Nuclear Test Ban Treaty, and later by further negotiations and treaties. By the mid-1960s the term 'détente' was being widely used to describe a new phase in the relations between the two superpowers. New issues were becoming more urgent as a degree of relative relaxedness about the Soviet threat was settling in. As far as the United States was concerned, the Vietnam war and student unrest in the late 1960s led to a very different intellectual climate.[162] One development was the abandonment, by one university after another, of the 'Western Civ' curricula that had emerged to great popularity since the end of the Great War. The causes for that abandonment were complex, and had to do as much with internal organisational changes (the modular system, for instance) and generational disputes (the role of Ph.D candidates as teaching assistants) as with 'culture wars';' but major shifts in cultural self-awareness and their historiographical repercussions were also involved. For '[m]uch of the deep structure of general education lay in a psychology developed during the half-century of U.S. involvement in the "crusade for democracy" in Europe'. Mixing patriotism and pedagogy, educators had 'equated core courses with common values, the need for unity in the republic with the need for unity in the curriculum, and the Western military alliance with Western civilization'. (In the first section of chapter 7 above we saw Walter Lippmann making that direct connection in 1940 and already lamenting its gradual decline due to the electives system). Now, America's 'new hegemony in the West' had come to undermine 'earlier notions of a common partnership with Europe', and simultaneously 'the rise of the Third World confronted the United States with an international environment of polycentrism and cultural diversity'. Quite simply, 'Europe was no longer the world'. Other peoples and their histories were emerging, 'a globe of historic diversity beyond the imagination of earlier Westerners, a cosmos where pluralism replaced the "oneness" of history and where human experience could not be ordered into a unilinear pattern of development'. A world seen in that way had no place for the 'Western Civ' course.[163]

Those unhappy with what was happening held strong views as to what was to blame. Very near the end of the Cold War, a book written by one of Leo Strauss's many former students, Allan Bloom (1930–1992), came to encapsulate the frustration of many American commentators at developments since the late 1960s. The 'Straussians' indeed became an important component of American intellectual as well as political life for decades.[164] As Mark Lilla has observed, after the implosion of universities in 1968, 'the Straussians took the student revolts, and all that followed in American society, particularly hard'. They had learnt from Strauss and his *Natural Right and History* 'to see the threat of "nihilism" lurking in the interstices of modern life, waiting to be released and to turn America into Weimar'. (Incidentally, that was the German-born Kissinger's anxiety as well, in the memoranda written in the early 1950s that we discussed above). According to Lilla, this was 'the premise underlying Allan Bloom's best seller *The Closing of the American Mind* (1987), and helps to explain why its genuine insights into American youth got buried in *Weltschmertz* and doomsaying'. Bloom had spent the 1960s at Cornell University, 'which had a particularly ugly experience with student violence, race-baiting, and liberal cowardice in the face of attacks on the university. [. . .] That moment seems to have been an apocalyptic revelation for Bloom.' Thus, after the 1960s, 'a new, more political catechism' developed among some of Strauss's disciples. Many of them, 'traumatized by the changes in American universities and society, began gravitating toward the circles of neoconservatives then forming in New York and Washington'.[165] Their message to their students started from the premise that the modern liberal West was in crisis, 'unable to defend itself intellectually against internal and external enemies, who are abetted by historical relativism'.[166]

In *The Closing of the American Mind* Allan Bloom complained that, in the post-1960s climate, one of the devices used for 'opening young people up' was to require 'a college course in a non-Western culture'. In his view, that requirement had 'a demagogic intention'. The aim was 'to force students to recognize that there are other ways of thinking and the Western ways are not better'. But 'if the students were ready to learn something of the minds of any of these non-Western cultures—which they do not—they would find that each and every one of these cultures is ethnocentric': that all of them 'think their way is the best way, and all others are inferior'. In fact, '[o]nly in the Western nations, i.e., those influenced by Greek philosophy, is there some willingness to doubt the identification of the good with one's own way'. A genuine study of non-Western cultures was bound to lead to the conclusion 'that not only to prefer one's own way but to believe it best, superior to all others, is [. . .] natural'—which was, Bloom commented, exactly the opposite of what was intended by the requirement in American universities during his time. 'What we are really doing is applying a Western prejudice—which we covertly take to indicate the superiority of our own culture—and deforming the evidence of those other cultures to attest to its validity.' In fact, to be consistent, 'professors of openness' ought to 'respect the ethnocentrism or closedness they find everywhere else'. However, instead, 'in attacking ethnocentrism', what they were actually doing, according to Bloom, was 'assert[ing] the superiority of their scientific understanding and the inferiority of the other cultures which do not recognize it at the same time that they reject all such claims to superiority. They both affirm and deny the goodness of their science.'

And yet, for Bloom, there was another way to pursue openness: 'Greek philosophers were the first men we know to address the problem of ethnocentrism. Distinctions between the good and one's own, between nature and convention, between the just and the legal are the signs of this movement of thought.' Those philosophers 'related the good to the fulfillment of the whole natural human potential and were aware that few, if any, of the nations of men had ways that allowed such fulfillment'. The philosophers in question 'were open to the good. *They had to use the good, which was not their own, to judge their own.*' That was 'a dangerous business', as it 'tended to weaken wholehearted attachment to their own, hence to weaken their peoples as well as to expose themselves to the anger of family, friends, and countrymen'. Clearly, then, '[l]oyalty versus quest for the good introduced an unresolvable tension into life. But the awareness of the good as such and the desire to possess it are priceless humanizing acquisitions.' That was 'the sound motive' contained in openness properly understood.

> Men cannot remain content with what is given them by their culture if they are to be fully human. This is what Plato meant to show by the image of the cave in the *Republic* and by representing us as prisoners in it. A culture is a cave. He did not suggest going around to other cultures as a solution to the limitations of the cave. Nature should be the standard by which we judge our own lives and the lives of peoples. That is why philosophy, not history or anthropology, is the most important human science.

On the other hand, the human or social sciences in the contemporary United States, Bloom complained, wanted 'to make us culture-beings with the instruments that were invented to liberate us from culture. Openness used to be a virtue that permitted us to seek the good by using reason. It now means accepting everything and denying reason's power.' Cultural relativism destroyed 'both one's own and the good'.

Bloom insisted that what was 'most characteristic of the West' was 'science, particularly understood as the quest to know nature and the consequent denigration of convention—i.e., culture or the West understood as a culture—in favor of what is accessible to all men as men through their common and distinctive faculty, reason'. Given that, the American social sciences' 'latest attempt to grasp the human situation—cultural relativism, historicism, the fact-value distinction' were 'the suicide of science. Culture, hence closedness, reigns supreme. *Openness to closedness is what we teach.*' As a result of what he was describing, Bloom argued, cultural relativism was succeeding in 'destroying the West's universal or intellectually imperialistic claims, leaving it to be just another culture. So there is equality in the republic of cultures.' But that was lethal in the case of that particular culture: '*Unfortunately the West is defined by its need for justification of its ways or values, by its need for discovery of nature, by its need for philosophy and science. This is its cultural imperative. Deprived of it, it will collapse.*'[167]

And the conclusion was not just theoretical. It was intimately tied to the very *raison d'être* of Bloom's own country: 'The United States is one of the highest and most extreme achievements of the rational quest for the good life according to nature.' What made its political structure possible was 'the use of the rational principles of natural right to found a people, thus uniting the good with one's own'. Differently put, Bloom claimed, 'the regime established here promised untrammeled freedom to reason—not to everything indiscriminately, but to reason, the essential freedom that justifies the other freedoms'. An 'openness' that denied 'the special claim of reason bursts the mainspring keeping the mechanism of this regime in motion'. And that regime, 'contrary to all claims to the contrary, was founded to overcome ethnocentrism, which is in no sense a discovery of social science'. It was important to emphasise that the lesson the students were drawing from their studies was 'simply untrue'; for '[h]istory and the study of cultures do not teach or prove that values or cultures are relative'. On the contrary, that was 'a philosophical premise that we now bring to our study of them. This premise is unproven and dogmatically asserted for what are largely political reasons.' Thus, history and culture were 'interpreted in the light of it, and then are said to prove the premise'. Bloom demurred: 'the fact that there have been different opinions about good and bad in different times and places in no way proves that none is true or superior to others. To say that it does so prove is as absurd as to say that the diversity of points of view expressed in a college bull session proves there is no truth.'[168]

As his German-born teacher had done more than three decades earlier, Bloom blamed the roots of '*value* relativism' on '[t]he German Connection': 'Our intellectual skyline has been altered by German thinkers even more radically than has our physical skyline by German architects.' Reiterating the point already made by Strauss in 1953, he continued, 'The great influence of a nation with a powerful intellectual life over less well endowed nations, even if the armies of the latter are very powerful, is not rare in human experience.' For Bloom, the best examples had been the influence of Greece on Rome and of France on Germany and Russia. The results in the more recent case of the German intellectual conquest of America had been the opposite, though: 'Greek and French philosophy were universalistic in intention and fact. They appealed to the use of a faculty potentially possessed by all men everywhere and at all times', whereas German philosophy after Hegel had cast doubt on such universalist aspirations. Instead, German historicism had taught that 'the mind is essentially related to history or culture': 'Germanness' was, 'according to later German philosophers, an essential part of them'. And 'For Nietzsche and those influenced by him, values are the products of folk minds and have relevance only to those minds. The possibility of translation itself [. . .] is doubted by Heidegger.' German thought tended 'not toward liberation from one's own culture, as did earlier thought, but toward reconstituting the rootedness in one's own, which has been shattered by cosmopolitanism, philosophical and political'. All this meant that Bloom's contemporary Americans had chosen 'a system of thought that, like some wines, does not travel; [. . .] a way of looking at things that could never be ours and had as its starting point dislike of us and our goals'. In the eyes of such a system of thought, the United States was 'a nonculture, a collection of castoffs from real cultures, seeking only comfortable self-preservation in a regime dedicated to superficial cosmopolitanism in thought and deed'.[169] Instead of the Americans 'Westernising' or 'civilising' the Germans, it had been the Germans who had sapped the basis of America's very existence: belief in natural right and rationality.

XV. Conclusion

By 1976, when the Greek prime minister Constantinos Caramanlis declared that Greece, 'in political, defence, economic [and] cultural terms' belonged to the West, he was not listing redundant terms.[170] He wanted to stress that Greece was Western in all these different senses, for by that time the concept of 'the West' had acquired the full range of political, military/defensive, economic and cultural/civilisational connotations. Some of these meanings or dimensions of 'the West' were older (the cultural/civilisational) and some were more recent and emerged or were intensified due to the Cold War: the economic sense was in contradistinction to the planned economies of Communist countries; the defensive-military dimension meant membership of NATO or close military alliance with the United States; the political sense referred to having a functioning liberal democratic political system. In Caramanlis's terms, Japan may have been said to belong to the West in the defensive, political and economic senses. The Greek prime minister wished to assert that Greece, after the restoration of democracy under his leadership, was Western in every possible sense.[171] The meanings of the Cold War 'West' had by then crystallised.

This chapter has shown that things had been very different three decades earlier, when the West and Western civilisation were talked of in quite different terms, and were even said to include Soviet Russia for a short while. We also saw that the notion of 'Western civilisation' could be used ambivalently, both to include the Americans when their help was desperately needed, and to exclude them when the 'spiritual' or 'moral' leadership of Western Europe was at stake— and claimed by the British in the late 1940s. We have seen too how widespread mistrust of the United States was in Europe in the late 1940s and early 1950s, as evidenced by the extraordinary popularity of a novel of questionable literary merit that happened to capture the anxieties of Europeans at the time; and that these negative attitudes towards America were so strong as to generate strategies to combat them in the United States. 'Western' or 'Occidental' civilisation was the umbrella concept chosen by the young German-Jewish émigré Henry Kissinger in deploying those strategies in order to 'swing the spiritual balance in favor of the US'.

We also followed some of the main arguments that made the British historian of civilisations and civilisational contacts Arnold Toynbee first a major global celebrity, and subsequently the object of much criticism and ridicule. We briefly discussed the role in the intellectual Cold War of cultural front organisations such as the Congress for Cultural Freedom, and the high stakes involved in winning over for 'the West' a critical mass of left-wing intellectuals. In that battle, the concept of 'totalitarianism' was crucial, and we followed the contribution of German-Jewish immigrants to the United States, and in particular Hannah Arendt. Besides her popularisation of the concept of totalitarianism, we noted Arendt's analysis of the misunderstandings between Europeans and Americans and her anxieties as to what they might lead to. Another German-Jewish refugee who marked American intellectual and political life, Leo Strauss, came to warn that what he called 'historicism', and the cultural relativism that it had introduced to American academic life, had disastrous consequences, blaming the trend upon German influences in his new country.

We then followed some of the arguments of Raymond Aron in relation both to the best strategy for the West and to his definition of what a Westerner was. The latter topic was of fundamental importance to the Afro-American novelist Richard Wright. We traced his agonised quest for a definition of what 'the West' meant, his original analysis of what the history of the encounter of the West with the rest of the world had resulted in, and his urgent pleas to the West to live up to its own principles and aid the Westernised elites of newly independent nations in modernising themselves—in the interest of sustaining a world based on the rationality that the modern West may well have preached, but not, he thought, fully embraced in practice. We also saw that Wright was not the only Afro-American writer to see himself as belonging to the West. James Baldwin did not just align himself on the side of the West in the Cold War divide, but envisaged a special role for African Americans as the interpreters of 'the West' to Africans and others outside it and as an indispensable bridge, in a manner reminiscent of Du Bois's 'double vision' and the special role with which it endowed Afro-Americans in particular. Then James Burnham (who had James Baldwin in mind when he charged that 'the liberal community not only flagellates itself with the abusive writings of a disoriented Negro homosexual, but awards him money, fame, and public honours') came in 1964 to denounce what he called the 'suicide of the West'; we followed his argument that the 'liberal community' was culpable, as liberalism was the ideology of Western suicide.

But we also considered the arguments of others, who were complaining about their countries having been forgotten by 'the West' to which they belonged, and which they wanted to (re)join. Milan Kundera, Czesław Miłosz and many other writers and thinkers from Central and Eastern Europe, exiled in Paris, London or America, had strong views on the matter. Their idea of the 'kidnapped West' was to prove crucial near and during the end of the Cold War, when, moreover, a Polish pope was in the Vatican.[172] Finally, we discussed the argument regarding what had gone wrong with American academic and intellectual life since the late 1960s contributed near the end of the Cold War by Allan Bloom. As Bloom's arguments reminded us, in terms of what it symbolised, the old battle of Arminius versus Varus was in some sense still going on.[173] It has been plausibly argued that it had been Du Bois's studies in Germany in 1892–94 that decisively shaped his subsequent enterprise, through notions of *Volksgeist*;[174] and it is beyond doubt that Leo Frobenius had a wide-ranging role in the 'revolt against the West'.[175] Nor is it a matter of dispute that an astonishing number of major thinkers raised in Weimar Germany decisively shaped twentieth-century American thought.[176] Leo Strauss, Allan Bloom and many other 'Straussians' thought that a pernicious 'historicism' and relativism of values imported from Germany had been destroying what the United States and the West stood for: thus the theme of Germany as the revolt against Rome, of German *Kultur* as an assertion of particularity versus 'Western' *Zivilisation* or universalism, as we saw it articulated by Dostoyevsky, Thomas Mann and many others since, was still a live one. Militarily defeated Germany had conquered its 'Western' victors by undermining their own belief in the possibility or value of universality.

Such debates about universality versus cultural specificity were only going to be intensified after the end of the Cold War, as we shall see in the next chapter. The most crucial of them all was to take place immediately: was the West offering a universalisable model for the whole world, or was it a distinct, unique, culture, that should look after itself and abandon universalist pretensions? Francis Fukuyama and his former teacher, Samuel Huntington, had different answers to that question.

9

What Is 'the West' after the Cold War?

'The universal civilization has been a long time in the making. It wasn't always universal; it wasn't always as attractive as it is today. The expansion of Europe gave it for at least three centuries a racial tint, which still causes pain. In Trinidad I grew up in the last days of that kind of racialism. And that, perhaps, has given me a greater appreciation of the immense changes that have taken place since the end of the war, the extraordinary attempt of this civilization to accommodate the rest of the world, and all the currents of that world's thought.'

V. S. NAIPAUL, 'OUR UNIVERSAL CIVILIZATION', *THE NEW YORK REVIEW OF BOOKS*, VOL. 38, NO. 3 (31 JANUARY 1991)

'The argument that the spread of pop culture and consumer goods around the world represents the triumph of Western civilization depreciates the strength of other cultures while trivializing Western culture by identifying it with fatty foods, faded pants, and fizzy drinks. The essence of Western culture is the Magna Carta, not the Magna Mac.'

SAMUEL P. HUNTINGTON, 'THE WEST UNIQUE, NOT UNIVERSAL', *FOREIGN AFFAIRS*, VOL. 75, NO. 6 (NOV.–DEC. 1996), PP. 28–46, AT P. 29

'No one in the West will ever be happy again, she also thought, never again; happiness today is nothing but an old dream, the past conditions for its existence are simply no longer being fulfilled. [...] [T]he third millennium had just begun, and for the West, which had previously been known as Judaeo-Christian [pour l'Occident antérieurement qualifié de judéo-chrétien], it was one millennium too many in the way that boxers have one fight too many.'

MICHEL HOUELLEBECQ, *SEROTONIN*, TRANSLATED BY SHAUN WHITESIDE (2019), P. 87 (HOUELLEBECQ, *SÉROTONINE* [2019], P. 102)

ONCE THE COLD WAR was over, it was inevitable that the meanings of 'the West' would change. And it was also probably inevitable that the very *raison d'être* for a 'West' would come to be questioned, at least to begin with. There soon arose widely differing prognoses as to its potential. Francis Fukuyama gained fame with his 'triumph of the West' and 'end of history' thesis early on. But the optimism (though with some provisos) that Fukuyama spread was duly challenged. An initial salvo was launched by the veteran historian and political insider Arthur Schlesinger, Jr., who focused on culture wars within the United States. But the most widely discussed and consequential response was that contributed by the political scientist Samuel Huntington, whose 'clash of civilization' thesis set a new tone. Huntington warned against the widespread complacency about a final victory of the West and the inevitable spread of its culture, models and values. He argued, instead, that 'the West' should be seen and cherished as a particular civilisation that had to learn how to live with other civilisations that were bound to become increasingly powerful and assertive. As well as addressing these contributions, this chapter will discuss the pronouncements on what was peculiar about the West by thinkers such as Cornelius Castoriadis, Jürgen Habermas and Heinrich August Winkler—the latter two in the context of German debates about their country's Western orientation or *Westbindung*, both during and after the German reunification that closely followed the end of the Cold War. The urgent question of whether America would continue to provide leadership of the West or was bound to abandon it after the end of the Cold War will then be analysed from various angles. In that regard attention will be paid to fascinating debates that arose following a controversial speech in Warsaw by US president Donald Trump in 2017—which in some sense turned out to be a sequel to the Fukuyama versus Huntington debates about whether the West should pursue the universalisation of its model and principles or, instead, regard itself as a particular and unique civilisation and look to itself and its own interests. Some of the most salient themes discussed not just in this chapter but in the book as a whole will be revisited in the final section of the chapter, through the prism of an analysis of Michel Houellebecq's novels during the past decades, and the theme of the end of Western civilisation that permeates them, as well as that author's public statements.

I. 'The Triumph of the West, of the Western *idea*' according to Francis Fukuyama

In an article published in the summer of 1989 and provocatively entitled 'The End of History?' the American political scientist and foreign policy establishment adviser Francis Fukuyama (b. 1952) announced more than the end of an era in world affairs. His title notwithstanding, he did not argue that history would end in a literal sense. But he explained that he was using the phrase 'the end of history' in the way it had been used by Hegel in the early nineteenth century to describe the end of serious alternatives after the victory of Napoleon over Prussia. After the collapse of Communism in Eastern Europe and Mikhail Gorbachev's reforms in the Soviet Union itself, Fukuyama explained, there was an exhaustion of ideological alternatives to the liberal democratic political and the liberal capitalist economic models that had prevailed in the West. The rest of the world would sooner or later adopt these systems—if they had not done so already. As he put it, '[t]he triumph of the West, of the Western *idea*, is evident first of all in the total exhaustion of viable systematic alternatives to Western liberalism'. The equation of 'Western liberalism' with 'the West', or 'the Western *idea*'—whatever that latter phrase means—already strikes one as rather facile. But worse was what followed:

> In the past decade, there have been unmistakable changes in the intellectual climate of the world's two largest communist countries, and the beginnings of significant reform movements in both. But this phenomenon extends beyond high politics and it can be seen also in the ineluctable spread of consumerist Western culture in such diverse contexts as the peasants' markets and color television sets now omnipresent throughout China, the cooperative restaurants and clothing stores opened in the past year in Moscow, the Beethoven piped into Japanese department stores, and the rock music enjoyed alike in Prague, Rangoon, and Tehran.[1]

That this all sounds like a caricature invoking superficial similarities, which may or may not amount to anything beyond a normal human appetite for consumer goods when available, did not seem to concern Fukuyama at the time. He meanwhile invested his theory with the intellectual veneer provided by Alexandre Kojève's analysis of Hegel and convinced some (though far from all) people of the profundity of his analysis. He would have done better, however, to have paid attention to an author who (by 1989) was far less fashionable than he once had been. For already in the first volume (1934) of his monumentally long (as well as tedious, admittedly) *Study of History*, Arnold J. Toynbee had put his finger on something crucial when he wrote that, 'in the struggle for existence', the West had 'driven its contemporaries to the wall and has entangled them in the meshes of its economic and political ascendancy, but it has not yet disarmed them of their distinctive cultures'. Instead, Toynbee argued, '[h]ard pressed though they are, they can still call their souls their own, and this means that the mental strife has not yet reached a decision'.[2] The announcement of the 'Westernisation' of the world was almost as premature in 1989 as it would have been in 1934. But then, Fukuyama found a way to admit as much, notwithstanding his grand, bold argument: in a footnote on Japan, which he had just used as an example of the trend expounded, he conceded, 'I use the example of Japan with some caution, since Kojève late in his life came to conclude that Japan, with its culture based on purely formal arts, proved that the universal homogenous state was not victorious and that history had perhaps not ended'. (Fukuyama referred his readers to 'the long note at the end of the second edition of *Introduction à la Lecture de Hegel*, 462–3'.)[3] Though he wanted to (and certainly did) make a splash with the sweepingness of his argument, Fukuyama embedded ambiguity into his claim from the beginning. This is how his 1989 article concluded:

> The end of history will be a very sad time. The struggle for recognition, the willingness to risk one's life for a purely abstract goal, the worldwide ideological struggle that called forth daring, courage, imagination, and idealism, will be replaced by economic calculation, the endless solving of technical problems, environmental concerns, and the satisfaction of sophisticated consumer demands. In the post-historical period there will be neither art nor philosophy, just the perpetual caretaking of the museum of human history. I can feel in myself, and see in others around me, a powerful nostalgia [...]. Even though I recognize its inevitability, I have the most ambivalent feelings for the civilization that has been created by Europe since 1945, with its north Atlantic and Asian offshoots. Perhaps this very prospect of centuries of boredom at the end of history will serve to get history started once again.[4]

II. Professor Schlesinger's Reflections on a Multicultural Society

On reading Burnham's *Suicide of the West* one would think that the main culprit responsible for the alleged 'suicide' was Professor Arthur M. Schlesinger, Jr. (1917–2007).[5] Others, meanwhile, have defended Schlesinger as one of the most sensible paragons of the American 'reformist Left'.[6] Both as a prolific Harvard academic and as adviser to President J. F. Kennedy and other politicians, Schlesinger certainly was a central figure in American intellectual and political life for decades.[7] But rather than fulfilling the undermining role that Burnham attributed to him, Schlesinger saw himself as a quintessential defender of what he considered Western institutions and values. In 1991 he published *The Disuniting of America:*

Reflections on a Multicultural Society. He began the book with a direct refutation of the Fukuyama thesis that had been widely discussed since two years earlier. 'The fading away of the cold war has brought an era of ideological conflict to an end. But it has not, as forecast, brought an end to history. One set of hatreds gives way to the next.' Instead, Schlesinger argued, humanity 'enters—or, more precisely, re-enters—a possibly more dangerous era of ethnic and racial animosity'. What disturbed him was that such ethnic or racial conflict was manifesting itself not only in the Balkans and the Soviet lands, but also within what he thought to be the most successful experiment of coexistence between people of different origins and religions: the United States. He evoked Hector St. John de Crèvecoeur's definition of what made 'this promiscuous breed' and that 'strange mixture of blood' one people, in the famous *Letters from an American Farmer*. And he evoked too the Swedish economist Gunnar Myrdal's description, in 1944, of the cluster of ideas, institutions and habits that united Americans as 'the American Creed'.[8]

The Disuniting of America pleased few people when it appeared.[9] Schlesinger castigated not just the betrayal of 'the American Creed' by white American racists, but also the 'use of history as therapy' by self-appointed leaders of oppressed or minority groups, which was inevitably resulting in 'the corruption of history as history'. But his plea was not only to leaders of separatist minority movements (such as Afrocentrists) to refrain from disuniting America. It was also to the majority: '[T]he burden to unify the country does not fall exclusively on the minorities. Assimilation and integration constitute a two-way street.' Racism, he repeatedly stressed, had been 'the great national tragedy'. Despite recently having 'at last begun to confront the racism so deeply and shamefully inbred in our history' he was adamant that 'white America' had a long way to go: 'When old-line Americans, for example, treat people of other nationalities and races as if they were indigestible elements to be shunned and barred, they must not be surprised if minorities gather bitterly unto themselves and damn everybody else.' It was clear to Schlesinger not only that '*they* [must] want assimilation and integration' but also that '*we* must want assimilation and integration too. The burden to make this a unified country lies as much with the complacent majority as with the sullen and resentful minorities.'[10]

One of the issues analysed in the book was the question of Eurocentrism in American education. 'Is Europe really the root of all evil? The crimes of Europe against lesser breeds without the law [...] are famous.' Nevertheless, 'these crimes do not alter the facts of history: that Europe was the birthplace of the United States of America, that European ideas and culture formed the republic, that the United

FIGURE 9.1. Arthur M. Schlesinger, Jr. watching the lift-off of Alan Shepherd in Mercury-Redstone 3 (the first US human space flight), with President Kennedy, Vice President Johnson, Jackie Kennedy and Admiral Arleigh Burke in the White House Office of the president's secretary, 5 May 1961. Photograph by Cecil W. Stoughton. White House Photographs, John F. Kennedy Presidential Library and Museum, Boston. *Source:* https://en.wikipedia.org/wiki/Arthur_M._Schlesinger
_Jr.#/media/File:Kennedy,_Johnson,_and_others_watching_flight_of_Astronaut
_Shepard_on_television,_05_May_1961.png

States is an extension of European civilization, and that 80 per cent of Americans are of European descent'. According to Schlesinger, it was '[t]hese humdrum historical facts, and not some dastardly imperialist conspiracy' that explained 'the Eurocentric slant in American schools'. Meanwhile, he stressed, '[o]f course the 20 percent and their contributions should be integrated into the curriculum too, which is the point of cultural pluralism'; but, 'self-styled "multiculturalists"' were very often 'ethnocentric separatists who see little in the Western heritage beyond Western crimes'. Furthermore, 'the assault on the Western tradition is conducted very largely with analytical weapons forged in the West'. Thus the '"unmasking," "demythologizing," "decanonizing," "dehegemonizing" blitz against Western culture depends on methods of critical analysis unique to the West—which surely testifies to *the internally redemptive potentialities of the Western tradition*'.[11] Schlesinger went on to ask, 'Is the Western tradition a bar to progress and a curse on humanity? Would it really do America and the world good to get rid of the

European legacy?' His answer was that while "[n]o doubt Europe has done terrible things, not least to itself",

> [t]here remains, however, a crucial difference between the Western tradition and the others. The crimes of the West have produced their own antidotes. They have produced great movements to end slavery, to raise the status of women, to abolish torture, to combat racism, to defend freedom of enquiry and expression, to advance personal liberty and human rights.
>
> Whatever the particular crimes of Europe, that continent is also the source—the *unique* source—of those liberating ideas of individual liberty, political democracy, the rule of law, human rights, and cultural freedom that constitute our most precious legacy and to which most of the world today aspires. These are *European* ideas, not Asian, nor African, nor Middle Eastern ideas, except by adoption.[12]

Schlesinger's point was that it was precisely because America was indeed a multicultural society that it desperately needed a unifying political creed. But he also argued that the creed had been—and it was to be hoped would go on—improving the realities on the ground, which were far from ideal: 'Our democratic principles contemplate an open society founded on tolerance of differences and mutual respect.' In practice, meanwhile, America had been 'more open to some than to others. But it is more open to all today than it was yesterday and is likely to be even more open tomorrow than today. The steady movement of American life has been from exclusion to inclusion.' He rehearsed the successive stages and claimed, 'Historically and culturally this republic has an Anglo-Saxon base; but from the start the base has been modified, enriched, and reconstituted by transfusions from other continents and civilizations.' That 'movement from exclusion to inclusion' had been causing 'a constant revision in the texture of our culture.' And he emphasised that

> Black Americans in particular have influenced the ever-changing national culture in many ways. They have lived here for centuries, and, unless one believes in racist mysticism, they belong far more to American culture than to the culture of Africa. *Their history is part of the Western democratic tradition, not an alternative to it.*

According to Schlesinger, '[n]o one does black Americans more disservice than those Afrocentric ideologues who would define them out of the West.'[13] Richard Wright and James Baldwin (Schlesinger quoted the latter in that part of the book) would have agreed.

III. Trotskyite (Critical) Defence of the West: Cornelius Castoriadis

What Schlesinger called 'the internally redemptive potentialities of the Western tradition' found defenders (critical, to be sure, but also convinced that, in some important sense, West is best) in what might at first sight appear surprising quarters. Cornelius Castoriadis (1922–1997) was one of the most important thinkers and intellectuals in the second half of the twentieth century in France. He was born in Constantinople/Istanbul, but his Greek father took the family to Athens at a time of troubles after Mustafa Kemal defeated the Greek army and abolished the Ottoman Empire. In 1945 the young Castoriadis left Greece with a scholarship for France. With Claude Lefort he founded the famous review *Socialisme ou Barbarie* (1949–65). The group going by the same name associated with the review is widely credited (or blamed) for the outbreak of social unrest in May 1968. Castoriadis was a fierce critic of capitalism; but he was also at the same time vociferously anti-Stalinist.[14] He relentlessly analysed concepts such as autonomy, the auto-determination of societies, the ills of the 'bureaucratic society' and the merits of ancient Greek (Athenian) democracy.[15] Few people were as caustic in their criticism of the flaws of his contemporary Western society and the 'historically unprecedented *privatization*' that characterised it—'the pursuit of trivial pleasures in a world devoid of projects and prospects other than people's petty individual well-being'—what he called 'consumerist, televisual onanism'. As he put it, '[o]urs is a lobby and hobby society. [...] Make as much money as you can and try to be seen on TV, that's the philosophy and morality of the system. What kind of individual, of human being, can that produce?' And he warned, 'It works, but for how long? We mustn't forget that capitalism's huge success rests, among other things, on the irreversible destruction of the biological resources accumulated on earth over a period of three billion years. That's a sort of wall against which we are being hurled at top speed.'[16] As he put it elsewhere, 'Western man doesn't believe in anything, except in the fact that he'll soon be able to buy a high-definition television set.' (Not that any of this would prevent him from opining, in 1991, that it was 'clear that capitalism, in its present Western form, is infinitely preferable to the Soviet "non-planning", which actually was total anarchy'.)[17]

Some of Castoriadis's most interesting comments were elicited by the 1991 Gulf War following Saddam Hussein's invasion of Kuwait in 1990 and reactions to it. On 5 February 1991 he published 'La Guerre du Golfe mise à plat' ('The Gulf War: Setting Things Straight') in the left-wing newspaper *Libération*. He did not mince his words and did not spare anyone (except perhaps the Palestinians and Kurds, whom he saw as the victims of multiple wrongs). 'Saddam Hussein doesn't give a damn about the Palestinians or about the Koran. [...] He doesn't represent the poor against the rich, or the South against the North. [...] He cuts his opponents to pieces, and gasses the Kurd minority.' Yet '"progressives" are prepared to forget all that because Saddam beautifully completes the collection of oppressors (Stalin, Mao, Castro, Pol Pot, and so on) they have always upheld so fervently'. On the other hand, '[t]he Western countries talk about "law." What a strange thing it is to uphold law, and human rights, in the company of Assad and King Fahd.' They talked, moreover about 'international law'. Castoriadis's comment was that '[t]hat infinitely elastic law was and still is left in abeyance where the West Bank, Lebanon, Cyprus, Grenada, or Panama is concerned'. Fanaticism, meanwhile, he thought to have reached an alarming point. He feared that 'the few Arab intellectuals who seemed to earnestly value criticism and reflection', until then, were 'presently actively contributing to a mythologized version of Arab history in which the Arabs have been doves, white as snow, over the past thirteen centuries, and all their ills have been inflicted on them by Western colonization'. Meanwhile, with 'few exceptions', Western intellectuals had not done much better. The vast majority were saying 'nothing'. Among those who did speak out, 'there are those who give in to the blackmail of "Arabism," "Islam," "the West's guilt," or give vent to their stupid hatred of the United States whatever it does'.[18]

Relentless criticisms of all and sundry continued, but the most serious issue for Castoriadis was that

> [b]y now the conflict has greatly exceeded the case of Iraq and Saddam Hussein. It's on the way to turning into a confrontation between societies in which the religious imaginary is still tenacious and even being strengthened in reaction, and Western societies which have more or less successfully rid themselves of that imaginary but have turned out to be incapable of transmitting anything other than techniques for warfare and for the manipulation of public opinion to the rest of the world. [...] What is important for us is that the present state of our society makes it unable to exert any influence other than material. A society that worships consumerism and zapping on TV cannot erode the anthropological hold of the Koran or of Hinduism. Peoples who are at a loss in the modern world and adhere tensely to their religious identity can't find any example worth imitating or any incitement to think for themselves in those apathetic citizens, huddled up in their petty private worlds, who leave government to the political, economic and cultural oligarchies, to the party apparatuses and the mass media.

His conclusion was, 'So what should we do? Should we get another people, as they say? Of course not. Should we get people to change? But who can do that? People themselves have to change, as a people.' Therefore, '[e]veryone can contribute to that change, all of us, within ourselves and around us whenever we can speak out. Without that change, there will be only false answers to monstrously wrongly posed problems.'[19]

Perhaps it was that, the possibility of speaking out and hoping to effect change through doing so, that distinguished 'the West', despite all its painful problems. This seems to emerge from Castoriadis's reply to the following question he was asked during an interview a few months after the publication of his *Libération* article: '"Colonialism was the Western world's main sin. However, I don't see any great leap forward in the vitality and plurality of cultures since its disappearance," says Claude Lévi-Strauss in *De près et de loin*. What do you think?' Castoriadis's reply was,

> The statement is historically false. The Greeks, the Romans, and Arabs all successfully undertook huge colonizing operations. Moreover, they assimilated or converted the people they conquered, whether they liked it or not. The Arabs now portray themselves as the eternal victims of the Western world. That's a grotesque myth. The Arabs have been conquerors ever since Muhammad's times, extending their nation into Asia, Africa, and Europe (look at Spain, Sicily, and Crete) by Arabizing the peoples they conquered. How many 'Arabs' were there in Egypt at the turn of the 7th century? The present expansion of the Arabs and of Islam is the outcome of the conquest and the more or less forced conversion to Islam of the peoples they subdued. Then they in turn were dominated by the Turks for over four centuries. Western semi-colonization lasted only one hundred thirty years in the worst case (Algeria), and much less in the others. And it was the Arabs who first introduced the trade in black slaves in Africa, three centuries before the Europeans.
>
> All that in no way lessens the weight of Western colonial crimes. But we must not overlook one essential difference. In the Western world, internal criticism of colonialism began very early (with Montaigne), and by the 19th century it had already led to the abolition of slavery (which actually still exists in some Muslim countries), and in the 20th century, to the refusal of the population of Europe and America to fight to retain the colonies (in Vietnam).[20]

The kind of extension of the scope of conflict beyond the context of Saddam Hussein's Iraq, and its 'turning into a confrontation between societies in which the religious imaginary is still tenacious [...] and Western societies', that Castoriadis was concerned about in 1991, was a worry for others as well. Soon one of them was to give it a name that stuck.

IV. 'The West Unique, Not Universal': Samuel Huntington and 'the Clash of Civilizations'

There is some irony in reading, after February 2022, the prediction that '[i]f civilization is what counts [...] the likelihood of violence between Ukrainians and Russians should be low. They are two Slavic, primarily Orthodox peoples who have had close relationships with each other for centuries.'[21] But then, the same author had conceded elsewhere that '[t]he record of past predictions by social scientists is not a happy one'. Samuel Huntington had criticised Fukuyama's thesis already in the autumn of 1989.[22] A more substantial airing of his own alternative prognosis came with an article in *Foreign Affairs* in 1993. There was a question mark in the title: 'The Clash of Civilizations?'. He would develop his arguments further in a book three years later.[23] During the same year that saw the publication of his book, Huntington also published an important article that should be read perhaps with greater attention than his 1993 one. It was entitled 'The West Unique, Not Universal'. And he was to come back during the following decade with an agonised book on the consequences of immigration and multiculturalism for American identity.[24]

In his 1989 article Huntington had already warned against 'the errors of endism'—the predictions of an end to war and the even more 'sweeping, dramatic, and provocative phrase', 'the end of history', as articulated by Fukuyama. It was erroneous, he retorted, 'to jump from the decline of communism to the global triumph of liberalism and the disappearance of ideology as a force in world affairs'. Among his several arguments, the most interesting from today's perspective is what he wrote in 1989 about China. To Fukuyama's statement that 'Chinese competitiveness and expansionism on the world scene have virtually disappeared', Huntington retorted that it was arguable (in 1989) 'that Chinese expansionism has yet to appear on the world scene'. It was in the wake of industrialisation that such expansionism had manifested itself in the histories of other powers so far. Huntington's warning was that while, '[m]aybe China will be different from all other major powers and not attempt to expand its influence and control as it industrializes', one could not predict that with any confidence. Meanwhile, if China were to follow the historical pattern, 'a billion Chinese engaged in imperial expansion are likely to impose a lot of history on the rest of the world'.[25]

In 'The Clash of Civilizations?' (1993) Huntington wrote that world politics was 'entering a new phase'. Many analysts had captured some aspects of that new phase. However, they all missed 'a crucial, indeed a central, aspect of what global politics is likely to be in the coming years'. It was his hypothesis 'that the fundamental source of conflict in this new world will not be primarily ideological or primarily economic'. Instead, '[t]he great divisions among humankind and the dominating source of conflict will be cultural'. Nation states would still be 'the most powerful actors in world affairs', but 'the principal conflicts of global politics will occur between nations and groups of different civilizations'. Time and again he repeated that '[t]he clash of civilizations will dominate global politics. The fault lines between civilizations will be the battle lines of the future.' All earlier conflicts since the Peace of Westphalia had been conflicts between princes, then between nation states, and then, as a result of the Russian Revolution, conflicts of ideology. Yet, '[t]hese conflicts between princes, nation states and ideologies were primarily conflicts within Western civilization, "Western civil wars"'. With the end of the Cold War, international politics was moving 'out of its Western phase', and 'its center-piece becomes the interaction between the West and non-Western civilizations and among non-Western civilizations'. In that 'politics of civilizations', the peoples and governments of 'non-Western civilizations' would, he predicted, 'no longer remain the objects of history as targets of Western colonialism but join the West as movers and shapers of history'. Given the centrality of 'civilizations' to his argument, definitions were in order:

> A Civilization is a cultural entity. Villages, regions, ethnic groups, nationalities, religious groups, all have distinct cultures at different levels of cultural heterogeneity. The culture of a village in southern Italy may be different from that of a village in northern Italy, but both will share in a common Italian culture that distinguishes them from German villages. European communities, in turn, will share cultural features that distinguish them from Arab or Chinese communities. Arabs, Chinese and Westerners, however, are not part of any broader cultural entity. They constitute civilizations. A Civilization is thus the highest cultural grouping of people and the broadest level of cultural identity people have short of that which distinguishes humans from other species. It is defined both by common objective elements, such as language, history, religion, customs, institutions, and by the subjective self-identification of people.

Huntington added a crucial qualification, which, perhaps, he did not sufficiently remember when he went on to enumerate actual civilizations and predict who might go to war with whom: '*People can and do redefine their identities and, as a result, the composition and boundaries of civilizations change.*' He predicted that '[c]ivilizational identity will be increasingly important in the future, and the world will be shaped in large measure by the interactions among seven or eight major civilizations'. These were 'Western, Confucian, Japanese, Islamic, Hindu, Slavic-Orthodox, Latin American and possibly African civilization'. In the future, the most important conflicts would 'occur along the cultural fault lines separating these civilizations from one another'. Why was that the case? First, he argued, because 'differences among civilizations are not only real; they are basic. Civilizations are differentiated from each other by history, language, culture, tradition, *and, most important, religion*'. As he went on to elaborate, '[t]he people of different civilizations have different views on the relations between God and man, the individual and the group, the citizen and the state, parents and children, husband and wife, as well as differing views on the relative importance of rights and responsibilities, liberty and authority, equality and hierarchy'. Those differences were 'the product of centuries. They will not soon disappear. They are far more fundamental than differences among political ideologies and political regimes'.[26]

Another of the several reasons Huntington gave for the salience of civilizational conflict that he predicted was that 'the growth of civilization-consciousness is enhanced by the dual role of the West'. On the one hand, the West was 'at a peak of power'. Simultaneously, however, 'and perhaps as a result, a return to the roots phenomenon is occurring among non-Western civilizations'. Consequently, '[a] West at the peak of its power confronts non-Wests that increasingly have the desire, the will and the resources to shape the world in non-Western ways'. As he explained, in former times, 'the elites of non-Western societies were usually the people who were most involved with the West, had been educated at Oxford, the Sorbonne or Sandhurst, and had absorbed Western attitudes and values'. Meanwhile, 'the populace in non-Western countries often remained deeply imbued with the indigenous culture'. That was no longer the case. In his own time, these relationships were being reversed. 'A de-Westernization and indigenization of elites is occurring in many non-Western countries at the same time that Western, usually American, cultures, styles and habits become more popular among the mass of the people.'[27]

Huntington criticised the suggestion that Western civilisation had gradually become 'our universal civilization'—articulated, for instance, by the Trinidadian novelist V. S. Naipaul in a widely discussed 1990 lecture.[28] It was only at a superficial level that 'much of Western culture has indeed permeated the rest of the world'. However, at a deeper level, 'Western concepts differ fundamentally from those prevalent in other civilizations'. Thus, 'Western ideas of individualism, liberalism, constitutionalism, human rights, equality, liberty, the rule of law, democracy,

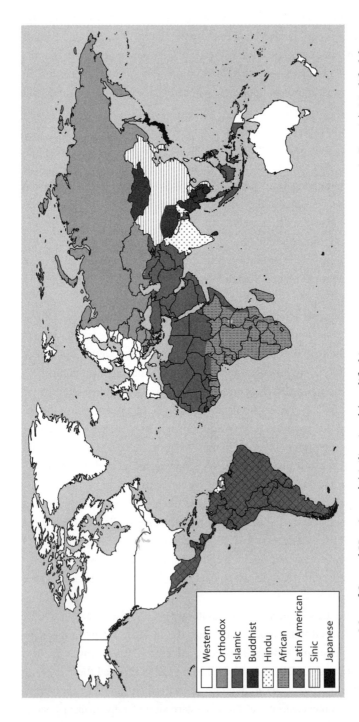

FIGURE 9.2. Map of Samuel Huntington's 'civilizations' (modified in response to contemporary events in Bosnia). Modified from Samuel P. Huntington, *The Clash of Civilizations and the Remaking of World Order*, Simon & Schuster, 1996, pp. 26–27. (Wikimedia: Kyle Cronan & Olahus). *Source*: https://en.wikipedia.org/wiki/Samuel_P._Huntington#/media/File:Clash_of_Civilizations_mapn2.png

free markets, the separation of church and state, often have little resonance in Islamic, Confucian, Japanese, Hindu, Buddhist or Orthodox cultures'; and 'Western efforts to propagate such ideas produce instead a reaction against "human rights imperialism" and a reaffirmation of indigenous values, as can be seen in the support for religious fundamentalism by the younger generation in non-Western cultures'. What was more, as he emphasised, '[t]he very notion that there could be a "universal civilization" is a Western idea, directly at odds with the particularism of most Asian societies'. (René Guénon would have fully agreed). The upshot of all this was that '[t]he central axis of world politics in the future' was likely to be 'the conflict between "the West and the Rest" and the responses of non-Western civilizations to Western power and values'.[29]

Most readers noticed Huntington's prediction of civilisational conflict and failed to notice by comparison his concluding recommendations in his initial famous article. He was certainly not calling for civilisational war: 'Hence the West will increasingly have to accommodate these non-Western modern civilizations whose power approaches that of the West but whose values and interests differ significantly from those of the West.' Such accommodation would require the West 'to maintain the economic and military power necessary to protect its interests in relation to those civilizations'. But that was not enough. The West would also need 'to develop a more profound understanding of the basic religious and philosophical assumptions underlying other civilizations and the ways in which people in those civilizations see their interests'. An effort would moreover be required 'to identify elements of commonality between Western and other civilizations. For the relevant future, there will be no universal civilization, but instead a world of different civilizations, each of which will have to learn to coexist with the others.' The major problem with Huntington's theory was, of course, that, as Stephen Walt put it appositely in a review of his 1996 book, it offered 'a dangerous, self-fulfilling prophecy: The more we believe it and make it the basis for action, the more likely it is to come true.'[30]

Three years later, as mentioned above, Huntington published another significant article, characteristically entitled 'The West Unique, Not Universal'. There he tried to combat the idea that Western civilisation was universal or universalisable and to urge Westerners to defend and preserve it as one among several different civilisations—and stop jeopardising it by insistence on universalist illusions. Modern societies had 'much in common', he conceded, 'but they do not necessarily merge into homogeneity. The argument that they do so rests on the assumption that modern society must approximate a single type, the Western type; that modern civilization is Western civilization, and Western civilization is modern civilization'. That, however, was 'a false identification'.

Huntington's response was that 'Western civilization emerged in the eighth and ninth centuries and developed its distinctive characteristics in the centuries that followed. It did not begin to modernize until the eighteenth century. *The West, in short, was Western long before it was modern*.' He went on (in a section entitled 'What Makes the West Western?') to identify 'the distinguishing characteristics of Western civilization during the hundreds of years before it modernized'. In his view, most scholars would agree on 'a number of institutions, practices, and beliefs that may be legitimately identified as the core of Western civilization'. These included 'the Classical legacy'; 'Western Christianity'; 'European languages'; 'separation of spiritual and temporal authority'; 'rule of law'; 'social pluralism and civil society'; 'representative bodies'; and 'individualism'. Huntington was of course sufficiently sophisticated to hasten to add, following this description of the 'core', that '[t]he above list is not an exhaustive enumeration of the distinctive characteristics of Western civilization. Nor is it meant to imply that those characteristics were always and everywhere present in Western society [. . . or] meant to suggest that none of these characteristics have appeared in other civilizations'. Admittedly, '[i]ndividually, almost none of these factors is unique to the West. But the combination of them is, and has given the West its distinctive quality.' In short, these 'concepts, practices, and institutions' had been 'far more prevalent in the West than in other civilizations. They form the essential continuing core of Western civilization. They are what is Western, but not modern, about the West'; and they also 'generated the commitment to individual freedom that now distinguishes the West from other civilizations'. Huntington approvingly quoted the argument of Arthur Schlesinger we encountered above, that Europe is '"the source—the *unique* source" of the "ideas of individual liberty [. . .]"'. Those 'concepts and characteristics' were 'also in large part the factors that enabled the West to take the lead in modernizing itself and the world. They make Western civilization unique, and Western civilization is precious not because it is universal but because it is unique.'[31]

All this meant that the time had come 'for the West to abandon the illusion of universality and to promote the strength, coherence, and vitality of its civilization in a world of civilizations'. The West's interests were not served 'by promiscuous intervention into the disputes of other peoples'.[32] (However, that may be a case of 'easier said than done'. Huntington rather contradicts himself; for one of his—many—concrete recommendations for the West in his earlier [1993] article had been, 'to support in other civilizations groups sympathetic to Western values and interests'.[33] He must have realised that doing so might well lead to ever-increasing involvement and 'interventions into the disputes of other peoples'.)

He stressed that '[p]romoting the coherence of the West means both preserving Western culture within the West and defining the limits of the West'. The former consideration required 'controlling immigration from non-Western societies [...] and ensuring the assimilation into Western culture of the immigrants who are admitted'. It also meant 'recognizing that in the post–Cold War world, NATO is the security organization of Western civilization and that its primary purpose is to defend and preserve that civilization'. That meant, in turn, that states that were 'Western in their history, religion, and culture should, if they desire, be able to join NATO'. According to Huntington's criteria, this meant that NATO membership should be open to 'the Visegrad states, the Baltic states, Slovenia, and Croatia, but not countries that have historically been primarily Muslim or Orthodox'. By the same token, he continued, 'While recent debate has focused entirely on the expansion rather than the contraction of NATO, it is also necessary to recognize that as NATO's mission changes, Turkish and Greek ties to NATO will weaken and their membership could either come to an end or become meaningless'. Indeed, '[w]ithdrawal from NATO is the declared goal of the Welfare Party in Turkey, and Greece is becoming as much an ally of Russia as it is a member of NATO'.[34]

The latter statement has of course proved completely off the mark, with hindsight; not to mention Huntington's prediction with regard to Ukrainians and Russians with which we began this section. It would hardly be uncharitable or unfair to comment that Huntington's over-reliance on religion as the main criterion of civilisational identity coloured his whole theory, and invested it with an undue inflexibility. Whether with reference to Ukraine or Greece or any other country, he seemed unwilling to accept the possibility of majorities and their governments in such countries opting to confirm their belonging to a civilisational alliance different from that to which their traditional religious affiliations would predispose him to allocate them.

V. '[A]uf die Seite des Westens': Jürgen Habermas, Heinrich August Winkler and the Western *Wertegemeinschaft*[35]

'Jürgen Habermas [...] gehört auf die Seite des Westens. So seltsam es klingt, *er* ist ein Enkel Adenauers' (Jürgen Habermas [...] belongs on the side of the West. As strange as it sounds, *he* is an heir of Adenauer's).

RALF DAHRENDORF, 'ZEITGENOSSE HABERMAS: JÜRGEN HABERMAS ZUM SECHZIGSTEN GEBURTSTAG', *MERKUR*, VOL. 43, NO. 484 (JUNE 1989), PP. 480–81

Jürgen Habermas has for some decades been universally acclaimed as 'the single most influential political thinker in Germany'. His 'moral stature is unique'. This, according to Mark Lilla, is because 'as with Sartre in the 1950s, Habermas' theoretical works and partisan engagements are meant to be read together and to be mutually reinforcing'.[36] He has been 'Germany's pre-eminent and most polarizing postwar social philosopher', who has 'participated in every major academic debate since the early 1960s, especially those controversies which touched on the political self-understanding of the Federal Republic'.[37] It has been rightly remarked that 'in the history of German culture there are few public intellectuals who have shaped social debate for as many decades' as has Habermas.[38] He was a major protagonist in the *Historikerstreit* (historians' dispute) of the late 1980s about the German past.[39] As Jan-Werner Müller has put it, 'In the *Historikerstreit* [... Habermas] fiercely opposed those whom he perceived as the proponents of a "sanitized" national identity and of cultural continuities with the pre-1933 past.' Habermas particularly resented the views of those (such as Michael Stürmer) whom he regarded as 'reducing the comprehensive "mental opening" and the establishment of firm political ties to the West, which Habermas saw as *the* historical achievement of the Federal Republic, to strategic military and economic considerations.'[40]

That attitude, and the importance of what was at stake, were both clear in a lecture Habermas had given in Denmark in 1987. There he referred to 'we Western Europeans, who are not only nourished by the heritage of European intellectual history but also share democratic forms of government and occidental forms of life'. He went on to emphasise that '[t]his "West" was given its definition by the first generation of states in modern Europe; it was taken for granted that Englishmen and Frenchmen as well as Danes and Swedes belonged to it.' However, '[o]nly in the decades since the end of World War II has it become a matter of course for Germans this side of the Elbe and the Werra to consider themselves a part of Western Europe'. Habermas reminded his audience of several facts that reflected 'the dream of a hegemony of the Central European powers and an ideology of "the middle" that had deep roots in *the "anti-civilizing, anti-Western undercurrent in the German tradition" from the Romantics to Heidegger*'. As he went on to note, '[t]he consciousness of having taken a *Sonderweg*, a special path that set Germany apart and gave it special privilege in relation to the West was discredited only by Auschwitz'. At any rate, after Auschwitz, it had 'lost its power to generate myths'. As a result, '[t]hat through which we Germans dissociated ourselves from Western civilization, and indeed from any and every civilization, set off a shock-wave; and though many citizens of the Federal Republic fended off this shock at first, they remained under its influence as they gradually abandoned their reservations about the political culture and social forms of the West. A mentality changed.' The change was indispensable: 'For it is only in the untroubled consciousness of a break with our disastrous traditions that the Federal Republic's unreserved openness to the political culture of the West will mean more than an opportunity that is economically attractive and inevitable in terms of power politics.' Habermas was 'concerned with this "more," the possibility of a greater meaning in the new intellectual orientation.' The explicitness of the question was crucial to him: 'Thus only now has the question of how to understand our orientation to the West come up for debate—whether we want to understand it pragmatically, as a matter of alliances, or intellectually as well, as a new beginning in political culture.' One could not simply reply, 'Both'; for that would be 'to evade the issue and turn an existential question into one of semantics'.[41]

Habermas is well known for his promotion of the idea of *Verfassungspatriotismus*, or 'constitutional patriotism'.[42] The idea had been earlier developed by the political scientist Dolf Sternberger, but Habermas appropriated it and caused it to be widely discussed in relation both to German debates and later to debates on the future of the EU. The concept became seriously popular in Germany. Constitutional patriotism would attach citizens to the constitution and its democratic institutions rather than to any national or ethnic links, and would direct their self-esteem as citizens to taking pride in the democratic institutions of the Federal Republic, and away from any *Volk*-ish attachments. To Habermas's mind, such a form of attachment was crucial for Germany's relationship to the West: 'Only such a form of patriotism, Habermas thought, would not alienate Germany from the West.'[43]

Habermas did not adopt a straightforward 'liberal' position. Instead he developed a radical democratic theory and agenda. Thus '[o]n the one hand, [he] was a relentless critic of the *Sonderweg* idea in German culture, arguing for full German participation in the Enlightenment culture of the West'. On the other hand, 'since no existing Western state was radically democratic enough, he remained opposed to the liberalism that Germany now shared with the West. Habermas, it seemed, refused to let Germany join any club that would have it as a member.'[44] But this critical attitude did not mean that he saw nothing good about the Federal Republic of (i.e., 'West') Germany. Rather, 'despite many disappointments and misgivings about the reality of democracy in West Germany', he 'always sought to stress that the Federal Republic had been a real historical achievement for the Germans. He unashamedly called himself a "product of 'Re-education'".'[45]

Habermas's attachment to the Westernisation of his country provoked in him an ambivalent attitude towards German reunification when it became an issue in 1990. As Jan-Werner Müller observes, 'it was remarkable for the leading West German social philosopher and political moralist to admit not having thought about the GDR as part of Germany at all, of never having included it on the road map to a post-national state.' The conclusion Müller draws is, 'Consequently, the GDR, as another country, clearly inferior to Habermas's idealized West, could merely be a detour on that route, or, worse, a setback.'[46]

It was not surprising then that, in 1989, another major German 'Westerner', Ralf Dahrendorf, suggested that Habermas was an heir of Adenauer (the architect of West Germany's drive towards the West), and that he emphatically 'belongs on the side of the West'.[47] But it is important to note, as Müller rightly does, that '[u]nlike many other leftist intellectuals, [...] Habermas did not just discover his attachment to the Federal Republic [i.e., what was up to then West Germany] at the very moment when it was to become part of a united Germany'. For '[d]espite his sometimes harsh criticisms of certain political aspects of the Federal Republic, Habermas had always sought to stress the real historical achievements in finally making West Germany a liberal democratic, *truly Western* polity'. This means that '[t]here was no newly found apologia-cum-nostalgia for the Federal Republic in 1990, precisely because there had been a long-lasting attachment'. The flipside, however, was that the attachment in question 'made 17 million East Germans who seemed to have just emerged from the 1950s appear as a threat'.[48]

Müller also notes that, after German reunification in 1990, Habermas 'perceived a further erosion of republican consciousness'. Intellectuals had been distancing themselves 'from the very West which Habermas cherished and, according to Habermas, argued that West Germany had been intellectually colonized by the West just as East Germany had been politically colonized by the Soviet Union'. Disturbed by this, he 'expressed concern that a reactionary alliance between West German anti-Westerners and embittered East German intellectuals might take the next logical step and call for a return to irrational German intellectual traditions'. As Müller remarks, such alarmism was not unfounded: 'In the years following unification, his concerns about the rise of a New Right were partly vindicated'. The New Right 'did question the cultural and political ties to the "victors of the West" (with Habermas as their prime polemical target), while East German intellectuals [...] espoused what often seemed like a rather crude anti-Western cultural pessimism.'[49]

The new tone that worried Habermas is exemplified in a characteristically titled collective volume published in early 1993, *Westbindung: Chancen und*

Risiken für Deutschland (Western orientation: opportunities and risks for Germany). The editors wrote as members of a new generation that did not have to apologise for the Third Reich or the 1960s and thus were 'free from the almost mystical glorification of "the West", as it had come to be a confession of faith [neuen politischen Religion] for many left-liberals and conservatives after 1945'. The major risk the editors warned against was the 'the utopia of a total integration of Germany in the West within a European federal state' (Utopie einer Totalwestintegration Deutschalnds in einer europäischen Bundesstaat). Habermas was a major target of the editors and of some of the contributors who were in sympathy with them.[50]

Habermas would continue to be preoccupied with his (now) reunited country's relationship with the West. The decision by US president George W. Bush to go to war in Iraq in 2003 led Habermas to emerge then as one of the leading European intellectuals commenting on 'the divided West', with (much of) continental Europe parting ways from the governments of the US and the UK on that issue. One of his best-known interventions was a letter he wrote (and signed jointly with the French philosopher Jacques Derrida), taking as a cue the day of huge simultaneous demonstrations in many European capitals, on 15 February 2003. The essay highlighted the factors that made for a distinctly European response to the international order and the chances of a European identity consolidating as a result. Most of it reads in retrospect like wishful thinking—and probably did so to many even at the time. (Habermas did also examine the countervailing factors. One of them was the universalisation of European experience, and another was the existence of a 'West' that was wider than Europe.)[51] Habermas was far from alone of course, at that historical moment, in thinking that George W. Bush's invasion of Iraq had deeply and perhaps irreparably divided the 'West' and that a distinctly European identity and allegiance could be reinforced by an awareness on the part of European public opinion of the—supposedly—common reflexes they were displaying on issues related to respect for international law and the international order more generally.[52] Developments such as the accession of ten new members to the European Union in 2004, eight of which were former Communist countries from Central and Eastern Europe (to be followed by more a few years later) caused such ideas to be more and more disputed. The end of the Bush presidency in 2008 and the accession of Barack Obama, who was particularly popular in Europe, also affected the latter's relationship with the US. Habermas nevertheless continued to propose constitutional blueprints for the EU.[53]

An interesting comparison can be pursued between the stances on German reunification of Habermas and of a fellow 'arch-Westerner', the historian Heinrich August Winkler. From the end of the Cold War and German reunification, Winkler published extensively.[54] His many, and lengthy, works are all part of a 'normative' project (and he often cites the term *Wertgemeinschaft* [community of values] in relation to 'the West').[55] This project has generated much debate among historians in Germany;[56] but its main target readership is the general public. His imposing four-volume *History of the West* is 'a performative act hard to ignore. It makes a statement no German is supposed to miss when browsing in the bookshop: Germans should care about the West because they belong to it.' Winkler had already made that point forcefully with his bestselling *Germany: The Long Road West*.[57] Published ten years after German reunification, it 'quickly gained the status of a master narrative of the Berlin Republic. After centuries of fateful deviation from the Western norm, climaxing in Nazism's "revolt against the political ideas of the West", Germans were to be congratulated on finally arriving in the Western heaven.'[58] Winkler's work is 'a heavily normative account—one that has been heaped with accolades in Germany'.[59] A supporter of the SPD (Social Democrats) since his early twenties, during the late 1980s *Historikerstreit* Winkler sided with Habermas against the conservative revisionists.

Winkler had started his battles in defence of the *westliche Wertegemeinschaft* (Western community of values) long before publication of *The Long Road West*. A year after the collective volume that we noted earlier, challenging Germany's *Westbindung*, came out in 1993,[60] Winkler wrote a polemical essay challenging that volume's 'attempt at revisionism'.[61] He detected a new *Historikerstreit* in the air, this time on the rights and wrongs of Germany's orientation towards the West. He criticised the editors and those of the contributors who agreed with them (or even outdid them, not least Panayiotis Kondylis). Here Winkler was already setting the agenda that would dominate the next three decades of his work. He concluded by deploring the lack of clarity on what the concept of 'the West' meant. After criticising one of the contributors for equating 'the West' with NATO and one side of the Cold War confrontation after World War II, Winkler offered his own light on the concept. 'It would presumably make sense', he noted, 'to draw a distinction between a narrower and a wider sense of "the West"' (Sinnvoll wäre es vermutlich, zwischen einem Westen im engeren und einem Westen im weiteren Sinn zu unterscheiden.) The former referred to the countries that had first established democratic political culture, notably the United States, 'England' and France. The latter—the West in a wider sense—coincided with the historical *Okzident*. To that West belonged all parts of Europe that, since the Middle Ages, had experienced the separation between *imperium* and *sacerdotium* and the resultant social pluralism, plus the parts of the New World formed out of that Europe. Not belonging to it, on the other hand, were the countries of Byzantine Caesaropapism, where the structures of a pluralistic society never developed or developed only in rudimentary form. Winkler hence declared that 'Germany and the new democrats of East-Central Europe' were a part of that wider West, the historical *Okzident*. Taking issue once more with the contributors to the *Westbindung* volume who pleaded for a mission for Germany as 'Macht der "Mitte"' or as a 'bridge between East and West', he concluded with the warning that 'it was nowhere more evident than here, where the supposed demythologization of the West ['die vermeintliche Entmythologisierung des Westens'] can lead: back to the German myths of the interwar period.' The echoes of the *konservative Revolution* of the years of the Weimar Republic, and its struggle against 'the West', were too obvious.[62]

Winkler stuck to his guns and went on to work hard to prove the case he had made in the early 1990s. In *The Long Road West* he built a long narrative of German history in which, in the end, Germany becomes a normal 'Western' country within NATO and the EU. His next step was 'to ground the German story in an overarching history of what he calls—his master-concept—the "normative project of the West", whose unfolding is humanity's greatest achievement'. This was 'the subject of his monumental tetralogy' *Geschichte des Westens* (*A History of the West*), which appeared between 2009 and 2016. The sociologist Dylan Riley has recently analysed Winkler's project:

> What then is 'the West'? Its goals are defined by Winkler in purely political terms: the realization of a national order combining separation of powers, the rule of law and representative democracy. But its project has a deeper meaning. Volume One roots the distinctiveness of the West in its religious history. 'In the beginning was a belief: a belief in *one* God.' Judaism provided a push toward rationalization and intellectualization. Christianity then threw two further concepts into the mix: the dignity of the individual and the separation of powers. According to Winkler, Jesus's quietist answer to the Pharisees—render unto Caesar that which is Caesar's and unto God that which is God's—laid the foundation for limited government and civil society. Subsequent milestones along the path to liberty and pluralism included the Investiture Conflict and Magna Carta, the Renaissance, Reformation and Enlightenment. It was an error to think that pagan Greece and Rome had played any significant role in the consummation of human freedom.[63]

In the end, Winkler's formula might be summarised as 'a healthy stew of Anglo-Saxon liberties ultimately based on Jesus's distinction between the religious and temporal realms, spiced up with a dash—but not more!—of Enlightenment universalism'.

VI. American Anticivilisation versus All Civilisations? Huntingtonism after Huntington

James Kurth picked up the torch of Huntingtonian civilisational analysis of 'the West' and America's relationship to 'Western civilisation' quite early on.[64] And his former supervisor gave his blessing, citing Kurth's article approvingly when he himself came to write the book sequel to his initial article.[65] Commenting on Huntington's list of seven or eight major civilisations, Kurth noted that all but one were characterised by their religious affiliation. 'The real anomaly in Huntington's list is the most powerful and most pervasive civilization of them all—Western civilization, which is identified with a term that is only a geographical direction.' Thus, rather than 'connoting the profound essence of the civilization,' the name ('Western') 'connotes something bland and even insipid, with no content at all'. What was more, the 'problematic quality of Western civilization' went 'deeper than an anomalous term'. It reached to 'the most fundamental character of the civilization, to its definition and direction'. According to Kurth, Western civilisation 'is the *only* civilization that is explicitly *non-religious* or post-religious'. That was 'the radical difference of the West from the other civilizations'. It helped to explain 'why there are new conflicts between the West and the rest'; and it led one to predict 'that these conflicts will become more intense in the future'. It also pointed to 'a possible fatal flaw within Western civilization itself'. This civilisation, 'unlike others, did not place religion at its core'.[66] (It is interesting to note that the very thing Kurth complains of here corresponds exactly to the intention of Comte in choosing the name 'the West'—as made explicit by Pierre Laffitte, quoted above in chapter 2, section X.)

Kurth then offered a sweeping analysis of the social and economic changes that had led to the rejection of 'Western civilization' by the American elites. The greatest movement of the second half of the twentieth century had been 'the movement of women from the home to the office'. That change resulted in 'political movements that are beginning to shape the history of our own time. One is feminism, with its political demands ranging from equal opportunity to academic deconstructionism to abortion rights.' And feminism had in turn provoked, in reaction to its excesses, 'a new form of conservatism. These new conservatives speak of "family values"; their adversaries call them "the religious right"'. The crux of the matter, for Kurth, was that the feminist movement was 'central to the multicultural coalition and its project'. It provided 'the numbers, having reached a central mass in academia and now in the media and the law'. The feminist movement promoted 'the theories, such as deconstructionism and postmodernism', and it also provided 'much of the energy, the leadership, and the political clout'. Thus, '[t]he overthrow of the Enlightenment by the post-Enlightenment is also the overthrow of the modern by the post-modern and therefore of the Western by the post-Western'. Paradoxically then, at 'the very moment of its greatest triumph, its defeat of the last great power opposing it, Western civilization is becoming non-Western'. Alluding to the title of his article, Kurth argued, 'The real clash of civilizations will not be between the West and one or more of the Rest. It will be between the West and the post-West, within the West itself'. That clash had 'already taken place within the brain of Western civilization, the American intellectual class. It is now spreading from that brain to the American body politic.' And his diagnosis applied to both sides of the political spectrum:

> The 1990s have seen another great transformation, this time in the liberal and conservative movements that have long defined American politics and that, whatever their differences, had both believed in the modern ideas represented by the American creed. Among liberals, the political energy is now found among multicultural activists. Liberalism is ceasing to be modern and becoming post-modern. Among conservatives, the political energy is now found among religious believers. Conservatism is ceasing to be modern and is becoming pre-modern. Neither these liberals nor these conservatives are believers in Western civilization. The liberals identify with multicultural society or a post-Western civilization (such as it is). The conservatives identify with Christianity or a pre-Western civilization.

This implies a definition of 'Western civilisation' different from that of Huntington, who differentiated (two years later, in 1996) between 'Western' and 'modern' and identified what was 'Western' in the West before the West became 'modern'. Western (Catholic plus Protestant) Christianity was a major constitutive part of what was 'Western' for Huntington. Kurth emphasises instead the secular and post-Christian character of Western civilisation. His inevitable concern was that '[a] question thus arises about who, in the United States of the future, will still

316 CHAPTER 9

FIGURE 9.3. Map of the North Atlantic Treaty Organization (NATO): membership in 2024. Created by Janitoalevic. *Source:* https://commons.wikimedia.org/wiki/File:North_Atlantic_Treaty_Organization_(orthographic_projection)_in_NATO_blue.svg

believe in Western civilization. Most practically, who will believe in it enough to fight, kill, and die for it in a clash of civilizations?'[67]

Three years later, in 1997, Kurth contributed an article reflecting on the imminent NATO expansion to three Central European countries and its relation to 'the Idea of the West'. There he reiterated that the 'multicultural coalition and its feminist core despise Western civilization, which they see as the work of "dead white European males" or "DWEMs"'. The 'multicultural project' of that coalition had 'already succeeded in marginalizing Western civilization in its very intellectual core, the universities, and the media of the United States'. As a result Kurth raised the question 'as to who in the United States still does believe in Western civilization?' He could see 'no large and powerful group that provides an obvious answer'. Hence the paradox that 'at the very moment of its greatest triumph', Western civilization had been 'abandoned by the great power which was long its principal defender.' This was far from being a theoretical question, given that it had 'practical consequences for any sustained American commitment to an enlarged NATO'. The question was, 'If NATO's original formation was buttressed by the idea of Western civilization, what idea can buttress NATO's current expansion?'[68] According to Kurth, there was 'a certain irony in the United States searching for a new legitimating idea for NATO to replace the old legitimating idea of Western civilization', since 'in some respects, the United States itself has become the great power that opposes much of what was once thought of as Western civilization, especially its cultural achievements and its social arrangements'. It was the American elites that 'attack and mock any traditional European authorities, such as religion, nations, families, and high culture'. Instead of any of these, the American elites 'promulgate the current American ideas of human rights, multiculturalism, expressive individualism, and popular culture'. And of these the principal culprit was

> the American popular culture that is especially destructive of what was once defined as Western civilization. American popular culture presents as its normative human types the star entertainer and athlete. It exalts the personal qualities of inherent talent, self-centeredness, frantic energy, and aggressiveness. These are the distinguishing qualities of an adolescent, not of a mature person. It is no accident that adults in America are increasingly adopting the qualities of adolescents—particularly self-centeredness and aggressiveness—even in the elite professions [...].
>
> Elite Americans imagine themselves as advancing the ideas of human rights, multiculturalism, and expressive individualism. They might even claim that these ideas are the best, perhaps the only worthy, legacy of Western civilization. In fact, they are subverting not only the traditions of the West, but of all civilizations. It is not surprising that some of these civilizations, especially the Islamic and Confucian ones, have mounted various forms of resistance to these American ideas. Samuel Huntington has referred to this as 'the clash of civilizations' involving 'the West against the rest.' But it also may be a clash between all civilizations: both the West and the rest on the one hand—and anticivilization, the actual behavior of many Americans today, on the other.

Now, that new and 'anti-Western character of the American elite' had implications for 'the grand project of a new and expanded NATO'. The new NATO would 'not be based upon any vision or idea comparable to the Western civilization of the old NATO'. That idea had 'helped to build conviction among NATO's most important support, the American people, and to build credibility with NATO's most important adversary, the Soviet Union'. However, the 'new NATO' was bound to lack 'the old vision and indeed will have no authentic and coherent union at all'. It was mainly 'the product of bureaucratic momentum and political calculations'. It would inevitably 'have little conviction among the American people and little credibility with a Russia that one day will regain the strength to assert its interests'.[69]

Kurth was an early analyst of what Michael Kimmage was later to call 'the abandonment of the West' among American foreign policy elites.[70] The same James Kurth, however, came later to enunciate proposals 'Toward a Renewed Western Civilization'.[71] Thus, in the immediate aftermath of a serious financial crisis, in 2009, he was writing, 'Despite the great and damaging transformations that we have discussed, there remains a real potential for a renewed Western civilization, and for a renewed American civilization within it.' His proposed solution was 'liberty with law'. Somehow the West and Western civilisation have a tendency to come back in new versions even among people who had buried them as irretrievably dead.

VII. A Tale of Three Speeches: Who Spoke Better in Warsaw—Bush or Trump?

No recent American president has shown himself more prepared to withdraw from 'Western civilisation' and 'the West' in the way James Kurth and Michael Kimmage have observed than Donald Trump. There is truth in the statement that, during his 2017–21 presidency, Trump was 'the first non-Western president of the United States'.[72] And yet, even he (or rather, his speechwriters) had something to say on 'Western civilization'—and the context is interesting. President Trump visited his Polish counterpart and gave a speech in Warsaw on 6 July 2017. The speech was widely discussed. It was immediately noted by commentators that Trump mentioned 'the West' ten times and 'civilization' and its defence at least five times.[73] American commentators focused on the purported messages for Trump's domestic audience but meanwhile forgot that the speech was delivered in Poland, to a Polish audience. Readers of this book cannot fail to appreciate that, given how sensitive Poles felt about their identity as members of a 'kidnapped West,' and given the long history of Poland's self-perception as a rampart of 'the West', the speech was designed to go down very well in Warsaw. Of course, I am not crediting Donald Trump with having the faintest idea about any of this; but

Steven Bannon and his team of speechwriters must have known very well what they were doing.

Trump mentioned 'terrorism and extremism' as 'dire threats to our security and to our way of life'. He declared that '[w]e are fighting hard against radical Islamic terrorism, and we will prevail'. Being in Poland, he could not of course ignore Russia, so he added, 'We urge Russia to cease its destabilizing activities in Ukraine and elsewhere,[74] and its support for hostile regimes—including Syria and Iran—and to instead join the community of responsible nations in our fight against common enemies and in defense of civilization itself.' (Applause followed, predictably.) Trump did not refrain from explicitly specifying where he saw the threats coming from: 'Americans, Poles, and the nations of Europe' valued 'individual freedom and sovereignty', he declared, and 'must work together to confront forces, whether they come from inside or out, from the South or the East, that threaten over time to undermine these values and to erase the bonds of culture, faith, and tradition that make us who we are'. He sounded a buoyant note: 'Our adversaries, however, are doomed because we will never forget who we are. And if we don't forget who [we] are, we just can't be beaten.' Bringing the two sides of the North Atlantic together, the speech went on, 'Americans will never forget. The nations of Europe will never forget. We are the fastest [*sic*] and the greatest community. There is nothing like our community of nations. The world has never known anything like our community of nations.'

Much of the speech concerned the Warsaw uprising against the Nazis, and parallels were repeatedly drawn:

> Because as the Polish experience reminds us, the defense of the West ultimately rests not only on means but also on the will of its people to prevail and be successful and get what you have to have. The fundamental question of our time is whether the West has the will to survive. Do we have the confidence in our values to defend them at any cost? Do we have enough respect for our citizens to protect our borders? Do we have the desire and the courage to preserve our civilization in the face of those who would subvert and destroy it? [Applause.]

Memories of those who had perished in the Warsaw Uprising 'remind us that the West was saved with the blood of patriots'. Coming to his own day, Trump asserted that '[o]ur own fight for the West does not begin on the battlefield—it begins with our minds, our wills, and our souls'; and thus, '[t]oday, the ties that unite our civilization are no less vital, and demand no less defense [...]. Our freedom, our civilization, and our survival depend on those bonds of history, culture, and memory.' The parallel with wartime Poland was pursued once more, and culminated in the declaration, 'Just as Poland could not be broken, I declare today for the world to hear that the West will never, ever be broken. Our values will prevail. Our people will thrive. And our civilization will triumph. [Applause.]'[75]

Some of the commentary on the speech in America was especially interesting. It was Peter Beinart who noted, in *The Atlantic*, that Trump 'referred ten times to "the West" and five times to "our civilization." His white nationalist supporters will understand exactly what he meant. It's important that other Americans do, too.'[76] Beinart undertook to explain to 'other Americans' what Trump's esoteric message to his 'white nationalist supporters' was. He noted that '[t]he West is not a geographic term. [...] The West is not an ideological or economic term either.' Rather, '[t]he West is a racial and religious term. To be considered Western, a country must be largely Christian (preferably Protestant or Catholic) and largely white.' Thus, '[w]here there is ambiguity about a country's "Westernness," it's because there is ambiguity about, or tension between, these two characteristics.' 'Is Latin America Western?' asked Beinart. 'Most of its people are Christian, but by U.S. standards, they're not clearly white. Are Albania and Bosnia Western? Maybe. By American standards, their people are white. But they are also mostly Muslim.' Beinart went on to note that 'Steve Bannon, who along with Stephen Miller has shaped much of Trump's civilizational thinking, has been explicit about this.' According to Beinart, in a 2014 speech, Bannon 'celebrated "the long history of the Judeo-Christian West struggle against Islam" and "our forefathers" who "bequeathed to [us] the great institution that is the church of the West".' (It is worth noting, however, that even were we to accept Bannon's highly debateable conception of 'the West', his statement as it stands made no specific reference to race.)

Beinart also noted that during the Cold War, 'American presidents sometimes contrasted the democratic "West" with the communist "East." But when the Cold War ended, they largely stopped associating America with "the West."' Instead, '[e]very president from George H. W. Bush to Barack Obama emphasized the portability of America's political and economic principles'. Their message was that 'democracy and capitalism were not uniquely "Western." They were not the property of any particular religion or race but the universal aspiration of humankind.' In that connection, Beinart compared Trump's Warsaw speech with two earlier speeches made in the same city by President George W. Bush, in 2001 and 2003 respectively. Bush had not mentioned 'the West' at all. Beinart commented that 'Bush's vision echoed Francis Fukuyama's. America and Europe may have been further along the road to prosperity, liberty, capitalism, and peace than other parts of the world, but all countries could follow their path.' And though he was '[i]n deeply Catholic Poland', Bush had 'sprinkled his speeches with religious references, but they were about Christianity as a universal creed, a moral imperative that knew no civilizational bounds'. On the other hand, Trump 'was talking not about Christianity but about Christendom: a particular religious civilization that must protect itself from outsiders'.[77] Beinart also noted that '[i]n his 2003 speech, Bush referred to democracy 13 times. Trump mentioned it once.'

Finally, in Beinart's opinion, the 'most shocking sentence in Trump's speech [...] was his claim that "The fundamental question of our time is whether the West has the will to survive."' Trump's sentence only made sense, according to Beinart, 'as a statement of racial and religious paranoia. The "south" and "east" only threaten the West's "survival" if by "West" you mean white, Christian (or at least Judeo-Christian).' That implied that 'anyone in the United States who is not white and Christian may not truly be American but rather [...] an impostor and a threat'. Given that 'America is racially, ethnically, and religiously diverse', the implication was that 'when Trump says being Western is the essence of America's identity', he is 'in part defining America in opposition to some of its own people. He's not speaking as the president of the entire United States. He's speaking as the head of a tribe.'[78]

Among the many critiques elicted by Beinart's article, one of the most interesting came from Daniel Foster, a commentator associated with the *National Review*, who wrote, also in *The Atlantic*, 'In Defense of "The West"'. Although Beinart was to complain in his later response that Foster failed to define what he means by 'the West', Foster did speak of it as 'a confederation of like-minded polities bound by common values' and took exception to Beinart's depiction of it as 'a mere demographic tribe'. Foster begged to disagree: '[the] phrase has always aimed at bigger, nobler referents than that'. He argued that, in his attempt 'to equate the idea of Western Civilization to Bannonism-Millerism, Beinart ends up performing the same facile reduction of that idea that Bannon and Miller do'; for, '[w]hen Beinart says "the West is a racial and religious term," this is a plain stipulation—the same stipulation made by so many in the dim-right'. Countries such as Morocco, Haiti, Egypt, Japan, India, and many other non-white, non-Christian places, Foster retorted, are 'well tangled up in the West—influencing and being influenced by it, acting on it and reacting to it'. He conceded that, 'if you'd like to point out that I've just described the fruits of so much colonial rapine, I'll say fine—but you can't have it both ways. The West can't be both a bloodthirsty cultural predator and a lilywhite provincial obsessed with its own purity.' When all is said and done, for Foster, '[t]he currents in the history of the West preoccupied with miscegenation and corruption of the blood are feeble in the face of the overwhelming tide of annexation, assimilation, and admixture. Sure, it's messy, but the West nets out as a mongrel civilization, to our everlasting credit.' The conclusion could only be that 'nobody who knows what they're talking about is talking about the racial and religious purity of the West, and nobody who is talking about the racial and religious purity of the West knows what they're talking about'.

Foster then granted 'a concession'—as well as raising a warning (an important idea that we will discuss further in chapter 10 below): 'There's a degree to which the worldview of Bannon and Miller—including the cheap bigotry [. . .] finds aid and comfort and a kind of respectability when dressed up in the language of Western Civilization. That's to be sniffed out and called out where it occurs.' There follows an even more serious challenge:

> To define the West the way such men as these [Steve Bannon and Stephen Miller] define it, to grant to them and their handlers the right to set the terms of the debate, is to have already lost it. And to hollow out the meaning of meaningful words because they once sat upon an especially odious set of lips is to let the bastards grind you down.

Foster also thought that Beinart's comparison between Trump's rhetoric and that used by former Republican president George W. Bush in two earlier speeches in Warsaw in 2001 and 2003 was 'inappropriate'. Post–Cold War presidents like Bush 'tended to speak more about universal human values than "Western" values [. . .] because the world then looked to be heading toward a Fukuyaman moment, with states converging on liberal democracy and free markets, and rival systems seemingly discredited once and for all'. Things had changed, however: 'Now [. . .] the world looks more Huntingtonian, with the return of all the old tribal and cultural rivalries, and plenty of novel ones', and it thus made sense to 'fall [. . .] back toward [a] more Cold War era vision of the West as bastion rather than universal order'. At any rate, 'the question whether Bush or Bannon is right, of whether the world is Fukuyaman or Huntingtonian' was 'an empirical one, and it exists quite apart from philosophical and normative questions about whether there is a coherent project called Western Civilization, and whether it's worth preserving'. Foster himself had no doubts: 'I happen to think there is and it is.'[79]

An often repeated theme follows: 'The strongest surviving Western impulse is the impulse to criticize the West, to feel shame and guilt over our collective inheritance.' Foster's comment was, 'I actually cherish this self-flagellating streak in the Western psyche, and I'd never want it completely to go away, not least because our long and uneven run at the top has given us plenty to think about.' (Seeking permission to misquote Mark Twain, he added that 'the West is the only civilization that blushes—or needs to.') That commendable impulse needed to be kept in perspective, though: '[s]o much time is wasted on disclaiming and caveating ourselves that we rarely allow even the blandest assertions of cultural solidarity, convinced they reek not just of chauvinism but of murder'. As a result, '[t]here are generations of Westerners now thinking and writing who don't think there is any other way to speak'. For Foster, that is not a healthy state of things:

> This autoimmune disorder of the West need not prove fatal if the West also has something to say for itself, an affirmative case for its values and vision. But if the West in its self-understanding is reduced, per Beinart, to mere self-loathing paired with the demographic accident of 'white, Christian hegemony,' how can it possibly defend itself—how can it possibly mean anything to anyone, not least to the 'non-white, non-Christian' migrants that it's meant to welcome with open arms? 'Diversity,' or 'pluralism,' long the empty signifiers at the other end of the argument, sure as hell won't cut it, as neither works as an end to itself. Diversity for what? Pluralism toward what? An assemblage of immigrants without a galvanizing ethos isn't a melting pot, it's a bus depot. Or the Calais Jungle.[80]

The latter point is reminiscent of the similar argument Arthur Schlesinger had advanced in 1991 (to the effect that that it was precisely because America was indeed a multicultural society that it desperately needed a unifying political creed).

Peter Beinart came back with a response.[81] He complained that Foster was 'trying to have it both ways': according to Foster, Morocco, Japan, Haiti, Egypt, 'and many other non-white, non-Christian places are right "well tangled with the West."' But, argued Beinart, 'Notice the slippery language. Are they Western or not? Saying no would require Foster to explain what excludes them from the club. Saying yes would render the term meaningless'—because, '[i]f being influenced by (and influencing) the West makes you part of the West, then the West is everything'. Foster wanted 'to associate the West with principles like democracy, freedom, tolerance, and equality'; the problem with that was that 'if the real test of a country's "Westernness" is its government's fidelity to liberal democratic ideals, then Japan, Botswana, and India are three of the most Western countries on Earth, Spain didn't become Western until it embraced democracy in 1975, and

FIGURE 9.4. NATO leaders: 'family photo' taken at the 2023 NATO summit in Vilnius, Lithuania. Photograph by Simon Dawson, No. 10 Downing Street (CC BY 2.0) ('Number 10', https://www.flickr.com/photos/number10gov/53038388599/), 11 July 2023. *Source:* https://commons.wikimedia.org/wiki/File:Family_photo_from_2023_NATO_Vilnius_summit_(53038388599).jpg

Hungary's slide towards authoritarianism means it is significantly less Western than it was a few years ago'. Therefore, '[a]lmost no one, including Foster, uses the term that way. And for good reason. *If* "Western" is synonymous with "democratic" or "free," then you don't need the term at all.'

Beinart's next argument was that a crucial part of 'the immigration debate in America and Europe' was the question of 'whether non-white, non-Christian immigrants will embrace values like tolerance, reason, and women's rights'. On that question there were two sides: 'Conservatives tend to be more pessimistic. Liberals—remembering that, in many countries, such principles were once considered alien to Catholics and Jews—are more optimistic.' In this regard, Beinart made the following point: the problem arose 'when conservatives ask not whether immigrants will embrace democratic or liberal values, but rather "Western" values. In doing so, they're conflating the universal and the particular. They're implying that being Muslim itself is incompatible with good citizenship.' His conclusion was that 'defending liberal democracy and defending "the West" are very different things'. In fact, he added, 'from Trump to Marine Le Pen to the leaders of Poland and Hungary, many of the people most loudly defending the latter represent the greatest threat to the former.'[82] Beinart's conclusion could also be turned against himself, however. As Foster had already commented, if 'the West' were to be left exclusively to Trump, Bannon & Co., then they win.

Though both Beinart and Foster propounded some odd claims, their debate undoubtedly points to a crucial dilemma, to which I will return in the concluding chapter. Meanwhile, whatever they—or the rest of us—may have thought of President Trump, in 2019 readers of *Harper's Magazine* were treated to the argument that 'Donald Trump is a good president'. It was signed by Michel Houellebecq. But that would be the least of the things Houellebecq would do to annoy the *bien-pensants*.

VIII. The End of the West, *version* Michel Houellebecq

'President Trump doesn't view Vladimir Putin as an unworthy interlocutor; neither do I. I don't believe that Russia has any role as a universal guide [...]; but I admire the resistance of Orthodoxy on its lands, I believe that Catholicism would do well to draw inspiration from it, that "ecumenical dialogue" could usefully be limited to a dialogue with the Orthodox, and that the schism of 1054 was, for the Christian world, the beginning of the end.'[83]

Michel Houellebecq has been for a long time widely seen as 'by any measure France's most significant contemporary writer'.[84] He is considered 'already notorious for taking the political temperature of both France and the West'.[85] On one of his most controversial novels, Mark Lilla commented, 'It will take some time for the French to appreciate *Submission* for the strange and surprising thing that it is.' That was because Houellebecq had 'created a new genre—the dystopian conversion tale. *Submission* [...] [a]t one level [...] is simply about a man who through suffering and indifference finds himself slouching toward Mecca'; yet '[a]t another level' it was a novel 'about a civilization that after centuries of a steady, almost imperceptible sapping of inner conviction finds itself doing the same thing'. According to Lilla, *Submission* is a classic novel in the European tradition of cultural pessimism and 'deserves a small place in whatever category we put books like Thomas Mann's *The Magic Mountain* and Robert Musil's *The Man Without Qualities*.' Lilla also argues that '[t]here is no doubt that Houellebecq wants us to see the collapse of modern Europe and the rise of a Muslim one as a tragedy'; for, as he had told an interviewer, it 'means the end, of what is, after all, an ancient civilization'. But, Lilla notes, 'that does not make Islam, in the novel at least, an evil religion, just a realistic one'.[86] Thus, whatever Houellebecq may think of Islam, Lilla argues that it is 'not the target of *Submission*'. Rather, it served 'as a device to express a recurring European worry that the single-minded pursuit of freedom—freedom from tradition and authority, freedom to pursue one's own ends—must inevitably lead to disaster'.

A recent critic who is less charitable to Houellebecq than Lilla agrees about the deeper meaning of *Submission*: 'Houellebecq's project has always been essentially reactionary, reacting against his hippy mother's abandonment of him as a child, blaming the *soixante-huitards*' lax morals and utopian fantasies for his own malaise'. His message had consistently been that 'it's better when people live under an authority'. It is here that the interesting comments on *Submission* come: 'As ever with Houellebecq, the real question is philosophical: what constitutes freedom, and does it necessarily bring happiness?' According to Nelly Kapriëlian, that was the question Houellebecq's *Soumission* (*Submission*) tackled. It attempted to imagine 'the return of a religious political order to France', and through that, 'to adopt the Grand Inquisitorial perspective that humans (or at least, men) would be happier under such a regime than they are in liberal Western societies that substitute mere consumer choice for any kind of existential freedom'.[87]

To return to Lilla, he also notices something else that is crucial (and congruent with Kapriëlian's interpretation):

> [Houellebecq's] breakout novel, *The Elementary Particles*, concerned two brothers who suffered unbearable psychic wounds after being abandoned by narcissistic hippie parents who epitomized the Sixties. But with each new novel it has become clear that Houellebecq thinks that the crucial historical turning point was much earlier. Our troubles, he now thinks, began with the Enlightenment attack on the organic wholeness of medieval society and the blind pursuit of technological advance. The qualities that Houellebecq projects onto Islam [in *Submission*] are no different from those that the religious right ever since the French Revolution has attributed to premodern Christendom: strong families, moral education, social order, a sense of place, a meaningful death, and, above all, the will to persist as a culture.[88]

All that is true. And it is surely no accident that Houellebecq repeatedly evokes the conversion to Islam of a figure we met in chapter 6 above, René Guénon. As we saw, even when Guénon and Massis were criticising each other, they were aware (or at least Guénon was) that they belonged to the same camp when it came to traditionalism versus modernity. In one of the several references to Guénon in *Submission*, François (the narrator of the novel) finds himself courted to convert to Islam so he could be allowed to return to university teaching. The person trying to persuade François is Professor Rediger—himself a convert to

WHAT IS 'THE WEST' AFTER THE COLD WAR? 327

Islam, and recently rewarded by the newly elected president of the French Republic, Ben Abbes (the leader of the Muslim Brotherhood), by being appointed president of the Islamic University of the Sorbonne:

> In an article for *Oumma*, Rediger raised the question whether Islam had been chosen for world domination. In the end he answered yes. He hardly bothered with Western societies, since to him they seemed so obviously doomed (liberal individualism triumphed as long as it undermined intermediate structures such as nations, corporations, castes, but when it attacked that ultimate social structure, the family, and thus the birth rate, it signed its own death warrant; Muslim dominance was a foregone conclusion). He had more to say about India and China: if India and China had preserved *their traditional civilisations*, he wrote, they might have remained strangers to monotheism and eluded the grasp of Islam. But from the moment they let themselves be contaminated by Western values, they, too, were doomed [...]. The article, cogent and well sourced, clearly betrayed the influence of Guénon, who drew the same basic distinction between *traditional societies*, considered as a whole, and *modern civilisation*.[89]

And, as if to din into readers that the whole thing is not about Islam, but something more, the novel goes on to inform the reader that in another article, Rediger had made 'a case for highly unequal wealth distribution'. This was because, although 'an authentic Muslim society would have to abolish actual destitution [...], it should also maintain a wide gap between the masses [...] and a tiny minority of individuals so fantastically rich that they could throw away vast, insane sums, thus assuring the survival of luxury and the arts'. The comment that follows is revealing: 'This aristocratic position came directly from Nietzsche; deep down, Rediger had remained remarkably faithful to the thinkers of his youth.'[90]

François later on confesses, 'Bizarrely enough, I found myself drawn to Rediger's Guénonian side'; and on another piece by Rediger in the *European Review*, François comments that 'the whole article was one long appeal to [Rediger's] old comrades, the traditional nativists'. He elaborates,

> It was a passionate plea. He called it tragic that their irrational hostility to Islam should blind them to the obvious: on every question that really mattered, the nativists and the Muslims were in perfect agreement. When it came to rejecting atheism and humanism, or the necessary submission of women, or the return of patriarchy, they were fighting exactly the same fight. And today *this*

fight, to establish a new organic phase of civilisation, could no longer be waged in the name of Christianity. Islam, its sister faith, was newer, simpler and more true *(why had Guénon, for example, converted to Islam?*—he was above all a man of science, and he had chosen Islam on scientific grounds, both for its conceptual economy and to avoid certain marginal, irrational doctrines such as the real presence of Christ in the eucharist), which is why Islam had taken up the torch. Thanks to the simpering seductions and the lewd enticements of the progressives, the Church had lost its ability to oppose moral decadence, to renounce homosexual marriage, abortion rights and women in the workplace. The facts were plain: Europe had reached a point of such putrid decomposition that it could no longer save itself, any more than fifth-century Rome could have done. This wave of new immigrants, with their traditional culture—of natural hierarchies, the submission of women and respect for elders—offered a historic opportunity for the moral and familial rearmament of Europe.

And the narrator concludes, 'He, Rediger, was the first to admit the greatness of medieval Christendom [...]; but little by little it had given way, it had been forced to compromise with rationalism [...] and so had sealed its own doom.'[91] The connection drawn between Guénon's thought and adherence to traditionalism is unmissable.[92]

Readers of the present volume are also in a position to appreciate the fact that Houellebecq has always declared himself to be an admirer of Auguste Comte. In the light of his frequently expressed enthusiasm for Comte, he was even asked by distinguished Comte scholars to contribute a preface to the volume *Auguste Comte aujourd'hui* in 2003. There he argued that 'it will be in our interest [...] to dive back to Comte. Because his real subject, his major subject, is religion; and, here, the least we can say is that he is an innovative thinker.'[93] There are many references to Comte in Houellebecq's interviews, and many more in several of his novels. Comte is omnipresent in *Atomised* (*Les Particules élémentaires* [1998]).[94] Joseph de Maistre also makes regular appearances (as do Nietzsche, Toynbee, Spengler and other figures familiar to readers of this book).[95]

Houellebecq's endlessly repeated message has been that Western civilisation has gone wrong and is dying ('a Western civilisation now ending before our very eyes').[96] In an interview in 2002 he said, 'It's true that my characters are all politically nihilistic. I'm forced to the realization that the society in which I live is moving towards goals that are not mine. The West isn't made for a human life. In fact, there's only one thing you can really do in the West, and that's to make

FIGURE 9.5. Michel Houellebecq, at the Fronteiras do Pensamento conference, Porto Alegre, Brazil, 7 November 2016. Photograph by Fronteiras do Pensamento/Luiz Munhoz. *Source:* https://en.wikipedia.org/wiki/Michel_Houellebecq#/media/File:Michel_Houellebecq_no_Fronteiras_do_Pensamento_Porto_Alegre_2016_(30895029365)_(cropped).jpg

money.' And when discussion turned to a character in *Atomised* ('Michel says that his ancestors had a project, believed in progress, in civilization and were attached to the idea of transmission. Your characters faithfully reflect the abandonment of all this'), Houellebecq commented, 'People are doing everything to bring the West to this position. For example, Berlusconi makes some remark and people immediately say that it's silly to classify civilizations on a scale of values'; to which Houellebecq's own response was, 'No, it's not silly. They want to discourage us from thinking that Western civilization may have been superior on certain points; suddenly, this civilization dissolves into cynicism.' And in response to another question, he replied, 'I don't think the West really wants to live. [. . .] People have limited capacities for emotional engagement. You can't start life all over again. Only the Americans think you can.' He also complained that '[t]he terrible thing is the extent to which you can't say anything anymore [. . .]. Nietzsche, Schopenhauer and Spinoza wouldn't be accepted today. Political correctness, in its current form, makes almost all of Western philosophy unacceptable. More and more things are becoming impossible to think. It's scary.' He confessed, 'Deep down, I don't give a damn about the future of the West; but it can become difficult to fight self-censorship.'[97]

IX. Conclusion: What 'West' for the Post-Post-Cold War Era?

James Kurth complained in 1994 that, compared with the rapidity with which the descriptor 'postwar' was replaced by 'Cold War' in the second part of the 1940s, continuing to speak of the post–Cold War era 'fully five years after the end of the Cold War' seemed 'to be stretching things a bit'. Yet, some thirty years later, we still do not have a universally accepted label for the era we live in.[98] Similar lack of agreement attaches to the very meaning of terms such as 'the West'—to say nothing of evaluation of, or normative attitudes towards, that West.

In his famous 1993 article Samuel Huntington stressed 'civilization consciousness'. It is striking, nevertheless, how partial—at best—such consciousness is among 'Westerners': members of what he calls 'Western civilization'. Meanwhile, despite the endless complaints about how weak it is, it is arguable (and perhaps hardly surprising, given the concerted efforts of EEC/EU institutions in that direction) that in recent decades a noticeable degree of 'European' identification has been built, especially among younger people. There is no comparable 'Western' identification across the board among the people Huntington would classify as 'Western'. However, there are notable exceptions. It was a Polish president of the European Council (and former and future premier of Poland), Donald Tusk, who declared that if Brexit happened it could be the beginning of the destruction of not only the EU but also 'Western political civilisation in its entirety'.[99] More generally, it is unmissable how often it is people from Kundera's and Miłosz's 'kidnapped West'—from Eastern and Central Europe, whose countries recently escaped the clutches of Soviet rule—who most explicitly and vociferously celebrate their (newly re-granted) membership of 'Western civilisation' or 'the West'. This explains the emphasis upon Western civilisation in Donald Trump's July 2017 speech in Warsaw—otherwise completely dissonant with his isolationist, 'America First' and anti-NATO rhetoric. Again today (or still today), 'the West' is evoked and needed by people who want to distance themselves from Russia: a Russia which cannot, however, be wished away from being part of 'Europe'. These are matters that can only perhaps be fully appreciated and assessed through the *longue durée* approach adopted in this book.

And yet, a version of a common 'Western' consciousness and civic identity was asserted as already existing during the very year when Huntington published his 'Clash of Civilizations?' article. It was very different from what he had in mind, however, as 'the West' in question included Japan, and its main cohesive glue was said to be 'business'. International relations academics Daniel Deudney and John Ikenberry published an essay in the winter of 1993 entitled 'The Logic of the West'. They raised the question as to whether the West (by which they meant, they clarified, 'western Europe, North America, and Japan') was 'destined to fragment into conflicting regional camps, with each acquiring the means for its own security and reasserting a power balance among them?' Or would it 'be able to sustain and expand its political community?' They criticised both what they called an 'anachronistic Realism' (of those who believed that 'nationalism is the dominant force in the West and predict a future riven by conflict') and a 'shallow Liberalism' (of those, like Fukuyama, who had 'articulated an optimistic vision of the triumph of liberal democratic institutions and the emergence of perpetual peace'). According to Deudney and Ikenberry, the West is 'a distinct political order—a civic "union"'. The 'logic' of the West was based on 'a neglected American political tradition of industrial liberalism [that] inspired and guided the founders of the Western system during the great crises of industrial capitalism in the 1930s and 1940s'. Thus the West 'has a distinct political logic. It is not a series of states in anarchy, but rather an integrated and functionally differentiated system.' It has, they claimed, 'three parts: private economic and social networks, a distinctive political culture and identity, and interstate public institutions'. They were adamant about the importance of the first of these: 'Make no mistake, the body of the civic union is capitalism. The business of the West is business. Western Europe, Japan, and the United States are thoroughly permeated by market relations, mentalities, and institutions.' The West's second pillar, they went on, was 'a common civic identity. Although impossible to quantify, what Montesquieu called "spirit" is an essential component of any political order. The West's "spirit"—common norms, public mores, and political identities—is the invisible sinew of the polity'. The third pillar was 'the public institutions that span states'. (The G7 forum and other Western-centric international organisations were mentioned in this context). Notwithstanding Deudney and Ikenberry's confident assertion that a Western 'civic union' already existed, their article ended with an exhortation to create one through various strategies (including school textbooks). Critics found many flaws with the optimism of 'The Logic of the West', especially its underestimation of the potency of nationalism.[100]

This assertion, in 1993, of the existence of a 'polity' and 'a common civic identity' shared by Western Europe, North America and Japan appears to have been an example of wishful thinking rather than a careful analysis of reality. Another way of putting it may be to remark that the authors may have been confusing the potential shared identities of a small international business and technocratic elite (the 'Anywheres', in David Goodhart's formulation) with the rest of the population (the 'Somewheres'). As Ivan Krastev has convincingly argued recently, such divisions, and the perception of a lack of loyalty on the part of the elites that comfortably self-identify as European, Western or cosmopolitan, account in large part for the perceived crisis of recent years.[101]

A decade after Deudney and Ikenberry's contribution, an attempt to describe some of the passionate divisions within Western countries in the aftermath of the 2003 Iraq war and the re-election of George W. Bush was offered by the Australian-born LSE political theorist Kenneth Minogue, in a 2004 review article. Minogue identified two different Wests: 'Our civilization has become the site of something not much less intense than a cultural civil war.' On the one hand there was 'the historical Western civilization deriving from Greece and Rome, developing into Christendom and modern times. Such a "Historic West" is to be found in the art, literature, architecture, music, philosophy and science we have inherited from the European past'. On the other hand there was 'the "Rationalist West", which believes itself to have emerged out of the Enlightenment and to have generated a universal civilization which in its doctrine of rights and its programme of internationalism has transcended the prejudice, superstitions and oppressions of the past.' According to Minogue, '[t]he essence of the Rationalist West is the belief in its immaculate conception as a pure birth of reason in the world'. Rationalism, he complained, 'is alarmingly deaf to the value of the past'.[102]

Much has happened since the Fukuyama–Huntington debate began; and yet, the *Atlantic* debate on the meaning, or lack thereof, of 'the West' in 2017 reminds one that the Fukuyama versus Huntington dilemma is still relevant. It is still not agreed whether 'the West' is one civilisation among several and must look to its own survival (Huntington), or is bound to become a universal civilisation and convert the world to its values (Fukuyama, more or less). Momentous events and developments have changed the world since the early 1990s: the first Gulf War in 1991; the '9/11' terrorist attacks in America in 2001; the second Gulf War in 2003; two decades of war in Afghanistan; Brexit; Donald Trump's election; authoritarian strongmen being elected in more and more 'illiberal democracies'; Russian intervention in Syria; the Russian annexation of Crimea in 2014; Chinese, Russian, Indian and other regimes challenging 'the West' and the international institutions that Huntington had described as designed to defend Western interests euphemistically in the name of the 'international community'; and much else. The term 'Westlessness' was coined to describe a new world where the West was perceived to be absent or in significant retreat. Last, but decidedly not least, the world has been a different place since the wholesale Russian invasion of Ukraine began in February 2022.

Of those who write on the matter, critics of the West in the post–Cold War era are far more numerous than those who defend it. The 2003 Iraq war led to heated debates. In more recent years in particular, events related to police brutality in the USA, not least after the death of George Floyd, have led to much criticism of what are seen as hypocrisy and persistent racism within the West. Even more recently, the support of most Western governments for Israel has led to strong accusations of double standards when it comes to the most recent war in Gaza (and, at the time or writing, escalation in Lebanon and potentially elsewhere). But the West has also had its defenders. Besides those that we have discussed in this chapter in some detail, Christopher Hitchens, Ian Buruma, Timothy Garton Ash, Anne Applebaum, Roger Scruton, Ayaan Hirsi Ali, Niall Ferguson ('a patriot of the West', according to a reviewer of his book *Civilization: The West and the Rest*), Douglas Murray and Susan Neiman, come to mind (although some of these, of course, have disagreed strongly with one another on particular issues and strategies; and while some of them defend what Minogue called the 'Historic West', others defend what he called the 'Rationalist West', and others still think that the two go together). The equivalent list of French authors, meanwhile, would be considerably longer; and though critics of their more recent positions would deny their left-wing credentials (and include them among the so-called *nouveaux réactionnaires*), writers such as Pascal Bruckner, Alain Finkielkraut, Régis Debray, and many more would reply that it is the eminently left-wing principles of the French republican and revolutionary tradition and its secular universalism that they have been defending.[103]

Similar things apply to thinkers in other national contexts. We have seen that Habermas and Winkler both come from the left of German politics (though I am not equating their political positions). In the English-speaking world it may appear to some, in the restricted conjuncture of the last few years, that those who say publicly that they are concerned about the state or future of 'the West' are positioned on the conservative side of politics (and according to increasing numbers of English-speaking academic classicists, any mention of 'Western civilisation' more or less equates to support for 'white supremacism'). Yet, there have also been many defenders of what they see as the West's Enlightenment legacy and universalist values who hail from various versions of the left of the political spectrum. Talk of 'the West' and its problems or future, as well as the defence of certain aspects of, or practices prevalent in, that West, are not appropriately seen simply in terms of party politics or right versus left. Such debates move fast and they are not now what they were in the aftermath of the Cold War in the 1990s, or even what they were five years ago. No doubt they will change again. Discussion and dispute among politicians and intellectuals in particular contexts notwithstanding, the idea of 'the West' is not one that neatly corresponds to left–right divides. Nor is it intrinsically a matter of 'race', 'white supremacy', 'imperialism', or any of the other contentious issues with which at various historical junctures certain users of the term have identified it. Taking the long view, it bears repeating, has its advantages.

The flow of books with 'the West' included in their titles shows no sign of diminishing. These do not all talk about the same thing, and some are more nuanced than others. But they certainly indicate that there is truth in the judgement that 'conceptual history teaches that "the West" has often been "in crisis" and "in decline", and that horizons of expectation attached to it have often faded only to reappear soon after. It may be safe to assume that its last chapter is yet to be written.'[104] Deciding what to make of it all may appear problematic, and it is the aim of this book's concluding chapter to provide some help.

10

Conclusion

WORDS, IDEAS, AND WHY THEY MATTER

'En vérité, on exige de l'Occident toutes les vertus, qu'il est souhaitable mais sans exemple de combiner.' (In truth, we demand of the West all the virtues whose combination is desirable but which has never yet been achieved anywhere.)

RAYMOND ARON, 'CONTRE LE DÉFAITISME', *LE FIGARO*,
3 MARCH 1950, IN ARON, *LES ARTICLES DU 'FIGARO'*,
VOL. 1: *LA GUERRE FROIDE 1947–1955* (1990), P. 361

'[M]y French and American friends [...] were surprised at my almost exaggerated sympathy for Russians taken individually. All of these attitudes did not seem to hang together. Regretfully I had to say that I did not possess a language that would allow me to carry through the necessary distinctions. But the lack of terminology is not only *my* lack. The twentieth century, panic-stricken in the face of nationalist and racist ravings, strains to fill up the chasm of time with production figures or the names of a few political-economic systems; meanwhile it has renounced investigations of the fine tissue of becoming, where no thread should be overlooked—even the ideas of forgotten Russian sects. What apparently disappears for ever is, in fact, imperceptibly transformed, and such remote phenomena as the character of Ancient Rome are still alive, simply because it was there, and nowhere else, that Catholicism took on a form. [...] The current fear of generalizing about racial and territorial groups is an honorable impulse because it protects us from falling into the service of people interested not so much in truth as in an expedient argument for a political battle. Only after the reasons for such a fear have disappeared will minds skilled in tracking down interdependencies penetrate what for wise men today is an embarrassing subject, fit only for table talk in a country tavern. They will not disappear until the appraisal of any civilization ceases to be a weapon against those human beings brought up within it—in other words, not soon.'

CZESŁAW MIŁOSZ, *NATIVE REALM: A SEARCH FOR SELF-DEFINITION*
(TRANSLATED BY CATHERINE S. LEACH) (1981 [1959]), PP. 146–47

IT WILL HAVE BECOME obvious by now that there is no one, single idea of 'the West'. And yet, it must also be obvious that 'names are not matters of indifference in politics'.[1] I have tried in this book to analyse the many different uses made of 'the West' across centuries, and in different linguistic traditions; how they changed and continue to change right up to the present, and what the implications of such changes have been and might be in the future. Such uses have been varied, confusing and often inconsistent. The meaning, the kind of entity referred to, the criteria for inclusion and the membership of what has been called 'the West' have changed very substantially indeed over time. But Czesław Miłosz was surely right in the passage quoted above as an epigraph; and that is why the history of the subject matters: many of the earlier meanings are still part of the potential repertoire of uses for the present and the future (even if sometimes in a dormant state). And such meanings do resurface, and sometimes prevail, depending on circumstances as well as on who uses the term, for which audience, and to what purposes.

To restrict the matter to recent times: for example, Japan came to be considered a member of 'the West' during the Cold War; but then it found itself—as far as many American commentators were concerned—regarded as the main (economic) threat to 'the West' immediately after the collapse of the Communist bloc in the late 1980s. Majority-Muslim Turkey became a member of NATO in 1952 and was considered—in some senses at least—a part of what was then called 'the West' until the end of the Cold War. One may wonder how many people now see Recep Tayyip Erdoğan as a 'Western' leader (he himself certainly does not). While President Putin has for long been defining Russia in opposition to 'the West', when his intervention in Syria began in 2015, various BBC journalists repeatedly wondered how local populations in the Middle East would react to 'yet another Western intervention', as they put it. That was not necessarily an inadvertent misuse of language. The BBC correspondents in the region were aware that, for Arabs and others in the Middle East, Russia was indeed perceived as part of 'the West', whatever the Russians might have thought of themselves (and what

FIGURE 10.1. Czesław Miłosz in mid-career. Photographer and date unknown. Photograph scanned from Aleksander Janta archive, *Lustra i reflektory* (Warsaw: Czytelnik, 1982). *Source:* https://commons.wikimedia.org/wiki/File:Czeslaw_Milosz.jpg

Americans or Western Europeans thought of the Russians). It is just one more reminder of how situational, contingent and contextual such usages are.

Even if we could leave aside what people far away have meant when referring to 'the West' (and we saw that we cannot leave aside all such utterances, as some closely interacted with Western self-perceptions and affected the latter)—even, that is, if it is studied only as a self-description—'the West' has meant and still means many different things to different users of the term. People often talk of the West as if it meant the same thing as 'Europe', as 'Christendom', as the English-speaking nations or 'Anglosphere', or the capitalist economies, to name but a few related and overlapping but differing concepts or groups. Most people, when asked what they think 'the West' means, stress particular moments, aspects, ingredients, at the expense of others. Some might say that the West began with the antagonism between freedom-loving ancient Greeks and despotic Orientals in the shape of the Persian empire; and others might think that, surely, 'the West' began in the late 1940s and early 1950s with the Cold War. In between there are several versions, enjoying varying degrees of popularity: the Roman Empire versus the rest of the world; the Western Roman Empire as opposed to the Eastern Roman Empire of Constantinople (as of 395 CE); Charlemagne's empire versus the rest; Christian Europeans versus Muslim invaders (Arabs/Saracens then Ottomans) in the Middle Ages and early modern times; Catholics versus Orthodox Christians after the schism of the eleventh century; Catholics versus Muslims (or versus Muslims as well as Orthodox Christians, not least in 1205) during the Crusades; European imperial powers versus 'the rest' from the sixteenth to the twentieth century; the list can go on. Like all self-identifications, 'the West' has been based on a juxtaposition with some 'other'. That rule at least remains stable. But what or who precisely that other entity might be has varied widely in the history of uses of 'the West'. Related to these distinctions are the following milestones:

- 395 CE: Division between 'Western' and 'Eastern' Roman empires
- Less than a century later (476 CE): Fall of the Western Roman Empire. Once that happened, what could an ambitious ruler who wanted to claim the mantle of the defeated empire do? He could not easily aspire to be the new Roman emperor, for there still was a Roman emperor and a Roman empire (the Eastern Roman Empire) in Constantinople. All he could plausibly try to claim was the succession to the western part of the empire. If the imperial throne in Constantinople happened to be occupied by a woman (Irene of Athens), so much the better: thus the king of the Franks was able to convince the pope (whose skin he had just saved in Paderborn) to crown him 'Emperor of the Romans' in Rome. Hence:
- 800 CE: Charlemagne is crowned Roman Emperor. But whatever the title he gave himself, he was routinely called 'Emperor of the West' (because there was another Roman emperor in Constantinople (and three years later this was a man again).
- 1054 CE: East–West 'Great Schism' of the Christian churches

Thus, at the very least, 'the West' has been used to describe:

- the western part of the Roman Empire as opposed to the eastern part of the empire with Constantinople as its capital
- Aspiring epigones of the Western Empire once it fell to the 'barbarian' invaders
- the Catholic Christian world as opposed to the Orthodox ('Greek') Christian world.

These earlier 'Wests' meant that the term was available and used, especially in historical works, to describe a part of Europe during a long historical period in the past. But the word was not used to describe a community in the present, or a projected or proposed community for the future, until the early nineteenth century. For the purposes of such self-identifications, 'Christendom' or 'Europe' were until then the prevalent terms. Now, we have already seen that the currently prevailing orthodoxy among academics who have written on the history of the idea of the West is that it emerged around the 1890s in the context of the needs of (British) high imperialism. I have criticised this consensus on the periodisation as well as the provenance of the idea of the West. Instead I argue, in the first place, that the term was used long before—though not always consistently—quite often in French and German, though less so in English; and, secondly, that the first detailed and sustained elaboration of an idea of the West as a desirable political entity based on common historical antecedents and a civilisational commonality was contributed by the French philosopher Auguste Comte before the middle of the nineteenth century, and was propagated by his loyal disciples in many countries in the second half of that century. Rather than serving the needs of high imperialism, moreover, Comte's Western Republic was aimed at abolishing empires and conquest and promoting altruism and peace. Many different—in some cases widely different—conceptualisations of the West (including later articulations that justified and promoted imperialism) were proposed by others; and we followed them in the pages above.

I. Alternatives at the Gates?

Is any of this important? It may be, if we reflect on some recent claims. The Portuguese former politician and writer Bruno Maçães has suggested the possibility that the Chinese 'belt and road' initiative may create a new alignment of countries as strong and successful as 'the West' has been.[2] The West, according to that logic, was an artificial edifice, and a new artificial edifice promoted by the

Chinese has every chance of being equally successful. To that extent, presumably any country that has been participating in the initiative animated by China, from China itself, through the Central Asian republics, to Greece and Italy, can as easily become a member of a new Chinese-led politico-cultural alliance as France and Britain and the United States have been members of 'the West'.

I find this reasoning unconvincing. Let me try to explain why. My attribution of the origins of an explicit and deliberate choice for an idea of the West to Comte in the 1840s is not merely a pedantic matter of timing. I argue, rather, that when Comte decided very deliberately to substitute the term 'the West' (*l'Occident*) for the term 'Europe', he chose 'Occident' because of the historical, cultural, religious and emotional baggage and associations that it carried. He expected to find an audience that would respond to the use of the term thanks to shared associations. Meanwhile, he also chose to reinterpret its history in order to promote his vision of a 'scientifically' based new sociopolitical entity or quasi-federation that he baptised 'the Western Republic'. In making that choice, even Comte, with all his 'cerebral hygiene' issues,[3] was more realistic and down to earth than Francis Lieber and his attempt to promote his coinage, 'Cis-Caucasian', as a self-description of the same civilisation (as we saw in chapter 4). The latter had geographical logic, precision and consistency on its side. Yet nobody besides Lieber used it. On the other hand, Comte's choice of 'West' had long and rich historical associations that could be exploited and evoked to inspire loyalty and affective attachments. That is precisely why a potential equation of the chances of consolidation of the 'belt and road' initiative to those of 'the West' is implausible. But which 'West' do we refer to here? For we have encountered many meanings of the term in the preceding chapters.

II. '[O]nly something which has no history can be defined.'[4]

One might usefully apply to the polysemy of 'the West' Nietzsche's dictum that you cannot define something that has a long history. The best course is rather to study its history in a genealogical fashion. According to the philosopher Raymond Geuss, giving a 'genealogy' was for Nietzsche 'the exact reverse of what we might call "tracing a pedigree"'. Talking of 'Paul's hijacking of the form of life embodied by Jesus', Geuss emphasises that it is crucial to understand that 'Paul's (successful) attempt to take over the Christian form of life by reinterpreting it' was 'only the first of a series of such episodes'. And each such event could be 'described as at the same time a new interpretation of Christianity-as-it-exists (at the given time) *and* as an attempt to take over or get mastery of that existing form of Christianity'. Thus, '[e]ach historically successive interpretation/*coup de main* gives the existing Christian way of life a new "meaning"'. Crucially, however,

> [Nietzsche thought that] such attempts to take over/reinterpret an existing set of practices or way of life will not in general be so fully successful that *nothing* of the original form of life remains, hence the continuing tension in post-Pauline Christianity between forms of acting, feeling, judging which still somehow eventually derive from aboriginal Christianity and Paul's theological dogmas.

Geuss then stresses that the same applied to any newcomer. Thus, once Paul's reading of Christian practice had given it 'a certain "meaning"', the 'historically *next* re-interpretation will in turn find the Pauline meaning already embedded in the form of life it confronts and will be unlikely in giving a new interpretation of that form of life to be able to abolish Pauline concepts and interpretations altogether.'[5] As a result, '[h]istorically, [...] successive layers of such "meanings" will be, as it were, deposited'. There would be 'some gradual change in the actual practices and form of life' as well as 'a rather more mercurial shift in the dominant "interpretation" given to the practice, but even the dominant interpretation won't have been able utterly to eradicate the "meanings" that have previously accumulated, i.e. that have been imposed upon "Christianity" by a series of past agencies.'[6]

So, in a genealogical perspective, the history of Christianity is 'a history of successive attempts on the part of a variety of different "wills" to take control of and reinterpret a complex of habits, feelings, ways of perceiving and acting, thereby imposing on this complex a "meaning"'. But crucially, although 'the "meaning" imposed at any time by a successful will may in some sense be superseded by a later "meaning" (imposed by a later will), the original meaning will in general not go out of existence altogether but will remain embedded in at least a modified form in the complex we call "Christianity"'. The result is that Christianity at any given point in time 'will be a "synthesis" of the various different "meanings" imposed on it in the past and which have succeeded in remaining embedded in Christian feeling, forms of action and belief, etc.' It is important to stress here that '[t]here will be nothing necessary or even particularly coherent about such a "synthesis"'. Rather, whatever 'meanings' it may contain and their mutual relations 'will be just the result of history, and this history will be contingent in a number of ways' (because it will be 'contingent which wills encounter and try to "interpret"/master Christianity at what times and under what circumstances, and it will be contingent how much force, energy, and success they will have in imposing their "meaning"'). As a result of all this, the history of Christianity will "crystallize itself into a kind of unity which is difficult to dissolve, difficult to analyse, and, it must be emphasized, utterly *undefinable*'.

Coming to the crux of the matter—of definition versus history—Geuss writes, 'One can't give a "definition" of Christianity *if* one means by that an account of a purported essential meaning (or purpose or function) which is invariably characteristic of Christianity'; because, as he quotes Nietzsche arguing, '[o]nly that which has no history is definable'. There is a clear reason why this is so: 'anything that has a history will partake, like Christianity, in the continuing struggle between wills attempting to impose their meaning or purpose on the item in question, a struggle with constantly shifting outcomes'. The upshot is that, rather than attempt to offer a definition, 'one must try to give an "analysis" of the contingent synthesis of "meaning" Christianity (for instance) represents'; and that 'process of disentangling the separate strands *will take the form of a historical account*'. The argument underlying this was that '"at an earlier stage that synthesis of 'meanings' presents itself in such a way as to be more easily dissolved" [...,] the individual elements, are more distinct'. Thus, '[t]he appropriate historical account is a genealogy'.[7]

Although a system of religious morality such as Christianity is not the same kind of entity as a sociopolitical concept such as 'the West', a historical account and genealogical analysis along the lines suggested by Geuss can and should be applied also to the study of that idea. If we attempt such an analysis of the idea of the West, both its current plethora of meanings and its potential for future meanings can be explained. Those who propose all sorts of divergent interpretations of what 'the West' means (who argue, for example, that the West began with Athenian democracy, who argue that the West began with medieval Catholicism, and who argue that the West began with European imperialism, as well as those who argue that it began with the divisions of the Cold War, or who favour different versions in between all these), can all be shown to be emphasising, selectively, disproportionately and often polemically, particular layers of the different meanings of the concept.[8] None of these different layers of meanings 'deposited' at various stages completely disappeared, even when other layers replaced them in the limelight. And some of the dormant layers and elements resurface depending on who uses the term, when, and why.

III. Why Does Any of This Matter?

'The West' is a term that evokes a number of historical, cultural, emotional and other associations. These were different in Comte's time from what they are today—but not unrecognisably different. It is just that more 'successive layers' of 'meanings' have been 'deposited' since the 1840s. The associations evoked by 'the

West' are many and at times bewilderingly confusing; but that is precisely why they can be rhetorically and politically useful and tempting (to various sides) as tools in debate, and why the term will not be jettisoned or abolished at any time soon, whatever many academics may say or write on the subject. And the fact that some of the associations or layers or meanings are incompatible with each other does not prevent them from being effectively used in political debates.[9]

Thus, the language related to 'the West' will not be abandoned in the foreseeable future. What I would argue should be avoided, however, is reference to so-called 'Western values' as being in any way owned by 'Western' peoples. If you tell other people that the institutions, practices, principles or values that you wish them to consider adopting are 'Western', what will the appellation imply, from their point of view? It is that they are losers of history, defeated; that what is good and commendable for everyone was invented by your own ('Western') ancestors, and has won; and they must adopt something that is alien to themselves, yet supposedly better in a normative sense. That expectation involves a hierarchical evaluation: if the question is framed in such a way, then from the point of view of the 'others', they must lose at least part of what they may see as their 'soul', in order to adopt something you have created.[10] It is this inevitable psychological conclusion and its repercussions that have led people since the nineteenth century into an endless search for the non-Western roots of Western civilisation, with varying degrees of scholarly credibility.

There may also be another way of dealing with this issue, however. If we wish people to consider adopting principles or institutions we may think are good for all peoples, we could begin by calling them by universal names. We could employ epithets that do not denote 'our' ownership. We may wish to argue that 'liberal' (another term that requires detailed definition/s of course!)—or egalitarian, or social-democratic, or utilitarian (happiness-promoting, consequentialist) or whatever else—principles, institutions, solutions, are worth considering or adopting; but that they deserve to be adopted not because they are 'Western', but rather because they are freedom-promoting, fair, equitable, conducive to justice, peace-promoting, happiness-enhancing, and so on, depending on what one's criteria of desirability are. (The 2017 debate in *The Atlantic* that we summarised in chapter 9 highlighted some of the dilemmas involved.)

If this book has shown anything beyond doubt, it is surely that attempts to give 'the West' an *essence*, an inherent and unchanging definition, nature or character, are misplaced. They are also psychologically ill-advised. Some examples may elucidate. We saw in chapter 2 how existential the question 'What is Greece, East or West?' was for Markos Renieris in 1842. If Greece was 'East', by receiving its institutions from Western Europe, the young country was 'committing political suicide, renouncing her national character and adopting alien features which would little by little stifle the innate ones, the end result being that Greece would henceforth live a borrowed life'. That is why he needed to prove that Greece was 'West', and thus simply reappropriating what was natural to its 'real essence'. Similarly, as we observed in chapter 6, Ernst Troeltsch was trying to reassure his compatriots in 1922 that Germans did not have to lose their 'soul' or 'essence' in order to accept the Weimar Republic: 'We are not required to retrace the whole of the path we have trod, or to renounce the quality of our national spirit'. Instead, he argued, 'we are only asked to recover ideas which we have allowed ourselves to lose, and to develop and adapt the thought of our stock to the vastly altered conditions of the modern world'.[11] (Heinrich August Winkler would try a similar approach at the beginning of the twenty-first century, as we saw in chapter 9.)

All sorts of historical and cultural acrobatics have been the stock in trade of intellectuals, historians and politicians in each and every country or group that, in the last two centuries, found itself regarded as 'backward' and in need of adopting institutions, technologies or models considered to have worked elsewhere. They needed to convince their fellow group members that, by doing so they would not be 'selling their soul' or betraying their 'essence'—for that perception is what the idea of the ownership of institutions or cultural models results in (and the last part of Miłosz's statement quoted in the epigraph above also seems relevant here).[12] The strategy Renieris adopted in 1842 was to be employed by many another. Fukuzawa Yukichi in Japan, Chinese reformers such as Liang Ch'i-ch'ao,[13] many Afro-American thinkers and activists, Turkish nationalist modernisers such as Ziya Gökalp,[14] and numerous others have tried versions of it. If 'ownership' of cultural achievements had not been so prominently claimed, much bad history and misplaced effort might have been avoided. (Some of Alain Locke's writings from the 1940s against the idea of anyone's ownership of cultural forms are surely pertinent here.)[15] It is politically counterproductive, historically problematic and even logically inconsistent to insist that, because certain things (cultural or political or intellectual achievements) were first developed or put together and articulated in a particular part of the world at a particular time (by the ancient Greeks, for instance, in the fifth and fourth centuries BCE), the people inhabiting that part of the world *now* are owners of the things in question. If that logic were to be followed, the narrow-minded Greek nationalists who claim that the world owes them everything because of what the ancient Greeks achieved—or appropriated and developed—at a particular time in their history, would have a point. I do not think they have a point, however; no one owes the modern

Greeks anything because of what the ancient Greeks did or did not do. But should not the same logic be applied to what has been achieved in recent centuries by Western Europe? Which is not to say that 'the West' has no meaning. It simply implies that meanings have to be more sensitively ascertained, and the ceaseless movement and inevitable mutability of history never lost sight of.

For meanwhile many people will go on being tempted to use 'West' and 'Western' to describe themselves or their proposals and projects while prescribing what being 'Western' means or ought to mean (inasmuch as reinterpretations amount simultaneously to interventions aimed at modifying the present and future, as described in Geuss's analysis of Nietzschean genealogy). The terms certainly cannot be abolished by the fiat of normative political philosophers or historians. There are some to whom 'West' or 'Western civilisation' will inevitably appeal, and if those on the left or centre or moderate centre right avoid the terms, they are no doubt all the more likely to be highlighted in justification of their proposals by extreme right groups—as has already happened from time to time, not least in France. (The number of times groups or magazines called *Occident* were formed in twentieth-century France is instructive here.) Again, the debate in the pages of *The Atlantic* in 2017 that we examined in chapter 9 is highly relevant to this issue. As we saw, one of the contributors argued (in relation to Donald Trump's speechwriters) that '[t]here's a degree to which the worldview of Bannon and Miller [...] finds [...] a kind of respectability when dressed up in the language of Western Civilization. That's to be sniffed out and called out where it occurs.' Otherwise, according to the same author, '[t]o define the West the way such men as these define it, to grant them [...] the right to set the terms of the debate, is to have already lost it. And to hollow out the meaning of meaningful words because they once sat upon an especially odious set of lips is to let the bastards grind you down.' (What was said in 2017 of Trump's speeches and speechwriters might equally be applied, or course, to Benjamin Netanyahu's reiterated declarations more recently that he is defending 'Western civilisation'.) All the above being the case, the best response I can think of to the idea of 'the West' is to submit it to meticulous and thorough historical scrutiny. 'The West' is neither more, nor less real or unreal, neither more nor less 'imagined', than other collective identities or entities (European, Mediterranean, Nordic, Pan-Islamic, Pan-Christian, etc.) that are meant to include people who are in many respects very different from each other.[16]

Academics have for a long time been keen to talk of 'the global South', and meanwhile the same term has become a favourite rhetorical tool used by India's prime minister Narendra Modi, and more recently has also been adopted by China's president Xi Jinping. Some of these academics may agree with Modi or Xi on some things, and not on others: is that a reason to stop talking of 'the global South'? Similar considerations apply to 'the West'. Strongly disagreeing with some of those who use the term or have used it in the past is no adequate reason to abolish it or to ignore its potentially different meanings (some of them widely divergent from those assigned to it by those one may disagree with); and the corollary is surely that one might well see the value in trying to explain that it means, in part, some of the different things that have been attached to it historically; and that the current conflicting definitions, understandings and 'membership lists' are all related to emphasising different layers of past meaning that have not been completely eclipsed, but have left their traces. Such a historically sensitive approach would, by definition, leave open the possibility (or rather underscore the certainty) of future redefinitions and reinterpretations of the past in the interests of various disputed projected futures.

When in July 2022 I gave a lecture related to the topic of this book in Tallinn, Estonia, an intelligent Ph.D student from the neighbouring Tartu University asked me a challenging question.[17] The timing was crucial. With the war in Ukraine having recently begun, people in the Baltic republics were intensely nervous about Russia's next moves. He asked me whether I was not worried that by exposing the many different and contradictory meanings of 'the West' and somehow 'deconstructing' the idea, I was bound to undermine our newfound unity? I took it that the unity in question referred to 'the West's' stance in solidarity with Ukraine since February that year. It seemed to me that the answer was somehow implicit in the question: I reminded my audience that the majority of Ukraine's population was Christian Orthodox. The vast majority of the definitions of 'the West' my lecture had gone through (and of the even greater number that this book has examined) would not have included Ukraine in 'the West'. (We saw in chapter 9 what Samuel Huntington predicted, and why). And yet at the time 'the West' was strongly supporting Ukraine. (Similar considerations could be applied to Greece, which Huntington was more or less proposing should be expelled from NATO in the 1990s.) Was that very situation not the best answer to the question? 'The West' was, once more, being redefined as we spoke.

IV. Classicists Bearing Gifts?

A particular issue meanwhile is the ongoing tendency to equate 'Western civilisation' with the flaws of a 'Plato to NATO' grand narrative and surreptitiously somehow to blame 'the classics' for what people in the nineteenth and twentieth centuries decided to do with Greek and Roman history, literature and thought.

That all sorts of people anachronistically co-opted parts of the classical past and distorted them into depictions of a pedigree for their preferred version of their own civilisation, or as proof of a purported 'eternal struggle between East and West', does not render the works those later people misread and misrepresented any less worthy of our reading and analysing them. It just makes it all the more imperative that we should read them more carefully. Works of ancient Greek philosophy and literature have inspired not just 'Westerners'. It is common knowledge that Muslim Arabs read them, cherished them and preserved some of them when they were much less familiar in what is now called 'the West'. Plato inspired Al-Farabi and many others, besides inspiring 'Westerners'. Aristotle was *'the teacher'* and appears innumerable times in Ibn Khaldun's *Muqaddimah*. The classics constitute an inheritance for the whole of humanity—not at all a peculiarly 'Western' possession that ought to be rejected by those who are upset about particular policies of particular 'Wests'. On 14 February 2021 the Pakistani Nobel Peace Prize laureate Malala Yousafzai was the guest on BBC Radio 4's 'Desert Island Discs',[18] and near the end was asked, as all guests on the programme are, to choose a book that she would like to take to the imaginary desert island. She replied that she would like to have Plato's complete works. She explained that she studied Plato's *Republic* at university, and since then she has become 'a big fan of Plato', so she wanted all his works with her. Malala is of course in very good company. In W.E.B. Du Bois's novel *The Quest of the Silver Fleece* (1911), the first book in the meaningful list of books to be found on Zora's shelves is Plato's *Republic*. Du Bois's own life and thought arguably provide one of the strongest arguments for studying the classics and for believing that the 'Western canon' can be employed as 'a liberatory tool for intellectual emancipation by all people'.[19] However, if some overzealous reformers of 'canons' continue the way they are going, Plato's *Republic* may not be taught for much longer, for future Malalas, Zoras or Du Boises to be inspired by it to want to read more of Plato. What an ultimate victory for the Taliban that would be!

If classicists, or social anthropologists, or practitioners of any other academic disciplines feel guilty about the origins of their disciplines and want to debunk their myths, they are most welcome to do so. Historians have for long been doing just that, and I grew up with a wave of critical scholarship exposing the nation-building myths of nineteenth-century nationalist historians. The exercise was very valuable; indeed, indispensable. But many practitioners seem to think that their works will be more interesting if they claim that 'Western civilisation' as a whole has to be demolished because of the sins of their predecessors. It has recently been argued that 'ever since those concepts ['West'/'Western civilisation'] emerged in the late nineteenth century the idea of the West—like other powerful constructs, such as race and gender—has had very real consequences'. Thus, the argument proceeds, they have been 'used to justify wars and colonization, calibrate stereotypes, and structure narratives of white supremacy; [...and] when "Westerners" set out to describe and account for the West, they typically identify ancient Greece—especially classical Athens—as its revered wellspring'. The reader is also told that '[a]cademics and others have nevertheless worked, since at least the mid-twentieth century, to question and even dismantle this picture'. An example is adduced, in the shape of 'George James, a historian from Guyana', who, in 'his landmark book' *Stolen Legacy: Greek Philosophy Is Stolen Egyptian Philosophy* (1954) 'opened a new direction in historical scholarship when he argued that Europe's greatest crime against Africa had been the ancient Greeks' theft and appropriation of African philosophy and civilization via the ancient Egyptians'.[20] Now, if the claim here is that ancient Greek cultural achievements were not the results of parthenogenesis, it is not particularly new (neither now, nor even in 1954). That Egypt was the major source of what the Greeks had found elsewhere, and that either the Egyptians themselves were Black Africans, or that, even if they were 'mixed', they had in turn received their civilisation from Black Ethiopia, were ideas widely discussed and disseminated by the early nineteenth century. Constantin-François Volney had already said as much more than two centuries ago. We saw too, in chapter 4 above, how Arnold Heeren's historical works were used by Afro-Americans who quoted him a century later. And as early as 1825, here is what one reads in the most prominent American magazine at the time, the *North American Review*: '[M]oreover, is it not true, that the East was the fountain of knowledge to the West? The very laws, that gave a semblance of stability to the Athenian democracies, were gleaned from Egypt.' Thus, the reviewer continued, '[t]he laws of Solon, and the philosophy of Plato, were little else than transcripts of what they had borrowed from the wise men of other countries'.[21] As we have seen (in chapter 4), such ideas had been widely discussed in German scholarship, and German scholarship had deeply impregnated the intellectual life of the young United States. It was more than a century prior to George James's book, furthermore—in 1850—that no less authoritative a figure in European cultural life than John Stuart Mill (in his attack against Thomas Carlyle's most recent racist rantings) wrote publicly, in one of the major Victorian magazines, that 'the earliest known civilization was, we have the strongest reason to believe, a negro civilization'. He went on, 'The original Egyptians are inferred, from the evidence of their sculptures, to have been a negro race: it was from negroes, therefore, that the Greeks learnt their first lessons in civilization.' And, as outstanding recent work by Suzanne Marchand has shown, some of the reasons that led German historians and philologists to begin focusing primarily or exclusively on the ancient Greeks in the early nineteenth century had at least as much to do with developments in terms of academic *wissenschaftlich* trends, increasing specialisation, acceptable professional standards and methods of proof, and the availability of sources that could be verified to meet those new standards, as with cultural prejudices.[22]

Talk of a conspiracy of silence about what the Greeks may have found in Africa or 'the East' has clearly, and repeatedly, been exaggerated. It would turn this Conclusion into a very long chapter were I to rehearse the instances in which Voltaire, Volney, Everett, Lieber, Spengler, Toynbee, Simone Weil, William W. McNeill and numerous others discussed in this book argued unequivocally that the first achievements in civilisation came from Africa and/or Asia. Criticisms of so-called 'grand narratives' of Western civilisation by recent scholars claiming to break new ground against a purportedly dominant monolithic account were in fact made long ago, and not least by many of the major figures discussed in this book as contributors to the development of the history of ideas on 'the West', who have castigated Eurocentrism, unilinear histories, historiographical biases and much more. (Twentieth-century thinking about civilisations in general and 'Western' civilisation in particular was shaped and defined by Spengler and Toynbee. Regarding the former, Massis had a point when he remarked that the whole philosophy of Spengler was 'a historico-metaphysical edifice, hastily constructed to liberate modern thought from Hellenism'.[23] Spengler very much criticised and undermined Western identification with the ancient Greeks, who were a separate 'Culture'. And given Toynbee's dominance for some decades, and how vociferous he was in opposing what is now being identified as 'the grand narrative', it is surprising to read that some of the claims now being advanced are new or original).[24] None of this changes the fact that some of the recent scholarship brings immense amounts and quality of research, new scientific methods, cultural openmindedness and critical analysis to discussion of the remote past on which the authors are specialists;[25] but some of the broader claims extrapolated in relation to modern history and 'the West' beg to be calmly discussed and sometimes challenged. Classicists are explicit about the extent to which what they are pursuing is a matter internal to their discipline.[26] We find ourselves at cross-purposes, however, when classicists set out to prove that the ancients did not think of themselves as 'Westerners' or 'white', and then assume that they have demolished the 'grand narrative' of Western civilisation and produced a more accurate history of the idea of the West. We have known these things for some time. The most persistent and authoritative narratives of 'the West' and 'Western civilisation', at any rate, have long been those that argue that 'it' began in the eighth, ninth or tenth century CE.

It is immensely welcome and most commendable that in recent years classicists have been expanding the pool of sources that they study, to contextualise and enrich our understanding of what earlier classicists focused upon. But meanwhile the texts, philosophical or literary, that the discipline of classics deals with constitute a baby that should not be thrown out along with the bathwater. The ideas or writings of Socrates, Thucydides, Plato, Sappho, Aristotle, Aeschylus, Euripides, Theophrastus, Plutarch, Cicero and other thinkers included in older 'canons' of the classics do not belong to any particular 'racial', cultural, linguistic, political or geographical group. They belong to the world.

V. What Is To Be Done?

Innumerable latter-day critics—or deniers of the very existence—of 'the West' or 'Western civilisation' take for granted one version of it, and thereby surreptitiously adopt the 'grand narrative' that they purportedly seek to deconstruct. To that extent, they begin by asking the wrong question. This book may serve as a reminder that there has been a plethora of definitions and redefinitions of 'the West'. Meanwhile, no matter how well-meaning the various studies exposing myths related to uses of 'Western civilisation' may be, Tristram Hunt surely had a point when he concluded in a recent review that if he was 'taking shelter in Kyiv, fearing another wave of [. . .] Russian bombardment, I think I might be hoping that "the west" did retain some sense of a historic identity and purpose in the world'.[27] Obviously, what the content of that historic identity and purpose in the world should be can be debated and redefined (potentially by every generation). This book has followed the story of such debates and redefinitions, and thereby demonstrated the potential for further debates still, and further redefinitions.

Liberal democracy with constitutional guarantees of what cannot be done to individuals or minorities, the rule of law, freedom of choice, meritocracy, toleration of different religions as well as of those who profess no religion, freedom of sexual orientation, and related norms, *are*, to my mind, to be preferred, and we should defend them against alarming alternatives. Most of us will miss them desperately if they are eclipsed. We may of course disagree as to the exact meanings of these norms and how to implement them in each case, but we obviously need to be allowed to continue disagreeing without being killed or otherwise silenced. Wherever such legal and moral principles and values are violated or threatened, be it in Vladimir Putin's 'Eastern' Russia, Viktor Orbán's 'Western' Hungary, Senator McCarthy's 'Western', or Donald Trump's 'Western' (or post-Western?), America, that should be denounced. If, meanwhile, the 'Westernness' of these models and principles is used by dictators and demagogues in Asia or Africa to persuade their people to reject them, that is obviously not the fault of the models or principles themselves. But when simply calling them 'Western' and therefore foreign, imposed by 'neo-colonialists', in itself does much of the work of decrying them for the dictators, one is reminded of how important it is to treat such ownership labels with caution.

The argument applies the other way round as well; for this discussion may be a useful reminder that, no matter how overstated his case may appear, Richard Wright had a point. To paraphrase: writing in the 1950s, he insisted that the West, so far, had never been 'Western' enough. The countries that were seen as constituting the West had not fulfilled the promise of their declared principles and values—those of a rational and enlightened civilisation of freedom and equality. And he warned that the irrationalism of one side reinforced the irrationalism of the other, and a vicious circle could ensue. Hence his plea for the West to live up to what he understood as its principles (summarised in his 'decalogue' quoted in chapter 8, section X), which Wright himself fully subscribed to.

I hope that we may be able to have more intelligent conversations about our past, present and future by being conscious of the multiple and changing meanings of 'essentially contested' and highly political concepts such as 'the West'— and of the alternative visions that each of these arose from, and stands for. The future depends, among other things, on the quality of our thinking and conversations, and clarity as to what the words we use mean, or might come to mean, will be among the most vital building blocks for enhancing that quality. There is no monolithic 'West' or unchanging 'Western' identity or essence. Like all identities, groups, histories, those referring to the West have often changed, and will go on changing. There are, understandably, Catholic narratives of the West, and Protestant narratives of the West. There are narratives of the West that define it as quintessentially secular, as did Richard Wright in the 1950s. There are further definitions and conceptions in between. Meanwhile, the existence of so many articulations certainly should not be taken to imply that there is in fact no such thing as 'the West'. It means rather that, like all identities, ideas, cultures, histories, those referred to as 'the West' are changing and evolving. People make choices. But what was there before is important for what follows and will follow thereafter: history matters. Yet history is, by definition, not static; it is ineluctably on the move, in the making, a constant process of becoming. (Controversial and lunatic though he was in many respects, Wyndham Lewis had a point when he complained that 'the West' was, for the people he was criticising (Massis included) '*a finished* thing, either over whose decay they gloat, or whose corpse they frantically "defend". What he proposed instead was '*a new West*, as it were, that we have to envisage'—'by an act of further creation.')[28]

This book is not a history of 'the West' as an entity, and therefore neither needs nor aspires to present a balance sheet of what 'it' has done in history. As a history of *the idea* of the West, it has been focused on the different meanings that the term 'the West' has come to assume during its history, and the implications of each meaning. The constitutional, political, cultural and moral models, principles and values prevalent in the West, are prevalent *now*, or have been in recent decades. They were not perennially or inherently present; they are not to be associated with any Western 'essence' or unchanging character. Many of them might well be seen as commendable and admirable, and most of us, despite all our passionate disagreements, might agree on the basic principles or rules of engagement in terms of which they exist and can operate. It is equally true that many of them are very recent acquisitions, and were not part of what 'the West' meant or stood for some centuries ago, or even some decades ago in some cases.

Does that mean that there is no such thing as a Western culture? Absolutely not. Studying these things historically shows that most of the models, institutions or principles in question evolved out of the history of a particular culture or society for particular combinations of reasons. The outcomes were not inevitable or 'providentially' predetermined, but they are equally far from being completely accidental. As Marx correctly noted and many have repeated, people make their own history, but they make it in circumstances that they do not choose; they have to make it within parameters already present in the contexts in which they find themselves. There exist cultures or societies, broader than the nation or nation state, that differ recognisably from each other; whether one wishes to call them 'civilisations' or by another term, one cannot deny the existence of such transnational units that share within themselves things that they do not share with the others. These transnational units, or civilisations or cultures or societies, are of course not static or eternal, but in constant flux. Nevertheless, at each of the phases of their history there are factors that reliably differentiate the civilisations or cultures of transnational societies such as 'the West' from those outside them—albeit these distinguishing traits too are not eternal, unchanging or inherent, but constantly susceptible to change. It is equally important to bear in mind that what comes later is affected by what was there before.

I think that Nietzsche was right, that you cannot offer a 'correct' definition of something with a long history, and I am not now going to contradict myself and attempt to define 'the West'. But some distinguishing tendencies that have been more pronounced in the history of particular groups than in those of others can be discerned and made explicit. It will hardly be disputed that belief in the use of science and technology for the conquest of nature in the (purported) interests of humanity has long been a thread in the history of the modern West.[29] (There Karl Marx, Auguste Comte, André Siegfried, Richard Wright, Hannah Arendt, Cornelius Castoriadis and many others have been in agreement.) To that extent, while the current ecological emergency is a problem for the whole of mankind, those who identify with the West must face it with the added urgency that goes with historical responsibility. Is the destruction of the planet to be the legacy of 'the West'? Or is the self-correcting quality that a number of the figures featured in this book identified as the most prominent trait of the West to come to the rescue? That is a key question.

When all is said and done, Raymond Aron's definition (substituting 'person' for 'man', obviously) seems apposite: 'The true "Westerner" is the man who accepts nothing unreservedly in our civilisation except the liberty it allows him to criticise it and the chance it offers him to improve it.'[30] As we saw in chapter 9, Cornelius Castoriadis, who stood at the opposite end of the political spectrum, would have agreed. Aron also wrote incisively that we demand of the West all the virtues which it is desirable but unexampled so far to combine. We may expect too much from this 'West': a set of qualities whose combination has been neither achieved nor even aspired to by any 'civilisation', 'culture' or wider 'society' anywhere to date, but which is nevertheless desirable. That is the West's predicament. It must deliver on a promise (or a series of promises) that is almost impossible completely to fulfil. Yet the aspiration to do so may be its main contribution to the world.

There is no doubt that after the Cold War (and the eclipse of the fear generated by an opposite pole) critics of 'the West' have proliferated. Whatever is wrong in the world is now habitually blamed on 'the West'. Even the opportunities afforded by the end of the Cold War were thought to have been squandered by arrogance or self-congratulation in the West. The critics are so numerous it would make little sense to name them; but, much of the time, reading between the lines, many essentially demand of the West that it do 'the Western thing', as it were: live up to proclaimed Western principles. What they criticise amounts to the practice, decisions and policies of various governments in the West, rather than the *idea* of the West. Much of the criticism is therefore a tribute to the (high) expectations raised by that idea. (Rabindranath Tagore's distinction—discussed in chapter 5, section IV—between 'the spirit of the West' on the one hand, and 'the Nation of the West' on the other, comes to mind here. As we saw, he told his Japanese audience that there was safety in the fact that Asians could 'claim Europe herself as our ally in our resistance to her temptations and to her violent encroachments; for she has ever carried her own standard of perfection, by which we can call her before her own tribunal and put her to shame'.) Of course, many unpalatable things have been justified in the name of 'Western civilisation'. But it is no less true that much of the critical and self-correcting reflection, argument and action against many of these and other ills has resulted from appeals to 'the West' and its principles. 'The West' (in particular understood as various Western governments and other agents) may have immense failings and much to answer for, but it is in terms of its own register of normative principles and values that it is found wanting in practice—not according to any impartial comparative universal standard.

There is not one, monolithic, evil West, and there is not one monolithic, benign, enlightened, just and liberal 'West'. And 'civilizations', furthermore, 'do not make decisions'.[31] That is reserved for states and their designated leaders and policy-making procedures. Meanwhile, there exists a group of peoples that share a broader society (call it a 'civilisation', 'culture', or what you will). The membership of the group is not static, but changes with additions, migration, conversions, political choices, enlargements and other historical processes. There exists also an idea of the West, onto which people project all sorts of desires, wishes, complaints, resentments or hopes. (And as Joseph Brodsky once put it, 'In choosing between a thing and an idea, the latter is always to be preferred, say I.')[32] That idea is more than likely to continue to be invoked by many and various actors in political and cultural debates, to reinforce their arguments and help them achieve what they wish to achieve. I hope that this book, by dissecting the many layers of the idea's meaning during its long history, may help diminish the confusions to which our dependence on the use of abstract terms often leads. Words, in their variety of meanings can, as Joseph Conrad and many others have warned, be treacherous. Their meanings change, and context matters a great deal. It is easy for people to be blinded by contemporary passions and debates in particular countries and political conjunctures; to be influenced by who uses what terms in their rhetoric at a given moment; to forget the many possible significations of a term or concept, and the potential for some of these to resurface, or mutate to mean something different in the future. A proper *longue durée* history of the concept in question could help to guard against this; hence the present book.

Whatever we choose to call them, a number of valuable principles and practices that came to be combined in what is called 'the West' in recent times should be cherished and encouraged to evolve, though various 'Western' governments or other agents may often fail to act in conformity with them—all the more reason, indeed, to defend those principles and practices and 'speak out', as Cornelius Castoriadis enjoined. The baby must not go out with the bathwater. For if we are not careful, as Richard Wright warned almost seven decades ago, 'the precious heritage—the freedom of speech, the secular state, the independent personality, the autonomy of science—which is not Western or Eastern, but human, will be snuffed out of the minds of men.'[33]

ACKNOWLEDGEMENTS

THIS BOOK TOOK MANY YEARS to complete and I have been blessed with the advice, help and friendship of many generous people on my way to writing it. (None of them is responsible for the shortcomings of this book of course, for which I am solely responsible). I first of all want to thank all my students, current and past, from undergraduates to Ph.D supervisees, who over many years have been inspiring, as well as teaching me a lot. Particular thanks are due to the students who took the intercollegiate London MA in 'History of Political Thought and Intellectual History' in the last couple of decades. I am also grateful to the students who took my Special Subject course 'The Idea of "the West": A History from the Nineteenth to the Twenty-First Century' over the past few years. And many thanks go also to the students who have, over many years, participated in the London Summer School in Intellectual History that I had the privilege to co-organise with a UCL colleague, sometimes with Angus Gowland and some with Avi Lifschitz (now at Oxford). I have furthermore had the privilege and luck to co-teach with each of them, depending on the year, on the core module of the MA in 'History of Political Thought and Intellectual History', and that experience taught me much, besides giving me enormous pleasure. The wider University of London is a wonderful community and I have been fortunate to work with and learn from many colleagues, among whom I thank in particular Valentina Arena, Adrian Blau, Kathleen Burk, Gregory Claeys, Stephen Conway, Hannah Dawson, Robin Douglass, Dina Gusejnova, Adela Halo, Humeira Iqtidar, Chloe Ireton, Leigh Jenco, Paul Kelly, Axel Körner, Michael Levin, Nicola Miller, Julia Nicholls, Niall O'Flaherty, Paul Sagar, Philip Schofield, Peter Schröder, William Selinger, Emily Steinhauer, Iain Stewart, Ian Stewart, Adam Sutcliffe, Lea Ypi and Samuel Zeitlin. Sam Zeitlin also provided very generous help through discussions on Carl Schmitt. My relationship with that community began long ago, when I studied at UCL with Fred Rosen, and my gratitude to him is immense. (It was also very important to me that Fred found the idea of this book convincing when I first spoke to him about it). I rejoined that community in 2006 when I came to Queen Mary, and I have been blessed with many wonderful colleagues there. I am grateful to them all; and for particular conversations, cooperation or advice I thank Caroline Ashcroft, Richard Bourke, Maks Del Mar, Thomas Dixon, Jean-François Drolet, Saul Dubow, James Ellison, Andrew Fitzmaurice, Katrina Forrester, Martyn Frampton, Patrick Higgins, Kimberly Hutchings, Joel Isaac, Maurizio Isabella, Engin Isin, Leslie James, Jeremy Jennings, Charlotte Johann, Colin Jones, Michael Lobban, Chris Moffat, Philip Ogden, Yossi Rapoport, Isobel Roele, Miri Rubin, Mira Siegelberg, Quentin Skinner, Gareth Stedman Jones, Barbara Taylor, Christina von Hodenberg and Waseem Yaqoob. I am grateful to the then vice-principal, Matthew Hilton, and successive heads of school Julian Jackson and Dan Todman for permission to take up in two different instalments a senior research fellowship at Göttingen; and also to the head of school under whose leadership this book was completed, Emma Griffin, for much appreciated support and encouragement and for the atmosphere that makes the School as special as it is. Julian Jackson also offered extremely valuable advice as my research mentor over several years while I was working on this book.

A senior fellowship at the Lichtenberg-Kolleg, at the Georg-August-Universität Göttingen, has already been mentioned. It was indispensable to 'breaking the back' of this book, regarding which I will always be immensely grateful to Martin van Gelderen for the fellowship and his very generous hospitality and friendship there. Martin's colleagues Dominik Hünniger and Kora Baumbach offered marvellous conditions and unstinting helpfulness that I very much appreciate. That I met Jyotirmaya Sharma at the Lichtenberg-Kolleg was one of its many blessings. Jyotirmaya's exceptional generosity in all respects made my experience of Göttingen most pleasantly memorable, notwithstanding the challenges of being there in the time of a scary pandemic. This book was completed under the auspices of a further generous fellowship, at the Institut für die Wissenschaften vom Menschen in Vienna. I could not have hoped for a better environment in which to reflect and write on the topic of this book. I am very grateful to the rector, Misha Glenny, and permanent fellows Clemena Antonova, Ayşe Çağlar, Ludger Hagedorn, Ivan Krastev and Ivan Vejvoda, and all others with whom I had marvellous conversations whilst at the IWM, not least Kristina Broučková, Rogers Brubaker, Jakub Čapek, Francesca De Benedetti, Katharina Hasewend, Evangelos Karagiannis, Julie Klinger, Malgorzata Mazurek, Anna Narinskaya, Katja Petrowskaja, Adam Shatz and Maria Todorova.

Kind invitations to speak on numerous occasions over many years have helped me think about and refine my arguments with regard to the topic of this book. I am very grateful to Isabella Thomas and the Axel and Margaret Ax:son Johnson

Foundation for an invitation to speak at their conference 'What is the West?' in 2007 and test some incipient arguments that were to grow over many years thereafter; to my colleagues at the QMUL School of Politics and International Relations for an invitation to speak to their seminar on the very early stages of my project—and to James Dunkerley for his considerate chairing; to Riccardo Bavaj and Martina Steber for an invitation to a related workshop at the University of St Andrews; to Shruti Kapila and Saul Dubow for an invitation to speak at the global intellectual history seminar at Cambridge; to Eva Piirimäe and Liisi Keedus for an invitation to an unforgettably pleasurable and fruitful workshop at the University of Tartu; to Liisi Keedues again for two more extremely welcome invitations to speak at Tallinn University; to Iain McDaniel for an invitation to deliver a public lecture at the Centre for Intellectual History, University of Sussex, and to Katharina Rietzler and Iain for their marvellous hospitality there; to Camille Creyghton, Annelien De Dijn, Lisa Kattenberg, René Koekkoek, Matthijs Lok and other convenors of the Amsterdam–Utrecht–Groningen 'Global Intellectual History' seminar for a most welcome first post-Covid invitation; to Anna-Louise Milne and the University of London Institute in Paris [ULIP] for an invitation to give the first ULIP-QMUL annual lecture (most appropriately Paris-centric, that one!); to Raf Geenens for an invitation to speak at the Research in Political Philosophy seminar in Leuven; to Maria Mälksoo and Albena Azmanova for an invitation to speak at the guest lecture series of the University of Kent's Brussels School of International Studies; to Jérémie Barthas and Arnault Skornicki for invitations to speak to their seminar in Paris; to Aurelie Knüfer for an invitation to the Université Paul Valéry, Montpellier; to Matthieu Renault for an invitation to speak at the Université Grenoble Alpes; to Antonio Massala for a kind invitation to Lucca; to Li Hongtu for an invitation to spend two unforgettable weeks at FuDan University, Shanghai, and speak to his colleagues and students—and to both Wenqin Sheng and Li Hongtu for their very generous hospitality and our discussions during those weeks; to Georgios Giannakopoulos for invitations to two different events where I spoke on topics related to this book—for one of these occasions I am also grateful to co-organiser Efi Gazi; to James Stafford for an invitation to speak as part of the 'Signaturen der Weltgesellschaft' lecture series, Universität Bielefeld; to Anne Thomson for an invitation to a most productive workshop at the European University Institute in Florence; to Ludmilla Lorrain for an invitation to speak at the *Séminaire d'histoire de la philosophie politique:'Pour une généalogie des concepts politiques'*, at the Université Paris 1–Panthéon-Sorbonne; to Alexander Schmidt for his invitation to speak at the University of Jena; to Christina Koulouri and Athena Leoussi for an invitation to Panteion University in Athens; to Antoine Lilti and Thomas Maissen for an invitation to speak at their Séminaire de recherche sur les Lumières at the German Historical Institute, Paris; to Thomas Maissen again, for a hugely welcome invitation to speak at the unforgettable conference that celebrated his ten years as director of the German Historical Institute in Paris, and for many conversations as highly fruitful as they have been enjoyable; to Michalis Sotiropoulos and the British School at Athens for the invitation to deliver the keynote lecture at a conference on the global history of Philhellenism; and to Dessy Gavrilova and all the organisers of the Vienna Humanities Festival for an invitation to speak at and participate in a hugely stimulating gathering in September 2024.

Parts of chapter 2 have appeared as an article in *Modern Intellectual History* and parts of chapter 3 in *History of European Ideas* (details of both are given in the Bibliography). I am very grateful to the respective editors and publishers of these journals for permission to use new versions of the work here. To the editor of the latter journal, Richard Whatmore, I am additionally indebted for many acts of kindness and generosity and marvellous conversations.

I owe an immense debt to David Labreure and the Maison d'Auguste Comte in Paris for their warm reception and consistently willing helpfulness during several years of repeated research visits to study the papers of Auguste Comte and his followers. I am also most grateful to Michel Bourdeau, *secrétaire* of the Maison d'Auguste Comte, for his warm welcome and many fruitful conversations. I am grateful to the staff at the British Library, LSE Library and Archives, Senate House Library, UCL Library, Queen Mary University of London Library, Bibliothèque nationale de France, Bibliothèque de l'Arsenal, Bibliothèque de la Sorbonne, the Library of Georg-August-Universität Göttingen, Firestone Library at Princeton University, and, not least, the London Library. When libraries did not have particular items I needed urgently and I could not be in France or Germany at the time, I was fortunate to be able to resort to the exceedingly kind Jérémie Barthas and Alexander Schmidt respectively. Both responded to my requests for articles or books in French or German that I could not find anywhere else, and sent them to me, on countless occasions, and my gratitude is correspondingly deep. The research I conducted in Paris, meanwhile, was accomplished thanks to the opportunity I had to stay in the marvellous flat of Patrizia Dogliani every year for several years; I am grateful to her, and to Glenda Sluga for recommending the idea.

For very helpful conversations, advice, assistance, tips or encouragement in relation to this book I am most grateful to David Armitage, Callum Barrell, Jérémie Barthas, Joe Coles, Aidan Fusco, Stefanos Geroulanos, Stuart Jones, Anna

Karakatsouli, Melissa Lane, Tony La Vopa, Olivia Leboyer, Antis Loizides, Karuna Mantena, Suzanne Marchand, John P. McCormick, Iain McDaniel, Jon Parry, John Robertson, Alexander Schmidt, Max Skjönsberg, Reto Speck, Michael Sutton, Maria Vassilaki, Nasia Yakovaki and Xinxian Zhu. I also thank, for their encouragement or/and stimulating conversations or exchanges, Andrew Apostolou, Michalis Avgoustianakis, Duncan Bell, Philippos Charalambous, Roger Crisp, Alexander Etkind, Indravati Félicité, Karsten Fischer, Olga Katsiardi-Hering, Jeremy Jennings, Duncan Kelly, Shiru Lim, Lilian Mitrou, Gregoris Molivas, Mark Philp, Jennifer Pitts, Vesna Popovski, Kostas Raptis, Ion de la Riva, Alan Ryan, Antoinette Saxer, Bart Schultz, Silvia Sebastiani, and Shang Yuan. I will always be very grateful to Paschalis Kitromilides for inspiring and encouraging me to study the history of political thought.

This book has benefited immensely from the generosity and wise advice of the two anonymous referees who read the initial proposal and then of the two anonymous referees who read the full manuscript. That one of the latter went to over-generous lengths of detailed and extremely helpful advice on how to shorten the book is something that I have no doubt the reader will be as grateful for as I am. I am most grateful too to Miri Rubin for her suggestion that I should talk with Al Bertrand of Princeton University Press about my new research project, and to Al for his gentle and patient reminders that he liked the idea of this book and looked forward to receiving a proposal. I took my time over that, and when it was sent, it was Al's successor in Europe, Ben Tate, who received it and most generously encouraged me to proceed. Meetings with Ben to discuss the book over the past several years have been among the major highlights of the whole experience. Josh Drake has been extremely helpful and most promptly and patiently responded to all my queries and requests in the final stages of submission of the text. I am grateful to my agent Toby Mundy for his encouragement and advice, and to Francis Eaves for unprecedented (in my experience) levels of thoroughness and professionalism, as well as patience, in his meticulous copy-editing of the book. Patience, gentle tolerance and generosity have been qualities Nathan Carr has displayed with me in abundance while overseeing the production of the book, and I thank him for that. To Richard Bourke my debts are so many that I cannot even begin to enumerate them here. Suffice it to say that I have almost literally learnt the job from him (though I am of course solely responsible for my shortcomings in it). I am very grateful that he read parts of the book at crucial stages and generously offered wise and subtle feedback on them. Richard's advice and encouragement over a long time with regard to this book have been crucial: literally indispensable.

I have benefited hugely from conversations about ideas and books (including this one) with my parents-in-law, Vanessa Thomas and the late Hugh Thomas, as well as with Inigo Thomas and Isambard Thomas (and I still remember that, when he found out that I was working on Comte, Hugh gave me his copy of the first English translation of *A General View of Positivism*). I am deeply grateful to them. My greatest debt is to Bella and Alexander, for their immense tolerance, patience and indulgence towards an antisocial, hermitic, absentee husband and father, and for their encouragement and belief in what I was trying to do. Bella read countless drafts of various chapters and offered crucial challenges, editorial suggestions and invaluable advice. Alexander has made more magnanimous and intelligent suggestions as well as jokes about this book than I will ever deserve. This book is dedicated to them.

NOTES

Chapter 1: Introduction

1. Aeschylus, *Persians*, pp. 104–5.
2. Kimmage, *Abandonment of the West*, p. 9.
3. Appiah, *Lies that Bind*, p. 200.
4. Montesquieu, *My Thoughts*, p. 270.
5. See Bowersock, 'East–West Orientation of Mediterranean Studies', pp. 167–78. On ideas related to orientation, see also Brotton, *Four Points of the Compass*.
6. [d'Alembert], 'Occident'; Larousse, *Grand dictionnaire universel*, vol. 11, pp. 1210–11. (Incidentally, the irrevocable division of the Roman Empire into Eastern and Western halves did not happen '[i]n the late third century', as stated in Mac Sweeney, *The West*, p. 56, but in the late fourth century CE.)
7. [M. W.] Lewis and Wigen, *Myth of Continents*, pp. 49–51. The third referent the authors identify has 'arisen since the 1960s' and stands as 'simply a proxy for the developed world', pp. 51, 53.
8. Novalis, 'Christianity or Europe'. Schulte Nordholt, *Myth of the West*.
9. This observation implies that the work of Edward Said is not relevant to my focus here, as we should be at cross-purposes. See Said, *Orientalism*; Said, *Culture and Imperialism*. Europeans were happy to treat 'the East' as 'the other' and continue to call themselves 'Christendom' or 'Europe', not 'the West'. The new term was due to (as well as further galvanised) subtle changes in the self-identification of those who used it, and to that extent generated a novel concept, overlapping to a great extent with 'Europe', but not identical with it. A recent contibution that talks of 'the West' over many centuries while conceding that the idea or term had not yet been invented is Mac Sweeney, *The West*: for both this book's merits and an analysis of the genre that it represents, see Thonemann, 'Know Thyself'.
10. GoGwilt, *Invention of the West*, pp. 1–2, 226–27.
11. GoGwilt, *Invention of the West*, pp. 226–27.
12. Heller, 'Russian Dawn'; Heller, 'Dawning of the West'.
13. Heller, 'Russian Dawn,' p. 47.
14. Billington, 'Intelligentsia and the Religion of Humanity'.
15. Heller, 'Russian Dawn,' pp. 37–38; Trautsch, 'Invention of the "West"'.
16. Walicki, *Slavophile Controversy*, pp. 83–117, esp. p. 87.
17. Note statements in Chaadaev's 'First Philosophical Letter', such as, 'The peoples of Europe have a common physiognomy, a family look. Despite their broad division into Latins and

Teutons, into Southerners and Northeners, there is a tie which binds them together into one and which is readily apparent to anyone who has studied their general history.' Chaadaev further noted that 'European society as it is today [...] contains the principle of continuous unlimited progress' (another major focus in Guizot's 1828 book). Chaadaev, 'Letters on the Philosophy of History: First Letter', pp. 164–65, 169, 171. (Cf. Guizot, *History of Civilization in Europe*, p. 30: 'notwithstanding their diversity, they have all a certain resemblance, a certain family likeness, which it is impossible to mistake'. Guizot had also used the expression 'the particular physiognomy of this [European] civilization', ibid., p. 27). See also Evtuhov, 'Guizot in Russia'.

18. Heller, 'Russian Dawn', p. 37. Trautsch, 'Invention of the "West"'; S. Conrad, 'Cultural History of Global Transformation', p. 455; Mac Sweeney, *The West*, p. 271.

19. See Quénet, *Tchaadaev et les Lettres philosophiques*, p. 157; Werth, *1837: Russia's Quiet Revolution*, pp. 43–58; Walicki, *Slavophile Controversy*, pp. 83–117; Kohn, *Mind of Modern Russia*, pp. 34–38; Berdyaev, *Origin of Russian Communism*, pp. 24–26; Miltchyna, 'Joseph de Maistre's Works in Russia', pp. 241–70. (Miltchyna calls Chaadaev 'the Russian de Maistre No. 1'.)

20. For the Russian context of Maistre's writing of *Du pape*, see Armenteros, *French Idea of History*, pp. 145–55.

21. Maistre, *The Pope*, p. 345. For other uses of 'the West' or 'western' see ibid., pp. 290–91, 304, 315, 326, 332–33. For the original, Maistre, *Du pape*.

22. Stourdza, *Considérations sur la doctrine*.

23. See Ghervas, *Réinventer la tradition*, pp. 191–202.

24. (French) original quoted in Latreille, *Joseph de Maistre et la papauté*, p. 35.

25. For a fascinating early example, see 'ΝΙΚΑΝΔΡΟΥ ΝΟΥΚΙΟΥ ΤΟΥ ΚΕΡΚΥΡΑΙΟΥ ΑΠΟΔΗΜΙΩΝ ΛΟΓΟΣ Α', in Nicandre de Corcyre, *Voyages*; for a recent French translation, Nicandre de Corcyre, *Voyage d'Occident*; and for a recent English translation, Muir, *Greek Eyes on Europe*.

26. Chaadaev, 'Letters on the Philosophy of History: First Letter', pp. 159–73.

27. Walicki, *History of Russian Thought*, pp. 273, 349–60, 362–70, 376, 387; Walicki, *Slavophile Controversy*, p. 426; Berdyaev, *Origin of Russian Communism*, pp. 63, 78; Billington, 'Intelligentsia and the Religion of Humanity'; Laurent, 'La Philosophie russe et le positivisme' (see too other articles in *La philosophie russe et le positivisme*, special issue, *Archives de philosophie* 79, no. 2 [(2016)]); Pickering, 'Conclusion'. For Comte's claim, see his letter to Czar Nicholas, 20 December 1852, in Comte, *Correspondance*, vol. 6, pp. 451–73, at 453–54; reprinted in Comte, *Système*, vol. 3, pp. xxix–xlvii, at p. xxxi; Comte, *System*, vol. 3, pp. xxiv–xli, at p. xxvi.

28. On Comte's admiration for Heeren, see Pickering, *Auguste Comte*, vol. 1, pp. 269, 289; vol. 2, pp. 383, 512. On Comte and Maistre, see Useche Sandoval, 'Auguste Comte's Reading of Maistre's *Du pape*'; Barth, 'Die Theologie Joseph de Maistres'.

29. Miłosz, 'Dostoevsky', p. 281.

30. Bonnett, *Idea of the West*, pp. 11, 14–39.

31. See Crook, *Benjamin Kidd*, pp. 3, 277, 283, 295, 375, 397 n.84. Kidd used the term 'the West' extensively in B. Kidd, *Social Evolution*, and B. Kidd, *Principles of Western Civilisation*.

32. Osterhammel, *Transformation of the World*, p. 86.

33. Herman, *Idea of Decline*, p. 4 (emphasis added).

34. Mac Sweeney, *The West*, p. 36; Appiah, *Lies that Bind*, p. 200.

35. For the classic warning against temptations to study 'unit ideas', see Skinner, 'Meaning and Understanding'. For the argument in favour of contextual study of ideas in *longue durée* studies, see Armitage, 'What's the Big Idea?'.

36. See Baritz, 'Idea of the West'; Schulte Nordholt, *Myth of the West*. Cf. Pocock, 'Historiography of the *translatio imperii*'. On changes in the conception of time, see Hartog, *Chronos*.

37. No. 10, rue Monsieur-le-Prince was the address of Comte's Paris flat and the centre of operations of the Comité occidental. It now houses the papers and archives of Comte and his disciples as the 'Maison d'Auguste Comte'.

38. Guizot, *Histoire de la civilisation en Europe*; Guizot, *History of Civilization in Europe*. See also Varouxakis, 'Guizot's Historical Works'.

39. Donoso Cortés, *Essays on Catholicism*, pp. 85–89.

40. Hegel, *Lectures on the Philosophy of World History—Introduction*, p. 197.

41. Bonnett, *Idea of the West*, p. 24. For a brilliant recent analysis of Hegel's thought, its context and its significance, see Bourke, *Hegel's World Revolutions*; for Hegel's focus on the 'Germanic peoples' and 'German' spirit of modern Europe, esp. pp. 123–30. For an analysis of Hegel's brief comments on America, written in 1830, see G. A. Kelly, 'Hegel's America'. Kelly argued that '[t]he United States is rather an inchoate part of what Hegel calls the "Germanic world". It reveals a tantalizing incompleteness': ibid., p. 3.

42. See Lemberg, 'Zur Entstehung des Osteuropabegriffs'; Speck, 'History and Politics of Civilisation'; Adamovsky, *Euro-Orientalism*.

43. Gibbon, *Decline and Fall*, vol. 3, Appendix 2, p. 1095.

44. Bodin, *Six Books of a Commonweale*, pp. 545–68. On the tradition Bodin was following, see Tooley, 'Bodin and the Mediaeval Theory of Climate'.

45. Lemberg, 'Zur Entstehung des Osteuropabegriffs'; Bavaj, '"The West"'; Struck, 'In Search of the "West"'; Schenk, 'Mental Maps'.

46. For an example, see Ghervas, *Réinventer la tradition*, p. 199.

47. Adamovsky, 'Euro-Orientalism'; also Adamovsky, *Euro-Orientalism*.

48. Mill to D'Eichthal, 3 March 1837, in Mill, *Collected Works*, vol. 12, p. 329 (emphases added).

49. Parry, 'Disraeli, the East and Religion'. (I am grateful to the author for making the article available to me before it was published.)

50. Laurens, *Orientales*, p. 16.

51. Condorcet, *Esquisse d'un tableau historique*; for an exhaustively critical edition, see Condorcet, *Tableau historique des progrès*. For recent critical commentaries, see Volpilhac-Auger, 'D'une histoire l'autre'; Minuti, 'L'Orient dans le *Tableau* de Condorcet'. For a comparison which does not, however, differentiate between 'l'Europe' and 'l'Occident', see De Boni, 'L'Idée de "république occidentale" et le positivisme'. See also De Boni, *Storia d'un utopia*.

52. Condorcet, *Political Writings*, pp. 55, 57, 58, 60, 62, 63, 66.

53. See Echeverria, *Mirage in the West*, p. 152.

54. Condorcet, *Écrits sur les États Unis*; Condorcet, *De l'influence de la Révolution d'Amérique*.

55. Diderot, *Œuvres*, vol. 3; see also Diderot, *Political Writings*.

56. Montesquieu, *Lettres persanes*, p. 52 (Lettre 22); p. 163 (Lettre 91).

57. Montesquieu, *My Thoughts*, p. 132.

58. Montesquieu, *My Thoughts*, p. 233. Herder, 'Another Philosophy of History', pp. 32–35, 40, 43, 75–77. See also Bourdieu, 'Le Nord et le Midi'.

59. Wolff, *Inventing Eastern Europe*, p. 200. For an important related contributon, see Todorova, *Imagining the Balkans*; also, Neumann, *Uses of the Other*.

60. Voltaire, *Lettres choisies*, pp. 429–31, 442–43, 450–52, 464–67, 516–17, 519–20. For Voltaire's importance to laudatory eighteenth-century accounts of the rise of Russia and its beneficent influence, see Nakhimovsky, *Holy Alliance*, p. 5.

61. Voltaire, *Essai sur les mœurs*, in *Les Œuvres complètes de Voltaire*, at vol. 22, pp. 26, 42; Voltaire, *Philosophie de l'histoire*, p. 57.

62. Voltaire, *Philosophie de l'histoire*, p. 73.

63. Voltaire, *Essai sur les mœurs*, in *Les Œuvres complètes de Voltaire*, at vol. 22, p. 149.

Chapter 2: 'The West' as an Alternative to 'Europe' in the Nineteenth Century

1. Volney, *Les Ruines*; Lilti, '"Et la civilisation deviendra générale"'; Lilti, *L'Héritage des Lumières*, pp. 155–90; Cook, 'Representing Humanity'; Osterhammel, *Unfabling the East*, pp. 191–96.

2. Schwab, *Renaissance orientale*, pp. 106–7; Schwab, *Oriental Renaissance*. For a brilliant analysis of the Anglo–French 'dispute of the Orient' between the time of the French Revolution and the 1840s (including an appreciation of Volney's significance), see C. Kidd, *World of Mr Casaubon*, pp. 131–75.

3. See Pitts, *Boundaries of the International*; Piirimäe, 'Russia, the Turks and Europe'.

4. Ghervas, *Conquering Peace*, pp. 106–16, 126. See also Sluga, *Invention of International Order*, pp. 179–82; Vick, *Congress of Vienna*. As Isaac Nakhimovsky has shown, the Holy Alliance had many liberal supporters. On the positive image of Russia during most of the eighteenth and the early decades of the nineteenth century more generally, see Nakhimovsy, *Holy Alliance*.

5. Cousin, *Souvenirs d'Allemagne*, p. 74.

6. On Heeren's contributions and significance as a historian, see Lok, *Europe against Revolution*, pp. 195–228, 261–70; also, Espagne, 'The *Universal- und Kulturgeschichte* at Göttingen'.

7. Heeren, *Reflections*, pp. 2–3. Russia was looked upon with favour in Göttingen, not least by some of Heeren's colleagues or former colleagues. See Golf-French, 'Limits of the Enlightenment Narrative'.

8. Heeren, *Ideen über die Politik*, p. 8.

9. Heeren, *Reflections*, pp. 8–9, 11 (emphasis added).

10. On Suzanne Curchod's intellectual contributions, see the fascinating analysis in La Vopa, *Labor of the Mind*.

11. Herold, *Mistress to an Age*, p. 384.

12. *Blackwood's Edinburgh Magazine*, December 1818.

13. Staël, *Ten Years of Exile*, p. 145; in the original French, Staël, *Dix années d'exil*, p. 210.

14. Milnes, 'The Marquis de Custine's Russia', p. 370.

15. Staël, *Ten Years of Exile*, pp. 145–46.

16. See Prochasson, *Saint-Simon ou l'anti-Marx*; Manuel, *Prophets of Paris*.

17. Saint-Simon and Thierry 'On the Reorganization of European Society', pp. 83–98.

18. Saint-Simon, *Œuvres complètes*, vol. 4, pp. 2764, 2767 (January 1822).

19. Saint-Simon, *Œuvres complètes*, vol. 4, pp. 2764, 2767 (January 1822), 2762, 2763, 2768.

20. Saint-Simon, *Œuvres complètes*, vol. 4, pp. 2764, 2767 (January 1822), 2764.

21. Saint-Simon, *Œuvres complètes*, vol. 4, p. 2826; vol. 1, pp. 123, 126, 583.

22. Saint-Simon, *Œuvres complètes*, vol. 1, pp. 582–84 ('Épître dédicatoire à mon neveu Victor de Saint-Simon').

23. See Laurens, *Orientales*, pp. 15–29; Laurens, 'Question d'Orient'.

24. See Lamartine, *Question d'Orient*, pp. 102, 154, 157–58, 183, 189, 202, 228, 230, 234, 249, 373, 375, 376.

25. Lamartine, *Question d'Orient*, 102, 117, 186, 187, 188, 190, 192, 193, 194, 195, 197, 201, 202–5, 218–20, 229, 231, 234, 238, 240, 246–47, 250–51, 373, 378, 381.

26. Chevalier, *Politique industrielle*; Musso, *Saint-Simonisme*; M. Drolet, 'Nineteenth-Century Mediterranean Union'; Figeac, 'Géopolitique orientale des saint-simoniens'; Régnier, 'Mythe oriental des Saint-Simoniens'; Levallois and Moussa, *L'Orientalisme des saint-simoniens*; Picon, *Saint-simoniens*, pp. 131–32, 153–62, 289–94.

27. See, for example, Maison d'Auguste Comte manuscripts, D. COM.40: 'Extrait des leçons de Hegel sur la philosophie de l'histoire—Annexe à la lettre de G. d'Eichthal du 18 Nov. 1824'.

28. Comte, *Correspondance*, vol. 1, pp. 78–85, 104–10, 133–38, 140–46, 160–61; Le Bret, *Frères d'Eichthal*, pp. 91–127; Ratcliffe and Chaloner, 'Gustave d'Eichthal'; Pickering, *Auguste Comte*, vol. 1, pp. 258–61, 275–303.

29. Comte to G. d'Eichthal, 23 October 1836, in Comte, *Correspondance*, vol. 1, p. 275.

30. Though his family had converted to Catholicism, d'Eichthal was of Jewish origin. He felt a deep attachment to what he often referred to as 'la race de mes Pères'. He advocated in *Les Deux Mondes* the emancipation of the Jews of the Austrian Empire and allocated to the Jews the role of religious mediators between East and West (with Metternich's Austria as the political mediator). See Peillon, *Jérusalem n'est pas perdue*, pp. 275–82; Le Bret, *Frères d'Eichthal*, pp. 229–47. See also, d'Eichthal, *Trois Grands Peuples méditerranéens*.

31. D'Eichthal, *Deux Mondes* (1836 edition), pp. 3–5.

32. D'Eichthal, *Deux Mondes* (1836 edition), pp. 23–31.

33. Chevalier, *Lettres sur l'Amérique du Nord*, vol. 1, pp. ix–x.

34. The first edition of *Les Deux Mondes* was published as a long introduction to the French translation of David Urquhart's *Turkey and Its Resources* [1833] in 1836. Then d'Eichthal had his long introduction published as a discrete volume in 1837.

35. Chevalier, *Lettres sur l'Amérique du Nord*, vol. 1, p. xiii.

36. Chevalier, *Politique industrielle*, p. 31.

37. Gustave d'Eichthal to Karl August Varnhagen von Ense, 25 January 1837, quoted in Le Bret, *Frères d'Eichthal*, p. 239.

38. Cf. Chevalier, *Lettres sur l'Amérique du Nord*, vol. 1, p. iii.

39. Grandeffe, *L'Empire d'Occident reconstitué*, p. 156.

40. See below, chapter 7.

41. For more on ideas of 'Latinity' in French debates at the time, see Thier, 'View from Paris'.

42. See Mazower, *Greek Revolution*, pp. 326–47; Beaton, 'Philhellenism'; Isabella, *Southern Europe*; Hatzis, *Ο ενδοξότερος αγώνας* (The most glorious struggle).

43. Constant, *Appel aux nations chrétiennes*, pp. 13–15 (emphasis added). See also Carrel, *Résumé de l'histoire des Grecs modernes*.

44. Pradt, *De la Grèce dans ses rapports avec l'Europe*; Pradt, *Parallèle de la puissance anglaise et russe*; Pradt, *L'Europe et l'Amérique en 1822 et 1823*; Pradt, *Vrai Système de l'Europe*; Pradt, *L'Europe par rapport à la Grèce*; Pradt, *Du système permanent de l'Europe*.

45. Osterhammel, *Unfabling the East*, p. 61. See also Bornholdt, 'Abbé de Pradt and the Monroe Doctrine'; Karakatsouli, 'La Guerre d'indépendance grecque'; Barau, 'What Independence for Greece?'. On de Pradt's broader geopolitical ambitions, see also D. Todd, *Velvet Empire*, pp. 33–44, 69–70. On early sources of anxiety about Russia, see Resis, 'Russophobia and the "Testament"'.

46. Pradt, *De la Grèce dans ses rapports avec l'Europe*, p. 25 (emphases added).

47. Pradt, *De la Grèce dans ses rapports avec l'Europe*, pp. 71–74.

48. Pradt, *Du système permanent de l'Europe*, p. viii.

49. Pradt, *Du système permanent de l'Europe*, pp. 29–31.

50. Pradt, *Du système permanent de l'Europe*, pp. 33–34.

51. For a very explicit evocation of a new distinction between Western and Eastern Europe emerging from the outcome of the French Revolution of 1830 (due to France having, as a result of it, become a constitutional monarchy like Britain), see Sirtema de Grovestins, *La Pologne, la Russie et l'Europe Occidentale*, pp. 216–18. For more on Britain, see chapter 3 below.

52. Custine, *Letters from Russia*. For the original, Custine, *La Russie en 1839*; Custine, *Lettres de Russie*.

53. Cadot, *La Russie dans la vie intellectuelle française*, pp. 173–278; Liechtenhan, *Astolphe de Custine*; Milčina, 'La Russie en 1839 du Marquis de Custine'; Platon, 'Astolphe de Custine's *Letters from Russia*'; Kennan, *Marquis de Custine*. The US diplomat George Kennan would ruminate on Custine's thoughts and predictions repeatedly at various stages of the Cold War: Kennan, *Kennan Diaries*, pp. 375, 483.

54. Fallmerayer, 'Marquis de Custine'. See also [Anon.], 'Custine's Rußland'. For reviews in Britain, see below, chapter 3.

55. Figes, *Crimea: The Last Crusade*, pp. 86–88.

56. Fallmerayer, *Geschichte der Halbinsel*.

57. Fallmerayer, 'Marquis de Custine'.

58. Clark, *Revolutionary Spring*.

59. Diezel, *Russia, Germany*, p. 5; in the German original, Diezel, *Rußland, Deutschland*, p. 3.

60. Diezel, *Russia, Germany*, pp. 5–6 / *Rußland, Deutschland*, p. 3.

61. Diezel, *Russia, Germany*, p. 8 / *Rußland, Deutschland*, p. 5.

62. Diezel, *Russia, Germany*, pp. 12–13. See also Diezel, *Deutchland und die abendländische Civilisation*; Diezel, *Die Bildung einer nationalen Partei*; Frantz, *Untersuchungen über das Europäische Gleichgewicht*.

63. Bavaj and Steber, 'Introduction', p. 13.

64. Quoted in Lehne, 'Glittery Fog of Civilization', p. 113.

65. Nietzsche, *Beyond Good and Evil*, p. 138 (aphorism 208). Hugo Drochon has argued that it was the Panjdeh Incident and Russian aggressiveness in Afghanistan in 1885 that led

Nietzsche to such formulations a year later in *Beyond Good and Evil*: Drochon, *Nietzsche's Great Politics*, pp. 2, 18–20, 153–65. On Nietzsche on international politics, see also J.-F. Drolet, *Beyond Tragedy*.

66. Nietzsche, *Beyond Good and Evil*, pp. 187–88 (aphorism 254).
67. Spengler, *Decline of the West*, vol. 1: *Form and Actuality*, p. 30.
68. Nietzsche, *On the Genealogy of Morality*, p. 56.
69. Nietzsche, *Twilight of the Idols*, pp. 65–66.
70. Doering-Manteuffel, 'Perceptions of the West', p. 83.
71. Nietzsche had of course read Comte, and famously agreed with the French thinker that God was 'dead', but levelled the charge against him that, by creating his elaborate Religion of Humanity, and particularly 'with his famous moral formula *vivre pour autrui*', he had 'indeed out-Christianised even Christianity'. See Cameron and Dombowsky, *Political Writings of Friedrich Nietzsche*, p. 123. On Nietzsche and Comte, see Young, *Friedrich Nietzsche*, pp. 242–44.
72. Chaadaev, 'Letters on the Philosophy of History: First Letter', pp. 162–64, 165, 167; Schimmelpenninck van der Oye, 'The East', p. 234. See also Khomiakov, 'On Humboldt'. On Khomiakov's importance, see Walicki, *History of Russian Thought*, pp. 92–96, 102–7; Walicki, *Slavophile Controversy*; Walicki, *Russia, Poland, and Universal Regeneration*, pp. 107–9, 124–26; Christoff, *K. S. Aksakov*, pp. 85–89, 92–94, 99–101, 108–10, 151–53, 155–62, 402–7, 425–32, 436–43. For the pronouncements of another prominent Slavophile in mid-century, see Kireevski, 'On the Nature of European Culture'; and for the views of a prominent Westerniser, Belinski, *Selected Philosophical Works*. See also Chamberlain, *Motherland*; Tolz, 'The West'.
73. [Renieris,] 'Τι είναι η Ελλάς;' ('What is Greece?'). For a brief analysis of Renieris's arguments in 1842 in context, see Varouxakis, 'Idea of "Europe"', pp. 20–23; also, Vallianos, 'Ways of the Nation'. Renieris was soon to cooperate with Gustave d'Eichthal in a campaign to promote the adoption of Greek as the international language. See S. Basch, *Le Mirage grec*, pp. 142–44.
74. [Renieris,] 'Τι είναι η Ελλάς;', pp. 189–90.
75. [Renieris,] 'Τι είναι η Ελλάς;', pp. 206–7.
76. On Koraïs's thought and significance, see Kitromilides, *Enlightenment and Revolution*.
77. [Renieris,] 'Τι είναι η Ελλάς;' pp. 209–10.
78. [Renieris,] 'Τι είναι η Ελλάς;' pp. 212–15.
79. [Renieris,] 'Le Dualisme grec'. For the context and Renieris's significance, see Dimaras [Δημαράς], *Κωνσταντίνος Παπαρρηγόπουλος* (Constantinos Paparrigopoulos), pp. 61, 64–66, 410–13.
80. [Renieris,] 'Le Dualisme grec', p. 34.
81. Toynbee, *Study of History: Abridgement*, vol. 1, p. 15.
82. [Renieris,] 'Le Dualisme grec', pp. 35–37.
83. [Renieris,] 'Le Dualisme grec', pp. 47–48.
84. The reader is then informed that the monument was erected on the initiative of Pierre Laffitte through international subscription. The inauguration of the statue on 18 May 1902 was attended by delegations from many parts of the world, and a senior French minister. (The statue was later moved slightly from its initial location.) See Lepenies, *Auguste Comte*; Wartelle, *L'Héritage d'Auguste Comte*, pp. 177–78.

85. Manuel and Manuel, *Utopian Thought in the Western World*, p. 717. Cf. Hayek, *Counter-Revolution of Science*, pp. 191–206; Schmitt, *Dictatorship*, p. 278 n. 22; Soloviev, 'L'Idée d'humanité chez Auguste Comte'; Nicolas, 'Critique et annexion'.

86. On the global reach of Comte's ideas, see Pickering, 'Conclusion'; also, Feichtinger, Fillafer and Surman, *Worlds of Positivism*.

87. I advanced an initial version of this argument in Varouxakis, 'Godfather of "Occidentality"'. See also Varouxakis, 'When did Britain Join the Occident?'.

88. GoGwilt, *Invention of the West*, p. 220.

89. On the staunch anti-imperialism of Comte's British disciples, see Claeys, *Imperial Sceptics*, pp. 47–123; also, Jones, 'Victorian Lexicon of Evil', pp. 126–43. On some French disciples, see Couderc-Morandeau, *Philosophie républicaine et Colonialisme*, pp. 35–53.

90. See Bourdeau, 'Auguste Comte'.

91. Laffitte, 'Conversations avec A. Comte'. See also Comte, *Correspondance*, vol. 3, pp. 78–86.

92. See, for example, Mill, 'Auguste Comte and Positivism', p. 367.

93. For the unity thesis, see Bourdeau, 'Auguste Comte'; Pickering, *Auguste Comte*, vol. 1, pp. 6, 691; vol. 2, p. 3; Petit, *Système d'Auguste Comte*, p. 269.

94. See Braunstein, *Philosophie de la médecine*, pp. 182–201; Wernick, *Auguste Comte and the Religion of Humanity*.

95. Comte, *Correspondance*, vol. 3, p. 62.

96. See Pickering, *Auguste Comte*, vol. 1, pp. 235–39, 439–43.

97. Comte came up with a dubious etymological connection between the verb *lier* and *religion*.

98. Braunstein, *Philosophie de la médecine*, p. 183.

99. Gilson, *Métamorphoses de la cité de Dieu*, p. 249. The subtitle of Annie Petit's book cited in n. 93 above implies the same idea: *De la science à la religion par la philosophie*.

100. Comte, *System*, vol. 4, p. 27; *Catechism*, pp. 74–77. For Comte's attempt to disseminate his religion, see also Comte, *Catéchisme positiviste*.

101. Comte, *System*, vol. 4, pp. 2, 322–23.

102. Auguste Comte, 'Huitième Circulaire Annuelle' (15 January 1857), in Comte, *Correspondance*, vol. 8, pp. 371–82, 374.

103. Comte, *System*, vol. 1, pp. 56.

104. See Brahami, 'Sortir du cercle'.

105. See, for an early example, Comte, *Early Political Writings*, p. 57.

106. See Bourdeau, *Les Trois États*; Schmaus, 'Reappraisal of Comte's Three-State Law'.

107. Laffitte, 'Conversations avec A. Comte,' p. 12 bis.

108. Comte, *System*, vol. 3, pp. 46–55; vol. 2, pp. 32–324.

109. On 29 April 1848 Comte told Pierre Laffitte that he would use from then onwards, instead of 'pouvoir spirituel', the far preferable 'pouvoir modérateur'. Laffitte, 'Conversations avec A. Comte,' pp. 20–21.

110. Comte, *Early Political Writings*, p. 211.

111. Comte, *Système*, vol. 4, pp. 420–22; *System*, vol. 4, p. 403.

112. Vernon, 'Comte and the Withering-away of the State'. See also Vernon, 'Auguste Comte's Cosmopolis of Care'.

113. Comte, *Système*, vol. 2, pp. 310, 319–20; vol. 4, p. 305.

114. Comte, *Système*, vol. 2, pp. 314–15.

115. Comte, *General View of Positivism*, pp. 88–90, 92–93. For the original, see Comte, *Discours sur l'ensemble du positivisme*.

116. Constantinople had long been seen as the ideal city in terms of uniting East and West, and the Saint-Simonians had focused much upon it. See Barrault, 'Une noce à Constantinople'; d'Eichthal, *Deux Mondes*.

117. Auguste Comte to Czar Nicholas, 20 December 1852, in Comte, *Correspondance*, vol. 6, pp. 451–73, at 467; reprinted in Comte, *Système*, vol. 3, pp. xxix–xlvii, at xlii.

118. Adamovsky, *Euro-Orientalism*, pp. 121, 130–31, 150, 256; Cadot, *La Russie dans la vie intellectuelle française*, pp. 514–16, 545.

119. D. Todd, 'Transnational Projects of Empire in France, c. 1815–c. 1870'. See also D. Todd, *Velvet Empire*. (There is no reference to Comte and his scheme in Todd's excellent article and subsequent book.) For many examples of how Francocentric the 'geopolitics of civilisation' was among French thinkers at the time, see Lochore, *History of the Idea of Civilization*.

120. 'Nationality and Cosmopolit[an]ism', in Mazzini, *Cosmopolitanism of Nations*, pp. 57–62, at p. 59.

121. Niebuhr, 'Irony of American History', p. 513.

122. Comte, *Correspondance*, vol. 1, p. 17.

123. See Rémond, *Les États Unis devant l'opinion française*, vol. 2, p. 495.

124. Comte, *System*, vol. 4, pp. 635–36 (n. 1) (emphasis added); Comte, *Système*, vol. 4, Appendix, p. 202 (n. 1).

125. These works mostly discuss Comte's writings as contributions to thinking on the idea of 'Europe'. See Petit, 'L'Europe positiviste'; Grange, 'La continuité de l'idée de l'Europe'; Braunstein, 'Auguste Comte, l'Europe et l'Occident'. For earlier attention paid to Comte in the context of the idea of 'Europe', see Gladwyn Jebb, *European Idea*, p. 39.

126. Useche Sandoval, 'L'Idée d'Europe'. For a work that charts the transition from *l'Europe* to *l'Occident* in Comte's vocabulary without attempting to situate Comte in the history of ideas of the West, see Tonatiuh Useche Sandoval's doctoral thesis, 'L'Idée d'Occident chez Auguste Comte'. (In his Conclusion Useche Sandoval complains of the absence of Comte from works dedicated to 'l'idée européenne' and says that his thesis was undertaken to make up for that neglect; whereas here I discuss Comte for his formulation of a separate concept of 'the West', rather than for his contribution to 'the European idea'.) See also Useche Sandoval, *L'Idée d'Occident chez Auguste Comte*; Useche Sandoval, 'L'Occident défini par Comte'.

127. Useche Sandoval, 'L'Idée d'Occident', p. 112.

128. Comte to Mill, 20 November 1841, in Comte, *Correspondance*, vol. 2, p. 22.

129. Comte, *Correspondance*, vol. 2, pp. 32, 37, 61.

130. Comte, *Correspondance*, vol. 2, p. 48.

131. Comte, *Correspondance*, vol. 2, pp. 57, 91.

132. Comte to Mill, 30 December 1842, in Comte, *Correspondance*, vol. 2, p. 125 (emphasis added).

133. Comte, *Correspondance*, vol. 2, pp. 142, 158, 203, 210, 248, 330; vol. 3, pp. 240, 244, 299; vol. 4, pp. 4, 8, 38.

134. Comte, *Correspondance*, vol. 4, pp. 20–21, 38.

135. Mill, *Collected Works*, vol. 13, p. 692.

136. Comte to Mill, 21 January 1846, in Comte, *Correspondance*, vol. 3, pp. 298–99 (emphasis added).

137. Saint-Simon, *Œuvres complètes*, vol. 4, pp. 2875–3016 ('Catéchisme des Industriels'), at p. 2974.

138. Comte, *System*, vol. 1, p. 314 (emphasis added.) In the original: 'Entre la simple nationalité, que le génie social de l'antiquité ne dépassa jamais, et l'Humanité définitive, le moyen âge a institué un intermédiaire trop méconnu aujourd'hui, en fondant une libre occidentalité. Notre premier devoir politique consiste maintenant à la reconstruire sur des bases inébranlables, en réparant l'anarchie suscitée par l'extinction du régime catholique et féodal.' Comte, *Système*, vol. 1, pp. 389–90.

139. Comte, *Système*, vol. 1, pp. 389–90.

140. Cf. Lepenies, *Auguste Comte*.

141. Mill, *Collected Works*, vol. 10, p. 366.

142. Jones, 'Introduction' (to Comte, *Early Political Writings*) p. vii. For the authoritative biography of Comte, see Pickering, *Auguste Comte*; also, Simon, *European Positivism in the Nineteenth Century*. On Positivism's impact in France, see Nicolet, *L'Idée républicaine en France*; on Britain, T. R. Wright, *Religion of Humanity*.

143. Forbes, *Positivism in Bengal*; Turnaoğlu, 'Positivist Universalism'; Fedi, *Réception germanique d'Auguste Comte*; Zea, *El positivismo en México*; Zea, *Apogeo y decadencia*; Harp, *Positivist Republic*; Cashdollar, *Transformation of Theology*.

144. Chirio, '1889: "Ordre et progrès" en terres tropicales'; Rohter, *Into the Amazon*, pp. 36–47, 74, 78–79.

145. The articles were then collected in Littré, *Conservation, révolution et positivisme*.

146. Émile Littré, 'République occidentale', *Le National*, 24 September 1849, reprinted in Littré, *Conservation, révolution et positivisme*, pp. 139–48.

147. Laffitte, 'Introduction' (to Richard Congreve's *L'Inde*), pp. xiii–lviii.

148. Laffitte, *Positive Science of Morals*, pp. 196–97; French original: Laffitte, *De la morale positive*, pp. 194–95.

149. Comte, *System*, vol. 4, pp. 635–36 (n. 1).

150. Laffitte, *General View of Chinese Civilization*, pp. iii–vii, 106 n. 1; in the original: Laffitte, *Considérations générales sur l'ensemble de la civilisation Chinoise*, pp. 5–9, 124 n. 1. See also Laffitte, *Grands Types de l'humanité*.

151. See d'Eichthal, *De l'unité européenne*; also d'Eichthal, *L'Italie, la papauté et la confédération européenne*.

152. Trautsch, 'Invention of the "West"', p. 89.

153. Comte, *System*, vol. 3, p. 2; vol. 4, pp. 322–23.

154. Congreve, 'The West', p. 37.

Chapter 3: Insular Britain Joins the West

1. The use of 'the West' to mean something other than their own shifting western frontier came later in the United States, as we will see in chapter 4.

2. Jürgen Fischer, *Oriens–Occidens–Europa*; Schulze Wessel, 'Westen; Okzident'; Bavaj and Steber, *Germany and 'The West'*; Gollwitzer, *Europabild und Europagedanke*; [d'Alembert], 'Occident'; Larousse, *Grand dictionnaire universel*, vol. 11, pp. 1210–11.

3. Dumons, *Un mot à propos de la question d'Orient*; Grandeffe, *L'Empire d'Occident reconstitué*.

4. Nicolet, *La Fabrique d'une nation*, pp. 145–53; see also Bryce, *Holy Roman Empire*, pp. 403–4.

5. Milton, 'Readie & Easie Way', p. 357.

6. A. Smith, 'History of Astronomy', p. 51.

7. Bacon, 'Novum Organum', pp. 186, 187.

8. Hobbes, *Leviathan*, p. 254.

9. Pocock, *Barbarism and Religion*, vol. 2, pp. 72–82, 395–96; Laurens, *Orientales*, pp. 17–19. There were many accounts of Russia in previous centuries, most of them negative. See Liechtenhan, 'La Russie, ennemi héréditaire de la chrétienté?'. For works comparing the periods before and after Peter the Great, see Groh, *Russland und das Selbstverständnis Europas*; M. B. Smith, *Russia Anxiety*, pp. 76–91; M. S. Anderson, *Britain's Discovery of Russia*. Anderson argues that Goldsmith's was one of two isolated exceptions to a generally positive attitude towards Russia at the time.

10. Goldsmith, *Citizen of the World*, vol. 1, pp. 180–85. On Goldsmith, see W. Irving, *Life of Oliver Goldsmith*.

11. Goldsmith, *Citizen of the World*, pp. 103–5 (emphasis added). See also M. S. Anderson, *Britain's Discovery of Russia*, pp. 123–24.

12. Pocock, *Barbarism and Religion*; Pocock, 'Barbarians and the Redefinition of Europe'; Pocock, 'Some Europes in Their History'.

13. Gibbon, *Decline and Fall*, vol. 2, pp. 508–16. The 'General Observations' were written several years before the composition of the third volume to which they were attached: see Pocock, *Barbarism and Religion*, vol. 2, pp. 392–96.

14. Gibbon, *Decline and Fall*, vol. 2, pp. 511–14.

15. Pocock, *Barbarism and Religion*, vol. 2, pp. 396 and 72–82.

16. Ellis, 'Comte's Conception', p. 89.

17. Ellis, 'Comte's Conception', p. 91.

18. K. O'Brien, *Narratives of Enlightenment*, pp. 167–203.

19. Cf. Pocock, 'Some Europes in Their History', pp. 62–67 ('The Enlightened Narrative'). On Edmund Burke's similar emphasis on 'Europe' as a 'commonwealth' or 'community' in the late eighteenth century, see Bourke, *Empire and Revolution*, pp. 911–13.

20. Malcolm, *Useful Enemies*, pp. 59–60; D. Hay, *Europe*.

21. Gollwitzer, 'Zur Wortgeschichte und Sinndeutung von "Europa"'; Burke, 'Did Europe Exist before 1700?'. See also Gollwitzer, *Geschichte des weltpolitischen Denkens*.

22. Schmidt, 'Establishment of "Europe" as a Political Expression'. See also Troost, '"To Restore and Preserve the Liberty of Europe"'; Stock, *Europe and the British Geographical Imagination*, p. 143.

23. Toland, 'To the Lord Mayor, Adelmen, Sherifs, and Common Council of London', p. viii.

24. Buckle, *History of Civilization in England*, passim.

25. See below, section VI.

26. Gielgud, *Memoirs of Prince Adam Czartoryski*, vol. 2, pp. 316–36; Kukiel, *Czartoryski and European Unity*, pp. 193–250; Czartoryski, *Essai sur la diplomatie*; J. H. Gleason, *Genesis of Russophobia*; Ziegler, *Duchess of Dino*.

27. Bitis, *Russia and the Eastern Question*, pp. 465–79; J. H. Gleason, *Genesis of Russophobia*, pp. 135–63.

28. Markovits, *Crimean War*. That by the time of the Crimean War Britain and France were to be referred to as 'the Occidental powers' should not be surprising. See Travers Twiss to Metternich, 1 October 1854, quoted in Fitzmaurice, *King Leopold's Ghostwriter*, p. 208. The unpopularity of Russia was to continue; see Sakowicz, 'Russia and the Russians'.

29. Quoted in Webster, *Foreign Policy of Palmerston*, vol. 1, p. 397.

30. On the first uses of 'the Eastern Question', see Case, *Age of Questions*, pp. 156, 290–91 n. 15; also, Laurens, 'Question d'Orient', pp. 18–20.

31. Kukiel, *Czartoryski and European Unity*, pp. 229–32.

32. Webster, *Foreign Policy of Palmerston*, p. 406.

33. See, e.g., [Rich,] 'History, Present Wrongs, and Claims of Poland', pp. 243, 246, 248, 266, 267, 268; [Urquhart,] 'Quadruple Treaty', pp. 227, 228, 236; Talleyrand, *Memoirs*, vol. 5, pp. 166–311.

34. J. H. Gleason, *Genesis of Russophobia*, pp. 153–57, 164–204, 257–66; Webster, 'Urquhart, Ponsonby, and Palmerston'; Lamb, 'Making of a Russophobe'; Parry, *Promised Lands*, pp. 175–82; Urquhart, *Turkey and Its Resources*; Urquhart, *Spirit of the East*.

35. Urquhart, *Recent Events in the East*, pp. 8, 22, 71, 99, 293.

36. Karl Marx to Ferdinand Lassalle, 1 June 1854, in *Marx and Engels Collected Works*, vol. 39, p. 455.

37. See Avineri, *Karl Marx on Colonialism*; Marx, *Dispatches for the 'New York Tribune'*; Marx and Engels, *Communist Manifesto*.

38. Jones, *Victorian Political Thought*, pp. 44–52, 57–58, 83.

39. Thomas Arnold to the archbishop of Dublin, 22 March 1835, in Stanley, *Life and Correspondence of Thomas Arnold*, vol. 1, p. 418. Cf. 'the ancient western world' (ibid., vol. 2, p. 315).

40. Semmel, *George Eliot*, pp. 117–32.

41. G. Eliot, *Daniel Deronda*, p. 443.

42. G. Eliot, *Daniel Deronda*, p. 445. The question of East and West was widely addressed in Zionist thought as well; see Saposnik, 'Europe and its Orients'.

43. D. A. Logan, *Collected Letters of Harriet Martineau*, vol. 3, p. 154. Martineau mentioned that she wanted to re-read the article for the purposes of her *History*. She duly made use of Milnes's review of Custine's book and of the language of 'Western civilisation' that she found there. See Martineau, *History of England during the Thirty Years' Peace*, vol. 2, pp. 361, 362, 366, 637. For more on Martineau, see D. A. Logan, *Hour and the Woman*.

44. [Milnes,] 'Marquis de Custine's Russia', pp. 369–70.

45. [Milnes,] 'Marquis de Custine's Russia', pp. 378–79 (emphasis added). Given such views on Russia, it is not surprising that later, as Lord Houghton, Milnes became president of the Literary Association of the Friends of Poland. See Gielgud, *Memoirs of Prince Adam Czartoryski*, p. 334.

46. [Murchison,] 'Tour in Russia'.

47. Pope-Hennessy, *Monckton Milnes*, pp. 52–61.

48. From 'The Flowers of Helicon', in Milnes, *Selections from the Works of Lord Houghton*, p. 142. Cf. 'St Mark's at Venice', ibid., p. 163.

49. Stock, *The Shelley-Byron Circle*, pp. 175–97.

50. See [Anon.,] 'German Pamphlet'.

51. Tzschirner, *The Cause of Greece the Cause of Europe* (translated from the German: Tzschirner, *Die Sache der Griechen, die Sache Europas*). On philhellenic agitation 'in the name of Europe', see also Conter, *Jenseits der Nation*, pp. 426–61.

52. Freeman, 'Review of my Opinions', pp. 155–57. Freeman had started by being in favour of the Crimean War against Russia, but during the course of the war he changed his mind. Stephens, *Life and Letters of Edward A. Freeman*, vol. 1, pp. 148–53.

53. Freeman, *History of Sicily*, vol. 1, p. 11; Freeman, *Chief Periods of European History*, pp. 5–6; Freeman, *History and Conquests of the Saracens*. On Freeman, see Morrisroe, '"Eastern History with Western Eyes"'; Morrisroe, '"Sanguinary Amusement"'; W. Kelley, 'Past History and Present Politics'; Koditschek, 'A Liberal Descent?'; Bell, 'Alter Orbis'.

54. Case, *Age of Questions*, p. 155.

55. Freeman, 'Byzantine Empire', p. 232 (emphasis added).

56. Freeman, 'Byzantine Empire', p. 275.

57. Freeman, 'Byzantine Empire', pp. 254–55.

58. On the 'Teutomaniacs', see Mandler, '"Race" and "nation" in Mid-Victorian Thought'; Mandler, *English National Character*.

59. Kingsley, *Roman and the Teuton*, pp. 304–5.

60. [Freeman,] 'Mr. Kingsley's Roman and Teuton', p. 448.

61. Freeman, 'Byzantine Empire', pp. 264–67, 272–73.

62. Freeman, *Ottoman Power in Europe*, pp. 5–7.

63. Stephens, *Life and Letters of Edward A. Freeman*, vol. 2, p. 406.

64. Freeman, 'English People in Its Three Homes'; Freeman, *Ottoman Power in Europe*, p. 8.

65. Freeman's friend Henry Maine also used 'West' and 'Western' more than most contemporaries, already in his bestselling *Ancient Law* (1861); see also Maine, *Village-Communities in East and West*, where his use of 'Western' in the 1870s comes much closer to later meanings: 'The view of land as merchantable property [...] seems to be not only modern but even now distinctly Western. It is most unreservedly accepted in the United States, with little less reserve in England and France, but, as we proceed through Eastern Europe, it fades gradually away, until in Asia it is wholly lost.' Maine, 'Effects of Observation of India', p. 228.

66. Congreve, 'The West'. On Congreve, see Wilson, *Richard Congreve*.

67. Congreve, 'Gibraltar'.

68. See Harrison's letters to Beesly in late 1856: Harrison Papers, box 1/4, 11, 25–35.

69. Harrison Papers, box 1/4, 35. Meanwhile, the author of 'the system' was very pleased with Congreve's *Gibraltar*: Comte, *Correspondance*, vol. 8, pp. 356–58.

70. T. R. Wright, *Religion of Humanity*, pp. 1, 5, 15, 72.

71. Jones, *Victorian Political Thought*, pp. 72–73; Vogeler, *Frederic Harrison*; Varouxakis, '"Patriotism", "Cosmopolitanism" and "Humanity"'. Some of Harrison's (many) contributions are: F. Harrison, 'England and France'; F. Harrison, *Order and Progress*; F. Harrison, *Memories and Thoughts*; F. Harrison, *National and Social Problems*; F. Harrison, *Autobiographic Memoirs*.

72. Seeley, *Expansion of England*; Haight, *Selections from George Eliot's Letters*, pp. 291, 318–19, 325, 331, 333; T. R. Wright, 'George Eliot and Positivism'; Hesse, *George Eliot and Auguste Comte*.

73. Congreve, 'The West', pp. 9–14 (emphasis added).

74. Congreve, 'The West', pp. 17–20. Congreve complained that '[i]n so valuable a book as Heeren's work on the Political State-system of Europe, it is assumed that Germany is the central state; and the idea is popular naturally in Germany, and fostered by certain tendencies in the minds of Englishmen.' Ibid., p. 19. The work Congreve refers to is Heeren, *History of the Political Systems of Europe*.

75. Congreve, 'The West', pp. 35–36.

76. Congreve, 'The West', pp. 44–49.

77. [Anon.,] '[Review of] International Policy'.

78. Mill, *Collected Works*, vol. 13, pp. 538, 561, 703.

79. [Anon.,] '[Review of] International Policy'.

80. Freemantle, 'M. Comte and His Disciples', p. 488.

81. *The Athenæum*, no. 2038 (17 November 1866), p. 642.

82. *The Saturday Review*, 11 August 1866, p. 176.

83. *The Westminster Review*, new series vol. 30, no. 2 (October 1866), pp. 484–85.

84. *The Reader*, 21 July 1866, p. 661.

85. Comte, *Cours*, vol. 2, pp. 694–96; Comte, *Positive Philosophy*, 'freely translated and condensed by Harriet Matrineau', vol. 2, pp. 493–95.

86. Comte, *Discours sur l'ensemble du positivisme*, p. 412; Comte, *Système*, p. 390.

87. Comte, *General View of Positivism*, p. 416 (emphasis added).

88. Heller, 'Russian Dawn,' pp. 47, 49 n. 17.

89. Mayer, 'Marvin, Francis Sydney' (*ODNB*); Desch, 'Francis Sidney Marvin'.

90. Marvin, *Unity of Western Civilization*. The authors of the essays included, besides Marvin, Ernest Barker, L. T. Hobhouse and J. A. Hobson. See also: Marvin, *Century of Hope*; Marvin, *Living Past*; Marvin, *Leadership of the World*.

91. Marvin, *Comte*, pp. 122–61, 187–212.

92. Bonnett, *Idea of the West*, pp. 28–31.

93. MacDonald, *Imperialism*; see also Claeys, *Imperial Sceptics*, p. 199.

94. Crook, *Benjamin Kidd*, pp. 3, 277, 283, 295, 375, 397 n. 84.

95. T. R. Wright, *Religion of Humanity*, pp. 122, 242–43, 246–48, 271.

96. For a brilliant analysis of the importance of Gibbon's personal experiences in continental Europe, see Whatmore, *End of Enlightenment*, pp. 135–60. On Monckton Milnes, see Pope-Hennessy, *Monckton Milnes*, pp. 26–27, 31–33. In the preface to his collection of poems inspired by a visit 'in the Levant and in Egypt in the winter of 1842–43', *Palm Leaves* (1844), two thirds of his references were to German sources, and the one that looms largest was Goethe's *West-oestliches Divan*. He also quotes from a related poem by the German orientalist poet Friedrich Rückert. Lamartine's *Voyage en Orient* is also cited. Uses of 'European' and 'Western' alternate in the text of the preface: Milnes, *Palm Leaves*, pp. viii, ix, xi, xiv, xviii, xx, xxii, xxiii n., xxvii n., xxix, xxx.

97. J. H. Gleason, *Genesis of Russophobia*, p. 153.

98. On Marx, see Stedman Jones, *Karl Marx*; on the strong and multiple connections between Arnold, Freeman and German philologists and historians, Steinberg, *Race, Nation, History*.

99. N. O'Brien, '"Something Older than Law Itself"'; Burrow, *Evolution and Society*, pp. 137–78; Mantena, *Alibis of Empire*, pp. 62–65, 98, 125, 128–29.

100. On Bunsen and Max Müller's central role regarding the 'Aryan idea' in Britain, see C. Kidd, *Forging of Races*, pp. 177, 181–85; on Freeman's 'comparative method', Freeman, *Comparative Politics*; Freeman, *Methods of Historical Study*. Besides George Eliot's immersion in Comte, her German influences (and translations) were crucial. See Ashton, *German Idea*, pp. 147–77.

Chapter 4: *Ex Germaniae lux?*

1. See Schulte Nordholt, *Myth of the West*; Baritz, 'Idea of the West'.
2. Ross, 'Historical Consciousness in Nineteenth-Century America', pp. 912, 913. For succinct analyses of the factors making for the set of ideas referred to as 'American exceptionalism', see also Ross, *Origins of American Social Science*, pp. 22–49; Pocock, *Machiavellian Moment*, pp. 506–52; Greenfeld, *Nationalism*, pp. 399–484; Kohn, *American Nationalism*; Weinberg, *Manifest Destiny*; Curti, *Roots of American Loyalty*. For a typical example of nineteenth-century works representing the message of westward progress, see Magoon, *Westward Empire*.
3. F. J. Turner, 'Problem of the West'.
4. Whitman, 'Democratic Vistas' p. 929.
5. 'West, The', *Encyclopædia Britannica* (1929), vol. 23, p. 521.
6. Though it is very rare, it is not impossible to find an American using, in the late eighteenth century, distinctions between 'the East' and 'West', and explicit juxtapositions between 'the Eastern & Western World', or references to 'the inferiority of the Eastern to the Western World'. See Watrous, *John Ledyard's Journey*, pp. 209–11, 223–25, 228–29. But all these were used interchangeably with juxtapositions between 'Asiatic & European manners', as well as references to the American author himself as a European (pp. 224–25). John Ledyard had spent many years as a sailor and traveller (including with Captain Cook); he cannot at all be seen as a typical American. (Besides its other strikingly idiosyncratic traits, his text is replete with French words and phrases). The very question, 'What is an American?' had only relatively recently been asked explicitly. See Crèvecoeur, 'Letters from an American Farmer', pp. 28–64 (Letter 3: 'What is an American?'). See also Schulte Nordholt, *Myth of the West*, pp. 111–12; Curti, *Roots of American Loyalty*, pp. 70–71. For more on Ledyard, see Wolff, *Inventing Eastern Europe*, pp. 343–55.
7. See Levine, *Allies and Rivals*; Diehl, *Americans and German Scholarship*; Diehl, 'Innocents Abroad'; Pochmann, *German Culture in America*; Tatlock and Erlin, *German Culture in Nineteenth-Century America*; Long, *Literary Pioneers*; Brooks, *Flowering of New England*, pp. 73–88; Mueller-Vollmer, *Transatlantic Crossings*.
8. Emerson, 'Anglo-American', p. 347.
9. Spencer, *Quest for Nationality*, p. 90. For a succinct analysis of the reasons that 'promoted this long-growing interest in German culture' after the War of 1812 in particular, see Curti, *Growth of American Thought*, pp. 242–44 and passim. The trend continued for the rest of the nineteenth century. One of the many Americans attracted to graduate study in Germany was W.E.B. Du Bois, in the early 1890s. The number of American classicists who studied in Göttingen and other German universities is impressive. See Winterer, *Culture of Classicism*, pp. 61, 152, 154–55 and passim.

10. [Bancroft,] 'Writings of Herder', p. 139. See also Mueller-Vollmer, *Transatlantic Crossings*, pp. 103–22.

11. Bancroft, 'Russia'.

12. Referring to the end of the eighteenth century, a recent historian of the Enlightenment wrote, 'The University of Göttingen was at this period the leading university in Europe.' Robertson, *Enlightenment*, p. 562. See also Shumway, 'American Students'.

13. Nye, *George Bancroft*, pp. 33–59; Long, *Literary Pioneers*, pp. 108–58; Howe, *Life and Letters of George Bancroft*, vol. 1, pp. 34–154.

14. Fred L. Burwick claimed that the review was written by Bancroft, anonymously reviewing his own translation: Burwick, 'Göttingen Influence'. This is incorrect, however: on 25 March 1824 the then–editor of the *North American Review*, Jared Sparks, wrote to Bancroft asking him to review a (different) book, and concluded, 'P.S. Prof. Everett has written a review of Heeren, which is printed.' See Bassett, *Correspondence of George Bancroft and Jared Sparks*, p. 76.

15. Obviously, Everett was referring to the Americas.

16. [Edward Everett,] '[Review of] *Reflections on the Politics of Ancient Greece*', pp. 393–94.

17. See Ross, *Origins of American Social Science*, pp. 37–42, 49–50, 64, 66–69, 85, 279–80; Adcock, *Liberalism and the Emergence*, pp. 1 (n. 2), 11–12, 67–102, 105–15, 139–41 and passim.

18. *Encyclopaedia Americana*. See also Freidel, *Francis Lieber*, p. 77; Weiss, 'Americanization of Franz Lieber'; De Kay, 'Encyclopedia Americana, First Edition'; Mueller-Vollmer, *Transatlantic Crossings*, pp. 227–43.

19. Pochmann, *German Culture in America*, pp. 125–27.

20. Freidel, *Francis Lieber*, p. 77. That the *Americana* 'certainly is much more than a translation or even adaptation of the German *Conversations-Lexicon*' is also affirmed in Weiss, 'Americanization of Franz Lieber', p. 282.

21. *Encyclopaedia Americana*, vol. 13, pp. 238–40, at p. 238. The quoted passage seems to have been confusingly associated with modern Greek developments in the recent work of a historian who writes that '[t]he Greek independence movement popularized "western civilization"': the assertion is unsubstantiated other than by misrepresented evidence from *Encyclopaedia Americana* that follows. We are told that 'Greece's transit into the West among American audiences was suggested by an encyclopaedia article of 1833, which described women in Greece, because they were "situated on the borders of Asia, then [. . .] qualities of Western civilization"'. (Roberts, 'Lajos Kossuth', pp. 798–99 and 799 n. 26, citing '*Encyclopaedia Americana*, ed. Francis Lieber, 13 vols. (Philadelphia, 1833), vol. 13, 238'). However, the article in question had nothing to do with modern Greece, and was referring to women's status in the ancient world. Roberts is in good company. Anachronistic projections were well established already in the early twentieth century, not least in the work of a scholar who was explicit about how much he resented the—pro-Greek, in his view—biases of American foreign policy in his own time, and what he saw as their causes: see Earle, 'American Interest in the Greek Cause'. However, the vociferous supporters of the Greeks in the United States did not invoke 'Western civilization' in their arguments. They were keen to stress that 'an *enlightened, free and Christian* nation like the people of the United States' was bound to 'take a deep interest in the present eventful struggle of that race of men who have been the Parents of Civilization and the Instructors of the rest of mankind in Letters and Arts—in the principles of Civil Liberty and the precepts of our Holy

Religion'. The sympathy was said to be shared 'with all the really civilized part of mankind'. The widely circulated declarations of the American philhellenes stated that they were resolved *as men, as republicans, as Christians*, no longer to remain inactive and apparently unconcerned spectators of a contest in which the interests of freedom, of knowledge and religion are so deeply involved. [...] It is to us *in common with other Christian nations* that the Greeks have looked for assistance.' For the Greeks presented 'the spectacle of a civilized and Christian people oppressed by the vengeance of barbarians, and persecuted by the bigotry of infidels'. See Cline, *American Attitude*, pp. 42–48 (emphases added). Meanwhile, it is worth noting that, in the context of what was by far the most significant contribution to American philhellenic agitation, in the hegemonic *North American Review*, its editor, Edward Everett, the most influential voice in American philhellenism (who was, moreover, the first professor of Greek literature at Harvard) did not merely avoid invocation of 'the classical debt' (later implied by Earle and many others to be a reason for the support of the Greeks that Everett was advocating), but specifically (if rhetorically astutely) drew attention to that forbearance: 'In the few remarks, which we have taken the liberty to make on this occasion, we have not insisted on the topic of the glorious descent of the Greeks; of the duty of hastening to the succor of those whose fathers were the masters of the world, in the school of civilization.' That was not because he was 'not sensible to the power of this appeal', but rather because he thought 'a much stronger appeal may be made'. Everett believed that the Greeks had 'more imperious claims upon us' than any that might derive from such associations: there was 'enough without these [ancient] names to awaken sympathy'. [Everett,] '[Review of] *The Ethics of Aristotle to Nicomachus*', pp. 421–22 (emphases added). On the phrase 'classical debt', see Hanink, *Classical Debt*. All in all, it cannot be said that the unprecedented agitation that took place in America in support of the Greek Revolution in the 1820s was instigated in the name of 'the West' or 'Western civilization' (*pace* Earle, Roberts and many others in between). Rather, the rhetoric used evoked *one*, undifferentiated, 'civilization', to which either the Greeks' ancestors were cited as major contributors (by many, though not by Everett), or towards which the (modern) Greeks were praised for making great and rapid strides (Everett's main argument). The fact that the Greeks were Christians was furthermore usually adduced as an argument in favour of supporting them.

22. [Lieber,] 'Turkey', p. 296.

23. Lieber, *Essays on Property and Labour*, pp. 18–19, 22–23 (cf. p. 94), 192–93 (emphases added). A recent work that seems to confound references by eighteenth-century American authors to 'the western world', in the geographical sense of the Western hemisphere, with allusion to a civilisational 'West' is Mac Sweeney, *The West* (pp. 239–41). The quotations adduced in fact refer to America simply as an area of the globe distinct from Europe, and not to anglophone America as 'the culmination of Western Civilisation' (ibid., p. 243) in the late eighteenth century. When Mac Sweeney quotes Benjamin Franklin in 1768 accusing the British 'of mistreating "us in the West"', or claiming, the following year, 'that the British were crushing liberty, or in any case "the first Appearance of it in the Western World"'; or George Washington writing about his concern for 'matters in the western world'; or John Hancock 'proudly stat[ing] that he looked forward to a time when there would be be liberty "in the western world"'; or a correspondent writing to John Adams that 'were it not for the efforts of men such as him, freedom "would long ere this have been banished from the western hemisphere"'; or a general writing to George

Washington wishing success 'in his work of "ensuring Freedom to the Western World"' (ibid., p. 240); or the lyrics of a song of the 1770s (Joseph Warren's 'Free America') that runs, 'beneath this western Sky / We form'd a new Dominion, a Land of Liberty'—these quotations do not prove any aim to 'embrace the idea of North America as constituting "the West"' (ibid.) in the sense of a sociopolitical concept of a West including America and Europe. They were obvious locative statements, as the Americans lived in the Western hemisphere and were claiming liberation from rule by people in the Old World to the east. The same applies to the quotation from Joseph Warren (1775) that serves as epigraph for the book's tenth chapter: 'Approving heaven beheld the favourite ark dancing upon the waves, and graciously preserved it until the chosen families were brought in safety to these western regions' (ibid., p. 223). Such talk of America as 'the western world' or 'western regions' is a matter of common-sense geography. Talk of America as succeeding or surpassing Europe in being the most free or enlightened country on earth, meanwhile, is an instance of the idea of *translatio imperii*, but does not mark the emergence in eighteenth-century America of the term 'the West' meaning what Mac Sweeney claims it does. Those who used it in this way were not referring to a West shared with Europe. They were leaving the Old World behind and building a new one, superseding Europe. And as this section and the next section will show, that was not what Francis Lieber, in the nineteenth century, was to mean by 'the Western World'.

24. Lieber to G. S. Hillard, April 1850, in T. S. Perry, *Life and Letters of Francis Lieber*, pp. 245–46.

25. Lieber to Charles Sumner, 22 February 1851, in T. S. Perry, *Life and Letters of Francis Lieber*, p. 249.

26. Lieber, *On Civil Liberty* (1853), pp. 30–31 (n. 4) (emphasis added).

27. Lieber, *On Civil Liberty* (2nd edition, 1859), p. 22 n. 2.

28. For one example among many, see Lieber, 'Latin Race', pp. 308–9.

29. Lieber, 'History and Uses of Athenæums', p. 299 and note.

30. Lieber, 'Nationalism and Internationalism', pp. 240–41 (emphasis added).

31. Lieber, 'History and Political Science Necessary Studies', p. 366, n. 1. It seems to me that a commentator is wrong to assert that, for Lieber, '[a] race was therefore largely synonymous with a nation' (Clinton, *Tocqueville, Lieber, and Bagehot*, pp. 48–49). As I hope the analysis above shows, Lieber was, like his contemporaries, using the term 'race' rather promiscuously, to refer to all sorts of groups. The Cis-Caucasian or Western Caucasian 'race' was composed of several 'advanced' and 'polished' nations, rather than being 'synonymous with a nation'.

32. Nor had the process to stop with what he called 'Cis-Caucasian' nations; for he added, 'And who will say that the time cannot arrive when that broad sea of history, as we just called it, this commonwealth of active and polished nations, shall extend over the face of our planet'. Lieber, 'Origin and Development', pp. 214–15.

33. Lieber to Privy-Councillor Mittermaier, 26 August 1867, in T. S.Perry, *Life and Letters of Francis Lieber*, p. 373; Lieber to Charles Sumner, 9 April 1867, in ibid., p. 371.

34. Lieber, 'Nationalism and Internationalism' p. 222.

35. Lieber to Judge Thayer, 22 July 1870, in T. S. Perry, *Life and Letters of Francis Lieber*, p. 397.

36. See Reclus, 'Progress', pp. 235–36; also Reclus, 'East and West'. On Reclus, see Siegrist, 'Cosmopolis and Community'; Ferretti, 'L'Occidente di Élisée Reclus'.

37. Lieber, 'Nationalism and Internationalism', pp. 222–23.

38. Armstrong, *E. L. Godkin*, pp. 116–17.
39. Lieber, 'Nationalism and Internationalism' pp. 242–43.
40. Herring, *From Colony to Superpower*, pp. 212–13; Hopkins, *American Empire*, pp. 237–38.
41. [Anon.,] 'Orientalism', pp. 487, 494.
42. [Anon.,] 'Orientalism', pp. 483, 484, 487.
43. [Anon.,] 'Orientalism', p. 494.
44. For Locke's importance in arguments for empire, see Armitage, *Foundations*, pp. 75–131; Armitage, *Ideological Origins*.
45. [Anon.,] 'Orientalism', pp. 494–95.
46. For the way in which what came to be known as the 'hitchhiking imperialism' of the US in China actually unfolded, see Herring, *From Colony to Superpower*, pp. 209–12.
47. [Anon.] 'Orientalism', p. 495.
48. Herring, *From Colony to Superpower*, p. 214.
49. L. H. Fischer, *Lincoln's Gadfly*, p. 271; Walicki, 'Adam Gurowski'; Walicki, *Russia, Poland, and Universal Regeneration*; Głębocki, *Disastrous Matter*, pp. 86, 195–96. On Gurowski's views on America's differences from Europe see: Gurowski, *America and Europe*.
50. L. H. Fischer, *Lincoln's Gadfly*, pp. 43–44, 271.
51. L. H. Fischer, *Lincoln's Gadfly*, pp. 45, 44, 56–57.
52. Gurowski, *Russia As It Is*; Gurowski, *Turkish Question*; Gurowski, *A Year of the War*. See also Golder, 'Russian–American Relations'; L. H. Fischer, *Lincoln's Gadfly*, pp. 58–66.
53. Gurowski, *Russia As It Is*, pp. x, xi–xii.
54. L. H. Fischer, *Lincoln's Gadfly*, pp. 65–67.
55. Gurowski, *Turkish Question*, pp. 8, 10. See also Walicki, 'Adam Gurowski', pp. 19–20.
56. See Marx and Engels, *Russian Menace to Europe*, pp. 247–51. For a translation of the two original Engels articles (before they were fatally interfered with by Gurowski), as they were published a couple of weeks earlier in a German newspaper, see ibid., pp. 84–90.
57. Marx and Engels, *Russian Menace to Europe*, p. 249.
58. L. H. Fischer, *Lincoln's Gadfly*, p. 63.
59. Francis Lieber to G. S. Hillard, 21 January 1855, in T. S. Perry, *Life and Letters of Francis Lieber*, p. 278.
60. Armstrong, *E. L. Godkin*, pp. 17–34, 37–53.
61. Godkin, 'Eastern Question' p. 109; see also pp. 115, 116, 117, 121, 122. For an example of positive comments on Russia and Russian–American relations (and a rebuttal of complaints in the British press against that American attitude) in 1864, see Everett, 'Russia and the United States'.
62. Wheeler, 'Greece and the Eastern Question', pp. 722–23.
63. Wheeler, 'Greece and the Eastern Question', pp. 723, 725, 726.
64. Wheeler, 'Greece and the Eastern Question', pp. 728–29.
65. See below, section VII.
66. Wheeler, 'Greece and the Eastern Question,' p. 731.
67. Wheeler, 'Greece and the Eastern Question', pp. 732, 733.
68. Wheeler, 'Modern Greek as a Fighting Man'; Wheeler, *Old World and the New*; Wheeler, *Alexander the Great*.

69. Pugach, 'Making the Open Door Work'.

70. See Fairbank and Goldman: *China*, pp. 230–34; Iriye, *From Nationalism to Internationalism*, pp. 168–71.

71. Reinsch, *World Politics*, pp. 236–38.

72. Reinsch, *World Politics*, pp. 238–39 (emphasis added).

73. Reinsch, *World Politics*, p. 240.

74. Reinsch, *World Politics*, p. 241.

75. Reinsch, *World Politics*, pp. 241–42.

76. On Vivekananda's thought, see Sharma, *Hindutva*, pp. 70–123. For Vivekananda's activities and influence in America and Europe during the previous decade, see Harris, *Guru to the World*; on Theosophy, Burrow, *Crisis of Reason*, pp. 221, 226–29.

77. Reinsch, *World Politics*, pp. 242–43.

78. Reinsch, *World Politics*, pp. 243–45.

79. Reinsch, *World Politics*, pp. 66–67, 211–14, 221–22. See also Reinsch, *Intellectual and Political Currents*.

80. For another example, see Foulke, *Slav or Saxon*. For examples of anxiety about Russia in American and British novels at the same time, see Bell, *Dreamworlds of Race*, pp. 211, 213, 215, 237–38.

81. H. Harrison, 'Russian Menace' (*New York Times*, 4 January 1904).

82. J. B. Perry, *Hubert Harrison*, pp. 66–67.

83. For a hypothesis, see J. B. Perry, *Hubert Harrison*, pp. 66–67. For Harrison's later book see H. H. Harrison, *When Africa Awakes*.

84. Du Bois, 'Color Line Belts of the World'.

85. Basbanes, *Cross of Snow*, pp. 256–58. For a discussion of the goal to establish a 'national literature' during this period, with close attention given to Longfellow's *Kavanagh*, see Frederick, 'American Literary Nationalism'.

86. Longfellow, *Kavanagh*, pp. 115, 117–18.

87. Wells et al., *The Reason Why*.

88. See Moses, *Alexander Crummell*; Moses, *Golden Age*, pp. 59–82; Moses, *Creative Conflict*.

89. Moses, *Golden Age*, pp. 76–77. See also Crummell, *Destiny and Race*.

90. Crummell, 'Destined Superiority of the Negro', pp. 343, 345, 346, 347.

91. Moses, *Golden Age*, pp. 76–78.

92. Ferris, *African Abroad*.

93. On the fascinating story of Frobenius's contribution to the change in the intellectual climate, see Marchand, 'Leo Frobenius'.

94. Moses, *Afrotopia*, pp. 185–86.

95. The work Ferris referred to in particular was the translated fourth volume of Heeren's *Historical Researches into the Politics, Intercourse, and Trade of the Principal Nations of Antiquity*, entitled *African Nations: Carthaginians. Ethiopians* (Oxford: D. A. Talboys, 1833). For the significance of Heeren and Göttingen 'universal history', see the brilliant recent analysis in Marchand, 'Herodotus and the Embarrassments', pp. 317–27.

96. Ferris, *African Abroad*, vol. 1, pp. 491–92 (emphasis added).

97. Moses, *Afrotopia*, p. 189.

98. See chapter 12 ('Of Alexander Crummell') in Du Bois, *Souls of Black Folk* (pp. 512–20).
99. For a recent appraisal, see Withun, *Co-workers*. See also Cook and Tatum, *African American Writers*.
100. Du Bois, 'Spirit of Modern Europe'.
101. Du Bois, 'Spirit of Modern Europe', pp. 50, 51, 56, 58.
102. Du Bois, 'Spirit of Modern Europe', pp. 59–60, 60–61 (emphasis added).
103. Du Bois, 'Spirit of Modern Europe', pp. 50, 62, 63–64 (emphasis added).
104. Du Bois, *Dusk of Dawn*, p. 555.
105. Du Bois, 'Ghana Calls'.
106. J. Turner, *Liberal Education of Charles Eliot Norton*, pp. 368–92; quotation at p. 384.
107. H. D. Croly, *Promise of American Life*.
108. See Harp, *Positivist Republic*, pp. 183–209; Stettner, *Shaping Modern Liberalism*, pp. 14–21. Croly's father had also written an interesting book: D. G. Croly, *Glimpses of the Future*.
109. For such examples, besides Wheeler's articles in the 1890s, see, among others, Fiske, *American Political Ideals*. For more cases, without particular reference to 'Occidentalism' or 'the West', but with a focus on projects or novels emphasising Anglo-American unity, see Bell, *Dreamworlds of Race*.

Chapter 5: The War of Words

1. For an analysis, see Ungern-Sternberg and Ungern-Sternberg, *Der Aufruf*; for the original 'Aufruf "An die Kulturwelt!"', ibid., pp. 156–60 (at p. 160 for the statement translated in the heading of this section: 'Glaubt, dass wir diesen Kampf zu Ende kämpfen werden als ein Kulturvolk'). For the French version, 'Au monde civilisé!', the first English version, 'To the Civilized World!' and the amended English version, see ibid., pp. 161–64.
2. 'To the Civilized World', reproduced in Chapman, *Deutschland Über Alles*, pp. 37–42.
3. Marchand, *German Orientalism*, p. 437.
4. Rudolf Eucken and Ernst Haeckel, Jena, 31 August 1914: 'GERMANY'S CULTURE: Philosophers Eucken and Haeckel Appeal to American Scholars: To the Universities of America', quoted in Chapman, *Deutschland Über Alles*, p. 51.
5. Rolland, 'Lesser of Two Evils', p. 57 (emphasis added).
6. Kohn, *Mind of Germany*, pp. 297–98; Casteel, *Russia in the German Global Imaginary*, pp. 77–81.
7. Scheler, *Der Genius des Krieges*, p. 185. See also Scheler, 'Europa und der Krieg'.
8. Scheler was to change his tune after the first months of the war and start blaming the mistrust in international relations before 1914 for the outbreak of war: see Harrington, *German Cosmopolitan Social Thought*, pp. 152–56.
9. Sombart, *Händler und Helden*. Sombart's anti-Western rhetoric is noted in Buruma and Margalit, *Occidentalism*, pp. 52–53.
10. Kohn, *Mind of Germany*, pp. 298–301.
11. 'To the Civilized World', quoted in Chapman, *Deutschland Über Alles*, p. 39.
12. Hanna, *Mobilization of Intellect*, p. 88. On the 'Controversy over Kant' in France, see ibid., pp. 106–41. See also V. Basch, 'La Philosophie et la Literature classiques'.

13. Hoeres, *Krieg der Philosophen*; Dewey, *German Philosophy and Politics*. See also Westbrook, *John Dewey and American Democracy*, pp. 195–227; Campbell, 'Dewey and German Philosophy'; Ryan, *John Dewey*; Cywar, 'John Dewey in World War I'; Farrell, 'John Dewey in World War I'; Kaplan, 'Social Engineers as Saviors'. For a critical response to such attribution of the war exclusively to German *Kultur*, see Bourne, 'American Use for German Ideals'.

14. Boutroux, 'L'Allemagne et la guerre: Lettre', pp. 387–88, 391–92, 389–90, 393–94.

15. Boutroux, 'L'Allemagne et la guerre: Lettre', pp. 399–401.

16. Boutroux, 'L'Allemagne et la guerre: Deuxième Lettre', p. 254; also pp. 248–49. On Barrès, see Brown, *Embrace of Unreason*, p. 22. See also V. Basch, 'La Philosophie et la Literature classiques'.

17. Bergson, *Signification de la guerre*, p. 15; Hanna, *Mobilization of Intellect*, pp. 91–92. Bergson came to be perceived as promoting a retrograde spiritualism contemptuous of science and reason: Pilkington, *Bergson and His Influence*, p. 207.

18. Walter Lippmann to Oliver Wendell Holmes, Jr., 21 February 1917, in Blum, *Public Philosopher*, pp. 62–63.

19. Élie Halévy to Xavier Léon, 19 October 1915, in Halévy, *Correspondance*, p. 500.

20. Suarès, *Occident*, p. 84.

21. See, for instance, 'Britain's Destiny and Duty. Declaration by Authors', *The Times*, 18 September 1914, p. 4. For more examples, see Hoeres, *Krieg der Philosophen*.

22. Marvin, *Unity of Western Civilization*, pp. 3, 4.

23. Hovey, *John Jay Chapman*, p. 223.

24. Chapman, *Deutschland Über Alles*, p. 89.

25. Howe, *John Jay Chapman*, pp. 278–79, 282–83.

26. Hovey, *John Jay Chapman*, pp. 221–22.

27. Thompson, *Reformers and War*, pp. 123–27.

28. Bergmann, 'American Exceptionalism'.

29. Quoted in Hovey, *John Jay Chapman*, p. 227 (emphasis added).

30. Chapman, 'Ode'.

31. Thompson, *Reformers and War*, p. 85.

32. See May, *End of American Innocence*, pp. 376–67; Temkin, 'Culture vs. *Kultur*', p. 169.

33. Thompson, *Reformers and War*, pp. 85–86. See also Gruber, *Mars and Minerva*.

34. *The New Republic*, 4 (9 October 1915; emphasis added), p. 245. See also Thompson, *Reformers and War*, p. 87.

35. [H. Croly,] 'End of American Isolation'. On Croly, his staff and *The New Republic* during the war, see Levy, *Herbert Croly of the New Republic*, pp. 218–62; Stettner, *Shaping Modern Liberalism*; Goldman, *Rendezvous with Destiny*, pp. 180–201; Lasch, 'The *New Republic* and the War'.

36. Schlesinger, 'Walter Lippmann', p. 126.

37. For just one example, see Audier, *Le Colloque Walter Lippmann*.

38. Runciman, *Confidence Trap*, p. 130.

39. On the concept of *Großraumordnung* (an order predicated on large spaces) rather later in Carl Schmitt's thought, see Hooker, *Carl Schmitt's International Thought*, pp. 126–55.

40. On the emergence of the 'Western Civ' course, see Allardyce, 'Rise and Fall'.

41. Lippmann, *Stakes of Diplomacy*, pp. 173–74.

42. Lippmann, *Stakes of Diplomacy*, pp. 175–77 (emphases added).

43. Lippmann, 'What Program', pp. 64–65.

44. Lippmann, 'What Program' pp. 66, 69.

45. Steel, *Walter Lippmann*, pp. 97, 339. On Mahan's theories, see Mahan, *Interest of America*; Westcott, *Mahan on Naval Warfare*.

46. Lippmann, 'What Program', p. 70.

47. Steel, *Walter Lippmann*, p. 111.

48. Lippmann, 'Defense of the Atlantic World', pp. 71, 72, 73 (emphases added).

49. Lippmann, 'Defense of the Atlantic World', pp. 73, 74, 75 (emphases added). The emphasis on 'liberalism' here shows Lippmann as a pioneer of the 'Liberalism' that was to emerge in the interwar period. See Bell, 'What Is Liberalism?'.

50. May, *End of American Innocence*, p. 364.

51. Adas, *Machines as the Measure of Men*, pp. 345–401; Adas, 'Contested Hegemony'; Moses, *Golden Age*, pp. 249–50.

52. Sen, 'Tagore and His India', p. 60.

53. S. N. Hay, 'Rabindranath Tagore in America'; S. N. Hay, *Asian Ideas of East and West*; Tagore, *'American Experience' & Other Articles*.

54. S. N. Hay, *Asian Ideas of East and West*, pp. 52–123; Aydin, *Politics of Anti-Westernism*, p. 121.

55. Tagore, *Nationalism*, pp. 1, 4, 5–6.

56. Tagore, *Nationalism*, pp. 8–9.

57. Gandhi, *'Hind Swaraj' and Other Writings*, pp. 60–63. For the deeper sources of Gandhi's thought, see Sharma, *Elusive Non-Violence*.

58. Tagore, *Nationalism*, pp. 12–14.

59. Tagore, *Nationalism*, pp. 28–31.

60. Tagore, *Nationalism*, p. 31.

61. Tagore, *Nationalism*, pp. 43, 46, 47, 50, 56.

62. Tagore, *Nationalism*, p. 71. See also Tagore, 'Nationalism in the West'.

63. Locke, 'Great Disillusionment'.

64. Locke, 'Great Disillusionment', pp. 106–7 (emphasis added).

65. For examples, see Chapman, *Deutschland Über Alles*, pp. 39, 47, 50, 60, 65–66, 72–73. One is an address delivered at a German–American meeting held in Berlin City Hall on 11 August 1914 (at a time Locke was in Berlin) by the general director of the Royal Library of Berlin, Professor Adolph von Harnack, who referred to the Russians as 'the Byzantine—I have to go back far—the Mongolian-Moscovite civilization'. Ibid., p. 72.

66. Stewart, *New Negro*, pp. 253–57.

67. Stewart, *New Negro*, p. 261.

68. In the 1900 lecture that we discussed in chapter 4, Du Bois said, 'No nation has treated subject peoples—black, white or yellow—with half the justice that England has.' Du Bois, 'Spirit of Modern Europe', p. 59.

69. Du Bois, 'World War and the Color Line' pp. 28–29.

70. Du Bois, 'African Roots of War' p.32. For the significance of this article, see the analysis in Getachew and Pitts, 'Democracy and Empire'.

71. Du Bois, 'Battle of Europe'.

72. Du Bois, 'Tagore'.
73. Du Bois, 'Close Ranks'.
74. For that fascinating story, see Williams, *Wounded World*.
75. See Hochschild, *American Midnight*.
76. Fauset, 'Negro on East St. Louis' (emphasis added). On Fauset, see Sylvander, *Jessie Redmon Fauset*.
77. Du Bois, 'Vive la France!'.
78. [Du Bois,] 'Returning Soldiers'. See also D. L. Lewis, *W.E.B. Du Bois*, pp. 368–82.
79. Du Bois, 'French and Spanish' (emphasis added). The highlighting of the very different way in which Black soldiers and Black people generally were treated in France (as compared to America) would continue during the 1920s and beyond. Among many examples, see Fauset, 'Impressions of the Second Pan-African Congress'; Locke, 'Black Watch on the Rhine'.
80. Moses, *Golden Age*, pp. 249–50.
81. Rolland, 'Pro Aris', p. 28 n. 1.
82. T. Mann, 'Thoughts in Wartime', pp. 493–95.
83. T. Mann, 'Thoughts in Wartime', pp. 498, 499.
84. T. Mann, 'Thoughts in Wartime', pp. 500, 503.
85. T. Mann, 'Thoughts in Wartime', pp. 505, 506. For the original, see Mann, 'Gedanken im Kriege'.
86. Thomas Mann to Peter Pringsheim, 10 October 1916, in T. Mann, *Letters of Thomas Mann*, p. 76 (emphasis added).
87. T. Mann, *Betrachtungen eines Unpolitischen*; T. Mann, 'Reflections'.
88. Kohn, *Mind of Germany*, p. 254.
89. For the translation 'literary prophet of civilization', see Lepenies, *Seduction of Culture*, p. 215 n. 7.
90. See Lilla, 'Introduction' (to T. Mann, *Reflections of a Nonpolitical Man*), pp. vii–xxi; Lepenies, *Seduction of Culture*, pp. 27–35.
91. T. Mann, 'Reflections', pp. 33–38.
92. Dostoievsky, *Diary of a Writer*, pp. 726–31.
93. T. Mann, 'Reflections', p. 33.
94. T. Mann, 'Reflections', p. 38 (emphasis added); Mann, *Betrachtungen*, pp. 7–8.
95. T. Mann, 'Reflections', pp. 38, 41, 42.
96. Thomas Mann to Gustav Blume, 5 July 1919, in Mann, *Letters of Thomas Mann*, pp. 90–91 (emphases added); for the original, Mann, *Briefe 1889–1936*, pp. 165–66.
97. See T. Mann, *Thomas Mann Diaries*, p. 61 (entry for 2 July 1919).

Chapter 6: From 'Decline of the West' to 'Defence of the West'

1. For details on the 'grand narrative', see McNeill, 'What We Mean by the West'; Gress, *From Plato to NATO*, pp. 29–48.
2. McNeill, 'What We Mean by the West', p. 520.
3. Toynbee, *Western Question*, p. 4. More will be said on Toynbee in chapter 8 below.
4. Toynbee, *Study of History: Abridgement*, vol. 1, p. 11.
5. Toynbee, *Civilization on Trial*, pp. 9–10.

6. Hughes, *Oswald Spengler*, p. 97. For some details on the biographical context of the composition of the book, see B. Lewis, *Oswald Spengler*, pp. 6–15.

7. Spengler, *Decline of the West*, vol. 1, p. 3.

8. Spengler, *Decline of the West*, vol. 1, pp. 7, 15.

9. On the importance of Joachim of Fiore, see Lubac, *La Postérité spirituelle de Joachim de Flore*.

10. Spengler, *Decline of the West*, vol. 1, pp. 19–20.

11. Spengler, *Decline of the West*, vol. 1, pp. 21, 23.

12. Homer, Heraclitus and Pythagoras were all from either Ionia in Asia Minor (Ephesus, in the case of Heraclitus) or from islands very close to the Asian coast (Samos, in the case of Pythagoras).

13. Spengler, *Decline of the West*, vol. 1, p. 16 and 16 n. 1 (emphases added). For the original, Spengler, *Der Untergang des Abendlandes*, p. 22 n. 1.

14. Spengler, *Decline of the West*, vol. 1, p. 31 (emphasis added).

15. Hughes, *Oswald Spengler*, p. 72. I am referring here obviously to Thomas Mann's distinction before he read Spengler in the summer of 1919 and, as we saw at the end of chapter 5, section VI above, began to adopt Spengler's language.

16. For that much more common distinction, best known through Mann, but widespread in German writings, see Lepenies, *Seduction of Culture*, pp. 27–55 and passim. See also the analysis of the distinction and the history of its emergence in Elias, *Civilizing Process*, pp. 5–11, 26–30; Elias, *The Germans*, pp. 123–34.

17. Spengler, *Decline of the West*, vol. 1, p. 31. For a recent book adopting Spengler's distinction between living, organic, culture and petrified civilisation, see Debray, *Civilisation* (translated as Debray, *Civilization*). See also Debray, 'Civilization: A Grammar'; Debray, Laurens and Sbaï, *Civilisations*.

18. Spengler, *Decline of the West*, vol. 1, p. 32.

19. See: Schoeps, *Vorläufer Spenglers*; Herman, *Idea of Decline*; B. Adams, *Law of Civilization and Decay*; H. Adams, *Letters of Henry Adams*, passim; Contosta, 'Henry Adams'; Contosta, *Henry Adams and the American Experiment*.

20. Danilevsky, *Russland und Europa*; Danilevsky, 'Russia and Europe'. See also Sorokin, *Social Philosophies*, pp. 49–112; Skupiewski, *Doctrine panslaviste*; Hughes, *Oswald Spengler*, pp. 44–50, 53–54.

21. For a sensitive analysis of the initial debate in German-speaking countries, see Schroeter, *Der Streit um Spengler*; for a contemporaneous British book propagating Spenglerism, Goddard and Gibbons, *Civilisation or Civilisations*; see also Wood, "German foolishness"'; Massingham, '[Review of] The Decline of the West'. For more general responses, see Gasimov and Duque, *Oswald Spengler als europäisches Phänomen*; Sorokin, *Social Philosophies*; Herman, *Idea of Decline*, pp. 221–55; Man, de, 'Germany's New Prophets'; Breuer, 'Retter des Abendlandes'; Frye, '*Decline of the West* by Oswald Spengler'; Bent and Keedus, 'Contesting German "Crisis Literature"'.

22. Stewart, *New Negro*, pp. 375–94; quotation at p. 379.

23. Cronon, *Black Moses*, pp. 177–83.

24. Locke, 'Apropos of Africa'.

25. Stewart, *New Negro*, pp. 384–85.

26. Stewart, *New Negro*, pp. 431–76, 504–20. The anthropologist Zora Neale Hurston was never convinced of Locke's credentials, however: see Hurston, 'Chick with One Hen'.

27. Marchand, 'Leo Frobenius'.

28. Moses, *Afrotopia*, pp. 30–31. For a fascinating analysis of why '[m]odernity identif[ied] with [p]rehistory', see Stavrinaki, *Transfixed by Prehistory*, pp. 177–213, and on Frobenius in particular, ibid., pp. 28, 50, 150–52, 209–12; see also Geroulanos, *Invention of Prehistory*.

29. Moses, *Afrotopia*, pp. 41–42.

30. Andrade, 'Manifesto of Pau-Brasil Poetry'; Rachum, 'Antropofagia against Verdamarelo'. More generally, all over the world, people who had earlier been pro-Western and keen to persuade their countries to modernise and 'Westernise' began to be more than sceptical about the West, in response to what had happened during the Great War. Liang Ch'i Ch'ao was a striking example. See Mishra, *From the Ruins of Empire*, pp. 124–83; Teng and Fairbank, *China's Response to the West*, pp. 267–74; Levenson, *Liang Ch'i Ch'ao*, pp. 199–219. The Turkish Comtist Positivist Ahmet Riza was another case. See Riza, *La Faillite morale*; Riza, *Moral Bankruptcy of Western Policy*; Turnaoğlu, 'Positivist Universalism'. Similarly, following the Great War, younger Zionists opposed Theodor Herzl's plan of establishing 'an outpost of the West in the midst of the East' and started seeing 'European civilization as decadent and in its death throes'—and consequently opting for a view of the Jews 'as Orientals and the Zionist movement as the vehicle returning them to their home in the East'. Brody, 'Judaism, Philosophy, and the Idea of the West', pp. 135–36. See also Adas, 'Contested Hegemony'.

31. Cf. Streckert, *Die Hauptstadt Lateinamerikas*.

32. For detailed studies of such contacts more generally, see B. H. Edwards, *Practice of Diaspora*; Dunstan, *Race, Rights and Reform*; Goebel, *Anti-Imperial Metropolis*.

33. Grant, *Passing of the Great Race*; Boas, 'Inventing a Great Race'; Chapman, 'Passing of a Great Bogey'. On Grant, see Spiro, *Defending the Master Race*.

34. King, *Reinvention of Humanity*, pp. 86–94, 111–12, 114, 306.

35. Vitalis, *White World Order*, pp. 62–66.

36. Du Bois, 'Americanization'; Du Bois, 'American Jew'. See also Du Bois, 'To the World'.

37. See Janken, *Rayford W. Logan*, p. 63; R. W. Logan, 'Confessions of Unwilling Nordic'; Boas, 'This Nordic Nonsense'.

38. Vasconcelos, *Cosmic Race*. See also Miller, *Rise and Fall of the Cosmic Race*; De Beer, *José Vasconcelos*.

39. Du Bois, *Dusk of Dawn*, p. 646.

40. See, for instance, T. Mann, 'On the Theory of Spengler' (originally published in *Allgemeine Zeitung*, 9 March 1924, and reprinted in 1925 as T. Mann, 'Über die Lehre Spenglers'); W. Lewis, *Time and Western Man*, pp. 226–33, 262–63, 268–307.

41. Several of these articles were later assembled in the volume Massis, *La Guerre de trente ans*, pp. 69–157. The article noticed by Eliot was Massis, 'Défense de l'Occident'.

42. Mazgaj, 'Defending the West'; Schurts, 'Safeguarding a "Civilization in Crisis"'; Kessler, *Histoire politique de la Jeune Droite*, p. 25; Foureau, '*Revue universelle*'. On Maurras (with a commendable emphasis on the importance to him of Auguste Comte), see Sutton, *Nationalism, Positivism and Catholicism*.

43. Sirinelli, *Intellectuels et passions*, pp. 28, 47–55, 66, 92–100.

44. Massis, 'Defence of the West, I', pp. 224–25.

45. Massis, 'Defence of the West, I', p. 231 (emphases added).
46. Massis, 'Defence of the West, I', pp. 231–32.
47. Massis, 'Defence of the West, I', pp. 232–33 (emphasis added).
48. Cf. Butler, *Tyranny of Greece*; Marchand, *Down from Olympus*.
49. Massis, 'Defence of the West, I', pp. 234–35. On Mann's ambivalent attitude, see Lepenies, *Seduction of Culture*, pp. 27–35 and passim.
50. Massis, 'Defence of the West, I', pp. 235–36.
51. Massis, 'Defence of the West, I', pp. 237–38, 239–42.
52. Massis, 'Defence of the West, II', pp. 482–84.
53. Massis, 'Defence of the West, II', p. 486.
54. Malraux, '[Review of] *Defense de l'Occident*'. John Cruickshank, however, in an otherwise brilliant analysis of André Malraux's works of the late 1920s, is incorrect in arguing that '*La Défense de l'Occident*, published by Massis in 1927 and reviewed by Malraux in the *Nouvelle Revue Française* [...], may be taken as echoing both Spengler and Malraux himself in its choice of title'. Cruickshank assumes that Malraux's 1926 epistolary book *La Tentation de l'Occident* (Paris: Grasset, 1926) influenced Massis's choice of title; but Massis had in fact already chosen 'Défense de l'Occident' as the title of an article he published in the *Revue universelle* (which was noticed by T. S. Eliot). For Cruickshank's fascinating treatment of Malraux's *La Tentation de l'Occident* of 1926 and 'D'une jeunesse européenne' of 1927, see: Cruickshank, *Variations on Catastrophe*, pp. 175–92.
55. Miłosz, 'Dictionary of Wilno Streets', p. 43.
56. Marchand, 'German Orientalism', p. 471–72. See also Marchand, *German Orientalism*; Marchand, 'Leo Frobenius'; Marchand, 'Eastern Wisdom'; Marchand, 'Philhellenism and the *furor orientalis*'.
57. Massis, *Défense de l'Occident*, pp. 25, 34–47, 53, 65, 117, 182 n. 1, 198–99 n. 1, 204 n. 1.
58. 'Pound and Eliot left what they regarded as barbarous America to come to civilized Europe [...]. Their poetry exalted the past which they had sought among the Georgian poets and found only embalmed in museums, and it derided the present, the decay of standards. They were, politically, Don Quixotes of the new world armed to rescue the Dulcinea of the old—whom they quickly discovered to be an old hag with rotten teeth. The aim of their polemical criticism was to re-invent the past, and convert it into a modern weapon against the arsenals of the dead men stuffed with straw.' Spender, *Thirties and After*, pp. 200–201.
59. On Eliot's agenda as editor of the *Criterion* and his attempts to promote 'Defence of the West', see Harding, *The Criterion*, pp. 202–26; also, Crawford, *Eliot after 'The Waste Land'*, pp. 13–19, 82, 95, 106, 294.
60. Eliot and Haughton, *Letters of T. S. Eliot*, vol. 2, p. 672; Eliot and Haffenden, *Letters of T. S. Eliot*, vol. 3, pp. 27–28n.
61. Massis, 'Defence of the West, I'; Massis, 'Defence of the West, II'.
62. Massis, *Défense de l'Occident*; Massis, *Defence of the West*. Among Indian contributions was Metta, 'In Defence of the East'; also Metta, 'Bias in History'. Meanwhile Metta publicised his views on relations between West and East elsewhere, too: Metta, 'What the East Is Thinking'. Another article by an Asian in Eliot's magazine was Shah, 'The Meeting of the East and the West'.
63. T. S. Eliot to Herbert Read, 20 January 1927, in Eliot and Haffenden, *Letters of T. S. Eliot*, vol. 3, p. 387 (emphases added).

64. T. S. Eliot to V. B. Metta, 12 August 1926, in Eliot and Haffenden, *Letters of T. S. Eliot*, vol. 3, p. 249.

65. T. S. Eliot to Geoffrey Faber, 4 September 1926, in Eliot and Haffenden, *Letters of T. S. Eliot*, vol. 3, p. 273.

66. Fletcher, 'Letter to the Editor', p. 748.

67. T. S. Eliot to John Gould Fletcher, 5 August 1927, in Eliot and Haffenden, *Letters of T. S. Eliot*, vol. 3, p. 612.

68. Fletcher, 'East and West'.

69. Fletcher, 'East and West', pp. 19–20 (emphasis added).

70. Fletcher, 'East and West', pp. 26, 32 (emphases added).

71. Lepenies, *Die Macht am Mittelmeer*, pp. 227–34, 237–39, 262–70, 313–318. See also Meaney, 'Fancies and Fears'.

72. For other US responses, see Troy, 'Defense of the Occident'; Kayden, 'Catholic Jazzmania'; R. B. Perry, 'West versus East'.

73. See Grant, *Passing of the Great Race* (1919 edition), pp. 184–87.

74. Krutch, 'What is the West?'.

75. 'Until further notice, we would like to remain Western.' Curtius, 'Französische Civilisation und Abendland,' p. 192.

76. Moeller van den Bruck, *Das dritte Reich*.

77. Moeller van den Bruck, *Germany's Third Empire*, pp. 263–64 (emphases added); original: Moeller van den Bruck, *Das dritte Reich*, p. 321.

78. Eliot and Haffenden, *Letters of T. S. Eliot*, vol. 3, pp. 240, 337.

79. Rychner, 'German Chronicle', pp. 726, 727, 728–31. Given the mention of Spengler here, it may be worth noting that in the early 1920s Rychner had met him and exchanged warm correspondence with him: Spengler, *Briefe*, pp. 246, 249, 348.

80. Rychner, 'German Chronicle', pp. 726–32.

81. Bem and Guyaux, *Ernst Robert Curtius*; G. Müller, *Europäische Gesellschaftsbeziehungen*, pp. 68–70, 98–103.

82. See Moras, *Ursprung und Entwicklung*; Lochore, *History of the Idea of Civilization*.

83. On Curtius's role in Weimar Germany's intellectual life, see Harrington, *German Cosmopolitan Social Thought*, pp. 95, 101–4, 115–15, 182, 205–8, 281–88.

84. Curtius, 'Französische Civilisation und Abendland', pp. 191–92.

85. Curtius, 'Restoration of the Reason', pp. 396–97 (emphasis added). (The essay had been first published as 'Restauration der Vernunft,' *Neue Schweizer Rundschau*, September 1927, pp. 856–62.)

86. Curtius, 'Restoration of the Reason', p. 390.

87. Curtius, *Französische Kultur*; translated in 1932 as Curtius, *Civilization of France*.

88. Curtius, *Civilization of France*, p. 13.

89. Curtius, *Civilization of France*, pp. 35–36. In terms of Curtius's definitions, the Turkish sociologist Ziya Gökalp was clearly following the German (and not the French) understanding of 'culture' when he insisted that the Turkish nation emerging from the ruins of the Ottoman Empire in the early 1920s had to adopt Western 'civilisation' while meanwhile preserving and enhancing its Turkish national 'culture'. See Gökalp, *Turkish Nationalism and Western Civilization*, pp. 268–90. But he also introduced an interesting further distinction, as he noted that

'[i]n French the term "culture" has two different meanings.' One of these was best expressed in Turkish by the word *hars*, which meant 'culture'; the other was best expressed in Turkish by the word *tehzib*, which stood more for 'refinement'. Gökalp's verdict was that '[m]any of the misconceptions regarding culture come from this dual meaning of the word *la culture*.' Ibid., p. 280.

90. Curtius, *Civilization of France*, p. 40.
91. Moenius, 'Einführung'.
92. Spengler to Paul Reusch, 30 June 1931, in Spengler, *Briefe*, pp. 626–27. On Moenius and his editorship of the *Allgemeine Rundschau*, see Munro, *Hitler's Bavarian Antagonist*; also Lehnert, 'Rome ou la solution'.
93. Kolnai, *War against the West*, p. 565; also pp. 258, 559.
94. See Moenius, 'Einführung', pp. 11–113; Moenius, 'Le Germanisme contre la Romanité' pp. 100 (Massis's preface), 114, 129. ('Le Germanisme contre la Romanité: Témoignage d'un Catholique allemand' was first published in Massis's *Revue universelle*, vol. 37, no. 6 [15 June 1929], pp. 641–58.)
95. Munro, *Hitler's Bavarian Antagonist*, p. 27.
96. Quoted in: Munro, *Hitler's Bavarian Antagonist*, pp. 27–28. On the concept of *Romanitas* among such intellectuals, see ibid., pp. 121–45.
97. Moenius, *Paris*.
98. See Platz, *Deutschland-Frankreich*; Conze, *Die Europa der Deutschen*, pp. 27–55; Conze, 'Facing the Future Backwards', pp. 72–89.
99. Massis, *Défense de l'Occident*, pp. 60–63 n. 1.
100. Troeltsch, 'Ideas of Natural Law' p. 202 (emphasis added).
101. Troeltsch, 'Naturrecht und Humanität' p. 500.
102. Troeltsch, 'Ideas of Natural Law', pp. 201–22. For more on Troeltsch, see Harrington, *German Cosmopolitan Social Thought*, pp. 114–20, 134–35, 159–63, 244–52. See also Troeltsch, *Deutscher Geist und Westeuropa*.
103. T. Mann, 'On the German Republic' (T. Mann, *Von Deutscher Republik*), p. 522 (emphases added); see also T. Mann, 'L'Esprit de l'Allemagne et son avenir'.
104. Antonio Gramsci to Giuseppe Berti, 8 August 1927, in Gramsci, *Letters from Prison* p. 94. Gramsci was to write more on Massis in his famous notebooks: Gramsci, *Further Selections*, pp. 92, 94–96, 118.
105. B. H. Edwards, *Practice of Diaspora*, p. 16. See also Dewitte, *Mouvements nègres en France*.
106. Nardal, 'Internationalisme noir' *La Dépêche africaine* (15 February 1928).
107. See B. H. Edwards, *Practice of Diaspora*, pp. 19–20; Sweeney, 'Resisting the Primitive'.
108. Gillouin, 'Problème de la colonisation'.
109. Gillouin, 'Destin de l'Occident', pp. 17–18, 19, 22, 24.
110. Gillouin, 'Destin de l'Occident', pp. 27–30, 52–53.
111. As a reviewer of an earlier work by Lewis put it, 'Anything that Wyndham Lewis writes is likely to prove fantastic and bizarre to the verge of lunacy. [...] But his mind is as keen as it is cranky, and as capacious as capricious.' L. P. Edwards, '[Review of] *The Art of Being Ruled*'.
112. W. Lewis, *Paleface*, pp. 252–55.
113. W. Lewis, *Paleface*, pp. 255–57.

114. Eliot and Haffenden, *Letters of T. S. Eliot*, vol. 3, pp. 768, 799.
115. Guénon, *Crisis of the Modern World*, p. 103; Guénon, *Crise du monde moderne*, p. 153.
116. See Sedgwick, *Against the Modern World*; Chacornac, *Simple Life of René Guénon*; Waterfield, *René Guénon and the Future of the West*; Irwin, *For Lust of Knowledge*, pp. 315–16; Hallaq, *Restating Orientalism*, pp. 143–78; Sablé, *René Guénon*.
117. Guénon, *East and West*, pp. 126–27. For the original, see Guénon, *Orient et Occident*.
118. Guénon, *Crisis of the Modern World*, pp. 100–101.
119. Guénon, *Crisis of the Modern World*, p. 101 n. 3 (Guénon, *Crise du monde moderne*, p. 151).
120. Guénon, *Crisis of the Modern World*, pp. 100–102.
121. Guénon, *Crisis of the Modern World*, p. 105.
122. In his manifesto 'Pour un parti de l'intelligence' of 1919, Massis had railed against 'le modernisme industriel' and its neglect of the moral reform of man: Massis, *La Guerre de trente ans*, pp. 72–73.
123. See Sedgwick, *Against the Modern World*, pp. 221–37; Sedgwick, *Traditionalism*; Teitelbaum, *War for Eternity*; Millerman, *Inside 'Putin's Brain'*, pp. x, 13, 72, 106, 180, 205; Shekhovtsov and Umland, 'Is Aleksandr Dugin a Traditionalist?'; Morson, 'Russian Exceptionalism'.
124. Sirinelli, *Intellectuels et passions*, pp. 92–100.
125. T. S. Eliot ['T.S.E.'], 'A Commentary'.
126. Gladwyn Papers, Ge/36/7: memorandum on 'Locarno and London', 13 March 1936.
127. Gladwyn Papers, Ge/36/21, 5 September 1936.
128. Lippmann, 'Watchman, What of the Night?', *New York Herald Tribune*,1 January 1935, quoted in Goodwin, *Walter Lippmann*, pp. 225–26.
129. Dietz, *Neo-Tories*; Dietz, 'Neo-Tories and Europe'.
130. Kolnai, *War against the West*.
131. Friedrich, '[Review of] Aurel Kolnai, *The War Against the West*'.
132. Schmitt, 'Donoso Cortés in Berlin', p. 61.
133. Schmitt, 'Age of Neutralizations', p. 80.
134. Schmitt, *Necessity of Politics*, pp. 77–82. (The original German edition was *Römischer Katholizismus und Politische Form* [Munich: Theatiner-Verlag, 1923]).
135. Schmitt, *Necessity of Politics*, pp. 80–81, 82. Among the very few works to have noted Schmitt's cultural antagonism to Russia, see McCormick, 'From Roman Catholicism to Mechanized Oppression'; McCormick, 'Introduction'; McCormick, 'Political Theory and Political Theology'; D. Kelly, *State of the Political*, p. 212; Schulman, 'Carl Schmitt and the Clash of Civilizations'.
136. Schmitt, *Crisis of Parliamentary Democracy*, pp. 74–75.
137. Quoted in Mehring, *Carl Schmitt*, pp. 198–99.
138. Schmitt, *Ex Captivitate Salus*, pp. 34–36; Schmitt, *Dialogues on Power and Space*, pp. 60–61, 67, 75–76, 101–2 (n. 26); Schmitt, 'Planetary Tension between Orient and Occident'.
139. Mehring, *Carl Schmitt*, p. 199. For examples of others (Woodrow Wilson and Harold Nicolson) being worried after the Great War about the potential formation of 'a Slav block' poised 'against the Western World', see Wolff, *Woodrow Wilson*, pp. 151–53.
140. Schmitt, *Leviathan*, p. 98.
141. Hughes, *Oswald Spengler*, p. 76 (emphasis added).

Chapter 7: The Second World War and Ideas of 'the West'

1. Maritain, 'To My American Friends'.
2. Blum, *Public Philosopher*, pp. 383–84.
3. Steel, *Walter Lippmann*, pp. 380–81.
4. Lippmann, *Some Notes on War and Peace*, pp. 46–47 (emphasis added).
5. Lippmann, 'Education vs. Western Civilization', pp. 184–85.
6. Lippmann, 'Education vs. Western Civilization', pp. 185, 186–87, 189.
7. Lippmann, 'Education vs. Western Civilization', pp. 190–92.
8. Quoted in Steel, *Walter Lippmann*, p. 519.
9. Reddick, 'Meditations'.
10. Achille, 'Upwards to Citizenship', p. 172.
11. Achille, 'Upwards to Citizenship', p. 173. It is worth noting in this connection that another Martinican, Frantz Fanon, volunteered to fight for France, and even as late as 1952, after painful experiences as a French soldier, was still writing that he wanted to be French and treated as French (though much was to change with the Algerian Revolution): see Fanon, *Black Skin, White Masks*.
12. *Life*, vol. 17, no. 10 (4 September 1944), editorial ('Paris: Everything that happens in its streets is symbolic, including way they were freed'), p. 26.
13. Grigg, *British Foreign Policy*, p. 125.
14. Arendt, 'Approaches to the "German Problem"', pp. 112–14.
15. See Bruneteau, *Les 'Collabos' de l'Europe nouvelle*, p. 166. For a brilliant study of French intellectual life during and in the aftermath of the war, see Sapiro, *French Writers' War*.
16. For German discourses on the new 'Europe' at the time, see Gassert, 'No Place for "the West"'.
17. On de Reynold, see Martin, 'Gonzague de Reynold'; also, Mattioli, *Gonzague de Reynold*.
18. Reynold, 'Qu'est-ce que l'Europe?', p. 95.
19. Bruneteau, *Les 'Collabos' de l'Europe nouvelle*, p. 167.
20. Guy-Grant, 'Civilisation occidentale'; Siegfried, ' Civilisation occidentale'; Siegfried, 'L'Occident et la direction spirituelle'; Germain, 'Le Duel éternel Orient–Occident'; Léon-Martin, 'Le Sentiment de l'Occident'; Combelle, 'Choisir l'Occident'; Benda, 'Occident et Extrême-Occident'.
21. S. Kennedy, 'Situating France'; Tillmann, *André Siegfried*.
22. Siegfried, *L'Occident et la direction spirituelle*; Siegfried, *What the British Empire Means*; Siegfried, ' Civilisation occidentale'; Siegfried, *Civilisation occidentale*.
23. Siegfried, ' Civilisation occidentale'. On the role, circulation and politics of the *Revue des deux mondes*, see Karakatsoulis, 'Une revue-entreprise'; Sapiro, *French Writers' War*.
24. Siegfried, 'Civilisation occidentale', pp. 129–30.
25. Sternhell, *Ni droite ni gauche*, pp. 32–60; S. Kennedy, 'Situating France'.
26. Bruneteau, *Les 'Collabos' de l'Europe nouvelle*, pp. 167–70.
27. Siegfried, ' Civilisation occidentale', p. 147.
28. Siegfried, ' Civilisation occidentale', p. 148.
29. For Weil's life, see Pétrement, *Vie de Simone Weil*.

30. Her immersion in original texts from both India and Greece is in evidence in Weil, *Œuvres Complètes*, tome 4: *Écrits de Marseille*, vol. 2: *(1941–1942) Grèce-Inde-Occitanie*.

31. See J. Jackson, *Certain Idea of France*.

32. Weil, *Need for Roots* (1952); for a better translation, see Weil, *Need for Roots* (2023).

33. Weil, 'Great Beast'.

34. Weil, 'Colonial Question', p. 110.

35. Césaire, *Discourse on Colonialism*, p. 36; Wilder, *Freedom Time*, pp. 82–83.

36. Weil, 'Colonial Question', pp. 113–14, 109.

37. Weil, 'Colonial Question', p. 113.

38. According to Camus (in a direct criticism of Charles Maurras), 'Toute l'erreur vient de ce qu'on confond Méditerranée et Latinité et qu'on place à Rome ce qui commença à Athènes.' Camus, 'Culture indigène' pp. 565–66 ('The fundamental error consists in confusing the Mediterranean with Latinity, and placing in Rome what began in Athens.' Camus, *Speaking Out*, p. 4). See also Foxlee, *Albert Camus's 'The New Mediterranean Culture'*.

39. Weil, 'Colonial Question', pp. 113, 114.

40. Weil, 'À propos de la question coloniale', p. 290.

41. Weil, 'Colonial Question', pp. 114–15. For the original, see Weil, 'À propos de la question coloniale', p. 290.

42. Weil, 'Colonial Question', pp. 115, 116.

43. Weil, *Need for Roots* (1952 translation), p. 164.

44. Camus, 'Letters to a German Friend', pp. 22, 23, 26.

45. Camus, *Camus at 'Combat'*, pp. 171–73. Camus was of course right to fear that the new international organisation was looking more like 'recognition of imperialism'. See Mazower, *No Enchanted Palace*.

46. On Aron's and many others' turn to thinking in global terms at the time, see Rosenboim, *Emergence of Globalism*.

47. Aron, 'Pour l'alliance de l'Occident', pp. 331–33, 335–36.

48. Aron, 'Remarques sur la politique étrangère' pp. 347–48.

49. See Filoni, *Philosophe du dimanche*; Lilla, 'Alexandre Kojève'; Nichols, *Alexandre Kojève*; Strauss, *On Tyranny*; Auffret, *Alexandre Kojève*; Scholz, 'Zwischen Vichy und Résistance'.

50. For an analysis of the essay, its context and its afterlives, see Lepenies, *Die Macht am Mittelmeer*, pp. 15–40, 69–71.

51. Kojève, 'Outline of a Doctrine of French Policy'. For the original, and for the dossier with articles found along with his notes for the 'Outline', see Kojève, 'Esquisse d'une doctrine' (dated 27 August 1945). The articles included Istel, 'Les Données d'un accord occidental'; and Don, 'L'Union occidentale vue de Londres'. The dossier also contained recent notes by the Resistance writer Jean Cassou on 'un projet d'union latine' (a project for Latin union). Kojève clearly sided with, and developed, that option.

52. Lippmann, *U.S. Foreign Policy*; see also Lippmann, *U.S. War Aims*.

53. Lippmann, *U.S. Foreign Policy*, pp. 70, 76, 80–83.

54. See Mariano, 'America as a Transatlantic Nation'; Mariano, 'Remapping America'.

55. Luce, 'American Century', published in *Life*, February 1941.

56. Lipmann, 'American Destiny' p. 73. For similar remarks on the displacement of the 'Occident' through a move from the old West to the new, see Schmitt, *Nomos of the Earth*, p. 290.

57. Locke, 'Unfinished Business', pp. 456, 457.
58. Locke, 'Unfinished Business', p. 458.
59. Stewart, *New Negro*, pp. 788–91.
60. Locke, 'Special Section', pp. 345, 348–49 (emphasis added).
61. Locke, 'Special Section', pp. 360, 379–80.
62. Locke, 'Cultural Relativism'. See also Kallen, 'Alain Locke and Cultural Pluralism'.
63. Kertzer, *Pope at War*; Kirby, 'From Bridge to Divide'.
64. Bullitt, 'World from Rome'. See also Etkind, *Roads Not Taken*.
65. Bullitt, 'World from Rome,' p. 95.
66. Kertzer, *Pope at War*, p. 469.
67. Hayek, *Road to Serfdom*, p. 73.
68. Gladwyn Jebb, *Memoirs*, pp. 118–20.
69. Crick, *George Orwell*, p. 273; see also Stansky, *Socialist Patriot*, pp. 62–64.
70. Orwell, 'Orwell's Proposed Preface', p. 109.
71. Valéry, 'War Economy for the Mind', p. 473.
72. Aldous Huxley to Julian Huxley, 27 May 1945, in Huxley, *Letters*, p. 528. For a succinct analysis of Huxley's thought both before and after he published *Brave New World*, see Claeys, *Dystopia*, pp. 357–89.
73. Stansky, *Socialist Patriot*, pp. 9, 10–11.
74. Stansky, *Socialist Patriot*, pp. 107–8.

Chapter 8: The Cold War and Its 'Wests'

1. D. L. Lewis, *W.E.B. Du Bois*, p. 683.
2. Jaspers, 'Is Europe's Culture Finished?', p. 518 (emphases added).
3. Siegfried, *Civilisation occidentale*, pp. 17–21.
4. Quoted in Greenwood, *Titan at the Foreign Office*, pp. 227–28 (emphasis added).
5. *FRUS*, 1947, vol. 2, doc. 317 (pp. 815–22); quotation at p. 815.
6. Orwell, 'Toward European Unity'.
7. See Pagden, *Pursuit of Europe*, pp. 209–46; Pistone, *Union of European Federalists*. On earlier, interwar ideas aiming at European federation, see Orluc, 'Caught between Past and Future'.
8. For a step-by-step analysis, see Thomas, *Armed Truce*.
9. It is indicative of Lippmann's importance that the whole affair assumed the dimensions that it did. As Dean Acheson was to comment much later, Kennan was in fact describing what was already happening, adding, 'The X article was a perfectly fine article. Then Walter Lippmann decided that he did not like it, well, it was as if God has looked over at George's shoulder and said "George, you shouldn't have written such a bad article."' Quoted in Aron, *République impériale*, p. 299.
10. Gaddis, *George F. Kennan*, pp. 272–75; Costigliola, *Kennan*, pp. 284–89, 301–11.
11. See Cooper, *Ambassadors*, pp. 192–201.
12. Lippmann, *Cold War*, pp. 14, 15, 24 (emphasis added).
13. Lippmann, *Cold War*, pp. 24–25 (emphasis added).
14. Du Bois, ['Introduction' to] 'An Appeal to the World', p. 245.

15. Radchenko, *To Run the World*, pp. 456–57.

16. It has been noted of the American secetary of state that 'Marshall recalled that the competition for leadership of the European response "became more or less of a race" between Bevin and French foreign minister Georges Bidault'. Toye, *Age of Hope*, p. 135.

17. For an analysis of the Suez debacle, see Thomas, *Suez Affair*.

18. Hennessy, *Never Again*, pp. 291–295.

19. Greenwood, *Titan at the Foreign Office*, p. 227 (emphases added).

20. Greenwood, *Titan at the Foreign Office*, pp. 228–29.

21. Bevin, 'Address' (22 January 1948) (emphases added).

22. Greenwood, *Titan at the Foreign Office*, pp. 234–36 (emphasis added). See also Gladwyn Jebb, *Memoirs*, pp. 211–12.

23. Even the magazine founded for the purposes of (and funded by) the Congress for Cultural Freedom in Britain, *Encounter*, was repeatedly accused by Americans of not standing up to British anti-Americanism and failing 'to offset the cliché that Americans are barbarians'. Coleman, *Liberal Conspiracy*, p. 72.

24. See Geppert, 'Bridge over Troubled Waters'; Bavaj, 'Cold War Liberalism in West Germany'; P. T. Jackson, *Civilizing the Enemy*; Strote, *Lions and Lambs*, pp. 197–219; Schildt, *Zwischen Abendland und Amerika*; Trentmann, *Out of the Darkness*, pp. 253–61; Bailey, 'Continuities', pp. 567–96; Bailey, *Between Yesterday and Tomorrow*.

25. See André Malraux's interview published on 15 February 1945 in the Geneva review *Labyrinthe* and reprinted in 'Lignes de Force' *Preuves*, no. 49, March 1955: Grémion, *Preuves*, pp. 132–38.

26. See Mathy, *Extrême-Occident*, pp. 137–62; Roger, *L'Ennemi américain*; Judt, *Past Imperfect*; Kuisel, *Seducing the French*; Chebel d'Appollonia, *Histoire politique*, pp. 135–69.

27. Miłosz, *Native Realm*, pp. 285, 290–93, 298; cf. ibid., pp. 274–75. See also Hoffman, *On Czesław Miłosz*, pp. 61–64.

28. Fowke, '[Review of] *The Twenty-Fifth Hour*', p. 255.

29. Kissinger Papers, box 132, folder 6, ('Seminar beginnings': 'Preliminary Statement of Objectives and Program of the Harvard Summer School Foreign Student Project').

30. Fowke, '[Review of] *The Twenty-Fifth Hour*', p. 256.

31. Frye, 'Novels on Several Occasions', p. 618.

32. The evocation of catacombs reminds one of the Fritz Lang film *Metropolis* (1927), which was in turn no doubt related to Spengler's recent denunciations of the dehumanising effects of machinery and the 'megalopolitan' civilisation of Western cities.

33. Gheorghiu, *Twenty-Fifth Hour*, pp. 495, 496 (emphasis added).

34. Gheorghiu, *Twenty-Fifth Hour*, pp. 399, 401 (emphasis added).

35. Gheorghiu, *Twenty-Fifth Hour*, pp. 391–92. Critics were divided. Everybody could see that the novel's artistic qualities left much to be desired, but many insisted that its grim message could not meanwhile be ignored. The German-born historian Golo Mann (Thomas Mann's son), at that time an émigré in America, did not like it at all: see G. Mann, 'America as Frankenstein'. But the Canadian literary critic Northrop Frye was much more sympathetic. He conceded that the book was 'humorless and preachy, but its subject is not amusing, and maybe we could do with a sermon'; and in any case, Gheorghiu's conviction that American democracy could 'bring nothing to Europe but a third invasion of stupid and

brutal officials makes *The Twenty-Fifth Hour* a document of great importance: it reflects an attitude too frequent among non-Communist Europeans to be shrugged off, and whatever reasons and evidence it presents need to be carefully examined'. Frye, 'Novels on Several Occasions', p. 619.

36. Miłosz, *Native Realm*, pp. 261–63. For subtle analyses of Miłosz's responses to America on the part of another Polish immigrant, see Hoffman, *On Czesław Miłosz*, pp. 87–89, 109–21, 135–38.

37. Siegfried, *Les États-Unis d'aujourd'hui*; Siegfried, *America Comes of Age*.

38. Siegfried, *Civilisation occidentale*, p. 17.

39. There had been an overabundance of theories on how America's huge extent, as well its climate and other geographical factors, made American humanity very different from European humanity. See Gerbi, *Dispute of the New World*. Similar comments abound in Camus, *Travels in the Americas*.

40. Siegfried, *Civilisation occidentale*, pp. 18–19, 21.

41. A. E. Benfield to Henry Kissinger, 6 October 1950: Kissinger Papers, part 2: series 1 (early career and Harvard University), box 132, folder 6 ('Seminar beginnings').

42. Kissinger Papers, part 2, series 1 (early career and Harvard University), box 132, folder 6 ('Seminar beginnings'): Henry A. Kissinger, 'Informal Memorandum for Professor Elliott', pp. 1–3 (emphases added).

43. Kissinger Papers, part 2, series 1 (early career and Harvard University), box 132, folder 6 ('Seminar beginnings'): 'Preliminary Statement of Objectives and Program of the Harvard Summer School Foreign Student Project' (emphasis added).

44. Ward, *Policy for the West*, p. 41 (emphasis added). See also Ward, *Five Ideas*.

45. Kissinger Papers, part 2, series 1 (early career and Harvard University), box 132, folder 6 ('Seminar beginnings'): 'Preliminary Statement of Objectives and Program of the Harvard Summer School Foreign Student Project'.

46. Kissinger Papers, part 2, series 1 (early career and Harvard University), box 132, folder 6 ('Seminar beginnings'), p. 3: Henry Kissinger, handwritten notes, c. 1951.

47. Kissinger Papers, part 2, series 1 (early career and Harvard University), box 132, folder 6 ('Seminar beginnings'): Henry A. Kissinger, 'Informal Memorandum for Professor Elliott', pp. 3–4.

48. Ferguson, *Kissinger 1923–1968*, p. 281. See also Wilford, *Mighty Wurlitzer*, pp. 123–28.

49. Elliott, 'Foreword' (emphases added).

50. Kissinger, 'Meaning of History'.

51. Toynbee, 'Unification of the World' p. 90.

52. McNeill, *Arnold J. Toynbee*, pp. 204–18; quotation at p. 216.

53. See Kimmage, *Conservative Turn*.

54. Quoted in McNeill, *Arnold J. Toynbee*, p. 213.

55. Toynbee, *World and the West*, pp. 1–3.

56. Toynbee, *Study of History*, vol. 1 (1934), pp. 51–181; on 'The Orthodox Christian Society', see ibid., pp. 63–67.

57. Toynbee, *World and the West*, pp. 11–15 (emphases added).

58. Toynbee, *World and the West*, pp. 15–17.

59. Toynbee, *World and the West*, pp. 85–99.

398 NOTES TO CHAPTER 8

60. For a particularly vociferous criticism, see Jerrold, *Lie about the West*; also Jerrold, 'Professor Toynbee, "The West" and the World'.

61. McNeill, *Arnold J. Toynbee*, p. 223.

62. *The Times*, 17 November 1952, p. 3.

63. [Anon.], 'As Others See Us'.

64. See the collected correspondence in the volume *'Counsels of Hope'*.

65. Arnold Toynbee, *TLS*, 16 April 1954: see *'Counsels of Hope'*, pp. 10–11.

66. Trevor-Roper, 'Arnold Toynbee's Millennium'.

67. 'Friends, freedom has taken the offensive!': Arthur Koestler on the final day of the Congress for Cultural Freedom, Berlin, 28 June 1950 (*Der Monat*, July–August 1950, p. 472), quoted in Coleman, *Liberal Conspiracy*, p. 1.

68. Saunders, *Who Paid the Piper?*; Wilford, *Mighty Wurlitzer*, pp. 70–98.

69. Hochgeschwender, *Freiheit in der Offensive?*; Hochgeschwender, *Intellectual as Propagandist*; Coleman, *Liberal Conspiracy*, pp. 1–32, 93–95; Grémion, *Intelligence de l'anticommunisme*; Lialiouti, 'The "Treason of the Intellectuals"'; Scott-Smith and Lerg, *Campaigning Culture*.

70. Coleman, *Liberal Conspiracy*, p. 13.

71. Berghahn, *America and the Intellectual Cold Wars*, pp. 139–40; Coleman, *Liberal Conspiracy*, pp. 199–205. For details on the ways the CCF worked on Africans, see Kalliney, *Aesthetic Cold War*, pp. 51–82.

72. Macdonald, 'I Choose the West'. See also Whitfield, *Critical American*.

73. On Mailer, see Joscelyne, 'Norman Mailer'.

74. Macdonald, 'I Choose the West,' pp. 197, 198, 199–200.

75. Lasch, 'Anti-Intellectualism of the Intellectuals' pp. 329–30. For much more recent criticism of Arendt on that and other counts, see Moyn, *Liberalism against Itself*, pp. 115–39.

76. Rorty, *Achieving Our Country*, pp. 55–71.

77. Arendt, 'What is Authority?' pp. 139–40; Arendt, *On Violence*, p. 69.

78. See Selinger, 'Politics of Arendtian Historiography'.

79. A much more systematic and 'academic' study was contributed five years later: Friedrich and Brzezinski, *Totalitarian Dictatorship and Autocracy*; but it did not capture intellectuals' imagination in the way Arendt's analysis did. See also A. Gleason, *Totalitarianism*.

80. Fabre, *Richard Wright*, p. 7; Fabre, *Unfinished Quest*, pp. 433–35 (where the impact of Arendt's book on the two most crucial lectures of what became Wright's *White Man, Listen!* is discussed). Wright had met Arendt in New York in 1944: ibid., p. 299.

81. Arendt, 'Dream and Nightmare' (10 September 1954), 'Europe and the Atom Bomb' (17 September 1954) and 'Threat of Conformism' (24 September 1954).

82. See Young-Bruehl, *Hannah Arendt*, pp. 280–86.

83. Arendt, 'Dream and Nightmare', pp. 411–12, 416–17.

84. Cf. what a highly intelligent European wrote later of his preconceptions: 'Like all Europeans I had painted for myself a false picture of technology's reign in America, imagining that nothing was left of nature.' Miłosz, *Native Realm*, p. 260.

85. On Arendt's and others' related concerns at the time, see Ashcroft, *Catastrophic Technology*; Yaqoob, 'Archimedean Point'.

86. Arendt, 'Europe and the Atom Bomb', pp. 418–19.

87. Arendt, 'Threat of Conformism', pp. 426–27.

88. For the background and broader context of such debates, see Kirby, 'Divinely Sanctioned'; Kirby, 'From Bridge to Divide'; Kirby, *Religion and the Cold War*.

89. Arendt, 'Religion and Politics', pp. 383–84 (originally published in *Confluence*, vol. 2, no. 3 [1953]).

90. For a fascinating brief analysis both of Strauss's main contributions and of what his American disciples made of them in the past five decades, see Lilla, 'Athens and Chicago'.

91. Strauss, 'Progress or Return?', pp. 29–30 (emphasis added).

92. Strauss, 'Progress or Return?', p. 33 (emphases added).

93. Strauss, 'Progress or Return?', pp. 44–45 (emphasis added).

94. Lilla, 'Athens and Chicago', p. 49.

95. Here Strauss cited 'Ernst Troeltsch on Natural Law and Humanity': i.e., Troeltsch, 'Ideas of Natural Law' (see chapter 6, section VII above).

96. Strauss, *Natural Right and History*, pp. 1–2.

97. Judt, *Burden of Responsibility*, p. 144. See also Craiutu, *Faces of Moderation*; Craiutu, 'Rediscovering Raymond Aron'; Jennings, *Revolution and the Republic*, pp. 504–5.

98. Leboyer, 'Raymond Aron'.

99. Aron, *La Société industrielle et la guerre*.

100. The subtitle of chapter 22 of his 1962 magnum opus is characteristic: in translation, 'To Survive Is to Conquer.' See Aron, *Peace and War*, pp. 665–702.

101. Aron, *Opium of the Intellectuals*, p. 57.

102. Aron, *Opium of the Intellectuals*, pp. 321–22.

103. Aron, *Peace and War*, p. 665.

104. Aron, *Peace and War*, p. 670.

105. Raymond Aron, 'L'Unité française en péril' (*Le Figaro*, 15 October 1955), pp. 102–3; Aron, *Peace and War*, pp. 474–75, 692–93, 728–29. See Bonfreschi, 'Le libéralisme face au processus de décolonisation'; Bonfreschi, 'Raymond Aron'.

106. R. Wright, *Pagan Spain*, pp. 3–4.

107. Robinson, *Black Marxism*, p. 182. Robinson was also right in accounting for the vicissitudes that Wright's reputation suffered as due to 'the several and remarkably extensive campaigns of vilification launched against him by [...] distinct and, in some instances, opposing political factions [who] concur[red] on the desirability of the suppression of his work and ideas'; ibid., p. 289. See also Gilroy, *Black Atlantic*, pp. 146–86; Kent, 'Richard Wright'; R.D.G. Kelley, 'How the West was One'. For an excellent recent analysis of Wright as a political thinker, see Shelby, 'Richard Wright'.

108. R. Wright, 'Richard Wright'.

109. Rowley, *Richard Wright*, p. 520.

110. W. G. Smith, 'Black Boy in France', p. 40.

111. R. Wright, *White Man, Listen!*, p. 633.

112. On Padmore and his friendship with Wright, see L. James, *George Padmore*.

113. Rowley, *Richard Wright*, p. 429.

114. Sartre, 'Préface', pp. 10–11; Sartre, 'Preface', pp. 8–9.

115. [Fanon,] 'Richard Wright's *White Man, Listen!*', p. 104 (originally published in *El Moudjahid*, no. 47 [3 August 1959]). For a recent judicious and highly perceptive assessment of the

relationship between Fanon and Wright, see Shatz, *Rebel's Clinic*, pp. 78–80, 113, 261–63; also, Shatz, 'Outcasts and Desperados'.

116. R. Wright, *Color Curtain*, pp. 592, 593. For an argument related to what Wright wrote on the French revolution that was used by leaders of the Algerian revolution at the time, see Mackinnon, 'Right to Rebel'.

117. R. Wright, *Color Curtain*, pp. 594–95 (emphases added).

118. One of the most interesting Afro-American academics in the field of international relations, and one of the very few females in the profession, did not find Wright's analysis of the Bandung Conference compelling: see Merze, '[Review of] *The Color Curtain*'.

119. On *Présence africaine* as 'probably the most resolutely nonaligned intellectual venue of the midcentury period', see Kalliney, *Aesthetic Cold War*, p. 33.

120. Proteau, '*Présence africaine*'.

121. Vaillant, *Black, French, and African*, pp. 252–59.

122. R. Wright, [contributions to] 'Débats', pp. 67–68.

123. R. Wright, 'Tradition and Industrialization: The Plight', pp. 347–348.

124. R. Wright, 'Tradition and Industrialization: The Historic Meaning', pp. 705–6. For an analysis (by a follower of Leo Strauss) crediting Afro-American thinkers with the kind of double vision Wright claimed here, see Storing, 'Introduction'; Storing, 'What Country Have I?'.

125. R. Wright, 'Tradition and Industrialization: The Historic Meaning', pp. 706–9 (emphasis added).

126. For the argument regarding lingering Marxism, see Fabre, *From Harlem to Paris*, pp. 191–93. Shklar is quoted in Moyn, *Liberalism against Itself*, p. 15. On 'Cold War liberalism', see ibid., passim.

127. R. Wright, 'Tradition and Industrialization: The Historic Meaning', pp. 709–11. For the chairman's opening speech, see Diop, 'Discours d'ouverture'; for the early Shklar's diagnosis, Moyn, *Liberalism against Itself*, pp. 13–37.

128. R. Wright, 'Tradition and Industrialization: The Historic Meaning', p. 712 (emphasis added).

129. R. Wright, 'Memories of My Grandmother'.

130. R. Wright, 'Tradition and Industrialization: The Historic Meaning', pp. 712–16.

131. R. Wright, 'Tradition and Industrialization: The Historic Meaning', pp. 716–18 (emphases added).

132. One cannot help noting the parallels with another statement, written more than a century earlier (1853): 'English interference [...] dissolved these small semi-barbarian, semi-civilized communities [...] and thus produced the greatest, and, to speak the truth, the only *social* revolution ever heard of in Asia.' Marx, 'British Rule in India', p. 93.

133. R. Wright, 'Tradition and Industrialization: The Historic Meaning', pp. 719–20.

134. R. Wright, 'Tradition and Industrialization: The Historic Meaning', pp. 721–22 (emphases added).

135. Cf. 'man, the sovereign of nature': Marx, 'British Rule in India', p. 94.

136. R. Wright, 'Tradition and Industrialization: The Historic Meaning', pp. 722–23 (emphases added).

137. R. Wright, 'Tradition and Industrialization: The Historic Meaning', pp. 723–25.

138. R. Wright, 'Tradition and Industrialization: The Historic Meaning', pp. 727–28 (emphasis added).

139. [E.] Wright and Fabre, *Richard Wright Reader*, pp. 110–11.

140. R. Wright, *Pagan Spain*, pp. 228–29.

141. Baldwin, 'Letter from Paris'; cf. later version, Baldwin, 'Princes and Powers'.

142. Baldwin, 'Princes and Powers', p. 27.

143. Du Bois, 'To the Congrès'. For more on Du Bois and the Cold War, see Horne, *Black and Red*.

144. In the later version of the text Baldwin changed the wording to read, 'Du Bois' extremely ill-conceived communication': Baldwin, 'Princes and Powers', pp. 27–28.

145. Baldwin, 'Letter from Paris,' p. 53.

146. Baldwin, 'Letter from Paris,' p. 53; Baldwin, 'Princes and Powers', pp. 29–30.

147. Baldwin, 'Princes and Powers', pp. 36–38, 44–46.

148. Baldwin to Sol Stein, undated; quoted in Menand, *Free World*, p. 420. On the Wright-Baldwin relationship, see Shatz, 'Introduction'.

149. A man who had been taught French by Jessie Fauset, Howard University's Professor Rayford W. Logan, was one of the most striking cases. Janken, *Rayford W. Logan*.

150. Orwell, 'Burnham's View', p. 321.

151. Burnham, *Suicide of the West*, pp. 3–5, 6–8.

152. Burnham, *Suicide of the West*, pp. 11–14, 15.

153. Burnham, *Suicide of the West*, pp. 345–46, 350–51.

154. For a distinguished example, among many, see Miłosz, 'L'Occident'.

155. Nora, 'Presentation'.

156. Kundera, *Kidnapped West*, pp. 36–37, 38–39 (emphasis added).

157. Kundera, *Kidnapped West*, pp. 44–45, 47–48.

158. Kundera, *Kidnapped West*, pp. 62–64, 72–73.

159. For a powerful analysis of this phenomenon, see Krastev and Holmes, *Light That Failed*, pp. 19–77.

160. Brodsky, 'Why Milan Kundera Is Wrong'. For some of Brodsky's own reflections on 'the West' and 'the East', see Brodsky, *Less than One*, pp. 123–63, 393–446; and for another interesting contribution, from Hungary, Bibó, *Misère des petits états d'Europe de l'Est*. Another Czechoslovak thinker had similar thoughts inside Communist Czechoslovakia: see Patočka, *Europa und Nach-Europa*; also, Hagedorn, 'Europa da Capo al Fine'; Hagedorn, 'Europe's Twentieth Century'.

161. Garton Ash, 'Where Is Central Europe Now?', p. 3.

162. On the significance of the Vietnam War for the American left's self-perceptions see Rorty, *Achieving Our Country*; Forrester, *In the Shadow of Justice*.

163. Allardyce, 'Rise and Fall', pp. 717–18. See also Weber, 'Western Civilization'; Segal, '"Western Civ"'; McNeill, 'What We Mean by the West'; Kimmage, *Abandonment of the West*. For examples of 'Western Civ' textbooks, see McNeill, *History of Western Civilization*; Hayes, Baldwin and Cole, *History of Western Civilization*; also, McNeill, *Rise of the West*; McNeill, *Pursuit of Truth*.

164. See Norton, *Leo Strauss*.

165. On the differences between the New York neoconservatives, as they emerged in the 1970s, and earlier Cold War conservatives of the kind represented by Whittaker Chambers, James Burnham and William F. Buckley, see Kimmage, *Abandonment of the West*, pp. 201–32. See also: J.-F. Drolet, *American Neoconservatism*.

166. Lilla, 'Athens and Chicago', pp. 59–61.

167. Bloom, *Closing of the American Mind*, pp. 35–39 (emphases added).

168. Bloom, *Closing of the American Mind*, pp. 35–39.

169. Bloom, *Closing of the American Mind*, pp. 141–56.

170. 'Η Ελλάς, πολιτικά, αμυντικά, οικονομικά, πολιτιστικά, ανήκει εις την Δύσιν.' Constantinos Caramanlis, speech to the Greek parliament, 12 June 1976.

171. That he had to assert it (and 'repeat it because I know it annoys the President of PASOK' [Andreas Papandreou], as he put it) is of course a strong reminder that it was disputed by some. This is how these things work.

172. On the role of Pope John Paul II, see Garton Ash, *Homelands*; Gaddis, *Cold War*, pp. 192–96, 217–23.

173. In a different context, Burnham had explicitly used the Arminius–Varus metaphor in 1964. Burnham, *Suicide of the West*, p. 345.

174. Herman, *Idea of Decline*, pp. 187–22.

175. Marchand, 'Leo Frobenius'.

176. Among many works, see Greenberg, *Weimar Century*.

Chapter 9: What Is 'the West' after the Cold War?

1. Fukuyama, 'End of History?', p. 3.

2. Toynbee, *Study of History*, vol. 1, p. 35.

3. Fukuyama, 'End of History?', p. 10 n. 12. For the footnote in question, see Kojève, *Introduction à la lecture de Hegel*, pp. 509–11; for the remarks on Japan, ibid., p. 511. (English translation: Kojève, *Introduction to the Reading of Hegel*.)

4. Fukuyama, 'End of History?' p. 18. For Fukuyama's responses to early criticisms, see Fukuyama, 'Reply to My Critics'; for the book version, Fukuyama, *End of History and the Last Man*. For critiques, see P. Anderson, *Zone of Engagement*; P. Anderson, *American Foreign Policy*.

5. Burnham, *Suicide of the West*, pp. xxix, 20, 22, 51, 81, 98–99, 131, 167–69, 228–29, 244, 282–83.

6. Rorty, *Achieving Our Country*, pp. 42–43, 45, 62, 70–71, 100.

7. See Aldous, *Schlesinger*.

8. Schlesinger, *Disuniting of America*, pp. 9–10, 11–12, 14–15, 26–27.

9. On the 'ferocious' reactions to Schlesinger's book at the time, see Aldous, *Schlesinger*, pp. 375–77.

10. Schlesinger, *Disuniting of America*, pp. 38–41, 53, 93, 19.

11. Schlesinger, *Disuniting of America*, pp. 122–23, 124 (emphasis added).

12. Schlesinger, *Disuniting of America*, pp. 126–27.

13. Schlesinger, *Disuniting of America*, pp. 134–35 (emphasis added).

14. For fascinating insights into Castoriadis's role in French intellectual life, see the recent autobiographical account of a contemporary: Morin, *Les Souvenirs viennent*; also Premat, 'New Generation'; Winock, *Siècle des intellectuels*, pp. 618, 630, 631, 745–46, 750.
15. See, for example, Castoriadis, 'Crisis of Western Societies'; Castoriadis, 'Greek Polis'.
16. Castoriadis, 'When the East Swings to the West' (interview published 1 November 1989), p. 159.
17. Castoriadis, 'Gorbachev', p. 181.
18. Castoriadis, 'Gulf War', pp. 171, 172, 173–74.
19. Castoriadis, 'Gulf War', pp. 174–75.
20. Castoriadis, 'On War, Religion, and Politics', p. 184.
21. Huntington, 'Clash of Civilizations?', p. 38.
22. Huntington, 'No Exit'; quotation at p 10.
23. Huntington, *Clash of Civilizations*.
24. Huntington, *Who Are We?*.
25. Huntington, 'No Exit', p. 8.
26. Huntington, 'Clash of Civilizations?', pp. 22, 23–24, 25 (emphases added).
27. Huntington, 'Clash of Civilizations?', pp. 26–27.
28. Naipaul, 'Our Universal Civilization'. For Huntington's criticisms, see Huntington, 'Clash of Civilizations?', p. 40; Huntington, *Clash of Civilizations*, p. 56.
29. Huntington, 'Clash of Civilizations?', pp. 40–41. See also Huntington, *Clash of Civilizations*, pp. 56–78.
30. Huntington, 'Clash of Civilizations?', p. 49. Walt, 'Building Up New Bogeymen', p. 189.
31. Huntington, 'The West Unique', pp. 30, 34–35 (emphasis added).
32. Huntington, 'The West Unique', p. 41.
33. Huntington, 'Clash of Civilizations?', p. 49.
34. Huntington, 'The West Unique' p. 45. Unlike Huntington, I hesitate to predict the future, and of course all things may change; but at the time of writing, in the context of the Russian attempted invasion of Ukraine, Greece has participated in all sanctions against Russia and in sending weapons to Ukraine (see, e.g., 'Russian Anger Builds as Greece Prepares a Military Deal with Ukraine', https://www.aljazeera.com/news/2024/7/16/russian-anger-builds-as-greece-prepares-a-military-deal-with-ukraine [accessed 16 October 2024])—and the Mitsotakis government that has pursued that policy was very comfortably re-elected in June 2023. Greece's military aligment with the USA and France has been steadily increasing in recent years.
35. *Wertegemeinschaft*: 'community of values'.
36. Lilla, 'Other Velvet Revolution', p. 144.
37. J.-W. Müller, *Another Country*, p. 90.
38. Hösle, *Short History*, p. 253.
39. Stirk, *Twentieth-Century German Political Thought*, pp. 167–68, 183–85.
40. J.-W. Müller, *Another Country*, p. 92.
41. Habermas, 'Historical Consciousness', pp. 249–50, 268 (emphases added).
42. J.-W. Müller, *Constitutional Patriotism*; J.-W. Müller, *Another Country*, pp. 90–119.
43. J.-W. Müller, *Another Country*, p. 97.
44. Lilla, 'Other Velvet Revolution', p. 146.

45. J.-W. Müller, *Another Country*, p. 104.
46. J.-W. Müller, *Another Country*, p. 111.
47. Dahrendorf, 'Zeitgenosse Habermas,' pp. 480–81.
48. J.-W. Müller, *Another Country*, pp. 111–12 (emphasis added).
49. J.-W. Müller, *Another Country*, p. 117.
50. Zitlemann, Weissmann and Grossheim, 'Einleitung'.
51. Derrida and Habermas, 'February 15', p. 44.
52. Levy, Pensky and Torpey, *Old Europe, New Europe, Core Europe*; Sloterdijk and Finkielkraut, *Les Battements du monde*, pp. 151–201.
53. Habermas, *Zur Verfassung Europas*; Habermas, *Crisis of the European Union*; Habermas, *Gespaltene Westen* (translated as Habermas, *Divided West*).
54. His longest work is Winkler, *Geschichte des Westens*; for the English translation of one of the volumes, see Winkler, *Age of Catastrophe*.
55. See, for example, Winkler, 'Was heißt westliche Wertgemeinschaft?'.
56. Doering-Manteuffel, 'Eine politische Nationalgeschichte'.
57. Winkler, *Germany: The Long Road West*, vols 1 and 2; originally Winkler, *Der Lange Weg nach Westen*, vols 1 and 2
58. Bavaj and Steber, 'Introduction', p. 2.
59. Riley, 'Metaphysicking the West', p. 125.
60. Zitlemann, Weissmann and Grossheim, *Westbindung*.
61. Winkler, 'Westbindung oder was sonst?'
62. Winkler, 'Westbindung oder was sonst?', pp. 114–15, 117.
63. Riley, 'Metaphysicking the West', p. 127.
64. Kurth, 'Real Clash'.
65. Huntington, *Clash of Civilizations*, p. 307.
66. Kurth, 'Real Clash,' pp. 9, 10.
67. Kurth, 'Real Clash,' pp. 11, 14–15.
68. Kurth, 'NATO Expansion', pp. 564–65.
69. Kurth, 'NATO Expansion', pp. 566–67.
70. Kimmage, *Abandonment of the West*. (Meanwhile Kurth is not mentioned in Kimmage's book.)
71. Kurth, *What are We Fighting For?*, pp. 12–14.
72. Kimmage, *Abandonment of the West*, p. 303.
73. Beinart, 'Racial and Religious Paranoia'. Some of the reactions are reported in Betts, *Ruin and Renewal*, pp. 446–47.
74. The Russians had annexed the Crimea by force in 2014.
75. Trump, 'Remarks'.
76. Beinart, 'Racial and Religious Paranoia'.
77. Beinart, 'Racial and Religious Paranoia'.
78. Beinart, 'Racial and Religious Paranoia'.
79. Foster, 'In Defense of "The West"'.
80. Foster, 'In Defense of "The West"'.
81. Beinart, 'Defending Liberal Democracy'.
82. Beinart, 'Defending Liberal Democracy'.

83. Houellebecq, 'Donald Trump', p. 224.
84. Lilla, 'Paris, January 2015', p. 109.
85. Kaprièlian, 'Cassandra of the Fifth Republic', p. 3.
86. Lilla, 'Paris, January 2015', pp. 116, 117, 125–27.
87. Kaprièlian, 'Cassandra of the Fifth Republic', p. 4.
88. Lilla, 'Paris, January 2015', pp. 127–28.
89. Houellebecq, *Submission*, pp. 226–27 (emphases added).
90. Houellebecq, *Submission*, p. 227.
91. Houellebecq, *Submission*, pp. 229, 230–31 (emphases added).
92. See Dickson, 'René Guénon'; François, 'Nouvelle Droite'.
93. Bourdeau, *Auguste Comte aujourd'hui*; the preface has been published in English as Houellebecq, 'Prolegomena to Positivism'; quotation at p. 135.
94. Houellebecq, *Atomised*, pp. 79, 309, 358. See also Houellebecq, *Platform* (originally *Plateforme*), pp. 178, 232, 299, 318.
95. Houellebecq, *Anéantir*, pp. 453, 695, 707, 709.
96. Houellebecq, *Submission*, p. 6.
97. Houellebecq, 'Interview with Christian Authier', pp. 103, 105, 107.
98. Ivan Krastev and Stephen Holmes have recently proposed 'Age of Imitation' for the thirty-year period from 1989 to 2019 (Krastev and Holmes, *Light That Failed*).
99. "'As a historian I fear Brexit could be the beginning of the destruction of not only the EU but also Western political civilisation in its entirety", [Donald Tusk] told the German newspaper *Bild*.' *BBC News*, 13 June 2016, https://www.bbc.co.uk/news/uk-politics-eu-referendum-36515680 (accessed 13 August 2024).
100. Deudney and Ikenberry, 'Logic of the West', pp. 17–21. For Stephen Walt's criticisms, see Cumings et al., 'Is There a Logic of the West?', pp. 117–20.
101. Goodhart, *Road to Somewhere*; Krastev, *After Europe*, pp. 86–93 and passim.
102. Minogue, 'Polls Apart', pp. 4, 6. For a recent analysis of Minogue's civilisational thinking, see S. Irving, 'Competitiveness, Civilizationism, and the Anglosphere'.
103. For a powerful analysis of the multiple reasons that have been conspiring of late towards a crisis of culture more generally, see Roy, *Crisis of Culture*. For a recent argument to the effect that criticisms of the West by 'what has come to be called the woke movement' are the culmination of a quintessentially Western 'hyper-liberalism' (or that 'the anti-Western creed of an antinomian intelligentsia [...] is ineffably Western'), see Gray, *New Leviathans*, pp. 109–15. For criticisms of Western attitudes to Gaza since October 2023, see Mishra, 'Shoah after Gaza'; Mações, 'Gaza and the End of Western Fantasy'. For some of the (vastly differing) defences mentioned, see Finkielkraut, *Undoing of Thought*; Scruton, *West and the Rest*; Bruckner, *Tyrannie de la pénitence* (translated as Bruckner, *Tyranny of Guilt*); Ferguson, *Civilization*; Murray, *War on the West*; Hirsi Ali, 'Why the West Is Best'; Hirsi Ali, 'Why I Am Now a Christian'; Neiman, *Left is not Woke*; Neiman, 'Fanon the Universalist'. The 'patriot of the West' characterisation applied to Ferguson appears in Bromwich, 'What Is the West?', p. 285.
104. Bavaj and Steber, 'Introduction', p. 25. Among the many further books or essays focusing on 'the West' and its future (or lack thereof) published in the past decades are: Coker, *Twilight of the West*; Gress, *From Plato to NATO*; Garton Ash, *Free World*; Nemo, *Qu'est-ce que l'Occident?* (translated as Nemo, *What Is the West?*); Manent, *Metamorphoses de la Cité*

(translated as Manent, *Metamorphoses of the City*); Marquand, *End of the West*; Debray and Girard, *Que reste-t-il de l'Occident?*; Debray, 'Decline of the West?'; Debray, 'L'Occident est-il en déclin?'; [David A.] Bell and Grafton, *The West*; Kurtz, *Lost History*; Emmott, *Fate of the West*; Joschka Fischer, *Abstieg des Westens*; E. Todd, *Défaite de l'Occident*.

Chapter 10: Conclusion

1. Heeren, *Reflections*, p. 152

2. According to Maçães, 'Past equivalents to the Belt and Road would have to be just as shapeless and ambitious. Perhaps concepts such as "the West" come the closest–even in the manner that a metaphor came to acquire epochal significance.' Maçães, *Belt and Road*, p. 30.

3. On Comte's decision to refrain from reading other people's works and newspapers (except poetry) for several years (and more generally on his attempts to isolate himself from his century), see Pickering, *Auguste Comte*, vol. 1, pp. 485–86, 503.

4. Nietzsche, *On the Genealogy of Morality*, p. 53.

5. Geuss, 'Nietzsche and Genealogy', pp. 280–81.

6. Here Geuss clarifies that in fact in this context Nietzsche doesn't speak of 'agencies', but of 'wills'.

7. Geuss, 'Nietzsche and Genealogy', pp. 281–82 (emphasis added).

8. A good example of what is meant here is David Gress's *From Plato to NATO: The Idea of the West and Its Opponents*. Despite its title, that book did not offer anything like a historical account of the idea of the West. Rather, it was a polemical attempt to debunk what the author considers a wrong account, 'the grand narrative' of 'Western Civilization', in order to substitute what has been aptly called 'a counter-narrative that is no less essentialist' (Bavaj, '"The West"'). See also P. T. Jackson, '"Civilization"on Trial'.

9. For significant recent examples, see the analysis in Brubaker, 'Between Nationalism and Civilizationism'.

10. For a brief but powerful argument related to what I am saying here, see Plamenatz, 'Two Types of Nationalism'. Plamenatz was born in Montenegro, though educated in Britain. For a fascinating, more recent analysis of related psychological reactions of 'feelings of inadequacy, inferiority, dependency, lost identity and involuntary insincerity' resulting from mimicking the West and resenting doing so, see Krastev and Holmes, *Light That Failed*, p. 71 and passim.

11. Troeltsch, 'Ideas of Natural Law', p. 221; original: Troeltsch, 'Naturrecht und Humanität', p. 500.

12. Ivan Krastev and Stephen Holmes convincingly argue that the recent appeal of illiberal leaders in Central and Eastern Europe, after two decades of perceived insults and humiliations at the hands of self-appointed 'Western' copyright-holders of a liberal model to be imitated, has to be understood primarily in psychological terms. Krastev and Holmes, *Light That Failed*.

13. Fukuzawa, *Outline of a Theory*; Craig, *Civilization and Enlightenment*; Teng and Fairbank, *China's Response*, pp. 153–57, 220–23; Levenson, *Liang Ch'i-ch'ao*; Chang, *Liang Ch'i-ch'ao*.

14. Moses, *Afrotopia*; Gökalp, *Türkçülüğün Esasları*; Gökalp, *Turkish Nationalism*; Gökalp, *Principles of Turkism*; Kedourie, 'Introduction'; Heyd, *Foundations of Turkish Nationalism*; Parla, *Social and Political Thought*.

15. Locke, 'Cultural Relativism', p. 552.

16. I am not including national 'imagined communities' in the list because, though they are very much 'imagined' in the way Benedict Anderson explains in his eponymous book (B. Anderson, *Imagined Communities*, p. 6), those 'nations' that have achieved statehood enjoy a relatively tangible existence, to the extent that they offer their members the legal status of citizenship. That there is no such thing as a nation state, and that states do not exactly coincide with nations I take for granted. Literally speaking, the 'nation state' is an aspiration, a self-fulfilling prophecy to which some states have approximated more than others. But France, being a state, has a more tangible existence than 'the West', nevertheless.

17. I am grateful to Henri Otsing for his stimulating question. Of course there might be dangers in the unity in question, since February 2022. For that argument, see Meaney, 'Putin Wants a Clash of Civilizations'.

18. https://www.bbc.co.uk/sounds/play/m000s84r (accessed 16 October 2024).

19. Du Bois, *Quest of the Silver Fleece*, p. 399; see also Withun, 'Zora's Bookshelf'; D. L. Lewis, *W.E.B. Du Bois*, pp. 294–96; for the quotation, Withun, *Co-Workers*, p. 214. For recent related arguments, see Montás, *Rescuing Socrates*; Montás, 'Martin Luther King, as Teacher'.

20. Hanink, *Classical Debt*, pp. 16, 18. For works advancing similar arguments before George James, see, for example, Parker, 'African Origins'; Parker, *Children of the Sun*.

21. [Anon.,] '[Review of] An Oration Pronounced at Cambridge', p. 433.

22. Mill, 'Negro Question', p. 93. Marchand, 'Herodotus and the Embarrassments'.

23. Massis, 'Defence of the West, I', p. 233.

24. Besides the lengthy books addressing the topic, there was immense coverage in the press. See, for examples, Toynbee, 'No Chosen People'; [Anon.,] 'Dr. Toynbee and his Critics'. For some among many recent estimates of Toynbee's work and influence, see Hall, '"Time of Troubles"'; Hall, '"Toynbee Convector"'; Kumar, 'Return of Civilization'. More recently the 'appropriation of the foreign' as the main characteristic of 'Western' or 'European' culture has been insisted upon in Brague, *Eccentric Culture*, pp. 92–109 and passim (for the original, Brague, *Europe, la voie romaine*, pp. 120–41 and passim).

25. For a notable recent example, see Quinn, *How the World Made the West*.

26. For some (among many) examples, see Mac Sweeney, *The West*, pp. 351–52; R. F. Kennedy, 'Classics and Western Civilization'; R. F. Kennedy, '"Western Civilization", White Supremacism'; Walden, 'Dismantling "the West"'. After the death of George Floyd in 2020, the Society for Classical Studies issued a statement that it 'recognizes and acknowledges the complicity of Classics as a field in constructing and participating in racist and anti-black educational structures and attitudes. [...] On the one hand, white supremacist and nationalist groups have misappropriated Classics and other pre-modern fields for their own hateful agendas. On the other, within the discipline and profession itself scholars have perpetuated racist attitudes and ideas. These attitudes and ideas include [...] the misleadingly reductive notion of a "Western Civilization" resulting from an allegedly linear transfer of knowledge from Greece to Rome to Western Europe; the whitewashing of ancient Mediterranean culture; [and] the uncritical use of Greece and Rome as ideals that serve as the foundations of the notion of American "exceptionalism"'. Society for Classical Studies, 'SCS Statement'.

27. Hunt, 'Myths of Our Civilisation', p. 10.

28. See above, chapter 6, section IX.

29. Cf. Charrier, *Scientisme et Occident*.
30. Aron, *Opium of the Intellectuals*, p. 57.
31. Walt, 'Building Up New Bogeymen', p. 187.
32. Brodsky, 'Flight from Byzantium', p. 435.
33. Castoriadis, 'Gulf War', p. 175; Wright, 'Tradition and Industrialization: The Historic Meaning', p. 728.

BIBLIOGRAPHY

Achille, Louis T. 'Upwards to Citizenship in the French Empire'. *The Crisis*, June 1940, pp. 172–73, 186.

Adamovsky, Ezequiel. 'Euro-Orientalism and the Making of the Concept of Eastern Europe in France, 1810–1880'. *The Journal of Modern History* 77, no. 3 (2005): 591–628.

Adamovsky, Ezequiel. *Euro-Orientalism: Liberal Ideology and the Image of Russia in France (c. 1740–1880)*. Bern: Peter Lang, 2006.

Adams, Brooks. *The Law of Civilization and Decay: An Essay on History*. New York: Alfred A. Knopf, 1943 [1895].

Adams, Henry. *The Letters of Henry Adams*, edited by Jacob C. Levenson, 6 vols. Cambridge, MA: Harvard University Press, 1982–88.

Adas, Michael. *Machines as the Measure of Men: Science, Technology and Ideologies of Western Dominance*. Ithaca, NY: Cornell University Press, 1989.

Adas, Michael. 'Contested Hegemony: The Great War and the Afro-Asian Assault on the Civilizing Mission Ideology'. *Journal of World History* 15, no. 1 (2004): 31–63.

Adcock, Robert. *Liberalism and the Emergence of American Political Science: A Transatlantic Tale*. Oxford: Oxford University Press, 2014.

Aeschylus. *Persians*, in *Aeschylus 1 (Persians, Seven against Thebes, Suppliants, Prometheus Bound)*, edited and translated by Alan H. Sommerstein (Loeb Classical Library 145). Cambridge, MA: Harvard University Press, 2009.

Aldous, Richard. *Schlesinger: The Imperial Historian*. New York: W. W. Norton & Co., 2017.

[d'Alembert, Jean Le Rond]. 'Occident', in *Encyclopédie ou Dictionnaire raisonné des sciences, des arts et des métiers* (facsimile reprint of the first edition of 1751–80), vol. 11, p. 331. Stuttgart-Bad Cannstatt: Frommann, 1988.

Allardyce, Gilbert. 'The Rise and Fall of the Western Civilization Course'. *The American Historical Review* 87, no. 3 (1982): 695–725.

Anderson, Benedict. *Imagined Communities: Reflections on the Origin and Spread of Nationalism*, revised edition. London: Verso, 1991.

Anderson, M[atthew] S. *Britain's Discovery of Russia 1553–1815*. London: Macmillan, 1958.

Anderson, Perry. *American Foreign Policy and Its Thinkers*. London: Verso, 2015.

Anderson, Perry. *A Zone of Engagement*. London: Verso, 1992.

Andrade, Oswald de. 'Manifesto of Pau-Brasil Poetry' [1924], translated by Stella M. de Sá Rego. *Latin American Literary Review* 14, no. 27 (1986): 184–87.

[Anon.] 'As Others See Us' [leading article]. *The Times*, 22 December 1952, p. 7.

[Anon.] 'Custine's Rußland'. *Zeitung für die elegante Welt*, no. 27 (5 July 1843), pp. 656–60.
[Anon.] 'Dr. Toynbee and his Critics'. *Times Literary Supplement*, no. 3100 (28 July 1961), pp. 457–58.
[Anon.] 'German Pamphlet: The Cause of Greece the Cause of Europe'. *The Calcutta Journal*, 25 January 1822.
[Anon.] 'Orientalism'. *The Knickerbocker: or, New York Monthly Magazine*, vol. 41, no. 6 (June, 1853), pp. 479–96.
[Anon.] '[Review of] An Oration Pronounced at Cambridge, before the Phi Beta Kappa Society, August 27, 1824, by Edward Everett; An Oration Delivered at Plymouth, December 22, 1824, by Edward Everett'. *The North American Review*, vol. 20, no. 47 (April 1825), pp. 417–40.
[Anon.] '[Review of] International Policy: Essays on the Foreign Policy of England. London: Chapman and Hall. 1866'. *The North American Review*, vol. 103, no. 213 (1866), pp. 608–9.
Appiah, Kwame Anthony. *The Lies that Bind: Rethinking Identity: Creed, Country, Colour, Class, Culture*. London: Profile Books.
Aragon, Louis. 'Fragments d'une conférence'. *La Révolution surréaliste*, no. 4 (15 July 1925), p. 25.
Arendt, Hannah. 'Approaches to the "German Problem"' [*Partisan Review*, vol. 12, no. 1 (Winter 1945)], in Arendt, *Essays in Understanding 1930–1954: Formation, Exile, and Totalitarianism*, edited by Jerome Kohn, pp. 106–20. New York: Harcourt, Brace & Co., 1994.
Arendt, Hannah. *The Burden of Our Time*. London: Secker & Warburg, 1951.
Arendt, Hannah. 'Dream and Nightmare' [1954], in Arendt, *Essays in Understanding 1930–1954: Formation, Exile, and Totalitarianism*, edited by Jerome Kohn, pp. 409–17. New York: Harcourt Brace and Company, 1994.
Arendt, Hannah. 'Europe and the Atom Bomb' [1954], in Arendt, *Essays in Understanding 1930–1954: Formation, Exile, and Totalitarianism*, edited by Jerome Kohn, pp. 418–22. New York: Harcourt Brace and Company, 1994.
Arendt, Hannah. *On Violence*. New York: Harcourt Brace Jovanovich, 1970 [1969].
Arendt, Hannah. *The Origins of Totalitarianism*. London: André Deutsch, 1986 [1952].
Arendt, Hannah. 'Religion and Politics' [1953], in Arendt, *Essays in Understanding 1930–1954: Formation, Exile, and Totalitarianism*, edited by Jerome Kohn, pp. 368–90. New York: Harcourt Brace and Company, 1994.
Arendt, Hannah. 'The Threat of Conformism' [1954], in Arendt, *Essays in Understanding 1930–1954: Formation, Exile, and Totalitarianism*, edited by Jerome Kohn, pp. 423–27. New York: Harcourt Brace and Company, 1994.
Arendt, Hannah. 'What is Authority?', in Arendt, *Between Past and Future: Eight Exercises in Political Thought*, pp. 91–141. London: Penguin, 2006 [1961; expanded edition 1968].
Armenteros, Carolina. *The French Idea of History: Joseph de Maistre and his Heirs, 1794–1854*. Ithaca, NY: Cornell University Press, 2011.
Armitage, David. *Foundations of Modern International Thought*. Cambridge: Cambridge University Press, 2013.
Armitage, David. *The Ideological Origins of the British Empire*. Cambridge: Cambridge University Press, 2000.
Armitage, David. 'What's the Big Idea? Intellectual History and the Longue Durée'. *History of European Ideas* 38, no. 4 (2012): 493–507.

Armstrong, William M. *E. L. Godkin: A Biography*. Albany, NY: State University of New York Press, 1978.

Aron, Raymond. 'Contre le défaitisme' [1950], in Aron, *Les Articles du Figaro*, vol. 1: *La Guerre froide 1947–1955*, pp. 359–63. Paris, Éditions de Fallois, 1990.

Aron, Raymond. *L'Opium des intellectuels*. Paris: Calmann-Lévy, 1955.

Aron, Raymond. *The Opium of the Intellectuals*. New Brunswick, NJ: Transaction Publishers, 2001 [1955].

Aron, Raymond. *Peace and War: A Theory of International Relations*. New Brunswick, NJ: Transaction Publishers, 2003 [*Paix et guerre entre les nations*, 1962].

Aron, Raymond. 'Pour l'alliance de l'Occident' [1944], in Aron, *L'Âge des empires et l'avenir de la France*, pp. 319–36. Paris: Éditions Défense de la France, 1945.

Aron, Raymond. 'Remarques sur la politique étrangère de la France' [1945], in Aron, *L'Âge des empires et l'avenir de la France*, pp. 337–54. Paris: Éditions Défense de la France, 1945.

Aron, Raymond. *République impériale: Les États-Unis dans le monde, 1945–1972*. Paris: Calmann-Lévy, 1973.

Aron, Raymond. *La Société industrielle et la guerre, suivi d'un tableau de la diplomatie mondiale en 1958*, 2nd edition. Paris: Plon, 1959.

Aron, Raymond. 'L'Unité française en peril' [1955], in Aron, *Les Articles du 'Figaro'*, vol. 2: *La Coexistence 1955–1965*, pp. 98–103. Paris, Éditions de Fallois, 1993.

Ashcroft, Caroline. *Catastrophic Technology in Cold War Political Thought*. Edinburgh: Edinburgh University Press, 2024.

Ashton, Rosemary. *The German Idea: Four English Writers and the Reception of German Thought 1800–1860*. London: Libris, 1994 [1980].

Audier, Serge (ed.). *Le Colloque Walter Lippmann: Aux origines du 'néo-libéralisme'*. Lormont: Éditions Le Bord de l'Eau, 2012.

Auffret, Dominique. *Alexandre Kojève: La philosophie, l'état, la fin de l'histoire*. Paris: Grasset, 1990.

Avineri, Shlomo (ed.). *Karl Marx on Colonialism and Modernization: His Despatches and Other Writings on China, India, Mexico, the Middle East and North Africa*. Garden City, NY: Anchor Books, 1969.

Aydin, Cemil. *The Politics of Anti-Westernism in Asia: Visions of World Order in Pan-Islamic and Pan-Asian Thought*. New York: Columbia University Press, 2007.

Bacon, Francis. 'Novum Organum' [1620], in Bacon, *The Works of Francis Bacon*, edited by James Spedding, Robert Leslie Ellis and Douglas Denon Heath, vol. 1: *Philosophical Works 1*, pp. 147–366. Cambridge: Cambridge University Press, 2011 [1872].

Bailey, Christian. *Between Yesterday and Tomorrow: German Visions of Europe 1926–1950*. New York: Berghahn, 2013.

Bailey, Christian. 'The Continuities of West German History: Conceptions of Europe, Democracy and the West in Interwar and Postwar Germany'. *Geschichte und Gesellschaft* 36, no. 4 (2010), pp. 567–96.

Baldwin, James. 'Letter from Paris: Princes and Powers'. *Encounter*, January 1957, pp. 52–60.

Baldwin, James. 'Princes and Powers', in Baldwin, *Nobody Knows My Name: More Notes of a Native Son*. London: Penguin, 1991 [1964].

Bancroft, George. 'Russia' [1829], in Bancroft, *Literary and Historical Miscellanies*, pp. 3128–33. New York: Harper & Brothers, 1855.

[Bancroft, George.] 'Writings of Herder'. *The North American Review*, vol. 20 (January 1825), pp. 138–47.

Barau, Denis. 'What Independence for Greece? Abbé de Pradt's Point of View'. *The Historical Review / La Revue historique* 18, no. 1 (2021): 135–47.

Baritz, Loren. 'The Idea of the West'. *The American Historical Review* 66, no. 3 (1961): 618–40.

Barrault, Émile. 'Une noce à Constantinople'. *Revue des deux mondes*, vol. 4, 3rd series (1834), pp. 152–73.

Barth, Hans. 'Die Theologie Joseph de Maistres als Urbild der Soziologie von Auguste Comte'. *Neue Züricher Zeitung*, 4 August 1956.

Basbanes, Nicholas A. *Cross of Snow: A Life of Henry Wadsworth Longfellow*. New York: Alfred A. Knopf, 2020.

Basch, Sophie. *Le Mirage grec: La Grèce moderne devant l'opinion française (1846–1946)*. Paris: Hatier, 1995.

Basch, Victor. 'La Philosophie et la Littérature classiques de l'Allemagne et les doctrines pangermanistes'. *Revue de métaphysique et de morale* 22, no. 6 (1914): 711–93.

Bassett, John Spencer (ed.). *Correspondence of George Bancroft and Jared Sparks, 1823–1832: Illustrating the Relation between Editor and Reviewer in the Early Nineteenth Century*. Northampton, MA: Department of History of Smith College, 1917.

Bavaj, Riccardo. 'Cold War Liberalism in West Germany: Richard Löwenthal and "Western civilization"'. *History of European Ideas* 49, no. 3 (2023): 607–24.

Bavaj, Riccardo. '"The West": A Conceptual Exploration'. *Europäische Geschichte Online*, https://www.ieg-ego.eu/en/threads/crossroads/political-spaces/riccardo-bavaj-the-west-a-conceptual-exploration (accessed 17 October 2024).

Bavaj, Riccardo and Martina Steber (eds). *Germany and 'The West': The History of a Modern Concept*. New York: Berghahn, 2015.

Bavaj, Riccardo and Martina Steber. 'Introduction: Germany and "the West"; the Vagaries of a Modern Relationship', in Bavaj and Steber (eds), *Germany and 'The West': The History of a Modern Concept*, pp. 1–37. New York: Berghahn, 2015.

Beaton, Roderick. 'Philhellenism', in Paschalis M. Kitromilides and Constantinos Tsoukalas (eds), *The Greek Revolution: A Critical Dictionary*, pp. 593–613. Cambridge, MA: Harvard University Press, 2021.

Beinart, Peter. 'Defending Liberal Democracy Is Not the Same as Defending "the West"'. *The Atlantic*, 11 July 2017, https://www.theatlantic.com/international/archive/2017/07/democracy-west-trump-poland/533208/ (accessed 17 October 2024).

Beinart, Peter. 'The Racial and Religious Paranoia of Trump's Warsaw Speech'. *The Atlantic*, 6 July 2017, https://www.theatlantic.com/international/archive/2017/07/trump-speech-poland/532866/ (accessed 17 October 2024).

Belinski, V. G. *Selected Philosophical Works*. Moscow: Foreign Language Publishing House, 1948).

Bell, David A. and Anthony Grafton. *The West: A New History*. New York: W. W. Norton, 2018.

Bell, Duncan. 'Alter Orbis: E. A. Freeman and Racial Destiny', in Bell, *Reordering the World: Essays on Liberalism and Empire*, pp. 321–40. Princeton, NJ: Princeton University Press, 2016.

Bell, Duncan. *Dreamworlds of Race: Empire and the Utopian Destiny of Anglo-America*. Princeton, NJ: Princeton University Press, 2020.

Bell, Duncan. 'What Is Liberalism?', *Political Theory* 42, no. 6 (2014): 682–715.

Bem, Jeanne and André Guyaux (eds). *Ernst Robert Curtius et l'idée d'Europe: Actes du Colloque de Mulhouse et Thann des 29, 30 et 31 janvier 1992*. Paris: Honoré Champion, 1995.

Benda, Julien. 'Occident et Extrême-Occident'. *Les Cahiers politiques*, no. 9 (April 1945), pp. 20–27.

Bent, Johannes and Liisi Keedus. 'Contesting German "Crisis Literature": Oswald Spengler in Interwar Hungarian and Romanian Reviews', in Balázs Trencsényi, Una Blagojević, Isidora Grubački and Lucija Balikić (eds), *East Central European Crisis Discourses in the Twentieth Century: A Never-Ending Story?*, pp. 55–77. London: Routledge, 2024.

Berdyaev, Nicolas. *The Origin of Russian Communism*. London: Geoffrey Bless: The Centenary Press, 1937.

Berghahn, Volker R. *America and the Intellectual Cold Wars in Europe: Shepard Stone between Philanthropy, Academy, and Diplomacy*. Princeton, NJ: Princeton University Press, 2001.

Bergmann, Peter. 'American Exceptionalism and German *Sonderweg* in Tandem'. *The International History Review* 23, no. 3 (2001): 505–34.

Bergson, Henri. *La Signification de la guerre*. Paris: Bloud et Gay, 1915.

Betts, Paul. *Ruin and Renewal: Civilising Europe after the Second World War*. London: Profile Books, 2020.

Bevin, Ernest. 'Address Given by Ernest Bevin to the House of Commons (22 January 1948)', available at https://www.cvce.eu/content/publication/2002/9/9/7bc0ecbd-c50e-4035-8e36-ed70bfbd204c/publishable_en.pdf (accessed 17 October 2024).

Bibó, István. *Misère des petits états d'Europe de l'Est*, translated (into French) by György Kassai. Paris: Albin Michel, 1993 [1946].

Billington, James H. 'The Intelligentsia and the Religion of Humanity'. *The American Historical Review* 65, no. 4 (1960): 807–21.

Bitis, Alexander. *Russia and the Eastern Question: Army, Government, and Society 1815–1833*. Oxford: Oxford University Press, 2006.

Bloom, Allan. *The Closing of the American Mind: How Higher Education Has Failed Democracy and Impoverished the Souls of Today's Students*. New York: Simon and Schuster, 1987.

Blum, John Morton (ed.). *Public Philosopher: Selected Letters of Walter Lippmann*. New York: Ticknor & Fields, 1985.

Boas, Franz. 'Inventing a Great Race'. *The New Republic*, 13 January 1917, pp. 305–7.

Boas, Franz. 'This Nordic Nonsense'. *The Forum*, October 1925, pp. 502–511.

Bodin, Jean. *The Six Books of a Commonweale: A Fascimile Reprint of the English Translation of 1606 [...]*, edited by Kenneth Douglas Mc Rae. Cambridge, MA: Harvard University Press, 1962 [1576].

Bonfreschi, Lucia. 'Raymond Aron: Nationalism and Supranationalism in the Years following the Second World War', in Julian Bourg (ed.), *After the Deluge: New Perspectives on the*

Intellectual and Cultural History of Postwar France, pp. 227–50. Lanham, MD: Lexington Books, 2004.

Bonfreschi, Lucia. 'Le Libéralisme face au processus de décolonisation: Le cas de Raymond Aron'. *Outre-mers* 94, no. 354/355 (2007): 271–84.

Bonnett, Alastair. *The Idea of the West: Culture, Politics and History*. Basingstoke: Palgrave Macmillan, 2004.

Bornholdt, Laura. 'The Abbé de Pradt and the Monroe Doctrine'. *The Hispanic American Historical Review* 24, no. 2 (1944): 201–21.

Bourdeau, Michel. 'Auguste Comte' in *Stanford Encyclopedia of Philosophy*, 1 October 2008, revised 27 January 2022, http://plato.stanford.edu/entries/comte/ (accessed 17 October 2024).

Bourdeau, Michel (ed.). *Auguste Comte aujourd'hui*. Paris: Kimé, 2003.

Bourdeau, Michel. *Les Trois États: Science, théologie et métaphysique chez Auguste Comte*. Paris: Éditions du CERF, 2006.

Bourdieu, Pierre. 'Le Nord et le Midi: Contribution à une analyse de l'effet Montesquieu'. *Actes de la recherche en sciences sociales* 35 (1980): 21–25.

Bourke, Richard. *Empire and Revolution: The Political Life of Edmund Burke*. Princeton, NJ: Princeton University Press, 2015.

Bourke, Richard. *Hegel's World Revolutions*, Princeton, NJ: Princeton University Press, 2023.

Bourne, Randolph. 'American Use for German Ideals'. *The New Republic*, 4 September 1915.

Boutroux, Émile. 'L'Allemagne et la guerre: Deuxième lettre'. *Revue des deux mondes*, vol. 33, no. 2 (15 May 1916), pp. 241–63.

Boutroux, Émile. 'L'Allemagne et la guerre: Lettre de M. Émile Boutroux'. *Revue des deux mondes*, vol. 23, no. 4 (15 October 1914), pp. 385–401.

Bowersock, G. W. 'The East–West Orientation of Mediterranean Studies and the Meaning of North and South in Antiquity', in W. V. Harris (ed.), *Rethinking the Mediterranean*, pp. 167–78. Oxford: Oxford University Press, 2005.

Brague, Rémi. *Eccentric Culture: A Theory of Western Civilization*, translated by Samuel Lester. South Bend, IN: St. Augustin Press, 2002.

Brague, Rémi. *Europe, la voie romaine*. Paris: Éditions Critérion, 1992.

Brahami, Frédéric. 'Sortir du cercle: Auguste Comte, la critique et les rétrogrades'. *Archives de philosophie* 70, no. 1 (2007) : 41–55.

Braunstein, Jean-François. 'Auguste Comte, l'Europe et l'Occident', in Françoise Chenet-Faugeras (ed.), *Victor Hugo et l'Europe dans la pensée*, pp. 193–206. Paris: Nizet, 1995.

Braunstein, Jean-François. *La Philosophie de la médecine d'Auguste Comte: Vaches carnivores, Vierge Mère et morts vivants*. Paris: Presses Universitaires de France, 2009.

Breuer, Stefan. 'Retter des Abendlandes: Spenglerkritik von rechts'. *Jahrbuch zur Kultur und Literatur der Weimarer Republik* 9 (2004): 165–95.

Brodsky, Joseph. 'Flight from Byzantium' [1985], in Brodsky, *Less than One: Selected Essays*, pp. 393–446. New York: Farrar, Straus and Giroux, 1986.

Brodsky, Joseph. *Less than One: Selected Essays*. New York: Farrar, Straus and Giroux, 1986.

Brodsky, Joseph. 'Why Milan Kundera Is Wrong About Dostoyevsky'. *The New York Times*, 17 February 1985.

Brody, Samuel Hayim. 'Judaism, Philosophy, and the Idea of the West'. *Harvard Theological Review* 111, no. 1 (2018): 135–43.

Bromwich, David. 'What is the West?' [2011], in Bromwich, *Moral Imagination: Essays*, pp. 273–86. Princeton, NJ: Princeton University Press, 2014.

Brooks, Van Wyck. *The Flowering of New England, 1815–1865*, revised edition. New York: E. P. Dutton, 1941.

Brotton, Jerry. *Four Points of the Compass: The Unexpected History of Direction*. London: Allen Lane, 2024.

Brown, Frederick. *The Embrace of Unreason: France, 1914–1940*. New York: Alfred A. Knopf, 2014.

Brubaker, Rogers. 'Between Nationalism and Civilizationism: The European Populist Moment in Comparative Perspective'. *Ethnic and Racial Studies* 40, no. 8 (2017): 1191–226

Bruckner, Pascal. *La Tyrannie de la pénitence: Essai sur le masochisme occidental*. Paris: Grasset, 2006.

Bruckner, Pascal. *The Tyranny of Guilt: An Essay on Western Masochism*, translated by Steven Rendall. Princeton, NJ: Princeton University Press, 2010 [2006].

Bruneteau, Bernard. *Les 'Collabos' de l'Europe nouvelle*. Paris: CNRS Éditions, 2016 [2003].

Bryce, James. *The Holy Roman Empire*, revised edition. London: Macmillan and Co., 1906 [first edition 1864].

Buckle, Henry Thomas. *History of Civilization in England*, 3 vols. London: Longmans, Green, and Co., 1857–67.

Bullitt, William C. 'The World from Rome: The Eternal City fears a Struggle between Christianity and Communism'. *Life*, vol. 17, no. 10 (4 September 1944), pp. 94–96, 98, 100, 103–4, 106, 109.

Burke, Peter. 'Did Europe Exist before 1700?'. *History of European Ideas* 1, no. 1: 21–29.

Burnham, James. *Suicide of the West: An Essay on the Meaning and Destiny of Liberalism*. New York: Encounter Books, 2014 [1964].

Burrow, J. W. *The Crisis of Reason: European Thought, 1848–1914*. New Haven, CT: Yale University Press, 2000.

Burrow, J. W. *Evolution and Society: A Study in Victorian Social Theory*. Cambridge: Cambridge University Press, 1966.

Buruma, Ian and Avishai Margalit. *Occidentalism: A Short History of Anti-Westernism*. London: Atlantic Books, 2004.

Burwick, Fred L. 'The Göttingen Influence on George Bancroft's Idea of Humanity'. *Jahrbuch für Amerikastudien* 11 (1966): 194–212.

Butler, Edith May. *The Tyranny of Greece over Germany*. Cambridge: Cambridge University Press, 1935.

Cadot, Michel. *La Russie dans la vie intellectuelle française, 1839–1856*. Paris: Fayard, 1967.

Cameron, Frank and Don Dombowsky (eds). *Political Writings of Friedrich Nietzsche: An Edited Anthology*. Basingstoke: Palgrave Macmillan, 2008.

Campbell, James. 'Dewey and German Philosophy in Wartime'. *Transactions of the Charles S. Peirce Society* 40, no. 1 (2004): 1–20.

Camus, Albert. *Camus at 'Combat': Writing 1944–1947*, edited by Jacqueline Lévi-Valensi, translated by Arthur Goldhammer. Princeton, NJ: Princeton University Press, 2006.

Camus, Albert. 'La Culture indigène: La nouvelle culture méditerranéenne', in Camus, *Œuvres complètes*, vol: 1: *1931–1944*, edited by Jacqueline Lévi-Valensi, pp. 565–72. Paris: Gallimard, 2006.

Camus, Albert. 'Letters to a German Friend' [1943–45], in Camus, *Committed Writings*, translated by Justin O'Brien and Sandra Smith, pp. 1–33. London: Penguin, 2020.

Camus, Albert. *Speaking Out: Lectures and Speeches, 1937–58*, translated by Quintin Hoare. London: Penguin, 2021.

Camus, Albert. *Travels in the Americas: Notes and Impressions of a New World*, edited by Alice Kaplan, translated by Ryan Bloom. Chicago: The University of Chicago Press, 2023.

Carrel, Armand. *Résumé de l'histoire des Grecs modernes, depuis l'envahissement de la Grèce par les Turcs jusqu'aux derniers événements de la Révolution actuelle*, 2nd edition. Paris: Lecointe, 1829 [1825].

Case, Holly. *The Age of Questions*. Princeton, NJ: Princeton University Press, 2018.

Cashdollar, Charles D. *The Transformation of Theology, 1830–1890: Positivism and Protestant Thought in Britain and America*. Princeton, NJ: Princeton University Press, 1989.

Casteel, James E. *Russia in the German Global Imaginary: Imperial Visions and Utopian Desires*. Pittsburgh, PA: Pittsburgh University Press, 2016.

Castoriadis, Cornelius. 'The Crisis of Western Societies' [1982], in Castoriadis, *The Castoriadis Reader*, edited and translated by David Ames Curtis, pp. 253–66. Oxford: Blackwell, 1997.

Castoriadis, Cornelius. 'Gorbachev: Neither Reform nor Backtracking' [1991], in Castoriadis, *A Society Adrift: Interviews and Debates 1974–1997*, edited by Enrique Escobar, Myrto Gondicas and Pascal Vernay, translated by Helen Arnold, pp. 176–82. New York: Fordham University Press, 2010.

Castoriadis, Cornelius. 'The Greek Polis and the Creation of Democracy' [1983], in Castoriadis, *The Castoriadis Reader*, edited and translated by David Ames Curtis, pp. 267–89. Oxford: Blackwell, 1997.

Castoriadis, Cornelius. 'The Gulf War: Setting Things Straight' [1991], in Castoriadis, *A Society Adrift: Interviews and Debates 1974–1997*, edited by Enrique Escobar, Myrto Gondicas and Pascal Vernay, translated by Helen Arnold, pp. 171–75. New York: Fordham University Press, 2010.

Castoriadis, Cornelius. 'On War, Religion, and Politics' [1991], in Castoriadis, *A Society Adrift: Interviews and Debates 1974–1997*, edited by Enrique Escobar, Myrto Gondicas and Pascal Vernay, translated by Helen Arnold, pp. 183–89. New York: Fordham University Press, 2010.

Castoriadis, Cornelius. 'When the East Swings to the West' [1989], in Castoriadis, *A Society Adrift: Interviews and Debates 1974–1997*, edited by Enrique Escobar, Myrto Gondicas and Pascal Vernay, translated by Helen Arnold, pp. 156–60. New York: Fordham University Press, 2010.

Césaire, Aimé. *Discourse on Colonialism*, translated by Joan Pinkham. New York: Monthly Review Press, 1972 [1955].

Chaadaev, Petr Iakovlevich. 'Letters on the Philosophy of History: First Letter' [1829/1836], in Marc Raeff (ed.), *Russian Intellectual History: An Anthology*, pp. 159–73. New York: Harcourt, Brace & World, 1966.

Chacornac, Paul. *The Simple Life of René Guénon*. Hillsdale, NY: Sophia Perennis, 2004 [1958].

Chamberlain, Lesley. *Motherland: A Philosophical History of Russia*. London: Atlantic Books, 2004.

Chang, Hao. *Liang Ch'i-ch'ao and Intellectual Transition in China, 1890–1907*. Cambridge, MA: Harvard University Press, 1971.

Chapman, John Jay. *Deutschland Über Alles or Germany Speaks: A Collection of Utterances of Representative Germans—Statesmen, Military Leaders, Scholars, and Poets—in Defence of the War Policies of the Fatherland*. New York: G. P. Putnam's Sons, 1914.

Chapman, John Jay. 'Ode: On the Sailing of Our Troops for France'. *The North American Review*, vol. 206, no. 744 (November 1917), pp. 682–87.

Chapman, John Jay. 'The Passing of a Great Bogey', *Vanity Fair*, October 1918, pp. 65 and 108.

Charrier, Jean-Paul. *Scientisme et Occident: Essais d'épistémologie critique*. Paris: Éditions Connaissances et Savoirs, 2005.

Chebel d'Appollonia, Ariane. *Histoire politique des intellectuels en France (1944–1954)*. Paris: Complexe, 1991.

Chevalier, Michel. *Lettres sur l'Amérique du Nord*, 2 vols. Paris: C. Gosselin, 1836.

Chevalier, Michel. *Politique industrielle et système de la Méditerranée*. Paris: Le Globe, 1832.

Chirio, Maud. '1889: "Ordre et progrès" en terres tropicales', in Patrick Boucheron (ed.), *Histoire mondiale de la France*, pp. 529–33. Paris: Seuil, 2017.

Christoff, Peter K. *K. S. Aksakov: A Study in Ideas* (= vol. 3 of Christoff, *An Introduction to Nineteenth-Century Russian Slavophilism*). Princeton, NJ: Princeton University Press, 1982.

Claeys, Gregory. *Dystopia: A Natural History; A Study of Modern Despotism, Its Antecedents, and Its Literary Diffractions*. Oxford: Oxford University Press, 2017.

Claeys, Gregory. *Imperial Sceptics*. Cambridge: Cambridge University Press, 2010.

Clark, Christopher. *Revolutionary Spring: Fighting for a New World 1848–1849*. London: Allen Lane, 2023.

Cline, Myrtle A. *American Attitude toward the Greek War of Independence 1821–1828*. Atlanta, GA: Higgins-McArthur, 1930.

Clinton, David. *Tocqueville, Lieber, and Bagehot: Liberalism Confronts the World*. New York: Palgrave Macmillan, 2003.

Coker, Christopher. *Twilight of the West*. Boulder, CO: Westview Press, 1998.

Coleman, Peter. *The Liberal Conspiracy: The Congress for Cultural Freedom and the Struggle for the Mind of Postwar Europe*. New York: The Free Press, 1989.

Combelle, Lucien. 'Choisir l'Occident'. *Révolution nationale*, 29 May 1943.

Comte, Auguste. *The Catechism of Positive Religion*, translated by Richard Congreve. London: John Chapman, 1858.

Comte, Auguste. *Catéchisme positiviste*, edited by Frédéric Dupin. Paris: Éditions du Sandre, 2012 [full title of original edition: *Catéchisme Positiviste, ou Sommaire Exposition de la religion universelle en onze entretiens systématiques entre une Femme et un Prêtre de l'HUMANITÉ*. Paris: Carilian-Goeury et V. Dalmont, 1852].

Comte, Auguste. *Correspondance générale et confessions*, 8 vols. Paris-La Haye: Mouton/Paris: Vrin, 1973–90.

Comte, Auguste. *Cours de philosophie positive*, edited by Jean-Paul Enthoven, 2 vols. Paris: Hermann, 1975 [originally 6 vols, 1830–42].

Comte, Auguste. *Discours sur l'ensemble du positivisme*, edited by Annie Petit. Paris: Flammarion, 1998 [1848].

Comte, Auguste. *Early Political Writings*, edited and translated by H. S. Jones. Cambridge: Cambridge University Press, 1998.

Comte, Auguste. *A General View of Positivism*, translated by J. H. Bridges. London: Trübner & Co., 1865.

Comte, Auguste. *The Positive Philosophy of Auguste Comte*, translated and condensed by Harriet Martineau, 2 vols. London: John Chapman, 1853.

Comte, Auguste. *System of Positive Polity; or Treatise on Sociology, Instituting the Religion of Humanity*, 4 vols. London, 1875–77 [1851–54].

Comte, Auguste. *Système de politique positive*, 5th edition, 4 vols. Paris: Carilian-Gœury et V. Dalmont, Société positiviste, 1929 [1851–54]).

Condorcet, Jean-Antoine-Nicolas, Marquis de. *De l'influence de la Révolution d'Amérique sur l'Europe*, edited by Pierre Musso. Houilles: Éditions Manucius, 2010.

Condorcet, Jean-Antoine-Nicolas, Marquis de. *Écrits sur les États Unis*, edited by Guillaume Ansart. Paris: Classiques Garnier, 2012.

Condorcet, Jean-Antoine-Nicolas, Marquis de. *Esquisse d'un tableau historique des progrès de l'esprit humain: Fragment sur l'Atlantide*, edited by Alain Pons. Paris: Flammarion, 1988 [1794].

Condorcet, Jean-Antoine-Nicolas, Marquis de. *Political Writings*, edited by Steven Lukes and Nadia Urbinati. Cambridge: Cambridge University Press, 2012.

Condorcet, Jean-Antoine-Nicolas, Marquis de. *Tableau historique des progrès de l'esprit humain: Projets, esquisse, fragments et notes (1772–1794)*, edited by Jean-Pierre Schandeler and Pierre Crépel. Paris: INED, 2004.

Congreve, Richard. 'Gibraltar: Or the Foreign Policy of England' [1857], in Congreve, *Essays: Political, Social, and Religious*, vol. 1, pp. 1–65. London: Longmans, Green & Co., 1874.

Congreve, Richard. 'The West', in Frederic Harrison (ed.), *International Policy: Essays on the Foreign Relations of England*, pp. 1–49. London: Chapman and Hall, 1866.

Conrad, Joseph. *Under Western Eyes*, edited by Jeremy Hawthorn. Oxford: Oxford University Press, 2003 [1911].

Conrad, Sebastian. 'A Cultural History of Global Transformation', in Conrad and Jürgen Osterhammel (eds), *An Emerging Modern World, 1750–1870*, pp. 411–581. Cambridge, MA: Harvard University Press, 2018.

Constant, Benjamin. *Appel aux nations chrétiennes en faveur des Grecs*. Paris: Treuttel et Würtz, 1825.

Conter, Claude D. *Jenseits der Nation—Das vergessene Europa des 19. Jahrhunderts: Die Geschichte der Inszenierungen und Visionen Europas in Literatur, Geschichte und Politik*. Bielefeld: Aisthesis, 2004.

Contosta, David R. *Henry Adams and the American Experiment*, edited by Oscar Handlin. Boston, MA: Little, Brown & Co., 1980.

Contosta, David R. 'Henry Adams and the Decline of the Modern West'. *Journal of Thought* 18, no. 1 (1983): 47–54.

Conze, Vanessa. *Das Europa der Deutschen: Ideen von Europa in Deutschland zwischen Reichstradition und Westorientierung (1920–1970)*. Munich: Oldenbourg, 2005.

Conze, Vanessa. 'Facing the Future Backwards: "Abendland" as an Anti-liberal Idea of Europe in Germany between the First World War and the 1960s', in Dieter Gosewinkel (ed.), *Anti-liberal Europe: A Neglected Story of Europeanization*, pp. 72–89. New York: Berghahn, 2015.

Cook, Alexander. 'Representing Humanity during the French Revolution: Volney's "General Assembly of Peoples"', in Cook, Ned Curthoys and Shino Konishi (eds), *Representing Humanity in the Age of Enlightenment*, pp. 15–26. London: Pickering & Chatto, 2013.
Cook, William W. and James Tatum. *African American Writers and Classical Tradition*. Chicago: The University of Chicago Press, 2010.
Cooper, Robert. *The Ambassadors: Thinking about Diplomacy from Machiavelli to Modern Times*. London: Weidenfeld & Nicolson, 2021.
Costigliola, Frank. *Kennan: A Life between Worlds*. Princeton, NJ: Princeton University Press, 2023.
Couderc-Morandeau, Stéphanie. *Philosophie républicaine et colonialisme: Origines, contradictions et échecs sous la IIIe République*. Paris: L'Harmattan, 2008.
'*Counsels of Hope*': *The Toynbee–Jerrold Controversy: Letters to the Editor of the Times Literary Supplement, with Leading Articles Reprinted*. London: Times Publishing Co., 1954.
Cousin, Victor. *Souvenirs d'Allemagne*. Paris: CNRS Éditions, 2011.
Craig, Albert M. *Civilization and Enlightenment: The Early Thought of Fukuzawa Yukichi*. Cambridge, MA: Harvard University Press, 2009.
Crawford, Robert. *Eliot after 'The Waste Land'*. London: Jonathan Cape, 2022.
Craiutu, Aurelian. *Faces of Moderation: The Art of Balance in an Age of Extremes*. Philadelphia: University of Pennsylvania Press, 2017.
Craiutu, Aurelian. 'Rediscovering Raymond Aron'. *Global Intellectual History* 7, no. 1 (2022): 144–51.
Crèvecoeur, J. Hector St. John de. '*Letters from an American Farmer*' [1782], in Crèvecoeur, *Letters from an American Farmer and Other Essays*, edited by Dennis D. Moore. Cambridge, MA: Harvard University Press, 2013.
Crick, Bernard. *George Orwell*. Boston, MA: Atlantic Monthly Press, 1980.
Croly, David Goodman. *Glimpses of the Future: Suggestions as to the Drift of Things; To Be Read Now and Judged in the Year 2000*. New York: G. P. Putnam's Sons, 1888.
Croly, Herbert David. *The Promise of American Life*. New York: Macmillan, 1909.
[Croly, Herbert.] 'The End of American Isolation'. *The New Republic*, 7 November 1914.
Cronon, Edmund David. *Black Moses: The Story of Marcus Garvey and the Universal Negro Improvement Association*. Madison, WI: University of Wisconsin Press, 1969.
Crook, D. P. *Benjamin Kidd: Portrait of a Social Darwinist*. Cambridge: Cambridge University Press, 1984.
Cruickshank, John. *Variations on Catastrophe: Some French Responses to the Great War*. Oxford: Oxford University Press, 1982.
Crummell, Alexander. 'The Destined Superiority of the Negro' [1877], in Crummel, *The Greatness of Christ and Other Sermons*, pp. 332–52. New York: Thomas Whittaker, 1882.
Crummell, Alexander. *Destiny and Race: Selected Writings, 1840–1898*, edited by Wilson Jeremiah Moses. Amherst, MA: The University of Massachusetts Press, 1992.
Crummell, Alexander. *The Greatness of Christ, and Other Sermons*. New York: Thomas Whittaker, 1882.
Cumings, Bruce, Richard Falk, Stephen M. Walt and Michael C. Desch. 'Is There a Logic of the West?'. *World Policy Journal* 11, no. 1 (1994): 113–24.
Curti, Merle. *The Growth of American Thought*, 2nd edition. New York: Harper & Brothers, 1951.

Curti, Merle. *The Roots of American Loyalty*. New York: Columbia University Press, 1946.
Curtius, Ernst Robert. *The Civilization of France: An Introduction*, translated by Olive Wyon. New York: The Macmillan Company, 1932 [1930].
Curtius, Ernst Robert. 'Französische Civilisation und Abendland'. *Europäische Revue*, vol. 3, no. 1 (June 1927), pp. 178–92.
Curtius, Ernst Robert. *Die Französische Kultur: Eine Einführung*. Bern: Francke, 1930.
Curtius, Ernst Robert. 'Restoration of the Reason', translated by William Sewart. *The Criterion*, vol. 6, no. 5 (November 1927), pp. 389–97.
Custine, Marquis [Astolphe] de. *Letters from Russia*, translated and edited by Robin Buss. London: Penguin, 1991.
Custine, Marquis [Astolphe] de. *Lettres de Russie*, edited by Pierre Nora. Paris: Gallimard, 1975.
Custine, Marquis [Astolphe] de. *La Russie en 1839*, 4 vols. Paris: Librairie d'Amyot, 1843.
Czartoryski, Adam. *Essai sur la diplomatie*. Lausanne: Les Éditions Noir sur Blanc, 2011 [1830].
Cywar, Alan. 'John Dewey in World War I'. *American Quarterly* 21 (1969): 578–95.
Dahrendorf, Ralf. 'Zeitgenosse Habermas: Jürgen Habermas zum sechzigsten Geburtstag'. *Merkur*, vol. 43, no. 484 (June 1989), pp. 478–87.
Dalberg-Acton, John Emerich Edward [Lord Acton]. *Selected Writings of Lord Acton*, vol. 3: *Essays in Religion, Politics, and Morality*, edited by J. Rufus Fears. Indianapolis: Liberty Classics, 1988.
Danilevsky, Nikolai. 'Russia and Europe', [extracts] in Hans Kohn (ed.), *The Mind of Modern Russia: Historical and Political Thought of Russia's Great Age*, pp. 195–211. New Brunswick, NJ: Rutgers University Press, 1955.
Danilevsky, N[ikolai] I. *Russland und Europa: Eine Untersuchung über die kulturellen und politischen Beziehungen der Slawischen zur Germanisch-Romanischen Welt*, translated (into German) by Karl Nötzel. Stuttgart: Deutsche Verlags-anstalt, 1920 [1869].
De Beer, Gabriella. *José Vasconcelos and His World*. New York: Las Americas Publishing Company, 1966.
De Boni, Claudio. 'L'Idée de "république occidentale" et le positivisme: de Condorcet à Comte', in Martha Petricioli, Donatella Cherubini and Alessandra Anteghini (eds), *Les Etats-Unis d'Europe: Un projet pacifiste*, pp. 195–212. Bern: Peter Lang, 2004.
De Boni, Claudio. *Storia di un'utopia: La religione dell'Umanità di Comte et la sua circolazione nel mondo*. Milan: Mimesis, 2013.
De Kay, Drake. 'Encyclopedia Americana, First Edition'. *The Journal of Library History* 3, no. 3 (1968): 201–20.
Debray, Régis. *Civilisation: Comment nous sommes devenus américains*. Paris: Gallimard, 2017.
Debray, Régis. 'Civilization: A Grammar'. *New Left Review*, 107 (September/October 2017), pp. 33–44.
Debray, Régis. *Civilization: How We All Became American*, translated by David Fernbach. London: Verso, 2019.
Debray, Régis. 'Decline of the West?'. *New Left Review*, 80 (March/April 2013), pp. 29–44.
Debray, Régis. 'L'Occident est-il en déclin?: Aux controverses du *Monde* en Avignon, l'écrivain Régis Debray interroge le devenir d'une aire géopolitique touchée par une crise d'identité'. *Le Monde*, 18 July 2014, pp. 18–19.
Debray, Régis and Renaud Girard. *Que reste-t-il de l'Occident?* Paris: Bernard Grasset, 2014.

Debray, Régis, Henry Laurens and Jalila Sbaï (eds). *Civilisations: Les entretiens de la Fondation des Treilles*. Paris: Gallimard, 2022.

Derrida, Jacques and Jürgen Habermas. 'February 15, or What Binds Europeans' [2003], in Habermas, *The Divided West*, edited and translated by Ciaran Cronin, pp. 39–48. Cambridge: Polity Press, 2006.

Desch, Cecil H. 'Francis Sidney Marvin, 1863-1943'. *Isis* 36 (1945), pp. 7–9.

Deudney, Daniel and John Ikenberry. 'The Logic of the West'. *World Policy Journal* 10, no. 4 (1993/1994): 17–25.

Dewey, John. *German Philosophy and Politics*. New York: Henry Holt & Co., 1915.

Dewitte, Philippe. *Les Mouvements nègres en France 1919–1939*. Paris: L'Harmattan, 1985.

Dickson, William Rory. 'René Guénon and Traditionalism', in Muhammad Afzal Upal and Carole M. Cusack (eds), *Handbook of Islamic Sects and Movements*, pp. 589–611. Leiden: Brill, 2021.

Diderot, Denis. *Œuvres*, vol. 3: *Politique*, edited by Laurent Versini. Paris: Robert Laffont, 1995.

Diderot, Denis. *Political Writings*, edited by John Hope Mason and Robert Wokler. Cambridge: Cambridge University Press, 1992.

Diehl, Carl. *Americans and German Scholarship 1770–1870*. New Haven, CT: Yale University Press, 1978.

Diehl, Carl. 'Innocents Abroad: American Students in German Universities, 1810–1870'. *History of Education Quarterly* 16, no. 3 (1976): 321–41.

Dietz, Bernhard. 'The Neo-Tories and Europe'. *Journal of Modern European History/Zeitschrift für moderne europäische Geschichte/Revue d'histoire européenne contemporaine* 15, no. 1 (2017): 85–108.

Dietz, Bernhard. *Neo-Tories: Britische Konservative im Aufstand gegen Demokratie und politische Moderne 1929–1939*. Munich: Oldenbourg, 2012.

Diezel, Gustav. *Die Bildung einer nationalen Partei in Deutschland: Eine Nothwendigkeit in der jetztigen Krisis Europas*. Gotha: Hugo Scheube, 1855.

Diezel, Gustav. *Deutschland und die abendländische Civilisation: Zur Läuterung unserer politischen und socialen Begriffe*. Stuttgart: Karl Göpel, 1852.

Diezel, Gustav. *Russia, Germany and the Eastern Question*, translated by Frederica Rowan. London: James Ridgway, 1854.

Diezel, Gustav. *Rußland, Deutschland, und die östliche Frage*. Stuttgart: Karl Göpel, 1853.

Dimaras, K. Th. [Κ. Θ. Δημαράς]. *Κωνσταντίνος Παπαρρηγόπουλος · Η Εποχή του—η Ζωή του—το Έργο του* (Constantinos Paparrigopoulos: his time, his life, his work). Athens: Μορφωτικό Ίδρυμα Εθνικής Τραπέζης, 1986.

Diop, Alioune. 'Discours d'ouverture', in *Le 1er Congrès international des écrivains et artistes noirs (Paris, Sorbonne, 19-22 Septembre 1956)*, special issue, *Présence africaine*, nos 8/9/10 (June–November 1956), pp. 9–19.

Doering-Manteuffel, Anselm. 'Perceptions of the West in Twentieth-Century Germany', in Riccardo Bavaj and Martina Steber (eds), *Germany and 'The West': The History of a Modern Concept*, pp. 81–93. New York: Berghahn, 2015.

Doering-Manteuffel, Anselm. 'Eine politische Nationalgeschichte für die Berliner Republik: Überlegungen zu Heinrich August Winklers *Der Lange Weg nach Westen*'. *Geschichte und Gesellschaft* 27, no. 3 (2001): 446–62.

Don, Léopold. 'L'Union occidentale vue de Londres'. *Le Monde*, 17 July 1945.

Donoso Cortés, Juan. *Essays on Catholicism, Liberalism, and Socialism: Considered in Their Fundamental Principles*, translated by William McDonald. Dublin: M. H. Gill & Son, 1879 [1851].

Dostoievsky, F. M. *The Diary of a Writer*, translated by Boris Brasol. Salt Lake City, UT: Peregrine Smith Books, 1985.

Drochon, Hugo. *Nietzsche's Great Politics*. Princeton, NJ: Princeton University Press, 2016.

Drolet, Jean-François. *American Neoconservatism: The Politics and Culture of a Reactionary Idealism*. London: Hurst & Co., 2011.

Drolet, Jean-François. *Beyond Tragedy and Eternal Peace: Politics and International Relations in the Thought of Friedrich Nietzsche*. Montreal and Kingston: McGill-Queen's University Press, 2021.

Drolet, Michael. 'A Nineteenth-Century Mediterranean Union: Michel Chevalier's *Système de la Méditerranée*'. *Mediterranean Historical Review* 30, no. 2 (2015): 147–68.

Du Bois, W.E.B. 'The African Roots of War' [*Atlantic Monthly*, 115 (May 1915), pp. 707–14], in Du Bois, *W. E. B. Du Bois: International Thought*, edited by Adom Getachew and Jennifer Pitts, pp. 23–35. Cambridge: Cambridge University Press, 2022.

Du Bois, W.E.B. 'The American Jew'. *The Crisis*, vol. 24, no. 4 (August 1922), p. 152.

Du Bois, W.E.B. 'Americanization'. *The Crisis*, vol. 24, no. 4 (August 1922), p. 154.

Du Bois, W.E.B. 'The Battle of Europe'. *The Crisis*, vol. 12, no. 5 (September 1916), pp. 216–17.

Du Bois, W.E.B. 'Close Ranks'. *The Crisis*, vol. 16, no. 3 (July 1918), p. 111.

Du Bois, W.E.B. 'The Color Line Belts of the World' [1906], in Du Bois, *W.E.B. Du Bois: A Reader*, edited by David Levering Lewis, pp. 42–43. New York: Henry Holt & Co., 1995.

Du Bois, W.E.B. *Dusk of Dawn: An Essay Toward an Autobiography of a Race Concept* [1940], collected in Du Bois, *Writings*, edited by Nathan Huggins, pp. 549–802. New York: The Library of America, 1986.

Du Bois, W.E.B. 'French and Spanish'. *The Crisis*, vol. 17, no. 6 (April 1919), pp. 269–70.

Du Bois, W.E.B. 'Ghana Calls' [1962], in Du Bois, *Creative Writings of W.E.B. Du Bois: A Pageant, Poems, Short Stories, and Playlets*, edited by Herbert Aptheker, pp. 52–55. White Plains, NY: Kraus-Thomson Organization, 1985.

Du Bois, W.E.B. ['Introduction' to] 'An Appeal to the World', in Du Bois, *W.E.B. Du Bois: International Thought*, edited by Adom Getachew and Jennifer Pitts, pp. 229–49. Cambridge: Cambridge University Press, 2022.

Du Bois, W. E.B. *The Quest of the Silver Fleece: A Novel*. Chicago: A. C. McClurg & Co., 1911.

[Du Bois, W.E.B.] 'Returning Soldiers'. *The Crisis*, vol. 18, no. 1 (May 1919), pp. 13–14

Du Bois, W.E.B. *The Souls of Black Folk* [1903], collected in Du Bois, *Writings*, edited by Nathan Huggins, pp. 357–547. New York: The Library of America, 1986.

Du Bois, W.E.B. 'The Spirit of Modern Europe' [1900?], in Du Bois, *Against Racism: Unpublished Essays, Papers, Addresses, 1887–1961*, edited by Herbert Aptheker, pp. 50–64. Amherst, NY: The University of Massachusetts Press, 1985.

Du Bois, W.E.B. 'Tagore'. *The Crisis*, vol. 13, no. 2 (December 1916), pp. 60–61.

Du Bois, W.E.B. 'To the Congrès des écrivains et artistes noirs', in *Le 1er Congrès international des écrivains et artistes noirs (Paris, Sorbonne, 19–22 Septembre 1956)*, special issue, *Présence africaine*, nos 8/9/10 (June–November 1956), p. 383.

Du Bois, W.E.B. 'To the World (*Manifesto of the Second Pan-African Congress*)'. *The Crisis*, vol. 23, no. 1 (November 1921), pp. 5–10.

Du Bois, W.E.B. 'Vive la France!'. *The Crisis*, vol. 17, no. 5 (March 1919), p. 216.

Du Bois, W.E.B. 'World War and the Color Line'. *The Crisis*, vol. 9, no. 1 (November 1914), pp. 28–30.

Duhamel, Georges. *Civilization 1914–1917*, translated by E. S. Brooks. New York: The Century Co., 1919 [French original: Denis Thévenin (pseud.), *Civilisation* (1918)].

Dumons, F. *Un mot à propos de la question d'Orient sur le devoir de la France et l'avenir de l'Europe*. Bordeaux: A. Pechade, 1840.

Dunstan, Sarah C. *Race, Rights and Reform: Black Activism in the French Empire and the United States from World War I to the Cold War*. Cambridge: Cambridge University Press, 2021.

Earle, Edward Mead. 'American Interest in the Greek Cause, 1821–1827'. *The American Historical Review* 33, no. 1 (1927): 44–63.

Echeverria, Durand. *Mirage in the West: A History of the French Image of American Society to 1815*. Princeton, NJ: Princeton University Press, 1968.

Edwards, Brent Hayes. *The Practice of Diaspora: Literature, Translation, and the Rise of Black Internationalism*. Cambridge, MA: Harvard University Press, 2003.

Edwards, Lyford P. '[Review of] *The Art of Being Ruled*. By Wyndham Lewis. New York and London: Harper & Bros., 1926'. *American Journal of Sociology* 32, no. 5 (1927): 858

d'Eichthal, Gustave. *De l'unité européenne*. Paris: Truchy, 1840.

d'Eichthal, Gustave. *Les Deux Mondes*. Leipzig: F. A. Brockhaus, 1837.

d'Eichthal, Gustave. *Les Deux Mondes: Servant d'introduction à l'ouvrage de M. Urquhart ; La Turquie et ses Ressources*. Paris: Arthur Bertrand, 1836.

d'Eichthal, Gustave. *Les Trois Grands Peuples méditerranéens et le Christianisme*. Paris: Hachette, 1865.

d'Eichthal, Gustave. *L'Italie, la papauté et la confédération européenne: Six articles publiés dans le journal 'Le Credit' les 12, 18, 25 Decembre 1848, et 1, 8, 22 et 23 Janvier 1849*. Paris, Bibliothèque de l'Arsenal, dossier 8-Z-4601.

Elias, Norbert. *The Civilizing Process: Sociogenetic and Psychogenetic Investigations*, translated by Edmund Jephott; revised edition edited by Eric Dunning, Johan Goudsblom and Stephen Mennell. Oxford: Blackwell, 2000 [1939].

Elias, Norbert. *The Germans: Power Struggles and the Development of Habitus in the Nineteenth and Twentieth Centuries*, edited by Michael Schröter, translated by Eric Dunning and Stephen Mennell. Cambridge: Polity Press, 1996 [1989].

Eliot, George. *Daniel Deronda*, edited by Caroline Jones. Ware: Wordsworth Classics, 2003 [1876]).

Eliot, T. S. 'A Commentary'. *The Criterion*, vol. 15, no. 59 (January 1936), pp. 265–69.

Eliot, Valerie and John Haffenden (eds). *The Letters of T. S. Eliot*, vol. 3: *1926–1927*. London: Faber and Faber, 2012.

Eliot, Valerie and Hugh Haughton (eds). *The Letters of T. S. Eliot*, vol. 2: *1923–1925*. London: Faber and Faber, 2009.

Elliott, William Y. 'Foreword' [to essays by various authors on 'The Issue: What Are the Bases of Civilization?'], *Confluence*, vol. 1, no. 1 (1952).

Ellis, Henry. 'Comte's Conception of Western Europe as a Republic'. *The Positivist Review*, vol. 6, no. 65 (1898), pp. 88–93.

Emerson, Ralph Waldo. 'The Anglo-American' [1852–55], in Emerson, *The Major Prose*, edited by Ronald A. Bosco and Joel Myerson, pp. 330–49. Cambridge, MA: Harvard University Press, 2015.

Emmott, Bill. *The Fate of the West: The Battle to Save the World's Most Successful Political Idea*. London: The Economist, 2017.

Encyclopaedia Americana: A Popular Dictionary of Arts, Sciences, Literature, History, Politics and Biography, brought down to the present time; including a copious collection of original articles in American biography; on the basis of the seventh edition of the German Conversations-Lexicon, edited by Francis Lieber, assisted by E. Wigglesworth, 13 vols. Philadelphia: Carey & Lea, 1829–33.

Espagne, Michel. 'The *Universal- und Kulturgeschichte* at Göttingen from Schlözer to Heeren', in Matthias Middell (ed.), *Cultural Transfers, Encounters and Connections in the Global 18th Century*, pp. 43–59. Leipzig: Leipzig Universitätsverlag, 2014.

Etkind, Alexander. *Roads Not Taken: An Intellectual Biography of William C. Bullitt*. Pittsburgh, PA: University of Pittsburgh Press, 2017.

[Everett, Edward.] '[Review of] *Reflections on the Politics of Ancient Greece, Translated from the German of Arnold H. L. Heeren* by George Bancroft [. . .]'. *The North American Review*, vol. 18, n. 43 (April 1824), pp. 390–406.

[Everett, Edward.] '[Review of] *The Ethics of Aristotle to Nicomachus, revised and edited by A. Coray, at the expense of the injured and oppressed Sciotes. Paris, 8vo. 1822*'. *The North American Review*, vol. 17, no. 41 (October 1823), pp. 389–424.

Everett, Edward. 'Russia and the United States' [1864], in Everett, *Orations and Speeches on Various Occasions*, vol. 4, pp. 674–83. Boston, MA: Little, Brown & Co., 1868.

Evtuhov, Catherine. 'Guizot in Russia', in Catherine Evtuhov and Stephen Kotkin (eds), *The Cultural Gradient: The Transmission of Ideas in Europe 1789–1991*, pp. 55–72. Lanham, MD: Rowman & Littlefield, 2003.

Fabre, Michel. *From Harlem to Paris: Black American Writers in France, 1840–1980*. Urbana, IL: University of Illinois Press, 1991.

Fabre, Michel. *Richard Wright: Books and Writers*. Jackson, MS: University Press of Mississippi, 1990.

Fabre, Michel. *The Unfinished Quest of Richard Wright*, 2nd edition. Champaign, IL: University of Illinois Press, 1993.

Fairbank, John King and Merle Goldman. *China: A New History*, 2nd enlarged edition. Cambridge, MA: Harvard University Press, 2006.

Fallmerayer, Jakob Philipp. *Geschichte der Halbinsel Morea wärend des Mittelalters*, 2 vols. Stuttgart: J. G. Cotta'schen Buchhandlung, 1830–36.

Fallmerayer, Jakob Philipp. 'Marquis de Custine: La Russie en 1839' [1843], in Fallmerayer, *Gesammelte Werke von Jakob Philipp Fallmerayer*, edited by Georg Martin Thomas, vol. 3, pp. 20–56. Leipzig: Wilhelm Engelmann, 1861.

Fanon, Frantz. *Black Skin, White Masks*, translated by Richard Philcox. London: Penguin Books, 2021.

Fanon, Frantz. *Les Damnés de la Terre*. Paris: François Maspero, 1961.

[Fanon, Frantz.] 'Richard Wright's *White Man, Listen!*' [1959], in Fanon, *The Political Writings from Alienation and Freedom*, edited by Jean Khalfa and Robert J. C. Young, translated by Steven Corcoran, pp. 101–4. London: Bloomsbury Academic, 2021.

Fanon, Frantz. *The Wretched of the Earth*, translated by Constance Farrington. London: Penguin, 1967.

Farrell, John C. 'John Dewey in World War I: Armageddon Tests a Liberal's Faith'. *Perspectives in American History* 9 (1975): 299–342.

Fauset, Jessie. 'Impressions of the Second Pan-African Congress'. *The Crisis*, vol. 23, no. 1 (November 1921), pp. 12–18.

Fauset, Jessie. 'A Negro on East St. Louis'. *The Survey*, vol. 38, no. 20 (18 August 1917), p. 448.

Fedi, Laurent (ed.). *La Réception germanique d'Auguste Comte*, special issue, *Les Cahiers philosophiques de Strasbourg* 35 (2014).

Feichtinger, Johannes, Franz L. Fillafer and Jan Surman (eds). *The Worlds of Positivism: A Global Intellectual History*. Cham: Palgrave Macmillan, 2018.

Ferguson, Niall. *Civilization: The West and the Rest*. London: Penguin Books, 2012.

Ferguson, Niall. *Kissinger 1923–1968: The Idealist*. London: Allen Lane, 2015.

Ferretti, Federico. 'L'Occidente di Élisée Reclus: L'invenzione dell'Europa nella *Nouvelle Géographie universelle* (1876–1894)'. Doctoral thesis, Università di Bologna, 2011.

Ferris, William Henry. *The African Abroad; or, His Evolution in Western Civilization, Tracing His Development under Caucasian Milieu*, 2 vols. New Haven, CT: The Tuttle, Morehouse & Taylor Press, 1913.

Figeac, Jean-François. 'La Géopolitique orientale des saint-simoniens'. *Cahiers de la Méditerranée* 85 (2012): 251–68.

Figes, Orlando. *Crimea: The Last Crusade*. London: Allen Lane, 2010.

Filoni, Marco. *Le Philosophe du dimanche: La vie et la pensée d'Alexandre Kojève*, translated (into French) by Gérald Larché. Paris: Gallimard, 2010 [2008].

Finkielkraut, Alain. *The Undoing of Thought*, translated by Dennis O'Keeffe. London: The Claridge Press, 1988.

Fischer, Joschka. *Der Abstieg des Westens: Europa in der neuen Weltordnung des 21. Jahrhunderts*. Cologne: Kiepenheuer & Witsch, 2018.

Fischer, Jürgen. *Oriens–Occidens–Europa: Begriff und Gedanke 'Europa' in der Späten Antike und im frühen Mittelalter*. Wiesbaden: Franz Steiner, 1957.

Fischer, LeRoy H. *Lincoln's Gadfly, Adam Gurowski*. Norman, OK: University of Oklahoma Press, 1964.

Fiske, John. *American Political Ideals: Viewed from the Standpoint of Universal History; Three Lectures Delivered at the Royal Institution of Great Britain in May, 1880*. Boston, MA: Houghton Mifflin, 1911 [1880].

Fitzmaurice, Andrew. *King Leopold's Ghostwriter: The Creation of Persons and States in the Nineteenth Century*. Princeton, NJ: Princeton University Press, 2021.

Fletcher, John Gould. 'East and West'. *The Criterion*, vol. 7, no. 4 (June 1928), pp. 18–36.

Fletcher, John Gould. 'Letter to the Editor'. *The New Criterion*, vol. 4, no. 4 (October 1926), pp. 746–50.

Forbes, Geraldine Hancock. *Positivism in Bengal: A Case Study in the Transmission and Assimilation of an Ideology*. Columbia, MO: South Asia Books, 1975.

Forrester, Katrina. *In the Shadow of Justice: Postwar Liberalism and the Remaking of Political Philosophy*. Princeton, NJ: Princeton University Press, 2019.

Foster, Daniel. 'In Defense of "The West"'. *The Atlantic*, 10 July 2017, https://www.theatlantic.com/international/archive/2017/07/defense-of-the-west/533163/ (accessed 18 October 2024).

Foulke, William Dudley. *Slav or Saxon: A Study of the Growth and Tendencies of Russian Civilization*, 2nd revised edition. New York: G. P. Putnam's Sons, 1899 [1887].

Foureau, Christine. 'La *Revue universelle* (1920–1940): Aux origines intellectuelles du pétainisme'. Doctoral dissertation, Princeton University, 1999.

Fowke, Edith. '[Review of] *The Twenty-Fifth Hour* by Virgil Gheorghiu'. *International Journal* 6, no. 3 (1951): 255–57.

Foxlee, Neil. *Albert Camus's 'The New Mediterranean Culture': A Text and Its Contexts*. Oxford: Peter Lang, 2010.

François, Stéphane. 'The Nouvelle Droite and "Tradition"'. *Journal for the Study of Radicalism* 8, no. 1 (2014): 87–106.

Frantz, Gustav Adolph Constanin. *Untersuchungen über das Europäische Gleichgewicht*. Berlin: Ferdinand Schneider, 1859.

Frederick, John T. 'American Literary Nationalism: The Process of Definition, 1825–1850'. *The Review of Politics* 21, no. 1 (1959): 224–38.

Freeman, Edward. A. 'The Byzantine Empire', in Freeman, *Historical Essays*, third series, pp. 231–77. New York: AMS Press, 1969 [1879].

Freeman, Edward A. *The Chief Periods of European History. Six Lectures read in the University of Oxford in Trinity Term, 1885*. London: Macmillan, 1886.

Freeman, Edward A. *Comparative Politics: Six Lectures Read before the Royal Institution in January and February, 1873 with 'The Unity of History', the Rede Lecture Read before the University of Cambridge, May 29, 1872*. London: Macmillan, 1896 [1873].

Freeman, Edward A. 'The English People in Its Three Homes', in Freeman, *Lectures to American Audiences*, pp. 1–204 (= lectures 1–6). Philadelphia: Porter & Coates/London: Trübner, 1882.

Freeman, Edward A. *The History and Conquests of the Saracens: Six Lectures Delivered before the Edinburgh Philosophical Institution*. London: Macmillan, 1876 [1856].

Freeman, Edward A. *The History of Sicily from the Earliest Times*, 4 vols. Oxford: The Clarendon Press, 1891–94.

Freeman, Edward A. *The Methods of Historical Study: Eight Lectures read in the University of Oxford in […] 1884*. London: Macmillan, 1886.

[Freeman, Edward A.] 'Mr. Kingsley's Roman and Teuton'. *The Saturday Review*, 9 April 1864, pp. 446–48.

Freeman, Edward A. *Ottoman Power in Europe: Its Nature, Its Growth, and Its Decline*. London: Macmillan, 1877.

Freeman, Edward A. 'A Review of my Opinions'. *The Forum*, vol. 13 (March–August 1892), pp. 145–57.

Freemantle, W. H. 'M. Comte and His Disciples on International Policy'. *The Contemporary Review*, 3 (1866), pp. 477–98.

Freidel, Frank. *Francis Lieber: Nineteenth-Century Liberal*. Baton Rouge, LA: Louisiana State University Press, 1947.

Friedrich, Carl J. '[Review of] Aurel Kolnai: *The War Against the West*, The Viking Press, New York 1938'. *The Review of Politics*, vol. 1, no. 1 (1939), p. 101.

Friedrich, Carl J. and Zbigniew K. Brzezinski. *Totalitarian Dictatorship and Autocracy*. Cambridge, MA: Harvard University Press, 1956.

FRUS [*Foreign Relations of the United States*], 1947, vol. 2: *Council of Foreign Ministers, Germany and Austria*, edited by William Slany, available at https://history.state.gov/historicaldocuments/frus1947v02 (accessed 18 October 2024).

Frye, Northrop. '*The Decline of the West* by Oswald Spengler'. *Daedalus* 103, no. 1 (1974): 1–13.

Frye, Northrop. 'Novels on Several Occasions'. *The Hudson Review*, vol. 3, no. 4 (1951), pp. 611–19.

Fukuyama, Francis. 'The End of History?'. *The National Interest*, no. 16 (Summer 1989), pp. 3–18.

Fukuyama, Francis. 'A Reply to My Critics'. *The National Interest*, no. 18 (Winter 1989/90), pp. 21–28.

Fukuyama, Francis. *The End of History and the Last Man*. London: Hamish Hamilton, 1992.

Fukuzawa, Yukichi. *An Outline of a Theory of Civilization*, translated by David A. Dilworth. New York: Columbia University Press, 2008 [1875].

Gaddis, John Lewis. *The Cold War*. London: Allen Lane, 2005.

Gaddis, John Lewis. *George F. Kennan: An American Life*. London: Penguin, 2011.

Gandhi, M. K. *'Hind Swaraj' and Other Writings*, edited by Anthony J. Parel. Cambridge: Cambridge University Press, 2009.

Garton Ash, Timothy. *Free World: America, Europe, and the Surprising Future of the West*. London: Random House, 2004.

Garton Ash, Timothy. *Homelands: A Personal History of Europe*. London: Vintage, 2023.

Garton Ash, Timothy. 'Where Is Central Europe Now?'. *Times Literary Supplement*, no. 6321 (24 May 2024), pp. 3–5.

Gasimov, Zaur and Carl Antonius Lemke Duque (eds). *Oswald Spengler als europäisches Phänomen: Der Transfer der Kultur- und Geschichtsmorphologie im Europa der Zwischenkriegszeit 1919–1939*. Göttingen: Vandenhoeck & Ruprecht, 2013.

Gassert, Philipp. 'No Place for "the West": National Socialism and the "Defence of Europe"', in Riccardo Bavaj and Martina Steber (eds), *Germany and 'The West': The History of a Modern Concept*, pp. 216–29. New York: Berghahn, 2015.

Geppert, Dominik. 'Bridge over Troubled Waters: German Left-Wing Intellectuals between "East" and "West", 1945–1949', in Riccardo Bavaj and Martina Steber (eds), *Germany and 'The West': The History of a Modern Concept*, pp. 262–76. New York: Berghahn, 2015.

Gerbi, Antonello. *The Dispute of the New World: The History of a Polemic, 1750–1900*, translated by Jeremy Moyle. Pittsburgh, PA: University of Pittsburgh Press, 2010 [1973].

Germain, José. 'Le Duel éternel Orient–Occident'. *Les Nouveaux Temps*, 2 February 1943.

Geroulanos, Stefanos. *The Invention of Prehistory: Empire, Violence, and Our Obsession with Human Origins*. New York: Liveright, 2024.

Getachew, Adom and Jennifer Pitts. 'Democracy and Empire: An Introduction to the International Thought of W.E.B. Du Bois', in W.E.B. Du Bois, *W.E.B. Du Bois: International*

Thought, edited by Adom Getachew and Jennifer Pitts, pp. xv–lvii. Cambridge: Cambridge University Press, 2022.
Geuss, Raymond. 'Nietzsche and Genealogy'. *European Journal of Philosophy* 2, no. 3 (1994): 274–92.
Gheorghiu, Constantin Virgil. *The Twenty-Fifth Hour*, translated by Rita Eldon. London: William Heinemann, 1950/New York: Knopf, 1950.
Gheorghiu, Constanin Virgil. *La Vint-cinquième Heure*, translated (into French) by Monique Saint-Côme. Paris: Plon, 1949.
Ghervas, Stella. *Conquering Peace: From the Enlightenment to the European Union*. Cambridge, MA: Harvard University Press, 2021.
Ghervas, Stella. *Réinventer la tradition: Alexandre Stourdza et l'Europe de la Sainte-Alliance*. Paris: Honoré Champion, 2008.
Gibbon, Edward. *The Decline and Fall of the Roman Empire* [1776–89], edited by David Womersley, 3 vols. London: Penguin, 1994.
Gielgud, Adam (ed.). *Memoirs of Prince Adam Czartoryski and His Correspondence with Alexander I; with Documents Relative to the Prince's Negotiations with Pitt, Fox, and Brougham, and an Account of his Conversations with Lord Palmerston and Other English Statesmen in London in 1832*, 2nd edition, 2 vols. London: Remington, 1888.
Gillouin, René. 'Le Destin de l'Occident', in Gillouin, *Le Destin de l'Occident, suivi de divers essais critiques*, pp. 13–56. Paris: Prométhée, 1929.
Gillouin, René. 'Le Problème de la colonisation', in Gillouin, *Le Destin de l'Occident, suivi de divers essais critiques*, pp. 69–84. Paris: Prométhée, 1929.
Gilroy, Paul. *The Black Atlantic: Modernity and Double Consciousness*. London: Verso, 1993.
Gilson, Étienne. *Les Métamorphoses de la cité de Dieu*. Paris: Vrin, 1952.
Gladwyn Jebb, Hubert Miles [Lord Gladwyn]. *The European Idea*. London: NEL Mentor, 1967 [1966].
Gladwyn Jebb, Hubert Miles [Lord Gladwyn]. *The Memoirs of Lord Gladwyn*. New York: Weybright and Talley, 1972.
Gladwyn Papers. Churchill College, Cambridge, Lord Gladwyn Papers.
Gleason, Abbott. *Totalitarianism: The Inner History of the Cold War*. New York: Oxford University Press, 1995.
Gleason, John Howes. *The Genesis of Russophobia in Great Britain: A Study in the Interaction of Policy and Opinion*. Cambridge, MA: Harvard University Press, 1950.
Głębocki, Henryk. *A Disastrous Matter: The Polish Question in the Russian Political Thought and Discourse of the Great Reform Age, 1856–1866*, translated by Teresa Bałuk-Ulewiczowa. Krakow: Jagiellonian University Press, 2017.
Goddard, E. H. and P. A. Gibbons. *Civilisation or Civilisations: An Essay in the Spenglerian Philosophy of History*. London: Constable, 1926.
Godkin, Edwin L. 'The Eastern Question'. *The North American Review*, vol. 124, no. 254 (January 1877), pp. 106–26.
Goebel, Michael. *Anti-Imperial Metropolis: Interwar Paris and the Seeds of Third World Nationalism*. Cambridge: Cambridge University Press, 2015.
GoGwilt, Christopher. *The Invention of the West: Joseph Conrad and the Double-Mapping of Europe and Empire*. Stanford, CA: Stanford University Press, 1995.

Gökalp, Ziya. *The Principles of Turkism*, translated by Robert Devereux. Leiden: E. J. Brill, 1968.

Gökalp, Ziya. *Türkçülüğün Esasları*, edited by Mehmet Kaplan. Istanbul: Devlet Kitapları, 1976 [1923].

Gökalp, Ziya. *Turkish Nationalism and Western Civilization: Selected Essays*, edited by Niyazi Berkes. London: Allen & Unwin, 1959.

Goldman, Eric F. *Rendezvous with Destiny: A History of Modern American Reform*, revised edition. New York: Vintage Books, 1977.

Goldsmith, Oliver. *The Citizen of the World: Or, Letters from a Chinese Philosopher, residing in London, to his Friends in the East*, 2 vols. London: R. Whiston, J. Woodfall, T. Baldwin, R. Johnston and G. Caddel, 1785 [1762].

Golf-French, Morgan. 'The Limits of the Enlightenment Narrative: Rethinking Europe in Napoleonic Germany'. *History of European Ideas* 46, no. 8 (2020): 1197–213.

Gollwitzer, Heinz. *Europabild und Europagedanke: Beiträge zur deutschen Geistesgeschichte des 18. Und 19. Jahrhunderts*. Munich: C. H. Beck, 1964.

Gollwitzer, Heinz. *Geschichte des weltpolitischen Denkens*, 2 vols. Göttingen: Vandenhoeck & Ruprecht, 1972–82.

Gollwitzer, Heinz. 'Zur Wortgeschichte und Sinndeutung von "Europa"'. *Saeculum* 2, no. JG (1951): 161–72.

Goodhart, David. *The Road to Somewhere: The Populist Revolt and the Future of Politics*. London: Hurst, 2017.

Goodwin, Craufurd D. *Walter Lippmann: Public Economist*. Cambridge, MA: Harvard University Press, 2014.

Gramsci, Antonio. *Letters from Prison*, edited and translated by Lynne Lawner. London: Jonathan Cape, 1975.

Gramsci, Antonio. *Further Selections from the Prison Notebooks*, edited and translated by Derek Boothman. London: Lawrence & Wishart, 1995.

Grandeffe, Arthur de. *L'Empire d'Occident reconstitué; ou, L'equilibre européen assuré par l'union des races latines*. Paris: Ledoyen, 1857.

Grange, Juliette. 'La continuité de l'idée de l'Europe', in Raphael Drai and Cao-Huy Thuan (eds), *Instabilités européennes: Recomposition ou décomposition?*, pp. 207–18. Paris: L'Harmattan, 1992.

Grant, Madison. 'Introduction', in Lothrop Stoddard, *The Rising Tide of Color against White World-Supremacy*, pp. xi–xxxii. New York: Charles Scribner's Sons, 1921.

Grant, Madison. *The Passing of the Great Race; or, The Racial Basis of European History*. New York: Charles Scribner's Sons, 1916.

Grant, Madison. *The Passing of the Great Race; or, The Racial Basis of European History*, revised and amplified edition. New York: Charles Scribner's Sons, 1919.

Gray, John. *The New Leviathans: Thoughts after Liberalism*. London: Allen Lane, 2023.

Greenberg, Udi. *The Weimar Century: German Émigrés and the Ideological Foundations of the Cold War*. Princeton, NJ: Princeton University Press, 2014.

Greenfeld, Liah. *Nationalism: Five Roads to Modernity*. Cambridge, MA: Harvard University Press, 1992.

Greenwood, Sean. *Titan at the Foreign Office: Gladwyn Jebb and the Shaping of the Modern World*. Leiden: Martinus Nijhoff, 2008.

Grémion, Pierre. *Intelligence de l'anticommunisme: Le Congrès pour la liberté de la culture à Paris, 1950–1975*. Paris: Fayard, 1995.

Grémion, Pierre (ed.). *Preuves: Une revue européenne à Paris*. Paris: Julliard, 1989.

Gress, David. *From Plato to NATO: The Idea of the West and its Opponents*. New York: The Free Press, 1998.

Grigg, Edward. *British Foreign Policy*. London: Hutchinson, 1944.

Groh, Dieter. *Russland und das Selbstverständnis Europas: Ein Beitrag zur europäischen Geistesgeschichte*. Neuwied: Hermann Luchterhand, 1961.

Gruber, Carol S. *Mars and Minerva: World War I and the Uses of the Higher Learning in America*. Baton Rouge, LA: University of Louisiana Press, 1975.

Guénon, René. *La Crise du monde moderne*. Paris: Éditions Allia, 2022 [1927].

Guénon, René. *The Crisis of the Modern World*, translated by Marco Pallis, Arthur Osborne and Richard C. Nicholson. Hillsdale, NY: Sophia Perennis, 2001 [1927].

Guénon, René. *East and West*, translated by William Massey. London: Luzac & Co., 1941.

Guénon, René. *Orient et Occident*. Paris: Éditions Didier et Richard, 1930 [1924].

Guizot, François. *Histoire de la civilisation en Europe: Depuis la chute de l'Empire romain jusqu'à la Revolution française*, edited by Pierre Rosanvallon. Paris: Hachette, 1985 [1828].

Guizot, François. *The History of Civilization in Europe*, translated by William Hazlitt [1846], edited by Larry Siedentop. London: Penguin, 1997.

Gurowski, Adam G. de. *America and Europe*. New York: D. Appleton & Co., 1857.

Gurowski, A[dam G.] de. *Russia As It Is*, 3rd edition. New York: D. Appleton & Co., 1854.

Gurowski, Adam [G.] de. *The Turkish Question*. New York: William Taylor & Co., 1854.

Gurowski, A[dam G.] de. *A Year of the War*. New York: D. Appleton & Co., 1855.

Guy-Grant, Georges. 'La Civilisation occidentale'. *L'Effort*, 18 October 1941.

Habermas, Jürgen. *The Crisis of the European Union: A Response*, translated by Ciaran Cronin. Cambridge: Polity Press, 2012.

Habermas, Jürgen. *The Divided West*, edited and translated by Ciaran Cronin. Cambridge: Polity Press, 2006.

Habermas, Jürgen. *Der gespaltene Westen*. Frankfurt am Main: Suhrkamp, 2004.

Habermas, Jürgen. 'Historical Consciousness and Post-Traditional Identity: The Federal Republic's Orientation to the West', in Habermas, *The New Conservatism: Cultural Criticism and the Historians' Debate*, edited and translated by Shierry Weber Nicholsen, pp. 247–61. Cambridge: Polity Press, 1989.

Habermas, Jürgen. *Zur Verfassung Europas: Ein Essay*. Berlin: Suhrkamp, 2011.

Hagedorn, Ludger. 'Europa da Capo al Fine: Jan Patočkas nacheuropäische Reflexionen; Zur Einfürung', in Jan Patočka, *Europa und Nach-Europa*, edited by Ludger Hegedorn and Klaus Nellen, pp. 7–22. Baden-Baden: Karl Albert, 2024.

Hagedorn, Ludger. 'Europe's Twentieth Century: History of Wars and War as History', in Francesco Tava and Darian Meacham (eds), *Thinking after Europe: Jan Patočka and Politics*, pp. 331–46. New York: Rowman & Littlefield, 2016.

Haight, Gordon S. (ed.). *Selections from George Eliot's Letters*. New Haven, CT: Yale University Press, 1985.

Halévy, Élie. *Correspondance (1891–1937)*, edited by Henriette Guy-Loë, annotated by Monique Canto-Sperber, Vincent Duclert and Henriette Guy-Loë, with a preface by François Furet. Paris: Éditions de Fallois, 1996.

Hall, Ian. '"Time of Troubles": Arnold J. Toynbee's Twentieth Century'. *International Affairs* 90, no. 1 (2014): 23–36.
Hall, Ian. 'The "Toynbee Convector": The Rise and Fall of Arnold J. Toynbee's Anti-Imperial Mission to the West'. *The European Legacy* 17, no. 4 (2012): 455–69.
Hallaq, Wael B. *Restating Orientalism: A Critique of Modern Knowledge*. New York: Columbia University Press, 2018.
Hanink, Johanna. *The Classical Debt: Greek Antiquity in an Era of Austerity*. Cambridge, MA: Harvard University Press, 2017.
Hanna, Martha. *The Mobilization of Intellect: French Scholars and Writers during the Great War*. Cambridge, MA: Harvard University Press, 1996.
Harding, Jason. *The Criterion: Cultural Politics and Periodical Networks in Inter-War Britain*. Oxford: Oxford University Press, 2002.
Harp, Gillis J. *Positivist Republic: Auguste Comte and the Reconstruction of American Liberalism, 1865–1920*. University Park, PA: The Pennsylvania State University Press, 1995.
Harrington, Austin. *German Cosmopolitan Social Thought and the Idea of the West: Voices from Weimar*. Cambridge: Cambridge University Press, 2016.
Harris, Ruth. *Guru to the World: The Life and Legacy of Vivekananda*. Cambridge, MA: Harvard University Press, 2022.
Harrison, Frederic. *Autobiographic Memoirs*, 2 vols. London: Macmillan, 1911.
Harrison, Frederic. 'England and France', in Harrison (ed.), *International Policy: Essays on the Foreign Relations of England*, pp. 51–152. London: Chapman and Hall, 1866.
Harrison, Frederic. *Memories and Thoughts: Men–Books–Cities–Art*. London: Macmillan, 1906.
Harrison, Frederic. *National and Social Problems*. London: Macmillan, 1908.
Harrison, Frederic. *Order and Progress*. London: Longmans, Green, and Co., 1875.
Harrison, Hubert H. 'The Black Man's Burden: Meditations of Mustapha as Translated by Hubert H. Harrison'. *The Negro World*, 20 September 1920.
Harrison, Hubert [H.]. '*The Rising Tide of Color against White World-Supremacy* by Lothrop Stoddard' (*Negro World*, 29 May 1920), in Jeffrey B. Perry (ed.), *A Hubert Harrison Reader*, pp. 305–9. Middletown, CT: Wesleyan University Press, 2001.
Harrison, Hubert [H.]. 'The Russian Menace' (letter to the editor). *New York Times*, 4 January 1904.
Harrison, Hubert H. *When Africa Awakes: The 'Inside Story' of the Stirrings and Strivings of the New Negro in the Western World*. Baltimore, MD: Black Classic Press, 1997 [1920].
Harrison Papers. British Library of Political and Economic Science (LSE) Archives, Frederic Harrison Papers
Hartog, François. *Chronos: L'Occident aux prises avec le Temps*. Paris: Gallimard, 2020.
Hatzis, Aristides N. *Ο ενδοξότερος αγώνας · Η Ελληνική Επανάσταση του 1821* (The most glorious struggle: the Greek Revolution of 1821). Athens: Εκδόσεις Παπαδόπουλος, 2021.
Hay, Stephen N. *Asian Ideas of East and West: Tagore and His Critics in Japan, China, and India*. Cambridge, MA: Harvard University Press, 1970.
Hay, Stephen N. 'Rabindranath Tagore in America'. *American Quarterly* 14, no. 3 (1962): 439–63.
Hayek, F[riedrich] A. *The Counter-Revolution of Science: Studies on the Abuse of Reason*. New York: The Free Press of Glencoe, 1955.

Hayek, Friedrich A. *The Road to Serfdom: Text and Documents. The Definitive Edition* [= *The Collected Works of F. A. Hayek*, vol. 2], edited by Bruce Caldwell. London: Routledge, 2008.

Hayes, Carlton J. H., Marshall Whithed Baldwin and Charles Woolsey Cole. *History of Western Civilization*, 2nd edition. New York: Macmillan, 1967.

Heeren, A[rnold] H. L. *Historical Researches into the Politics, Intercourse, and Trade of the Principal Nations of Antiquity*, translated by D[avid] A[lphonso] Talboys, 4 vols, vol. 4: *African Nations: Carthaginians. Ethiopians*. Oxford: D. A. Talboys, 1833.

Heeren, A[rnold] H. L. *History of the Political Systems of Europe, and Its Colonies, from the Discovery of America to the Independence of the American Continent*, translated by George Bancroft. Northampton, MA: S. Butler and Son/New York: G. and C. Carvill/Boston, MA: Richardson and Lord, 1929.

Heeren, Arnold H. L. *Ideen über die Politik, den Verkehr und den Handel der vornehmsten Völker der alten Welt*. Uppsala: Bruzelius, 1818.

Heeren, A[rnold] H. L. *Reflections on the Politics, Intercourse, and Trade of the Ancient Nations of Africa*, translated by D[avid] A[lphonso] Talboys, 2 vols. Oxford: D. A. Talboys, 1832.

Heeren, Arnold H. L. *Reflections on the Politics of Ancient Greece*, translated by George Bancroft. Boston, MA: Cummings, Hilliard & Co., 1824.

Hegel, Georg Wilhelm Friedrich. *Lectures on the Philosophy of World History—Introduction: Reason in History* [1837], translated by by H. B. Nisbet, with an introduction by Duncan Forbes. Cambridge: Cambridge University Press, 1975.

Heidegger, Martin. 'The Nature of Language', in Heidegger, *On the Way to Language*, pp. 57–108. New York: HarperCollins, 1982.

Heller, Kathleen Margaret [Peggy]. 'The Dawning of the West: On the Genesis of a Concept'. Doctoral dissertation, Union Institute and University, Cincinnati, Ohio, 2007.

Heller, Peggy. 'The Russian Dawn: How Russia Contributed to the Emergence of "the West" as a Concept', in Christopher S. Browning and Marko Lehti (eds), *The Struggle for the West: A Divided and Contested Legacy*, pp. 33–52. London: Routledge, 2010.

Hennessy, Peter. *Never Again: Britain 1945–51*. London: Jonathan Cape, 1992.

Herder, Gottfried Johann. *'Another Philosophy of History' and Selected Political Writings*, edited and translated by Ioannis D. Evrigenis and Daniel Pellerin. Indianapolis: Hackett, 2004.

Herman, Arthur. *The Idea of Decline in Western History*. New York: The Free Press, 1997.

Herold, J. Christopher. *Mistress to an Age: A Life of Madame de Staël*. London: Hamish Hamilton, 1959.

Herring, George C. *From Colony to Superpower: U.S. Foreign Relations since 1776*. Oxford: Oxford University Press, 2008.

Hesse, David Maria. *George Eliot and Auguste Comte: The Influence of Comtean Positivism on the Novels of George Eliot*. Frankfurt am Main: Peter Lang, 1996.

Heyd, Uriel. *Foundations of Turkish Nationalism: The Life and Teachings of Ziya Gökalp*. Westport, CT: Hyperion Press, 1979.

Hirsi Ali, Ayaan. 'Why I Am Now a Christian: Atheism Can't Equip Us for Civilisational War'. *UnHerd*, 25 December 2023, https://unherd.com/2023/12/why-i-am-now-a-christian-2/ (accessed 16 October 2024).

Hirsi Ali, Ayaan. 'Why the West *Is Best*', [first published in] *The Spectator World*, 23 June 2021, available at https://ayaanhirsiali.com/articles/why-the-west-is-best (accessed 15 October 2024).

Hobbes, Thomas. *Leviathan*, edited by Richard Tuck. Cambridge: Cambridge University Press, 1996 [1651].

Hochgeschwender, Michael. *Freiheit in der Offensive? Der Kongreß für kulturelle Freiheit und die Deutschen*. Munich: Oldenbourg, 1998.

Hochgeschwender, Michael. *The Intellectual as Propagandist: 'Der Monat', the Congress for Cultural Freedom, and the Process of Westernization in Germany*. Washington, DC: German Historical Institute, 1999.

Hochschild, Adam. *American Midnight: The Great War, a Violent Peace and Democracy's Forgotten Crisis*. New York: Mariner Books, 2022.

Hoeres, Peter. *Krieg der Philosophen: Die deutsche und die britische Philosophie im Ersten Weltkrieg*. Paderborn: Ferdinand Schöningh, 2004.

Hoffman, Eva. *On Czesław Miłosz*. Princeton, NJ: Princeton University Press, 2023.

Hooker, William *Carl Schmitt's International Thought: Order and Orientation*. Cambridge: Cambridge University Press, 2009.

Hopkins, A. G. *American Empire: A Global History*. Princeton, NJ: Princeton University Press, 2018.

Horne, Gerald. *Black and Red: W.E.B. Du Bois and the Afro-American Response to the Cold War, 1944–1963*. Albany, NY: State University of New York Press, 1986.

Hösle, Vittorio. *A Short History of German Philosophy*, translated by Steven Rendall. Princeton, NJ: Princeton University Press, 2017.

Houellebecq, Michel. *Anéantir*. Paris: Flammarion, 2022.

Houellebecq, Michel. *Atomised*, translated by Frank Wynne. London: Vintage Books, 2001.

Houellebecq, Michel. 'Donald Trump Is a Good President' [2019], in Houellebecq, *Interventions 2020*, translated by Andrew Brown, pp. 220–26. Cambridge: Polity Press, 2022.

Houellebecq, Michel. 'Interview with Christian Authier' [2002], in Houellebecq, *Interventions 2020*, translated by Andrew Brown, pp. 98–108. Cambridge: Polity Press, 2022.

Houellebecq, Michel. *Les Particules élémentaires*. Paris: Flammarion, 1998.

Houellebecq, Michel. *Platform*, translated by Frank Wynne. London: William Heinemann, 2002.

Houellebecq, Michel. *Platforme*. Paris: Flammarion, 1999.

Houellebecq, Michel. 'Prolegomena to Positivism', in Houellebecq, *Interventions 2020* pp. 131–37. Cambridge: Polity Press, 2022.

Houellebecq, Michel. *Serotonin*, translated by Shaun Whiteside. London: William Heinemann, 2019.

Houellebecq, Michel. *Sérotonine*. Paris: Flammarion, 2019.

Houellebecq, Michel. *Soumission*. Paris: Flammarion, 2015.

Houellebecq, Michel. *Submission*, translated by Lorin Stein. London: William Heinemann, 2015.

Hovey, Richard B. *John Jay Chapman: An American Mind*. New York: Columbia University Press, 1959.

Howe, M. A. DeWolfe. *John Jay Chapman and His Letters*. Boston, MA: Houghton Mifflin Co., 1937.

Howe, M. A. DeWolfe. *The Life and Letters of George Bancroft*, 2 vols. London: Hodder & Stoughton, 1908.

Hughes, H. Stuart. *Oswald Spengler: A Critical Estimate*. New York: Scribner, 1952.

Hunt, Tristram. 'The Myths of Our Civilisation'. *Financial Times* 'Life & Arts' section, 2/3 March 2024, p. 10.

Huntington, Samuel P. 'The Clash of Civilizations?'. *Foreign Affairs*, vol. 72, no. 3 (1993), pp. 22–49.

Huntington, Samuel P. *The Clash of Civilizations and the Remaking of World Order*. New York: Simon & Schuster, 2011 [1996].

Huntington, Samuel P. 'No Exit: The Errors of Endism'. *The National Interest*, no. 17 (Fall 1989), pp. 3–11.

Huntington, Samuel P. 'The West Unique, Not Universal'. *Foreign Affairs*, vol. 75, no. 6 (1996), pp. 28–46.

Huntington, Samuel P. *Who Are We? America's Great Debate*. London: Simon & Schuster, 2004.

Hurston, Zora Neale. 'The Chick with One Hen' [1937], in Hurston, *You Don't Know Us Negroes and Other Essays*, edited by Henry Louis Gates, Jr. and Genevieve West, pp. 131–33. London: HarperCollins, 2022.

Huxley, Aldous. *Letters of Aldous Huxley*, edited by Grover Smith. London: Chatto & Windus, 1969.

Iriye, Akira. *From Nationalism to Internationalism: US Foreign Policy to 1914*. London: Routledge & Kegan Paul, 1977.

Irving, Sean. 'Competitiveness, Civilizationism, and the Anglosphere: Kenneth Minogue's Place in Conservative Thought'. *Modern Intellectual History* 21, no. 2 (2024): 469–88.

Irving, Washington. *Life of Oliver Goldsmith*. New York: Thomas Y. Crowell, 1849.

Irwin, Robert. *For Lust of Knowledge: The Orientalists and their Enemies*. London: Penguin, 2006.

Isabella, Maurizio. *Southern Europe in the Age of Revolutions*. Princeton, NJ: Princeton University Press, 2023.

Istel, André. 'Les Données d'un accord occidental'. *Le Monde*, 7 June 1945.

Jackson, Julian. *A Certain Idea of France: The Life of Charles de Gaulle*. London: Allen Lane, 2018.

Jackson, Patrick Thaddeus. '"Civilization" on Trial'. *Millennium* 28 (1999): 141–53.

Jackson, Patrick Thaddeus. *Civilizing the Enemy: German Reconstruction and the Invention of the West*. Ann Arbor, MI: The University of Michigan Press, 2006.

James, George G. M. *Stolen Legacy: Greek Philosophy is Stolen Egyptian Philosophy*. New York: Philosophical Library, 1954.

James, Leslie. *George Padmore and Decolonization from Below: Pan-Africanism, the Cold War, and the End of Empire*. Basingstoke: Palgrave Macmillan, 2015.

Janken, Kenneth Robert. *Rayford W. Logan and the Dilemma of the African American Intellectual*. Amherst, MA: University of Massachusetts Press, 1993.

Jaspers, Karl. 'Is Europe's Culture Finished? Paths Toward a New Creativity'. *Commentary*, vol. 4, no. 6 (December 1947), pp. 518–26.

Jennings, Jeremy. *Revolution and the Republic: A History of Political Thought in France since the Eighteenth Century*. Oxford: Oxford University Press, 2011.

Jerrold, Douglas. *The Lie about the West: A Response to Professor Toynbee's Challenge*. London: J. M. Dent, 1954.

Jerrold, Douglas. 'Professor Toynbee, "The West"' and the World'. *The Swanee Review*, vol. 62, no. 1 (January–March 1954), pp. 56–83.

Jones, H. S. 'Introduction', in Auguste Comte, *Early Political Writings*, edited and translated by H. S. Jones, pp. vii–xxviii. Cambridge: Cambridge University Press, 1998.

Jones, H. S. 'The Victorian Lexicon of Evil: Frederic Harrison, the Positivists and the Language of International Politics', in Tom Crook, Rebecca Gill and Bertrand Taithe (eds), *Evil, Barbarism and Empire: Britain and Abroad, c. 1830–2000*, pp. 126–43. Basingstoke: Palgrave Macmillan, 2011.

Jones, H. S. *Victorian Political Thought*. Basingstoke: Macmillan, 2000.

Joscelyne, Sophie. 'Norman Mailer and American Totalitarianism in the 1960s'. *Modern Intellectual History* 19, no. 1 (2022): 241–67.

Judt, Tony. *The Burden of Responsibility: Blum, Camus, Aron, and the French Twentieth Century*. Chicago: The University of Chicago Press, 1998.

Judt, Tony. *Past Imperfect: French Intellectuals, 1944–1956*. New York: New York University Press, 2011.

Kallen, H[orace]. M. 'Alain Locke and Cultural Pluralism'. *The Journal of Philosophy* 54, no. 5 (1957): 119–27.

Kalliney, Peter J. *The Aesthetic Cold War: Decolonization and Global Literature*. Princeton, NJ: Princeton University Press, 2022.

Kaplan, Sidney. 'Social Engineers as Saviors: Effects of World War I on Some American Liberals'. *Journal of the History of Ideas* 17 (1956): 247–69.

Kaprièlian, Nelly. 'Cassandra of the Fifth Republic: Houellebecq flirts with the Extreme Right in His Latest Novel'. *Times Literary Supplement*, no. 6207 (18 March 2022), pp. 3–4.

Karakatsouli, Anne. 'La Guerre d'indépendance grecque en tant que lutte anticoloniale: La pensée radicale et moderne de l'abbé Dominique de Pradt', in Chryssanthi Avlami, Franck Salaün and Jean-Pierre Schandeler (eds), *De l'Europe ottomane aux nations balkaniques: Les Lumières en question / From Ottomane Europe to the Balkan Nations: Questioning the Enlightenment* (Turnhout: Brepols, 2023).

Karakatsoulis, Anne. 'Une revue-entreprise: *La Revue des Deux Mondes* pendant l'entre-deux-guerres'. *La Revue des revues* 22 (1996): 17–44.

Kayden, Eugene M. 'Catholic Jazzmania'. *The Sewanee Review*, vol. 37, no. 4 (October 1929), pp. 504–6.

Kedourie, Elie. 'Introduction', in Kedourie (ed.), *Nationalism in Asia and Africa*, pp. 1–152. London: Frank Cass, 1974 [1970].

Kelley, Robin D. G. 'How the West Was One: The African Diaspora and the Re-Mapping of U.S. History', in Thomas Bender (ed.), *Rethinking American History in a Global Age* pp. 123–47. Berkeley, CA: University of California Press, 2002.

Kelley, William. 'Past History and Present Politics: E. A. Freeman and the Eastern Question', in G. A. Bremner and Jonathan Conlin (eds), *Making History: Edward Augustus Freeman and Victorian Cultural Politics*, pp. 119–35. Oxford: Oxford University Press, 2015.

Kelly, Duncan. *The State of the Political: Conceptions of Politics and the State in the Thought of Max Weber, Carl Schmitt and Franz Neumann*. Oxford: Oxford University Press, 2003.

Kelly, G. A. 'Hegel's America'. *Philosophy and Public Affairs* 2, no. 1 (1972): 3–36.

Kennan, George F. *The Kennan Diaries*, edited by Frank Costigliola. New York: W. W. Norton, 2014.

Kennan, George F. *The Marquis de Custine and His Russia in 1839*. London: Hutchinson, 1972.

Kennedy, Rebecca [Futo]. 'Classics and Western Civilization: The Troubling History of an Authoritative Narrative', in Juliana Bastos Marques and Federico Santangelo (eds), *Authority and History: Ancient Models, Modern Questions*, pp. 87–108. London: Bloomsbury Academic, 2023.

Kennedy, Rebecca Futo. '"Western Civilization", White Supremacism and the Myth of a White Ancient Greece', in Elisabeth Niklasson (ed.), *Polarized Past: Heritage and Belonging in Times of Political Polarization*, pp. 88–109. Oxford: Berghahn Books, 2023.

Kennedy, Sean. 'Situating France: The Career of André Siegfried, 1900–1940,' *Historical Reflections / Reflexions historiques* 30, no. 2 (2004): 179–203.

Kent, George E. 'Richard Wright: Blackness and the Adventure of Western Culture'. *CLA Journal* 12, no. 4 (1969): 322–43.

Kerlin, Robert T. *Negro Poets and Their Poems*. Washington, DC: Associated Publishers, 1923.

Kertzer, David I. *The Pope at War: The Secret History of Pius XII, Mussolini, and Hitler*. Oxford: Oxford University Press, 2022.

Kessler, Nicolas. *Histoire politique de la Jeune Droite (1929–1942): Une révolution conservatrice à la française*. Paris: L'Harmattan, 2001.

Keyserling, Hermann. *The Travel Diary of a Philosopher*, translated by J. Holroyd Reece, 2 vols. London: Jonathan Cape, 1925.

Khomiakov, Aleksei Stepanovich. 'On Humboldt' [1849], in Marc Raeff (ed.), *Russian Intellectual History: An Anthology*. New Jersey: Humanities Press, 1978 (repr.), pp. 208–29.

Kidd, Benjamin. *Principles of Western Civilisation*. London: Macmillan, 1902.

Kidd, Benjamin. *Social Evolution*. London: Macmillan, 1894.

Kidd, Colin. *The Forging of Races: Race and Scripture in the Protestant Atlantic World, 1600–2000*. Cambridge: Cambridge University Press, 2006.

Kidd, Colin. *The World of Mr Casaubon: Britain's Wars of Mythography, 1700–1870*. Cambridge: Cambridge University Press, 2016.

Kimmage, Michael. *The Abandonment of the West: The History of an Idea in American Foreign Policy*. New York: Basic Books, 2020.

Kimmage, Michael. *The Conservative Turn: Lionel Trilling, Whittaker Chambers, and the Lessons of Anti-Communism*. Cambridge, MA: Harvard University Press, 2009.

King, Charles. *The Reinvention of Humanity: How a Circle of Renegade Anthropologists Remade Race, Sex and Gender*. London: Vintage, 2020.

Kingsley, Charles. *The Roman and the Teuton: A Series of Lectures delivered before the University of Cambridge*, with a preface by F. Max Müller. London: Macmillan, 1901 [1864].

Kinnamon, Keneth and Michel Fabre (eds). *Conversations with Richard Wright*. Jackson, MS: University Press of Mississippi, 1993.

Kirby, Dianne. 'Divinely Sanctioned: The Anglo-American Cold War Alliance and the Defence of Western Civilization and Christianity, 1945–1948'. *Journal of Contemporary History* 35, no. 3 (2000): 385–412.

Kirby, Dianne. 'From Bridge to Divide: East–West Relations and Christianity during the Second World War and Early Cold War'. *The International History Review* 36, no. 4 (2014): 721–44.

Kirby, Dianne (ed.). *Religion and the Cold War*. New York: Palgrave Macmillan, 2003.

Kireevski, Ivan Vasil'evich. 'On the Nature of European Culture and its Relation to the Culture of Russia: Letter to Count E. E. Komarovskii' [1852], in Marc Raeff (ed.), *Russian Intellectual History: An Anthology*. New Jersey: Humanities Press, 1978 (repr.), pp. 175–207.

Kissinger, Henry A. 'The Meaning of History (Reflections on Spengler, Toynbee, and Kant)'. Harvard senior thesis, Harvard University, 1950.

Kissinger Papers. Yale University Library, Manuscripts and Archives, Henry A. Kissinger Papers.

Kitromilides, Paschalis M. *Enlightenment and Revolution: The Making of Modern Greece*. Cambridge, MA: Harvard University Press, 2013.

Koditschek, Theodore. 'A Liberal Descent? E. A. Freeman's Invention of Racial Traditions', in G. A. Bremner and Jonathan Conlin (eds), *Making History: Edward Augustus Freeman and Victorian Cultural Politics*, pp. 199–216. Oxford: Oxford University Press.

Kohn, Hans. *American Nationalism: An Interpretative Essay*. New York: Macmillan, 1957.

Kohn, Hans. *The Mind of Germany: The Education of a Nation*. London: Macmillan, 1965 [1960].

Kohn, Hans (ed.). *The Mind of Modern Russia: Historical and Political Thought of Russia's Great Age*. New Brunswick, NJ: Rutgers University Press, 1955.

Kojève, Alexandre. 'Esquisse d'une doctrine de la politique française [27/VIII/45]'. Bibliothèque nationale de France, Fonds 'Alexandre Kojève', NAF 28320 (13).

Kojève, Alexandre. *Introduction à la lecture de Hegel: Leçons sur la 'Phénoménologie de l'Esprit' professées de 1933 à 1939 à l'École des Hautes Études*, edited by Raymond Queneau. Paris: Gallimard, 1968 [1947].

Kojève, Alexandre. *Introduction to the Reading of Hegel: Lectures on the Phenomenology of Spirit*, assembled by Raymond Queneau, edited by Allan Bloom, translated by James H. Nichols, Jr. Ithaca, NY: Cornell University Press, 1980.

Kojève, Alexandre. 'Outline of a Doctrine of French Policy', translated by Erik de Vries. *Policy Review*, no. 126 (2004), available at https://web.archive.org/web/20070929083759/http://www.hoover.org/publications/policyreview/3436846.html (accessed 19 October 2024).

Kolnai, Aurel. *The War against the West*, with a preface by Wickham Steed. London: Victor Gollancz, 1938.

Krastev, Ivan. *After Europe*, updated edition. Philadelphia: University of Pennsylvania Press, 2020.

Krastev, Ivan and Stephen Holmes. *The Light That Failed: A Reckoning*. London: Penguin, 2019.

Krutch, Joseph Wood. 'What is the West?'. *The Nation*, vol. 126, no. 3268 (22 February 1928), pp. 214–16.

Kuisel, Richard F. *Seducing the French: The Dilemma of Americanization*. Berkeley, CA: University of California Press, 1993.

Kukiel, M[arian]. *Czartoryski and European Unity, 1770–1861*. Princeton, NJ: Princeton University Press, 1955.

Kumar, Krishan. 'The Return of Civilization—and of Arnold Toynbee?'. *Comparative Studies in Society and History* 56, no. 4 (2014): 815–43.

Kundera, Milan. *A Kidnapped West: The Tragedy of Eastern Europe*, translated by Linda Asher and Edmund White. London: Faber & Faber, 2023.

Kundera, Milan. 'The Tragedy of Eastern Europe'. *The New York Review of Books*, 26 April 1984.

Kurth, James. 'NATO Expansion and the Idea of the West'. *Orbis*, vol. 41, no. 4 (1997), pp. 555–67.

Kurth, James. 'The Real Clash'. *National Interest*, no. 37 (Fall 1994), pp. 3–15.

Kurth, James. *What are We Fighting For? Western Civilization, American Identity, and U.S. Foreign Policy*. Philadelphia: Foreign Policy Research Institute, 2009.

Kurtz, Stanley. *The Lost History of Western Civilization*. Princeton, NJ: National Association of Scholars, 2020.

La Vopa, Anthony J. *The Labor of the Mind: Intellect and Gender in Enlightenment Cultures*. Philadelphia: University of Pennsylvania Press, 2017.

Laffitte, Pierre. *Considérations générales sur l'ensemble de la civilisation chinoise et sur les relations de l'Occident avec la Chine*, 2nd edition. Paris: Société Positiviste, 1900 [1861].

Laffitte, Pierre. 'Conversations avec A. Comte: Notes manuscrites de P. Laffitte sur des conversations entre 1845 et 1850', Maison d'Auguste Comte manuscripts, p. 12 bis.

Laffitte, Pierre. *De la morale positive*. Paris: Hachette Livre–BnF, 2018 [1881].

Laffitte, Pierre. *A General View of Chinese Civilization and of the Relations of the West with China*, translated by John Carey Hall. London: Trübner & Co., 1887 [1861].

Laffitte, Pierre. *Les Grands Types de l'humanité: Appréciation systématique de l'évolution humaine*, 2nd edition, 2 vols. Paris: Société Positiviste, 1932 [1875].

Laffitte, Pierre. 'Introduction: Des opinions actuelles sur les relations de l'Occident avec le reste de la terre', in Richard Congreve, *L'Inde*, pp. xiii–lviii. Paris: P. Jannet, 1858.

Laffitte, Pierre. *The Positive Science of Morals: Its Opportuneness, Its Outlines, and Its Chief Applications*, translated by J. Carey Hall. London: Watts & Co., 1908 [1881].

Lamartine, Alphonse de. *La Question d'Orient: Discours et articles politiques (1834–1861)*, edited by Sophie Basch and Henry Laurens. Paris: André Versaille, 2011.

Lamb, Margaret. 'The Making of a Russophobe: David Urquhart; the Formative Years, 1825–1835'. *The International History Review* 3, no. 3: 330–57.

Larousse, Pierre. *Grand dictionnaire universel du XIXe siècle*, vol. 11. Paris: Administration du Grand Dictionnaire, 1874.

Lasch, Christopher. 'The Anti-Intellectualism of the Intellectuals', in Lasch, *The New Radicalism in America (1889–1963): The Intellectual as a Social Type*, pp. 286–349. London: Chatto & Windus, 1966.

Lasch, Christopher. 'The *New Republic* and the War: "*An Unanalyzable Feeling*"', in Lasch, *The New Radicalism in America (1889–1963): The Intellectual as a Social Type*, pp. 181–224. London: Chatto & Windus, 1966.

Latreille, Camille. *Joseph de Maistre et la papauté*. Paris: Hachette, 1906.

Laurens, Henry. 'La Question d'Orient', in Alphonse de Lamartine, *La Question d'Orient: Discours et articles politiques (1834–1861)*, edited by Sophie Basch and Henry Laurens, pp. 7–58. Paris: André Versaille, 2011.

Laurens, Henry. *Orientales*. Paris: CNRS Éditions, 2007.

Laurent, Jérôme. 'La Philosophie russe et le positivisme', in *La philosophie russe et le positivisme*, special issue, *Archives de philosophie* 79, no. 2 (2016): 229–31.
Le Bret, Hervé. *Les Frères d'Eichthal: Le saint simonien et le financier au XIXe siècle*. Paris : Presses de l'Université Paris-Sorbonne, 2012.
Leboyer, Olivia. 'Raymond Aron, lecteur d'Auguste Comte, avec un inédit d'Aron de 1928'. *Revue européenne des sciences sociales* 54, no. 2 (2016) : 113–44.
Lehne, Jakob. 'The Glittery Fog of Civilization: Great Britain, Germany, and International Politics, 1854–1902'. Doctoral thesis, European University Institute, Florence, 2015.
Lehnert, Joris. 'Rome ou la solution à tous les problèmes européens: Georg Moenius et le concept de romanité durant l'entre-deux-guerres'. *Amnis* 11 (2012): 1–12.
Lemberg, Hans. 'Zur Entstehung des Osteuropabegriffs im 19. Jahrhundert Vom "Norden" zum "Osten" Europas'. *Jahrbücher für Geschichte Osteuropas* 33, no. 1 (1985): 48–91.
Léon-Martin, Louis. 'Le Sentiment de l'Occident'. *Les Nouveax Temps*, 30 March 1943.
Lepenies, Wolf. *Auguste Comte: Die Macht der Zeichen*. Munich: Carl Hanser, 2010.
Lepenies, Wolf. *Die Macht am Mittelmeer: Französische Träume von einem anderen Europa*. Munich: Carl Hanser, 2016.
Lepenies, Wolf. *The Seduction of Culture in German History*. Princeton, NJ: Princeton University Press, 2006.
Levallois, Michel and Sarga Moussa (eds). *L'Orientalisme des saint-simoniens*. Paris: Maisonneuve & Larose, 2006.
Levenson, Joseph R. *Liang Ch'i-ch'ao and the Mind of Modern China*. Cambridge, MA: Harvard University Press, 1953.
Levine, Emily J. *Allies and Rivals: German-American Exchange and the Rise of the Modern Research University*. Chicago: The University of Chicago Press, 2021.
Levy, Daniel, Max Pensky and John Torpey (eds). *Old Europe, New Europe, Core Europe: Transatlantic Relations After the Iraq War*. London: Verso, 2005.
Levy, David W. *Herbert Croly of the New Republic: The Life and Times of an American Progressive*. Princeton, NJ: Princeton University Press, 1985.
Lewis, Ben. *Oswald Spengler and the Politics of Decline*. New York: Berghahn, 2022.
Lewis, David Levering. *W.E.B. Du Bois: A Biography*. New York: Henry Holt, 2009.
Lewis, Martin W. and Kären E. Wigen. *The Myth of Continents: A Critique of Metageography*. Berkeley, CA: University of California Press, 1997.
Lewis, Wyndham. *Paleface: The Philosophy of the 'Melting-Pot'*. London: Chatto & Windus, 1929.
Lewis, Wyndham. *Time and Western Man*. London: Chatto & Windus, 1927.
Lialiouti, Zinovia. 'The "Treason of the Intellectuals": The Shadowy Presence of the Congress for Cultural Freedom in Greece, 1950–1963'. *Intelligence and National Security* 33, no. 5 (2018): 687–704.
Lieber, Francis. *Essays on Property and Labour as Connected with Natural Law and the Constitution of Society*. New York: Harper & Brothers, 1841.
Lieber, Francis. 'History and Political Science Necessary Studies in Free Countries: An Inaugural Address Delivered on the 17th of February, 1858, on Assuming the Chair of History and Political Science, in Columbia College, New York', in Lieber, *Miscellaneous Writings*, vol. 1: *Reminiscences, Addresses, and Essays*, pp. 329–68. Philadelphia: J. B. Lippincott & Co., 1881.

Lieber, Francis. 'The History and Uses of Athenæums: A Lecture Delivered at the Request of the Columbia Athenæum, March 17, 1856', in Lieber, *The Miscellaneous Writings of Francis Lieber*, vol. 1: *Reminiscences, Addresses, and Essays*, pp. 297–327. Philadelphia: J. B. Lippincott & Co., 1881.

Lieber, Francis. 'The Latin Race' [1871], in Lieber, *The Miscellaneous Writings of Francis Lieber*, vol. 2: *Contributions to Political Science*, pp. 306–10. Philadelphia: J. B. Lippincott & Co., 1881.

Lieber, Francis. 'Nationalism and Internationalism' [1868], in Lieber, *The Miscellaneous Writings of Francis Lieber*, vol. 2: *Contributions to Political Science*, pp. 221–43. Philadelphia: J. B. Lippincott & Co., 1881.

Lieber, Francis. *On Civil Liberty and Self-Government*, 2 vols. Philadelphia: Lippincott, Crambo, & Co., 1853.

Lieber, Francis. *On Civil Liberty and Self-Government*, 2nd edition (in one volume). Philadelphia: J. B. Lippincott & Co., 1859.

Lieber, Francis. 'Origin and Development of the First Constituents of Civilization: A Lecture Delivered at Columbia, South Carolina, 1845', in Lieber, *The Miscellaneous Writings of Francis Lieber*, vol. 1: *Reminiscences, Addresses, and Essays*, pp. 205–23. Philadelphia: J. B. Lippincott & Co., 1881.

[Lieber, Francis.] 'Turkey'. *The North American Review*, vol. 31, no. 69 (October 1830), pp. 291–308.

Lieber, Francis. *The West: A Metrical Epistle*. New York: Putnam, 1848.

Liechtenhan, Francine-Dominique. *Astolphe de Custine, voyageur et philosophe*. Paris: Honoré Champion, 1990.

Liechtenhan, Francine-Dominique. 'La Russie, ennemi héréditaire de la chrétienté? La diffusion de l'image de la Moscovie en Europe occidentale aux XVIe et XVIIe siècles'. *Revue historique* 285, no. 577 (1991): 77–103.

Lilla, Mark. 'Alexandre Kojève', in Lilla, *The Reckless Mind: Intellectuals in Politics*, pp. 113–36. New York: New York Review Books, 2001.

Lilla, Mark. 'Athens and Chicago: Leo Strauss', in Lilla, *The Shipwrecked Mind: On Political Reaction*, pp. 43–63. New York: New York Review Books, 2016.

Lilla, Mark. 'Introduction', in Thomas Mann, *Reflections of a Nonpolitical Man*, pp. vii–xxi. New York: New York Review Books, 2021.

Lilla, Mark. 'The Other Velvet Revolution: Continental Liberalism and Its Discontents'. *Daedalus* 123, no. 2 (1994): 129–57.

Lilla, Mark. 'Paris, January 2015', in Lilla, *The Shipwrecked Mind: On Political Reaction*, pp. 105–29. New York: New York Review Books, 2016.

Lilti, Antoine. '"Et la civilisation deviendra générale": L'Europe de Volney, ou l'orientalisme à l'épreuve de la Révolution'. *La Révolution française* 4 (2011) ('Dire et faire l'Europe à la fin du XVIIIe siècle'), https://journals.openedition.org/lrf/290 (accessed 29 July 2024).

Lilti, Antoine. *L'Héritage des Lumières: Ambivalences de la modernité*. Paris: Seuil/Gallimard, 2019.

Lippmann, Walter. 'The American Destiny'. *Life*, vol. 6, no. 23 (5 June 1939), pp. 47 and 72–73.

Lippmann, Walter. *The Cold War: A Study in U.S. Foreign Policy*. New York: Harper & Brothers, 1947.

Lippmann, Walter. 'The Defense of the Atlantic World' [*New Republic*, 17 February 1917], in Lippmann, *Early Writings*, with an introduction and annotations by Arthur Schlesinger, Jr., pp. 69–75. New York: Liveright, 1970.

Lippmann, Walter. 'Education vs. Western Civilization'. *The American Scholar*, vol. 10, no. 2 (Spring 1941), pp. 184–93.

Lippmann, Walter. *Some Notes on War and Peace*. New York: The Macmillan Company, 1940.

Lippmann, Walter. *The Stakes of Diplomacy*. New York: Henry Holt & Co., 1915.

Lippmann, Walter. *U.S. Foreign Policy: Shield of the Republic*. Boston, MA: Atlantic–Little, Brown & Co., 1943.

Lippmann, Walter. *U.S. War Aims*. Boston, MA: Atlantic–Little, Brown & Co., 1944.

Lippmann, Walter. 'What Program Shall the United States Stand for in International Relations?'. *Annals of the American Academy of Political and Social Science* 66 ('Preparedness and America's International Program') (July 1916): 60–70.

Littré, Émile. *Conservation, révolution et positivisme*. Paris: Ladrange, 1852.

Lochore, R. A. *History of the Idea of Civilization in France (1830–1870)*. Bonn: Ludwig Röhrscheid, 1935.

Locke, Alain [LeRoy]. 'Apropos of Africa'. *Opportunity: A Journal of Negro Life*, vol. 2, no. 14 (February 1924), pp. 37–40 and 58.

Locke, Alain [LeRoy]. 'The Black Watch on the Rhine'. *Opportunity: A Journal of Negro Life*, vol. 2, no. 13 (January, 1924), pp. 6–9.

Locke, Alain [LeRoy]. 'Cultural Relativism and Ideological Peace' [1944], in Locke, *The Works of Alain Locke*, edited by Charles Molesworth, pp. 548–54. Oxford: Oxford University Press, 2012.

Locke, Alain LeRoy. 'The Great Disillusionment' [lecture delivered on 26 September 1914], Appendix, in Locke, *Race Contacts and Interracial Relations: Lectures on the Theory and Practice of Race*, edited by Jeffrey C. Stewart, pp. 105–10. Washington, DC: Howard University Press, 1992.

Locke, Alain [LeRoy]. 'Special Section: When Peoples Meet: A Study in Race and Culture Contacts' [fifteen interchapters from *When Peoples Meet: A Study in Race and Culture Contacts*, edited by Alain Locke and Bernhard Stern (1942)], in Locke, *The Works of Alain Locke*, edited by Charles Molesworth, pp. 343–418. Oxford: Oxford University Press, 2012.

Locke, Alain [LeRoy]. 'The Unfinished Business of Democracy'. *Survey Graphic*, vol. 31, no. 11 (November 1942), pp. 455–59.

Locke, Alain and Bernhard J. Stern (eds). *When Peoples Meet: A Study in Race and Culture Contacts*. New York: Progressive Education Association, 1942.

Logan, Deborah Anna (ed.). *The Collected Letters of Harriet Martineau*, 5 vols. London: Pickering & Chatto, 2007.

Logan, Deborah Anna. *The Hour and the Woman: Harriet Martineau's 'Somewhat Remarkable' Life*. DeKalb, IL: Northern Illinois University Press, 2002.

Logan, Rayford W. 'The Confessions of an Unwilling Nordic' [1927], in Sterling Brown (ed.), *The Negro Caravan*, pp. 1043–50. New York: The Dryden Press, 1941.

Lok, Matthijs. *Europe against Revolution: Conservatism, Enlightenment, and the Making of the Past*. Oxford: Oxford University Press, 2023.

Long, Orie William. *Literary Pioneers: Early American Explorers of European Culture*. Cambridge, MA: Harvard University Press, 1935.

Longfellow, Henry Wadsworth. *Kavanagh: A Tale*. Boston, MA: Ticknor, Reed, and Fields, 1849.

Lubac, Henri de. *La Postérité spirituelle de Joachim de Flore*, edited by Michael Sutton. Paris: Les Éditions du Cerf, 2014.

Luce, Henry R. 'The American Century'. *Life*, vol. 10, no. 7 (17 February 1941), pp. 61–65.

Mac Sweeney, Naoíse. *The West: A New History of an Old Idea*. London: W. H. Allen, 2023.

Maçães, Bruno. *Belt and Road: A Chinese World Order*. London: Hurst, 2019.

Maçães, Bruno. 'Gaza and the End of Western Fantasy'. *Time*, 10 January 2024, https://time.com/6553708/gaza-end-of-western-hypocrisy-essay/ (accessed 16 October 2024).

Macdonald, Dwight. 'I Choose the West' [1952], in Macdonald, *Memoirs of a Revolutionist: Essays in Political Criticism*, pp. 197–200. New York: Farrar, Straus & Cudahy, 1957.

MacDonald, James Ramsay. *Imperialism: Its Meaning and Its Tendency*. London: Independent Labour Party, 1900.

Mackinnon, Emma Stone. 'The Right to Rebel: History and Universality in the Political Thought of the Algerian Revolution', in John Robertson (ed.), *Time, History, and Political Thought*, pp. 285–307. Cambridge: Cambridge University Press, 2023.

Magoon, E[lias] L. *Westward Empire; or, The Great Drama of Human Progress*. New York: Harper & Brothers, 1856.

Mahan, Alfred Thayer. *The Interest of America in Sea Power, Present and Future*. Boston, MA: Little, Brown and Co., 1898.

Maine, Henry Sumner. *Ancient Law: Its Connection with the Early History of Society and Its Relation to Modern Ideas*. London: John Murray, 1905 [1861].

Maine, Henry Sumner. 'The Effects of Observation of India on Modern European Thought' [1875], in Maine, *Village-Communities in the East and West: Six Lectures Delivered at Oxford*, 7th edition. London: John Murray, 1895), pp. 203–39.

Maine, Henry Sumner. *Village-Comunities in the East and West: Six Lectures Delivered at Oxford*, 7th edition. London: John Murray, 1895.

Maison d'Auguste Comte manuscripts. Maison d'Auguste Comte, 10, rue Monsieur-le-Prince, Paris.

Maistre, Joseph de. *Du pape*. Paris: Garnier, 2021 [1819]

Maistre, Joseph de. *The Pope; Considered in his Relations with the Church, Temporal Sovereignties, Separated Churches, and the Cause of Civilization*, translated by the Aeneas McD. Dawson. New York: Howard Fertig, 1975 (with an introduction by Richard A. Lebrun) [1850].

Malcolm, Noel. *Useful Enemies: Islam and the Ottoman Empire in Western Political Thought, 1450–1750*. Oxford: Oxford University Press, 2019.

Malraux, André. '[Review of] *Défense de l'Occident*, par Henri Massis (Plon)'. *Nouvelle Revue française*, vo l. 28 (1927), pp. 813–18.

Malraux, André. *La Tentation de l'Occident*. Paris: Grasset, 1926.

Man, Henry [Henri/Hendrik] de. 'Germany's New Prophets'. *The Yale Review*, series 2, vol. 13 (1923–24), pp. 665–83.

Mandler, Peter. *The English National Character: The History of an Idea from Edmund Burke to Tony Blair*. New Haven, CT: Yale University Press, 2006.

Mandler, Peter. '"Race" and "nation" in Mid-Victorian Thought', in Stefan Collini, Richard Whatmore and Brian Young (eds), *History, Religion, and Culture: British Intellectual History 1750–1950*, pp. 224–44. Cambridge: Cambridge University Press, 2000.

Manent, Pierre. *Les Metamorphoses de la cité: Essai sur la dynamique de l'Occident*. Paris: Flammarion, 2010.

Manent, Pierre. *Metamorphoses of the City: On the Western Dynamic*, translated by Marc LePain. Cambridge, MA: Harvard University Press, 2013.

Mann, Golo. 'America as Frankenstein: *The Twenty-Fifth Hour*, by C. Virgil Gheorghiu' [review article]. *Commentary*, vol. 11 (January 1951), pp. 99–101.

Mann, Thomas. *Betrachtungen eines Unpolitischen*. Berlin: G. Fischer, 1918.

Mann, Thomas. *Briefe, 1889–1936*, edited by Erika Mann. Frankfurt am Main: S. Fischer, 1961.

Mann, Thomas. 'L'Esprit de l'Allemagne et son avenir entre la mystique slave et la latinité occidentale'. *L'Europe Nouvelle*, no. 369 (14 March 1925), pp. 333–37.

Mann, Thomas. 'Gedanken im Kriege' [1914], in Mann, *Von Deutscher Republik: Politische Schriften und Reden in Deutschland*, pp. 7–25. Frankfurt am Main: S. Fischer, 1984.

Mann, Thomas. *Letters of Thomas Mann, 1889–1955*, selected and translated by Richard Winston and Clara Winston. London: Penguin, 1975.

Mann, Thomas. 'On the German Republic' [1922], translated by Lawrence Rainey, in Mann, *Reflections of a Nonpolitical Man*, edited by Mark Lilla, pp. 507–47. New York: New York Review Books, 2021.

Mann, Thomas. 'On the Theory of Spengler', in Mann, *Past Masters and Other Papers*, translated by H. T. Lowe-Porter, pp. 215–27. London: Martin Secker, 1933.

Mann, Thomas. 'Reflections of a Nonpolitical Man' [1918], translated by Walter D. Morris, in Mann, *Reflections of a Nonpolitical Man*, edited by Mark Lilla, pp. 1–489. New York: New York Review Books, 2021.

Mann, Thomas. *Thomas Mann Diaries, 1918–1939*, translated by Richard Winston and Clara Winston. London: Robin Clark, 1984.

Mann, Thomas. 'Thoughts in Wartime' [1914], translated by Cosima Mattner and Mark Lilla, in Mann, *Reflections of a Nonpolitical Man*, edited by Mark Lilla, pp. 493–506. New York: New York Review Books, 2021.

Mann, Thomas. 'Über die Lehre Spenglers' [1924], in Mann, *Bemühungen: Neue Folge der Gesammelten Abhandlungen und kleinen Aufsätze*, pp. 239–48. Berlin: G. Fischer, 1925.

Mann, Thomas. 'Von Deutscher Republik: Gerhart Hauptmann zum sechzigsten Geburtstag' [1922], in Mann, *Von Deutscher Republik: Politische Schriften und Reden in Deutschland*, pp. 118–59. Frankfurt am Main: S. Fischer, 1984.

Manuel, Frank E. *The Prophets of Paris: Turgot, Condorcet, Saint-Simon, Fourier, and Comte*. New York: Harper & Row, 1965.

Manuel, Frank E. and Fritzie P. Manuel, *Utopian Thought in the Western World*. Oxford: Basil Blackwell, 1979.

Maran, René. *Batouala, véritable roman nègre*. Paris: Albin Michel, 1921.

Marchand, Suzanne L. *Down from Olympus: Archaeology and Philhellenism in Germany, 1750–1970*. Princeton, NJ: Princeton University Press, 1996.

Marchand, Suzanne [L.]. 'Eastern Wisdom in an Era of Western Despair: Orientalism in 1920s Central Europe', in Peter E. Gordon and John P. McCormick (eds), *Weimar Thought: A Contested Legacy*, pp. 341–60. Princeton, NJ: Princeton University Press, 2013.

Marchand, Suzanne [L.]. 'German Orientalism and the Decline of the West'. *Proceedings of the American Philosophical Society* 145, no. 4 (2001): 465–73.

Marchand, Suzanne L. *German Orientalism in the Age of Empire: Religion, Race, and Scholarship*. Cambridge: Cambridge University Press, 2009.

Marchand, Suzanne L. 'Herodotus and the Embarrassments of Universal History in Nineteenth-Century Germany'. *The Journal of Modern History* 95, no. 2 (2023): 308–48.

Marchand, Suzanne [L.]. 'Leo Frobenius and the Revolt against the West'. *Journal of Contemporary History* 32, no. 2 (1997): 153–70.

Marchand, Suzanne [L.]. 'Philhellenism and the *furor orientalis*'. *Modern Intellectual History* 1, no. 3 (2004): 331–58.

Mariano, Marco. 'America as a Transatlantic Nation: Henry Luce, *Life*, and the West in the 1940s', in Ferdinando Fasce, Maurizio Vaudagna and Raffaella Baritono (eds), *Beyond the Nation: Pushing the Boundaries of US History from a Transatlantic Perspective*, pp. 255–71. Turin: Otto, 2013.

Mariano, Marco. 'Remapping America: Continentalism, Globalism, and the Rise of the Atlantic Community, 1939–1949', in Mariano (ed.), *Defining the Atlantic Community: Culture, Intellectuals, and Politics in the Mid-Twentieth Century*, pp. 71–87. London: Routledge, 2010.

Maritain, Jacques. 'To My American Friends'. *Commonweal*, vol. 30 (13 October 1939), pp. 551–52.

Markovits, Stefanie. *The Crimean War in the British Imagination*. Cambridge: Cambridge University Press, 2009.

Marquand, David. *The End of the West: The Once and Future Europe*. Princeton, NJ: Princeton University Press.

Martin, Marie-Madeleine. 'Gonzague de Reynold'. *Revue des deux mondes*, 15 December 1960, pp. 692–95.

Martineau, Harriet. *The History of England during the Thirty Years' Peace: 1816–1846*, 2 vols. London: Charles Knight, 1849–1850.

Marvin, F. S. *The Century of Hope: A Sketch of Western Progress from 1815 to the Great War*. Oxford: The Clarendon Press, 1919.

Marvin, F. S. *Comte: The Founder of Sociology*. London: Chapman and Hall, 1936.

Marvin, F. S. *The Leadership of the World*. London: Humphrey Milford/Oxford University Press, 1914).

Marvin, F. S. *The Living Past*. Oxford: The Clarendon Press, 1913.

Marvin, F. S. (ed.). *The Unity of Western Civilization*. London: Henry Milford/Oxford University Press, 1915.

Marx, Karl. 'British Rule in India' [*New York Daily Tribune*, 25 June 1853], in Shlomo Avineri (ed.), *Karl Marx on Colonialism and Modernization: His Despatches and Other Writings on China, India, Mexico, the Middle East and North Africa*, pp. 88–95. Garden City, NY: Anchor Books, 1969.

Marx, Karl. *Dispatches for the 'New York Tribune': Selected Journalism of Karl Marx*, edited by James Ledbetter. London: Penguin, 2007.

Marx, Karl and Friedrich Engels. *The Communist Manifesto*, edited by Gareth Stedman Jones. London: Penguin, 2002 [1848].

Marx, Karl and Frederick Engels. *Marx and Engels Collected Works*, vol. 39: *Letters 1852–55*. London: Lawrence & Wishart.

Marx, Karl and Friedrich Engels. *The Russian Menace to Europe: A Collection of Articles, Speeches, Letters and News Despatches*, selected and edited by Paul W. Blackstock and Bert F. Hoselitz. London: George Allen and Unwin, 1953.

Massingham, H. J. '[Review of] The Decline of the West: Perspectives of World History. By Oswald Spengler. Authorized Translation by C. A. Atkinson. Vol. 2 (Allen & Unwin.)'. *The Criterion*, vol. 9, no. 37 (July 1930), pp. 731–37.

Massis, Henri. 'Défence de l'Occident', *La Revue universelle*, vol. 23, no. 14 (15 October 1925), pp. 145–59.

Massis, Henri. *Défense de l'Occident*. Paris: Plon, 1927.

Massis, Henri. *Defence of the West*, translated by F. S. Flint, with a preface by G. K. Chesterton. London: Faber & Gwyer, 1927.

Massis, Henri. 'Defence of the West, I', translated by F. S. Flint. *The New Criterion*, vol. 4, no 2 (April 1926), pp. 224–43.

Massis, Henri. 'Defence of the West, II', translated by F. S. Flint, *The New Criterion*, vol. 4, no 3 (June 1926), pp. 476–93.

Massis, Henri. *La Guerre de trente ans: Destin d'un âge, 1909–1939*. Paris: Plon, 1940.

Massis, Henri. *Verteidigung des Abendlandes; mit einer Einführung von Georg Moenius*, translated (into German) by Georg Moenius. Hellerau: Jakob Hegner, 1930 [1927].

Mathy, Jean-Philippe. *Extrême-Occident: French Intellectuals and America*. Chicago: The University of Chicago Press, 1993.

Mattioli, Aram. *Gonzague de Reynold: Idéologue d'une Suisse autoritaire*. Fribourg: Éditions Universitaires Fribourg Suisse, 1997.

May, Henry F. *The End of American Innocence: A Study of the First Years of Our Time 1912–1917*. London: Jonathan Cape, 1960.

Mayer, Anna-K. 'Marvin, Francis Sydney (1863–1943)', in *Oxford Dictionary of National Biography*, published online 17 September 2015, https://doi.org/10.1093/ref:odnb/52397

Mazgaj, Paul. 'Defending the West: The Cultural and Generational Politics of Henri Massis'. *Historical Reflections / Réflexions historiques* 17, no. 2 (1991): pp. 103–23.

Mazower, Mark. *The Greek Revolution: 1821 and the Making of Modern Europe*. London: Allen Lane, 2021.

Mazower, Mark. *No Enchanted Palace: The End of Empire and the Ideological Origins of the United Nations*. Princeton, NJ: Princeton University Press, 2009.

Mazzini, Giuseppe. *A Cosmopolitanism of Nations: Giuseppe Mazzini's Writings on Democracy, Nation Building, and International Relations*, edited by Stefano Recchia and Nadia Urbinati. Princeton, NJ: Princeton University Press, 2009.

McCormick, John P. 'From Roman Catholicism to Mechanized Oppression: On Political-Theological Disjunctures in Schmitt's Weimar Thought'. *Critical Review of International Social and Political Philosophy* 13, no. 2 (2010): 391–98.

McCormick, John P. 'Introduction to Schmitt's "The Age of Neutralizations and Depoliticizations"'. *Telos* 96 (1993): 119–29.

McCormick, John P. 'Political Theory and Political Theology: The Second Wave of Carl Schmitt in English'. *Political Theory* 26, no. 6 (1998): 830–54.
McNeill, William H. *Arnold J. Toynbee: A Life*. Oxford: Oxford University Press, 1989.
McNeill, William H. *History of Western Civilization: A Handbook*. Chicago: University of Chicago Press, 1949.
McNeill, William H. *The Pursuit of Truth: A Historian's Memoir*. Lexington, KY: The University Press of Kentucky, 2005.
McNeill, William H. *The Rise of the West: A History of the Human Community*. Chicago: The University of Chicago Press, 1963.
McNeill, William H. 'What We Mean by the West'. *Orbis*, 41, no. 4 (1997), pp. 513–24.
Meaney, Thomas. 'Fancies and Fears of a Latin Europe'. *New Left Review*, 107 (September/October 2017), pp. 117–29.
Meaney, Thomas. 'Putin Wants a Clash of Civilizations: Is "the West" Falling for It?'. *The New York Times*, 11 March 2022, available at https://www.nytimes.com/2022/03/11/opinion/nato-russia-the-west-ukraine.html (accessed 19 October 2024).
Mehring, Reinhard. *Carl Schmitt: A Biography*, translated by Daniel Steuer. Cambridge: Polity Press, 2014.
Menand, Louis. *The Free World: Art and Thought in the Cold War*. London: Fourth Estate, 2021.
Metta, Vasudeo B. 'Bias in History'. *The Criterion*, vol 6, no. 5 (November 1927), pp. 418–25.
Metta, Vasudeo B. 'In Defence of the East'. *The New Criterion*, vol 5, no. 1 (January 1927), pp. 100–105.
Metta, Vasudeo B. 'What the East Is Thinking'. *The Spectator*, 179, no. 5 (1 October 1927), p. 496.
Mill, John Stuart. 'Auguste Comte and Positivism' [1865], in Mill, *The Collected Works of John Stuart Mill*, vol. 10: *Essays on Ethics, Religion, and Society*, edited by John M. Robson, pp. 261–368. Toronto: University of Toronto Press/London: Routledge & Kegan Paul, 1985.
Mill, John Stuart. *The Collected Works of John Stuart Mill*, vol. 12: *The Earlier Letters 1812–1848, Part 1*, edited by Francis E. Mineka. Toronto: University of Toronto Press/London: Routledge & Kegan Paul, 1963.
Mill, John Stuart. 'The Negro Question' [*Fraser's Magazine*, 41 (January 1850), pp. 25–31], in Mill, *The Collected Works of John Stuart Mill*, vol. 21: *Essays on Equality, Law, and Education*, edited by John M. Robson, pp. 85–95. Toronto: University of Toronto Press/London: Routledge & Kegan Paul, 1984.
Miller, Marilyn Grace. *Rise and Fall of the Cosmic Race: The Cult of Mestizaje in Latin America*. Austin, TX: University of Texas Press, 2004.
Millerman, Michael. *Inside 'Putin's Brain': The Political Philosophy of Alexander Dugin*. Montreal: Millerman School, 2022.
[Milnes, Richard Monckton.] 'The Marquis de Custine's Russia'. *The Edinburgh Review*, vol. 79, no. 160 (April 1844), pp. 351–96.
Milnes, Richard Monckton. *Palm Leaves*. London: Edward Moxon, 1844.
Milnes, Richard Monckton. *Selections from the Works of Lord Houghton*. London: Edward Moxon, 1868.
Miłosz, Czesław. 'Dictionary of Wilno Streets', in Miłosz, *To Begin Where I Am: Selected Essays*, edited by Bogdana Carpenter and Madeline G. Levine, pp. 27–51. New York: Farrar, Straus and Giroux, 2001.

Miłosz, Czesław. 'Dostoevsky', in Miłosz, *To Begin Where I Am: Selected Essays*, edited by Bogdana Carpenter and Madeline G. Levine, pp. 281–83. New York: Farrar, Straus and Giroux, 2001.

Miłosz, Czesław. *Native Realm: A Search for Self-Definition*, translated by Catherine S. Leach. Berkeley, CA: University of California Press, 1981 [1959].

Miłosz, Czesław. 'L'Occident'. *Preuves*, vol. 33 (November 1953), pp. 9–23.

Milčina, Vera. '*La Russie en 1839* du Marquis de Custine et ses Sources contemporaines'. *Cahiers du monde russe* 41, no. 1: 151–63.

Miltchyna, Vera. 'Joseph de Maistre's Works in Russia: A Look at Their Reception', in Richard A. Lebrun (ed.), *Joseph de Maistre's Life, Thought and Influence: Selected Studies*, pp. 241–70. Montreal and Kingston: McGill-Queen's University Press, 2001.

Milton, John. 'The Readie & Easie Way to Establish a Free Commonwealth' [1660], in *The Complete Prose Works of John Milton*, vol. 7: *1659–1660*, edited by Robert W. Ayers. New Haven, CT: Yale University Press, 1980, pp. 351–88 and 405–463.

Minuti, Rolando. 'L'Orient dans le *Tableau* de Condorcet: Notes de lecture', in Bertrand Binoche (ed.), *Nouvelles lectures du 'Tableau historique' de Condorcet*, pp. 171–98. Paris: Hermann, 2013.

Mishra, Pankaj. *From the Ruins of Empire: The Revolt against the West and the Remaking of Asia*. London: Allen Lane, 2012.

Mishra, Pankaj. 'The Shoah after Gaza'. *London Review of Books*, vol. 46, no. 6 (21 March 2024), pp. 5–10.

Moeller van den Bruck, Arthur. *Das dritte Reich*. Hamburg: Hanseatische Verlagsanstalt, 1931 [1923].

Moeller van den Bruck, Arthur. *Germany's Third Empire*, translated by E. O. Lorimer. London: George Allen & Unwin, 1934.

Moenius, Georg. 'Einführung', in Henri Massis, *Verteidigung des Abendlandes*, pp. 11–113. Hellerau: Jakob Hegner, 1930.

Moenius, Georg. 'Le Germanisme contre la Romanité', in Henri Massis, *'Allemagne d'hier et d'après-demain', suivi de 'Germanisme et Romanité' par Georg Mœnius*, pp. 98–146. Paris: Éditions du Conquistador, 1949.

Moenius, Georg. *Paris: Frankreichs Herz*. Munich: Limes, 1928.

Montás, Roosevelt. 'Martin Luther King, as Teacher: What the Civil Rights Icon Found in Texts That Are Falling Out of Favour with American Academics'. *FT Weekend Magazine*, no. 960 (26/27 February 2022), pp. 16–19.

Montás, Roosevelt. *Rescuing Socrates: How the Great Books Changed My Life and Why They Matter for a New Generation*. Princeton, NJ: Princeton University Press, 2021.

Montesquieu, Charles-Louis de Secondat. *Lettres persanes*, edited by Jacques Roger. Paris: Flammarion, 1992 [1721].

Montesquieu, Charles-Louis de Secondat. *My Thoughts*, translated and edited by Henry C. Clark. Indianapolis: Liberty Fund, 2012.

Montesquieu, Charles-Louis de Secondat. *Persian Letters*, translated and edited by Christopher J. Betts. London: Penguin, 1973.

Moras, Joachim. *Ursprung und Entwicklung des Begriffs der Zivilisation in Frankreich (1756–1830)*. Hamburg: Hans Christians, 1930.

Morin, Edgar. *Les Souvenirs viennent à ma rencontre*. Paris: Fayard, 2019.

Morrisroe, Vicky L. '"Eastern History with Western Eyes": E. A. Freeman, Islam and Orientalism'. *Journal of Victorian Culture* 16, no. 1 (2011): 25–45.

Morrisroe, Vicky L. '"Sanguinary Amusement": E. A. Freeman, the Comparative Method and Victorian Theories of Race'. *Modern Intellectual History* 10, no. 1 (2013): 27–56.

Morson, Gary Saul. 'Russian Exceptionalism'. *The New York Review of Books*, vol. 71, no. 3 (22 February 2024), pp. 38–41.

Moses, Wilson Jeremiah. *Afrotopia: The Roots of African American Popular History*. Cambridge: Cambridge University Press, 1998.

Moses, Wilson Jeremiah. *Alexander Crummell: A Study of Civilization and Discontent*. Oxford: Oxford University Press, 1989.

Moses, Wilson Jeremiah. *Creative Conflict in African American Thought: Frederick Douglass, Alexander Crummell, Booker T. Washington, W.E.B. Du Bois and Marcus Garvey*. Cambridge: Cambridge University Press, 2004.

Moses, Wilson Jeremiah. *The Golden Age of Black Nationalism, 1850–1925*. Hamden, CT: Archon Books, 1978.

Moyn, Samuel. *Liberalism against Itself: Cold War Intellectuals and the Making of Our Times*. New Haven, CT: Yale University Press, 2023.

Mueller-Vollmer, Kurt. *Transatlantic Crossings and Transformations: German–American Transfer from the 18th to the End of the 19th Century*. Frankfurt am Main: Peter Lang, 2015.

Muir, John (trans.). *Greek Eyes on Europe: The Travels of Nikandros Noukios of Corfu*. London: Routledge, 2023.

Müller, Guido. *Europäische Gesellschaftsbeziehungen nach dem Ersten Weltkrieg: Das Deutsch-Französische Studienkomitee und der Europäische Kulturbund*. Munich: Oldenbourg, 2005.

Müller, Jan-Werner. *Another Country: German Intellectuals, Unification and National Identity*. New Haven, CT: Yale University Press, 2000.

Müller, Jan-Werner. *Constitutional Patriotism*. Princeton, NJ: Princeton University Press, 2007.

Munro, Gregory. *Hitler's Bavarian Antagonist*. Lewiston, NY: Edwin Mellen Press, 2006.

[Murchison, Roderick Impey.] 'Tour in Russia by the Marquis de Custine'. *The Quarterly Review*, vol. 73, no. 146 (March 1844), pp. 324–74.

Murray, Douglas. *The War on the West*. London: HarperCollins, 2022.

Musso, Pierre (ed.). *Le Saint-Simonisme, L'Europe et la Méditerranée*. Houilles (Paris): Éditions Manucius, 2008.

Naipaul, V. S. 'Our Universal Civilization'. *The New York Review of Books*, vol. 38, no. 3 (31 January 1991).

Nakhimovsky, Isaac. *The Holy Alliance: Liberalism and the Politics of Federation*. Princeton, NJ: Princeton University Press, 2024.

Nardal, Jane [Jeanne]. 'Internationalisme noir'. *La Dépêche africaine*, 15 February 1928.

Nehring, Holger. '"Westernization": A New Paradigm for Interpreting West European History in a Cold War Context'. *Cold War History* 4, no. 2 (2004): 175–91.

Neiman, Susan. 'Fanon the Universalist'. *The New York Review of Books*, vol. 71, no. 10 (6 June 20024), pp. 19–21.

Neiman, Susan. *Left is not Woke*. Cambridge: Polity Press, 2023.

Nemo, Philippe. *Qu'est-ce que l'Occident?*. Paris: PUF, 2004.

Nemo, Philippe. *What is the West?*, translated by Kenneth Casler. Pittsburgh, PA: Duquesne University Press, 2004.

Neumann, Iver B. *Uses of the Other: 'The East' in European Identity Formation*. Minneapolis: University of Minnesota Press, 1999.

Nicandre de Corcyre. *Le Voyage d'Occident*, translated by Paolo Odorico, annotated by Joël Schnapp. Paris: Anacharsis, 2002.

Nicandre de Corcyre. *Voyages*, edited by J.-A. Foucault. Paris: Les Belles Lettres, 1962.

Nichols, James H., Jr. *Alexandre Kojève: Wisdom at the End of History*. Lanham, MD: Rowman & Littlefield, 2007.

Nicolas, Rambert. 'Critique et annexion de la doctrine positiviste: Soloviev lecteur de Comte', in *La Philosophie russe et le positivisme*, special issue, *Archives de philosophie* 79, no. 2 (2016): 233–44.

Nicolet, Claude. *La Fabrique d'une nation: La France entre Rome et les Germains*. Paris: Perrin, 2006.

Nicolet, Claude. *L'Idée républicaine en France (1789–1924): Essai d'histoire critique*, 2nd edition. Paris: Gallimard, 1994.

Niebuhr, Reinhold. 'The Irony of American History', in Niebuhr, *Major Works on Religion and Politics*, edited by Elisabeth Sifton, pp. 459–589. New York: The Library of America, 2015.

Nietzsche, Friedrich. *Beyond Good and Evil: Prelude to a Philosophy of the Future*, translated by R. J. Hollingdale, with an introduction by Michael Tanner. London: Penguin, 2003 [1973; original 1886].

Nietzsche, Friedrich. *On the Genealogy of Morality*, translated by Carol Diethe, edited by Keith Ansell-Pearson. Cambridge: Cambridge University Press, 2007 [1994; original 1887].

Nietzsche, Friedrich. *Twilight of the Idols: or How to Philosophize with a Hammer*, translated by Duncan Large. Oxford: Oxford University Press, 1998 [1889].

Nora, Pierre. 'Presentation: A Kidnapped West, or The Tragedy of Central Europe, 1983', translated by Linda Asher, in Milan Kundera, *A Kidnapped West: The Tragedy of Eastern Europe*, translated by Edmund White, pp. 31–33. London: Faber & Faber, 2023.

Norton, Anne. *Leo Strauss and the Politics of American Empire*. New Haven, CT: Yale University Press, 2004.

Novalis [Friedrich von Hardenberg]. 'Christianity or Europe: A Fragment' [1799], in Frederick C. Beiser (ed.), *The Early Political Writings of the German Romantics*, pp. 59–79. Cambridge: Cambridge University Press, 1996.

Nye, Russell B. *George Bancroft: Brahmin Rebel*. New York: Octagon Books, 1972.

O'Brien, Karen. *Narratives of Enlightenment: Cosmopolitan History from Voltaire to Gibbon*. Cambridge: Cambridge University Press, 1997.

O'Brien, Nick. "Something Older than Law Itself": Sir Henry Maine, Niebuhr, and "the Path Not Chosen"'. *Journal of Legal History* 26, no. 3 (2005): 229–51.

Orluc, Katiana. 'Caught between Past and Future: The Idea of Pan-Europa in the Interwar Years', in Hans-Ake Persson and Bo Strath (eds), *Reflections on Europe: Defining a Political Order in Time and Space*, pp. 95–120. Brussels: Peter Lang, 2007.

Orwell, George [Eric Blair]. 'Orwell's Proposed Preface to *Animal Farm*', included in Orwell, *Animal Farm: A Fairy Story*, pp. 103–13. London: Penguin Books, 2021.

Orwell, George [Eric Blair]. 'Toward European Unity' [1947], in Orwell, *The Collected Essays, Journalism and Letters of George Orwell*, edited by Sonia Orwell and Ian Angus, 4 vols, vol. 4, pp. 370–75. London: Secker & Warburg, 1968.

Osterhammel, Jürgen. *The Transformation of the World: A Global History of the Nineteenth Century*, translated by Patrick Camiller. Princeton, NJ: Princeton University Press, 2014.

Osterhammel, Jürgen: *Unfabling the East: The Enlightenment's Encounter with Asia*, translated by Robert Savage. Princeton, NJ: Princeton University Press, 2018.

Pagden, Anthony. *The Pursuit of Europe: A History*. Oxford: Oxford University Press, 2022.

Paine, Thomas. *The Writings of Thomas Paine*, edited by Moncure Daniel Conway, 4 vols. New York: G. P. Putnam's Sons, 1894–96.

Parker, George Wells. 'The African Origins of the Grecian Civilization'. *The Journal of Negro History* 2, no. 3 (1917): 334–44.

Parker, George Wells. *Children of the Sun*. Omaha, NE: Hamitic League of the World, 1918.

Parry, J[onathan] P. 'Disraeli, the East and Religion: *Tancred* in Context'. *The English Historical Review* 132, no. 556 (2017): 570–604.

Parry, Jonathan [P.]. *Promised Lands: The British and the Ottoman Middle East*. Princeton, NJ: Princeton University Press, 2022.

Patočka, Jan. *Europa und Nach-Europa*, edited by Ludger Hegedorn and Klaus Nellen. Baden-Baden: Karl Albert, 2024.

Peillon, Vincent. *Jérusalem n'est pas perdue: La philosophie juive de Joseph Salvador et le judéo-républicanisme français*. Lormont: Le Bord de l'Eau, 2022.

Perry, Jeffrey B. (ed.). *A Hubert Harrison Reader*. Middletown, CT: Wesleyan University Press, 2001.

Perry, Jeffrey B. *Hubert Harrison: The Struggle for Equality, 1918–1927*. New York: Columbia University Press, 2021.

Perry, Jeffrey B. *Hubert Harrison: The Voice of Harlem Radicalism, 1883–1918*. New York: Columbia University Press, 2009.

Perry, Ralph Barton. 'West versus East'. *The Saturday Review of Literature*, 7 July 1928, pp. 1015–16.

Perry, Thomas Sergeant. *The Life and Letters of Francis Lieber*. Boston. MA: James R. Osgood & Co., 1882.

Petit, Annie. 'L'Europe positiviste: La "République occidentale"'. *Revue de la Société d'histoire des révolutions du XIXe siècle*, no. 7 (1991) : 19–35.

Petit, Annie. *Le Système d'Auguste Comte: De la science à la religion par la philosophie*. Paris: Vrin, 2016.

Pétrement, Simone. *La Vie de Simone Weil, avec des lettres et d'autres textes inédits de Simone Weil*. Paris: Librairie Anthème Fayard, 1973.

Pickering, Mary. *Auguste Comte: An Intellectual Biography*, 3 vols. Cambridge: Cambridge University Press, 1993–2009.

Pickering, Mary. 'Conclusion: The Legacy of Auguste Comte', in Michel Bourdeau, Mary Pickering and Warren Schmaus (eds), *Love, Order, and Progress: The Science, Philosophy, and Politics of Auguste Comte*, pp. 250–304. Pittsburgh, PA: University of Pittsburgh Press.

Picon, Antoine. *Les Saint-simoniens: Raison, imaginaire et utopie*. Paris: Belin, 2002.

Piirimäe, Pärtel. 'Russia, the Turks and Europe: Legitimations of War and the Formation of European Identity in the Early Modern Period'. *Journal of Early Modern History* 11, nos 1–2 (2007): 63–86.

Pilkington, A[nthony] E. *Bergson and His Influence: A Reassessment*. Cambridge: Cambridge University Press, 1976.

Pistone, Sergio. *The Union of European Federalists: From the Foundation to the Decision on Direct Election of the European Parliament (1946–1974)*. Milan: Giuffrè Editore, 2008.

Pitts, Jennifer. *Boundaries of the International: Law and Empire*. Cambridge, MA: Harvard University Press, 2018.

Plamenatz, John. 'Two Types of Nationalism', in Eugene Kamenka (ed.), *Nationalism: The Nature and Evolution of an Idea*, pp. 22–36. Canberra: Australian University Press, 1973.

Platon, Mircea. 'Astolphe de Custine's *Letters from Russia* and the Defense of the West: Patterns of Prejudice from Henri Massis to Walter Bedell Smith'. *Russian History* 43, no. 2 (2016): 142–80.

Platz, Hermann. *Deutschland-Frankreich und die Idee des Abendlandes*. Cologne: Verlag der Rheinischen Zentrums-Partei, 1924.

Pochmann, Henry A. *German Culture in America: Philosophical and Literary Influences*. Madison, WI: The University of Wisconsin Press, 1957.

Pocock, J.G.A. 'Barbarians and the Redefinition of Europe: A Study of Gibbon's Third Volume', in Larry Wolf and Marco Cipolloni (eds), *The Anthropology of the Enlightenment*, pp. 35–70. Stanford, CA: Stanford University Press.

Pocock, J.G.A. *Barbarism and Religion*, 6 vols. Cambridge: Cambridge University Press, 1999–2015.

Pocock, J.G.A. *Barbarism and Religion*, vol. 2: *Narratives of Civil Government*. Cambridge: Cambridge University Press, 2001.

Pocock, J.G.A. 'The Historiography of the *translatio imperii*', in Pocock, *Barbarism and Religion*, vol. 3: *The First Decline and Fall*, pp. 127–50. Cambridge: Cambridge University Press, 2005.

Pocock, J.G.A. *The Machiavellian Moment*. Princeton, NJ: Princeton University Press, 1975.

Pocock, J.G.A. 'Some Europes in Their History', in Anthony Pagden (ed.), *The Idea of Europe: From Antiquity to the European Union*, pp. 55–71. Cambridge: Cambridge University Press.

Poesche, Theodore and Charles Goepp. *The New Rome; or, The United States of the World*. New York: G. P. Putnam & Co., 1853.

Pope-Hennessy, James. *Monckton Milnes: The Years of Promise, 1809–1851*. London: Constable, 1949.

Pradt, Dominique de. *De la Grèce dans ses rapports avec l'Europe*. Paris: Béchet aîné, 1822.

Pradt, Dominique de. *L'Europe et l'Amérique en 1822 et 1823*, 2 vols. Paris: Béchet aîné, 1824.

Pradt, Dominique de. *L'Europe par rapport à la Grèce et la réformation de la Turquie*. Paris: Béchet aîné, 1826.

Pradt, Dominique de. *Parallèle de la puissance anglaise et russe relativement à l'Europe, suivi d'un aperçu sur la Grèce*. Paris: Béchet aîné, 1823.

Pradt, Dominique de. *Vrai Système de l'Europe relativement à l'Amérique et la Grèce*. Paris: Béchet aîné, 1825.

Pradt, Dominique de. *Du système permanent de l'Europe à l'égard de la Russie et des affaires de l'Orient*. Paris: Pichon et Didier, 1828.
Premat, Christophe. 'A New Generation of Greek Intellectuals in Postwar France', in Julian Bourg (ed.), *After the Deluge: New Perspectives on the Intellectual and Cultural History of Postwar France*, pp. 103–23. Lanham, MD: Lexington Books, 2004.
Prochasson, Christophe. *Saint-Simon ou l'anti-Marx: Figures du saint-simonisme français XIXe– XXe siècles*. Paris: Perrin, 2005.
Proteau, Laurent. '*Présence africaine*', in Jacques Julliard and Michel Winock (eds), *Dictionnaire des intellectuels français: Les personnes, les lieux, les moments*, pp. 915–97. Paris: Seuil, 1996.
Pugach, Noel. 'Making the Open Door Work: Paul S. Reinsch in China, 1913–1919'. *Pacific Historical Review* 38, no. 2 (1969): 157–75.
Quénet, Charles. *Tchaadaev et les Lettres philosophiques: Contribution à l'étude du mouvement des idées en Russie*. Paris: H. Champion, 1931.
Quinn, Josephine. *How the World Made the West: A 4,000-Year History*. London: Bloomsbury, 2024.
Rachum, Ilan. 'Antropofagia against Verdamarelo'. *Latin American Literary Review* 4, no. 8 (1976): 67–81.
Radchenko, Sergey. *To Run the World: The Kremlin's Cold War Bid for Global Power*. Cambridge: Cambridge University Press, 2024.
Ratcliffe, Barrie M. and W. H. Chaloner. 'Gustave d'Eichthal: An Intellectual Portrait', in Ratcliffe and Chaloner (eds), *A French Sociologist Looks at Britain: Gustave d'Eichthal and British Society in 1828*, pp. 109–61. Manchester: Manchester University Press, 1986.
Reclus, Élisée. 'East and West'. *The Contemporary Review*, October 1894, pp. 475–87.
Reclus, Élisée. 'Progress' [1905], in John P. Clark and Camille Martin (eds), *Anarchy, Geography, Modernity: The Radical Social Thought of Elisée Reclus*, pp. 223–47. Lanham, MD: Lexington Books, 2004.
Reddick, Lawrence D. 'Meditations upon the War and Democracy in America'. *The Crisis*, August 1940, p. 263.
Régnier, Philippe. 'Le Mythe oriental des Saint-Simoniens', in Magali Morsy (ed.), *Les Saint-Simoniens et l'Orient: Vers la modernité*, pp. 29–49. Aix-en-Provence: Édisud, 1989.
Reinsch, Paul S. *Intellectual and Political Currents in the Far East*. Boston, MA: Houghton Mifflin Company, 1911.
Reinsch, Paul S. *World Politics at the End of the Nineteenth Century as Influenced by the Oriental Situation*. London: Macmillan & Co., 1900.
Rémond, René. *Les États Unis devant l'opinion française, 1815–1852*, 2 vols. Paris: A. Colin, 1962.
[Renieris, Markos (signed: 'R')]. 'Le Dualisme grec'. *Le Spectateur de l'Orient*, vol. 2 (10/22 September 1853), pp. 33–49.
[Renieris, Markos.] 'Τι είναι η Ελλάς; Ανατολή ή Δύσις;' (What is Greece? East or west?). *Eranistis* 1, no. 3 (1842): 189–215.
Resis, Albert. 'Russophobia and the "Testament" of Peter the Great, 1812–1980'. *Slavic Review* 44, no. 4 (1985): 681–93.
Reynold, Gonzague de. 'Qu'est-ce que l'Europe?'. *Revue universelle*, new series, no. 2 (15 January 1941), pp. 86–95.

[Rich, Henry.] 'History, Present Wrongs, and Claims of Poland'. *The Edinburgh Review*, vol. 55, no. 109 (April 1832), pp. 220–70.
Riley, Dylan. 'Metaphysicking the West'. *New Left Review*, 113 (September/October 2018), pp. 125–38.
Riza, Ahmet. *La Faillite morale de la politique occidentale en Orient*. Paris: Picart, 1922.
Riza, Ahmet. *The Moral Bankruptcy of Western Policy towards the East*, translated by Adair Mill. Ankara: Ministry of Culture and Tourism, 1988.
Roberts, Tim. 'Lajos Kossuth and the Permeable American Orient of the Mid-Nineteenth Century'. *Diplomatic History* 39, no. 5 (2015): 793–818.
Robertson, Ritchie. *The Enlightenment: The Pursuit of Happiness, 1680–1790*. London: Allen Lane, 2020.
Robinson, Cedric J. *Black Marxism: The Making of the Black Radical Tradition*. London: Penguin, 2020 [1983].
Roger, Philippe. *L'Ennemi américain: Généalogie de l'antiaméricanisme français*. Paris: Seuil, 2002.
Rohter, Larry. *Into the Amazon: The Life of Cândido Rondon, Trailblazing Explorer, Scientist, Statesman, and Conservationist*. New York: W. W. Norton, 2023.
Rolland, Romain. 'The Lesser of Two Evils: Pangermanism, Panslavism' [*Journal de Genève*, 10 October 1914], in Rolland, *Above the Battle*, translated by C. K. Ogden, pp. 56–75. Chicago: Open Court Publishing, 1916.
Rolland, Romain. 'Pro Aris' [October 1914], in Rolland, *Above the Battle*, translated by C. K. Ogden, pp. 23–36. Chicago: Open Court Publishing, 1916.
Rorty, Richard. *Achieving Our Country: Leftist Thought in Twentieth-Century America* (The William E. Massey Sr. Lectures in the History of American Civilization, 1997). Cambridge, MA: Harvard University Press, 1998.
Rosenboim, Or. *The Emergence of Globalism: Visions of World Order in Britain and The United States, 1939–1950*. Princeton, NJ: Princeton University Press, 2017.
Ross, Dorothy. 'Historical Consciousness in Nineteenth-Century America'. *The American Historical Review* 89, no. 4 (1984): 909–28.
Ross, Dorothy. *The Origins of American Social Science*. Cambridge: Cambridge University Press, 1991.
Rowley, Hazel. *Richard Wright: The Life and Times*. New York: Henry Holt, 2001.
Roy, Olivier. *The Crisis of Culture: Identity Politics and the Empire of Norms*, translated by Cynthia Schoch and Trista Selous. London: Hurst, 2024.
Runciman, David. *The Confidence Trap: A History of Democracy in Crisis from World War I to the Present*. Princeton, NJ: Princeton University Press, 2013.
Ryan, Alan. *John Dewey and the High Tide of American Liberalism*. New York: W. W. Norton, 1995.
Rychner, Max. 'German Chronicle'. *The New Criterion*, vol. 4, no. 4 (October 1926), pp. 726–32.
Rynning, Sten. *NATO: From Cold War to Ukraine, a History of the World's Most Powerful Alliance*. New Haven, CT: Yale University Press, 2024.
Sablé, Erik. *René Guénon: Le visage de l'éternité*. Paris: Éditions Point, 2013.
Said, Edward W. *Culture and Imperialism*. London: Vintage, 1994 [1993].

Said, Edward W. *Orientalism*. London: Penguin, 2003 [1978].

Saint-Simon, Henri de. *Œuvres complètes*, edited by Juliette Grange, Pierre Musso, Philippe Régnier and Frank Yonnet, 4 vols. Paris: Presses Universitaires de France, 2012.

Saint-Simon, Henri de and Augustin Thierry. 'On the Reorganization of European Society' [October 1814], in Ghita Ionescu (ed.), *The Political Thought of Saint-Simon*, pp. 83–98. Oxford: Oxford University Press, 1976).

Sakowicz, Iwona. 'Russia and the Russians: Opinions of the British Press during the Reign of Alexander II (Dailies and Weeklies)'. *Journal of European Studies* 35, no. 3 (2005): 271–82.

Sapiro, Gisèle. *The French Writers' War, 1940–1953*, translated by Vanessa Doriott Anderson and Dorrit Cohn. Durham, NC: Duke University Press, 2014 [1999].

Saposnik, Arieh Bruce. 'Europe and its Orients in Zionist Culture before the First World War'. *The Historical Journal* 49, no. 4 (2006): 1105–23.

Sartre, Jean-Paul. 'Préface', in Frantz Fanon, *Les Damnés de la terre*, pp. 9–26. Paris: François Maspero, 1961.

Sartre, Jean-Paul. 'Preface', in Frantz Fanon, *The Wretched of the Earth*, pp. 7–26. London: Penguin, 1967.

Saunders, Frances Stonor. *Who Paid the Piper? The CIA and the Cultural Cold War*. London: Granta Books, 1999.

Scheler, Max. *Der Genius des Krieges und der deutsche Krieg* [1915], collected in Scheler, *Gesammelte Werke*, vol. 4: *Politisch-pädagogische Schriften*, pp. 7–250. Bern: Francke, 1982.

Scheler, Max. 'Europa und der Krieg' [1915], in Scheler, *Gesammelte Werke*, vol. 4: *Politisch-pädagogische Schriften*, pp. 251–66. Bern: Francke, 1982.

Schenk, Frithjof Benjamin. 'Mental Maps: Die Konstruktion von geographischen Räumen in Europa seit der Aufklärung'. *Geschichte und Gesellschaft* 28, no. 3 (2002): 493–514.

Schildt, Axel. *Zwischen Abendland und Amerika: Studien zur westdeutschen Ideenlandschaft der 50er Jahre*. Munich: Oldenbourg, 1999.

Schimmelpenninck van der Oye, David. 'The East', in William Leatherbarrow and Derek Offord (eds), *A History of Russian Thought*, pp. 217–40. Cambridge: Cambridge University Press, 2010.

Schlesinger, Arthur M., Jr. 'Walter Lippmann: The Intellectual vs. Politics' [1959], in Schlesinger, *The Politics of Hope*, pp. 126–54. London: Eyre & Spottiswoode, 1964.

Schlesinger, Arthur M., Jr. *The Disuniting of America: Reflections on a Multicultural Society*. New York: W. W. Norton, 1992 [1991].

Schmaus, Warren. 'A Reappraisal of Comte's Three-State Law'. *History and Theory* 21, no. 2 (1982): 248–66.

Schmidt, H. D. 'II. The Establishment of "Europe" as a Political Expression'. *The Historical Journal* 9, no. 2 (1966): 172–78.

Schmitt, Carl. 'The Age of Neutralizations and Depoliticizations' [1929], in Schmitt, *The Concept of the Political*, translated and with an introduction by George Schwab, expanded edition, pp. 80–96. Chicago: The University of Chicago Press, 2007.

Schmitt, Carl. *The Crisis of Parliamentary Democracy*, translated by Ellen Kennedy. Cambridge, MA: The MIT Press, 1985.

Schmitt, Carl. *Dialogues on Power and Space*, edited by Andreas Kalyvas and Federico Finchelstein, translated by Samuel Garrett Zeitlin. Cambridge: Polity Press, 2015.

Schmitt, Carl. *Dictatorship: From the Origin of the Modern Concept of Sovereignty to Proletarian Class Struggle*, translated by Michael Hoelzl and Graham Ward. Cambridge: Polity Press, 2014 [1921].

Schmitt, Carl. 'Donoso Cortés in Berlin (1849)', in Schmitt, *Donoso Cortés in gesamteuropäischer Interpretation: Vier Aufsätze*, pp. 41–66. Cologne: Greven, 1950.

Schmitt, Carl. *Ex Captivitate Salus: Experiences, 1945–47*, edited by Andreas Kalyvas and Federico Finchelstein, translated by Matthew Hannah. Cambridge: Polity Press, 2017 [1950].

Schmitt, Carl. *The Leviathan in the State Theory of Thomas Hobbes: Meaning and Failure of a Political Symbol*, translated by George Schwab and Erna Hilfstein. Chicago: The University of Chicago Press, 2008 [1938].

Schmitt, Carl. *The Necessity of Politics: An Essay on the Representative Idea in the Church and Modern Europe*, translated by E. M. Codd. London: Sheed & Ward, 1931 [1923].

Schmitt, Carl. *The Nomos of the Earth in the International Law of the Jus Publicum Europaeum*, translated and annotated by G. L. Ulmen. New York: Telos Press, 2006 [1950].

Schmitt, Carl. 'The Planetary Tension between Orient and Occident and the Opposition Between Land and Sea' [*Revista de estudios políticos* 81 (1955): 3–28]. *Política Común* 5 (2014), https://quod.lib.umich.edu/p/pc/12322227.0005.011?view=text;rgn=main (accessed 19 October 2024).

Schoeps, Hans Joachim. *Vorläufer Spenglers: Studien zum Geschichtspessimismus im 19. Jahrhundert*. Leiden: Brill, 1995.

Scholz, Danilo. 'Zwischen Vichy und Résistance: Alexandre Kojève im Krieg'. *Zeitschrift für Ideengeschichte* 13, no. 3 (2019): 23–35.

Schroeter, Manfred. *Der Streit um Spengler: Kritik seiner Kritiker*. Munich: C. H. Beck, 1922.

Schulman, Alex. 'Carl Schmitt and the Clash of Civilizations: The Missing Context'. *Journal of Political Ideologies* 17, no 2 (2012): 147–67.

Schulte Nordholt, Jan Willem. *The Myth of the West: America as the Last Empire*, translated by Herbert H. Rowen. Grand Rapids, MI: William B. Ferdmans, 1995.

Schulze Wessel, M[artin]. 'Westen; Okzident', in Joachim Ritter, Karlfried Gründer and Gottfried Gabriel (eds), *Historisches Wörterbuch der Philosophie*, vol. 12, pp. 661–72. Darmstadt: Wissenschaftliche Buchgesellschaft.

Schurts, Sarah. 'Safeguarding a "Civilization in Crisis": *La Revue Universelle*'s Conceptualization of Western Civilization and its Renewal, 1920–1935'. *Journal of Modern European History / Zeitschrift für moderne europäische Geschichte / Revue d'histoire européenne contemporaine* 15, no. 1 (2017): 48–71.

Schwab, Raymond. *The Oriental Renaissance: Europe's Rediscovery of India and the East, 1680–1880*, translated by Gene Patterson-Black and Victor Reinking. New York: Columbia University Press, 1984.

Schwab, Raymond. *La Renaissance orientale*. Paris: Payot, 1950.

Scott-Smith, Giles and Charlotte A. Lerg (eds). *Campaigning Culture and the Global Cold War: The Journals of the Congress for Cultural Freedom*. London: Palgrave Macmillan, 2017.

Scruton, Roger. *The West and the Rest: Globalization and the Terrorist Threat*. London: Continuum, 2002.

Sedgwick, Mark. *Against the Modern World: Traditionalism and the Secret Intellectual History of the Twentieth Century*. Oxford: Oxford University Press, 2004.

Sedgwick, Mark. *Traditionalism: The Radical Project for Restoring Sacred Order.* London: Pelican, 2023.
Seeley, J. R. *The Expansion of England*, edited by John Gross. Chicago: The University of Chicago Press, 1971 [1883].
Segal, Daniel A. '"Western Civ" and the Staging of History in American Higher Education'. *The American Historical Review* 105, no. 3 (2000): 770–805.
Selinger, William. 'The Politics of Arendtian Historiography: European Federation and the Origins of Totalitarianism'. *Modern Intellectual History* 13, no. 2 (2016): 417–46.
Semmel, Bernard. *George Eliot and the Politics of National Inheritance.* Oxford: Oxford University Press, 1994.
Sen, Amartya. 'Tagore and His India'. *The New York Review of Books*, 26 June 1997, pp. 55–63.
Shah, Sirdar Ikbal Ali. 'The Meeting of the East and the West'. *The Criterion*, vol. 7, no. 4 (June 1928), pp. 37–53.
Sharma, Jyotirmaya. *Elusive Non-Violence: The Making and Unmaking of Gandhi's Religion of Ahimsa.* Chennai: Context, 2021.
Sharma, Jyotirmaya. *Hindutva: Exploring the Idea of Hindu Nationalism.* New Delhi: Penguin-Viking, 2003.
Shatz, Adam. 'Introduction: A Stranger in Paris', in William Gardner Smith, *The Stone Face*, pp. vii–xxv. New York: New York Review of Books Classics, 2021.
Shatz, Adam. 'Outcasts and Desperados'. *London Review of Books*, vol. 43, no. 19 (7 October 2021).
Shatz, Adam. *The Rebel's Clinic: The Revolutionary Lives of Frantz Fanon.* New York: Farrar, Straus and Giroux, 2024.
Shekhovtson, Anton and Andreas Umland. 'Is Aleksandr Dugin a Traditionalist? "Neo-Eurasianism" and Perennial Philosophy'. *The Russian Review* 68, no 4 (2009): 662–78.
Shelby, Tommie. 'Richard Wright: Realizing the Promise of the West', in Melvin L. Rogers and Jack Turner (eds), *African American Political Thought: A Collected History*, pp. 413–38. Chicago: The University of Chicago Press, 2021.
Shumway, Daniel Bussey. 'The American Students of the University of Göttingen'. *German American Annals* n.s. 8 (1910): 171–254.
Siegfried, André. *America Comes of Age: A French Analysis*, translated by H. H. Hemming and Doris Hemming. London: Jonathan Cape, 1927.
Siegfried, André. 'La Civilisation occidentale'. *Revue des deux mondes*, vol. 65, no. 2 (15 September 1941), pp. 129–48.
Siegfried, André. *La Civilisation occidentale: The Romanes Lecture Delivered in the Sheldonian Theatre, 5 June 1945.* Oxford: The Clarendon Press, 1945.
Siegfried, André. *Les États-Unis d'aujourd'hui*, 3rd edition. Paris: Armand Colin, 1927.
Siegfried, André. *L'Occident et la direction spirituelle du monde.* Neuilly: La Cause, 1932.
Siegfried, André. 'L'Occident et la direction spirituelle du monde'. *Le Figaro*, 12 February 1942.
Siegfried, André. *What the British Empire Means to Western Civilization*, translated by George M. Wrong. Toronto: Oxford University Press, 1940.
Siegrist, Pascale. 'Cosmopolis and Community: Élisée Reclus and Pëtr Kropotkin on Spatial and Moral Unity, 1870s to 1900s'. *Global Intellectual History* 7, no. 2 (2022): 47–64.

Simon, W. M. *European Positivism in the Nineteenth Century: An Essay in Intellectual History*. Ithaca, NY: Cornell University Press, 1963.
Sirinelli, Jean-François. *Intellectuels et passions françaises: Manifestes et pétitions au XXe siècle*. Paris: Fayard, 1990.
Sirtema de Grovestins, Charles-Frédéric. *La Pologne, la Russie et l'Europe occidentale; ou, De la nécessité de résoudre la question russo–polonaise dans une conférence des Grandes Puissances*. Paris: Amyot, 1847.
Skinner, Quentin. 'Meaning and Understanding in the History of Ideas', in Skinner, *Visions of Politics*, vol. 1: *Regarding Method*, pp. 57–89. Cambridge: Cambridge University Press, 2002.
Skupiewski, Józef Julian. *La Doctrine panslaviste d'après N. J. Danilewsky (La Russie et l'Europe: Coup d'œil sur les rapports politiques entre le monde slave et le monde germano-roman)*. Bucharest: Bureaux de la ' Liberté Roumaine', 1890.
Sloterdijk, Peter and Alain Finkielkraut. *Les Battements du monde: Dialogue*. Paris: Arthème Fayard, 2003.
Sluga, Glenda. *The Invention of International Order: Remaking Europe after Napoleon*. Princeton, NJ: Princeton University Press, 2021.
Smith, Adam. 'History of Astronomy', in Smith, *Essays on Philosophical Subjects*, edited by W.P.D. Wightman and J. C. Bryce (The Glasgow Edition of the Works and Correspondence of Adam Smith, vol. 3; general editors D. D. Raphael and A. S. Skinner), pp. 33–105. Indianapolis: Liberty Fund, 1982.
Smith, Mark B. *The Russia Anxiety and How History Can Resolve It*. London: Allen Lane, 2019.
Smith, William Gardner. 'Black Boy in France: America's Most Famous Negro Author Finds Freedom, Relaxation Living in Voluntary Exile in Paris to Escape from U.S. Racism'. *Ebony*, 8 (July 1953), pp. 32–42.
Society for Classical Studies. 'SCS Statement on Police Brutality, Systemic Racism, and the Death of George Floyd', https://classics.ufl.edu/news/2020/statement-on-police-brutality-systemic-racism-and-the-death-of-george-floyd/ (accessed 16 October 2024).
Soloviev, Vladimir. 'L'Idée d'humanité chez Auguste Comte' [1898], in *La Philosophie russe et le positivisme*, special issue, *Archives de philosophie* 79, no. 2 (2016): 245–270.
Sombart, Werner. *Händler und Helden: Patriotische Besinnungen*. Munich: Duncker & Humblot, 1915.
Sorokin, Pitirim A. *Social Philosophies of an Age of Crisis*. London: Adam & Charles Black, 1952.
Speck, Reto. *The History and Politics of Civilisation: The Debate about Russia in French and German Historical Scholarship from Voltaire to Herder*. Doctoral thesis, Queen Mary University of London, 2010.
Spencer, Benjamin T. *The Quest for Nationality: An American Literary Campaign*. Syracuse, NY: Syracuse University Press, 1957.
Spender, Stephen. 'The Intellectuals and Europe's Future: Reopening the Lines of Communication in Western Culture'. *Commentary*, vol. 3, no. 1 (January 1947), pp. 7–12.
Spender, Stephen. *The Thirties and After: Poetry, Politics, People (1933–75)*. London: Fontana/Collins, 1978.
Spengler, Oswald. *Briefe, 1913–1936*, edited by Anton M. Koktanek with Manfred Schröter. Munich: C. H. Beck, 1963.

Spengler, Oswald. *The Decline of the West*, vol. 1: *Form and Actuality*, translated by Charles Francis Atkinson. New York: Alfred A. Knopf, 1926 [1918].

Spengler, Oswald. *The Decline of the West*, vol. 2: *Perspectives of World-History*, translated by Charles Francis Atkinson. New York: Alfred A. Knopf, 1928 [1922].

Spengler, Oswald. *Der Untergang des Abendlandes*. Munich: C. H. Beck, 1980 [1918–22; definitive edition 1923].

Spiro, Jonathan Peter. *Defending the Master Race: Conservation, Eugenics, and the Legacy of Madison Grant*. Burlington, VT: University of Vermont Press, 2009.

Staël, Mme [Anne-Louise-Germaine] de. *Dix Années d'exil*. Paris: Payot & Rivages, 2012 [1821].

Staël, Mme [Anne-Louise-Germaine] de. *Ten Years of Exile*. London: Centaur Press, 2005 (repr.).

Stanley, Arthur Penrhyn. *The Life and Correspondence of Thomas Arnold*, 5th edition, 2 vols. London: B. Fellowes, 1845.

Stansky, Peter. *The Socialist Patriot: George Orwell and War*. Stanford, CA, Stanford University Press, 2023.

Stavrinaki, Maria. *Transfixed by Prehistory: An Inquiry into Modern Art and Time*. New York: Zone Books, 2022.

Stedman Jones, Gareth. *Karl Marx: Greatness and Illusion*. London: Penguin, 2016.

Steel, Ronald. *Walter Lippmann and the American Century*. New Brunswick, NJ: Transaction Publishers, 1999 [1980].

Steinberg, Oded Y. *Race, Nation, History: Anglo-German Thought in the Victorian Era*. Philadelphia: University of Pennsylvania Press, 2019.

Stephens, W[illiam] R. W. *The Life and Letters of Edward A. Freeman*, 2 vols. London: Macmillan, 1895.

Sternhell, Zeev. *Ni droite ni gauche: L'idéologie fasciste en France*, 4th edition. Paris: Gallimard, 2012.

Stettner, Edward A. *Shaping Modern Liberalism: Herbert Croly and Progressive Thought*. Lawrence, KS: University Press of Kansas, 1993.

Stewart, Jeffrey C. *The New Negro: The Life of Alain Locke*. New York: Oxford University Press, 2018.

Stirk, Peter M. R. *Twentieth-Century German Political Thought*. Edinburgh: Edinburgh University Press. 2006.

Stock, Paul. *Europe and the British Geographical Imagination, 1760–1830*. Oxford: Oxford University Press, 2019.

Stock, Paul. *The Shelley-Byron Circle and the Idea of Europe*. New York: Palgrave Macmillan.

Stoddard, Theodore Lothrop. *The Rising Tide of Color against White World-Supremacy*, with an introduction by Madison Grant. New York: Charles Scribner's Sons, 1921 [1920].

Storing, Herbert J. 'Introduction', in Storing (ed.), *What Country Have I? Political Writings by Black Americans*, pp. 1–12. New York: St. Martin's Press, 1970.

Storing, Herbert J. 'What Country Have I? Political Writings by Black Americans' [1970], in *Toward a More Perfect Union: Writings of Herbert J. Storing*, edited by Joseph M. Bessette, pp. 206–20. Washington, DC: The AEI Press, 1995.

Stourdza, Alexandre de. *Considérations sur la doctrine et l'esprit de l'église orthodoxe*. Stuttgart: J. G. Cotta, 1816.

Strauss, Leo. *Natural Right and History*. Chicago: The University of Chicago Press, 1953.

Strauss, Leo. *On Tyranny*, corrected and expanded edition, including the Strauss–Kojève correspondence, edited by Victor Gourevitch and Michael S. Roth. Chicago: The University of Chicago Press, 2013.
Strauss, Leo. 'Progress or Return? The Contemporary Crisis in Western Civilization' [1952]. *Modern Judaism* 1, no. 1 (1981): 17–45.
Streckert, Jens. *Die Hauptstadt Lateinamerikas: Eine Geschichte der Lateinamerikaner im Paris der Dritten Republik (1870–1940)*. Cologne: Böhlau, 2013.
Strote, Noah Benezra. *Lions and Lambs: Conflict in Weimar and the Creation of Post-Nazi Germany*. New Haven, CT: Yale University Press, 2017.
Struck, Bernhard. 'In Search of the "West": The Languages of Political, Social and Cultural Spaces in the *Sattelzeit*, from about 1770 to the 1830s', in Riccardo Bavaj and Martina Steber (eds), *Germany and 'The West': The History of a Modern Concept*, pp. 41–54. New York: Berghahn, 2015.
Suarès, André. *Occident*. Paris: Émile-Paul Frères, 1915.
Sutton, Michael. *Nationalism, Positivism and Catholicism: The Politics of Charles Maurras and French Catholics, 1890–1914*. Cambridge: Cambridge University Press, 1982.
Sweeney, Carole. 'Resisting the Primitive: The Nardal Sisters, *La Revue du Monde Noir* and *La Dépêche Africaine*'. *Nottingham French Studies* 43, no. 2 (2004): 45–55.
Sylvander, Carolyn Wedin. *Jessie Redmon Fausset, Black American Writer*. Troy, NY: The Whitston Publishing Company, 1981.
Tagore, Rabindranath. *'American Experience' and Other Articles*. New Delhi: Rupa & Co., 2006.
Tagore, Rabindranath. *Nationalism*. London: Penguin Books, 2010 [1917].
Tagore, Rabindranath. 'Nationalism in the West'. *The Atlantic Monthly*, March 1917, pp. 289–301.
Talleyrand-Périgord, Charles Maurice de. *Memoirs of the Prince de Talleyrand*, edited by the Duc de Broglie, translated by Mrs Angus Hall, 5 vols. New York: G. P. Putnam's Sons, 1892.
Tate, Merze. '[Review of] *The Color Curtain: A Report on the Bandung Conference*. By Richard Wright'. *The Journal of Negro History* 41, no. 3 (1956): 263–65.
Tatlock, Lynne and Matt Erlin (eds). *German Culture in Nineteenth-Century America: Reception, Adaptation, Transformation*. Rochester, NY: Camden House, 2005.
Teitelbaum, Benjamin R. *War for Eternity: The Return of Traditionalism and the Rise of the Populist Right*. London: Penguin, 2020.
Temkin, Moshik. 'Culture vs. *Kultur*, or a Clash of Civilizations: Public Intellectuals in the United States and the Great War, 1917–1918'. *The Historical Journal* 58, no. 1 (2015): 157–82.
Teng, Ssu-yü and John K. Fairbank (eds). *China's Response to the West: A Documentary Survey, 1839–1923*. Cambridge, MA: Harvard University Press, 1954.
Thier, Maike. 'The View from Paris: "Latinity", "Anglo-Saxonism", and the Americas, as Discussed in the *Revue des races latines*, 1857–64'. *The International History Review* 33, no. 4 (2011): 627–44.
Thomas, Hugh. *Armed Truce: The Beginnings of the Cold War 1945–46*. London: Hamish Hamilton, 1986.
Thomas, Hugh. *The Suez Affair*. London: Weidenfeld and Nicolson, 1966.
Thompson, John A. *Reformers and War: American Progressive Publicists and the First World War*. Cambridge: Cambridge University Press, 1987.

Thonemann, Peter. 'Know Thyself: A Civilization That Questions Its First Principles'. *Times Literary Supplement*, no. 6267 (12 May 2023), pp. 3–4.

Tillmann, Serge. 'André Siegfried 1875–1959: L'Odyssée de l'Occident; la construction d'une histoire des identités'. Doctoral thesis, Université Le Havre Normandie, 2018.

Todd, David. 'Transnational Projects of Empire in France, c. 1815–c. 1870'. *Modern Intellectual History* 12, no. 2 (2015): 265–93.

Todd, David. *A Velvet Empire: French Informal Imperialism in the Nineteenth Century*. Princeton, NJ: Princeton University Press, 2021.

Todd, Emmanuel. *La Défaite de l'Occident*. Paris: Gallimard, 2024.

Todorova, Maria. *Imagining the Balkans*. Oxford: Oxford University Press, 2009.

Toland, John. 'To the Lord Mayor, Aldermen, Sherifs, and Common Council of London', in Toland (ed.), *The Oceana of James Harrington and His Other Works [...]*. London, 1700.

Tolz, Vera. 'The West', in William Leatherbarrow and Derek Offord (eds), *A History of Russian Thought*, pp. 197–216. Cambridge: Cambridge University Press, 2010.

Tooley, Marian J. 'Jean Bodin and the Mediaeval Theory of Climate'. *Speculum* 28, no. 1 (1953): 64–83.

Toye, Richard. *Age of Hope: Labour, 1945, and the Birth of Modern Britain*. London: Bloomsbury Continuum, 2023.

Toynbee, Arnold J. *Civilization on Trial*. London: Oxford University Press, 1948.

Toynbee, Arnold J. 'No Chosen People, No Unique Truth'. *The Observer Weekend Review*, 16 April 1961, p. 21.

Toynbee, Arnold J. *A Study of History*, 12 vols. Oxford: Oxford University Press, 1934–61.

Toynbee, Arnold J. *A Study of History: Abridgement*, abridged and edited by D. C. Somervell, 2 vols. London: Oxford University Press, 1960.

Toynbee, Arnold J. 'The Unification of the World and the Change in Historical Perspective' (The Creighton Lecture, Senate House, University of London, 17 November 1947), in Toynbee, *Civilization on Trial*, pp. 62–96, London: Oxford University Press, 1948.

Toynbee, Arnold J. *The Western Question in Greece and Turkey: A Study in the Contact of Civilisations*. Boston, MA: Houghton Mifflin Company, 1922.

Toynbee, Arnold J. *The World and the West: The BBC. Reith Lectures 1952*. London: Oxford University Press, 1953.

Trautsch, Jasper M. 'The Invention of the "West"'. *Bulletin of the GHI* (German Historical Institute, Washington, DC) 53 (Fall 2013): 89–102.

Trentmann, Frank. *Out of the Darkness: The Germans, 1942–2022*. London: Allen Lane, 2023.

Trevor-Roper, H[ugh] R. 'Arnold Toynbee's Millennium'. *Encounter*, June 1957, pp. 14–27.

Troeltsch, Ernst. *Deutscher Geist und Westeuropa*. Tübingen: Mohr, 1925.

Troeltsch, Ernst. 'The Ideas of Natural Law and Humanity in World Politics' [1922], in Otto Gierke, *Natural Law and the Theory of Society 1500 to 1800, with a Lecture on 'The Ideas of Natural Law and Humanity' by Ernst Troeltsch*, pp. 201–22. Boston, MA: Beacon Press, 1957 [1934].

Troeltsch, Ernst. 'Naturrecht und Humanität in der Weltpolitik'. *Weltwirtschaftliches Archiv*, vol. 18 (1922), pp. 485–501.

Troost, Wout. '"To Restore and Preserve the Liberty of Europe": William III's Ideas on Foreign Policy', in David Onnekink and Gijs Rommelse (eds), *Ideology and Foreign Policy in Early Modern Europe (1650–1750)*, pp. 283–303. Farnham: Ashgate, 2011.

Troy, William. 'A Defense of the Occident'. *The New Republic*, 18 April 1928, pp. 277–78.

Trump, Donald. 'Remarks by President Trump to the People of Poland', Krasiński Square, Warsaw, 6 July 2017, available at https://trumpwhitehouse.archives.gov/briefings-statements/remarks-president-trump-people-poland/ (accessed 19 October 2024).

Turnaoğlu, Banu. 'The Positivist Universalism and Republicanism of the Young Turks'. *Modern Intellectual History* 13, no. 3 (2017): 777–805.

Turner, Frederick J. 'The Problem of the West'. *The Atlantic Monthly*, vol. 78 (September 1896), pp. 289–97.

Turner, James. *The Liberal Education of Charles Eliot Norton*. Baltimore, MD: The Johns Hopkins University Press, 1999.

Tzschirner, Heinrich Gottlieb. *The Cause of Greece the Cause of Europe*. London: J. Ridgeway, 1821.

Tzschirner, Heinrich Gottlieb. *Die Sache der Griechen, die Sache Europas*. Leipzig: Vogel, 1821.

Ungern-Sternberg, Jürgen von and Wolfgang von Ungern-Sternberg. *Der Aufruf 'An die Kulturwelt!' Das Manifest der 93 und die Anfänge der Kriegspropaganda im Ersten Weltkrieg*. Stuttgart: Franz Steiner, 1996.

[Urquhart, David.] 'Quadruple Treaty'. *The British and Foreign Review or European Quarterly Journal*, vol. 1, no. 1 (July 1835), pp. 217–37.

Urquhart, David. *Recent Events in the East: Being a Reprint of Mr. Urquhart's Contributions to the 'Morning Advertiser' during the Autumn of 1853*. London: Trübner, 1854.

Urquhart, David. *The Spirit of the East: Illustrated in a Journal of Travels through Roumeli during an Eventful Period*, 2 vols. London: Henry Colburn, 1838.

Urquhart, David. *Turkey and Its Resources: Its Municipal Organization and Free Trade; the State and Prospects of English Commerce in the East, the New Administration of Greece, Its Revenue and National Possessions*. London: Saunders and Otley, 1833.

Useche Sandoval, Tonatiuh. 'Auguste Comte's Reading of Maistre's *Du pape*: Two Theories of Spiritual Authority', in Carolina Armenteros and Richard A. Lebrun (eds), *Joseph de Maistre and his European Readers: From Friedrich von Gentz to Isaiah Berlin*, pp. 75–92. Leiden: Brill, 2011.

Useche Sandoval, Tonatiuh. 'L'Idée d'Europe dans la politique positive d'Auguste Comte'. *Philonsorbonne* 3 (2008–9): 51–73.

Useche Sandoval, Tonatiuh. 'L'Idée d'Occident chez Auguste Comte'. Doctoral thesis, Université Paris I–Panthéon-Sorbonne, 2013.

Useche Sandoval, Tonatiuh. *L'Idée d'Occident chez Auguste Comte*. Villeneuve-d'Ascq: ANRT, 2014.

Useche-Sandoval, Tonatiuh. 'L'Occident défini par Comte: Un européocentrisme anticolonial?' *Cahiers philosophiques*, no. 166 (3e trimestre 2021), pp. 63–77.

Vaillant, Janet G. *Black, French, and African: A Life of Léopold Sédar Senghor*. Cambridge, MA: Harvard University Press, 1990.

Valéry, Paul. 'War Economy for the Mind' [1939], in Valéry, *The Collected Works of Paul Valéry*, vol. 10: *History and Politics*, translated by Denise Folliot and Jackson Mathews, pp. 471–74. London: Routledge & Kegan Paul.

Vallianos, Pericles S. 'The Ways of the Nation: Messianic and Universalist Nationalism in Renieris, Zambelios and Paparrigopoulos'. *The Historical Review / La Revue historique* 15, no. 1 (2018): 161–92.

Varouxakis, Georgios. 'The Godfather of "Occidentality": Auguste Comte and the Idea of "the West"'. *Modern Intellectual History* 16, no. 2 (2019): 411–41.

Varouxakis, Georgios. 'Guizot's Historical Works and J. S. Mill's Reception of Tocqueville'. *History of Political Thought* 20, no. 2 (1999): 292–312.

Varouxakis, Georgios. 'The Idea of "Europe" in Nineteenth-Century Greek Political Thought', in Philip Carabott (ed.), *Greece and Europe: Aspects of a Troubled Relationship*, pp. 16–37. London: Centre for Hellenic Studies, King's College London, 1995.

Varouxakis, Georgios. '"Patriotism", "Cosmopolitanism" and "Humanity" in Victorian Political Thought'. *European Journal of Political Theory* 5, no. 1 (2006): 100–118.

Varouxakis, Georgios. 'When Did Britain Join the Occident? On the Origins of the Idea of "the West" in English'. *History of European Ideas* 46, no. 5 (2020): 563–81.

Vasconcelos, José. *The Cosmic Race: A Bilingual Edition*, translated by Didier T. Jaén. Baltimore, MD: The Johns Hopkins University Press, 1997 [1925].

Vernon, Richard. 'Comte and the Withering-away of the State'. *Journal of the History of Ideas* 45, no. 4 (1984): 549–66.

Vernon, Richard. 'Auguste Comte's Cosmopolis of Care', in Vernon, *Friends, Citizens, Strangers: Essays on Where We Belong*, pp. 81–97. Toronto: University of Toronto Press, 2005.

Vick, Brian E. *The Congress of Vienna: Power and Politics after Napoleon*. Cambridge, MA: Harvard University Press, 2014.

Vitalis, Robert. *White World Order, Black Power Politics: The Birth of American International Relations*. Ithaca, NY: Cornell University Press, 2015.

Vogeler, Martha S. *Frederic Harrison: The Vocations of a Positivist*. Oxford: Clarendon Press, 1984.

Volney, Constantin-François. *Les Ruines: ou Méditation sur les révolutions des empires* [1791], in Volney, *Œuvres*, collected and revised by Anne Deneys and Henry Deneys, 3 vols, vol. 1: *1788–1795*, pp. 165–440 (Paris: Fayard, 1989).

Volpilhac-Auger, Catherine. 'D'une histoire l'autre: Voltaire, Condorcet et l'Europe', in Bertrand Binoche (ed.), *Nouvelles Lectures du 'Tableau historique' de Condorcet*, pp. 155–69. Paris: Hermann, 2013.

Voltaire [François-Marie Arouet]. *Essai sur les mœurs et l'esprit des nations (I–IX)*, in Voltaire, *Les Œuvres complètes de Voltaire*, vols 21–27, edited by Bruno Bernard, John Renwick, Nicholas Cronk and Janet Godden. Oxford: Voltaire Foundation, 2009-19.

Voltaire [François-Marie Arouet]. *Lettres choisies*, edited by Nicholas Cronk. Paris: Gallimard, 2017.

Voltaire [François-Marie Arouet]. *La Philosophie de l'histoire*. Amsterdam: Changuion, 1765.

Walden, Daniel. 'Dismantling the "West"'. *Current Affairs*, 28 June 2018.

Walicki, Andrzej. 'Adam Gurowski: Polish Nationalism, Russian Panslavism and American Manifest Destiny'. *The Russian Review* 38, no. 1 (1979): 1–26.

Walicki, Andrzej. *A History of Russian Thought: From the Enlightenment to Marxism*, translated by Hilda Andrews-Rusiecka. Stanford, CA: Stanford University Press, 1979.

Walicki, Andrzej. *Russia, Poland, and Universal Regeneration: Studies on Russian and Polish Thought of the Romantic Epoch*. Notre Dame, IN: University of Notre Dame Press, 1991.

Walicki, Andrzej. *The Slavophile Controversy: History of a Conservative Utopia in Nineteenth-Century Russian Thought*, translated by Hilda Andrews-Rusiecka. Oxford: The Clarendon Press, 1975.

Walt, Stephen M. 'Building Up New Bogeymen'. *Foreign Policy*, no. 106 (Spring 1997), pp. 176–89.

Ward, Barbara. *Five Ideas That Change the World: The Aggrey-Fraser-Guggisberg Lectures* (published for the University College of Ghana). London: Hamish Hamilton, 1959.

Ward, Barbara. *Policy for the West*. Harmondsworth: Penguin Books, 1951.

Wartelle, Jean-Claude. *L'Héritage d'Auguste Comte: Histoire de 'l'église positiviste' (1849–1946)*. Paris: L'Harmattan, 2001.

Waterfield, Robin. *René Guénon and the Future of the West: The Life and Writings of a 20th-Century Metaphysician*, 2nd edition. Hillsdale, NY: Sophia Perennis, 2002.

Watrous, Stephen D. (ed.). *John Ledyard's Journey through Russia and Siberia 1787–1788: The Journal and Selected Letters*. Madison, WI: The University of Wisconsin Press, 1966.

Weber, Eugen. 'Western Civilization', in Anthony Molho and Gordon S. Wood (eds), *Imagined Histories: American Historians Interpret the Past*, pp. 206–21. Princeton, NJ: Princeton University Press, 1998.

Webster, Charles. *The Foreign Policy of Palmerston 1830–1841: Britain, the Liberal Movement and the Eastern Question*, 2 vols. London: G. Bell, 1951.

Webster, Charles. 'Urquhart, Ponsonby, and Palmerston'. *The English Historical Review* 62, no. 244 (1947): 327–51.

Weil, Simone. 'À propos de la question coloniale dans ses rapports avec le destin du peuple français', in Weil, *Œuvres complètes*, tome 5, *Écrits de New York et de Londres*, vol. 1: *(1942–1943) Questions politiques et religieuses*, edited by Robert Chenavier, Jean Riaud and Patrice Rolland, pp. 280–95. Paris: Gallimard, 2019.

Weil, Simone. 'The Colonial Question and the Destiny of the French People' [1943], in Weil, *Simone Weil on Colonialism: An Ethic of the Other*, edited and translated by J. P. Little, pp. 105–19. Lanham, MD: Rowman & Littlefield, 2003.

Weil, Simone. 'The Great Beast: Some Reflections on the Origins of Hitlerism' [1939–40], in Weil, *Selected Essays, 1934–1943: Historical, Political, and Moral Writings*, chosen and translated by Richard Rees, pp. 89–144. Eugene, OR: Wipf & Stock, 2015.

Weil, Simone. 'The *Iliad* or The Poem of Force', in Weil, *Simone Weil: An Anthology*, edited by Siân Miles, pp. 182–215. London: Penguin, 2005. (First published as 'L'Iliade ou le poème de la force', *Cahiers du Sud*, December 1940–January 1941; translation by Mary McCarthy, *Politics* [New York], November 1945).

Weil, Simone. *The Need for Roots: Prelude to a Declaration of Duties towards Mankind*, translated by Arthur Wills, with a preface by T. S. Eliot. London: Routledge, 1952.

Weil, Simone. *The Need for Roots: Prelude to a Declaration of Obligations towards the Human Being*, translated by Ros Schwartz, with an introduction by Kate Kirkpatrick. London: Penguin, 2023.

Weil, Simone. *Œuvres complètes*, tome 4: *Écrits de Marseille*, vol. 2: *(1941–1942) Grèce–Inde–Occitanie*, edited by Anissa Castel-Bouchouchi and Florence de Lussy. Paris: Gallimard, 2009.

Weinberg, Albert K. *Manifest Destiny: A Study of Nationalist Expansionism in American History*. Gloucester, MA: Peter Smith, 1958 [1935].

Weiss, Gerhard. 'The Americanization of Franz Lieber and the *Encyclopedia Americana*', in Lynne Tatlock and Matt Erlin (eds), *German Culture in Nineteenth-Century America: Reception, Adaptation, Transformation*, pp. 273–87. Rochester, NY: Camden House, 2005.

Wells, Ida B., Frederick Douglass, Irvine Garland Penn and Ferdinand L. Barnett. *The Reason Why the Colored American Is Not in the World's Columbian Exposition: The Afro-American's Contribution to Columbian Literature*, edited by Robert W. Rydell. Urbana: University of Illinois Press, 1999 [1893].

Wernick, Andrew. *Auguste Comte and the Religion of Humanity: The Post-Theistic Program of French Social Theory*. Cambridge: Cambridge University Press, 2009.

Werth, Paul W. *1837: Russia's Quiet Revolution*. Oxford: Oxford University Press, 2021.

Westbrook, Robert B. *John Dewey and American Democracy*, Ithaca, NY: Cornell University Press, 1991.

Westcott, Allan (ed.). *Mahan on Naval Warfare: Selections from the Writings of Rear Admiral Alfred T. Mahan*. London: Sampson Low, Marston & Co., 1919.

Whatmore, Richard. *The End of Enlightenment: Empire, Commerce, Crisis*. London: Allen Lane, 2023.

Wheeler, Benjamin Ide. *Alexander the Great: The Merging of East and West in Universal History*. New York: G. P. Putnam's Sons, 1900.

Wheeler, Benjamin Ide. 'Greece and the Eastern Question'. *The Atlantic Monthly*, vol. 79 (June 1897), pp. 721–33.

Wheeler, Benjamin Ide. 'The Modern Greek as a Fighting Man'. *The North American Review* 164, no. 486 (1897): 609–16.

Wheeler, Benjamin Ide. *The Old World and the New* (address delivered at the commencement of exercises of the University of Michigan, 30 June 1898; reprinted from the *Atlantic Monthly* for August 1898). Houghton, Miflin & Co., 1898.

Whitfield, Stephen J. *A Critical American: The Politics of Dwight Macdonald*. Hamden, CT: Archon Books, 1984.

Whitman, Walt. 'Democratic Vistas' [1867/1870], in Whitman, *Complete Poetry and Complete Prose*, edited by Justin Kaplan, pp. 929–94. New York: The Library of America, 1982.

Wilder, Gary. *Freedom Time: Negritude, Decolonization, and the Future of the World*. Durham, NC: Duke University Press, 2015.

Wilford, Hugh. *The Mighty Wurlitzer: How the CIA Played America*. Cambridge, MA: Harvard University Press, 2008.

Williams, Chad L. *The Wounded World: W.E.B. Du Bois and the First World War*. New York: Farrar, Straus and Giroux, 2023.

Willkie, Wendell L. *One World*. New York: Simon & Schuster, 1943.

Wilson, Matthew. *Richard Congreve, Positivist Politics, the Victorian Press, and the British Empire*. Cham: Palgrave Macmillan, 2021.

Winkler, Heinrich August. *The Age of Catastrophe: A History of the West, 1914–1945*, translated by Stewart Spencer. New Haven, CT: Yale University Press, 2015.

Winkler, Heinrich August. *Germany: The Long Road West*, vol. 1: *1789–1933*, translated by Alexander J. Sager. Oxford: Oxford University Press, 2006.

Winkler, Heinrich August. *Germany: The Long Road West*, vol. 2: *1933–1990*, translated by Alexander J. Sager. Oxford: Oxford University Press, 2007.

Winkler, Heinrich August. *Geschichte des Westens: Von den Anfängen in der Antike bis zum 20. Jahrhundert*, 4 vols. Munich: C. H. Beck, 2009–15.

Winkler, Heinrich August. *Der Lange Weg nach Westen*, vol. 1: *Deutsche Geschichte vom Ende des Alten Reiches bis zum Untergand der Weimarer Republik*. Munich: C. H. Beck, 2000.

Winkler, Heinrich August. *Der Lange Weg nach Westen*, vol. 2: *Deutsche Geschichte vom 'Dritten Reich' bis zur Wiedervereinigung*. Munich: C. H. Beck, 2000.

Winkler, Heinrich August. 'Was heißt westliche Wertgemeinschaft?', in Winkler, *Auf ewig in Hitlers Schatten? Anmerkungen zur deutschen Geschichte*, pp. 180–201. Munich: C. H. Beck, 2007.

Winkler, Heinrich August. 'Westbindung oder was sonst? Bemerkungen zu einem Revisionsversuch'. *Politische Vierteljahresschrift* 35, no. 1 (1994): 113–17.

Winock, Michel. *Le Siècle des intellectuels*, 2nd edition. Paris: Seuil, 1999.

Winterer, Caroline. *Culture of Classicism: Ancient Greece and Rome in American Intellectual Life*. Baltimore, MD: Johns Hopkins University Press, 2004.

Withun, David. *Co-workers in the Kingdom of Culture: Classics and Cosmopolitanism in the Thought of W.E.B. Du Bois*. Oxford: Oxford University Press, 2022.

Withun, David. 'Zora's Bookshelf in *The Quest of the Silver Fleece* by W.E.B. Du Bois'. *The Explicator*, vol. 77, no. 3–4 (2019), pp. 124–27.

Wolff, Larry. *Inventing Eastern Europe: The Map of Civilization on the Mind of the Enlightenment*. Stanford, CA: Stanford University Press, 1994.

Wolff, Larry. *Woodrow Wilson and the Reimagining of Eastern Europe*. Stanford, CA: Stanford University Press, 2020.

Wood, John Carter. '"German foolishness" and the "prophet of doom": Oswald Spengler and the Interwar British Press', in Zaur Gasimov and Carl Antonius Lemke Duque (eds), *Oswald Spengler als europäisches Phänomen: Der Transfer der Kultur- und Geschichtsmorphologie im Europa der Zwischenkriegszeit 1919–1939*, pp. 157–84. Göttingen: Vandenhoeck & Ruprecht, 2013.

Wright, Ellen and Michel Fabre (eds). *Richard Wright Reader*. New York: Da Capo Press, 1997.

Wright, Richard. *Black Power: A Record of Reactions in a Land of Pathos* [1954], collected in Wright, *Black Power: Three Books from Exile*, pp. 1–427. New York: Harper Perennial, 2008.

Wright, Richard. *The Color Curtain: A Report on the Bandung Conference* [1956], collected in Wright, *Black Power: Three Books from Exile*, pp. 429–629. New York: Harper Perennial, 2008.

Wright, Richard. [contributions to] 'Débats', in *Le 1er Congrès international des écrivains et artistes noirs (Paris, Sorbonne, 19–22 Septembre 1956)*, special issue, *Présence africaine*, nos 8/9/10 (June–November 1956), pp. 67–69.

Wright, Richard. 'Memories of My Grandmother', in Wright, *The Man Who Lived Underground: A Novel*, pp. 161–211. New York: A Library of America Special Publication, 2021.

Wright, Richard. *Pagan Spain*. New York: Harper Perennial, 1995 [1957].

Wright, Richard. 'Richard Wright' [originally 'I Tried to be a Communist' (1944)], in Richard Crossman (ed.), *The God That Failed: Six Studies in Communism*, pp. 121–66. London: Hamish Hamilton, 1950.

Wright, Richard. 'Tradition and Industrialization: The Historic Meaning of the Plight of the Tragic Elite in Asia and Africa', in Wright, *White Man, Listen!* [1957], collected in Wright, *Black Power: Three Books from Exile*, pp. 631–812. New York: Harper Perennial, 2008.

Wright, Richard. 'Tradition and Industrialization: The Plight of the Tragic Elite in Africa', in *Le 1er Congrès international des écrivains et artistes noirs (Paris, Sorbonne, 19–22 Septembre 1956)*; special issue, *Présence africaine*, nos 8/9/10 (June–November 1956), pp. 347–60.

Wright, Richard. *White Man, Listen!* [1957], collected in Wright, *Black Power: Three Books from Exile*, pp. 631–812. New York: Harper Perennial, 2008.

Wright, T. R. 'George Eliot and Positivism: A Reassessment'. *The Modern Language Review* 76, no. 2 (1981): 257–72.

Wright, T. R. *The Religion of Humanity: The Impact of Comtean Positivism on Victorian Britain*. Cambridge: Cambridge University Press, 1986.

Yaqoob, Waseem. 'The Archimedean Point: Science and Technology in the Thought of Hannah Arendt, 1951–1963'. *Journal of European Studies* 44, no. 3 (2014): 1–26.

Young, Julian. *Friedrich Nietzsche: A Philosophical Biography*. Cambridge: Cambridge University Press, 2010.

Young-Bruehl, Elisabeth. *Hannah Arendt: For Love of the World*. New Haven, CT: Yale University Press, 1982.

Zea, Leopoldo. *Apogeo y decadencia del positivismo en México*. México: El Colegio de México, 1944.

Zea, Leopoldo. *El positivismo en México*. México: El Colegio de México, 1943.

Ziegler, Philip. *The Duchess of Dino*. London: Collins, 1962.

Zitlemann, Rainer, Karlheinz Weissmann and Michael Grossheim. 'Einleitung: Wir Deutschen und der Westen', in Zitlemann, Weissmann and Grossheim (eds), *Westbindung: Chancen und Risiken für Deutschland*, pp. 9–17. Frankfurt am Main: Propyläen, 1993.

Zitlemann, Rainer, Karlheinz Weissmann and Michael Grossheim (eds). *Westbindung: Chancen und Risiken für Deutschland*. Frankfurt am Main: Propyläen, 1993.

INDEX

The Abandonment of the West (Kimmage), 318
Abd al-Wāḥid Yaḥyá (René Guénon), 22, 24, 187, 194, 195–97, 305, 326–28
Abendland, 5, 39, 164, 167–71, 177, 182, 188, 190–91
Acheson, Dean, 395n9
Achille, Louis T., 22, 207–8
Achilles of the West, 203, 221–24
Action Française movement, 177, 190
Acton, Lord (John Dalberg-Acton), 69, 93, 95–96
Adams, John, 379n23
Adenauer, Konrad, 233, 307, 310
Aeschylus, 2, 350
Afghanistan, 333, 368n65
Africa: Afro-Americans' relation to, 121–25, 151–56, 165, 171–76, 227, 263–69, 275–76, 289; Communism in, 248; as origin of Western civilisation, 122–25, 172–74, 214–16, 343, 348–49
The African Abroad: Or, His Evolution in Western Civilization, Tracing His Development under Caucasian Mileu (Ferris), 124–25
African Orthodox Church, 172
'The African Roots of War' (Du Bois), 154
Afro-Americans: soldiers during Great War, 154–56; as Western, 122–28, 267–77, 289, 297, 401n149
Afro-American thinkers: African links, 121–25, 171–74, 263–64, 276, 289, 348; Harlem Renaissance, 156, 171–75, 221; on ownership of culture, 221–24, 344; on Russian menace, 119–21; World War I, 21, 151–56, 163; interwar period, 171–75, 192–93; Cold War, 23, 230–31, 261–77, 289; after Cold War, 24, 295–97, 320–23, 333, 407n26. *See also specific person*
Afrocentrism, 124–25, 171–74, 295
Afro-Latinity, 192–93
After Utopia (Shklar), 269–70
age of questions (Case), 82
aim of the West (Congreve), 89
d'Alembert, Jean le Rond, 5
Alexander I, Czar, 11, 26, 31
Al-Farabi, 347
Allgemeine Rundschau, 190
Alpine (white) alleged racial group, 175
alternatives to the West, 4, 14–18, 25–26, 30–31, 72–75, 175–76, 209–10, 212–20, 233–37, 339–40
America: Afro-Americans (*see* Afro-Americans); anti-Americanism, 214–15, 231–41, 252–53, 288, 299, 396n23; Civil War in, 89, 129; Communists in, 249, 261, 269–70; Congreve on, 89–90; culture wars in, 23, 278–80, 283–87, 292, 294–97, 301, 314–18, 320–25; Declaration of Independence, 256–57; European expansion into, 7–9; Europe's image of, 236–37, 251–53, 257, 288; exceptionalism, 20–21, 95–96, 110, 128; German intellectual influence on, 20, 95–107, 113–15, 125, 283–88, 348; invasion of Iraq, 311, 332; isolationism, 131, 142, 331; manifest destiny, 110, 221; 9/11 terrorist attacks, 333; as Pacific nation, 141; philhellenism in,

467

468　INDEX

America (*continued*)
　378n21; Positivist view of, 52, 57–58, 60, 65; power of (*see* American leadership); race relations in, 175–76, 222–24, 260, 275–76, 295, 320–22, 333; student revolts (1960s), 23, 283–84; Tagore's lectures in, 149–51; universities in, 94, 140, 166, 205–6, 237–40, 283–84; Vietnam War, 283–84; as Western, 7–9, 17, 20–21, 34–35, 69, 83–84, 166, 183, 210–11, 232, 314; in Western alliance, 217–20, 232; Western civilisation rejected by, 314–25, 331; the West used in (*see* American use of 'the West'); westward expansion within, 95–96, 104, 109; World War I, 21, 131, 136–39, 142–43, 162–63, 166; interwar years, 166, 175–76, 185–86; World War II, 22, 203–4, 210–11, 225; Cold War, 228–31, 283–87 (*see also* Cold War); post-Cold War, 314–18

American Association for the Advancement of Science, 205

'The American Century' (Luce), 221

American Creed, 295–97, 317

American Hunger (Wright), 263

Americanisation of Europe, 210–12, 214–16, 228, 231–39, 253

'Americanization' (Du Bois), 175–76

American leadership: origins of, 98–99, 108–10, 113–15, 129; World War I, 131, 137–45, 150–51; interwar period, 166; World War II, 203, 214–15, 220–22; Cold War, 228–31, 237–43, 250–53, 256–57, 275–78, 283; after Cold War, 24, 292, 314–18

'American Negro Academy,' 122, 125

American use of 'the West,' 7, 20, 21, 94–129; overview, 20, 94–96, 128–29; Afro-American attitudes, 119–28; Eastern Question, 107–15; European immigration, 20, 94, 95, 99–103, 109–13, 121–22; fear of Russia, 113–20; German influence, 20, 94–107, 110, 113–15, 125; need for distinct name, 103–7; Orientalism *versus* Occidentalism, 107–10, 113–15; Orient-Occident meeting, 115–19

Amery, Leo, 225

Ancient Law (Maine), 375n65

Anderson, Benedict, 407n16

Anglo-Saxon civilisation: Nordic supremacists, 175–76, 184–85; *versus* Slav, 111–15, 119–20, 129, 151–52, 187–89, 219

Animal Farm (Orwell), 225

anthropomorphism, 32

anti-Americanism, 214–15, 231–41, 243, 252–53, 288, 299, 396n23

anti-modernist paradox, 174

Anywheres (Goodhart), 332

Apollinian (Classical) culture (Spengler), 168, 171

'Apopos of Africa' (A. Locke), 172–73

'An Appeal to Americans' (Chapman), 137

'An Appeal to the Civilized World' (German academics' manifesto), 131

'An Appeal to the World' (Du Bois), 230–31

Appel aux nations chrétiennes en faveur des Grecs (Constant), 35

Appiah, Kwame Anthony, 2, 13

Applebaum, Anne, 333

Appleton's American Encyclopedia, 100

Arabism, 299–300

Aragon, Louis, 165

Arendt, Hannah: on science and technology, 353; World War II, 22, 208–9, 398n80; Cold War, 23, 249–54, 258, 288

Arminius (Hermann), 4, 134, 160, 163, 402n173

Armitage, David, 365n35, 381n44

Arnold, Thomas, 19, 77, 92

Aron, Raymond: on what distinguished 'the West,' 24, 257–61, 289, 335, 353; World War II, 22, 203, 212, 217–18, 220; Cold War, 23, 233, 257–61, 289

art, 158

Aryan people, 83

'As Others See Us' (*The Times*), 246

Atatürk (Mustafa Kemal), 298

The Atlantic, 154, 261, 320, 321, 332, 343, 345

INDEX 469

Atlantic Community, 143–44, 203, 218, 220–21, 226, 229–31
atomic bombs, 253
Atomised (Les Particules élémentaires) (Houellebecq), 326–29, 405n94
Auch eine Philosophie der Geschichte zur Bildung der Menschheit (Herder), 18
Auguste Comte aujourd'hui, 328
Augustine, 53, 253
Australia, 58, 84, 109, 141
Austria, 76, 88, 198
authority, 126

Bacon, Francis, 19, 71
Baldwin, James, 23, 231, 275–77, 289, 297
Bancroft, George, 97–98
Bandung Conference (1955), 264–65, 272, 276
Bannon, Steve, 197, 319–22, 345
barbarism: Roman Empire, 339; World War I, 133–35; interwar period, 171, 200; World War II, 204, 214; Cold War, 233–37, 243, 254–55
Barker, Ernest, 136
Barrault, Émile, 31
Barrès, Maurice, 134, 177
Batouala, véritable roman nègre (Maran), 146, 174–75, 193
'The Battle of Europe' (Du Bois), 154
BBC, 243–47, 336, 347
Bebel, August, 40
Beesly, Edward Spencer, 84
Beinart, Peter, 320–25
Belgium, 217, 220
Benedict, Ruth, 223
Bergson, Henri, 134–35
Betrachtungen eines Unpolitischen (Reflections of a Nonpolitical Man) (Mann), 159–62
Bevin, Ernest, 228–29, 231–33
Beyond Good and Evil (Nietzsche), 368n65
Biblical origins of the West, 193, 255–56. See also Christianity as Western basis
Bidault, Georges, 225, 396n16

Bismarck, Otto von, 161
Black Americans. *See* Afro-Americans
Black Boy (Wright), 261, 263
Black Power: A Record of Reactions in a Land of Pathos (Wright), 263, 264
Black Skin, White Masks (Fanon), 393n11
Blackwood's Edinburgh Magazine, 78
Blair, Eric (George Orwell), 22, 225, 226, 229, 278
Blavatsky, Helena, 117
bloc latin (Latin bloc), 217–20
Bloom, Allan, 23, 284–87, 289–90
Bluntschli, Johann Caspar, 134
Boas, Franz, 124, 174, 223
Bodin, Jean, 16
Bohemia (Czechoslovakia), 233, 278, 280–82
Bolshevik revolution, 10, 177, 180, 198, 199, 278
de Bonald, Louis, 67
Bonaparte (Napoléon I), 25, 26, 28, 36, 71
Bonnett, Alastair, 13, 15–16, 91, 92
Boston Society of Useful Knowledge, 100
Botswana, 323
Bourke, Richard, 365n41, 373n19
Bourne, Randolph, 138
Boutroux, Émile, 133–34, 162–63
Boxer Rebellion, 116
Brazil, 53, 64, 174
Brexit, 330, 333
Brezhnev, Leonid, 231
Bridges, John Henry, 84, 91
'A Brief Genealogy of the West' (GoGwilt), 50–51
Britain: Brexit, 330, 333; Comtists in, 70, 74, 84–93, 135–36, 162; imperialism, 51, 91–93, 339; India ruled by, 25, 27, 108–9, 116, 145, 266, 400n132; insularity of, 70–71; as leading power, 115, 231–33; philhellenism in, 80–81; Positivist view of, 52, 57; in Western alliance, 38, 217–20, 231–33; World War I, 21, 132–36, 142–43, 152, 162; interwar years, 182–85, 194, 198; World War II, 225; Cold War, 231–33, 243–47, 288

British use of 'the West', 69–93; overview, 19, 69–70, 93; anti-imperialist role of, 91–93; early instances, 71–72; English terminology, 70–71, 90–93; Freeman's work, 81–84; Gibbon's work, 72–75; 'others' (Russia, Jews, Turkey), 75–81; Positivists, 84–93

Brockhaus *Conversations-Lexicon*, 100

Brodsky, Joseph, 282, 354

Broglie, Duc de, 76

Bruckner, Pascal, 333

Bruneteau, Bernard, 210

Buckle, Henry Thomas, 19, 75

Buckley, William F., 402n165

Bulgarian crisis (Eastern question), 81, 112–13

Bullitt, William C., 224–25

Bunsen, Christian von, 92–93

The Burden of Our Time (Origins of Totalitarianism) (Arendt), 249–50

Burke, Arleigh, 296

Burke, Edmund, 373n19

Burlingame, Anson, 107

Burnham, James, 23, 277–80, 283, 289, 294, 402n165

Buruma, Ian, 333

Burwick, Fred L., 378n14

Bush, George H. W., 320–21

Bush, George W., 311, 320–22, 332

Byzantine (Eastern Roman) Empire, 3, 5–7, 11–12, 16, 17, 45–46, 48, 73, 82–83, 152, 172, 280, 385n65

Calvin, John, 270

Camus, Albert, 22, 212, 214, 216–17, 394n38

Canada, 141

capitalism, 298, 305, 320, 331–32, 338

Caramanlis, Constantinos, 287–88

Carlyle, Thomas, 348

Carolingian Empire, 5, 8, 31, 56–57, 338–39. See also Charlemagne's empire

Carter, Jimmy, 231

Case, Holly, 81–82

Castoriadis, Cornelius, 24, 292, 298–301, 353, 355

Catherine the Great, 18

Catholic Church: *versus* Orthodox Church, 5–9, 11–12, 14, 26, 42–48, 66–67, 280; political role of, 200, 224–25; Positivist view of, 54–55, 57, 59, 65, 67, 74, 87, 91; Stourdza's criticism of, 11; as Western core, 22, 26, 38, 42–48, 351 (*see also* Christianity as Western basis)

Catholic intellectuals, 177, 183–85, 189–91, 193, 195, 203–4. *See also specific person*

Caucasian 'race,' 102–7, 128–29, 380n31 and 32

The Cause of Greece, the Cause of Europe, 80

Ceauşescu, Nicolae, 234

Central Europe: in European Union, 311; in NATO, 316; as Western, 4, 23, 278, 280–82, 289, 330–31. *See also specific country*

Césaire, Aimé, 213, 265

Chaadaev, Petr (Peter), 10–13, 42–43, 180, 363n17

Chambers, Whittaker, 242–43, 402n165

Chapman, John Jay, 21, 136–38, 162, 166, 175, 198

Charlemagne's empire: Britain not part of, 71, 73; Comte's project based on, 67; France as centre of, 17, 35, 57, 71; Saint-Simon as descendant of, 31; as successor of Roman Empire, 5, 9, 71, 338; unity under, 59, 61, 65

Chevalier, Michel, 19, 31, 33–35

Chicago Exhibition (1893), 121

China: American immigrants from, 109; belt and road initiative, 339–40; Boxer Rebellion, 116; Communism in, 245; as Eastern, 33, 72, 183; as global South, 345–46; during Great War, 132, 141–42; international relations, 107, 278; as pivotal to world politics, 115–20, 142; post-Cold War potential expansionism, 293, 301; racial prejudice against, 222; reformers' strategies, 344

Chou En-lai, 265, 273

Christianity: Catholicism (*see* Catholic Church); civilisation differentiated by,

303–4, 320–22; Crusades, 17, 45, 73, 338; d'Eichthal on, 32; East-West division of, 338–39; Greece as part of, 35–36, 48, 80–81; history of, 341–42; Orthodoxy (*see* Orthodox Church); Positivist view of, 58–59, 65; secular versions of, 75, 90–91, 254, 315; Wright on, 270–71

Christianity as Western basis: origins of, 3, 5–9, 11–14, 17, 26, 106, 118, 338–39; World War II, 205, 215; Cold War, 243–47, 255–59, 280; post-Cold War, 303–4, 315, 320–22

'Christianity or Europe' (Novalis), 9

Church of Humanity, 53, 86

CIA, 247, 276

Cicero, 5, 350

Cis-Caucasian (as self-description proposed by Lieber), 103–7, 128–29, 340, 380n31 and 32

Citizen of the World (Goldsmith), 71–72, 92

City of God (Augustine), 53

civic union, West as, 331–32

civilisation: clash of civilisations thesis, 23–24, 292, 301–7, 315–17, 331; contested during Great War, 131, 133–34, 151–64; *versus* 'culture' (according to Mann, Curtius and other Germans), 157–60, 187–89, 290; *versus* 'culture' (according to Spengler), 161–64, 170–71; definition of, 167, 244, 302–3, 315; politics of, 302–5; religion as differentiation, 303–7, 313–18, 320–22; Western (*see* Western civilisation). See also *Zivilisation*

civilisation occidentale. See *l'Occident*

Civilization, the Primal Need of the Race (Crummell), 122

Civilization: The West and the Rest (Ferguson), 333

civilization consciousness (Huntington), 330

civil war: American, 89, 129; Western, 205, 302, 315–16

clash of civilisations thesis, 23–24, 292, 301–7, 315–17, 331

Classical (Apollinian) culture (Spengler), 168, 171

classical past. See Greco-Roman roots of the West

classicists on 'Western civilisation,' 346–50

Claudel, Paul, 193

Clausewitz, Carl von, 258

climate change, 353

The Closing of the American Mind (Bloom), 284

Cocteau, Jean, 188

Cold War, 227–90; overview, 4, 22–23, 228–29, 287–90; American domination, 237–42, 283–87; Arendt's work, 249–54; Aron's work, 257–61; Atlantic Community, 229–31; Baldwin's work, 275–77; British leadership in Western Europe, 231–33; East-West conflict, 233–37; first uses of term, 226, 229; kidnapped West, 280–82, 289, 318, 330–31; liberalism as Western 'suicide,' 278–80, 283, 289, 294; period after (*see* post-Cold War); rejection of Soviet ideology, 247–49; Toynbee's work, 242–47; Western principles, 254–57; Wright's work, 261–75

The Cold War (Lippmann), 229

colonialism: alleged benefits of, 207–8, 246; British India, 25, 27, 108–9, 116, 145, 266, 400n132; decolonisation, 248, 260–61, 264–67; Nazism, 213; neo-colonialists, 351; as Western sin, 300

The Color Curtain: A Report on the Bandung Conference (Wright), 263, 272

Color Line, 120–21, 153, 222

Combat, 216

Commonweal, 203–4, 250

Communism: American interest in, 249, 261, 269–70; in China, 245; Eastern Europe, 232–33, 293, 311; fear of, 203–4, 224–25, 249 (*see also* Cold War); French interest in, 233–34, 258; Italian interest in, 233; *versus* religion, 253–54, 258; spiritual resistance to, 238–40, 244–47, 253–54, 288; spread of, 278; in Third World, 248

Communist Party of the United States, 261

Comte, Auguste: Aron's study of, 257–58; British followers of, 70, 84–93, 135–36, 162; cerebral hygiene, 340; correspondence with Mill, 52–53, 61–63, 90; d'Eichthal as disciple of, 32–33; Houellebecq's admiration of, 328; as link for English use of the West, 92; *longue durée* approach and, 24; political project of, 52–60, 67, 92, 339–40; portrait of, 15; prominence of, 49, 63–64, 84–85, 201; religious theory of, 52–55, 369n71; Russian interest in philosophy of, 12–13; as Saint-Simon's secretary, 31; on science and technology, 353; sociological laws, 58–59; sociopolitical concept of 'the West' introduced by, 3, 8–9, 14, 19, 49, 66–68, 314, 339–40; substitution of *Occident* for *Europe*, 48–52, 66–67, 90–91, 169; translated works, 84, 91; tributes to, 48–50, 365n37; on Western unity, 16, 135; work phases, 52; Wright's (serendipitous) association with, 261
Concert of Europe, 88
Condorcet, (Marquis) Nicolas de, 12, 17
Confluence, 238, 240, 253
conformism, 211
Congrès international des écrivains et artistes noirs, 265–77
Congress for Cultural Freedom (CCF), 23, 247–48, 276, 288, 396n23, 398n67
Congress of Vienna, 2, 26, 31
Congreve, Richard, 19, 64, 69, 75, 84–90, 135
Conrad, Joseph, 354
conservatism, 315, 324, 334
'Considerations on the Spiritual Power' (Saint-Simon), 60
Constant, Benjamin, 13, 19, 25, 35–36, 81
Constantinople: capital of Eastern Roman/Byzantine Empire, 11, 45–46, 48, 73, 82–83, 172, 280, 338–39; as East-West link, 57, 371n116; as future capital of Humanity according to Comte, 57; Russian interest in, 76, 111, 114; and significance of Eastern Roman Empire, 338–39

constitutionalism, 303
constitutional patriotism (*Verfassungspatriotismus*), 309
containment policy, 229–30
Cornell University, 284
cosmic race, 176
Cours de philosophie positive (Comte), 52, 60–61, 91
Crèvecoeur, Hector St. John de, 295, 377n6
Crimea, Russian annexation of, 333, 404n74
Crimean War, 38, 40, 46, 76, 88, 111–13, 374n28
The Crisis, 127, 146, 152, 154–56, 206–7
crisis of modernity, 255
The Criterion, 182–83, 186, 195, 197, 198
Croly, D. G., 383n108
Croly, Herbert, 129, 138–39
Crossman, Richard, 261–62
Cruickshank, John, 389n54
Crummell, Alexander, 122–24, 127
Crusades, 17, 45, 73, 338
Cuban missile crisis (1962), 283
cultural diversity, 224, 283, 296, 323–24
cultural relativism, 174, 284–90
culture: American popular, 317; *versus* civilisation, 131, 157–58, 164, 170–71, 187–89, 290, 302–5, 352–54; crisis of, 405n103; ownership of, 343–45, 351; *versus* race, 223–24. See also *Kultur*
culture wars, 23, 283–87, 292
Curchod-Necker, Suzanne, 28
Curtius, Ernst Robert, 22, 187–89
Custine, Marquis (Astolphe) de, 19, 29, 38, 43, 80, 180, 368n53
customs union, 231
cyclical theory of history, 14
Czartoryski, Adam, 4, 76
Czechoslovakia (Bohemia), 233, 278, 280–82

Dahrendorf, Ralf, 4, 307, 310
Daily News, 113
Dalberg-Acton, John E.E. (Lord Acton), 69, 93, 95–96

Les Damnés de la Terre (The Wretched of the Earth) (Fanon), 264
Dana, Charles A., 112
Daniel Deronda (Eliot), 77–78
Danilevsky, Nikolai Iakovlevitch, 12, 171
Le Débat, 280
Debray, Régis, 333, 387n17, 406n104
Declaration of Independence: America, 256–57; Greece, 81
decline of the civilizationistic pattern (Moses), 156
The Decline of the West (Spengler), 21–22, 161–64, 166–71, 176–82, 191, 199, 249, 254
decolonisation, 248, 260–61, 264–67
deconstructionism, 315
'The Defence of the West' (Jebb), 198
Défense de l'Occident (Massis), 22, 146, 176–97, 201
definition: of civilisation, 167, 244, 302–3, 315; *versus* history, 342. See also *Zivilisation*
De Gaulle, Charles, 140, 212
democracy: Cold War issues, 229, 252–53, 283, 320; Habermas' theory, 309; as Western value, 67–70, 118, 203, 297, 303, 320–24, 350–51
Democracy in America (Tocqueville), 251–53
Democratic Vistas (Whitman), 96
Denmark, 220
De près et de loin (Lévi-Strauss), 300
Derrida, Jacques, 311
'The Destined Superiority of the Negro' (Crummell), 123
Destiny, 168, 171, 221
détente, 283
Deudney, Daniel, 331–32
Deutschland Über Alles or Germany Speaks (Chapman), 137
Les Deux Mondes (d'Eichthal), 16–17, 32–34, 71, 367nn30 and 34
dewesternisation of Germany, 177–82, 186–92
Dewey, John, 133
dictatorship, 229, 351

Diderot, Denis, 17
Die Französische Kultur: Eine Einfürung (Curtius), 188–89
Die geistesgeschichtliche Lage des heutigen Parlamentarismus (Schmitt), 200
Diezel, Gustav, 19, 39–40
Diop, Alioune, 265, 270
Discours sur l'ensemble du positivisme (Comte), 56–57, 60–63
Disraeli, Benjamin, 17
The Disuniting of America: Reflections on a Multicultural Society (Schlesinger), 294–97
divided West, 311
Dix années d'exil (de Staël), 29
Donoso Cortés, Juan, 14, 199–201
Dostoyevsky, Fyodor, 12, 160, 290
double vision (double-consciousness of Afro-Americans), 122, 267–68, 289
Douglass, Frederick, 122
Drochon, Hugo, 368n65
dual role of the West (Huntington), 303
Du Bois, W.E.B.: background of, 125, 347, 377n9; on European civilization, 125–28, 172, 385n68; passport refusal, 275–76; portrait of, 157; on Russo-Japanese War, 120–21; World War I, 21, 146, 151–57, 163; interwar period, 22, 175–76; Cold War, 23, 228, 230–31, 267, 275–76, 289
Du contrat social (Rousseau), 72
Dugin, Aleksandr, 197
Duhamel, Georges, 130
Du pape (de Maistre), 11, 54
DWEMs (dead white European males), 316

the East, 29, 31–34, 146–50, 181–82, 195–97, 213–16, 245–47, 249; Anglo-French rivalry over, 25; characteristics of, 32–33, 116–18; religious division from 'West,' 42–48. See also *l'Orient*
'East and West' (Fletcher), 183
East and West (Guénon), 195–97
Eastern civilisation, rivalry with Western civilisation, 23–24, 47–48, 115–19

Eastern Europe: Communism in, 232–33, 293, 311; invention of, 18; Positivist view of, 57–58; as Western, 4, 23, 232–33, 278, 289, 330–31. *See also specific country*
Eastern Orthodox Church. *See* Orthodox Church
Eastern Powers (Palmerston), 76
Eastern Question: American views on, 107–15; Freeman on, 81–84; meaning of, 47–48, 76; prominence of, 26, 31, 33. *See also* Ottoman Empire
'The Eastern Question' (Godkin), 113
Eastern religions, 195–97, 246–47; civilisation differentiated by, 303–4. *See also* Islam
Eastern Roman Empire, 5–6, 11, 73, 82–83, 93, 172, 338–39
East-West division: of Christianity, 7, 11–12, 14, 17, 325, 338–39; debate over Greece, 5, 7, 11, 35–39, 43–48, 114–15, 134, 287–88, 343–44, 346; d'Eichthal's theory of, 32–35; within Europe, 34, 37–38, 71–72, 280–82, 343–44; within Germany, 134; during Great War, 141–42, 145–51; kidnapped West, 280–82, 289, 318, 330–31; purported ancient concepts of, 1–2, 5–7; religion in, 32, 42–48, 66–67, 195–97, 246–47, 253–54; of Roman Empire, 5–7, 9, 14, 17, 35, 73–74, 82–83, 93, 172, 338–39; Russia and, 18, 22, 26, 29, 36–42, 66; versions of, 15–16; Weil's theory of, 214–16; Wright's theory of, 265, 272–74
Ecevit, Bülent, 240
Economist, 239
education: Eurocentrism in America, 295–97; German universities, 20, 95, 96–99, 113–15, 125; Western civilisation curricula, 94, 140, 166, 205–6, 238–40, 283
Egypt: civilisational origins in, 124, 172–73, 215, 348; French interest in, 25, 35–36; Guénon in, 195–97
d'Eichthal, Gustave, 16, 19, 31–33, 66–67, 71, 367nn30 and 34, 369n73

Eliot, George (Mary Ann Evans), 19, 77–78, 86, 87, 93, 377n100
Eliot, T. S., 22, 182–84, 186, 195–98, 252, 389n58
Elliott, William Yandell, 238–40
Emerson, Ralph Waldo, 96–97
Encounter, 247, 248, 275, 276, 396n23
Encyclopaedia Americana (Lieber), 100, 378n21
Encyclopaedia Britannica, 96
end of history thesis, 23–24, 292–94, 301, 325–30, 334
end of ideology thesis, 248, 258
Engels, Friedrich, 112, 200, 244
English language, use of the West, 69–71, 90–93, 338. *See also* America; Britain
The English Review, 198
L'Enracinement (The Need for Roots) (Weil), 212–13, 216
entente occidentale (Western entente), 217–18
Erdoğan, Recep Tayyip, 336
Esquisse (Condorcet), 17
Ethiopia, 124, 172, 197
ethnocentrism, 59, 285, 295–97, 349
Europäische Revue, 188
Europa Occidens, 7–9
Europe: Americanisation of, 214–16, 253; as civilisation, 2–3, 8–9, 14, 18, 169–70; Comte's substitution of *Occident* for, 48–52, 66–67, 90–91; as conceptual term (*see* Europe *versus* the West); as cultural entity, 70; East-West division within, 34, 37–38, 71–72, 280–82, 343–44; Germany as centre of, 3–4, 89; image of America, 236–37, 251–53, 257, 288; North-South division within, 5, 16–18, 27–29, 34, 41, 66, 185; racist theory in, 223–24; as secular version of Christendom, 75, 254; unification of (*see* European federation)
European Council, 330
European expansion, 7–9, 51
European federation, 217–18, 229; Arendt on, 208–9, 250, 253; d'Eichthal on, 66–67; European Union, 311, 313, 330; fear of

Russia prompting, 38–42; Gibbon on, 73–74; de Pradt on, 37–38; Saint-Simon on, 30–31; as third force, 233–37
européanisme (Comte), 62
European superiority, Heeren's theory of, 26–28
European Union, 311, 313, 330
Europe *versus* the West, 25–68; overview, 2–4, 10, 14–17, 25–26, 66–68; British influence on, 70, 88; Christianity and, 42–48; Greek role in, 35–38; Heeren on, 26–28; Kundera on, 280–82; *Occident* substitution, 48–52, 66–67, 90–91; Positivist theory on, 52–65, 84 (*see also* Comte, Auguste); Saint-Simon on, 30–35; World War II, 203, 209–17, 226, 237; after World War II, 231–37, 240, 250–53, 280–82; post-Cold War, 311, 330
Evans, Mary Ann (George Eliot), 19, 77–78, 86, 87, 93, 377n100
Everett, Edward, 97–99, 106, 349, 379n21
exceptionalism, 20–21, 95–96, 110, 128
expansionism, 301
The Expansion of England (Seeley), 86–87
Extreme West, 212–17, 233
extremism, 319

Fallmerayer, Jakob Philipp, 19, 39, 368n56 and 57
family values, 315
fanaticism, 299, 305, 315
Fanon, Frantz, 264, 393n11, 399n115
fascism, 197–98. *See also* Nazism
Fauset, Jessie Redmond, 22, 151, 153, 155, 386n79, 401n149
Faustian (Western) culture (Spengler), 168
feminism, 314–16
Ferguson, Niall, 333
Ferris, William H., 124–25
feudalism, 59, 65, 88, 101
Fichte, Johann Gottlieb, 133–34
Le Figaro, 177, 209, 260
Finkielkraut, Alain, 333
Finland, 204

'First Philosophical Letter' (Chaadaev), 10, 12, 13, 42–43, 180, 363n17
First World War. *See* Great War
Fletcher, John Gould, 22, 183–85
Floyd, George, 333, 407n26
Foreign Affairs, 301
Foreign Student Project (Harvard), 234, 238–49
Fortune, 243
Foster, Daniel, 321–25, 345
France: Black intellectuals in, 174–75, 262–77; central role of (*see* France as centre of the West); Charlemagne's empire, 17, 35, 57, 71; as Christian, 32; Communists in, 233–34, 258; interest in the East, 25; July Revolution (1830), 38; as Latin, 35; *nouveaux réactionnaires*, 333; as origin of Positivism, 92; ownership of culture, 345; philhellenism in, 35–36; Poland supported by, 76; in Western alliance, 38, 217–20; World War I, 21, 155–56; interwar period, 174–89; World War II, 22, 206–17; Cold War, 231, 233–34, 257–61. *See also* Paris
France as centre of the West: origins of, 3–4, 41, 56–59, 89; World War I, 135, 162; interwar years, 22, 174–89; World War II, 206–9, 212, 219–20; Cold War, 231
la France eternelle, 212
Franco-Prussian War, 40
Franklin, Benjamin, 379n23
'Französische Civilisation und Abendland' (Curtius), 188
Frederick of Prussia, 158
freedom. *See* liberty
Free French, 212, 217
Freeman, Edward Augustus, 19, 43, 81–84, 93, 113
free world, 250, 253
'French and Spanish' (Du Bois), 156
French language, the West used early in, 8, 19, 31–38, 49–52, 60–65, 70–71, 92–93. See also *l'Occident*
French Revolution, 54, 59, 368n51

Freud, Sigmund, 172, 174
Friedrich, Carl J., 199
Frobenius, Leo, 22, 124, 172, 175, 182, 289
frontier thesis, 95–96
Frye, Northrop, 387n21, 396n35
Fukuyama, Francis, 23, 290, 292–94, 301, 320, 322, 331–33
Fukuzawa Yukichi, 344
fureur antigérmanique, 193
furor orientalis (Marchand), 181
Fyvel, Tosco, 225

Gallimard, 216
Gandhi, M. K., 118, 145, 148, 150, 180–81
Garton Ash, Timothy, 282, 333, 401n161, 402n172, 405n104
Garvey, Marcus, 125, 172, 175
Gaza, 333
genealogical analysis, 340–42, 345
'General Observations' (Gibbon), 74
geographical concept of 'the West': overview, 5–9; in America, 95–96, 101; in Britain, 71, 75; *versus* Comte's concept, 5–9, 49, 58, 65, 340
Germanic World (Hegel), 15–16
German language, the West used early in, 8, 19, 26–28, 39–42, 70–71, 92–93. See also *Abendland*
German Social Democrats, 40, 233, 312
Germany: American fear of, 136–39, 198; American immigrants from, 95, 99–103, 110; as centre of Europe, 3–4, 57, 89, 134, 204, 209, 308–14, 376n74; as Christian, 32; cultural debate about, 131–36, 156–59, 162–64, 170, 290, 292; dewesternisation of, 177–82, 186–92; dualism within, 134, 144, 162–63, 186–87, 201, 344; as eternal 'protest' and resistance against Rome and 'the West' (Mann), 159–60, 163; fear of Russia, 39–42, 132–33, 152; *Historikerstreit*, 308, 312; inimical to 'civilisation' and instead attached to 'culture' (Mann), 156–59; intellectual influence on America, 20, 95–99, 113–15, 125, 283–88, 348;
'mission' against 'imperialism of civilization' (Mann), 160; reunification of, 24, 292, 310–12; Russian alliance with, 204, 224; universities in, 20, 95, 96–99, 113–15, 125; Westernisation of, 137, 247, 278, 307–14; World War I (*see* Great War); interwar years, 186–92 (*see also* interwar period); World War II (*see* Nazism; Second World War); Cold War, 228–29, 233, 247
Germany: The Long Road West (Winkler), 312–13
Geschichte des Westens (A History of the West) (Winkler), 313
Geuss, Raymond, 340–41, 345
Gheorghiu, Virgil, 234–37, 239, 252
Gibbon, Edward, 16, 19, 45, 72–75, 92
Gibraltar (Congreve's pamphlet), 84
Gillouin, René, 22, 193
Gilson, Étienne, 53, 205
Giscard d'Estaing, Valéry, 240
global South, 345–46
glory, Roman idea of, 212–13
Gobineau, Arthur de, 266
Godkin, Edwin Lawrence, 112–13
The God That Failed: Six Studies in Communism (Crossman), 261–62
Goepp, Charles, 110
Goethe, 376n96
GoGwilt, Christopher, 10, 12, 13, 50–51, 91
Gökalp, Ziya, 1, 344, 390n89
Goldsmith, Oliver, 19, 71–72, 92, 373n9
Goodhart, David, 332
Gorbachev, Mikhail, 293
Gramsci, Antonio, 22, 192
La Grande Illusion (film), 161
grand narratives of Western civilisation, 346–50
Grant, Madison, 22, 94, 175, 185
'Great Disillusionment' lecture (A. Locke), 152
Greater Eastern Question (Wheeler), 113–15
Great War, 130–64; overview, 20–21, 130–31, 162–64; Afro-American views on, 151–56;

American reactions to, 136–39; anti-imperialism during (Marvin), 92; German cultural debate, 131–36, 156–59, 170; Lippmann on, 139–45; Mann on, 156–62; period after (*see* interwar period); Tagore on, 145–51

Greco-Roman roots of the West: overview, 338–39; early theories of, 43–48, 57, 59, 65; American theories of, 98, 124; British theories of, 71, 80–83, 88, 90; ownership of culture issue, 344–45; Plato to NATO narrative, 9, 346–50, 406n8; projections of the West onto ancient Greece and/or Rome, 1–2, 5, 45, 81–82, 113–15, 134, 159–60, 177, 193, 205–6, 210–11, 214–16, 250, 254–56, 284–85; World War I, 160, 163; interwar period, 22, 168, 171–72, 177, 183–85, 190, 193; World War II, 205–6, 210–15; Cold War, 245, 250, 255–56, 280–81, 284–87; post-Cold War, 300, 332

Greco-Turkish War (1897), 113

Greece: American protection of, 229, 242, 378n21; Byzantine Empire and, 5, 11, 45–46, 48, 82–83, 172; East-West debate over, 5, 7, 11–13, 35–39, 43–48, 57, 80–81, 108, 113–15, 134, 287–88, 343–44, 346, 378n21; Positivist view of, 57; as potential Russian ally (Huntington), 307, 403n34; as Western inspiration (*see* Greco-Roman roots of the West)

Greek Orthodox Church. *See* Orthodox Church

Greek Revolution, 13, 25–26, 31, 35–38, 46, 66, 80–81, 378n21

Greeley, Horace, 110–11

Gress, David, 406n8

Grigg, Edward, 208

Groß-deutsch, 190

Großräume thinking, 140

Großraumordnung, 384n39

Guénon, René (Abd al-Wāḥid Yaḥyá), 22, 24, 187, 194, 195–97, 305, 326–28

Guizot, François, 10, 14, 122, 364n17

Gulf War (1991), 298–301, 333

Gulf War (2003), 298–301, 311, 332, 333

Gurowski, Adam, 110–12

Habermas, Jürgen, 4, 24, 292, 307–12, 334

Haffner, Sebastian, 225

Halévy, Élie, 130, 131, 135

Händler und Helden (Sombart), 133

Hapgood, Norman, 138

Harlem Renaissance, 156, 171–75, 221

Harnack, Adolph von, 385n65

Harper's Magazine, 325

Harrison, Frederic, 19, 84–86

Harrison, Hubert, 94, 119–20, 165

Harvard International Seminar, 234, 237–38

Harvard Summer School, 23, 234, 238–40

Hayek, Friedrich, 225

Hebraic origins of the West/Western civilisation, 193, 255–56. *See also* Christianity as Western basis

Hedge, Frederic Henry, 97

Heeren, Arnold Hermann Ludwig: overview, 26–28; on centrality of Germany, 89, 376n74; influence of, 12, 19, 124, 348, 382n95; on monogamy, 27, 101; quoted, 336; *Reflections on the Politics of Ancient Greece,* 98, 106

Hegel, Georg Wilhelm Friedrich: on east-west flow, 15–16; on end of history, 293–94; influence of, 32, 49, 168, 365n41; *Kultur* movement, 133–34

Heidegger, Martin, 1, 287

heliotropic myth *(translatio imperii),* 14, 28, 95, 98, 106, 115, 380n23

Hell, fear of, 254

'Hellenic Civilisation' (Toynbee), 47–48

Heller, Peggy, 10, 91

Heraclitus, 170

Herder, Johann Gottfried, 18, 97–98, 169, 174

Herman, Arthur, 13

Hermann (Arminius), 4, 134, 160, 163

Herodotus, 124, 214–15

Hertz, Fanny, 84

Herzl, Theodor, 388n30

Hesse, Hermann, 181, 187

High Imperialism, 146
Hind Swaraj (Gandhi), 118, 148, 181
Hirsi Ali, Ayaan, 333
Histoire de la civilisation en Europe (Guizot), 10, 14, 364n17
Histoire de l'Empire de Russie sous Pierre le Grand (Voltaire), 18, 74
historical process, 255
historical relativism, 284–90
historical term, 'the West' as, 7–9, 72–74
Historic West, 332–34
Historikerstreit (1980s German historians' dispute), 308, 312
history: active process of, 351–52; cyclical theory of, 14; *versus* definition, 342; end of (thesis), 23–24, 292–94, 301, 325–30, 334; importance of, 336–37, 340–46, 354; labelling of eras, 330, 340–42; linear theory of, 14; *longue durée* approach, 24, 331; as therapy, 295; Western schemes of, 168–71
History of Civilization in England (Buckle), 75
History of Civilization in Europe (Guizot), 10, 14, 364n17
History of England during the Thirty Years' Peace (Martineau), 374n43
History of the Decline and Fall of the Roman Empire (Gibbon), 45, 72–75
A History of the West (Geschichte des Westens) (Winkler), 313
History of the West (Winkler), 312
Hitchens, Christopher, 333
hitchhiking imperialism, 381n46
Hitler, Adolf: agreement with Stalin, 204, 224; defeat of, 201; influenced by American racist theories, 175; invasion of Soviet Union, 22, 203; rise to power, 198–99. *See also* Nazism; Second World War
Hobbes, Thomas, 19, 71, 92
Hobhouse, L. T., 136
Hobson, J. A., 136
Holland (Netherlands), 92, 217, 220

Holmes, Stephen, 406n12
Holy Alliance, 26, 66, 76
Holy Alliance (Nakhimovsky), 366n4
Homer, 124, 170
Houellebecq, Michel, 24, 197, 291, 292, 325–30
Houghton, Lord (Richard Monckton Milnes), 19, 78–81, 92, 374n45
Hughes, Stuart, 170, 201
human evolution, laws of, 55, 63
human rights, 69–70, 118, 126, 303, 305
Hungary, 278, 324, 351
Hunt, Tristram, 350
Huntington, Samuel, 23, 282, 290–92, 301–7, 314, 330–33, 346
Hurston, Zora Neale, 388n26
Hutton, Henry Dix, 84
Huxley, Aldous, 22, 226
hyper-liberalism (Gray), 405n103

Ibn Khaldun, 347
Iceland, 220
Ikenberry, John, 331–32
Imagined Communities (Anderson), 407n16
immigration, 95, 99–103, 109–13, 122, 324
Immigration Act (1924), 175
imperialism, 266, 271; American, 108–9; anti-imperialism, 91–93; British, 51, 91–93, 339; Chinese, 301; Comte's attitude toward, 55, 59; Great War and, 132, 146, 152–53, 160, 163. *See also* colonialism
'In Defence of the East' (Metta), 182–83
'In Defense of "the West"' (Foster), 321321
India: British rule of, 25, 27, 108–9, 116, 145, 266, 400n132; as Eastern, 29, 33, 183; as genesis of civilisation, 25, 116–17; as global South, 345–46; positivism in, 64; racial prejudice against, 222; religious influence of, 212, 214–15, 246–47; Tagore's lectures on, 149–51
indigenous values, 303–5
individualism, 54, 67, 118, 225, 298, 303, 317
industrialisation, 258, 301

INDEX

international law, 105–7, 109, 132, 142–43, 299
International Policy: Essays on the Foreign Relations of England, 84, 87, 92
interwar period, 165–201; overview, 21–22, 166–67, 199–201; Afro-American thinkers, 171–75, 192–93; Anglo-American responses to Massis, 182–86, 195–96; French responses to Massis, 192–93; German east-mania, 181–82; German responses to Massis, 186–92; Guénon's response to Massis, 195–97; lead up to war (1930s), 197–99; Massis affair, 176–81; 'A New West' concept (Lewis), 194–95; Nordic supremacists, 175–76, 184–85; Spengler affair, 167–71
Introduction à la Lecture de Hegel (Kojève), 294
Inventing Eastern Europe (Wolff), 18
'The Invention of Western Civilization' (Turner), 128
Iran, 319
Iraq, 298–301, 311, 332
Irene of Athens, 5, 338
Islam: civilisation differentiated by, 299–300, 303–4, 320; classical influences on, 347; Crusades, 17, 45, 73, 338; Guénon's work, 195–97; in Houellebecq's work, 325–28
Islamic terrorism, 319
isolationism, 131, 142, 225, 331
Israel, 78, 333
Italy: Communists in, 233; criticism of Massis in, 192; as cultural centre, 183–85 (*see also* Greco-Roman roots of the West); fascism in, 197; in Latin bloc, 35, 57, 219
'I Tried to Be a Communist' (Wright), 261

James, George, 348
Japan: as beacon of hope, 119–21; as Eastern, 33, 336; Fukuyama on, 294; international relations, 107–9; racial prejudice against, 222; Tagore's lectures in, 146–49; as Western, 288, 323, 331, 336, 354; World War I, 132, 141–42, 162; World War II, 228
Jaspers, Karl, 228
Jebb, Gladwyn, 198, 225, 231–33, 243
Jerrold, Douglas, 198, 246
Jewish people: American immigrants, 249–50, 288; as East-West bridge, 77–78; Hebraic origins of the West, 193, 255–56 (*see also* Christianity as Western basis); as 'other,' 93, 247; racial prejudice against, 175; religious belief, 256, 367n30; Zionist movement, 388n30. *See also specific person*
Joachim of Fiore, 168
John Reed Book Club, 261
Johnson, Lyndon B., 296
Josselson, Michael, 247
July Revolution (1830), 38
justice, 126

Kant, Immanuel, 133, 134, 241
Kaprièlian, Nelly, 326
Kavanagh: A Tale (Longfellow), 121
Kennan, George, 229–30, 368n53
Kennedy, Jackie, 296
Kennedy, John F., 294, 296
Keshub Chunder Sen, 117
Keyserling, Hermann Graf, 146, 181–82
Khomyakov, Aleksei, 19, 43–44, 83
Kidd, Benjamin, 9, 13, 19, 92, 364n31
kidnapped West, 23, 280–82, 289, 318, 330–31
Kimmage, Michael, 318
Kingsley, Charles, 83
Kipling, Rudyard, 168
Kissinger, Henry, 23, 234, 237–42, 253, 284, 288
The Knickerbocker, 108, 110, 112
knowledge, 126
Koestler, Arthur, 398n67
Kohn, Hans, 223
Kojève, Alexandre, 22, 35, 217–20, 293–94
Kolnai, Aurel, 22, 198–99
Kondylis, Panayiotis, 312

Koraïs, Adamantios, 46
Krastev, Ivan, 332, 405n98 and 101, 406n10 and 12
Krutch, Joseph Wood, 185–86
Kultur, 131; German *Kultur* as root of German militarism, 133–35, 136–37; German *versus* French use of *Kultur/Culture* and *Zivilisation/Civilisation* (explained by Curtius), 187–89; Mann adopts Spengler's new use of *Kultur* and *Zivilisation* (1919), 161–62, 163–64; Mann's juxtaposition between *Kultur* and *Zivilisation,* 156–60; new distinction *Kultur* versus *Zivilisation* introduced by Spengler, 170–71
Kundera, Milan, 4, 23, 280–82, 289–90, 330
Kunze, Otto, 190
Kurth, James, 314, 318, 330
Kuwait, 298–301

'La Civilisation occidentale' (Siegfried), 210
Laffitte, Pierre, 19, 64–65, 314, 369n84, 370n109
'La Guerre du Golfe mise à plat' ('The Gulf War: Setting Things Straight') (Castoriadis), 298–99
Lamartine, Alphonse de, 31
Lang, Fritz, 396n32
languages, different uses of the West, 70–71, 90–93, 338
Larousse dictionary, 5
Lasch, Christopher, 249
Laski, Melvin, 247
Lassalle, Ferdinand, 200
Latin America, 174–76, 232, 248, 263, 320. *See also specific country*
Latin Church. *See* Catholic Church
Latinity, 51–52, 176–79, 183–85, 188, 192–94, 218–20, 380n28, 394n38
Latin nations, 35, 47–48, 51–52, 57, 217–20. *See also specific country*
Laurens, Henry, 17
law of the three states (Comte), 55
leadership: American (*see* American leadership); Anglo-Saxon *versus* Slav, 114–15, 119–20, 129, 151–52, 187–89, 219; British, 115, 231–33, 288; French (*see* France as centre of the West); German, 3–4, 57, 89, 134, 204, 209, 308–14, 376n74; Soviet, 228
League of Nations, 92, 197
League of Peace, 143
Lebanon, 333
'Le Destin de l'Occident' (Gillouin), 193
Ledyard, John, 377n6
Lefort, Claude, 298
Leibnitz, 134
Lemming, George, 276
Lepenies, Wolf, 185, 386n89 and 90, 387n16, 389n49
'Letter LXXXVII' (Goldsmith), 72
Letters from an American Farmer (Crèvecoeur), 295, 377n6
Letters to a German Friend (Camus), 216
Lettres persanes (Persian Letters) (Montesquieu), 17–18
Leviathan (Hobbes), 71, 92
Lévi-Strauss, Claude, 300
Lewis, Martin, 7–8
Lewis, Wyndham, 22, 194–95, 352
Liang Ch'i-ch'ao (Qichao), 344, 388n30
liberalism, 67, 293, 303, 309, 324, 331, 350–51; as ideology of Western suicide, 23, 278–80, 283, 289, 294, 315; radical, 269–70
Libération, 298
liberties of Europe, 70, 75
liberty: with law, 318; as Western value, 69–70, 126, 148–49, 277, 303, 306
'L'Idée d'Occident chez Auguste Comte' (Useche Sandoval), 371n126
The Lie about the West (Jerrold), 246
Lieber, Francis (Franz): on Americans siding with Russia, 112; Arendt's similarity to, 250; Comte compared to, 340; Gurowski, 112; on monogamy, 27; overview, 20, 99–103, 110, 128–29
Liebknecht, Wilhelm, 40
Life, 208, 221, 224–25, 243

Lilla, Mark, 256, 284, 308, 325
linear theory of history, 14
Lippmann, Walter: on Russian-American relations, 114; World War I, 21, 134–35, 138–45, 162–63, 166; interwar period, 198; World War II, 22, 203–6, 218–26, 283; Cold War, 229–31
The Listener, 243–47
Literary Association of the Friends of Poland, 374n45
Littré, Émile, 19, 64
Lobb, Samuel, 84
Locke, Alain LeRoy: visits Africa, 172; World War I, 21, 22, 138, 151–52; interwar period, 171–73, 192; World War II, 22, 203, 221–24, 344
Locke, John, 5, 109, 381n44
Logan, Rayford W., 401n149
logic of space (Spengler), 168
'The Logic of the West' (Deudney & Ikenberry), 331–32
logic of time (Spengler), 168
Longfellow, Henry Wadsworth, 110, 121
longue durée approach, 3, 24, 331, 334, 354
Louis-Napoléon Bonaparte (Napoléon III), 64
Luce, Henry, 203, 221, 224, 242–43
Lushington, Godfrey, 84
Lushington, Vernon, 84
Luther, Martin, 161, 270

Maçães, Bruno, 339, 405n103
Macdonald, Dwight, 248–49
MacDonald, James Ramsay, 19, 92
machine society, 234–35, 244, 252–53
Macmillan, Harold, 227, 231
Mac Sweeney, Naoíse, 13, 363n9, 379n23
The Magic Mountain (Mann), 325
Mahan, Alfred Thayer, 143
Mahatir bin Mohamad, 240
Maĭkov, Valerian, 12
Mailer, Norman, 248
Maine, Henry, 19, 93, 375n65
Maistre, Joseph de, 11, 12, 24, 54, 67, 199, 328
maladie occidentale (the Western disease), 54

Malraux, André, 181, 233, 389n54
The Managerial Revolution (Burnham), 278
manifest destiny, 110, 221
Mann, Golo, 396n35
Mann, Heinrich, 159–60, 163
Mann, Thomas: attacks on Francophiles, 159–60, 163; German cultural debates, 3–4, 21, 133, 156–63, 170, 290; juxtaposition between 'culture' *(Kultur)* and 'civilisation' *(Zivilisation)*, 156–60, 290; *The Magic Mountain*, 325; Massis's criticism of, 181; 'On the German Republic' *(Vom Deutscher Republik)*, 191–92; *Reflections of a Nonpolitical Man*, 159–62; Spengler's influence on use of 'culture' and 'civilisation' by (after 1919), 161–64, 387n15; 'Thoughts in Wartime' *(Gedanken im Kriege)*, 156–59; Weimar Republic defended by, 192
The Man Without Qualities (Musil), 325
Maran, René, 22, 146, 174–75, 193
Marchand, Suzanne, 174, 181–82, 348–49, 383n3
Maritain, Jacques, 22, 177, 193, 203–4, 224–25
marriage metaphor, 34
Marshall, George C., 228–29, 231–32
Marshall Plan, 231
Martineau, Harriet, 19, 78–79, 91, 374n43
Marvin, Francis Sydney, 19, 91, 92, 135–36
Marx, Karl: as contributor in British and American debates, 19, 49, 77, 92, 110; on European imperialism, 266, 400n132; French interest in, 257; on history making, 352; on Panslavism, 112; on science and technology, 353; Westernness of, 200, 244
Marxism, 233, 248, 252, 261, 269. See also Communism
Massis, Henri: overview, 22, 166, 176–81; Anglo-American responses to, 182–86; attack on Tagore, 146, 178, 180–81; French responses to, 192–93, 209; German responses to, 186–92; Guénon's response to, 195–97, 326; Lewis on, 352; on Spengler, 349

materialism, 118, 180, 197, 244
Maurer, Georg Ludwig von, 93
Maurras, Charles, 177, 183, 190, 209, 394n38
May, Henry, 145
Mazzini, Giuseppe, 59
McCarthy, Joseph, 249, 351
McNeill, William W., 166, 349
Mead, Margaret, 223
Meaney, Thomas, 390n71, 407n17
meaning, importance of, 336–37, 340–46, 354
Mediterranean: as alleged racial group (Grant), 175; as cradle of Western civilisation, 22, 34, 209–10, 215, 230, 394n38; French use of, 177–79, 183–85
Mehmet Ali, 35–36, 76
'Memorandum on Compulsory Disarmament' (Chapman), 137
metaphysical state (Comte), 55
Metropolis (Lang), 396n32
Metta, Vesudeo B., 182–83, 389n62
Mexico, 175–76
Middle Power: Britain as, 231–33; Germany as, 186, 313
Militarism (German), 133–34, 156–59
Mill, John Stuart, 5, 16–17, 32, 52, 61–63, 90, 96, 348
Miller, Stephen, 320–22, 345
Milnes, Richard Monckton (Lord Houghton), 19, 78–81, 92, 374n45
Miłosz, Czesław: on America, 236–37; on Dostoyevsky, 12; French intellectuals' hostility toward, 233; influence of, in the West, 4; kidnapped West, 4, 23, 280–82, 289, 330; Massis's early impression on, 181; *Native Realm*, 281, 335–36; portrait of, 337
Milton, John, 19, 71
Minogue, Kenneth, 332
minority groups: cultural diversity, 224, 283, 296, 323–24; multiculturalism, 294–97, 317; in Western civilisation, 263–75, 295, 323–24. *See also specific group*
misdating of questions (Freeman), 82
Mitsotakis, Kyriakos, 403n34

modernisation, 253, 263–75, 289; *versus* traditionalism, 325–30; *versus* Westernisation, 146, 197, 305–6
Modernism, 174
Modi, Narendra, 345
Moeller van den Bruck, Arthur, 186
Moenius, Georg, 22, 190
Moldavia, 29
Molotov-Ribbentrop Pact (August 1939), 22, 203, 224
Der Monat, 247
Le Monde, 218
monogamy, 27, 101
Montaigne, Michel de, 300
Montesquieu, 3, 17–18, 331
moral principles, 255, 261–75, 288, 350–51
Morley, John, 87
Moses, Wilson Jeremiah, 123–24, 156, 174
Moyn, Samuel, 269
Mr. X (George Kennan), 229–30
Müller, Friedrich Max, 93
Müller, Jan-Werner, 308–10
multiculturalism, 294–97, 317, 323
Muqaddimah (Ibn Khaldun), 347
Murray, Douglas, 333
Murray, Gilbert, 92
Musil, Robert, 325
Myrdal, Gunnar, 250, 295

Naipaul, V. S., 291, 303
Nakasone, Yasuhiro, 240
Nakhimovsky, Isaac, 366n4
Napoléon I (Bonaparte), 25, 26, 28, 36, 71
Napoléon III (Louis-Napoléon Bonaparte), 64
Nardal, Jane (Jeanne), 22, 192–93, 207
Nardal, Paulette, 207
Nasser, Gamal Abdel, 273
Le National, 64
nationalism, 145–51, 331–32
'Nationalism in India' (Tagore), 150–51
'Nationalism in the West' (Tagore), 149–50
Nationalism (Tagore), 145–51
National Review, 321

The Nation (Krutch), 185–86
Native Realm (Miłosz), 281, 335–36
Native Son (Wright), 261
NATO (North Atlantic Treaty Organization): as American alliance, 288, 317–18; expansion of, 316–18, 336; Huntington's proposed expulsion of Greece from, 346; leadership group, 324; map of, 316; Plato to NATO narrative, 9, 346–50; the West as more than, 240; as Western, 307, 312–13
Natural Right and History (Strauss), 256–57, 284
Nazism: Arendt's work on, 250; colonial aims of, 213; New Europe aim, 203, 209–11, 216; revolt against Western ideas, 198–99, 202, 312–13; rise of, 198–99, 204. *See also* Second World War
Necker, Jacques, 28
The Need for Roots (L'Enracinement) (Weil), 212–13, 216
'Negro Society for Historical Research,' 151
Negro World, 125, 175
Nehru, Jawaharlal, 273
Neiman, Susan, 333
neo-colonialists, 351
néomédiévalistes, 193
Netanyahu, Benjamin, 345
Netherlands (Holland), 92, 217, 220
Neue Rundschau, 156
Neutralism (during Cold War), 233, 237, 252–53, 260
New Criterion, 183
New Europe, 203, 209–11, 216
The New Negro: An Interpretation (A. Locke), 173–74, 192, 221
The New Republic, 129, 138–39, 141
The New Rome; Or, The United States of the World (Poesche & Goepp), 110
New York Daily Tribune, 110–12
New York Herald Tribune, 229
New York Review of Books, 280
New York Times, 119–20
New York Times Magazine, 239

New Zealand, 58
Νίκανδρος (Nicandre de Corcyre), 364n25
Nicholas I, Czar, 26, 57–58
Nicolson, Harold, 392n139
Niebuhr, Barthold Georg, 92
Niebuhr, Reinhold, 59
Nietzsche, Friedrich: overview, 40–42; *Beyond Good and Evil*, 368n65; on Comte, 369n71; genealogical study according to, 340–42, 345, 353; on German spirit, 133; Houellebecq on, 327, 328, 330; influence of, 191, 287; mentioned by T. Mann, 161; use of the West, 19, 41, 66
nihilism, 238–41, 284
9/11 terrorist attacks, 333
Nkrumah, Kwame, 273
Nora, Pierre, 280
Nordic supremacists, 175–76, 184–85
North American Review, 97, 101, 113, 138, 348, 378n14, 379n21
Northern Powers (Palmerston), 76
North-South division, within Europe, 5, 16–18, 27–29, 34, 41, 66, 185
Norton, Charles Eliot, 128
Norway, 220
'Note on the United States of America' (Congreve), 89–90
nouveaux réactionnaires, 333
Nouvelle Revue française, 177, 181
Novalis, 9
Nuclear Test Ban Treaty, 283

Obama, Barack, 311, 320
O'Brien, Karen, 74
The Observer, 226
l'Occident: Comte's substitution of, for Europe, 48–52, 66–67, 90–91, 340; Laffitte's clarification of, 65; Massis's use of, 177; Suarès's rejoicing at creation of, thanks to Great War, 135; 18th-century use of, 5; 19th-century use of, 11, 13, 16–19, 31–35, 38, 80. *See also* the West
occidentalisme, 62

occidentalité, 50, 62–63, 65, 91
oceans, Lippmann's focus on, 140–44
'Ode on the Sailing of Our Troops for France' (Chapman), 138
Oeuvres (Diderot), 17
der Okzident, 70, 170, 190
One World (Willkie), 220
On the Genealogy of Morality (Nietzsche), 41, 340–42
L'Opium des intellectuels (Aron), 258
opuscules de jeunesse (Comte), 52, 59–60
Ora 25 (Gheorghiu), 234–37, 239
Orbán, Viktor, 282, 351
Order (going together with progress, according to Comte), 54, 64
l'Orient: 19th-century use of, 16–18, 31–35. *See also* the East
Orientalism, in America, 107–10, 113–19
Origins of Totalitarianism (Arendt), 249–50
Ortega y Gasset, 187
'Orthodox Christian Civilisation' (Toynbee), 47–48, 244
Orthodox Church: African, 172; civilisation differentiated by (Huntington), 303–4; Eastern/Greek, 5–9, 11–12, 14, 26, 42–48, 66–67, 280–82, 346
Orwell, George, 22, 225, 226, 229, 278
Osterhammel, Jürgen, 13, 366n1, 368n45
Otsing, Henri, 407n17
Ottoman Empire: American view on, 108–9, 111–13; East-West division and, 33–37, 66, 88–89, 93; during Great War, 132; Greece and, 35–38, 46–47; Russia and, 76–78, 88–89; Slavs and, 83. *See also* Eastern Question
'An Outline of a Doctrine of French Policy' (Kojève), 218
ownership of culture, 221–24, 343–45, 351

Pacific rim, 141–42
Padmore, George, 207, 264
Pagan Spain (Wright), 261, 263, 274–75
Paine, Thomas, 94, 121
Paix et guerre entre les nations (Peace and War) (Aron), 260

Paleface: The Philosophy of the 'Melting-Pot' (Lewis), 194–95
Palmerston, Lord, 19, 76
Pan-African Congresses, 155, 275, 386n79
Panslavism, 110–12
pantheism, 32
Papandreou, Andreas, 402n171
Paris: Aron tribute in, 259; Baldwin in, 275–77; as capital of Latin America/Latin civilisation, 174, 176; as capital of the West/Western civilisation, 56–57, 176–81, 208; Communists in, 233–34; Comte tribute in, 48–50; Du Bois on, 125; Wright in, 262–63; Wright tribute in, 266
Les Particules élémentaires (Atomised) (Houellebecq), 326–29, 405n94
Partisan Review, 208, 229
The Passing of the Great Race; or, The Racial Basis of European History (Grant), 175, 185
patriotism, 55, 212–13, 309
Peace and War (Paix et guerre entre les nations) (Aron), 260
Peace of Vienna, 88
Perry, Matthew C., 107–8
Persian empire, 1–2, 338
Peter the Great, 18, 19, 26, 58, 70, 72, 74, 78–79, 170, 180, 244, 278
philhellenism, 35–39, 80–81, 378n21
philosophia perennis, 197
Pius XII, Pope, 224–25
Plamenatz, John, 406n10
Plato, 5, 250, 253, 285, 347, 348, 350
Plato to NATO narrative, 1–2, 9, 346–50
From Plato to NATO: The Idea of the West and Its Opponents (Gress), 406n8
Poesche, Theodore, 110
Poland: German invasion of, 203, 319–20; Russian suppression of, 75–76; Warsaw speeches (Bush vs Trump), 318–25, 331, 345; as Western, 4, 57, 58, 278, 280–82, 318–219, 330–31
politics: American political science, 99, 115–19; of civilisations, 302–5; importance

of terms in, 336–37, 340–46, 354; left-right divides, 334
polygamy, 27
Portugal, 65–67, 76, 220, 270
positive state (Comte), 55
Positivism: after Comte, 63–65; in Britain, 70, 74, 84–93, 135–36, 162; Comte's theory of, 52–63, 67–68
Positivist Review, 92
post–Cold War, 291–334; overview, 23–24, 292, 330–34; Castoriadis's views, 298–301; Fukuyama's work, 292–94; Habermas's activism, 307–12; Houellebecq's work, 325–30; Huntington's work, 301–7; Huntingtonism after Huntington, 314–18; Schlesinger's work, 294–97; Warsaw speeches (Bush vs Trump), 318–25, 345; Winkler's work, 312–14
postmodernism, 315
Pound, Ezra, 389n58
'Pour l'alliance de l'Occident' (Aron), 217–18
'Pour un parti de l'intelligence' (Massis), 177
Pradt, Dominique de, 13, 19, 25, 36–38, 66, 81
Présence africaine, 265
Preuves, 248, 280
Primitivism, 174
Privatization in Western society (Castoriadis), 298
Progress (going together with order, according to Comte), 54, 64
Progressive Education Association, 222
'Progress or Return? The Contemporary Crisis in Western Civilization' (Strauss), 254–55
The Promise of American Life (Croly), 129, 139
property rights, 101
Protestantism, 26, 48, 57, 95, 122, 191, 193, 270, 351
Prussia, 3, 76, 88, 132. *See also* Germany
Putin, Vladimir, 197, 325, 336, 351, 407n17
Pythagoras, 170

'Qu'est-ce que l'Europe?' (de Reynold), 209
The Quest of the Silver Fleece (Du Bois), 347

race: Black (*see* Afro-Americans); Color Line, 120–21, 153, 222; *versus* culture, 223–24; whiteness (*see* white supremacism/whiteness); World War I, 151–54; interwar period, 175–76, 184–85; World War II, 210, 221–24; Cold War, 230–31, 260, 262–77; post–Cold War, 295, 333–34
racist theories and reactions to them, 119–28, 145–56, 175–76, 222–24, 261–77, 295, 334
radical liberalism (Shklar), 269–70
Ram Mohan Roy, Raja, 117
Rathenau, Walter, 178, 187
Rationalist West, 332–33
reactionary forces, 54, 118
Read, Herbert, 183, 252
Reclus, Élisée, 106
Reddick, Lawrence D., 206–7
Reden an die Deutsche Nation (Fichte), 134
Reflections of a Nonpolitical Man (Mann), 159–62
Reflections on the Politics of Ancient Greece (Heeren), 98, 106
Reinsch, Paul S., 115–19, 142
Reith Lectures (BBC), 243–47
relativism, 257, 284–87, 289–90
religion: civilisation differentiated by, 303–7, 314–18, 320–22; *versus* Communism, 253–54, 258; in East-West division, 32, 42–48, 66–67, 195–97, 246–47, 253–54; fanaticism, 300–301, 305, 315; Wright's view on, 270–75. *See also* Christianity; *specific religion*
religion of Humanity (Comte), 52–55, 67–68, 86, 129, 369n71
Renieris, Markos, 19, 43–48, 343–44
Renoir, Jean, 161
Republic of the West (Positivist concept), 51–60, 64–65, 92
Republic (Plato), 285, 347
république occidentale, 64–65
retrograde party, 54
Revista de Occidente, 187
revolt against the West (Frobenius), 124, 181–82, 289–90

revolutionary principles, 54, 59, 88
Revue des deux mondes, 210
Revue universelle, 176–77, 182, 197, 209
Reynold, Gonzague de, 22, 209
Riley, Dylan, 313
The Rising Tide of Color: The Threat against White World-Supremacy (Stoddard), 175
Riza, Ahmet, 388n30
Robinson, Cedric, 261
Rolland, Romain, 132, 156
Roman Empire: east-west division in, 5–7, 9, 14, 17, 35, 73–74, 82–83, 93, 172, 338–39; as Western inspiration (*see* Greco-Roman roots of the West)
Romania, 234
Roosevelt, Franklin D., 224
Rousseau, Jean-Jacques, 72, 181
Rückert, Friedrich, 376n96
rule of law, 303
Runciman, David, 139
Russell, Charles Edward, 138
Russia: American fear of, 113–21, 198; annexation of Crimea, 333; Bolshevik revolution, 10, 177, 180, 198, 199, 278; British dislike of, 75–78, 93; Burnham on, 278; de Staël on, 29; Eastern nature of (*see* Russia as Eastern); European federation and, 38–42, 66, 233–37; German alliance with, 204, 224; German fear of, 39–42, 132–33, 152; importance for the West, 3–4, 10–13, 19, 26; invasion of Ukraine, 4, 24, 301, 307, 319, 333, 346, 351, 403n34; opposition to the West, 336; Positivist view of, 57–58, 65; religion in (*see* Orthodox Church); Western nature of (*see* Russia as Western); World War I, 132–33, 152; interwar period, 177, 180, 183, 198–201; World War II, 22, 203, 228. *See also* Soviet Union
Russia as Eastern: origins of, 18, 22, 26, 29, 36–48, 66, 88–89, 116–19; interwar period, 177, 180, 183, 199–201; Cold War, 244, 278, 281

Russia as Western: origins of, 16, 18, 27, 70–74, 108, 201; Cold War, 4, 201, 203, 224, 226, 235, 244, 246, 281, 288; post–Cold War, 336
Russia As It Is (Gurowski), 111–12
'The Russian Menace' (Harrison), 119–20
La Russie en 1839 (de Custine), 29, 38, 80, 368n54
Russo-Japanese war (1904–5), 120
Russo-Turkish War (1877–78), 81
Rychner, Max, 22, 186–87, 195

Saddam Hussein, 298
Said, Edward, 363n9
Saint-Simon, Henri de, 12, 19, 30–35, 60, 62, 67
Saint-Simonians, 12, 19, 30–33, 185
samaj (society), 146
Santayana, George, 139, 206
Sarkozy, Nicolas, 185
Sartre, Jean-Paul, 258, 264, 308
Savigny, Friedrich Carl von, 93
Scheler, Max, 132–33
Schlesinger, Arthur, Jr., 23, 292, 294–98, 306, 323
Schmitt, Carl, 22, 199–201
School of wisdom (Schule der Weisheit), 146, 182
Schopenhauer, Arthur, 116, 330
Schule der Weisheit (School of wisdom), 146, 182
Scottish Enlightenment, 74
Scruton, Roger, 333
SDAP (Social Democratic Workers' Party of Germany), 40
sea power, 143
Searchlight Books, 225
'Second Discourse' (Rousseau), 181
Second World War, 202–26; overview, 22, 203, 224–26; Atlantic Community, 220–21, 226; education issue, 203–6; Extreme West, 212–17; France as centre, 206–9; occupation of France, 209–12; period before (*see* interwar period); race

issue, 203–4, 210, 221–24; Western alliance, 217–20; Westernisation after, 4, 7
secularisation, 75, 90–91, 197, 254, 274, 315, 351
secular universalism, 333
Seeley, J. R., 86–87, 92
self-description, the West as, 9–12, 69–70, 93, 95, 337–39, 345
Sen, Amartya, 145
Sen, Keshub Chunder, 117
Senghor, Léopold Sédar, 265–67, 270–71, 276
Seven Years' War, 72
the shadow of the West (Toynbee), 167
Shils, Edward, 247
Shklar, Judith, 269–70
Siegfried, André, 22, 209–12, 228, 237, 252, 353
Six Books of the Republic (Bodin), 16
Skinner, Quentin, 365n35
Slav civilisation, 48, 83, 146, 171, 180; versus Anglo-Saxon, 111–15, 119–20, 129, 151–52, 187–89, 219
Slavophiles, in 19th-century Russia, 10–13, 42–43, 146, 170, 180, 369n72
Smith, Adam, 19, 71
social equality, 69–70, 118, 126
Socialisme ou Barbarie, 298
Socialist United States of Europe (Orwell), 229
social organisation: frontier thesis, 95–96; units of, 87–88, 167, 352
Society for Classical Studies, 407n26
society *(samaj)*, 146
sociology, Positivist laws of, 58–59
sociopolitical concept of 'the West': alternatives to, 339–40; American use of (*see* American use of 'the West'); British use of (*see* British use of 'the West'); Comte's introduction of, 3, 8–9, 14, 19, 49, 58, 66–68; future of, 350–55; versus geographical use (*see* geographical concept of 'the West'); gradual emergence of, 19, 66, 128; history overview, 338–39; importance of, 336–37, 340–46, 354–55;

modern use of, 23–24, 67–69; post–Cold War, 331–32; purported Russian origin of, 9–13, 91–92; as self-description, 9–12, 69–70, 93, 95, 337–39, 345; 19th-century development of, 13–18
Socrates, 166, 198, 250, 350
Sombart, Werner, 133
Somewheres (Goodhart), 332
Sonderweg, 308–9
Sophia Perennis (publishing house), 197
Sorbonne conference *(Congrès international des écrivains et artistes noirs)* (1956), 265–77
The Souls of Black Folk (Du Bois), 267
Soumission (Houellebecq), 325–30
Soviet Union: Cold War, 228, 247–49, 260 (*see also* Cold War); Finland threatened by, 204; Hitler's invasion of, 22, 203; leadership by, 228; as NATO adversary, 318; post–Cold War reforms in, 293; racial equality in, 260; as Western, 4, 201, 203, 224, 226, 228, 235, 244, 288. *See also* Russia
space, logic of (Spengler), 168
Spain: British alliance with, 76; Christianity in, 270, 274–75; in Latin bloc, 35, 57, 219, 220; as Western, 323; Wright in, 261, 266, 274–75
Sparks, Jared, 378n14
Le Spectateur de l'Orient, 47
Spender, Stephen, 227, 389n58
Spengler, Oswald: on boundaries of the West, 3, 10, 13, 187, 191, 201, 245; *Decline of the West*, 21–22, 161–64, 166–71, 176–82, 191, 199, 249, 254; on Europe's image of America, 252; in Houellebecq's work, 328; influence of, 349; introduces novel use of 'culture' and 'civilisation,' 170–71; Kissinger's study of, 241; Mann's adoption of his distinction between 'civilisation' and 'culture,' 161–64; on Moenius, 190; proposes to strike the word 'Europe' out of history, 169–70
Spinoza, Baruch, 330

spirit, 158, 202–47, 331, 354
spiritual survival of Western civilisation, 231–33, 238–40, 244–47, 253–54, 288
spiritual-temporal division (Comte), 55–56, 67–68
Staël-Holstein, Louise Germaine de (Mme de Staël), 19, 25–30, 35, 66
The Stakes of Diplomacy (Lippmann), 141
Stalin, Joseph, 204, 224, 244, 250
Steffens, Lincoln, 138
Stein, Gertrude, 261, 274
Stein, Sol, 276
Stern, Bernhard, 222
Sternberger, Dolf, 309
Sternhell, Zeev, 210
Stewart, Jeffrey, 172
Stoddard, T. Lothrop, 22, 175
Stolen Legacy: Greek Philosophy Is Stolen Egyptian Philosophy (James), 348
Stourdza, Alexander, 11, 16
Strauss, Leo, 23, 254–57, 284, 287, 288–90
Stuart, Reginald, 110
student revolts (1960s), 23, 283–84
A Study of History (Toynbee), 167, 242, 244, 293
Stürmer, Michael, 308
Suarès, André, 130, 135, 162, 177
Submission (Houellebecq), 325–30
Suez crisis (1956), 231, 278
The Suicide of the West (Burnham), 278–80, 294
Sukarno, 273
Sumner, William Graham, 174
The Survey, 155
Survey Graphic, 173, 221
symbols, Positivist use of, 63–64
sympathy, 89, 118
Syria, 319, 333, 336
Système de politique positive (Comte), 52–63
System of Positive Polity, 84

Tagore, Rabindranath, 21, 117, 145–51, 154, 163, 178, 180–81, 354
Talleyrand, 76

Tallinn University, 346
Tancred (Disraeli), 17
Tartu University, 346
technological civilisation, 234–35, 244, 252–53
temporal-spiritual division (Comte), 55–56, 67–68
Le Temps, 131, 209
La Tentation de l'Occident (Malraux), 389n54
terrorism, 319, 333
Teutonic people, 82–84, 175–76
'The Colonial Question and the Destiny of the French People' (Weil), 213–16
Theodosius, Emperor, 5–6
theological state (Comte), 55
Theosophy (Blavatsky), 117
Third World: Communism in, 248; rise of, 283, 303, 333; Westernisation of, 263–75, 289, 303. *See also specific region or country*
Thompson, John A., 138
'The Threat to Western Civilization' (Jebb), 233
Ticknor, George, 97
Time, 242–43
time, logic of (Spengler), 168
The Times, 137, 202, 246
Times Literary Supplement (TLS), 246
Tindemans, Leo, 240
Tocqueville, Alexis de, 251–52, 258
'Today and Tomorrow' column (Lippmann), 139, 204
Todd, David, 59, 368n45
Toland, John, 19, 75
'To My American Friends' (Maritain), 203–4
Totalitarian Dictatorship and Autocracy (Friedrich & Brzezinski), 398n79
totalitarianism, 203, 249–50, 288
'Toward a Renewed Western Civilization' (Kurth), 318
Toynbee, Arnold: Cold War, 23, 231, 233, 241–47, 288, 293, 328, 349; influence of, 349; origins of the West, 10, 13, 47–48;

interwar period, 166–67; World War II, 223, 225
traditionalism, 195–97, 326–28
'The Tragedy of Central Europe' (Kundera), 280
translatio imperii (heliotropic myth), 14, 28, 95, 98, 106, 115, 380n23
Travel Diary of a Philosopher (Keyserling), 182
Treaty of Unkiar Skelessi (Hünkâr İskelesi), 76
Treaty of Vienna, 76
Treitschke, Heinrich von, 134
Trevor-Roper, Hugh, 247
tribe, 'the West' as, 321–22
triumph of the West (Fukuyama), 23–24, 292–94
Troeltsch, Ernst, 22, 191, 257, 344
Truman, Harry, 242
Truman doctrine, 229
Trump, Donald, 24, 197, 292, 318–25, 331, 333, 345, 351
Turkey: American protection of, 229, 242; as Eastern, 89; nationalist modernisers, 344, 390n89; NATO membership, 307, 336; Ottoman (*see* Ottoman Empire); Positivism in, 64–65
The Turkish Question (Gurowski), 111
Turner, Frederick Jackson, 95–96, 115, 137
Turner, James, 128
Tusk, Donald, 330
Tutankhamun's (Tut's) tomb, 172
Twain, Mark, 323
The Twenty-Fifth Hour (Gheorghiu), 234–37, 239
Twilight of the Idols (Nietzsche), 41–42
'Two Types of Nationalism' (Plamenatz), 406n10

Ukraine, 4, 24, 301, 307, 319, 333, 346, 350, 403n34
'The Unfinished Business of Democracy' (Locke), 221–22
United States. *See* America

unit ideas, 365n35
The Unity of Western Civilization (Marvin), 92
'The Unity of Western Civilization' (Woodbrooke Settlement), 135
universalisability of Western civilisation, 23–24, 290, 292, 303–7, 311, 320–21, 324, 332
Der Untergand des Abendlandes (The Decline of the West) (Spengler), 21–22, 161–64, 166–71, 176–82, 199, 249, 254
Urbain, Ismaÿl (Thomas), 31
Urquhart, David, 19, 77, 92
U.S. Foreign Policy (Lippmann), 220
Useche Sandoval, Tonatiuh, 61

Valéry, Paul, 22, 226
value relativism, 286–87
vanguard of Humanity (Comte), 58–59, 62–63, 67, 84, 135
Vasconcelos, José, 22, 175–76
Vaux, Clothilde de, 52
Venezuela, dispute over, 115
Verfassungspatriotismus (constitutional patriotism), 309
Verteidigung des Abendlandes (Moenius), 190
Vichy-ruled France, 209–12
Vietnam War, 283–84
Village-Communities in East and West (Maine), 375n65
La Vint-cinquième Heure (Gheorghiu), 234–37, 239
'vitalist orientalism' (Marchand), 181
Vivekananda, Swami, 117
Volney, Constantin-François, 25, 124, 348
Voltaire, 18, 27, 74, 158
Voyages (Νίκανδρος/ Nicandre de Corcyre), 364n25

Walt, Stephen, 305
The War against the West (Kolnai), 198
Warburg, Fredric, 225
Ward, Barbara, 239, 397n44

Warren, Joseph, 380n23
Warsaw speeches (Bush vs Trump), 318–25, 331, 345
Washington, George, 379n23
Weil, Simone, 22, 202, 203, 212–16, 237, 252, 349
Wertgemeinschaft, 307, 312
The West: A Metrical Epistle (Lieber), 104
The West: A New History of an Old Idea (Mac Sweeney), 13, 363n9, 379n23
Westbindung, 24, 233, 292, 307–14
Westbindung: Chancen und Risiken für Deutschland (Zitlemann, et al.), 310–13
'The West' (Congreve), 69, 84, 87–90
Western alliance: after World War II, 229–32, 283, 288; Aron's concept of, 217–18; Lippmann's concept of, 141–44; Palmerston's concept of, 76; proposed in 1820s, 36–38; proposed in 1830s–1840s and thereafter, 38–42, 48–65, 69, 75–81, 84–90, 106; proposed during Great War, by Lippmann, 141–45; proposed during World War II: by Aron, 217–18; by Lippmann, 220–21
Western civilisation: African origin of, 122–25, 172–74, 348–49; American rejection of, 314–25, 331; classical origins of (*see* Greco-Roman roots of the West); commonality as basis of, 14, 18, 47–48, 106–7; end of, 278–80, 292, 294, 301, 315–18, 325–30, 334; essence of, 343–44, 351–55; failings of, 351–54; grand narratives of, 349–50; minority groups in, 263–75; rivalry with Eastern civilisation, 23–24, 47–48, 115–19; spiritual survival of, 231–33, 238–40, 244–47, 253–54, 288; superiority of, 21, 131; technicalisation, 234–35, 244, 252–53; universalisability of, 23–24, 290, 292, 303–7, 311, 320–21, 324, 332; university curricula about, 94, 140, 166, 205–6, 238–40, 283; World War I, 131, 133–34, 151–64; interwar period, 167–71, 198; World War II, 203–6, 214–16, 224–26; Cold War, 234–42, 244, 252–57, 263–75, 288; post–Cold War (*see* post–Cold War)
Western civil wars, 205, 302, 315–16
Western disease *(maladie occidentale)*, 54
Western entente *(entente occidentale)*, 217–18
Westerner: Aron's definition of, 257–61, 289, 353; Baldwin's definition of, 275–77, 289, 297; Wright's definition of, 23–24, 267–75, 289, 297, 351
Western Europe (term): Comte's use of, 61, 74; Goldsmith's use of, 72; Saint-Simon's use of, 31
Westernisation: of Germany, 137, 247, 278, 307–14; *versus* modernisation, 146; of Third World, 263–75, 289, 303
Westernisers, in 19th-century Russia, 10–13, 42–43, 170, 180, 369n72
Westernized Easterners, 196, 264–65
Western Navy (Comte), 63
Westernness *(occidentalité)*, 50, 62–63, 65, 91
The Western Question in Greece and Turkey: A Study in the Contact of Civilizations (Toynbee), 167
Western Republic (Positivist concept), 51–60, 65, 92, 339–40
Western Roman Empire, 5–7, 9, 14, 17, 35, 73–74, 82–83, 338–39
Western schemes of history, 168–71
Western suicide, 23, 278–80, 283, 289, 294, 315
Western Union policy, 232
Western values: *versus* American popular culture, 317; failure to live up to, 351–54; not unique to Westerners, 343–44, 350–51, 355; origins of, 67–70, 93, 116–18, 126; World War I, 148–49, 163; interwar period, 168, 180, 197; Cold War, 254–57, 286; post–Cold War, 293, 297, 303–7, 318–25, 331–32
Westlessness, 333
Westminster Review, 77, 90
West-oestliches Divan (Goethe), 376n96
'The West Unique, Not Universal' (Huntington), 301, 305–7

'What is Greece, East or West?' (Renieris), 43–48, 343–44
Wheaton's Law of Nations, 107
Wheeler, Benjamin Ide, 113–15, 119
When Peoples Meet (Locke), 222–24
Whigs (Britain), 70, 75
White Man, Listen! (Wright), 263, 267–74, 398n80
white supremacism/whiteness: Caucasian race theories rejected by Lieber, 102–7, 380n31 and 32; narratives of, 13, 210, 222–24, 295, 320–22, 334, 349, 407n26; Nordic supremacists, 175–76, 184–85
Whitman, Walt, 96, 110
Wigen, Kären, 7–8
Wilhelm II, 182
William III, 70, 75
William IV, 77
Willkie, Wendell L., 220
Wilson, Woodrow, 392n139
Winkler, Heinrich August, 4, 24, 292, 312–14, 334, 344
wissenschaftlich, 349
Wolff, Larry, 18, 377n6
women: in ancient world, 378n21; feminism, 314–16; Wright's complaint on absence of, at 1956 Sorbonne conference, 267
Woodbrooke Settlement, 135
The World and the West (Toynbee), 243–47
World Politics at the End of the Nineteenth Century as Influenced by the Oriental Situation (Reinsch), 115–19
World War I: period after (*see* interwar period). *See* Great War

World War II. *See* Second World War
Worringer, Wilhelm, 187
The Wretched of the Earth (Les Damnés de la Terre) (Fanon), 264
Wright, Richard: overview, 261–76; on Arendt, 250; Arendt's influence on, 398n80; Cold War, 23; on history, 93; quote about Afro-Americans' difference from Asian and African writers, 227; on science and technology, 353; Westernness definition, 23–24, 267–75, 289, 297; on Western principles *versus* practice, 270–74, 351, 355
Wright, Terence, 84–85

Xi Jinping, 345

Yousafzai, Malala, 347

Zivilisation, 189, 290; German soul 'too deep for civilization to be its highest value' (T. Mann), 158; Germans' refusal to succumb to the civilising process (T. Mann), 159; Germany as fighting against, in Great War, 156–57; Germany as 'protest' and resistance against (T. Mann), 160; *versus Kultur* (T. Mann), 157–60; not as attractive to Germans as to the French or English (T. Mann), 158; Paris as the 'Mecca of civilization' (T. Mann), 158; Spengler's novel distinction between *Kultur* and, 161–62, 163–64, 170–71
Zivilisationsliterat, 159–61